Alexandre Verkinderen
Anders Bengtsson
Patrik Sundqvist
David Pultorak

with Kurt Van Hoecke,
Travis Wright,
Maarten Goet, and
Oskar Landman

System Center Service Manager 2010

UNLEASHED

SAMS | 800 East 96th Street, Indianapolis, Indiana 46240 USA

System Center Service Manager 2010 Unleashed

ISBN-13: 978-0-672-33436-8
ISBN-10: 0-672-33436-4

Library of Congress Cataloging-in-Publication Data:
System center service manager 2010 unleashed / Kerrie Meyler ... [et al.].
    p. cm.
  Includes index.
  ISBN-13: 978-0-672-33436-8
  ISBN-10: 0-672-33436-4
  1. Electronic data processing—Management. 2. Microsoft Windows server.
3. Computer systems. I. Meyler, Kerrie.
  QA76.9.M3S98 2012
  005.4'476—dc23

                          2011027819

Printed in the United States of America

First Printing: August 2011

Trademarks

Warning and Disclaimer

Bulk Sales

Pearson offers excellent discounts on this book when ordered in quantity for bulk purchases or special sales. For more information, please contact:

U.S. Corporate and Government Sales
1-800-382-3419
corpsales@pearsontechgroup.com

For sales outside of the U.S., please contact:

International Sales
+1-317-581-3793
international@pearsontechgroup.com

Editor-in-Chief
Greg Wiegand

Executive Editor
Neil Rowe

Development Editor
Mark Renfrow

Managing Editor
Kristy Hart

Project Editor
Lori Lyons

Copy Editor
Keith Cline

Indexer
Lisa Stumpf

Proofreader
Water Crest
Publishing

Technical Editor
Anders Ravnholt

**Publishing
Coordinator**
Cindy Teeters

Interior Designer
Gary Adair

Cover Designer
Gary Adair

Compositor
Nonie Ratcliff

Contents at a Glance

Table of Contents

About the Authors

Kerrie Meyler, MVP, is the lead author of numerous System Center books in the Unleashed series, including *System Center Operations Manager 2007 Unleashed* (2008), *System Center Configuration Manager 2007 Unleashed* (2009), *System Center Operations Manager 2007 R2 Unleashed* (2010), and *System Center Opalis Integration Server 6.3 Unleashed* (2011). She is an independent consultant and trainer with more than 15 years of Information Technology experience. Kerrie was responsible for evangelizing SMS while a Sr. Technology Specialist at Microsoft, and has presented on System Center technologies at TechEd and MMS.

Alexandre Verkinderen, MVP, is a Principal Consultant and trainer at Infront Consulting Group, a Microsoft Gold Certified Partner. Alexandre is an industry expert in the systems management area, and actively consults to large organizations helping them architect, implement, configure, and customize System Center technologies by integrating them into their business processes. Alexandre founded the System Center Users Group Belgium, and was a contributing author for *System Center Operations Manager 2007 R2 Unleashed* (Sams, 2010). Alexandre was an early tester in the Service Manager 2010 TAP.

Anders Bengtsson is a Microsoft senior premier field engineer, focusing on System Center. He was involved in the Service Manager TAP with one of the largest Service Manager TAP customers. Anders has written a number of System Center training courses, including the Service Manager and Operations Manager advanced courses for Microsoft Learning. Before joining Microsoft, Anders was a Microsoft MVP from 2007-2010 for his work in the System Center community, including more than 10,000 posts in news groups and forums. Anders has presented and worked at numerous Microsoft conferences and events, including Microsoft Techdays and Microsoft TechEd EMEA.

Patrik Sundqvist is a senior consultant working as a solution architect, focusing on developing automated solutions for IT processes on the System Center platform. Since the early beta of Service Manager, Patrik has worked with the Service Manager product team to develop community solutions for Service Manager. Over the past eight years, Patrik has developed custom System Center solutions for some of Europe's largest companies. Patrik was also one of the authors of the level 400 Service Manager course for Microsoft Learning. He often speaks at Microsoft events and is a member of the Microsoft Extended Expert Team.

David Pultorak is founder and principal consultant of Acceleres, specializing in Service Manager implementation and training, and Pultorak & Associates, providing ITIL and MOF consulting and training. David is a recognized leader in the field of IT Service Management with more than 24 years of IT experience. He has completed numerous Service Manager implementations and has contributed to ITIL, MOF, and COBIT. His most recent books are *Microsoft Operations Framework* (2008) and the *ITIL V3 Foundation Exam Study Guide* (2011).

About the Contributors

Kurt Van Hoeke, managing consultant at inovativ Belgium, focuses on the System Center product suite, including Service Manager, Configuration Manager, and Opalis. Kurt has been working with Service Manager beginning with the beta versions and has a number of Service Manager deployments to his credit.

Travis Wright is a Senior Program Manager on the Service Manager engineering team responsible for incubating new projects/partnerships and enabling customers and partners to harness the full potential of Service Manager. Travis was previously responsible for many different areas of the Operations Manager product, going back to Operations Manager 2000.

Maarten Goet, MVP, is a managing consultant at inovativ in The Netherlands, helping customers to implement System Center, Forefront, and Hyper-V solutions. As a strong supporter of the community, Maarten regularly speaks at conferences such as the Microsoft Management Summit and TechEd North America.

Oskar Landman, MVP, a consultant at inovativ in The Netherlands, has more than ten years of IT consulting experience. Oskar focuses on Service Manager and Operations Manager, designing complex monitoring solutions and writing management packs and reports.

Dedication

To Eric, Dawn, and Ethan.

Acknowledgments

Writing a book is an all-encompassing and time-consuming project, and this book certainly meets that description. The authors and contributors would like to offer their sincere appreciation to all those who helped with *System Center Service Manager 2010 Unleashed*. This includes Acceleres for dedicating lab resources, Bryan Anthony for his assistance with the lab, Sean Christensen and Chris Lauren of Microsoft, Peter Quagliariello, Anders Ravnholt, and Pete Zerger.

We would also like to thank our spouses and significant others for their patience and understanding during the many hours spent on the book. Thank you Helene Daamen, Ilse Klaassen, Karolien Botterman, Malin Bengtsson, Maria Sundqvist, Mary Clare Henry, Monique Landman, Nichole Wright, and Stan Liebowitz.

In addition, a very special thanks to Oskar Landman for his work at the 11th hour, so to speak; and to his wife Monique, and children Noah and Maya for their support.

Thanks also go to the staff at Pearson, in particular to Neil Rowe, who has worked with us since *Microsoft Operations Manager 2005 Unleashed* (Sams, 2006).

We Want to Hear from You!

As the reader of this book, *you* are our most important critic and commentator. We value your opinion and want to know what we're doing right, what we could do better, what areas you'd like to see us publish in, and any other words of wisdom you're willing to pass our way.

You can email or write me directly to let me know what you did or didn't like about this book—as well as what we can do to make our books stronger.

Please note that I cannot help you with technical problems related to the topic of this book, and that due to the high volume of mail I receive, I might not be able to reply to every message.

When you write, please be sure to include this book's title and author as well as your name and phone or email address. I will carefully review your comments and share them with the author and editors who worked on the book.

Email: feedback@samspublishing.com

Mail: Neil Rowe
         Executive Editor
         Sams Publishing
         800 East 96th Street
         Indianapolis, IN 46240 USA

Reader Services

Visit our website and register this book at informit.com/register for convenient access to any updates, downloads, or errata that might be available for this book.

Foreword

Service Manager 2010 is without a doubt the most customizable and extensible product in the System Center suite. The ability to customize and extend the product is enabled by the common technology platform born in Operations Manager that now underlies other Microsoft products such as System Center Essentials, Windows InTune, Virtual Machine Manager, and now Service Manager. The platform was substantially extended in the Service Manager 2010 development lifecycle to meet the requirements of an IT service management product. Thus, while Service Manager 2010 itself is a first generation product, the core platform is fifth generation, preceded by MOM 2000, MOM 2005, Operations Manager 2007, and Operations Manager 2007 R2. This book is all about how to harness the power of that rich platform and unleash Service Manager.

In the past four years, I have visited with many customers and heard the requirements of many others by speaking with our implementation partners. One requirement is universal—customizability! Some customers will use Service Manager for incident management. Other will use it just for change or configuration management. One thing for certain: No two customers have the same processes, the data storage requirements, or regulations. No one uses Service Manager as is out of the box without substantial modification.

When I first joined the product team, there was a debate whether Service Manager was a platform or a set of solutions—configuration, incident, change, and problem management. Knowing every customer was different; the platform proponents wanted to spend most of our time building a highly customizable platform and very little time providing for solutions out of the box. The solutions proponents felt we just needed to build a product with lots of features designed around ITIL or MOF best practices. The reality— we needed to do both! We needed to provide immediate value out of the box to enable customers to adopt ITIL and MOF, but also needed to be adaptable to match the customers' processes and configuration management database (CMDB) data storage requirements.

Early in the development cycle, Microsoft hired David Pultorak (one of the authors of this book) to write a marketing white paper about Service Manager 2010 for an upcoming Microsoft Management Summit. Being new to the product, David stopped by to get an idea of what it was all about. On my whiteboard, I drew two boxes, one on top of the other. I labeled the bottom box "Platform" and the top box "Solutions." Inside the Platform box I drew several smaller boxes and labeled them model-based database, extensible data warehouse, reporting platform, role based security, notification platform, workflow engine, application programming interface (API), and management pack infrastructure. In the Solutions box, I drew circles for configuration, incident, problem, knowledge, and change management. (Today, as we are working on Service Manager 2012, I would add circles for release and service request management.) David produced a Visio diagram of this whiteboard drawing that was included in the white paper and many other PowerPoint presentations. I still see this diagram in many presentations today. It is the essence of Service Manager—customizable platform + solutions on top.

This book covers each of the solutions provided out of the box in detail, but more importantly shows you how to use the platform capabilities to extend and adapt the solutions to meet your requirements.

You can do just about anything with Service Manager provided you have the skills and knowledge to do it. One Microsoft product engineering team adapted Service Manager to be their test automation platform. They use the workflow engine to automatically execute their tests, and extended the database and user interface to store and display test results and to schedule test runs. Custom reports were written on top of the data warehouse and reporting platform to show test results over time. The possibilities are endless, and I'm excited to see what possibilities become realities after you become more knowledgeable and skillful from reading this book.

Service Manager is what it is today because of an extraordinarily dedicated engineering team. Developers, testers, and program managers alike put in many, many long nights and weekends to deliver Service Manager as soon as possible, with the highest quality and maximum capability possible. It has been my pleasure and honor to work with these passionate professionals these last four years. As individuals, we may not always have agreed on how to do something or what was most important, but one thing was always for sure—we all cared deeply about the product we were working on and wanted to do the best we could for our customers and partners. Out of that constant conflict of ideas and opinions, we forged a v1 product—something not many people can lay claim to. I'm proud of the product we built and even prouder of the way we all worked diligently together as a team. I'm very excited about the future of Service Manager as we continue to build on top of a solid foundation.

Lastly, I would like to thank the co-authors and contributors of this book—all Service Manager superstars in the community. Service Manager would not be as successful as it is today without them sharing their knowledge freely in the community and helping others get started. Gathering all of their collective knowledge into one place like this book will make it even easier to do amazing things with Service Manager.

See you out there in the Service Manager community!

Travis Wright, Senior Program Manager
Microsoft Corporation

Introduction

In May 2010, Microsoft announced the release of Service Manager 2010. This first version of the product was a long time in coming, having been revamped considerably since early testing in 2006 as the previously code-named Service Desk product. Service Manager 2010 rounds out System Center's focus on Information Technology Information Library (ITIL) and Microsoft Operations Framework (MOF) by adding centralized incident, problem, and change management capabilities to the product suite. Service Manager's level of integration with ITIL and MOF is unique in the System Center suite.

Service Manager is unique for other reasons: the fact that it touches so many different types of individual in an organization, and because of its high level of integration with other products in the System Center suite in addition to Active Directory. Service Manager 2010 offers the potential of an integrated configuration management database (CMDB) through connectors with Active Directory, Operations Manager, and Configuration Manager, enabling it to become a centralized repository of information. By unifying knowledge across System Center, Service Manager can help IT align to business needs while lowering time to resolution. Service Manager provides built-in processes based on industry best practices for incident and problem resolution, change control, and asset life cycle management.

Service Manager delivers integration, efficiency, and business alignment of the data center's IT services by

- ▶ Optimizing processes and ensuring their use through templates guiding IT analysts through best practices for Incident, Process, and Change Management

- ▶ Reducing resolution times by cutting across organizational silos, ensuring the right information from incident, problem, change, or asset records is accessible through a single pane

- ▶ Extending the value of the Microsoft platform with automated generation of incidents from alerts and coordinating activities among System Center products

- ▶ Enabling decision making through its data warehouse, integrating knowledge from disparate systems, delivering out-of-the-box reporting, and providing flexible data analysis through SQL Server Reporting Services

When work first commenced on this book, Service Manager 2010 was released and had its first service pack in the offing. Microsoft planned to round out the product with a R2 release in 2011, which would also be covered as part of the book. Things changed. At the 2011 Microsoft Management Summit, Microsoft announced that Service Manager 2010 R2 would be renamed and released as Service Manager 2012, thus aligning the Service Manager product cycle with the rest of the System Center suite. This announcement led the authoring team to rethink the book, removing topics planned with the R2 release and material that would be changing significantly with the 2012 version. *System Center Service Manager 2010 Unleashed* focuses on the core components of Service Manager 2010: its relationship to MOF and ITIL, integration with other System Center components, design, planning, installation, how it works, and extensibility. Because of the high level of integration with ITIL, you will find that a number of chapters focus on process.

This book is divided into six sections:

Part I, "Service Manager Overview and Concepts," introduces service management and the product and discusses its history, concepts, its relationship to MOF and ITIL, and architectural design. These topics are discussed in Chapter 1, "Service Management Basics," Chapter 2, "Service Manager 2010 Overview, Chapter 3, "MOF, ITIL, and Service Manager," and Chapter 4, "Looking Inside Service Manager."

Part II, "Planning and Installation," steps through product design, planning, and installation. Chapter 5, "Designing Service Manager," discusses envisioning and planning for Service Manager 2010, including licensing considerations. Chapter 6, "Planning Complex Configurations," delves into more advanced physical design considerations; and Chapter 7, "Installing Service Manager 2010," steps through the installation process.

Part III, "Service Manager Operations," focuses on Service Manager operations and processes in your environment. This includes Chapter 8, "Using Service Manager," Chapter 9, "Business Services," Chapter 10, "Incident Management," Chapter 11, "Problem Management," Chapter 12, "Change Management," and Chapter 13, "IT Management: Governance, Risk Management, and Compliance," which discusses the IT GRC Process management pack.

Part IV, "Administering Service Manager," includes Chapter 14, "Notification," and Chapter 15, "Service Manager Security." These chapters discuss those key functionalities and their use in Service Manager.

Part V, "Beyond Service Manager," looks at going beyond the box. As Travis Wright mentions in the Foreword, Service Manager is extremely customizable and extensible, with no two installations using it the same way. This section includes Chapter 16, "Planning Your Customization," Chapter 17, "Management Packs," Chapter 18, "Customizing Service Manager," Chapter 19, "Advanced Customization Scenarios," and Chapter 20, "Reports, Dashboards, and Data Analysis."

By this time, you should have at your disposal all the tools necessary to become a Service Manager expert. **Part VI** of the book includes two appendixes. Appendix A, "Reference URLs," incorporates useful references you can access for further information, and Appendix B, "Available Online," is a guide to supplementary resources offered with the book that you can download from Pearson's website at http://www.informit.com/store/product.aspx?isbn=0672334364.

Throughout, this book provides in-depth reference and technical information about System Center Service Manager 2010, as well as information about other products and technologies on which its features and components depend.

PART I

Service Manager
Overview and Concepts

IN THIS PART

Service Management Basics

System Center Service Manager 2010, a new addition to the Microsoft System Center suite, is an integrated platform for automating and adapting Information Technology service management (ITSM) best practices, such as those found in the Information Technology Infrastructure Library (ITIL) and Microsoft Operations Framework (MOF), to your organization's requirements. Service Manager provides built-in processes for incident resolution, problem resolution, change control, and configuration management.

Service Manager is a help desk and change management tool. By using its configuration management database (CMDB) and process integration, Service Manager automatically connects knowledge and information from System Center Operations Manager (OpsMgr), System Center Configuration Manager (ConfigMgr), and Active Directory (AD) Domain Services. Service Manager provides the following capabilities to deliver integration, efficiency, and business alignment for your Information Technology (IT) services:

▶ **Integrating process and knowledge across the System Center suite:** Through its integration capabilities with Operations Manager and Configuration Manager, Service Manager provides an integrated service management platform. This helps to reduce downtime and improve the quality of services in the data center.

▶ **Providing an accurate and relevant knowledge base:** Knowledge base information resides in the CMDB and contains the product and user knowledge to enable IT analysts to quickly identify and resolve incidents. Users can use the Self-Service portal (SSP) to search the knowledge base for information to help find solutions to issues. An organization can create and manage its own knowledge base articles and make this information accessible to both IT analysts and end users.

▶ **Lowering costs and improving responsiveness:** Service Manager's capabilities can improve user productivity and satisfaction, while reducing support costs using the SSP and increasing confidence in meeting compliance requirements with the IT GRC (governance, risk, and compliance) Process management pack.

▶ **Improving business alignment:** Service Manager helps your organization align to its business goals and adapt to new requirements through its configuration management, compliance, risk management, reporting, and analysis capabilities.

▶ **Delivering immediate value with built-in process management packs:** Included with Service Manager are core process management packs for incident and problem resolution, change control, and configuration and knowledge management.

This chapter introduces System Center Service Manager 2010. Various abbreviations for the product include SCSM, SM, Service Manager, and SvcMgr; this book uses the nomenclature of Service Manager and SvcMgr. Service Manager provides user-centric support, enables data center management efficiency, and enables you to align to your organization's business goals and adapt to ever-changing business requirements.

Ten Reasons to Use Service Manager

Why should you use Service Manager 2010 in the first place? How does this make your daily life easier? Although this book covers the features and benefits of Service Manager in detail, it definitely helps to have a general idea about why Service Manager is worth a look!

Let's look at 10 compelling reasons why you might want to use Service Manager:

1. Your support desk is overwhelmed with manually entering user requests (24x7).

2. You realize help desk management would be much simpler if you had visibility and information for all your systems on a single console.

3. You discover email is down when upper management calls the help desk. Although this mechanism is actually quite effective in getting your attention, it is somewhat stress inducing and not particularly proactive.

4. You would be more productive if you weren't dealing with user issues all day... and night... and during lunch and vacation.

5. The bulk of your department's budget pays for teams of contractors to manage user support and the help desk.

6. You are tired of going through each of your servers looking for reports you need on your client, server, physical, and virtual environments.

7. Your system admins are patching and updating production systems during business hours, often bringing down servers in the process.

8. By the time you update your user documentation, everything has changed, and you have to start all over again!

9. You can't stay on top of adapting to your organization's business needs when you're not sure of your current capabilities.

10. You don't have the time to write down all the troubleshooting information that is in your brain, and your boss is concerned you might be hit by a truck (or want to take that vacation). This probably is not the best way to support end users.

While somewhat tongue-in-cheek, these topics represent very real problems for many IT managers and support staff. If you are one of those individuals, you owe to it yourself to explore how you can leverage Service Manager to solve many of these common issues. These pain points are common to almost all users of Microsoft technologies to some degree, and Service Manager holds solutions for all of them.

However, perhaps the most important reason for using Service Manager is the peace of mind it can bring you, knowing that you have complete visibility and control of your IT systems. The productivity this can bring to your organization is a tremendous benefit as well.

The Problem with Today's Systems

With increasing operational requirements unaccompanied by linear growth in IT staffing levels, organizations must continually find ways to streamline administration through tools and automation. Today's IT systems are prone to a number of problems from the perspective of service management, including the following:

▶ Configuration "shift and drift"

▶ System isolation

▶ Lack of historical information

▶ Not enough expertise

▶ Missing incidents and information

▶ Lack of process consistency

▶ Not meeting service level expectations

This list should not be surprising, because these problems manifest themselves in all IT shops with varying degrees of severity. In fact, Forrester Research estimates that 82% of larger shops are pursuing service management, and 67% are planning to increase Windows management. Let's look at what the issues are.

Why Do Systems Go Down?

Let's start with examining reasons why systems go down. Figure 1.1 illustrates reasons for system outages, based on the authors' personal experiences and observations, and the following list describes some of these reasons:

- ▶ **Software errors:** Software is responsible for somewhat less than half the errors. These errors include software coding errors, software integration errors, data corruption, and such.

- ▶ **User errors:** End users and operators cause just fewer than half the errors. This includes incorrectly configuring systems, failing to catch warning messages that turn into errors, accidents, unplugging the power cord, and so on.

- ▶ **Miscellaneous errors:** This last category is fairly small. Causes of problems here include disk crashes, power outages, viruses, natural disasters, and so on.

As Figure 1.1 demonstrates, the vast majority of failures result from software-level errors and user errors. It is surprising to note that hardware failures account for only a small percentage of problems, which is a tribute to modern systems such as redundant array of independent disks (RAID), clustering, and other mechanisms deployed to provide server and application redundancy.

The numbers show that to reduce system downtime, you need to attack the software and user error components of the equation. That is where you will get the most "bang for the buck."

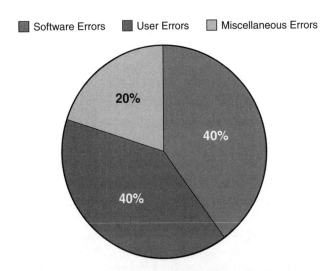

FIGURE 1.1   Causes of System Outages. D. Scott, in a May 2002 presentation titled *Operation Zero Downtime*, discussed similar statistics at a Gartner Group Security Conference.

Configuration "Shift and Drift"

Even in IT organizations with well-defined and documented change management, procedures fall short of perfection. Unplanned and unwanted changes frequently find their way into the environment, sometimes as an unintended side effect of an approved, scheduled change.

You might be familiar with an old philosophical question: If a tree falls in a forest and no one is around to hear it, does it make a sound?

Here's the change management equivalent: If a change is made on a system and no one is around to hear it, does identifying it make a difference?

The answer to this question is absolutely "yes." After all, every change to a system can potentially impact the functionality or security of a system, or that system's adherence to corporate or regulatory compliance.

For example, adding a feature to a web application component may affect the application binaries by potentially overwriting files or settings replaced by a critical security patch. Or perhaps the engineer implementing the change sees a setting he thinks is misconfigured and decides to just "fix" it while already working on the system. In an e-commerce scenario, where sensitive customer data is involved, this could have potentially devastating consequences. Not to mention that troubleshooting something you don't know was changed is like looking for the proverbial needle in a haystack.

At the end of the day, your management platform must bring a strong element of baseline configuration monitoring and enforcement to ensure configuration standards are implemented and maintained with the required consistency.

System Isolation

Microsoft Windows Server and the applications that run on it expose a wealth of information with event logs, performance counters, and application-specific logs. However, this data is isolated and typically server centric—making it difficult to determine what and where a problem really is. To get a handle on your systems, you need to take actions to prevent the situation shown in Figure 1.2, where you have multiple islands of information.

Here are places you might find isolated information:

- ▸ **Event logs:** Events are generated by the Windows operating system, components, and applications. The logs include errors, warnings, information, and security auditing events. These event logs are stored locally on each server.

- ▸ **Performance counters:** The Windows operating system and multiple applications expose detailed performance information through performance counters. The data includes processor utilization, memory utilization, network statistics, disk free space, and thousands of other pieces of information. This information can help with forecasting performance trends and identifying response issues that can affect application availability.

▶ **Windows Management Instrumentation (WMI):** WMI provides access to an incredible amount of information, ranging from high-level status of services to detailed hardware information.

▶ **Expertise:** Consultants, engineers, and subject matter experts have information locked up in their heads or written down on whiteboards and paper napkins. This is as much an island of information as the statistics and data stored on any computer.

FIGURE 1.2   Multiple islands of information.

Although system information is captured through event logs, performance counters, file-based logs, and experiences, it is typically lost over time. Most logs roll over, are erased to clear space, or eventually overwritten. Even if the information is not ultimately lost or forgotten, it typically is not reviewed regularly.

Most application information is also server centric, typically stored on the server, and specific to the server where that application resides. There is no built-in, systemwide, cross-system view of critical information.

Having islands of information, where data is stranded on any given island, makes it difficult to get to needed information in a timely or effective manner. Not having that information can make managing user satisfaction a difficult endeavor.

Lack of Historical Information

Sometimes you may capture information about problems but are unable to look back in time to see whether this is an isolated instance or part of a recurring pattern. An incident can be a onetime blip or can indicate an underlying issue. Without having a historical context, it is difficult to understand the significance of any particular incident.

Here's an example: Suppose that a consultant is brought in to review why a database application has performance problems. To prove there is an issue, the in-house IT staff points out that users are complaining about performance but the memory and CPU on the database server are only 50% utilized. By itself, this does not indicate anything. It could be that memory and the CPU are normally 65% utilized and the problem is really a network utilization problem, which in turn is reducing the load on the other resources. The problem could even be a newly implemented but poorly written application! A historical context could provide useful information.

As an expert, the consultant develops a hypothesis and tests it, which takes time and costs money. Instead of trying to solve a problem, many IT shops just throw more hardware resources at it—only to find that this does not necessarily improve performance. With historical records, they would see that system utilization actually dropped at the same time that users started complaining, and could look elsewhere to find the problem. Ideally, you would have historical information for troubleshooting and detecting trends.

Lack of Expertise

Do you lack the in-house expertise needed to support users calling the help desk? Is your documentation inadequate, and do you lack the knowledge to keep it current? Do you pay an arm and a leg to have contractors manage user support and expectations?

If the expertise you need is not available for those areas needing attention, you can incur additional costs and even potential downtime. This can translate to loss of user productivity, system outages, and ultimately higher operational costs if emergency measures are required to resolve problems.

Missing Incidents and Information

Sometimes problems are detected by what occurred elsewhere. The information being reported to your operations and change management systems can affect system availability and user satisfaction. If that information is not available to the help desk, it might as well be an isolated island of information.

One of the primary jobs of support personnel is incident detection and recording. A complete service management solution needs the capability to capture information occurring throughout your data center to generate trouble tickets as appropriate and manage user expectations as necessary, providing efficient and responsive support for end users. The CMDB must provide the information required for analysts to resolve issues quickly. Without the capability to integrate information from throughout your IT organization, the help desk is severely handicapped in the quality of support it can provide to its customers.

Reported incidents can also disappear from sight by not being assigned to an owner. Your service management solution must be able to track information from the time it enters the system until the problem is resolved and the issue closed.

Lack of Process Consistency

Many IT organizations still "fly by the seat of their pants" in terms of identifying and resolving problems. Using standard procedures and a methodology helps minimize risk and solve issues faster.

A *methodology* is a framework of processes and procedures used by those who work in a discipline. You can look at a methodology as a structured process that defines the who, what, where, when, and why of your operations, and the procedures to use when defining problems, solutions, and courses of action.

When employing a standard set of processes, it is important to ensure that the framework that is adopted adheres to accepted industry standards or best practices and takes into account the requirements of the business to ensure continuity between expectations and the services delivered by the IT organization. Consistent use of a repeatable and measurable set of practices allows an organization to quantify their progress more accurately to facilitate adjustment of processes as necessary to improve future results. The most effective IT organizations build an element of self-examination into their service management strategy to ensure processes can be incrementally improved or modified to meet the changing needs of the business.

With IT's continually increased role in running successful business operations, having a structured and standard way to define IT operations aligned to the needs of the business is critical when meeting expectations of business stakeholders. This alignment results in improved business relationships where business units engage IT as a partner in developing and delivering innovations to drive business results.

Not Meeting Service Level Expectations

What is customer satisfaction? It's all about perception. Customer satisfaction is not necessarily about objective quality of service; it is how your customer (end user and the business) sees that quality. There will be times that your users see the service as much better than it is, and also times when that service is perceived as much worse than it is in reality—usually due to bad communication or from isolated cases that have high visibility.

Keeping your end users satisfied is about providing excellent services, but it is also about managing their expectations about what excellent services actually are.

```
End-user satisfaction = Perception - Expectation
```

The expectation part of this equation is managed by your service level agreements (SLAs) and how well you meet them. The goal of service level management is ensuring that the agreed level of IT service is provided and that any future services will be delivered as agreed upon. An SLA is just a document; service level management—the process that creates that document—helps IT and the business you support understand each other.

If you have not established expectations, you will not be able to satisfy your end users as to the quality of the service IT is providing, and you will not be perceived as a valuable part of the business.

What It's All About

It can be intimidating when you consider the fact that the problems described to this point could happen even in an ostensibly "managed" environment. However, these examples just serve to illustrate that the very processes used for service management must themselves be reviewed periodically and updated to accommodate changes in tools and technologies employed from the desktop to the data center. By not correlating data across systems, being aware of potential issues, maintaining a history of past performance and problems, and so on, IT shops open themselves up to putting out fires and fighting time bombs (see Figure 1.3) that could be prevented by using a more systematic approach to service management, which is described in the next section.

FIGURE 1.3   Fighting fires.

Service Management Defined

ITSM is a discipline for managing information IT systems, philosophically centered on the customer's perspective of IT's contribution to the business. As such, it stands in deliberate contrast to technology-centered approaches to IT management and business interaction.

ITSM is process focused and has ties and common interests with process improvement movement (for example, Total Quality Management [TQM], Six Sigma, Business Process Management, and Capability Maturity Model Integration [CMMI]) frameworks and methodologies. Instead of being concerned with the details of how to use a particular vendor's product or the technical details of the systems under management, service management focuses on providing a framework to structure IT-related activities and the interactions of IT technical personnel with business customers and users. Achieving this calls for coordination between technology, processes, and people, resulting in improved quality and productivity, as depicted in the IT service triangle shown in Figure 1.4.

FIGURE 1.4   The IT service triangle.

Evolution of the CMDB

A configuration management database is a repository of information related to all the components of an information system. Configuration management itself focuses on establishing and maintaining consistency of a system or product's performance and its functional and physical attributes with its requirements, design, and operational information throughout its life cycle. A CMDB contains configuration item (CI) information and is used to understand the CI relationships and track their configuration.

The term CMDB stems from ITIL v2 (in ITIL v3, it is now known as a *configuration management system*, or CMS), where it represents the authorized configuration of the significant components of the IT environment. A CMDB helps an organization understand the relationships between these components and track their configuration. The CMDB is a fundamental component of the ITIL framework's Configuration Management process. CMDB implementations often involve federation, the inclusion of data into the CMDB from other sources. Information in a CMDB is typically used for planning, identification, control, monitoring, and verification.

The Service Manager CMDB is a database containing details of configuration items and details of the important relationships between the configuration items. These CIs have relationships that capture, record, and provide output about the status, urgency, historical changes, and the impact of data between CIs.

Service Manager uses its CMDB and process integration to connect knowledge and information from Operations Manager, Configuration Manager, and Active Directory Domain Services. In this manner, it orchestrates and unifies knowledge across the System Center suite.

Strategies for Service Management

Microsoft uses a multifaceted approach to service management. This strategy includes advancements in the following areas:

▶ Adoption of a model-based management strategy (a component of the Dynamic Systems Initiative, discussed in "Microsoft's Dynamic Systems Initiative," the next section of this chapter) to implement synthetic transaction technology. Service Manager 2010 is intended to deliver a service-based monitoring set of scenarios, enabling you to define models of services to deliver to end users using a *service map*: a combination of Operation Manager's distributed application functionality with Service Manager business services.

▶ Using an Infrastructure Optimization (IO) Model as a framework for aligning IT with business needs and as a standard for expressing an organization's maturity in service management. The "Optimizing Your Infrastructure" section of this chapter discusses the IO Model further. The IO Model describes your IT infrastructure in terms of cost, security risk, and operational agility.

▶ Supporting a standard Web Services specification for system management. WS-Management is a specification of a Simple Object Access Protocol (SOAP)-based protocol, based on Web Services, used to manage servers, devices, and applications. The intent is to provide a universal language that all types of devices can use to share data about themselves, which in turn makes them more easily managed. Microsoft has included support for WS-Management beginning with Windows Vista and Windows Server 2008, and it is leveraged by multiple System Center components.

▶ Building complete management solutions on this infrastructure, either through making them available in the operating system or by using management products such as Service Manager, Operations Manager, Configuration Manager, and other components of the System Center family.

▶ Continuing to make Windows easier to manage by providing core management infrastructure and capabilities in the Windows platform itself, allowing business and management application developers to improve their infrastructures and capabilities. Microsoft believes that improving the manageability of solutions built on Windows Server System will be a key driver shaping the future of Windows management.

Microsoft's Dynamic Systems Initiative

A large percentage of IT departments' budgets and resources typically focuses on mundane maintenance tasks such as applying software patches or monitoring the health of a network, without leaving the staff with the time or energy to focus on more exhilarating (and more productive) strategic initiatives.

The Dynamic Systems Initiative, or DSI, is a Microsoft and industry strategy intended to enhance the Windows platform, delivering a coordinated set of solutions that simplify simplifies and automates how businesses design, deploy, and operate their distributed systems. Using DSI helps IT and developers create operationally aware platforms. By designing systems that are more manageable and automating operations, organizations can reduce costs and proactively address their priorities.

DSI is about building software that enables knowledge of an IT system to be created, modified, transferred, and operated on throughout the life cycle of that system. It is a commitment from Microsoft and its partners to help IT teams capture and use knowledge to design systems that are more manageable and to automate operations, which in turn reduces costs and gives organizations additional time to focus proactively on what is most important. By innovating across applications, development tools, the platform, and management solutions, DSI will result in the following:

▶ Increased productivity and reduced costs across all aspects of IT

▶ Increased responsiveness to changing business needs

▶ Reduced time and effort required to develop, deploy, and manage applications

Microsoft positions DSI as the connector of the entire system and service life cycles.

Microsoft Product Integration

DSI focuses on automating data center operational jobs and reducing associated labor though self-managing systems. Here are several examples where Microsoft products and tools integrate with DSI:

▶ Operations Manager uses the application knowledge captured in management packs to simplify identifying issues and their root causes, facilitating resolution and restoring services or preventing potential outages, and providing intelligent management at the system level.

▶ Configuration Manager uses model-based configuration baseline templates in its Desired Configuration Management feature to automate identification of undesired shifts in system configurations.

▶ Service Manager uses model-based management packs. You can easily add new models describing your own configuration items or work items to track their life cycle. Each data model is stored in one or more management packs that make up the model.

▶ Visual Studio is a model-based development tool that leverages Service Modeling Language (SML), enabling operations managers and application architects to collaborate early in the development phase and ensure applications are modeled with operational requirements in mind.

▶ Windows Server Update Services (WSUS) enables greater and more efficient administrative control through modeling technology that enables downstream systems to construct accurate models representing their current state, available updates, and installed software.

SDM AND SML: WHAT'S THE DIFFERENCE?

Microsoft originally used the System Definition Model (SDM) as its standard schema with DSI. SDM was a proprietary specification put forward by Microsoft. The company later decided to implement SML, which is an industrywide published specification used in heterogeneous environments. Using SML helps DSI adoption by incorporating a standard that Microsoft's partners can understand and apply across mixed platforms. SML is discussed later in the section "The Role of Service Modeling Language in IT Operations."

DSI focuses on automating data center operations and reducing total cost of ownership (TCO) though self-managing systems. Can logic be implemented in management software so the software can identify system or application issues in real time and then dynamically take actions to mitigate the problem? Consider the scenario where, without operator intervention, a management system moves a virtual machine running a line-of-business application because the existing host is experiencing an extended spike in resource utilization. This is actually a reality today, delivered in the quick migration feature of Virtual Machine Manager. DSI aims to extend this type of self-healing and self-management to other areas of operations.

In support of DSI, Microsoft has invested heavily in three major areas:

▶ **Systems designed for management:** Microsoft is delivering development and authoring tools, such as Visual Studio, that enable businesses to capture the knowledge of everyone from business users and project managers to the architects, developers, testers, and operations staff using models. By capturing and embedding this knowledge into the infrastructure, organizations can reduce support complexity and cost.

▶ **An operationally aware platform:** The core Windows operating system and its related technologies are critical when solving everyday operational and service challenges. This requires designing the operating system services for manageability. In addition, the operating system and server products must provide rich instrumentation and hardware resource virtualization support.

▶ **Virtualized applications and server infrastructure:** Virtualization of servers and applications improves the agility of the organization by simplifying the effort involved in modifying, adding, or removing the resources a service utilizes in performing work.

THE MICROSOFT SUITE FOR SYSTEM MANAGEMENT

End-to-end automation could include update management, availability and performance monitoring, change and configuration management, and rich reporting services. Microsoft's System Center is a family of system management products and solutions that focuses on providing you with the knowledge and tools to manage and support your IT infrastructure. The objective of the System Center family is to create an integrated suite of systems management tools and technologies, thus helping to ease operations, reduce troubleshooting time, and improve planning capabilities.

The Importance of DSI

Three architectural elements underpin the DSI initiative:

▶ That developers have tools (such as Visual Studio) to design applications in a way that makes them easier for administrators to manage after those applications are in production

▶ That Microsoft products can be secured and updated in a uniform way

▶ That Microsoft server applications are optimized for management, to take advantage of System Center

DSI represents a departure from the traditional approach to systems management. DSI focuses on designing for operations from the application development stage, rather than a more customary operations perspective that concentrates on automating task-based processes. This strategy highlights the fact that the DSI is about building software that enables knowledge of an IT system to be created, modified, transferred, and used throughout the life cycle of a system. DSI's core principles of knowledge, models, and the life cycle are key in addressing the challenges of complexity and manageability faced by IT organizations. By capturing knowledge and incorporating health models, DSI can facilitate easier troubleshooting and maintenance, and thus lower TCO.

The Role of Service Modeling Language in IT Operations

A key underlying component of DSI is the eXtensible Markup Language (XML)-based specification called the Service Modeling Language. SML is a standard developed by several leading IT companies that defines a consistent way for infrastructure and application architects to define how applications, infrastructure, and services are modeled in a consistent way.

SML facilitates modeling systems from a development, deployment, and support perspective with modular, reusable building blocks that eliminate the need to reinvent the wheel when describing and defining a new service. The end result is systems that are easier to develop, implement, manage, and maintain, resulting in reduced TCO to the organization. SML is a core technology that will continue to play a prominent role in future products developed to support the ongoing objectives of DSI.

IT Infrastructure Library and Microsoft Operations Framework

ITIL is widely accepted as an international standard of best practices for operations management. MOF is closely related to ITIL, and both describe best practices for IT service management processes. The next sections introduce you to ITIL and MOF, described in greater detail in Chapter 3, "MOF, ITIL, and Service Manager." Warning: Fasten your seatbelt, because this is where the fun really begins!

What Is ITIL?

As part of Microsoft's management approach, the company relied on an international standards-setting body as its basis for developing an operational framework. The British Office of Government Commerce (OGC) provides best practices advice and guidance on using IT in service management and operations. The OGC also publishes the IT Infrastructure Library, commonly known as ITIL.

ITIL provides a cohesive set of best practices for ITSM. These best practices include a series of books giving direction and guidance on provisioning quality IT services and facilities needed to support IT. The documents are maintained by the OGC and supported by publications, qualifications, and an international users group.

Started in the 1980s, ITIL is under constant development by a consortium of industry IT leaders. The ITIL covers a number of areas and is primarily focused on ITSM; its ITIL is considered to be the most consistent and comprehensive documentation of best practices for ITSM worldwide.

ITSM, introduced in the "Service Management Defined" section, is a business-driven, customer-centric approach to managing IT. It specifically addresses the strategic business value generated by IT and the need to deliver high-quality IT services to one's business organization. Here are the key objectives of ITSM:

▶ Align IT services with current and future needs of the business and its customers

▶ Improve the quality of IT services delivered

▶ Reduce long-term costs of providing services

MORE ABOUT ITIL

The core books for version 3 (ITIL v3) were published on June 30, 2007. With v3, ITIL has adopted an integrated service life cycle approach to ITSM, as opposed to organizing itself around the concepts of IT service delivery and support.

ITIL v2 was a more targeted product, explicitly designed to bridge the gap between technology and business, with a strong process focus on effective service support and delivery. The v3 documents recognize the service management challenges brought about by advancements in technology, such as virtualization and outsourcing, and emerging challenges for service providers. The v3 framework emphasizes managing the life cycle of the services provided by IT and the importance of creating business value, rather than just executing processes.

There are five core volumes of ITIL v3:

- ▶ **Service Strategy:** This volume identifies market opportunities for which services could be developed to meet a requirement on the part of internal or external customers. Key areas here are service portfolio management and financial management.

- ▶ **Service Design:** This volume focuses on the activities that take place to develop the strategy into a design document that addresses all aspects of the proposed service and the processes intended to support it. Key areas of this volume are availability management, capacity management, continuity management, and security management.

- ▶ **Service Transition:** This volume centers on implementing the output of service design activities and creating a production service (or modifying an existing service). There is some overlap between Service Transition and Service Operation, the next volume. Key areas of the Service Transition volume are change management, release management, configuration management, and service knowledge management.

- ▶ **Service Operation:** This volume involves the activities required to operate the services and maintain their functionality as defined in SLAs with one's customers. Key areas here are incident management, problem management, and request fulfillment.

- ▶ **Continual Service Improvement:** This volume focuses on the ability to deliver continual improvement to the quality of the services that the IT organization delivers to the business. Key areas include service reporting, service measurement, and service level management.

Updates to ITIL v3 are currently expected the latter part of 2011.

Philosophically speaking, ITSM focuses on the customer's perspective of IT's contribution to the business, which is analogous to the objectives of other frameworks in terms of their consideration of alignment of IT service support and delivery with business goals in mind.

Although ITIL describes the what, when, and why of IT operations, it stops short of describing how a specific activity should be carried out. A driving force behind its development was the recognition that organizations are increasingly dependent on IT for satisfying their corporate objectives relating to both internal and external customers, which increases the requirement for high-quality IT services. Many large IT organizations realize that the road to a customer-centric service organization runs along an ITIL framework.

ITIL also specifies keeping measurements or metrics to assess performance over time. Measurements can include a variety of statistics, such as the number and severity of service outages, along with the amount of time it takes to restore service. These metrics or key performance indicators (KPIs) can be used to quantify to management how well IT is performing. This information can prove to be particularly useful for justifying resources during the next budget process!

What Is MOF?

ITIL is generally accepted as the "best practices" for the industry. Being technology agnostic, it is a foundation that can be adopted and adapted to meet the specific needs of various IT organizations. Although Microsoft chose to adopt ITIL as a standard for its own IT operations for its descriptive guidance, Microsoft designed MOF to provide prescriptive guidance for effective design, implementation, and support of Microsoft technologies.

MOF is a set of publications providing both descriptive (what to do, when, and why) and prescriptive (how to do) guidance on ITSM. The key focus in developing MOF was providing a framework specifically geared toward managing Microsoft technologies. Microsoft created the first version of the MOF in 1999. The latest iteration of MOF (version 4) is designed to further

- ▶ Update MOF to include the full end-to-end IT service life cycle.

- ▶ Let IT governance serve as the foundation of the life cycle.

- ▶ Provide useful, easily consumable best practice-based guidance.

- ▶ Simplify and consolidate service management functions (SMFs), emphasizing workflows, decisions, outcomes, and roles.

MOF v4 now incorporates Microsoft's previously existing Microsoft Solutions Framework (MSF) in its Deliver Phase, providing guidance for application development solutions. The combined framework provides guidance throughout the IT life cycle, as shown in Figure 1.5.

At its core, the MOF is a collection of best practices, principles, and models. It provides direction to achieve reliability, availability, supportability, and manageability of mission-critical production systems, focusing on solutions and services using Microsoft products and technologies. MOF extends ITIL by including guidance and best practices derived from the experience of Microsoft's internal operations groups, partners, and customers worldwide. MOF aligns with and builds on the ITSM practices documented within ITIL, thus enhancing the supportability built on Microsoft's products and technologies.

MOF uses a model that describes Microsoft's approach to IT operations and the service management life cycle. The model organizes the ITIL volumes of service strategy, service design, service transition, service operation, and continual service improvement, and includes additional MOF processes in the MOF components, which are illustrated in Figure 1.6.

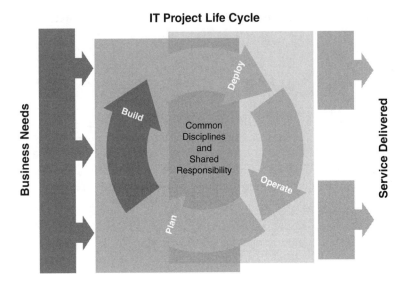

FIGURE 1.5   The IT life cycle.

FIGURE 1.6   The IT life cycle, as described in MOF v4, has three life cycle phases and one functional layer operating throughout all the other phases.

TIP: USING MOF FOR SERVICE MANAGER DEPLOYMENT

Microsoft uses MOF to describe IT operations and uses the System Center suite as a tool to put that framework into practice. However, products such as Service Manager 2010 are also applications and, as such, best deployed using a disciplined approach. Although the MOF Deliver Phase is geared toward application development, it can be adapted to support infrastructure solution design and deployment, as discussed in Chapter 5, "Designing Service Manager."

It is important to note that the activities pictured in Figure 1.6 can occur simultaneously within an IT organization. Each area has a specific focus and tasks, and within each area are policies, procedures, standards, and best practices that support specific service management-focused tasks.

Service Manager 2010 can be employed to support tasks in the different top-level MOF components. Let's look briefly at each of these areas and see how one can use Service Manager to support MOF:

▶ **Plan:** This phase covers activities related to IT strategy, standards, policies, and finances. This is where the business and IT collaborate, to determine how IT can most effectively deliver services enabling the overall organization to succeed.

   Service Manager delivers services that support the business, enabling IT to change to meet business strategy and support the business in becoming more efficient.

▶ **Deliver:** This phase represents activities related to envisioning, planning, building, testing, and deploying IT service solutions. It takes a service solution from vision through deployment, ensuring you have a stable solution inline with business requirements and customer specifications.

   Using connectors, Service Manager can integrate information from other areas of System Center. The Configuration Manager connector integrates configuration item data about computers managed by Configuration Manager, while using the Operations Manager connector ensures that alerts reported by Operations Manager are tracked in Service Manager as incidents.

▶ **Operate:** This phase focuses on activities related to operating, monitoring, supporting, and addressing issues with IT services. It ensures that IT services function in line with SLA targets.

   Configuring incident SLAs in Service Manager provides a mechanism to set up customized reporting, notification, and escalation for incidents nearing an SLA breach. Service Manager also helps to ensure compliance and lower the risk of configuration errors with functionality that detects and remediates noncompliant configurations.

By implementing and automating trouble ticketing best practices, Service Manager provides the tools to streamline incident and problem management.

▶ **Manage:** This layer, operating continuously though the three phases, covers activities related to managing governance, risk, compliance, changes, configurations, and organizations. It promotes consistency and accountability in planning and delivering IT services, providing the basis for developing and operating a flexible and durable IT environment.

  The Manage layer establishes an approach to ITSM activities, which helps to coordinate the work of the SMFs in the three life cycle phases.

  Service Manager can assist IT with governance, risk management, and compliance through implementation of the IT GRC Process management pack, discussed in Chapter 13, "IT Management: Governance, Risk Management, and Compliance."

You can find additional information about the MOF at http://go.microsoft.com/fwlink/ ?LinkId=50015.

MOF Does Not Replace ITIL

Microsoft believes that ITIL is the leading body of knowledge of best practices. For that reason, it uses ITIL as the foundation for MOF. Instead of replacing ITIL, MOF complements it and is similar to ITIL in several ways:

▶ MOF (incorporating MSF) spans the entire IT life cycle.

▶ Both MOF and ITIL are based on best practices for IT management, drawing on the expertise of practitioners worldwide.

▶ The MOF body of knowledge is applicable across the business community (from small businesses to large enterprises). MOF also is not limited only to those using the Microsoft platform in a homogenous environment.

▶ As is the case with ITIL, MOF has expanded to be more than just a documentation set. In fact, MOF is now intertwined thoroughly with several System Center components, Service Manager, Configuration Manager, and Operations Manager!

In addition, Microsoft and its partners provide a variety of resources to support MOF principles and guidance, including self-assessments, IT management tools that incorporate MOF terminology and features, training programs and certification, and consulting services.

COBIT: A Framework for IT Governance and Control

Control Objectives for Information and related Technology (COBIT) is an IT governance framework and toolset developed by ISACA, the Information Systems Audit and Control Association. COBIT enables managers to bridge the gap between control requirements, technical issues, and business risks. It emphasizes regulatory compliance and helps organizations increase the value they obtain from IT. COBIT was first released in 1996, and is now at level 4.1, with COBIT 5 set for release in late 2011. Service Manager, which is the focal point in System Center for IT compliance, implements IT governance and compliance through the IT GRC Process management pack, discussed in Chapter 13.

Total Quality Management: TQM

The goal of Total Quality Management (TQM) is to continuously improve the quality of products and processes. It functions on the premise that the quality of the products and processes is the responsibility of everyone involved with the creation or consumption of the products or services offered by the organization. TQM capitalizes on the involvement of management, workforce, suppliers, and even customers, to meet or exceed customer expectations.

Six Sigma

Six Sigma is a business management strategy, originally developed by Motorola, which seeks to identify and remove the causes of defects and errors in manufacturing and business processes. The Six Sigma process improvement originated in 1986 from Motorola's drive toward reducing defects by minimizing variation in processes through metrics measurement. Applications of the Six Sigma project execution methodology have since expanded to incorporate practices common in TQM and Supply Chain Management; this includes customer satisfaction and developing closer supplier relationships.

CMMI

Capability Maturity Model Integration (CMMI) is a process improvement approach providing organizations with the essential elements of effective processes. It can be used to guide process improvement—across a project, a division, or an entire organization—thus helping to integrate traditionally separate organizational functions, set process improvement goals and priorities, provide guidance for a quality processes, and provide a point of reference for appraising current processes. Here are some benefits you can realize from CMMI:

- Linking your organization's activities to your business objectives
- Increasing your visibility into your organization's activities, helping to ensure that your service or product meets the customer's expectations
- Learning from new areas of best practice, such as measurement and risk

Business Process Management

Business Process Management (BPM) is a management approach focused on aligning all aspects of an organization with the wants and needs of clients. It is a holistic management approach, promoting business effectiveness and efficiency while striving for innovation, flexibility, and integration with technology. BPM attempts to improve processes continuously and can be considered a process-optimization process. It is argued that BPM enables organizations to be more efficient, more effective, and more capable of change than a functionally focused, traditional hierarchical management approach. BPM can help organizations gain higher customer satisfaction, product quality, delivery speed, and time-to-market speed.

Service Management Mastery: ISO 20000

You can think of ITIL and ITSM as providing a framework for IT to rethink the ways in which it contributes to and aligns with the business. ISO 20000, which is the first international standard for ITSM, institutionalizes these processes. The ISO 20000 helps companies to align IT services and business strategy and create a formal framework for continual service improvement and provides benchmarks for comparison to best practices.

Published in December 2005, ISO 20000 was developed to reflect the best practice guidance contained within ITIL. The standard also supports other ITSM frameworks and approaches, including MOF, CMMI, and Six Sigma. ISO 20000 consists of two major areas:

▶ Part 1 promotes adopting an integrated process approach to deliver managed services effectively that meets business and customer requirements.

▶ Part 2 is a "code of practice" describing the best practices for service management within the scope of ISO 20000-1.

These two areas—what to do and how to do it—have similarities to the approach taken by the other standards, including MOF.

ISO 20000 goes beyond ITIL, MOF, Six Sigma, and other frameworks in providing organizational or corporate certification for organizations that effectively adopt and implement the ISO 20000 code of practice.

Optimizing Your Infrastructure

According to Microsoft, analysts estimate that more than 70% of the typical IT budget is spent on infrastructure—managing servers, operating systems, storage, and networking. Add to that the challenge of refreshing and managing desktop and mobile devices, and there's not much left over for anything else. Microsoft describes an Infrastructure Optimization (IO) Model that categorizes the state of one's IT infrastructure, describing the impacts on cost, security risks, and the ability to respond to changes. Using the model shown in Figure 1.7, you can identify where your organization is and where you want to be:

▶ **Basic:** Reactionary, with much time spent fighting fires

▶ **Standardized:** Gaining control

▶ **Rationalized:** Enabling the business

▶ **Dynamic:** Being a strategic asset

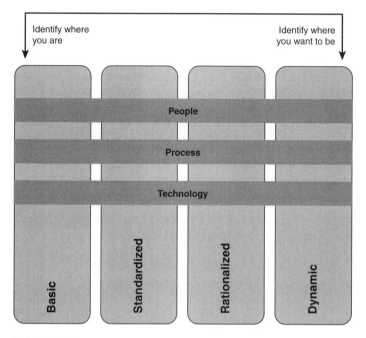

FIGURE 1.7   The Infrastructure Optimization Model.

Although most organizations are somewhere between the basic and standardized levels in this model, typically one would prefer to be a strategic asset rather than fighting fires. Once you know where you are in the model, you can use best practices from ITIL and guidance from MOF to develop a plan to progress to a higher level. The IO Model describes the technologies and steps organizations can take to move forward, whereas the MOF explains the people and processes required to improve that infrastructure. Similar to ITSM, the IO Model is a combination of people, processes, and technology.

You can find more information about Infrastructure Optimization at http://www.microsoft.com/technet/infrastructure.

ABOUT THE IO MODEL

Not all IT shops will want or need to be dynamic. Some will choose, for all the right business reasons, to be less than dynamic! The IO Model includes a three-part goal:

- ▶ Communicate that there are levels
- ▶ Target the desired levels
- ▶ Provide reference on how to get to the desired levels

Realize that infrastructure optimization can be by application or by function, rather than a single ranking for the entire IT department.

Items that factor into an IT organization's adoption of the IO Model include cost, ability, and whether the organization fits into the business model as a cost center versus being an asset, along with a commitment to move from being reactive to proactive.

From Fighting Fires to Gaining Control

At the basic level, your infrastructure is hard to control and expensive to manage. Processes are manual, IT policies and standards are either nonexistent or not enforced, and you don't have the tools and resources (or time and energy) to determine the overall health of your applications and IT services. Not only are your desktop and server management costs out of control, but you are also in reactive mode when it comes to security threats and user support. In addition, you tend to use manual rather than automated methods for applying software deployments and patches.

Does this sound familiar? If you can gain control of your environment, you may be more effective at work! Here are some steps to consider:

- ▶ Develop standards, policies, and controls.

- ▶ Alleviate security risks by developing a security approach throughout your IT organization.

- ▶ Adopt best practices, such as those found in ITIL, and operational guidance found in the MOF.

- ▶ Build IT to become a strategic asset.

If you can achieve operational nirvana, this will go a long way toward your job satisfaction and IT becoming a constructive part of your business.

From Gaining Control to Enabling the Business

A standardized infrastructure introduces control by using standards and policies to manage desktops and servers. These standards control how you introduce machines into your network. For example, you could use directory services to manage resources, security policies, and access to resources. Shops in a standardized state realize the value of basic standards and some policies but still tend to be reactive. Although you now have a managed IT infrastructure and are inventorying your hardware and software assets and starting to manage licenses, your patches, software deployments, and desktop services are not yet automated. Security-wise, the perimeter is now under control, although internal security may still be a bit loose. Service management becomes a recognized concept and your organization is taking steps to implement it.

To move from a standardized state to the rationalized level, you need to gain more control over your infrastructure and implement proactive policies and procedures. You might also begin to look at implementing service management. At this stage, IT can also move more toward becoming a business asset and ally, rather than a burden.

From Enabling the Business to Becoming a Strategic Asset

At the rationalized level, you have achieved firm control of desktop and service management costs. Processes and policies are in place and beginning to play a large role in supporting and expanding the business. Security is now proactive, and you are responding to threats and challenges in a rapid and controlled manner.

Using technologies such as lite-touch and zero-touch operating system deployment helps you to minimize costs, deployment time, and technical challenges for system rollouts. Because your inventory is now under control, you have minimized the number of images to manage, and desktop management is now largely automated. You also are purchasing only the software licenses and new computers the business requires, giving you a handle on costs. Security is now proactive with policies and control in place for desktops, servers, firewalls, and extranets. You have implemented service management in several areas and are taking steps to implement it more broadly across IT.

Mission Accomplished: IT as a Strategic Asset

At the dynamic level, your infrastructure is helping run the business efficiently and stay ahead of competitors. Your costs are now fully controlled. You have also achieved integration between users and data, desktops and servers, and the different departments and functions throughout your organization.

Your IT processes are automated and often incorporated into the technology itself, allowing IT to be aligned and managed according to business needs. New technology investments are able to yield specific, rapid, and measurable business benefits. Measurement is good—it helps you justify the next round of investments!

Using self-provisioning software and quarantine-like systems to ensure patch management and compliance with security policies allows you to automate your processes, which in turn improves reliability, lowers costs, and increases your service levels. Service management is implemented for all critical services with SLAs and operational reviews.

According to IDC Research (October 2006), very few organizations achieve the dynamic level of the Infrastructure Optimization Model—due to the lack of availability of a single toolset from a single vendor to meet all requirements. Through execution on its vision in DSI, Microsoft aims to change this. To read more about this study, visit http://download.microsoft.com/download/a/4/4/a4474b0c-57d8-41a2-afe6-32037fa93ea6/IDC_windesktop_IO_whitepaper.pdf.

MICROSOFT INFRASTRUCTURE OPTIMIZATION HELPS REDUCE COSTS

The April 21, 2009, issue of *BizTech* magazine includes an article by Russell Smith about Microsoft's Infrastructure Optimization Model. Russell makes the following points:

Although dynamic or fully automated systems that are strategic assets to a company sometimes seem like a far-off dream, infrastructure optimization models and products can help get you closer to making IT a valuable business asset.

Microsoft's Infrastructure Optimization is based on Gartner's Infrastructure Maturity Model and provides a simple structure to evaluate the efficiency of core IT services, business productivity, and application platforms.

Though the ultimate goal is to make IT a business enabler across all three areas, you will need to concentrate on standardizing core services: moving your organization from a basic infrastructure (in which most IT tasks are carried out manually) to a managed infrastructure with some automation and knowledge capture.

A 2006 IDC study of 141 enterprises with 1,000 to 20,000 users found that PC standardization and security management could save up to $430 per user annually; standardizing systems management servers could save another $46 per user.

For additional information and the complete article, see http://www.biztechmagazine.com/article.asp?item_id=569.

Overview of Microsoft System Center

At the Microsoft Management Summit (MMS) in 2003, Microsoft announced System Center, envisioned as a future solution for providing customers with complete application and system management for enterprises of all sizes. (See http://www.microsoft.com/press-pass/press/2003/mar03/03-18mssystemcenterpr.mspx for the original press release.) The first phase was anticipated to include Microsoft Operations Manager (MOM) 2004—later released as MOM 2005—and Systems Management Server (SMS) 2003.

WHAT IS SYSTEM CENTER?

System Center is an umbrella or brand name for Microsoft's systems management family of products, and as such has new products and components added over time. System Center is not a single integrated product; it represents a means to integrate system management tools and technologies to help you with systems operations, troubleshooting, and planning.

Different from the releases of Microsoft Office (another Microsoft product family), Microsoft has released System Center in "waves"; the components are not released simultaneously. The first wave initially included SMS 2003, MOM 2005, and System Center Data Protection Manager 2006; 2006 additions included System Center Reporting Manager 2006 and System Center Capacity Planner 2006.

The second wave included Operations Manager 2007, Configuration Manager 2007, System Center Essentials 2007, Virtual Machine Manager 2007, and new releases of Data Protection Manager and Capacity Planner. Next released were updates to Virtual Machine Manager (version 2008) Operations Manager 2007 R2, Configuration Manager 2007 R2 and R3, DPM 2010, System Center Essentials 2010, and Service Manager 2010. Think of these as rounding out the second wave.

Microsoft has also widened the System Center product suite with recent acquisitions of Opalis and AVIcode. Organizations licensed for Microsoft System Center Server Management Suite Enterprise (SMSE) or Microsoft System Center Server Management Suite Datacenter (SMSD) may obtain Opalis and AVIcode as part of that license. AVIcode 5.7 is also available without charge to companies with the Core Infrastructure Server

Enterprise and/or to those with a Core Infrastructure Server Datacenter license with Software Assurance.

A third wave includes the "v.Next" versions of System Center products: Operations Manager 2012, Configuration Manager 2012, and Virtual Machine Manager 2012. The wave also includes a new version of Opalis, rebranded as System Center Orchestrator, and Service Manager 2012. System Center Advisor, previously code-named Atlanta, promises to offer configuration-monitoring cloud service for Microsoft SQL Server and Windows Server deployments. Expect the list of monitored products to grow over time.

System Center builds on Microsoft's DSI, introduced in the "Dynamic Systems Initiative" section, which is designed to deliver simplicity, automation, and flexibility in the data center across the IT environment. Microsoft System Center products share the following DSI-based characteristics:

- Ease of use and deployment
- Based on industry and customer knowledge
- Scalability (both up to the largest enterprises and down to the smallest organizations)

Figure 1.8 illustrates the relationship between the System Center components and MOF.

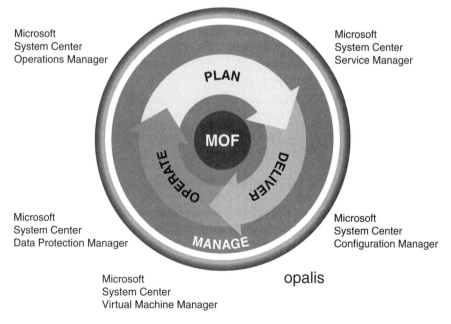

FIGURE 1.8   MOF with System Center applications.

Reporting and Trend Analysis

The data gathered by the System Center products is collected in self-maintaining data warehouses, enabling numerous reports to be viewable. By using the SQL Server Reporting Services (SRS) engine, you can export reports to a Report Server file share. SRS's Web Archive format retains links. You are also able to schedule and email reports, enabling users to open these reports without accessing the product console.

The Service Manager data warehouse is installed in a management group separate from the other Service Manager components, leading to speculation that this will ultimately be a unified data warehouse used by all products in the System Center suite.

Operations Management

The design pillars of Operations Manager 2012, currently in development, include a holistic view of application health, reduced TCO, and decreased time to value for partners:

▶ Taking a holistic view of application health means OpsMgr 2012 will not only monitor an application from inside the infrastructure up to the application itself but also from the end-user perspective. Microsoft's acquisition of AVIcode will help in this endeavor, telling one where the problems are down to the specific line of code in the application.

▶ TCO is reduced through a simplified infrastructure with elimination of the root management server (RMS), reliable monitoring, increased scale and performance, and operational continuity.

▶ To achieve decreased time to value for partners, Microsoft is looking at module extensibility, downloading dependencies required by management packs, adding templates, and additional dashboards.

Operations Manager 2012 also adds extensively to those network monitoring capabilities available with OpsMgr 2007 R2 by incorporating EMC Smarts technology.

In 2010, Gartner Group placed Operations Manager in its Magic Quadrant for IT Event Correlation and Analysis.

Configuration and Change Management

System Center Configuration Manager is Microsoft's systems management solution for change and configuration management. In 2009, Gartner Group placed Configuration Manager in its Magic Quadrant for software change and configuration management for distributed platforms.

With ConfigMgr 2012, Microsoft's first foray into systems management gets a new look and feel by replacing its MMC console with the standard System Center UI Framework (Outlook-style user interface), similar to other products in the System Center suite. In addition, Microsoft redesigned software distribution and the site server hierarchy, making it easier to implement and use Configuration Manager. The 2012 release also targets management at the user, not the device—delivering the right application in the right way to the right user under the right condition. This enables the user to be productive anywhere and anytime, yet maintains IT control while balancing the need for end-user empowerment.

Service Management

Using System Center Service Manager implements a single point of contact for all service requests, knowledge, and workflow. Service Manager 2010 incorporates processes such as incident, problem, change, and change management.

Service Manager fills a gap in Operations Manager: What occurs when OpsMgr detects a condition that requires human intervention and tracking for resolution? Until Service Manager, the answer was to create a ticket or incident in one's help desk application. Now, within the System Center framework, OpsMgr can hand off incident management to Service Manager.

Protecting Data

System Center's Data Protection Manager (DPM) is a disk-based backup solution for continuous data protection supporting Windows servers such as SQL Server, Exchange, SharePoint, virtualization, and file servers—as well as Windows desktops and laptops. DPM provides byte-level backup as changes occur, utilizing Microsoft's Virtual Disk Service and Shadow Copy technologies.

DPM 2010 includes the ability for roaming laptops to get centrally managed policies around desktop protection. It also provides native site-to-site replication for disaster recovery to another DPM server or an off-site cloud provider. DPM includes centrally managed system state and bare metal recovery.

To support virtual machines, DPM supports host-based backups of virtual machines using a single agent on the host. To support branch office and low-bandwidth scenarios, DPM's advanced de-duplication technology and block-level filter technology only moves changed data during full backups. Additional cloud capabilities are planned for DPM 2012.

Virtual Machine Management

System Center Virtual Machine Manager (VMM) is Microsoft's management platform for heterogeneous virtualization infrastructures. VMM provides centralized management of virtual machines across several popular platforms, specifically Windows Server 2008 and 2008 R2 Hyper-V, VMware ESX 3.x, and Citrix XenServer. VMM enables increased utilization of physical servers, centralized management of a virtual infrastructure, delegation of administration in distributed environments, and rapid provisioning of new virtual machines by system administrators and users via a self-service portal.

VMM 2012 will have the ability to build both Hyper-V hosts and host clusters as it moves to being a private cloud product in terms of management and provisioning rather than just a virtualization management solution. This provisioning will involve deploying services using service templates, in addition to simply configuring storage and networking.

Concero (code-named), a self-service portal built on Silverlight, will allow IT managers to more easily deploy and manage applications in cloud infrastructures. Concero enables administrators to manage multiple private and public clouds while provisioning virtual machines and services to individual business units. Using Concero with VMM 2012, data center administrators will be able to provision not only virtual machine OS deployments but also, leveraging App-V, deploy and manage down to the application level, minimizing the number of virtual hard disk (VHD) templates necessary to maintain.

Orchestration and Automation

System Center Orchestrator 2012 will be based on Opalis Integration Server (OIS), acquired by Microsoft in December 2009. The product provides an automation platform for orchestrating and integrating IT tools to drive down the cost of one's data center operations while improving the reliability of IT processes. Orchestrator enables organizations to automate best practices, such as those found in MOF and ITIL, by using workflow processes that coordinate the System Center platform and other management tools to automate incident response, change and compliance, and service life cycle management processes.

The IT process automation software reduces operational costs and improves IT efficiency by delivering services faster and with fewer errors. Orchestrator replaces manual, resource-intensive, and potentially error-prone activities with standardized, automated processes. The product can orchestrate tasks between Operations Manager, Configuration Manager, Virtual Machine Manager, Data Protection Manager, and third-party management tools. (OIS came with integration packs for BMC, CA, EMC, FTP, HP, IBM, Symantec, and VMware.) This positions it to automate any IT process across a heterogeneous environment, providing full solutions for incident management, change and configuration management, and provisioning and service management.

System Center Essentials

System Center Essentials 2010 (Essentials, for short) is a System Center application targeted to the medium-sized business that combines the monitoring features of OpsMgr with the inventory and software distribution functionality found in ConfigMgr, along with VMM 2008 R2 technology built in. This gives you a single console to manage a broad range of tasks against your physical and virtual servers, clients, hardware, software, and IT services.

The monitoring function utilizes the form of the OpsMgr 2007 engine that uses OpsMgr 2007 management packs, and Essentials brings additional network device discovery and monitoring out of the box. The VMM technology enables Essentials 2010 to provide a management solution for managing both your physical and virtual servers. The platform provides systems management functionality, software distribution, update management, and hardware and software inventory, all performed using the native Automatic Updates client and WSUS 3.0. Using Essentials, you can centrally manage Windows-based servers and PCs, as well as network devices, by performing the following tasks:

▶ Discovering and monitoring the health of computers and network devices and view summary reports of computer health

▶ Converting physical servers to virtual machines, including support for live migration

▶ Centrally distributing software updates, tracking installation progress, and trouble-shooting problems using the update management feature

▶ Centrally deploying software, tracking progress, and troubleshooting problems with the software deployment feature

▶ Collecting and examining computer hardware and software inventory using the inventory feature

Essentials lacks the granularity of control and extensibility to support distributed environments and enterprise scalability. The flip side of this reduced functionality is that Essentials greatly simplifies many functions compared to its OpsMgr counterparts. Customization and connectivity options for Essentials are limited, however. An Essentials deployment supports only a single management server; all managed devices must be in the same AD forest. Reporting functionality is included, but only accommodates about a 40-day retention period.

Essentials 2010 also limits the number of managed objects per deployment to 50 Windows server-based computers and 500 Windows non-server-based computers. There is no limit to the number of network devices.

System Center Advisor

System Center Advisor promises to offer configuration-monitoring cloud service for Microsoft Windows Server and SQL Server deployments. Microsoft servers in the Advisor cloud analyze the uploaded data, and then provide feedback to the customer in the Advisor console in the form of alerts about detected configuration issues. System Center Advisor's mission statement is to be a proactive tool to help Microsoft customers avoid configuration problems, reduce downtime, improve performance, and resolve issues faster. The web-based console itself is written with Silverlight and is very similar to the look and feel of the Microsoft InTune console, Microsoft's cloud-based management service for PCs.

The Value Proposition of Service Manager 2010

IT organizations must provide efficient and effective services while contending with pressures to reduce operating costs, ensure compliance, and add value to the business. Service Manager orchestrates people, process, and technology across the Microsoft platform. By integrating information, knowledge, processes, activities, and workflows, System Center Service Manager reduces the cost and improves the quality of IT services.

The value of Service Manager lies in these areas:

▶ Delivering efficient and responsive support through the Self-Service portal for provisioning, self-help, and managing requests

▶ Optimizing processes and ensuring their use through templates that guide IT analysts through best practices for change and incident management

▶ Reducing resolution times by cutting across organizational silos, ensuring that the right information from incident, problem, change, or asset records is accessible through a single pane

▶ Extending the value of the Microsoft platform by connecting the processes and activities among System Center products, and using reporting as a driver for KPIs

Summary

This chapter introduced you to service management. You learned that service management is a process that touches many areas within ITIL and MOF, such as change and configuration management, asset management, security management, and indirectly, release management. You learned about the functionality delivered in Service Manager that can be leveraged to meet these challenges more easily and effectively.

Microsoft's management approach, which incorporates the processes and software tools of MOF and DSI, is a strategy or blueprint intended to build automation and knowledge into data center operations. Microsoft's investment in DSI includes building systems designed for operations, developing an operationally aware platform, and establishing a commitment to intelligent management software.

Service Manager drives integration, efficiency, and IT business alignment. Together with Operations Manager, Configuration Manager, and the other members of the System Center family of products, Service Manager is a critical component in Microsoft's approach to system management that can increase your organization's agility in delivering on its service commitments to the business.

The next chapter looks at the technology and terminology used by the product, and looks at product features, including changes in Service Pack 1.

CHAPTER 2

Service Manager 2010 Overview

System Center Service Manager (SvcMgr or SCSM) 2010 delivers an integrated platform for automating and adapting IT Service Management best practices to your organization's requirements, such as those found in Microsoft Operations Framework (MOF) and Information Technology Infrastructure Library (ITIL), which are discussed in Chapter 3, "MOF, ITIL, and Service Manager." Service Manager provides built-in processes for incident and problem resolution, change control, and configuration management.

What this means is Microsoft's System Center suite now provides the capability to manage the system life cycle defined by MOF. MOF uses a model that describes Microsoft's approach to IT operations and the service management life cycle. The model organizes the ITIL areas of service strategy, service design, service transition, service operation, and continual service improvement; and includes additional MOF processes in phases of the IT life cycle, as introduced in Chapter 1, "Service Management Basics."

This chapter looks at the history of Service Manager. It discusses the development of the product leading to Service Manager 2010, the technology and terminology used by the product, and looks at product features. It provides information about tools and utilities you can use with Service Manager, and includes a summary of what is included in Service Pack (SP) 1.

The History of Service Manager

Microsoft's System Center Service Manager product has the somewhat dubious distinction of being completely rewritten from its initial prerelease code. The first version of Service Manager, code-named Service Desk, went into early testing in 2006 with release planned for the second half of 2008. Service Desk was written to run on a 32-bit version of Windows Server 2003 Service Pack (SP) 1, using Internet Information Services (IIS) 6.0, .NET Framework 2.0 and 3.0, SQL Server 2005 SP 2 with Reporting Services, Internet Explorer 7.0, and Office SharePoint Server 2007 Enterprise, and could be installed on a single server during the beta.

ITIL DEFINITION OF SERVICE DESK

ITIL defines *service desk* as a function that serves as a single point of contact between the users and IT service management. It is closely linked with incident management; its intent is to restore the normal service to the users as quickly as possible, with reasonable costs. The term service desk is part of the Operating phase of MOF v4. A code name of Service Desk was entirely reasonable for the product that eventually became Service Manager.

Initial design plans were to include capabilities of Reporting Manager 2006 to extract data from Microsoft Operations Manager (MOM) 2005, Systems Management Server (SMS) 2003, and Active Directory installations, consolidate that information into a data warehouse, and generate canned and custom reports using SQL Server Reporting Services. The design evolved as Microsoft released Operations Manager 2007 and Configuration Manager 2007 and eliminated a Reporting Manager product.

In early 2007, Microsoft held a contest to officially name the product. After much deliberation, Service Manager became the official name, although given the fact that most System Center products include the word *Manager* as part of their name, calling the software Service Manager should not have been much of a surprise. This first version of Service Manager used solution packs rather than management packs. The solution packs contained objects such as workflows, forms, and reports that determined the behaviors of the various features of Service Manager. Beta 1 included incident management, change and asset management, knowledge management, and a self-service portal with self-service provisioning.

In the first part of 2008, Microsoft announced it was delaying Service Manager until 2010. Testing revealed performance and scalability problems, so the product at that point was scrapped and rewritten, with a new beta at the end of 2008 and release rescheduled for the first half of 2010. Microsoft made good on the new release date; they announced availability of Service Manager 2010 at MMS 2010 April 21, 2010.

Because Service Manager 2010 is a v1 product, it does not necessarily include all the features and functionality that you might find in a more mature product. Microsoft was quick to follow up on the initial release, with a first service pack in December 2010. Service Manager 2012 is currently slated to release after the 2012 versions of other System Center products such as Operations Manager 2012 and Configuration Manager 2012.

Service Manager's key strength is the ease in which you can integrate it with Operations Manager and Configuration Manager. For those customers currently holding System Center Server Management Suite Enterprise (SMSE) and System Center Server Management Suite Datacenter (SMSD) licenses, Server Manager can be acquired at a nominal cost. (The Microsoft Enterprise CAL [Client Access License] provides rights for the Service Manager Client Management License.)

Introducing Service Manager 2010

With Service Manager 2010, Microsoft continues to round out System Center's ITIL- and MOF-focused architecture by adding centralized incident and problem management capabilities to the product suite. Through connectors provided with the product, Service Manager 2010 can import data from Operations Manager, Configuration Manager, and Active Directory—enabling it to become a centralized repository of information.

Service Manager is all about ITIL and MOF. Regardless of whether your organization plans full implementation of the various IT operational frameworks discussed in Chapter 1 (ITIL, MOF, and so on), there are always fundamental issues to address. One such area requiring appropriate processes and procedures revolves around IT service management, which includes functions such as incident tracking and resolution, configuration management, and change management.

In its most simple form, service management encompasses aspects of Information Technology (IT) management involving the end user. With its wide span of potential issues, end-user support is perhaps one of the most critical and most challenging aspects of IT operations. In addition, without processes in place for users to address some of their own support needs, the IT service desk can become overwhelmed performing common and repeated tasks.

Service Manager endeavors to improve and simplify IT service desk operations and has the capability to simplify and normalize support processes across your entire IT organization. In addition to providing end users with a support submission tool and self-service tools, Service Manager integrates with other System Center products with an objective of improving IT operations. For example, when Operations Manager generates an alert for a server access issue, Service Manager can automatically create an incident and assign it to support staff. The automation between the products eliminates the requirement to go through a manual ticket-creation process.

This automation, in addition to removing manual procedures and operations, ensures that any request, whether created by a user or automatically generated due to a server issue, generates an activity log. This helps to prevent situations where requests are not addressed. Tracking all tasks also helps IT management to gauge workloads and make informed decisions regarding budgets and staffing.

Technology and Terminology

Pillars of Service Manager 2010 include user-centric support, data center management efficiency, and business alignment:

▶ **User-centric support:** With its Self-Service portal (SSP) and integration with Configuration Manager (ConfigMgr), Service Manager can improve user productivity (and thus increase satisfaction) while reducing support costs.

▶ **Data center management efficiency:** Service Manager facilitates centralized incident, problem, and change management, helping to restore service quickly and reduce downtime while it improves the reliability of IT services running in your data center.

▶ **Business alignment:** By optimizing your organization's resources to align to its business goals and requirements, Service Manager 2010 works to lower the high costs of IT compliance, and provides integrated knowledge and reporting.

Service Manager uses terminology that is unique and specific to its management infrastructure and the actions that it carries out. The next sections describe some of these terms, providing a foundation to understand how these objects interact with one another and the infrastructure.

Configuration Items

ITIL defines a configuration item (CI) as *any component that needs to be managed in order to deliver an IT Service.* These could be a piece of hardware, software, documentation, a user or group, location, or network.

CIs are the fundamental structural unit in a configuration management system such as Service Manager 2010, and are a way to store information in the Service Manager database about services and IT assets such as computers, software, software updates, users, and other objects. These CIs can then be selected when you submit forms, such as an incident form, a change request form, or a work item form.

Work Items

Incidents, change requests, and problems are represented as work items and stored in the Service Manager database.

Queue

In Service Manager, a queue is a container that contains work items. When you change the support group on an incident in Service Manager, you are sending the incident to another queue. By default, there are three support groups, tier 1 to tier 3. Permissions on a queue can be controlled for users and roles for those actions they can perform on a work item in a queue; see Chapter 15, "Service Manager Security," for additional information.

Incident Management

The Incident Management process is responsible for managing the life cycle of all incidents; the goal is to restore to a normal service operation as quickly as possible and minimize the business impact.

Problem Management

Problem Management is the process that will identify the root cause of one or more incidents. The process will also find a workaround or a fix to the root cause. An example can be that a number of end users have problems logging in to Active Directory. The Problem Management process can identify that the root cause is an incorrect domain controller setting in one branch office. Proactive Problem Management aims to identify and solve problems and known errors before the incidents occur. (This is one of the functions of monitors in Operations Manager.)

Change Management

Change Management is the process responsible for controlling the life cycle of all changes, where a change is the addition, modification, or removal of anything that could affect IT services.

Connector

A connector is a software component that connects Service Manager with an external system. Connectors are used to transfer data between Service Manager and external systems. Out of the box, Service Manager contains connectors for Active Directory, Operations Manager, and Configuration Manager. To illustrate the use of a connector, the Active Directory connector transfers information about users, computers, groups, and printers into the Service Manager database.

Configuration Management Database

The configuration management database (CMDB) stores all CIs, information about how they are configured, the relationships they have, and their properties. It also includes work items and knowledge, as depicted in Figure 2.1. The Service Manager CMDB is a SQL Server database, given the name ServiceManager by default.

NOTE: ITIL V3 CHANGES THE NAME OF THE CMDB TO CMS

Although not reflected in Service Manager 2010, ITIL v2 used the term *CMDB* to refer to its configuration management database. ITIL v3 uses the nomenclature of configuration management system (CMS). History is tracked for each configuration item and work item.

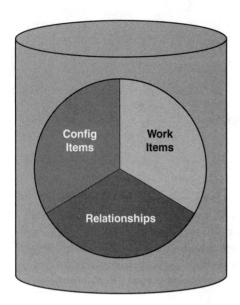

FIGURE 2.1   The Service Manager CMDB includes configuration items, work items, and knowledge.

Data is also populated using connectors, which synchronize with external systems. Data from multiple sources can be merged into the same item.

Data Warehouse Databases

Service Manager 2010's data warehouse is a logical database. It physically consists of three separate databases:

- ▶ DWStagingAndConfig
- ▶ DWRepository
- ▶ DWDataMart

These are described in the next sections, and illustrated in Figure 2.2. The data warehouse resides in a separate management group from the other Service Manager components. Chapter 20, "Reports, Dashboards, and Data Analysis," discusses the Extract, Transform, and Load (ETL) process.

DWStagingAndConfig Database

When data is moved from the Service Manager database to the data warehouse, it is first moved to this database. Here is where the data is transformed into a new format.

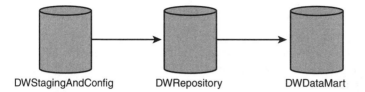

DWStagingAndConfig   DWRepository   DWDataMart

FIGURE 2.2   CMDB data movement through the data warehouse.

DWRepository Database
Once the data is reformatted in the DWStagingAndConfig database, it is written to the DWRepository database. The data is then inserted into the DWDataMart database.

DWDataMart Database
The DWDataMart is the database used when running reports; this database includes all the report data. Data is stored long term in the DWDataMart, 1 year by default.

Grooming (Data-Retention Policy)

Grooming is the process where Service Manager moves data from the Service Manager database (CMDB) over to the data warehouse, where it ends up in the DWDataMart database. This helps keep the Service Manager database at a reasonable size and with acceptable response times. All data is copied to the data warehouse for long-term reporting.

Service Manager automatically grooms incident, problem, and change request work items from the CMDB, with default retention periods of 90, 365, and 365 days, respectively. You can configure these values in the Service Manager console. Setting a value to 0 days signifies there is no retention for that type of work item, and it is deleted the next time the grooming workflow runs. You can find information on how grooming works in an article by Travis Wright at http://blogs.technet.com/b/servicemanager/archive/2009/09/18/data-retention-policies-aka-grooming-in-the-servicemanager-database.aspx.

Incident

An incident is an event that is not part of the normal standard operation of the IT service. This event causes interruption and affects the quality of the service in a negative way. Examples of incidents include a hardware failure or a printer that no longer can print correctly. Service Manager's process for managing incidents is discussed in Chapter 10, "Incident Management."

Service Request

A service request is an incident that is not a failure in the IT infrastructure. An example is a login reset request.

Change Request

A change request is a document that contains a proposal of a change to any component in an IT environment or an IT service. The change request includes what needs to be done, but not how to do it. It most often also includes a deadline, affected component, risk priority, and a rollback plan.

Activity

An activity is a stage or task carried out as part of managing an incident, problem, or change request. For example, an activity could be creating an account in a change request or a troubleshooting step when working with an incident. An activity could also be related to any other work item. For example, a problem can obtain an activity such as a manual step to perform. Activities can include review activities and manual activities.

Review Activity

A review activity is a step in a review process in which a user approves or denies a change request.

Workflow

A workflow consists of a number of activities automatically carried out. An example is a notification workflow that sends notification or a workflow that automatically changes severity on an incident if the affected user is an important (VIP) user.

Problem

Problems are unknown errors and the underlying cause of one or more incidents. A problem in Service Manager is a type of work item.

Known Error

A known error is a problem for which a root cause and permanent fix or workaround are identified but the fix has not yet implemented.

Workaround

This is a temporary fix or technique. A workaround eliminates the end user's reliance on the faulty service component.

Business Service

A business service is a number of objects that together enable a business process (IT service). One example of a business service could be your messaging environment. The business service object in Service Manager then shows you CIs such as Windows services and servers, metadata, and people associated with the service. Associated people can consist of the service owner, contact person, and affected users.

Service Map

A service map shows you relationships between services and service ownership. It also shows you components, dependencies, and settings. In Service Manager, service maps are seen as business services. These are discussed in Chapter 9, "Business Services."

Role-Based Security

Service Manager 2010 supports role-based security. This makes it possible to scope the console in a number of ways. For example, if you are working in the network expert team, you only want to see incidents related to your team. The Service Manager administrators can configure a user role for your team and limit the number of views and items you can see and access. Chapter 15 includes a discussion of role-based security.

User Role

Based on a user role profile, the user role limits and defines what users see in the console. For example, a user role for the Microsoft Exchange expert team would only show Exchange-related work items and objects.

User Role Profile

User role profiles are a number of preexisting user role templates that can be used when creating a new user role. These templates control what the user can and cannot do.

Management Pack

Management packs (MPs) are eXtensible Markup Language (XML) files containing definitions that define not only data models but also objects such as views for the Service Manager console, workflows, groups, queues, tasks, forms, connectors, and so on. All customizations are stored in MPs. For example, if you want to modify the incident form, you save your modification from the Authoring Tool in an MP and then import it into Service Manager.

MPs used by Service Manager 2010 are referred to as version 1.1, to distinguish them from Operations Manager 2007 MPs (version 1.0). The MP schema for Service Manager is extended from that in version 1.0, but includes all the functionality in version 1.0. More information on this is available in Chapter 4, "Looking Inside Service Manager."

Class

A Service Manager class is the name of a type of objects that share the same common properties. For example, all logical hard disks are members of the `logical disk` class. Properties of the `logical disk` class include `size`, `file system`, and `defrag level`. Other attributes members of a class can share are relationships and behaviors.

Knowledge

Knowledge articles in Service Manager are objects that provide knowledge and guidance for Service Manager users. A knowledge article could be a guideline for troubleshooting a specific issue, which would be used by service desk operators or engineers. It could also be a step-by-step guide for end users to read in the SSP.

Service Manager Console

The Service Manager 2010 console is used by all different roles working with the product. The console supports role-based security; based on your role you see a different set of objects in the console. The console is similar in look and feel to other System Center products. Figure 2.3 shows the Service Manager console. Chapter 8, "Using Service Manager," discusses the console in depth.

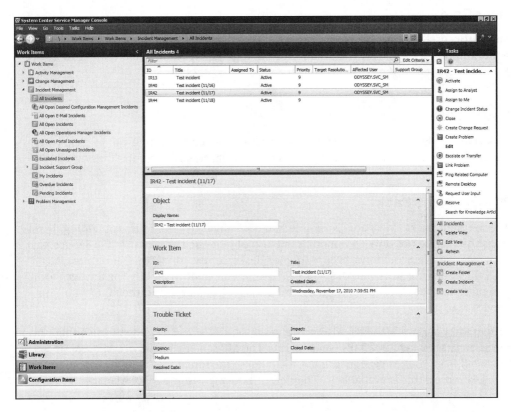

FIGURE 2.3   The Service Manager 2010 console.

Service Manager Self-Service Portal

The SSP is a web portal where end users can search for knowledge, create support requests, and read IT announcements.

Service Manager Analyst Portal

Analysts can use a portion of the SSP, known as the Analyst portal, to work on change requests (for example, to review and approve change requests). They can also get an overview of the number of active changes and the changes within their area. The Analyst portal can also be used to assign activities to a user.

Service Manager Management Server

This server is where the primary software part of Service Manager is installed and running. You connect your console to this server role. This is also the server hosting the System Center Management (HealthService) service, which runs all workflows, and the System Center Management Configuration service. The first management server installed is also referred to as the workflow server.

Service Manager Reporting Server

This is the SQL Server Reporting Services installation used by the data warehouse and reporting components of Service Manager.

Management Group

A management group represents the data store and the management servers as a whole. The data warehouse is installed into its own management group.

Management group names must be unique, cannot be changed, and are case sensitive. The name is entered when you install Service Manager. The name of the Server Manager and data warehouse management server is stored in the Windows Registry, in a key under `HKEY_LOCAL_Machine\SOFTWARE\Microsoft\Microsoft Operations Manager\3.0\Server Management Groups`. The key is under the Operations Manager section of the Registry; this is because Service Manager uses a common platform that underlies multiple System Center products.

Software Provisioning

Software provisioning delivers software to a computer. Service Manager lets an end user request software from the SSP. After approval, if needed, Configuration Manager delivers the software.

Tools and Utilities

A number of tools and utilities are available for Service Manager 2010. This section includes information about several of the online and downloadable tools and utilities for Service Manager 2010 and its components.

These tools are not part of the Service Manager product and, except where noted, are not officially supported by Microsoft, even if you download the software from a Microsoft.com address.

EnumCreator.xlsx

This Excel spreadsheet lets you create a list item structure in Excel that is automatically generated into an MP. You can then copy the MP XML out of the spreadsheet, paste it into a XML file, and import it into Service Manager.

Figures 2.4 and 2.5 show how you can input information in the Excel spreadsheet. Figure 2.4 shows some basic MP information, and Figure 2.5 shows the structure of your list item. Figure 2.6 shows the result of the XML code generated by the tool.

Management Pack ID:	MyCustomMP
Management Pack Version:	1.0.0.0
Management Pack Name:	My Custom MP
Dependent MP Info (optional)	
Root Enum MP ID	System.WorkItem.I
Root Enum MP Version:	7.0.5244.0
Root Enum MP Public Key Token:	31bf3856ad364e35

FIGURE 2.4   Input of basic MP information.

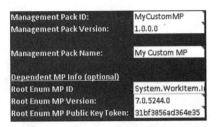

Root Level (if from another MP)	Level 1	Level 2	Level 3	Level 4	Level 5
IncidentClassificationEnum	Coffee Machine				
	Coffee Machine	Filters			
	Coffee Machine	Drain			
	Coffee Machine	Drain	Pipe		
	Coffee Machine	Drain	Fitting		
	Coffee Machine	Coffee			
	Coffee Machine	Coffee	Out of Coffee		
	Coffee Machine	Coffee	Coffee Tastes Bad		
	Coffee Machine	Coffee	Coffee Tastes Bad	Tastes Watered Down	
	Coffee Machine	Coffee	Coffee Tastes Bad	Too Cold	
	Coffee Machine	Coffee	Coffee Tastes Bad	Doesn't Taste Like Starbucks"	
IncidentResolutionCategoryEnum	Called Coffee Machine Repair Technician				

Enter Valid Data
Allowed characters:
A-Z, a-z, 0-9
`~!@#$%^&*()_+-=[]{}\|\;':"<>,.?/`

FIGURE 2.5   Building the list item structure.

FastSeal.exe

MPs in Service Manager can have two formats: sealed and unsealed. An unsealed MP is an XML file that can be modified, and a sealed MP is an MP file that cannot be modified.

FastSeal.exe is a tool that helps you seal an MP. You can find additional information about fastSeal and sealed and unsealed MPs in Chapter 17, "Management Packs."

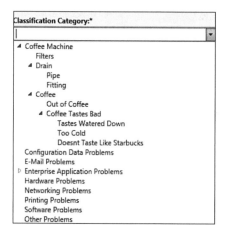

FIGURE 2.6   The new incident classification list in the Service Manager console.

SecureStorageBackup

When installing the Service Manager components, several encryption keys are generated:

▶ An encryption key between your Service Manager management server and the database. This key encrypts the data traffic between Service Manager and the database warehouse management servers and their databases.

▶ An encryption key between your SSP and the Service Manager database. This encrypts the data traffic between the SSP and the Service Manager database.

Should it become necessary to recover your Service Manager installation from a disaster such as a software or hardware failure, you will need the encryption keys. After you back up the encryption key, store it in a safe location. On the installation media for Service Manager, in the SecureStorageBackup folder, you will find the SecureStorageBackup tool to use both for export of the key and restore of the key.

Exchange Connector

Connecting to a mail server and handling incoming email were among the first big topics in the Service Manager forums when the product released. Out of the box, Service Manager can handle incoming email regarding incidents, but there are some challenges. By default, one incident is generated for each email message; even if the email message is a response to an already existing incident, there is no capability to update an incident, only to create new incidents. The addition of the Exchange connector addresses this issue by communicating directly with Microsoft Exchange 2007 and 2010. The Exchange connector connects Service Manager to the Exchange server for processing incoming email related to work items, such as incidents and change requests. The connector also includes a SendEmail solution that enables analysts to email messages to end users directly from the Service Manager console.

The Exchange connector contains the following features:

▶ Create incident from email

▶ Update incident action log from email

▶ Resolve or close incident from email

▶ Approve or reject change requests from email

▶ Update change request "action log" from email

▶ Mark manual activities completed from email

▶ Add email file attachment to work items as attachments

▶ Send notification to users from the console

Opalis Integration Pack for Service Manager

Opalis Integration Server (OIS) is an automation platform for orchestrating and integrating IT tools. OIS is part of the System Center suite and supported by Microsoft. It is available at no cost to customers with System Center Suite Datacenter or Enterprise (SMSD/E) licenses. A 180-day trial version is available, as well.

OIS enables IT organizations to automate processes and ensure they use best practices and do so in a reliable way. The current version, OIS 6.3, includes a large number of integration packs. An integration pack is a collection of objects, used to integrate with a specific product. Figure 2.7 shows an OIS policy that, among others, includes Service Manager, Operations Manager, and Virtual Machine Manager (VMM) objects.

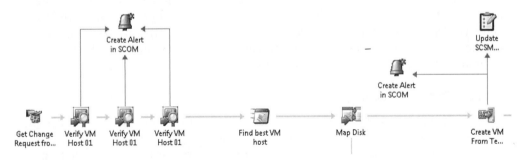

FIGURE 2.7   Part of a Opalis policy, including Service Manager activities.

If you need to integrate with tools outside of Service Manager, consider using the Opalis product. OIS does not require any code writing or development skills; instead, it is drag and drop to build workflows. Each activity for all integration packs outputs all results to a data bus. All data on the data bus can be used as input in another activity. For example, if you use the Get Object activity to get all old inactive incidents, you can use the Update

Object to resolve each one of them, without keeping track of which incidents the first object returns, simply by telling the engine to use the output from Get Object as input in Update Object.

The Service Manager integration pack includes the following objects:

▶ **Create Change with Template:** This object is used to create a change request based on a template that already exists in Service Manager.

▶ **Create Object:** This object can be used to create a new instance of a class in Service Manager. This object can, for example, be used to create a new change request or a new incident and to create a new project in a custom class.

▶ **Create Incident with Template:** This object is used to create an incident based on a template that already exists in Service Manager.

▶ **Created Related Object:** This object is used to create a new object that is related to other existing objects. This activity supports both membership relationship and hosted relationship.

▶ **Create Relationship:** This object is used to create a relationship between two already existing objects (for example, between a computer and an incident).

▶ **Delete Relationship:** This object is used to delete a relationship between two objects.

▶ **Get Activity:** This object is used to query for an activity record based on a set of criteria.

▶ **Get Object:** This object is used to query for a record based on a set of filter criteria. For example, this object can be used to get all incidents with a specific category and severity.

▶ **Get Relationship:** This object is used to generate a list of related objects for the source object and criteria that you specify in the activity in OIS.

▶ **Monitor Object:** This object looks for either new objects that fulfill the criteria or for updated objects that fulfill the criteria. For example, it can trigger a workflow if a new incident is created with a specific category or if special activities in a change request update the status.

▶ **Update Activity:** This object is used to update an object of the selected activity class—for example, a step in a change request that OIS carries out and afterward updates the activity in Service Manager. Figure 2.8 displays the dialog box of the Update Activity object.

▶ **Update Object:** The Update object is used to change the values of an existing object in Service Manager.

For additional information about Opalis Integration Server and the Service Manager integration pack, see *System Center Opalis Integration Server 6.3 Unleashed* (Sams, 2011).

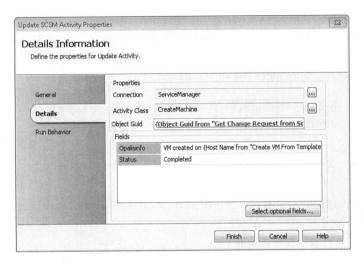

FIGURE 2.8   Settings of an Update SCSM Activity object in an OIS policy.

Overview of SP 1

Service Manager 2010 was released to production (RTM) in April 2010. Service Pack (SP) 1 followed rather quickly, released in December of the same year, generally available Q1 2011. As is expected with SPs, there were no new features. SP 1 included bug fixes, additional languages, and support for SQL Server 2008 Release 2 (R2). The main features in the SP 1 release included the following:

- ▶ Support for 10 additional languages

- ▶ Performance enhancements

- ▶ Updates in the Operations Manager CI connector around support for distributed applications

- ▶ Updates related to notification

- ▶ Localizability and globalization updates

- ▶ Support for SQL Server 2008 R2

- ▶ Fixing a memory leak in the console

- ▶ Updates to the data warehouse and reporting

Bug fixes included those fixes in cumulative updates (CUs) 1, 2, and 3. You can install SP1 after any of these CUs or you can install SP 1 directly on the Service Manager 2010 RTM version. You can also install SP 1 directly without any earlier version of Service Manager 2010.

Language Support

Many organizations have a policy and requirement that all software-facing end users must be in the local language, and many government organizations in Europe have this requirement. Service Manager 2010 did not support many of the European languages when first released. Many customers worked around this by implementing a third-party self-service console that provided other languages. (English in the Service Manager console itself was never an issue.) SP 1 adds 10 additional languages to Service Manager:

- Danish
- Finnish
- Swedish
- Greek
- Turkish
- Dutch
- Norwegian
- Portuguese (Portugal)
- Polish

Updated Service Manager Authoring Tool

The System Center Service Manager Authoring Tool is used to customize and extend Service Manager. Along with the SP 1 release, there was also a new version of the Authoring Tool. The SP 1 version of the Authoring Tool feature list includes the following:

- Form customization
- Creating new simple forms to support custom classes
- Class editor to create and extend classes and relationships in the CMDB
- Creation of workflows with detailed trigger criteria and extensible library of actions
- Support for sealing MPs
- Class browser and form browser to easy locate classes and forms from all MPs

Summary

This chapter introduced Service Manager 2010. It discussed its history and commonly used terms and provided an overview of the product and changes in Service Pack 1. The next chapter discusses MOF and ITIL and how Service Manager is built on these frameworks.

CHAPTER 3

MOF, ITIL, and Service Manager

This chapter discusses the service management processes specified in the Microsoft Operations Framework (MOF) and Information Technology Information Library (ITIL) supported by System Center Service Manager, including Incident, Problem, Change, and Configuration Management. The focus is to describe the goals and objectives, key terminology, concepts, and activity workflows of these processes, because they are the ideas behind the functionality found in Service Manager. Understanding these ideas is critical to ensuring a successful implementation that provides the intended value to the business, for several reasons:

▶ Understanding the goals and objectives of each process is necessary to ensure that your implementation helps your organization achieve them.

▶ Without a firm understanding of these concepts, you put your implementation at risk—either by spending cycles trying to sort the distinctions between terms such as *Incident, Problem, Known Error,* and *Service Request* or through missteps, rework, or suboptimal implementation because these concepts aren't understood.

This chapter includes a high-level mapping of MOF and ITIL concepts to Service Manager, but detailed implementation guidance is left for subsequent chapters.

Introduction to MOF and ITIL

Service Manager is different from Microsoft's other System Center products. It is more like SAP, which encodes business processes in software. For Service Manager, those processes are a subset of the service management processes of MOF and ITIL: Incident, Problem, Change, and Configuration Management. That is why an understanding of MOF and ITIL is particularly useful for Service Manager, and why getting full value from the product requires not only adequate technical knowledge but also an appropriate level of knowledge of the processes the Service Manager product supports.

The sections that follow describe what MOF and ITIL are, the value they provide, and how to get started with them in the context of implementing Service Manager.

MOF and ITIL Are IT Service Management Frameworks

Both MOF and ITIL are service management frameworks. *Service management* is the concept of organizing and presenting Information Technology (IT) to the business as a set of services. MOF and ITIL employ a set of interrelated terminology, concepts, and process workflows based on best practices for supporting and delivering services to the customers and users. MOF and ITIL are models for how to run IT as a service provider (as opposed an IT organization that is technology centric and views itself and conducts its business primarily as one that cares for and feeds technology).

MOF and ITIL are written guidance specifying how to organize and manage around a set of services to optimize value for customers and users of those services. An enormous corollary to this idea (at least for the IT organization) is that to consistently and sustainably provide the levels of service the business needs, IT must have the wherewithal it requires to deliver those services consistently. The intention here is to do something good both for IT and the customers and users it serves.

BUSINESS SERVICES IN SERVICE MANAGER

Service Manager's business service definition functionality directly supports the idea of managing IT as a service provider with defined services supported by IT processes.

Through it, Service Manager provides a place for you to define services and to describe their components and how they relate to one another—as a basis for managing Incidents, Problems, Changes, and configuration items (CIs).

Here is an example of how an IT organization's approach will differ if they are technology centered versus service centered:

▶ With a technology-centered model, the organization and what it does and provides for its customers and end users is organized around technology (for example, Microsoft Exchange).

▶ In a service management model, this is organized around messaging.

This is more than just semantics. A messaging service consists of Microsoft Exchange along with a number of other associated components and mechanisms such as service level agreements (SLAs) required to consistently deliver a service to customers and users at the expected levels of quality. These things might be missed or go unmanaged when the focus is just on the technology, and might then result in an overall lower quality of service.

Think about the difference between how a company that offers messaging as a service over the Internet and how a traditional IT shop offers it, and you start to get the idea of service management. If you are provisioning messaging over the Internet, you must

- Determine the services you want to provide. You might have different service packages with different features (email, instant messaging, teleconferencing, shared workspaces, LiveMeeting, and so on) in each package.

- Establish service level packages (different levels of features and support for each service package), such as the level of availability, capacity and performance, security, and service continuity (disaster recovery).

- Set pricing and establish charging models and mechanisms for each service and service level package combinations.

- Present your services (including quality of service and cost) in a catalog to customers and potential customers so that they can easily understand which services and service level packages are right for them.

- Separate the service provided (messaging) from the technologies that make it possible (the specific infrastructure and applications; for example, Microsoft Exchange and Lync) so that you have agility and choice in how to provide the service.

Why might an internal IT shop want to adopt such a model? For the same reasons a vendor would:

- The value of the service is made more explicit, so it is clear that the service either has or does not have the right price-to-performance characteristics.

- It is obvious what is and is not included in the service.

- Available service levels and their cost are made explicit.

- Most important for the service provider, what it takes (the wherewithal required) to provide the services consistently to agreed service levels is made explicit in terms of infrastructure, applications, organization, contracts, vendors, processes, subservices, and service levels. The roles and responsibilities of the provider and users and customers are also made explicit.

Put another way, organizing around services helps you avoid overcommitting—for example, to providing five nines (99.999%) of availability on a network technology that can provide only 99% uptime. Organizing around services forces you to think through what people, processes, and technology are required for each service to meet its objectives and to staff and procure accordingly (or, with explicit agreement from your customer, to back off to a lesser service with lower service levels).

The idea is that each service is managed for value individually and that IT can make explicit and strive to put in place and maintain the resources required to consistently make, and keep, good commitments. A related idea is that the focus keeps the end in mind (the service itself: what is provided and to what service level) rather than the means (the particular technologies chosen). This separation of ends and means is vital in allowing both IT and the organization it serves to have the level of agility modern businesses require. This is the essence of any IT management framework, which is as follows:

▶ To provide key principles, models, and organizing principles that provide a better capability than alternatives for ensuring customers get what they need

▶ For IT to have all the underpinning mechanisms to ensure the levels of quality of service required and agreed for each service, including infrastructure, applications, and processes

Organizing around services brings together what the customer needs (the features and the levels of service) with the technology wherewithal required to deliver on that need consistently. In the end, your aim with service organizations is to be able to say, with confidence, "Yes, Mr./Ms. Customer, this can be done, and this is what it costs." A service management framework helps you get there because it provides the set of concepts and constructs that work together to make it happen.

One such useful service management construct is the service map. *Service maps* provide a graphical way to define the components and dependencies of a service that are inputs into the service catalog and SLAs for the service. Microsoft, via service maps, provides a great start with IT Service Management (ITSM). These maps are logical diagrams of services, which are useful for understanding and communicating the components that make up services and how they relate to one another. They provide documentation of architecture, are useful in troubleshooting, and function as a basis for automating services and their associated monitoring and control processes. For example, you can take a service map and translate it into a distributed application in Operations Manager (OpsMgr). This is described in Chapter 9, "Business Services."

TIP: BEST PRACTICES FOR CREATING BUSINESS SERVICES IN SERVICE MANAGER

Creating distributed applications in Operations Manager is the preferred way to establish business services in Service Manager. It is important to note that only the name of the IT service is synchronized across the connector. If you want the relationships to show between CIs in the service, you must export the distributed application from Operations Manager and import it into Service Manager.

The big bet of MOF and ITIL is that organizing around and managing to a set of services is a superior way to provide value to customers.

Imagine two IT organizations with the exact same resources—IT infrastructure, applications, people (including vendors and suppliers), money, agreements, contracts, documents, and anything else needed to deliver an IT service—yet with widely different results in terms of the value they create for their customers. What makes the difference in their results? A key factor is how they organize themselves and manage the important things (what they do, manage, and deliver), including the processes they follow, how they use knowledge, the people they have, and how they leverage them to create value in the form of goods and services.

MOF and ITIL specify, among other things, that IT service providers should

▶ Create a service catalog (see http://blogs.technet.com/b/randyy/archive/2005/07/25/408206.aspx).

A *service catalog entry* is a service description that helps communicate what the service is, what it costs, and how performance is measured. Table 3.1 is a portion of a service catalog entry for messaging for a fictitious company (Odyssey.com).

TABLE 3.1   Service Catalog Excerpt (Adapted from MOF Job Aid "SIP Service Catalog")

Service Name	Messaging Service
Service Description	Odyssey's IT department hosts the entire messaging service infrastructure, enabling Odyssey employees to send and receive email and to synchronize their work schedules.
Business Alignment	This service is funded as part of Odyssey's IT operational budget. The service benefits all users by providing a centralized facility for synchronizing data from Microsoft Outlook, email filtering and caching, web-based access to email, and free/busy schedule synchronization.
Business Owner	The Human Resources (HR) division is the business owner for this application.
Service Qualification	This service is available to all regular employees of Odyssey, at all locations worldwide. Each data center has a Microsoft Exchange server that provides for the servers at that location, and each of these servers is connected to the corporate backbone for data synchronization.
Service Manager	Dave Pultorak.
Service Initiation Contact	Service is initiated by the HR department for each new employee given approval to use company's email.
External Dependencies	Internet communication facilities, VeriSign security certificate services.

TABLE 3.1   Service Catalog Excerpt (Adapted from MOF Job Aid "SIP Service Catalog")

Service Name	Messaging Service
Service Elements	Service desk/incident management.
	Application availability and metric reporting.
	Application SLA.
	Hours of service.
	Problem management.
	Tier 2 escalations and proactive root-cause analysis.
	Change management.
	Change management and control.
	Technology upgrades.
	Patch management.
	Security management.
	Security protection: intrusion detection, locked-down security policies.
	Internet-specific security protection: antivirus, antiphishing, antispam.
	Additional service features.
	Proactive health monitoring.
	High-availability management.
	Nightly server data backup.

▶ Present themselves to the business through that service catalog (using customer-oriented terminology abstracted from the technology used to deliver the service—for example, using *messaging* as the name for the service instead of Microsoft Exchange).

▶ Define service levels in SLAs.

An SLA is an agreement between an IT service provider and customer specifying the service, service level targets, and provider and customer responsibilities. Table 3.2 is an example of service quality measurements and performance targets excerpted from "MOF Job Aid - Service Level Agreement," available from Microsoft.

▶ Use these and other mechanisms required to manage the quality, cost, and ultimately the value provided to the business by every service.

Although this version of Service Manager does not support service catalogs or SLAs, it is important to understand what they are because they are at the center of the service management ecosystem that Service Manager supports.

You can get examples and templates for service catalogs, SLAs, and other service management mechanisms in the "MOF Job Aid" collections, available for download from Microsoft.

TABLE 3.2   SLA Excerpt

Service Quality Measurements

Measurement	Definition	Performance Target
Service availability percentage	Percent of time the application is available during normal schedule minus the impact time from any scheduled or unexpected events	Target percentage. Example: 99.6%.
Incident resolution time	Time between recording and resolution of an incident: Priority 1 = < 30 minutes Priority 2 = < 2 hours Priority 3 = < 4 hours	X% of transactions of type Y to be completed within Z minutes or hours or days. Example: 95% of all Priority 1 email incidents are resolved within 30 minutes.
Root-cause analysis reports	Production of reports describing root cause of a particular incident or problem	Timeframe for report to be delivered. Example: 100% of all root-cause analysis reports will be delivered within 24 hours of when the incident occurred.
SLA review	Review of service to determine whether any changes are required	% of reviews to be completed. Example: 100%.

TIP: FOCUS ON ENDS, NOT MEANS, TO ENSURE BUSINESS VALUE FROM SERVICE MANAGER IMPLEMENTATION

You can argue about the level of formality required from organization to organization. You can use different terminology. You can vary from the basic processes described in this chapter. In the end, however, you cannot argue against the primary objectives of MOF and ITIL processes described on Table 3.3. This is an important point because the processes are means and the primary objectives are outcomes or ends that you seek by investing in them. They are, in the end, how you will be measured by the business and how you should measure yourself and others. This is vital to understand and keep in mind while implementing the Service Manager tool and the processes it underpins—what organizations are aiming to gain is some end typically satisfied or described by the primary objective.

Said another way, you are not done when the tool is stood up. You are done when the use of the tool is producing the measurable improvements the organization set out to gain when choosing to implement the tool.

TABLE 3.3   Subset of MOF and ITIL Processes That Underpin Services

Process	Responsible For	Primary Objective
Incident Management	Managing the life cycle of all Incidents, where an *Incident* is an unplanned interruption to an IT service or a reduction in the quality of an IT service. Failure of a CI that has not yet impacted a service is also an Incident. The primary objective of Incident Management is to return the IT service to users as quickly as possible.	Minimize the business disruption of incidents by getting individual instances of a user or service being down back up and running as quickly as possible.
Problem Management	Managing Problems, which are the root cause of one or more Incidents, by ensuring these are identified and that workarounds or permanent fixes are found.	Get to the root cause of problems. Know and be able to articulate clearly what the top problems are, what you have done so far to mitigate them, and what you will do next.
Change Management	Controlling the life cycle of all Changes, where a *Change* is the addition, modification, or removal of anything that could impact IT services. The scope should include all IT services, CIs, processes, documentation, and so on. The primary objective of Change Management is to enable beneficial Changes to be made with minimum disruption to IT services.	Minimize the business disruption of Changes and ensure you can answer this question: What changed?
Configuration Management	Maintaining information about CIs required to deliver an IT service, including relationships among CIs, where a configuration item is any component that needs to be managed to deliver an IT service.	Ensure a logical model of the live environment is defined, controlled, maintained, and kept accurate as a source of fact-based management of IT services and to comply with corporate governance requirements.

Determining the Value of MOF and ITIL

MOF and ITIL terminology, concepts, and mechanisms are embedded in Service Manager, and the product supports service management services and processes. This is one very good reason to care about MOF and ITIL. However, there are other reasons, which are important for you to consider as a basis for understanding and articulating the value the product can bring (and to whom). What is in it for you, your team, your IT organization and its suppliers, your customers and end users, and the business? Consider WIIFM (*What's In It For Me?*) for MOF and ITIL for all stakeholder audiences: the IT individual contributor, the IT team, the IT organization, its suppliers, its customers and end users, and the business as a whole:

▶ **For the individual contributor:** Service management certification is becoming a "basic and expected" criterion and is also a top certification in terms of salary. (Much of what IT professionals do each day is handle changes, troubleshoot incidents, seek the root cause of problems, and so on.) The training for that lies in MOF and ITIL. Other professions have long-established common terminology (accountants, for example, don't argue over what an *asset* or *liability* is) and mechanisms (accountants can expect to see a general ledger when they start work at a company). MOF and ITIL provide these for IT professionals.

▶ **For the IT team:** It is not unusual for teams of highly intelligent individuals to devolve into a communal idiot, especially when a significant issue arises. (Just about anyone who has spent more than a few minutes in IT can attest to this!) For teams to function well, they need shared ideas and standards for "how things are done around here." MOF and ITIL provide these for IT teams.

▶ **For the IT provider:** The IT provider as a whole needs "a" method to organize, and that method needs to be fully worked out with enough interlocking concepts and supporting templates and examples to stand on its own legs. It also helps (greatly) if these methods are adopted widely, because it then can be expected that new starters and vendors who come and go need less ramp-up time. MOF and ITIL provide these.

LEARN CONCEPTS BEHIND THE TOOL TO HELP ENSURE THE RESULTS YOU SEEK BY IMPLEMENTING IT ARE REALIZED

By far, the most important reason to care about MOF as it pertains to Service Manager is that MOF and ITIL are the concepts behind the configuration parameters. Experience in implementing ITSM tools shows that where people (and tooling implementations) get stuck is the concepts behind the tools.

Service Manager is like SAP: It's not just software, it is a new mindset and new way of working (service management), with its own set of processes, key principles, models, and terminology. There is a certain entry-level understanding of these you need to configure and use the tool effectively. You can't just sit down and play a board game without understanding the layout of the board, the pieces, the play, and rules, however basic. Similarly, you and your organization will make a grave error if you just install the tool and shout "mission accomplished," or just as bad, try to shoehorn the tool into your old ways of thinking and working.

Said another way, as with SAP, if your organization tries to jam its old way of working into the tool, results will be suboptimal, and everyone will be sorry. The resulting tool configuration will be suboptimal, as will the use of the tool. The end result will be the value the organization sought to gain by implementing the tool (remember, the "ends in mind" or primary objectives in Table 3.3?) will not be fully realized. There is an old saying in service management circles: A fool with a tool is still a fool. You need to understand the concepts behind the software.

MOF and ITIL Compared

Table 3.4 compares MOF and ITIL along a number of key dimensions. You can use it as a starting point for determining where to invest your time in learning more about these frameworks.

TABLE 3.4   Comparison of MOF and ITIL

Features	MOF	ITIL
Form factor and cost	Publication. MOF is available for free download.	Publication. ITIL publications are available in book form and a variety of other formats for purchase.
Training and certification	Both MOF and ITIL have training and certification paths. MOF is limited to one course and certification at the Foundation level.	ITIL has a Foundation-level certification, along with Intermediates, all the way up to Expert- and Master-level certification.
Mapping to generally accepted IT management frameworks	Both MOF and ITIL provide mapping to other generally accepted IT management frameworks, including each other as well as ISO 20000 and COBIT. Both support these generally accepted frameworks and even provides a map to them. So, you can be assured that what you do with MOF and ITIL will not be out of line with other frameworks.	
Cost, features, restrictions	MOF is free to download and use, and includes not just guidance but also examples and templates, with creative commons licensing.	ITIL is owned by the U.K. Office of Government Commerce, with associated restrictions and costs for use.
Writing style and purpose	MOF is written in a checklist, prescriptive style, to be applied directly. It features clear outcomes, key questions, inputs, outputs, goals, and measures in a concise, relevant checklist style. This is a refreshing departure from more academic treatments of service management ideas.	ITIL is written in a textbook style, describing service management activities, deliverables, processes, functions, roles, key concepts, and models, with comprehensive coverage and many more pages of core content than MOF.

TABLE 3.4   Comparison of MOF and ITIL

Features	MOF	ITIL
Intention	MOF provides navigation into Microsoft's service management assets—the additional guidance, training, solution accelerators, services, and products—that help you implement service management concepts on the Microsoft platform *and* the products and technologies that make up that platform. Because the Microsoft platform is a key part of most IT shops, you need to understand what Microsoft has to offer, and MOF helps organization these assets so that you can quickly discover, grasp, and apply them.	ITIL is technology agnostic.
Content (processes, functions, and management reviews)	MOF covers a set of processes and functions, and includes management reviews, as driven by Microsoft's ecosystem of customers and partners	ITIL includes processes and functions as driven by the membership of the IT Service Management Forum (itSMF), the ITIL user group.

The conclusion here is that although there are differences between ITIL and MOF, and to some extent because of these differences, some knowledge of both MOF and ITIL are necessary as background and context for a successful Service Manager implementation.

IMPLEMENTING SERVICE MANAGER (THE TECHNOLOGY) IS ONLY PART OF WHAT IS NECESSARY IN A SERVICE MANAGEMENT TOOL IMPLEMENTATION

It is vital to understand the service management triad introduced in Chapter 1, "Service Management Basics:" people, processes, and technology. Although this is an old saw, it is a good one. The key point here is that implementing service management requires effort and action in all three dimensions. Standing up the tool is only one-third of the equation. You must also organize and train people to understand the concepts behind the tool and the processes it supports to encourage the new way of working. The Service Manager product is only part of the equation. Only a portion of what needs to be implemented lies within the tool. The rest lies in people (what's between their ears and what new behaviors they take on) and in processes. For more information, see Chapters 10, "Incident Management," 11, "Problem Management," and 12, "Change Management."

Here are some examples: To implement Change Management, you have to decide policies on what is and is not a major, minor, or significant Change; and what qualifies as
a standard Change or an emergency Change. You have to decide whether you are going
to have a CAB, who will be on it, and how often they will meet. You must decide who
owns and who manages the Change process and what reports will be generated (and
by whom, for whom, at what interval, and to what end).

Much of this lies outside the tool (technology) in people and processes, and only some
is directly supported by the tool, and yet it is all important and part of what needs to
be considered, decided, and delivered in a service management tool implementation.

Getting Started with MOF and ITIL

This section outlines some ideas and resources for getting started with MOF and ITIL.
Once you have a clear vision of what you want to do with MOF and ITIL, it is important
to know how to get started.

Take the following steps to get started with MOF (additional information available at
http://www.microsoft.com/mof):

▶ Download MOF core content. Skim the contents so that you get a feel for what is
  included and then keep it near for reference. Read the MOF overview to familiarize
  yourself with MOF, and read the MOF Glossary to understand the terminology.

▶ Download and review the IT Pro Quick Start Kit for a great introduction to MOF,
  including podcasts, PowerPoint files, and training and certification information.

▶ Download the "Getting Started with MOF" implementation guide and read it to
  determine your highest potential, most relevant jumping-off point for getting started.

▶ Download "Bridging from MOF Guidance to Microsoft Products - A Companion
  Guide" and read it to understand how Microsoft products support MOF IT service
  management concepts.

▶ Review and download other MOF guidance and job aids as you see fit where there is
  a direct hit for a problem or opportunity you see on the job.

▶ Optionally, take an MOF Foundation course and pass the MOF Certification
  examination.

Here are some ways to get started with ITIL:

▶ Read "An Introductory Overview of ITIL V3," from the IT Service Management
  Forum to get a feel for ITIL's structure and content.

▶ Read Van Haren Publishing's excellent *ITIL V3: A Pocket Guide*, which provides
  process details left out of IT Service Management Forum's "An Introductory
  Overview of ITIL V3," which is more concerned with providing a high-level
  overview of the service life cycle.

▶ Download and review the ITIL Glossary to understand the terminology.

▶ Take an ITIL Foundation course, and take and pass the ITIL Foundation examination.

▶ Optionally, read the five core ITIL publications. These books are available from a wide variety of sources and in a number of formats, such as PDF, eBook, hardcopy publication, and HTML-based DVD.

▶ Optionally, take additional ITIL courses and examinations leading to ITIL Expert or Master status.

MOF and ITIL Processes Supported by Service Manager

MOF and ITIL specify a set of IT processes deemed necessary to ensure consistent quality of delivery of IT services. The core set of processes tend to be those most closely associated with end users (that is, the processes that if missing or broken tend to evoke loud complaints most quickly). This version of Service Manager supports the most important end user-facing processes: Incident, Problem, Change, and Configuration Management.

The following sections discuss these processes, looking at the following for each process:

▶ Definition, goals, and objectives

▶ Key terminology

▶ Why the process matters (its value)

▶ Key performance indicators (KPIs)

▶ Reporting

▶ Scope

▶ Integration with other processes and functions

▶ Process activity workflow

▶ Key roles and responsibilities

▶ Key inputs and outputs

▶ High-level considerations for implementing with Service Manager

The key decisions to make when implementing the processes include people and process decisions that in some cases sit outside the Service Manager tool and in other cases drive configuration values for the tool.

Incident Management

Incident Management refers to the process responsible for managing the life cycle of all Incidents, where an *Incident* is an unplanned interruption to an IT service or a reduction in the quality of an IT service. Failure of a CI (any component that needs to be managed to deliver an IT service, including IT services, hardware, software, buildings, people, and formal documentation such as process documentation and SLAs) that has not yet impacted service is also an Incident. The primary objective of Incident Management is to return the IT service to users as quickly as possible. For more information, see Chapter 10, which covers Incident Management in detail.

Incident Management is the process of managing deviations from normal service, restoring normal service operation quickly with minimum business disruption, and getting individual Users back up and running. Incident Management utilizes Configuration Management data to enable efficient and effective resolution of Incidents and to identify where Change releases have caused Incidents.

The goal of Incident Management is to restore normal service operation as quickly as possible with minimum disruption to the business and to ensure that the best achievable levels of availability and service are maintained.

Objectives of Incident Management include the following:

▶ Restoring normal service as quickly as possible.

▶ Minimizing the negative impact of Incidents on the business.

▶ Ensuring that Incidents are processed consistently and that none are lost

▶ Directing support resources where most required.

▶ Providing information that allows support processes to be optimized, the number of Incidents to be reduced, and management planning to be carried out.

Table 3.5 presents Incident Management key terminology.

TABLE 3.5   Key Terminology in Incident Management

Term	Explanation
Incident	Any event that is not part of the standard operation of a service and that causes, or may cause, an interruption to, or a reduction in, the quality of that service.
Problem	An unknown error, the underlying cause of one or more Incidents.
Known Error	A Problem for which a root cause and permanent fix or workaround are identified but where the fix has not been implemented.
Workaround	A temporary fix or technique that eliminates the customer's reliance on the faulty service component.
Impact	The likely effect on the business service, often equal to the extent of distortion of agreed or expected service levels.
Urgency	The speed of resolution required, based on impact and the business needs of the customer.

TABLE 3.5   Key Terminology in Incident Management

Term	Explanation
Priority	This is the relative sequence of resolution required, based on impact and urgency, and other relevant factors such as resource availability, and calculated based on impact and urgency.
Escalation	The mechanism that assists with timely resolution of an Incident. There are two types: functional escalation (transfer of an Incident between n-tier support departments) and hierarchical escalation (calling on management to assist in handling of an Incident).

Incident Management helps IT professionals, teams, and organizations achieve a critical outcome: minimizing the business disruption of Incidents by getting individual "hands on the keyboard"—users back up and running and restoring service as quickly as possible.

Because resources are to be allocated to the Incident Management process, the value of that process to the business has to be determined so that the resources allocated can be justified. To determine the value an organization places on Incident Management, consider the following:

▶ What mechanisms are in place to reduce the business disruption of incidents and help ensure user satisfaction, especially when multiple Incidents arrive at the same time?

▶ Who handles Incidents when they arrive, and what does good handling look like as measured by impact on user satisfaction? What are expected service levels and resolve times, and how do you ensure performance is satisfactory?

▶ How do you ensure quick, consistent resolution of Incidents and keep Incidents from getting lost?

▶ How can you organize around Incidents in a way that fosters the productivity of both users and IT analysts?

▶ How do you minimize the impact of Incidents on service quality, either by preventing them in the first place or minimizing their impact when they do occur?

▶ Who are the stakeholders of Incident Management? What is their stake?

The value of Incident Management should drive all further discussions and decisions on scope, priority, resources allocated to, and automation of the Incident Management process with Service Manager.

Reporting is a means of understanding and managing the performance of the Incident Management process. Although Service Manager includes out-of-the-box reporting functionality for Incident Management, you can look to MOF and ITIL for further guidance and what to report, when, and why (including the KPIs that are important to Incident

Management). This includes first-call fix rate, the number of Incidents raised based on a Change, number of escalated Incidents, number of Incidents not meeting SLA targets, and Operations Manager alert to Incident ticket ratio.

INCIDENT MANAGEMENT AND OTHER PROCESSES AND FUNCTIONS

The service desk plays a key role in Incident Management. The service desk is a function, organizational unit, or department. It is the end users' principal interface to the IT service provider, and handles Incidents and Service Requests. It provides an interface for the end user to other ITSM processes and plays the key role in the Incident Management process, recording and monitoring the progress of incidents and retaining ownership of incidents until they are resolved. However, it is important to understand that even though the service desk plays a key role in the Incident Management process, it is not equivalent to it. The Incident Management process involves many organizational units (for example, Tier 1+ support groups).

Problem and Change Management depend on Incident Management for Incident data. Incident Management depends on Change Management to control Incidents; the service desk function to own, record, and track Incident progress; Problem Management for root-cause resolution and Problem, Known Error, and workaround knowledge bases; and Configuration Management for an accurate configuration management database (CMDB).

The Request Fulfillment process is responsible for managing the life cycle of all *Service Requests*, which are requests from users for information, or advice, or for a standard change or for access to an IT service. An example is a request to reset a password, or to set up standard IT services for a new user. Service Requests are usually handled by a service desk and do not require a request for change (RFC) to be submitted. They have a separate workflow from Incidents and Incident Management, and often have different IT analysts involved in performing and reviewing the associated activities. This version of Service Manager does not directly support service request processing as its own separate workflow. See the System Center Engineering Team blog for some examples of how to customize Service Manager for service request processing.

Figure 3.1 shows the activities in the Incident Management process.

Incident Management roles include the following:

▶ The incident manager, who owns the results of the Incident Management process

▶ The service desk manager, who owns the results of the service desk function

▶ IT managers and analysts in first, second, and third-tier support groups, including specialist support groups and external suppliers

▶ The problem manager, for major Incident handling

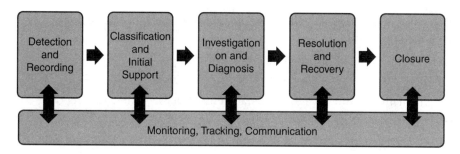

FIGURE 3.1   Incident Management process activities.

Table 3.6 shows inputs and outputs of the Incident Management process.

TABLE 3.6   Inputs and Outputs in Incident Management

Input	Output
Incident details (from the service desk, networks, or computer operations)	Updated Incident records, including resolution/workarounds.
Configuration details from the CMDB	RFC for Incident resolution.
Response from Incident matching against Problems and Known Errors	Update, resolved, and closed Incidents. Communication to customers.
Resolution details	Management information (reports): service reports, incident statistics, audit reports.
Response or result of RFC to effect resolution for Incident(s)	Update, resolved, and closed Incidents. Communication to customers.

The following key questions must be answered to drive decisions when implementing the Incident Management process with Service Manager:

▶ What is the value of Incident Management to the business?

▶ Which Incidents are within scope for the process, and what target resolution times have you identified?

▶ What values should be assigned to Incident record fields/drop-down (enumeration) list values?

▶ What are your Incident escalation procedures, and how do they relate to the Escalated tick box and Assigned to field in the Incident form?

▶ What Incident prioritization scheme will you use?

▶ How will you use the Incident process in conjunction with Problem, Change, and Configuration Management? What are the expected interfaces?

▶ What roles and responsibilities will be assigned for the Incident Management processes, and to whom?

▶ Will auto-ticketing be used (for example, for events trapped by Configuration Manager's Desired Configuration Management [DCM] or Operations Manager alerts)?

▶ What requirements do you have for automatic escalation or flexible routing of Incidents?

▶ Will the Self-Service portal and email ticketing be used to reduce inbound call volume?

▶ What requirement do you have for automated, rule-based Incident notification?

▶ Which metrics will you track, and which reports will you produce as a basis for managing performance? Will custom reports be required?

▶ Who needs to be informed and when throughout the life cycle of an Incident?

▶ What role will announcements and knowledge articles play in the Incident Management process?

Problem Management

Problem Management refers to the process by which Problems, which are the root cause of one or more Incidents, are identified and by which a workaround or a permanent fix is found, enabling the organization to reduce the number and impact of Incidents over time. Chapter 11 covers the Problem Management process in detail.

The goal of Problem Management is twofold—reactive and proactive:

▶ Being reactive minimizes the adverse effect on the business of Incidents and Problems caused by errors in the infrastructure, including supporting Incident Management, identifying and diagnosing Problems, escalating Problems, and monitoring Known Errors through the Change process.

▶ Being proactive preempts the occurrence of Incidents, Problems, and, including identifying potential Problems, initiating Change so that Problems don't (re)occur, and tracking problems and analyzing trends.

Here are the objectives of Problem Management:

▶ Minimize the negative impact of problems on the business

▶ Identify and correct the root cause of problems

Table 3.7 lists the key terminology of Problem Management.

It is important to understand that a Problem is not the same as an Incident. A Problem is the root cause of one or more Incidents. Problems are unknown errors; once the cause is known, they are flagged as Known Errors.

TABLE 3.7   Key Terminology in Problem Management

Term	Explanation
Incident	Any event that is not part of the standard operation of a service and that causes, or may cause, an interruption to, or a reduction in, the quality of that service.
Problem	An unknown error, the underlying cause of one or more Incidents.
Known Error	A Problem for which a root cause and permanent fix or workaround are identified but where the fix has not been implemented.
Work-around	A temporary fix or technique that eliminates the customer's reliance on the faulty service component.

Similarly, the Problem Management process is related to but distinct from the Incident Management process, so much so that MOF and ITIL recommend against combining Incident and Problem Management in the same function because they have conflicting interests. The imperative of Incident Management is to get the service and user back up and running, whatever it takes. It is not to go after the root cause of multiple Incidents. Problem Management, on the other hand, pulls up the zoom level and focuses on the root cause of multiple Incidents, seeking to eliminate and minimize the negative business impact of them by going after the root cause and by sharing information about Problems, Known Errors, and Workarounds. These imperatives conflict because, for example, eliminating Problems typically results in a lower first-call closure rate, because a whole set of Incidents have been eliminated as a result of eliminating the Problem. Problem Management helps IT professionals, teams, and organizations achieve a critical outcome: getting to the root cause of Problems and knowing and articulating what the top Problems are, what has been done to advance them, and what will be done next.

Because resources are to be allocated to the Problem Management process, the value of that process to the business has to be determined so that the resources allocated can be justified. To determine the value of an organization places on Problem Management, consider these questions:

▶ What mechanisms are in place to reduce the impact of chronic Problems on service availability and reliability?

▶ What mechanisms are in place to reduce Incident volume and resolution time and the negative impact on the business for related sets of Incidents?

▶ What mechanisms are in place to reduce Change volume as driven by the need to address chronic Problems and the associated negative impact of on the business?

▶ How can you achieve a good balance between reactive root-cause analysis efforts and proactive efforts to preempt Problems in the first place?

▶ How can service availability be guaranteed if there are outstanding Problems left unresolved? What are the potential issues with having Problems bypassed and not actually resolved?

▶ How can you help ensure that the time spent on investigation and diagnosis of multiple related Incidents and their root cause is as productive as possible for IT analysts?

▶ What mechanisms are in place to permanently solve chronic or recurring issues and reduce their number and negative impact on the business over time?

▶ What mechanisms are in place to ensure organizational learning occurs so that each day isn't another "Groundhog Day?" What means do you have to feed the organization with historical data to identify trends, root-cause resolutions, and workarounds to prevent and reduce problems?

▶ What means do you have of ensuring quicker, more consistent Incident resolution and a better first-time fix rate at the service desk? Who is going to make sure the workarounds, Known Error records, and knowledge articles required for this exist, are current, and are made available to the service desk when it makes a difference for them?

▶ Who are the stakeholders of Problem Management? What is their stake?

The value of Problem Management should drive all further discussions and decisions on scope, priority, resources allocated to, and automation of the Incident Management process with Service Manager.

Reporting is a means of understanding and managing the performance of the Problem Management process. Although Service Manager includes out-of-the-box reporting functionality for Problem Management, you can look to MOF and ITIL for further guidance and what to report, when, and why. This can include top Problems, what has been done to advance them so far, and what will be done next, percentage reduction of repeat Incidents, and percentage reduction in SLA targets being missed that are attributable to Problems.

PROBLEM MANAGEMENT AND OTHER PROCESSES AND FUNCTIONS

It is important to understand the differences between Problem and Incident Management. The main goal of Problem Management is detection of the underlying cause of Incidents and their subsequent resolution and prevention. In some cases, this goal directly conflicts with that of Incident Management, where the objective there is to restore service as quickly as possible through a workaround rather than a permanent Change. Prevention of future interruptions rather than recovery speed is of primary concern, although the speed of recovery is also an important consideration.

Problem Management is depended on by Incident Management for root-cause resolution and to help identify trends and take remedial action. Problem Management depends on Incident Management for Incident data, Change Management for Changes to resolve Known Errors, and Configuration Management for CI data in the CMDB.

Figure 3.2 shows the activities in the Problem Management process.

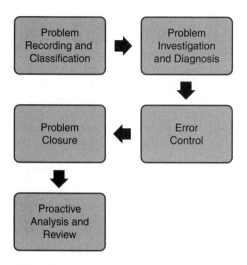

FIGURE 3.2   Problem Management process activities.

It is vital to identify who does what relative to Problem Management. Otherwise, there is no ownership, no one who can be held accountable for its results, and no or unclear responsibility for carrying out the process activities. Problem Management roles that you should make sure are identified and assigned in your organization include the following:

- ▶ The problem manager, who owns the results of the Problem Management, assigns Problems, and handles major Problems

- ▶ Support groups, which are second- and third-line support groups, specialist support groups, and external suppliers who own normal Problems, progress Problems through resolution, assign Problems to resolver group, create teams to resolve Problems, and monitor and track Problems and ensure resolution

- ▶ Problem resolvers, who are the IT analysts who investigate and diagnose Problems

Table 3.8 shows Problem Management inputs and outputs.

Several vital questions need to be answered to drive decisions when implementing the Problem Management process with Service Manager. Without getting these questions answered, you and the organization will get stuck somewhere along the way (in design, deployment, or operation of Service Manager) as you seek to accomplish the objectives set out by the business.

TABLE 3.8   Inputs and Outputs in Problem Management

Input	Output
Incident details	Known Errors
Configuration details	Fix/Workaround
Failed Change details	Management reports
Defined workarounds	Major Problem reviews
Potential Problem reported	RFC
Trends reported	Updated and closed Problem and Known Error records
Annual survey results	Improvements for procedures, documentation, training needs
Anecdotal evidence from users	

The following key questions must be answered to drive decisions when implementing the Problem Management process with Service Manager:

▶ What is the value of Problem Management to the business?

▶ Which Problems are within scope for the process, and what target resolution times have you identified?

▶ What values should be assigned to Problem record fields/drop-down (enumeration) list values?

▶ What is your policy and procedure regarding ticking the Known Error box in the Problem Form, indicating that the root cause of the Problem has been identified? In other words, who can do this, and what else do they need to do in conjunction with it (for example, update knowledge articles, make announcements, and close related tickets).

▶ What provisions have you made to ensure that bugs that come out of development are transferred into Service Manager as Problems and Known Errors along with any associated workarounds and knowledge articles when the systems are moved to production?

▶ What problem prioritization scheme will you use?

▶ How will you use the Problem process in conjunction with Incident, Change, and Configuration Management? What are the expected interfaces?

▶ What roles and responsibilities will be assigned for the Problem Management processes and to whom?

▶ What requirements do you have for correlation of multiple Incidents to Problems and related Workarounds, Changes, and knowledge articles, and what procedures will you adopt for resolving and closing Incidents when the related Problem is resolved or closed?

▶ Which metrics will you track, and which reports will you produce as a basis for managing performance? Will custom reports be required?

▶ What provisions have you made to ensure that a post-implementation review is made after major Problems?

▶ Who needs to be informed and when throughout the life cycle of a Problem?

▶ What role will announcements and knowledge articles play in the Problem Management process?

Change Management

Change Management refers to the process responsible for controlling the life cycle of all Changes, where a *Change* is the addition, modification, or removal of anything that could affect IT services. Change Management is about controlling proposed and actual Change to all CIs in the live environment and minimizing the business disruption from Changes the business requires. It is about ensuring the question "what changed?" can be answered effectively. For information about implementation of Change Management in Service Manager 2010, see Chapter 12.

The goals of the Change Management process are to ensure that standardized methods and procedures are used for efficient and prompt handling of all Changes, to minimize the impact of Change-related Incidents on service quality, and consequently to improve the day-to-day operations of the organization.

Table 3.9 presents Change Management key terminology.

TABLE 3.9   Key Terminology in Change Management

Term	Explanation
Change	Any new IT component deliberately introduced or modified to the IT environment that may affect an IT service level, the functioning of the environment, or one of its components.
Normal/Basic Change	Any deliberate action that alters the form, fit, or function of CIs (typically, an addition, modification, movement, or deletion that affects the IT infrastructure).
Standard Change	Change that is recurrent and well known and has been proceduralized to follow a predefined and relatively risk-free path and is the accepted response to a specific requirement of set of circumstances, where approval is effectively given in advance by policy.
Emergency Change	A Change that must be introduced as soon as possible to alleviate or avoid detrimental impact on the business.
Unauthorized Change	A Change made to the IT infrastructure that violates defined and agreed Change policies.

TABLE 3.9   Key Terminology in Change Management

Term	Explanation
Change category (major, significant, minor)	Measure of a Change's deployment impact on IT and the business. This is determined by measuring complexity, resources required (including people, money, and time), and risk of the deployment (including potential service downtime).
Major Change	Major impact or resources required or impact on other parts of the organization. The change manager seeks authorization from the CAB or top IT management for approval.
Significant Change	Moderate impact or moderate resources required. The change manager consults the CAB before authorizing or rejecting the change.
Minor Change	Minor impact and few resources required. The change manager authorizes or rejects, and informs the CAB.
Change priority	A change classification that determines the speed with which a requested Change is to be approved and deployed.
Configuration item (CI)	Any component of an IT infrastructure, including a documentary item such as a SLA or an RFC, which is (or is to be) under the control of Configuration Management and therefore subject to formal Change control.
Change record	This is a record containing details of which CIs are affected by an authorized Change (planned or implemented) and how. It is created from an accepted RFC.
Change log	Log of RFCs raised showing information about each Change; for example, its evaluation, what decisions have been made, and its current status (for example, raised, reviewed approved, implemented, or closed).
Change Advisory Board (CAB)	Cross-functional group set up to evaluate Change Requests for business need, priority, cost/benefit, and potential impacts to other systems or processes. The CAB makes recommendations for implementation, further analysis, deferment, or cancellation of Changes.
Emergency Change Advisory Board (ECAB)	A subset of the CAB who makes decisions about high-impact emergency Changes.
Change schedule or forward schedule of change (FSC)	A document that lists all approved Changes and their planned implementation dates. A change schedule is sometimes called a forward schedule of change, even though it also contains information about Changes that have already been implemented.
Request for change (RFC)	A formal proposal for a Change to be made. An RFC includes details of the proposed Change, and may be recorded on paper or electronically. The term RFC is often misused to mean a Change record or the Change itself.

Change Management helps IT professionals, teams, and organizations achieve a critical outcome: minimizing the business disruption of IT changes and ensuring the question "what changed?" can be answered.

Because resources are to be allocated to the Change Management process, the value of that process to the business has to be determined so that the resources allocated can be justified. To determine the value the organization places on the Change Management process, consider these questions:

▶ What mechanism do you have in place to ensure that you can handle spikes in the quantity and complexity of Changes efficiently, promptly, and consistently?

▶ What mechanism do you have in place to ensure that the change schedule and impact of Changes is visible and communicated to the business?

▶ What mechanism do you have in place to ensure that there is a balance between the business getting the Changes it needs when it needs them for agility/speed to market and IT ensuring Changes are planned, with adequate resourcing, fewer emergencies, fewer surprises, risk mitigation and contingency planning, and fewer disruptive and failed changes?

▶ What provisions have you made to ensure the productivity of users, customers, and IT analysts in relation to changes?

▶ What mechanism do you have to determine the number of Changes implemented in a given period, broken down by the reasons for the Change, by CI, by service, and so on? Do you know trends in RFCs and where they are coming from, such as the number of RFCs rejected, Changes driven by Incident, unauthorized Changes, Changes completed on schedule, Changes in backlog, Changes that go badly and must be backed out, and emergency Changes?

▶ What mechanism do you have in place to reduce the number of Problems and Incidents caused by Changes?

▶ What mechanism do you have to reduce the cost and effort required to make Changes, including the cost of failed Changes and associated rework? What provisions have you made to ensure estimated and actual time, cost, and resources required for Changes match?

▶ What is the negative impact on service quality of Changes, and what mechanism do you have to reduce it?

▶ What provisions have you made to ensure that poor Changes do not move forward, and that badly done Changes are reviewed after implementation so that mistakes are not repeated?

The value of Change Management should drive all further discussions and decisions on scope, priority, resources allocated to, and automation of the Change Management process with Service Manager.

Reporting is a means of understanding and managing the performance of the Change Management process. Although Service Manager includes out-of-the-box reporting functionality for Change Management, you can look to MOF and ITIL for further guidance and what to report, when, and why (such as the number and trend of Changes requiring backout, unauthorized Changes, number of rejected Changes, and percentage reduction in downtime due to scheduled and unscheduled Changes).

The activities in the Change Management process are shown in Figure 3.3.

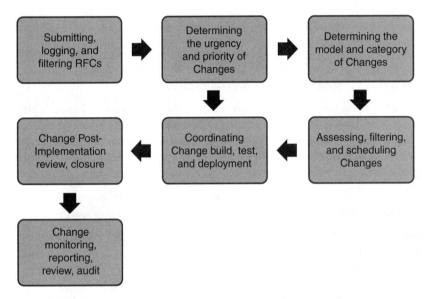

FIGURE 3.3   Change Management process activities.

CHANGE MANAGEMENT AND OTHER PROCESSES AND FUNCTIONS

Change Management is not the same as project change management. Change Management controls changes to CIs in the live environment. The project change management process controls changes within ongoing solution development projects. Although a close liaison between the change manager and development project managers is expected, Change Management and project change management are not the same.

Change Management depends on Configuration Management for raising RFCs, accurate CMDB information, the configuration management system, and contribution to Configuration and Change Management planning. Change Management is depended on by Configuration Management for the change schedule, RFC handling, communication of impact of Changes on service and CI availability, contribution to Configuration and Change Management planning, and maintaining the physical production environment in a controlled state so that it matches as closely as possible the logical model captured in the CMDB.

Change Management depends on Incident Management for raising RFCs, especially for break/fix situations and Change-related Incident status updates. Change Management is depended on by Incident Management for the change schedule, RFC handling, urgent Change procedures and standard Change models, and maintaining the physical production environment in a controlled state so that the number of Incidents caused by Changes is kept to a minimum.

Change Management depends on Problem Management for raising RFCs and for Change-related Problem status. Change Management is depended on by Problem Management for the change schedule, RFC handling, a history of backed-out Changes, urgent Change procedures and standard Change models, and maintaining the physical production environment in a controlled state so that the number of Problems caused by Changes is kept to a minimum.

Table 3.10 lists roles in Change Management and associated activities as the Change process moves from start to finish.

TABLE 3.10   Change Categories and Descriptions

Role	Activity
Change initiators/requestors	Submits RFCs.
Change manager	Filters (assesses—for impact, resource ($ and staff), and schedule requirements—and authorizes or rejects) RFCs. Accepted RFCs become Change records.
Configuration manager	Logs RFCs.
Change manager	Allocates initial priority to Change records.
Change manager	Chooses urgent, standard, or normal path for the Change.
Configuration manager	Updates Change log.
Change builder	Builds Change and devises back-out and test plans.
Configuration manager	Updates log with progress reports.
Independent tester	Tests the Change. If failure, it goes to the Change builder; if success, the process proceeds.
Configuration manager	Updates log.
Change manager	Coordinates implementation of the change.
Configuration manager	Informs users, updates log.
Change builder	If implementation fails, implements the back-out (that is, the reversion to a previous trusted state).
Configuration manager	Updates log.

TABLE 3.10   Change Categories and Descriptions

Role	Activity
Change manager	Reviews Change. If failed, the procedure restarts; if success, closes the Change.
Configuration manager	Updates log, associates any new RFC with an old one, and closes the Change in the log.

Table 3.11 describes key inputs and outputs for Change Management.

TABLE 3.11   Change Management Key Inputs and Outputs

Input	Output
RFCs	Change schedule or forward schedule of changes (FSC)
Incidents	CAB minutes
Problem reports	Management reports, Change statistics
	Change post implementation review (PIR) reports
	Change process review and audit reports

The following key questions must be answered to drive decisions when implementing the Change Management process with Service Manager:

▶ What is the value of Configuration Management to the business?

▶ What is the appropriate scope of Change Management (which CIs should be under control of Change Management)?

▶ Who can initiate Changes, and is there any prior screening or approval required (for example, by the submitter's manager) before an RFC can be submitted?

▶ What mechanism do you have in place to screen Changes, and under what circumstances are RFCs rejected?

▶ What fields and drop-down (enumeration) list values will you have in your RFC form?

▶ What prioritization scheme will be used for Changes?

▶ What is your Change model? (In other words, what is your policy for what will pass as a standard, major, minor, significant, emergency, or unauthorized Change?)

▶ What Change categories will you use?

▶ Will you have a CAB and an ECAB, and if so, who will be members, when will they meet, and what is the agenda?

▶ Who will manage the change schedule and make sure it and the impact of Changes on service availability are communicated effectively?

▶ Will the Self-Service portal be used for Change submittal?

▶ What requirement do you have for automated, rule-based change notification?

▶ Which metrics will you track, and which reports will you produce as a basis for managing performance? Will custom reports be required?

▶ What role will announcements and knowledge articles play in the Change Management process?

Configuration Management

Configuration Management refers to the process responsible for maintaining information about CIs (where a *configuration item* is any component that needs to be managed to deliver an IT service, including IT services, hardware, software, buildings, people, and formal documentation such as process documentation and SLAs) required to deliver an IT service, including their relationships.

The goal of Configuration Management is to provide accurate information about the IT infrastructure, including CIs and how they relate to other CIs, and identify, control, maintain, and verify the versions of all CIs in the IT infrastructure.

The objectives of Configuration Management are to bring all IT services and infrastructure components, with their associated documentation, under control, and to provide an information service to facilitate the effective and efficient planning, release, and implementation of Changes to the IT services.

Although Service Manager does not include workflows for the Configuration Management process, it does support Configuration Management functionality, through the Configuration Items workspace and the connectors, which provide an instant CMDB (database) and configuration management system (CMS) (tool) functionality.

Table 3.12 lists the key terminology of Configuration Management.

TABLE 3.12   Key Terminology in Configuration Management

Term	Explanation
Configuration Item (CI)	A component of an IT infrastructure, or an item associated with an IT infrastructure, that is or will be under the control of Configuration Management. CIs include not just hardware and software, but documentation, procedures, and role charts. CIs vary in complexity, size, and type, from an entire system to a single software module or minor hardware component.
CI attribute	A piece of information about a CI. Examples are name, location, version number, and cost. Attributes of CIs are recorded in the CMDB.

TABLE 3.12   Key Terminology in Configuration Management

Term	Explanation
Configuration Management System	A set of tools used to manage an IT service provider's Configuration data. Compare with the CMDB; the CMS is the tool or system that provides access and presents data; the CMDB is the single logical database that may consist of multiple physical databases that stores the CI data.
Configuration management database	A database that stores all relevant information about IT components (CIs) throughout their life cycle.

Configuration Management helps IT professionals, teams, and organizations achieve a critical outcome: knowing what CIs they have, where they are, what their status is, and how they relate to the other CIs they have.

Because resources are to be allocated to the Incident Management process, the value of that process to the business has to be determined so that the resources allocated can be justified. To determine the value the organization places on the Configuration Management process, consider these questions:

▶ What is the value of knowing the detailed configuration of the IT infrastructure is at any given point in time? How can this help in resolving Problems or performing system upgrades?

▶ What mechanism do you have in place to ensure you have good information on the number, type, location, and status of CIs you have and how they relate to one another, and when there is drift between what is and what should be, to correct this?

▶ What mechanism do you have in place to track growth, capacity, and rate of change of CIs?

▶ What mechanism do you have in place to keep your Configuration under control, with fewer errors and less unauthorized equipment and better support for the delivery of quality IT services and more cost-effective service provision?

▶ What provisions have you made to reduce the number of Change failures due to inaccurate Configuration data and improve Incident resolution time due to availability of complete and accurate Configuration data?

▶ How do you ensure you have accurate information about CIs and control of them, and how are they updated when changed?

▶ What provision have you made to ensure adherence to legal (such as licensing), security, and regulatory obligations related to CIs? To reduce the instances where unauthorized software is in use causing risk to the business and Incidents caused by unauthorized CIs?

▶ How does your knowledge and lack thereof of your Configuration help or hinder your financial and expenditure planning?

▶ You cannot recover what you do not know about. How comfortable are you that your current Configuration is known so that it can be recovered in the event of a disaster?

▶ How in control are you of the number of versions of CIs that are in use, and what is the impact does that have on your ability to enforce IT security and protect your information assets?

▶ How certain are you that the CI data you have enables you to perform impact analysis and schedule Changes safely, efficiently, and effectively?

▶ Do you have a mechanism in place to provide Problem Management with data on CI trends so that the chronic issues can be identified and eliminated?

▶ To what extent does control of your Configuration or lack thereof contribute or take away from cost-effective provision of quality IT service?

The value of Configuration Management should drive all further discussions and decisions on scope, priority, resources allocated to, and automation of the Configuration Management process with Service Manager.

Reporting is a means of understanding and managing the performance of the Configuration Management process. Although Service Manager includes out-of-the-box reporting functionality for Configuration Management, you can look to MOF and ITIL for further guidance and what to report, when, and why. This can include percentage reduction in unauthorized CIs detected, percentage reduction of CIs out of compliance with desired Configuration baselines and regulatory compliance, and reduction in the number of failed Changes resulting from incorrect CI information.

CONFIGURATION MANAGEMENT AND OTHER PROCESSES AND FUNCTIONS

Configuration Management is depended on by Incident, Problem, and Change Management for accurate Configuration information as a basis for impact and trend analysis data.

Configuration Management depends on Incident, Problem, Change, and Release Management for accurate Configuration information as the basis for "to be" CI data.

Figure 3.4 shows the process activity workflow for Configuration Management.

Configuration Management roles include the following:

▶ The incident manager, who owns the results of the Incident Management process

▶ The service desk manager, who owns the results of the service desk function

▶ IT managers and analysts in first-, second-, and third-tier support groups, including specialist support groups and external suppliers

▶ The problem manager, for major incident handling

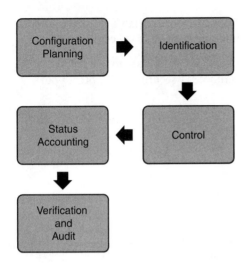

FIGURE 3.4   Configuration Management process activities.

Table 3.13 lists key inputs and outputs of Configuration Management.

TABLE 3.13   Key Inputs and Outputs for Configuration Management

Input	Output
Change Management requests to update CIs	IT service continuity management relationships for continuity plans
Release Management audit of infrastructure	Financial management for capturing key financial information on assets
	Change Management for identifying impact of Changes

The following key questions must be answered to drive decisions when implementing the Configuration Management process with Service Manager:

▶ What is the value of Configuration Management to the business?

▶ What CIs are within scope for Configuration Management, and what CI levels (depth of detail on CIs) are to be kept for each?

▶ What CI attributes must be tracked and what CI record fields and drop-down (enumeration) list values will you require?

▶ What are your CI naming conventions?

▶ What will your CMDB design include? What will be brought over from Active Directory (AD), Operations Manager, and Configuration Manager? Will you need to extend the schema to allow for additional fields, or purchase a third-party product such as Provance to get the functionality you need?

▶ Who will own the Configuration Management process?

▶ Which metrics will you track, and which reports will you produce as a basis for managing performance? Will custom reports be required?

▶ What provisions have you made to ensure a PIR is made after major Problems?

▶ What role will announcements and knowledge articles play in the Configuration Management process?

Summary

A basic understanding of MOF and ITIL concepts will greatly enhance how quickly you get Service Manager going and how effectively you utilize it. How do MOF and ITIL map to Service Manager? They are the ideas behind the business service and Incident, Problem, Change, and Configuration Management processes in Service Manager. It is vital for you to understand these ideas and the goals behind them when planning, deploying, and using Service Manager, too, so that your organization can aim for these outcomes in their work with the tool.

This chapter covered MOF and ITIL, including what they are, their value, and how they map to the Service Manager product. It provided information about how to get started with MOF and ITIL. Consider this chapter context for what is to come in subsequent chapters, which will help you to map these concepts to Service Manager features and provide a reference for planning and deployment tasks at a more granular level.

CHAPTER 4

Looking Inside Service Manager

System Center Service Manager (also referred to as SvcMgr or SCSM) 2010 is a newcomer to the Microsoft System Center suite and completes Microsoft's approach to operations and the service management life cycle. In Chapter 3, "MOF, ITIL, and Service Manager," you learned how Service Manager supports the IT Infrastructure Library (ITIL) areas of Incident, Problem, Change, Knowledge, and Information Technology (IT) management. This chapter looks at how Service Manager 2010 works by presenting an architectural overview and discussing the Service Manager components.

If you are familiar with the architecture of System Center Operations Manager (OpsMgr), you will recognize many similarities in the Service Manager architecture, because the product was built from the OpsMgr platform. In fact, while Operations Manager, Service Manager, Virtual Machine Manager, and System Center Essentials were originally developed using separate code platforms, Microsoft in 2008 made a strategic decision to unify the product platforms. Going forward, each of the products is able to benefit from the development of the other products. This decision has provided value to both Microsoft and its customers in several areas:

▶ Speeding up the product development cycle by utilizing common functionality, enabling each product to provide additional features more quickly.

▶ Reusing code that has already been tested and proven in other products, giving higher quality to new features in products reusing that code.

▶ Customers familiar with one of the products (OpsMgr as an example) feel at home and have less of a learning curve when administrating/using one of the other products (Service Manager, Virtual Machine Manager, or System Center Essentials).

Architectural Overview

Service Manager 2010 is often referred to as an integrated platform for IT Service Management (ITSM). The word *integrated* in this context refers to the product leveraging the capabilities of other System Center products, using connectors that can dynamically import and maintain information updated in the Service Manager database (also known as the Service Manager configuration management database, or CMDB).

Figure 4.1 presents an overview of the Service Manager architecture. The main component is the CMDB (titled SM DB in the graphic). The CMDB tracks configuration items as computers and work items, such as incidents, and how these items relate to each other through their life cycle.

Above the Database Layer (Platform Infrastructure) shown in Figure 4.1 is the Data Access Layer. This Data Access Layer is a set of assemblies that understands how to communicate with the database. Using these assemblies for read/write operations against the database ensures consistency of the database data. Responsible for securing access to the Data Access Layer is a Windows Communication Foundation (WCF) service, hosted in the System Center Data Access Service, and a set of assemblies that consumes the WCF service and simplifies the communication with the service. To use the Service Manager Software Development Kit (SDK) when developing your own solutions, you will reference these assemblies and use the methods and classes provided in them.

TIP: USING THE SERVICE MANAGER SDK

For information about getting started with the Service Manager SDK, see http://blogs. msdn.com/b/jakuboleksy/archive/2008/12/03/getting-started-with-the-service-manager-sdk.aspx.

Service Manager uses connectors to integrate information from Active Directory, Operations Manager, and Configuration Manager. For information on these connectors, see the "Connectors" section, later in this chapter.

Service Manager 2010 uses three Windows services:

▶ System Center Data Access Service

▶ System Center Management

▶ System Center Management Configuration

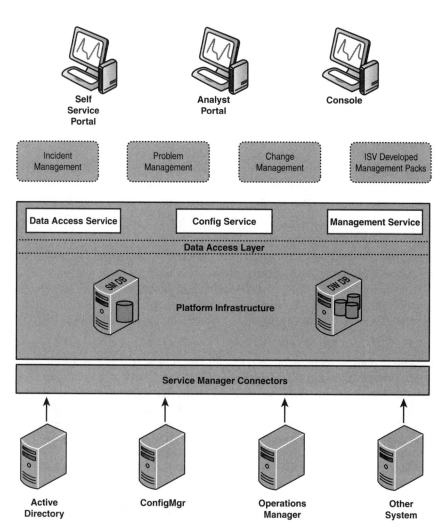

FIGURE 4.1   Architectural overview of Service Manager 2010.

The System Center Data Access Service is the component that provides data access to Service Manager for clients such as the Service Manager console. Other clients can be workflows, the Service Manager web portals, and third-party-developed solutions such as PowerShell scripts. Even the internal workflows within Service Manager use the System Center Data Access Service to read and manipulate data in the CMDB.

The Service Manager workflow engine, the System Center Management service, is what makes the product tick; it is used to automate internal jobs such as calculating target resolution time for an Incident and for executing user-defined workflows such as automating a Change Request. Read more about how the System Center Management service executes workflows and the services used by Service Manager in the "Windows Services" section of this chapter.

The System Center Management Configuration service is responsible for updating the System Center management services if workflows or rules are modified. It accomplishes this by reading workflow configuration data in the Service Manager database and then passing on instructions based on this information to the System Center Management service.

Management Group Defined

As mentioned at the beginning of this chapter, another component in the System Center family is Operations Manager, introduced in Chapter 1, "Service Management Basics." Those readers familiar with Operations Manager may recognize that Operations Manager also uses those service names used by Service Manager. The same is true regarding the concept of a management group:

▶ An Operations Manager management group is an instance of Microsoft's end-to-end Operations Manager 2007 service management solution. It includes at a minimum a root management server (RMS) and a database. It can also include the Operations Manager data warehouse, agents, and a web console. You can deploy multiple management groups within your organization. These management groups can be based on areas of responsibility or geographic location.

▶ A Service Manager management group is conceptually similar to an Operations Manager management group, but the data warehouse components are deployed in their own management group. The data warehouse solution delivered with Service Manager is ultimately intended as the data warehouse for multiple System Center products. For this reason, it is not bound to a specific Service Manager installation (or Service Manager management group). Instead, you can configure multiple Service Manager installations to work with the same data warehouse.

NOTE: ABOUT MANAGEMENT GROUP NAMES

Management group names must be unique. Do not use the same management group name when deploying a Service Manager management group and a Service Manager Data Warehouse management group. Furthermore, do not use the management group name you are using for your Operations Manager installation. Note that management group names are also case sensitive.

A Service Manager implementation will have two management groups:

▶ A management group for Service Manager

▶ A management group for the data warehouse components

The management group for Service Manager must include a management server and a database, the Service Manager database. It can include multiple management servers and consoles as necessary. The management group for the data warehouse will include the data warehouse management server and the data warehouse databases.

You connect these management groups to each other through an internal connector.

TIP: ABOUT REGISTERING TO THE DATA WAREHOUSE

The internal connector used within Service Manager is not visible through the Service Manager console, except from the Connect to data warehouse page in the console. If you need to remove a connector, you can use the "unregister" feature on the Connect to a data warehouse page.

Most organizations, regardless of size, deploy a Service Manager environment that includes one management group for Service Manager and one for the data warehouse. This is analogous to a single Active Directory (AD) forest or a single Exchange organization.

Very large organizations may choose to deploy multiple Service Manager management groups to distribute the workload and administration responsibilities.

Because the Service Manager data warehouse is built using the same platform as the rest of Service Manager, it is not possible to host all Service Manager roles on the same machine, as the data warehouse management server and the service manager management server share the same Windows services, specifically the following:

▶ System Center Data Access Service

▶ System Center Management Configuration

▶ System Center Management

These services are discussed in the "Windows Services" section of this chapter.

Server Components

Six main components comprise Service Manager 2010. Some components are optional, and in some enterprise scenarios, you might need to deploy multiple instances of one component (management servers, for example).

Here are the Service Manager 2010 components:

▶ Service Manager management server

▶ Service Manager database

▶ Data Warehouse management server

▶ Data Warehouse database

▶ Service Manager console

▶ Self-Service portal

NOTE: ACTIVE DIRECTORY REQUIREMENT FOR SERVER COMPONENTS

All computers hosting any Service Manager 2010 components must be members of a domain.

Minimum Installation

If your organization does not require reporting capabilities, you can create a minimum installation by installing Service Manager on a single computer hosting both the Service Manager management server and the Service Manager database. Figure 4.2 shows an example of a minimum installation of Service Manager 2010.

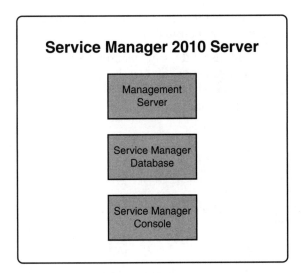

FIGURE 4.2   Minimum installation of Service Manager 2010 installation on a single physical server.

Adding Reporting Capabilities

Installing reporting services requires two management groups, one for Service Manager and one for the data warehouse; you then connect them to each other. Because both management groups use the same components from the common System Center platform (services being an example mentioned in the previous section), you cannot install all components on a single server.

Figure 4.3 shows a Service Manager 2010 installation including the data warehouse and reporting components. This installation is based on two servers; these can be two physical servers or a physical server running two virtual guest systems. If you have a large organization, you want to scale out Service Manager 2010 components over multiple physical servers (for example, dividing the data warehouse and report components between one server for databases and a second server for SQL Server Reporting Services [SRS], which would include the data warehouse management server).

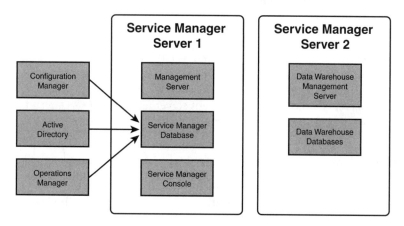

FIGURE 4.3   Minimum installation of Service Manager 2010 when including the data warehouse components.

Service Manager uses connectors to feed the Service Manager database with configuration items from external systems. Out of the box, Service Manager 2010 includes five connectors:

- ▶ Active Directory connector
- ▶ Configuration Manager connector
- ▶ Operations Manager Alert connector
- ▶ Operations Manager CI connector
- ▶ CSV connector

These connectors are discussed in the "Connectors" section.

NOTE: MINIMIZING SQL SERVER LICENSES

You can minimize the number of SQL Servers required by sharing one SQL Server installation (properly sized) between your data warehouse databases and your Service Manager database.

The next sections discuss the different server components.

Service Manager Management Server

The Service Manager management server is where the primary software portion of Service Manager is installed and running. The Service Manager console connects to this server role. This server is also the server hosting the System Center Management service (HealthService), which runs all workflows, and the Configuration service, which updates and configures the System Center Management service.

The Service Manager management server is the first management server you install. It is also referred to as the *workflow server* and handles all workflows in your Service Manager 2010 environment. Any additional Service Manager 2010 servers deployed are used to load balance Service Manager 2010 console connections. Because workflows run only on the first installed management server, should that management server fail—perhaps as a result of a major hardware issue—you can promote another management server to run workflows.

Service Manager Database (ServiceManager)

The ServiceManager database contains all configuration and operating data for the management group and Service Manager 2010 installation. This database is also the Service Manager 2010 implementation of the CMDB. The CMDB contains Service Manager configuration items such as computers and printers. It also contains all work items, including objects such as incidents and change requests.

Data Warehouse Management Server

The data warehouse management server controls the workflow processes associated with the data warehouse. There are three main processes:

► Management pack (MP) synchronization

► Data warehouse schema and report deployment

► Extract, Transform, Load

These jobs are described in Table 4.1. These workflows transfer data from the CMDB database to the data warehouse database.

Data Warehouse Database

Service Manager 2010 uses the data warehouse for long-term storage of data, such as incidents. The data warehouse is therefore used as the data source for reports, since old data is groomed from the Service Manager database on a recurring interval to maintain performance and keep the database at a manageable size.

TABLE 4.1   Workflows That Populate the DWDataMart Database

Process	Workflow Description
MPSync	MPSync manages inserts, updates, and deletes of management packs between the ServiceManager and DWStagingAndConfig databases.
Extract	The Extract job retrieves data from the Service Manager database. It queries the Service Manager database for the delta data from its last run and writes this new data into the DWStagingAndConfig database in the data warehouse. There are two extract jobs in Service Manager: –A job for the Service Manager management group –A job for the Data Warehouse management group
Transform	This job takes the raw data from the staging area and does any cleansing, reformatting, and aggregation required to get it into the final format for reporting. This transformed data is written into the DWRepository database.
Load	The Load job queries the data from the DWRepository database and inserts it into the DWDataMart database. The DWDataMart is the database used for all end-user reporting needs.

The data warehouse is a logical database. It actually consists of three databases with different roles:

▸ DWStagingAndConfig

▸ DWRepository

▸ DWDataMart

Data is automatically transferred from the ServiceManager database to the DWDataMart database with a 30- to 60-minute latency delay. The process responsible for populating the datamart with data is divided into three parts; these jobs were listed in Table 4.1.

The primary reason to have three different databases is to enable organizations to optimize their hardware environments more easily. In high-volume environments, you will want to place the DWStagingAndConfig and DWRepository databases on hardware optimized for read and write input/output (I/O), whereas you should optimize the DWDataMart for read I/O only. By using separate databases, organizations can separate out the DWDataMart to a different server and drive from the DWStagingAndConfig and DWRepository. The DWStagingAndConfig and DWRepository databases must be located on the same server.

HOW LONG DOES IT TAKE FOR DATA TO APPEAR IN REPORTS?

The three categories of jobs listed in Table 4.1 work together to populate the datamart, which is where you run reports. Each job runs independently of each other:

- ▶ The Extract job runs every 45 minutes.
- ▶ The Transform job runs every 30 minutes.
- ▶ The Load job runs every 30 minutes.

In a normally operating Service Manager 2010 environment, it takes approximately two hours before you will see the data in the reports.

Service Manager Console

The Service Manager 2010 console is used by all different roles that work with the product. This component is automatically installed when you install a Service Manager 2010 management server. You can install the console on a separate computer, as well (for example, a service desk operator's workstation). The console experience is controlled by role-based security, which gives each security role a common set of views, tasks, templates, and objects. Service Manager administrators can view everything when they open the console. The console is discussed in detail in Chapter 8, "Using Service Manager," with prerequisites covered in Chapter 7, "Installing Service Manager." Role-based security is discussed in Chapter 15, "Service Manager Security."

There is also an Authoring Tool, sometimes called the *Authoring console*. The Authoring Tool is used to author MPs and customize the product. For additional information about the Service Manager Authoring Tool, see Chapter 17, "Management Packs," and Chapter 18, "Customizing Service Manager."

Self-Service Portal

The Self-Service portal (SSP) is a web-based portal divided into two main parts, one for end users and one for analysts:

- ▶ Analysts can use a section of the portal to work with change requests (for example, to review and approve change requests). They can also get an overview of the number of active changes and changes within their area. IT analysts can also use the analyst portal to view and complete manual activities.

- ▶ The end user portion of the portal enables users to submit requests, read announcements and IT-related news, search knowledge base articles, and request software. Service Manager 2010's software provisioning components require for it is be connected to System Center Configuration Manager (ConfigMgr), which manages the end user's computer. If you run Forefront Identity Lifecycle Management 2010 and connect it to Service Manager, an end user can also reset his password via the portal.

Windows Services

Computers running Service Manager components also host particular Windows services in specific configurations depending on their functions. The next sections describe services that exist when Service Manager components are deployed.

System Center Data Access Service

The System Center Data Access Service (OMSDK), which is also referred to as the SDK Service, can be considered the core service for Service Manager 2010. This service is installed on all management servers. All data flowing to and from the database is transported via the System Center Data Access Service. Between the System Center Data Access Service and the database is a layer known as the Data Access Layer (DAL), previously shown in Figure 4.1.

The DAL is a set of dynamic link libraries (DLLs) used internally in the platform. The DAL is transparent to the Service Manager administrator and operator. The DAL uses ADO.NET to communicate with the database, with a default communication port of 1433. ADO.NET is a set of software components you can use to access data and data services. You configure the System Center Data Access Service account as the Service Manager account during installation.

You can verify which account is used by looking at the Properties page of the System Center Data Access Service in services.msc, the Services application. Figure 4.4 shows the portion of the Services application displaying the services used by Service Manager 2010. Clicking a particular service and selecting the **Log On** tab identifies the account being used.

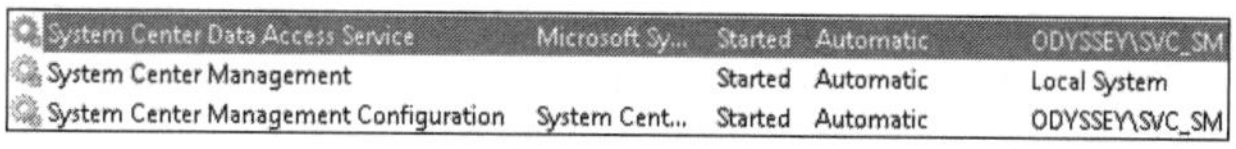

System Center Data Access Service	Microsoft Sy...	Started	Automatic	ODYSSEY\SVC_SM
System Center Management		Started	Automatic	Local System
System Center Management Configuration	System Cent...	Started	Automatic	ODYSSEY\SVC_SM

FIGURE 4.4   Configuration of account settings for Service Manager services.

NOTE: WHAT SERVICES RUN ON WHICH MANAGEMENT SERVERS

Figure 4.4 shows only the System Center Management service running. The other services are installed on all management servers but only run on the first management server installed.

Figure 4.5 shows the SDK service components.

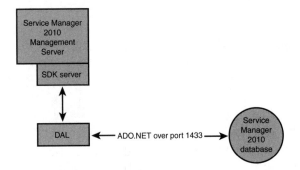

FIGURE 4.5   SDK service components.

The System Center Data Access Service is a Windows service with a WCF interface that exposes all programmatic web service application program interfaces (APIs) for the Service Manager platform. WCF is a framework for building service-oriented applications. You can use WCF to send data as asynchronous messages from one endpoint to another.

All communication with the ServiceManager database is through the System Center Data Access Service, which authenticates and authorizes users using Authorization Manager. Authorization Manager (AzMan) is a role-based security architecture for Windows. You can find additional information about AzMan at http://msdn.microsoft.com/en-us/library/bb897401.aspx.

System Center Management Service (HealthService)

The System Center Management service is a component that provides a general execution environment for modules. Different modules form different workflows, enabling workflows such as database grooming, incident workflows, and report deployment. A typical workflow contains a source model, a condition module, and an action module:

▶ The *data source module* defines the condition that triggers the workflow to run.

▶ The *condition module* is an optional module.

▶ The *write action module* defines the workflow actions.

The functionality of this service is primarily defined by the MPs installed. The Health Service is extended by installing new and additional MPs. Future versions of these MPs containing new functionality provide updates to the agent health services by means of the management server pushing out the required updates. MPs are discussed in the "Modeling and Management Pack Schema" section of this chapter.

The System Center Management service does not run the workflows directly. Instead, it starts an instance of healthservice.exe that runs the workflows. You may occasionally see a large number of healthservice.exe instances running at your management server; this is normal. The System Center Management service runs each workflow separately from each other to ensure they cannot interrupt one another. Another benefit of running in isolated instances is that each instance can use different credentials and be monitored individually by the management server. If one workflow is hanging or using an unusual amount of hardware resources, it can be terminated without interrupting another workflow. Figure 4.6 shows the Service Manager 2010 workflow.

FIGURE 4.6   The Service Manager 2010 workflow.

System Center Management (OMCFG)

The OMCFG service manages the relationships and running configuration of the Service Manager 2010 environment. This service is responsible for providing the configuration to each health service (System Center Management service). It sends sensitive data as part of the data used to configure the health service. The sensitive data is stored and maintained by the ServiceManager database. The SDK API prevents the System Center Management service from viewing the data and forces the data to be passed to the System Center Data Access Service in an encrypted form that uses the public key of the target health service. In this process, the System Center Data Access Service acts as an intermediary for delivering the encrypted configuration from the database to the target health service on a management server.

The configuration that a System Center Management service receives consists of workflows. These workflows can be tasks, discoveries, and rules. Each workflow is built up from a number of modules. The most common workflow in Service Manager 2010 is a rule. Examples of rules are MP synchronization to the data warehouse, connectors, and incident workflows. For more information about workflows, see Chapter 18.

Connectors

Using connectors for the initial load of data to the CMDB gives you a jump-start when setting up the Service Manager database. After the initial load, the connectors run periodically and update the CMDB with changes from each source system. This functionality gives Service Manager what has been called a dynamic CMDB, because it is a CMDB that is updated automatically. Here are the connectors provided out of the box:

▶ **Active Directory connector:** Use the Active Directory connector to import information about users, groups, printers, and computers.

▶ **Configuration Manager connector:** Use the Configuration Manager connector to import hardware and software information from Configuration Manager.

▶ **Operations Manager Alert connector:** This connector registers incidents in Service Manager based on alerts in Operations Manager.

▶ **Operations Manager Configuration Item (CI) connector:** The Operations Manager CI connector imports objects into the Service Manager database that are discovered by Operations Manager. The MPs used in Operations Manager that contain the class definitions for the CIs must be imported into Service Manager before importing the associated objects.

▶ **CSV connector:** Use a comma-separated value (CSV) file to import any type of object defined in the CMDB.

CAUTION: DELETING A CONNECTOR

Every object, configuration object, or work item in the CMDB has *discovery sources*, which may be connectors or other registered discovery sources. For each object or work item, the system will track those sources that created or updated the object during its lifetime. If a given object is added by connector A and later updated by a user and connector B, it has a reference count of 3. If connector A eventually says the object should be deleted, the reference to connector A's discovery source is removed and the reference count decremented to 2. Once all discovery sources say an object should be deleted, it is actually deleted.

A Service Manager administrator has the right to delete an object including all of its discovery references.

In general, it is best to disable the connector rather than delete it. The connector will no longer run but no objects are deleted.

An unsupported connector for Exchange, developed by the Service Manager product team, was released in early 2011. The connector enables a deeper integration with Exchange, allowing end users to create, update, resolve, or close incidents (and more). For detailed information about the Exchange Connector, see http://www.microsoft.com/downloads/en/details.aspx?FamilyID=0b48d1f1-434a-4ee6-8017-fc13f4c16785.

Integration with Opalis (being rebranded as System Center Orchestrator) is available via the product's System Center Service Manager Integration Pack. Opalis does a great job in helping customers integrate Service Manager with systems not covered by the out-of-the-box connectors. Information about Opalis is available at http://www.microsoft.com/systemcenter/en/us/opalis.aspx.

The Exchange Connector and Opalis Integration Pack for Service Manager are discussed in Chapter 2, "Service Manager 2010 Overview."

Modeling and Management Pack Schema

The core of the Service Manager architecture is the highly modular database, the Service Manager database (also known as the Service Manager CMDB). The term *modular* is appropriate in that you can create your own models or extend existing ones. The next sections introduce data modeling and the MP schema.

Data Modeling

Service Manager 2010 lets you easily add new models that describe your own CIs or work items to track their life cycle. A data model in the CMDB consists of class types, properties, and relationships (describing how objects relate to each other).

Each data model is stored in one or several MPs that together make up the model. When you import MPs (through the System Center Data Access Service) into Service Manager using the console or PowerShell, the Service Manager DAL reads the content of the MP and creates a representation of the data model within the database. Here's how the data model is populated in the database:

▶ A new class type in the MP results in a new table in the Service Manager database.

▶ A column is added to the table for each property defined in the class type in the MP.

▶ For each relationship defined between class types in an MP, a relationship entry is added to the database that represents the relationship and its constraints.

▶ For each object of a given class type (for example, a Windows computer) added to the Service Manager database, a line is added in a matching table, created when importing the MP into the Service Manager database.

If you delete an MP in Service Manager using the console or another method, this results in deletion of the associated database objects such as tables and relationship entries.

The fact that everything is stored in MPs provides you with a simple process of transferring models between different environments; it is as simple as exporting and importing the MP from one management group to another, such as from a test environment to a production environment.

TIP: MORE ABOUT MANAGEMENT PACKS

MPs can be seen as eXtensible Markup Language (XML) files containing definitions that define not only data models but also objects such as views for the Service Manager console, workflows, groups, queues, tasks, connectors, and so on. Chapters 17, 18, and 19, "Advanced Customization Scenarios," provide additional detail on this topic and information about how to define these objects.

When defining a new data model for Service Manager 2010, you define class types, properties, and how the classes relate to each other. Defined classes are used (and should be reused) to define specialized models using inheritance. Figure 4.7 provides an example of inheritance, displaying the `Microsoft.Windows.Computer` class type as a specialized type of a `System.ConfigItem`, which is a specialized type of `System.Entity`. Each new specialized type can add new properties that are unique for that specialized type but inherits the common properties from parent class types. The figure also shows an example of how the

System.User relates to the System.ConfigItem. This effectively means that all class types that derive from the System.ConfigItem can be related to a System.User using the System.ConfigItem.OwnedByUser relationship.

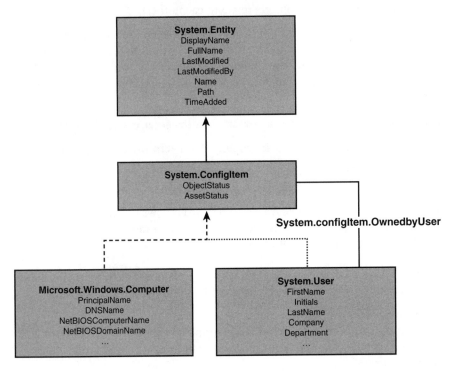

FIGURE 4.7   Data model inheritance and relationships example.

Chapters 16, "Planning Your Customization," 17, 18, and 19 describe in more detail how you can create your own data models and implement them into the Service Manager CMDB.

Management Pack Schema

The modeling schema for Service Manager 2010 comes from Operations Manager 2007, referred to here as version 1.0. The newer MP schema for Service Manager (version 1.1) has been extended with features such as class extensions and categories, but includes all the functionality and experience previously acquired by Operations Manager 2007. The MP sample code shown in Listing 4.1 demonstrates an MP based on the schema version 1.1, which contains a class type definition for a simple CI. The class type has a base class defined, and the attribute Extension equals "false", which means this defines a new type of object that can be stored in the CMDB. Had there been a class type attribute saying Extension equals "true", this would just have extended the class type declared as Base with the new properties defined.

LISTING 4.1   Management Pack Example

```
<ManagementPack ContentReadable="true" SchemaVersion="1.1"
xmlns:xsd="http://www.w3.org/2001/XMLSchema"
xmlns:xsl="http://www.w3.org/1999/XSL/Transform">
<Manifest>
  <Identity>
    <ID>Oddysey.CI</ID>
    <Version>1.0.0.0</Version>
  </Identity>
    <Name>Odyssey Configuration Items</Name>
  <References>
    <Reference Alias="System">
      <ID>System.Library</ID>
      <Version>7.0.5826.216</Version>
      <PublicKeyToken>31bf3856ad364e35</PublicKeyToken>
    </Reference>
  </References>
</Manifest>
<TypeDefinitions>
  <EntityTypes>
    <ClassTypes>
      <ClassType ID="Odyssey.CI.Phone" Accessibility="Public" Abstract="false"
Base="System!System.ConfigItem" Extension="false">
        <Property ID="SerialNumber" Type="string" Key="true" CaseSensitive="false"
MaxLength="256" MinLength="0" Required="true" />
        <Property ID="Make" Type="string" MaxLength="256" MinLength="0"
Required="false" />
        <Property ID="Model" Type="string" MaxLength="256" MinLength="0"
Required="false" />
        <Property ID="PurchaseDate" Type="datetime" Required="true" />
      </ClassType>
    </ClassTypes>
  </EntityTypes>
    </TypeDefinitions>
    </ManagementPack>
```

The modular schema primarily used by the Service Manager database is also used in the DWStagingAndConfig database in the data warehouse. The purpose of the DWStagingAndConfig database is to store configuration information for the data warehouse and act as a temporary place to stage the data moving from the ServiceManager database into the other parts of the data warehouse (DWRepository and DWDataMart).

NOTE: MANAGEMENT PACK SCHEMA VERSION 1.1

Management packs written for System Center Service Manager 2010 can take advantage of the new version of the MP schema (version 1.1), although you can still import older MPs (version 1.0) into Service Manager. This makes it possible to import older MPs from your Operations Manager 2007 environment that already contain data models. Doing so automatically extends the CMDB with the known objects that are defined in Operations Manager so that these can be synced into the Service Manager database.

Workflow

When discussing workflows in Service Manager, you should not translate that into pure Windows Workflow Foundation workflows. As mentioned earlier in the "System Center Management Service (HealthService)" section of this chapter, a typical Service Manager workflow includes the following components:

▶ Data source module

▶ Condition module (optional)

▶ Write action module

Looking at these three components, a Windows Workflow Foundation workflow is typically executed by the write action module if an event occurs in the data source module that fulfills the condition in the condition module. The write action does not necessarily need to execute a Windows Workflows Foundation workflow. It could execute a number of different things, including PowerShell scripts/commands. The action taken depends on which write action module is being used.

As mentioned in the "Data Modeling" section, adding a new workflow to Service Manager consists of importing an MP (which has a workflow defined) along with deploying any necessary files such as assembly files containing Windows Workflow Foundation workflows—referenced in the MP—to the Service Manager installation folder on the management server. When the MP is imported through the System Center Data Access Service, which passes it over to the DAL, the workflow definition is stored in the Service Manager database.

When a new workflow definition is imported into Service Manager, the System Center Configuration service picks up information about the new workflow (through the DAL) and passes instructions over to the System Center Management service. The System Center Management service spawns a new MonitoringHost process that uses the defined subscription to listen for matching events (let's say a new incident created) that fulfills the defined criteria ("Incident classification equals Printing Problem," in this example).

When the MonitoringHost receives an event matching the criteria it submits the defined task to the System Center Data Access Service, which uses the Data Access Layer to store the task submission in the JobStatus table inside the ServiceManager database.

The System Center Management Configuration service picks up a new task request (based on the JobStatus data) via the Data Access Layer, which hands over the task request to the System Center Management service.

The System Center Management service spawns a new MonitoringHost process to execute the task. After executing defined write actions, the task executes a Windows Workflow Foundation module, which calls the System Center Data Access Service to update the Service Manager database (JobStatus table) via the Data Access Layer. See Figure 4.8 for an illustration of how the Service Manager platform makes use of a workflow definition.

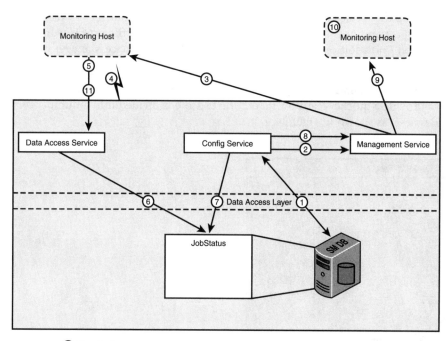

① Config Service retrieves information about new mp

② Config Service passes workflow information to Management Service

③ Management Service spawns a new Monitoring Host

④ Event received

⑤ Passes task submission to Data Access Service

⑥ Data Access Service stores the information in JobStatus

⑦ Config Service picks up a new task request

⑧ Confg Service hands over task instructions to Management Service

⑨ Management Service spawns a new Monitoring Host

⑩ Monitoring Host executes the task

⑪ Monitoring Host executes WF that updates JobStatus –"Completed"

FIGURE 4.8   Workflow communications.

Chapter 18 includes a detailed description of how to add custom workflows to Service Manager that utilize the process described in this section.

Service Manager Console

Regardless of your role in the Service Manager environment, you will most likely work with the Service Manager 2010 console on a daily basis. What you can see and do in the console is controlled by security roles configured by Service Manager administrators. If you are a service desk analyst, you might only need to see all incidents assigned to you or your team. If you are the service desk manager, you might need to see all active incidents for all levels of support and possibly need to run reports to make sure the unit is working as expected. You can find additional information about security in Service Manager in Chapter 15.

The layout of the Service Manager console is similar to other System Center products, the intent being to provide a quicker learning curve. The console is divided into a number of areas and workspaces, as shown in Figure 4.9.

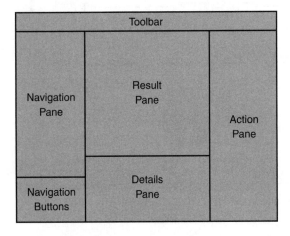

FIGURE 4.9   Layout of the Service Manager 2010 console.

Figure 4.10 shows the Service Manager console after initial installation. Figure 4.11 displays the navigation sections of the console.

The navigation buttons (wunderbars) in the lower-left side of the console let you quickly switch between workspaces. Here is a quick introduction to each workspace (also referred to as a *space* or *node*):

> ▶ **Administration:** Enables configuring high-level settings of the Service Manager 2010 management group. Examples of tasks that can be carried out in this workspace are notification configuration, working with MPs, working with accounts, and configuring connectors. Only administrators have access to this workspace.

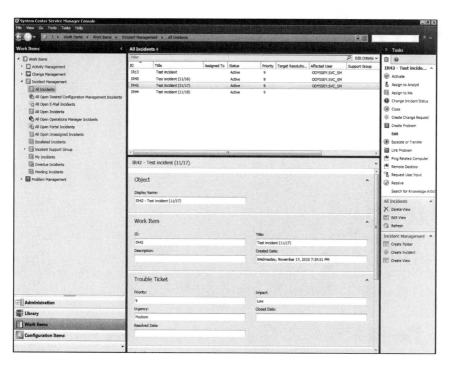

FIGURE 4.10   The Service Manager 2010 console after installation.

▶ **Library:** This workspace enables working with templates, tasks, queues, groups, knowledge, and lists. In general, this is where you configure values that will be shared between a number of objects in the other workspaces. For example, you can create templates here for use in change requests or incidents. You also manage your groups and queues here, which you can use with security roles.

▶ **Work Items:** This is where you create work items and work with work items, such as change requests, incidents, and problems. You can scope down this workspace using different security roles to fit your organization's requirements.

▶ **Configuration Items:** In this workspace, you can look at all your CIs. This is where you can see all computers and open the Properties page of a specific computer to see how many CPUs it has (for example). You can extend Service Manager 2010 with more CI classes, such as one for projects; these additional classes can be shown in this workspace.

▶ **Data Warehouse:** This workspace is visible if you have installed the Service Manager data warehouse. In this workspace, you can work with data warehouse settings and configure high-level settings of the data warehouse management group. The Data Warehouse component is optional.

▶ **Reporting:** If you have installed the Service Manager data warehouse, this workspace is visible. It enables you to run reports against your data warehouse, such as the number of incidents last week or the most common change category. The Reporting component is an optional component.

FIGURE 4.11   The Navigation pane and Navigation buttons of the Service Manager 2010 console.

NOTE: EXTENDING THE CONSOLE

You can extend the console with more workspaces. For example, third-party asset management solutions extend the console with an additional workspace named IT Asset Management.

The Result and Details panes of the console are displayed in Figure 4.12. Figure 4.13 focuses on the Tasks pane, which is on the right side of the Service Manager console. Content of the Tasks pane is dynamic; it changes based on the type of work item you have selected and what view is selected in which folder of the Navigation pane.

PowerShell

PowerShell plays a key role in Service Manager 2010. In addition to helping administrators perform administrative tasks, it is a flexible tool you can use to automate IT processes within workflows and enable powerful tasks to be executed within the Service Manager

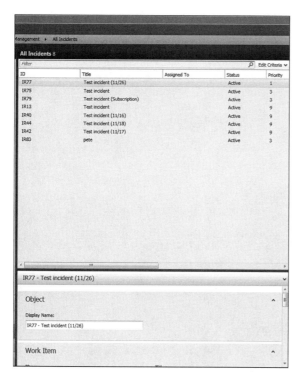

FIGURE 4.12   The Result and Details panes of the Service Manager 2010 console.

console. Currently, there are two resources for PowerShell commands for Service Manager 2010:

▶ Service Manager cmdlets (SMCmdletsSnapIn)

▶ SMLets

These are discussed in the following two sections.

Service Manager Cmdlets for Windows PowerShell

Installed with the Service Manager 2010 product are the Service Manager cmdlets for Windows PowerShell. To start using these cmdlets, complete these steps:

1. Open a PowerShell window on your Service Manager management server.

2. Enter the following:

```
Add-PSSnapIn SMCmdletsSnapIn
```

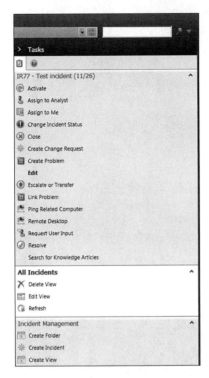

FIGURE 4.13   The Tasks pane of the Service Manager 2010 console.

This loads the Service Manager snap-in. The commands available in the SMCmdletsSnapIn are described in this section. As an administrator working with Service Manager, you have use of the PowerShell cmdlets that ship with the product, giving you the capability to automate your administrative workload and make it more efficient.

> **TIP: GETTING STARTED WITH SERVICE MANAGER CMDLETS FOR WINDOWS POWERSHELL**
>
> A great place to start exploring the Service Manager cmdlets for Windows PowerShell is the *System Center Service Manager Administrator's Guide* on TechNet. Here is a link that takes you directly to the chapter "Using the Service Manager Cmdlets for Windows PowerShell": http://technet.microsoft.com/en-us/library/ff461199.aspx.

Here are the cmdlets included in the snap-in:

▶ **Add-SCDWMgmtGroup**

   The Add-SCDWMgmtGroup cmdlet registers a Service Manager management group and its servers as the source for the Service Manager data warehouse.

▶ **Add-SCSMAllowListClass**

The Add-SCSMAllowListClass cmdlet adds the specified classes to the allowed list of classes used by the Operations Manager 2007 CI connector during synchronization. The specified classes must already be defined in existing MPs.

▶ **Disable-SCDWJob**

The Disable-SCDWJob cmdlet enables data warehouse administrators to disable jobs to prevent the jobs from running. This means that the jobs cannot be run according to their defined schedule and they cannot be run manually. To reenable the jobs, use the Enable-SCDWJob cmdlet.

▶ **Disable-SCDWJobSchedule**

The Disable-SCDWJobSchedule cmdlet disables a data warehouse job schedule, which causes the job schedule to stop initiating jobs. If the job schedule was previously enabled, disabling the job schedule retains the job schedule settings. To modify the job schedule settings, run the Set-SCDWJobSchedule cmdlet.

▶ **Enable-SCDWJob**

The Enable-SCDWJob cmdlet allows data warehouse administrators to enable jobs so that the jobs can run according to their specified schedule or run manually. To disable the jobs, use the Disable-SCDWJob cmdlet.

▶ **Enable-SCDWJobSchedule**

The Enable-SCDWJob cmdlet allows data warehouse administrators to enable job schedules so that jobs run according to their specified schedule. If the job schedule was previously disabled, enabling the job schedule retains the job's schedule settings. To disable the job schedule, use the Disable-SCDWJobSchedule cmdlet. To modify the job's schedule, use the Set-SCDWJobSchedule cmdlet.

▶ **Export-SCSMManagementPack**

The Export-SCSMManagementPack cmdlet exports an MP as a valid XML-formatted file that you can later import into Service Manager. All the MP's information is included in the file as XML data. You can use this cmdlet to save or to archive MP information.

▶ **Get-SCDWJob**

The Get-SCDWJob cmdlet returns job status for all recurring data warehouse jobs.

▶ **Get-SCDWJobModule**

Each data warehouse job consists of multiple subprocesses known as *modules*. Modules perform the individual work items associated with their parent job. The Get-CDWJobModule cmdlet enables you to retrieve the status of a job's constituent modules.

▶ **Get-SCDWJobSchedule**

The Get-SCDWJobSchedule cmdlet displays scheduling information for data warehouse jobs. You can use the JobName parameter to specify a job for which to display scheduling information. Otherwise, the Get-SCDWJobSchedule cmdlet displays scheduling information for all data warehouse jobs.

▶ **Get-SCDWMgmtGroup**

The Get-SCDWMgmtGroup cmdlet returns all the Service Manager installations that are registered with the data warehouse.

▶ **Get-SCSMAllowList**

The Get-SCSMAllowList cmdlet gets the allowed list of classes that is used by the Operations Manager 2007 CI connector during synchronization. The connector imports only the instances of the class types that are included on this allowed list.

▶ **Get-SCSMConnector**

The Get-SCSMConnector cmdlet retrieves the connectors that are currently installed on the system. If the Name parameter is omitted, all connectors are retrieved. If the Name parameter is specified, the specified value is interpreted as a regular expression. All connectors whose Name or DisplayName property matches the regular expression are returned. For each returned connector, the cmdlet displays type, name, and status information.

▶ **Get-SCSMManagementPack**

The Get-SCSMManagementPack cmdlet gets the Service Manager MPs that have been imported into the system named by the ComputerName parameter. The MPs are listed in the order in which they are detected.

The Name parameter specifies the name of the MP to retrieve. This parameter is interpreted as a regular expression. Get-SCSMManagementPack returns all MPs that have a Name or a DisplayName property that matches the specified regular expression.

▶ **Get-SCSMRunAsAccount**

Retrieves the Run As Accounts available in the Service Manager environment. Run As Accounts contain the user credentials under which workflows run. These accounts allow Service Manager to act on behalf of a specific user. If the RunAsProfileName parameter is omitted, all Run As Accounts are returned. If the RunAsProfileName parameter is specified, the specified value is interpreted as a regular expression. All Run As Accounts whose Name or DisplayName property matches the regular expression are returned.

▶ **Import-SCSMInstance**

The Import-SCSMInstance cmdlet imports objects and relationships into Service Manager. Several parameters must be set to import instances in bulk into Service Manager:

- ▶ DataFileName, which must contain the file path of a CSV file that contains the instance data.

- ▶ FormatFileName, which must contain the file path of an XML file that defines the format of the CSV file.

- ▶ There is an optional BatchSize parameter that specifies the number of object or projection instances that will be committed on each database write. If specified, this parameter must be an integer value between 1 and 5000. The default value is 50.

▶ **Import-SCSMManagementPack**

The classes managed by Service Manager must be defined in an MP. MPs consist of an XML manifest that defines metadata about objects and references to resources that the objects use. An unsealed MP is an XML file that can be modified, and a sealed MP is an MP file that cannot be modified. You can find sample MPs at *<SvcMgrInstallPath>*\Microsoft System Center Service Manager 2010.

The Service Manager server into which the MP is imported will try to validate the MP before importing it. If the MP contains XML code that is not valid, the MP is not imported, and an error is returned.

▶ **Remove-SCDWMgmtGroup**

The Remove-SCDWMgmtGroup cmdlet removes a Service Manager management group and its associated servers as a registered data warehouse data source.

▶ **Remove-SCSMAllowListClass**

The Remove-SCSMAllowListClass removes the specified classes from the allowed list of classes used by the Operations Manager 2007 CI connector during synchronization. An ArgumentException is displayed if the classname cannot be found or if the classname is not present on the allowed list.

▶ **Reset-SCSMAllowList**

The Reset-SCSMAllowList cmdlet replaces the existing allowed list of classes to be synchronized by the Operations Manager 2007 CI connector with the default allowed list. Table 4.2 lists the default allowed list and classes.

TABLE 4.2   Default Allowed List Classes for Operations Manager Connector Synchronization

Name	Management Pack
System.Service	System.Library
System.Database	System.Library
Microsoft.Windows.ApplicationComponent	Microsoft.Windows.Library
Microsoft.Windows.ComputerRole	Microsoft.Windows.Library
System.Computer	System.Library
System.OperatingSystem	System.Library
Microsoft.Windows.LogicalDevice	Microsoft.Windows.Library
System.SoftwareInstallation	System.Library
System.WebSite	System.Library

▶ **Resume-SCDWJob**

The `Resume-SCDWJob` cmdlet enables data warehouse administrators to resume jobs that have been suspended. All job modules that were queued when the job was suspended will run.

▶ **Set-SCDWJobSchedule**

The `Set-SCDWJobSchedule` cmdlet configures the schedule for data warehouse jobs. The schedule can be configured on a daily basis or on a weekly basis. For a daily schedule, you must specify the time interval at which the job recurs (`DailyFrequency`) and the time of day at which this recurrence starts (`DailyStart`). For a weekly schedule, you must specify the time of day (`WeeklyStart`) at which the job should run and the list of days for which this start time is effective (`WeeklyFrequency`).

▶ **Set-SCSMConnector**

The `Set-SCSMConnector` cmdlet enables or disables connectors.

If the `Name` parameter is specified, all the connectors whose `Name` or `DisplayName` property matches the specified regular expression are set to the state specified in the `State` parameter. If connector objects are passed via the `ConnectorObject` parameter, the state of these connectors is set to the state specified in the `State` parameter. Either the `Name` parameter or the `ConnectorObject` parameter (but not both) must be specified.

The `State` parameter assumes one of two values:

▶ Enabled

▶ Disabled

▶ **Set-SCSMRunAsAccount**

The `Set-SCSMRunAsAccount` cmdlet sets the credentials for a Run As Account. The cmdlet enables you to change the stored credentials for a Run As Account when that account's user name or password changes. Passwords are securely stored in Service Manager so that impersonation can take place for workflows and other operations.

▶ **Start-SCDWJob**

The `Start-SCDWJob` cmdlet enables data warehouse administrators to start jobs that are not running. When a job is started, its associated job modules run in the order prescribed by the job. To pause the job, use the `Suspend-SCDWJob` cmdlet.

▶ **Suspend-SCDWJob**

The `Suspend-SCDWJob` cmdlet enables data warehouse administrators to suspend a job that is currently running. When a job is suspended, all its running job modules continue to be processed, but its queued job modules do not run. When the job resumes, the job modules continue to run from the point of suspension, and all previously queued job modules run.

To learn about each command, simply execute the `get-help` cmdlet on the cmdlet you are interested in, as shown in Figure 4.14.

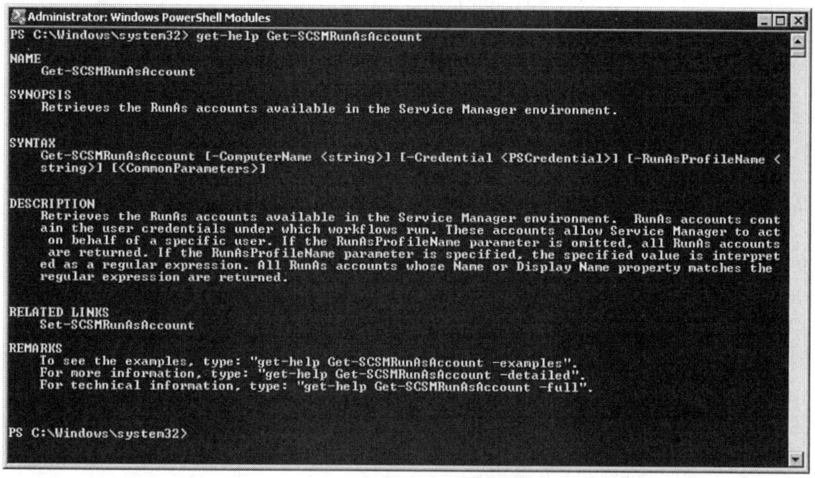

FIGURE 4.14   Help shown for the **Get-SCSMRunAsAccount** cmdlet.

SCSM PowerShell Cmdlets: SMLets

Whereas the cmdlets provided with the product focus on administrating the Service Manager 2010 infrastructure, the SMLets PowerShell module (further referred to as *the module*) found at http://smlets.codeplex.com provides functionality related to creating and maintaining configuration and work items.

GETTING STARTED WITH SCSM POWERSHELL CMDLETS (SMLETS)

SMLets is an open source code project available on Codeplex, where you can download the latest version (including source code). See http://smlets.codeplex.com for more information.

Using the module, you can create objects of any type defined in the Service Manager CMDB using the generic commands provided. An example is shown in Listing 4.2, which is also available in the online material accompanying this book at http://www.informit.com/store/product.aspx?isbn=0672334364.

LISTING 4.2   PowerShell Script: Creating a Change Request

```
#Make sure smlets imported
Import-Module smlets -Force


#Get change class
```

```
$changeClass = Get-SCSMClass System.WorkItem.ChangeRequest$

#Get enum values for Impact, Priority and Risk
$impactEnum = Get-SCSMEnumeration ChangeImpactEnum.Major
$priorityEnum = Get-SCSMEnumeration ChangePriorityEnum.Medium
$riskEnum = Get-SCSMEnumeration ChangeRiskEnum.Medium

#Define properties
$props = @{
ID="CR{0}";
Title="Change of disk in SAN";
Description="Receiving failures...";
Impact=$impactEnum;
Risk=$riskEnum;
Priority=$priorityEnum;}

#Create new Change Request using class and defined properties
New-SCSMObject $changeClass $props
```

Extending the Service Manager Console

The Service Manager console can be extended with custom tasks (further discussed in Chapter 18) so that it executes anything that can be executed from the command line and more. This means you incorporate PowerShell scripts in console tasks and thus provide console users with powerful tasks unavailable out of the box.

PowerShell in Service Manager Workflows

A common place to use PowerShell for Service Manager is when creating workflows that automate common IT processes in Service Manager (for example, when creating a workflow that automates a change request involving a new Active Directory user account). Using PowerShell scripts and the Authoring Tool for Service Manager, you can easily create a workflow that uses data registered with the change request to create the user account automatically in Active Directory. Read more on how to accomplish this in Chapter 18.

Communications

Service Manager 2010 uses a variety of network ports that are optimized for security and performance. Communication with the Service Manager database and the data warehouse databases always occurs via standard SQL client/server protocols.

For communications between servers and the console, the primary Transmission Control Protocol (TCP) port used by Service Manager 2010 is 5724.

The initial Service Manager management server hosts data access, workflow services, and authorization services. This management server executes workflows and sends notifications. If this server is unavailable, most features of Service Manager will be inaccessible. The management server depends completely on its connection to the Service Manager database to function.

Both the Service Manager database and a management server must be continuously available to provide uninterrupted continuity of management functions. This requirement makes clustering the Service Manager database and load balancing the management server top considerations when designing a highly available management solution for your organization. For management servers, you can deploy additional management servers to the same Service Manager management group to provide failover. See Chapter 6, "Planning Complex Configurations," for information about planning for complex configurations.

Table 4.3 lists communications paths and ports, but it does not illustrate the need for Remote Procedure Call/Distributed Component Object Model (RPC/DCOM) communication between the management server, console, or the end-user workstation. Depending on how you work, you might need to allow network traffic to workstations for service desk operators to run tasks and recovery tools against end-user workstations.

TABLE 4.3   Communication Paths and Ports

From Component	Port Number and Direction	To Component
Service Manager console	5724 >	Service Manager management server
Service Manager console	5724 >	Data warehouse management server
Service Manager management server	1433 >	Remote service manager database
Service Manager management server	5724 >	Data warehouse server
Service Manager management server	5724 >	Operations Manager 2007 Alert and CI connectors
Service Manager management server	389 >	Active Directory connector
Service Manager management server	1433 >	Configuration Manager 2007 CI connector
Service Manager management server	RPC dynamic ports >	Configuration Manager 2007 Software Provisioning connector
Data warehouse server	1433 >	Remote data warehouse database server
SQL Reporting service server	1433 >	Remote data warehouse database server
Data warehouse server	1433 >	Remote service manager database server

TABLE 4.3   Communication Paths and Ports

From Component	Port Number and Direction	To Component
Web browser	443 >	Self-Service portal
Self-Service portal	1433 >	Service Manager database
Web browser	80 >	SQL Server Reporting Services

In addition, note that new extensions to Service Manager may require additional network ports.

Summary

This chapter provided a look inside Service Manager 2010, from a general overview down to macro perspectives. It first described how Service Manager components are deployed in a minimum installation of two machines, and then discussed an installation that included multiple machines and adding the data warehouse component. This chapter also presented a first look at management packs and workflow. In addition, the chapter discussed the Service Manager 2010 console, portal, and PowerShell. The chapter also looked at the ports used between product components and the different Windows services used by Service Manager 2010.

With this background, you are now ready for the following chapters, which delve deeper into the components and capabilities of Service Manager 2010.

PART II

Planning and Installation

IN THIS PART

CHAPTER 5

Designing Service Manager

Although Service Manager (SvcMgr) is a completely new product and an addition to the System Center suite, what is not new is the requirement of planning your deployment before rushing into production; this is the scope of design.

Design is capturing the specifications for what will be built and why, enabling you to proceed to the build, test, and ultimately to the deploy stage of your solution. Many Information Technology (IT) projects fail because of missed expectations and finger pointing. Avoid these problems by creating a high-level design document as a means to drive decisions and agree on expectations, and involving all the stakeholders or sponsors in your organization.

This chapter discusses design; it discusses capturing the scope and specification of what ultimately will be implemented. It lists what to capture in a Vision / Scope and Functional Specification for Service Manager to ensure that you set the scope properly and have what is necessary for a successful implementation. The chapter also covers whom you should talk to and why, and how to go about getting specifications efficiently and effectively.

The activities and deliverables of the Service Manager design stage are included in the Microsoft Operations Framework (MOF) Deliver Phase—specifically the Envision and Project Planning stage functions of the Deliver Phase. The deliverables of this stage are the Vision / Scope and Functional Specification documents, which include the business drivers for the solution along with the physical design (technical specifications) and logical design (configuration parameters and values) components. A configured system is the deliverable of the MOF Build, Stabilize, and

Deploy phases, the result of which should flow down from the Vision / Scope and Functional Specification set out in the Deliver Phase.

Envisioning Service Manager

Microsoft has incorporated into Service Manager guidance from MOF as it pertains to IT implementation projects (in addition to application development projects). The MOF Deliver Phase consists of five stages or functions:

▶ **Envision:** Development of the Vision / Scope document that clearly communicates the project's vision and the scope of that vision for this project.

▶ **Project Planning:** Development of the Functional Specification and preparing work plans, cost estimates, and schedules.

▶ **Build:** Actual development of a solution, including creating a development and test lab, or the preparation of an IT service solution for pilot deployment.

▶ **Stabilize:** Testing and remediation in preparation for release.

▶ **Deploy:** Releasing a stable IT service solution into the production environment, including stabilizing the solution in that environment and transferring responsibility for the solution from the project team to the operations and support teams.

This chapter focuses on the first two stages of the MOF Deliver Phase. You can find additional information about the MOF Deliver Phase at http://technet.microsoft.com/en-us/library/cc506047.aspx.

The first step in designing and deploying a Service Manager solution is to document and obtain agreement from key stakeholders on a clear vision and scope for what is to be accomplished, and why. Accomplishing this requires gaining an understanding of overall business drivers, how a successful implementation contributes to these drivers, and the value the business expects to get from the solution—as this will be how they will measure success. It also includes obtaining agreement on a precise statement of what is (and is not) to be included in the scope, given resources, schedule, and other constraints. Typically, solutions contribute to only a portion of the overall vision a company has; the Vision / Scope document should indicate precisely the portion that will be provided. Here are some questions to ask stakeholders to define the scope and vision:

▶ What benefit do you seek to gain by implementing Service Manager?

    ▶ Lower cost?

    ▶ Faster time to incident and problem resolution and change implementation?

    ▶ Less failed changes?

    ▶ Better regulatory compliance?

    ▶ Higher customer satisfaction?

- Which part of the organization will be participating in the implementation of Service Manager?

- Which part of the organization will use Service Manager?

- Which part of the organization will be maintaining and administering Service Manager?

- Do you have any Information Technology Infrastructure Library (ITIL) process currently implemented within your organization?

- Are you subject to any legal constraints or other regulations (for example, concerning service desks and the handling of user information)?

- Are there key features and workflows, custom or out of the box, that are required for your implementation? If so, what are they?

TIP: DOCUMENTATION ON THE MOF ENVISION SMF

You can find additional information about the MOF Envision Service Management Function (SMF) at http://technet.microsoft.com/en-us/library/cc531013.aspx.

For the vision (where you want to go) to be realistic and achievable, it is important in the Envision Stage to also establish a baseline (where you are now). This starts with understanding the current environment.

Using Assessment to Understand the Current Environment

An Assessment document is the result of gathering a variety of detailed information from various sources. Performing an assessment helps ensure there is a complete and correct understanding of the environment, so that you can identify where you are starting from and determine issues and remediation necessary for a successful implementation of Service Manager.

You use a variety of sources to gather information for an Assessment document, including the following:

- Active Directory (AD), Exchange, Internet Information Services (IIS), Simple Mail Transport Protocol (SMTP), and SharePoint (where applicable)

- Monitoring solution, such as System Center Operations Manager (OpsMgr)

- Deployment solution, such as System Center Configuration Manager (ConfigMgr)

- Service desk solution, and User and IT Analyst self-service portals

- Password reset solution, such as Forefront Identity Manager (FIM) or Identity Lifecycle Manager (ILM)

- ▶ Business services

- ▶ IT processes, including Incident, Event, Problem, Knowledge, Change, and Configuration Management

- ▶ SQL Server and SQL Server Reporting Services (SRS)

- ▶ Virtualization

- ▶ High availability, backup, and disaster recovery

For each of these areas, you need to determine the following:

- ▶ **What it is:** You should assess and collect information for various different sources to ensure that you have a complete and correct understanding of the environment and have identified all stakeholders.

- ▶ **What is to be accomplished:** For each source, determine what or how you want to use it in Service Manager. For example, if you have a deployment solution such as Configuration Manager, how do you package your software, and is self-service available; if not, do you want that capability?

The next sections discuss the questions to ask and the answers you need to document in each of these areas.

NOTE: NEED TO ASSESS HEALTH OF SOURCES

Information from AD, Operations Manager, and Configuration Manager flows into Service Manger via connectors. If the data in the source is not clean or healthy, what comes across to Service Manager will also not be clean. Here are some examples:

- ▶ If the AD structure does not reflect the organization or AD is missing objects you want carried over to Service Manager across the connector, you will have difficulty cleanly mapping user roles in Service Manager, and you may not have the data required to drive and complete workflows.

- ▶ If the Alert to Ticket ratio is not well-tuned in Operations Manager, or Desired Configuration Management (DCM) settings are not well-tuned in Configuration Manager, this could lead to a lot of spurious tickets being generated in Service Manager.

Active Directory, Exchange, IIS, and SMTP

Determine whether Service Manager will integrate with AD to automatically populate the Service Manager configuration management database (CMDB) with data from Active Directory Users and Computers. If this is the case, you must establish which AD forests are in scope. You can automatically import the entire AD domain or by specific organizational units (OUs). Each Service Manager management group can have multiple AD connectors; trusts are not required. Before configuring the AD connectors, it is best to also perform an assessment of AD health and remediate any issues to prevent the Service Manager console from being cluttered with irrelevant data, and address any issues. For example, a self-service software request workflow in Service Manager requires manager approval when the user requests software that requires disbursement of funds. Service Manager depends on the approving manager information being properly recorded in AD in the record for that user. If the manager information is missing or incorrect in AD, the workflow will break in Service Manager.

Service Manager uses Microsoft Exchange, IIS, and SMTP for inbound and outbound notification. You should determine which version of each is in use and on which servers. Knowing the version in use is important because different versions require different configuration methods for inbound and outbound email settings. Also key is determining whether you will be using a self-signed certificate or one from a trusted Secure Sockets Layer (SSL) provider for the self-service portals.

Monitoring Solutions

Establish whether a monitoring solution is installed, such as Operations Manager. These products may include server, network, application, or hardware monitoring products. Here is the information you want to gather:

- What monitoring solutions are being used to monitor the production environment, and what versions of that software?
- What servers are the monitoring solutions running on?
- What is being monitored by the products?
- Can configuration items (CIs) be automatically imported from the monitoring solution into the Service Manager CMDB?
- Who are the users of the product?
- Can you forward alerts from the monitoring solution to Service Manager?

If you require some method of communication between Service Manager and your monitoring solution, such as automated alert forwarding, you need to have a good understanding of this monitoring solution.

Here are questions to ask regarding the current monitoring solutions:

- What type of monitoring is implemented?
- Do you have health-state monitoring or only alert monitoring?
- Are you monitoring on a server or on a business services/application level?
- Who are the product owners?
- What is the current alert-to-ticket ratio?

Deployment Solutions

Determine whether a deployment solution such as Configuration Manager is currently installed. These products may include software and patch management, operating system deployment, desired configuration management, and so on. Here are examples of the type of information you want to gather:

▶ What products are used for software deployment? What version is in use?

▶ Can the deployment solution be used to deploy software requested through the Self-Service portal (SSP)?

▶ Can the CMDB be populated with the deployment solution?

If you require communication between Service Manager and your deployment solution, such as automated configuration item import into the Service Manager CMDB, you must have a good understanding of this deployment solution.

Here are questions to ask as a starting point for understanding the current deployment solution:

▶ Who are the product owners?

▶ Is it possible to import data to Service Manager from the deployment solution?

▶ Can this deployment solution be used through the SSP?

Service Desk Solution and User and IT Analyst Self-Service Portals

Establish whether a service desk solution is installed in the environment and whether IT Analyst and End User portals are in use. These products may include Incident and Problem Management solutions, CMDB products, and so on. You want to gather information about the following:

▶ Can work items from an existing service desk solution be imported or migrated into Service Manager, and is this a requirement?

▶ Can the Service Manager CMDB be populated from the existing CMDB?

If you require communication between Service Manager and your service desk solution, such as CI import into the CMDB, you must have a good understanding of this service desk solution.

Password Reset Solution

Although Service Manager includes a link for a password reset solution on the Self-Service portal, it is only a link; you must provide your own password reset solution, such as Forefront Identity Manager (FIM) or Identity Lifecycle Manager (ILM). Therefore, you need to ask the following:

▶ Is there a password reset solution in place?

▶ If not, will a solution be acquired and implemented on the portal?

Business Services

Are business services defined in the organization? Service Manager lets you create business services that visualize the different IT components of that business service. You can merge data from other System Center products such as Operations Manager and Configuration Manager and import OpsMgr distributed applications into Service Manager.

For example, you can create a distributed application (DA) in OpsMgr for your IT messaging application. This distributed application contains all the objects (such as a mail server, router, Outlook client, storage, authentication services, and so on) that make up the IT messaging application; you can then import this DA into Service Manager. Note that the connector only imports the DA object, not the relationships between the objects. To get relationships between objects into Service Manager, you must export the management pack containing the DA and import it into Service Manager.

CAUTION: SERVICE MANAGER LIMITATIONS FOR COMPONENTS IN A BUSINESS SERVICE

Service Manager is currently not designed to handle a large number of components in a business service. You may experience slow console response time if you have more than 100 components and go more than five levels deep.

You can find more information about business services in Chapter 9, "Business Services."

IT Processes

Determine which IT processes are in use in the organization, who owns them, and what their relative state of health is. This includes Incident, Event, Problem, Knowledge, Change, and Configuration Management, because these are all in scope for functionality supported by Service Manager out of the box. You can find more information about the different IT processes in Service Manager in Chapter 10, "Incident Management," Chapter 11, "Problem Management," and Chapter 12, "Change Management."

SQL Server and SQL Server Reporting Services

It is important to document the SQL and SQL Server Reporting Services (SRS) architecture underpinning Service Manager, for two reasons:

▶ The performance of Service Manager is in large part a function of the performance of SQL Server.

▶ The type of configuration your organization has standardized on has implications for your Service Manager configuration (for example, whether you have a shared SQL Server environment and whether SRS is on a separate server).

Virtualization

If Service Manager will be deployed in a virtual environment, determine the implications and the provisions that need to be put in place to ensure adequate performance. For example, certain virtualization technologies limit the number of processor cores per virtual machine (VM), which in term limits the number of concurrent console sessions available per Service Manager management server. You also want to follow best practices for using SQL Server in a virtualized environment to ensure proper performance of Service Manager.

High Availability, Backup, and Disaster Recovery

Determine the provisions being made to ensure availability (such as clustering, RAID, and so on) of Service Manager and what will be done for backup and disaster recovery of Service Manager.

Deliverables

The deliverable of the Envision stage is a Vision / Scope document that includes an Executive Summary and Assessment sections. The Executive Summary captures the business reasons and requirements for the Service Manager solution. The Assessment document is a backgrounder providing insight into the current environment and the motivation to move to Service Manager.

PLAN FOR DIFFERENT STAKEHOLDERS FOR ENVISIONING AND ASSESSMENT

Service Manager is unique in the System Center suite because of the many different types of people interacting with the product; essentially, everyone in the organization interacts with Service Manager at some point. This chapter discusses designing Service Manager and capturing specifications. One of the first steps in designing a solution is to document and obtain agreement from the key stakeholders in your environment. Consulting with a number of stakeholders is often required to obtain a clear vision and scope for what has to be accomplished and why. The key stakeholders who can help define the vision and scope in the Envision stage will not be technical system administrators but most likely IT managers, chief technology officers (CTOs), chief information officers (CIOs), technical decision makers, and so on.

Once the stakeholders agree on the scope and vision of Service Manager in the Envision stage, you start with the Assessment. In the Assessment, you will most likely talk to a different set of stakeholders than you did in the Envision stage. When assessing various sources such as AD, OpsMgr, ConfigMgr, and others, you must gather detailed information about those sources, as discussed in the "Using Assessment to Understand the Current Environment" section of this chapter. You can obtain this detailed information from the AD architect, OpsMgr architect, and others. For a successful Service Manager implementation, it is important that you not skip this step in the process. Without speaking to the different stakeholders, it is impossible to have a good envisioning/assessment document. The Vision / Scope document provides the goal of your implementation. The Assessment document provides the background that will help that vision and scope to reach the ground in the planning stage that follows.

The Assessment document provides a realistic grounding in "where you are now" to complement the "where you want to go" of the vision statement; this ensures that the vision and the scope for the Service Manager implementation are aligned with both current realities and where the business wants to go. All appropriate personnel in the organization should review this document to validate that the collected information is correct and accurate. Do not expect that this document will be completely correct the first time. Plan to organize review sessions with each stakeholder, and based on feedback, you will improve the accuracy of the Assessment document. After reaching agreement on the accuracy of the document content, you can move to the next stage: Planning and Design.

Planning Service Manager

The Vision / Scope and Assessment documents created in the Envision stage now provide you with all required vision and background to design your new Service Manager solution. In the Project Planning stage, you move from vision and background and a solution concept to the precise articulation of what will be delivered in the form of a Functional Specification. This design is sized and configured to deliver a solution meeting the business requirements discovered in the Assessment and Envisioning stage. A best practice approach when creating your design document is to evaluate your technical decisions against the following design principles:

- Keep it simple (KIS)

- Keep it scalable and available (KISA)

- You ain't gonna need it (YAGNI)

- Vendor best practices followed (BP)

Do not add complexity to the solution just because it is cool or fun. Only add complexity to the design to meet the business requirements, which is the first step of the Planning and Design stage.

Whereas the Vision / Scope document captures the background, vision, and high-level solution concept, the deliverable from this stage is the Functional Specification, which precisely describes what you will and will not deliver in the solution. For example, the Vision / Scope may specify that the SSP is needed. But, will the portal include password reset, self-service software provisioning, and other functionality, and to what extent? The scope of the solution for the SSP could include simply hiding the password reset link, or it could include identifying, testing, selecting, and installing a password reset utility and adding it to the portal. The Functional Specification spells out the details of precisely what will and will not be included in scope, which helps ensure that expectations are set and that your estimates for schedule and resources for the implementation will be on target.

A Functional Specification for Service Manager consists of two distinct design specifications: physical and logical.

Functional Specification: Physical Design

Physical design results in the technical specification of the implementation. Ideally, the specification includes the default or required values where applicable, shown next to the chosen values and best practice notes, with annotations wherever the organization is varying from these values. For example, an organization may choose to use less memory or storage or fewer processors than recommended or required because they are moving to a new virtualized platform in a few months and don't want to spend on the legacy hardware. The idea is to show where chosen values vary from or align with both default and best practice values. Physical design components of the Functional Specifications for Service Manager include the following:

▶ Hardware, software, network, and database specifications, along with the Service Manager sizing parameters and notes, and SQL Server and virtualization configuration for performance and notes, and prerequisite/supported configuration specifications that drive them.

▶ Versions specifications for components related to Service Manager (typically, AD, Exchange, SMTP, IIS, SQL/SRS, Operations Manager, Configuration Manager, SharePoint where applicable, and whatever password reset utility is used, such as FIM or ILM) along with the prerequisite/supported configuration specifications that drive them.

▶ Installation parameters (literally, what to type into dialog boxes in the installation screens).

▶ Specifications for installation and Run As Accounts, and groups and users and associated access rights, along with the sizing parameters and prerequisite/supported configuration specifications driving them.

▶ Fault tolerance, high availability, backup and restore, and disaster recovery provisions specification.

▶ Specification of which complementary solutions (for example, the Service Manager Dashboard) are in or out of scope for the implementation.

▶ Specifications for any custom user roles and mapping to AD groups and the organization chart.

▶ IT analyst specification, including a table depicting who will get the Service Manager console, and what their user role will be.

MAPPING IT GROUPS AND ANALYSTS TO USER ROLES, GROUPS, AND QUEUES IN SERVICE MANAGER

The roles and functions that make up your organization must be mapped into Service Manager. This is accomplished through user roles, groups, and queues.

A *user role* is a method of granting permissions to specific users for groups of data. These permissions are based on a user role profile, which is a set of permitted operations and classes of data that users need access to so they can perform specific job duties.

Groups are collections of configuration items, which are any components that need to be managed to deliver a service. In Service Manager, CIs might include services, hardware, software, buildings, people, and formal documentation, such as process documentation and service level agreements (SLAs). Groups can contain members of different configuration item classes (for example, a computer and a user).

Queues are collections of work items. Members of a queue must be of the same work item class (for example, only incidents).

Who should get a copy of the Service Manager console loaded on their desktop, and what should they see and be able to do (and to what) when they log in to that console? These questions need to be answered during design. For more information about mapping user roles, see Chapter 15, "Service Manager Security." You can find user roles in Service Manager 2010 in the console, in the Administration workspace under Security. See Chapter 15 for a full explanation of user roles in Service Manager.

Here are some questions you might have when considering how to map users and groups in your organization to user roles in Service Manager:

▶ What is the full set of permitted operations a user role can have?

   Create, edit, and delete. You can see that Activity Implementers have permission to edit manual activities within their queue scope but cannot create or delete them; their set of permitted operations is limited to edit.

▶ What is the full set of possible scopes?

   Queues, groups, console tasks, runtime tasks, views, templates, and classes.

▶ What is the full set of classes of objects/data that can be the target of permitted operations in Service Manager?

   Knowledge articles, work items, configuration items, notifications, and subscriptions.

User roles provide a means to limit what different classes of users can do, and to what, within Service Manager. For example, you would not want a service desk operator to have the same rights as a system administrator, and vice versa. You place users in user roles so that they can only perform the operations their job requires, to the classes of objects and data that job requires.

The Service Manager administrator assigns personnel in the organization user roles in Service Manager, which give them rights (such as read, create, edit, and delete) to a set scope of objects (such as incident tickets and knowledge base articles).

> **TIP: MAPPING USER ROLES TO ACTIVE DIRECTORY GROUPS**
>
> A best practice is to create a corresponding set of groups in AD for each of the built-in user roles in Service Manager. Then, include that AD group in the Users section of each user role. When an individual needs to be added to Service Manager as a user, instead of entering that person's user name directly into Service Manager, you add him or her to the corresponding group in AD. This keeps user administration clean and in one place: Active Directory.
>
> Follow this approach for each additional group you might create in Service Manager.

Here are key questions to ask to ensure that the design is complete:

▶ Are all prerequisites (hardware, software, operating system roles, features, hotfixes, applications, and so on) met by the specification? Does this check out against what is specified in the Service Manager Sizing Helper tool and the planning and deployment guides?

▶ Are all values required for installation of each Service Manager component specified (the values you will type into each dialog box for each installation)?

▶ Are the groups and accounts required for Service Manager installation and operation specified, along with their required access rights, and have you checked these against the planning and deployment guides?

▶ Do you know who will have access to the console and the user role (including custom roles) they will be assigned in Service Manager? Who will need access to the Authoring Tool?

As part of the physical design process, you specify the technical requirements. The physical design produces a specification documenting decisions regarding technical requirements settings. Here are list and setting values to capture in the physical design:

▶ Physical requirements

▶ The number of management groups

▶ The number of Data Warehouse management groups

▶ Design the Service Manager server infrastructure environment

▶ The placement of the Service Manager components

▶ The number of Service Manager servers needed

▶ Fault-tolerance requirements

▶ Required hardware

Determine the Physical/Technical Requirements

In this step, you must speak to the technical business decision makers in the organization to determine the technical requirements of the Service Manager solution. This step expands and elaborates on what is understood about the business domain and the proposed solution. Here are some questions you want answered:

- ▶ What is the appropriate number of computers that will be included?

- ▶ How will the SSP be used?

- ▶ How many IT analysts are in each location, and what support groups do they belong to?

- ▶ Will connectors be used, and if so, in what way?

In this step, you need to determine the expected response time, user load, fault-tolerance requirements, and the estimated size of your Service Manager databases, which can be determined by the Service Manager Sizing Helper tool. (Information about sizing your Service Manager environment is discussed in Chapter 6, "Planning Complex Configurations.")

To determine the technical physical requirements, you must speak to the stakeholders who are responsible for the administration, including the following:

- ▶ Service Manager administrators

- ▶ Operations Manager administrators

- ▶ Configuration Manager administrators

- ▶ Exchange and network administrators for Exchange, AD, IIS, and SMTP

- ▶ SQL Server/SRS administrators

- ▶ IT management associated with each of these technology streams

Here are some questions you can ask the administrators to determine the physical technical requirements:

- ▶ What is the expected response time?

- ▶ What is the user load?

- ▶ Is there any network latency?

- ▶ Are there any specific provisions to make for availability, capacity, security, and disaster recovery?

Determine the Number of Management Groups

Based on discussions with the business decision makers to determine the business requirements and the technical decision makers to determine the technical requirements, you can now determine and design the Service Manager management groups.

Service Manager utilizes two types of management groups:

▶ Service Manager management groups

▶ Data Warehouse management groups

Although there is no limit to the number of management groups that can exist in an organization, remember the KIS (keep it simple) and YAGNI (you ain't gonna need it) design principles. Each additional management group adds complexity and cost because each requires new licenses, new servers, and databases. Service Manager management groups exist as separate entities that cannot connect to or communicate with each other, other than the Data Warehouse management group for historical reporting. You can have up to five Service Manager management groups connecting to a Data Warehouse management group.

Determine the Number of Service Manager Management Groups
Service Manager management groups are used (similar to OpsMgr) to define an administrative boundary for managed devices. An organization could have one or more Service Manager management groups to define an administrative boundary for the managed devices. For most cases, a single management group is the simplest configuration to implement, support, and maintain, although in some cases you may have multiple management groups in an organization:

▶ **Exceeding management group support limits:** One reason to add extra Service Manager management groups is if you have more than 50,000 users or computers. This is more a support limit than a technical limit. The product group has tested and validated a working Service Manager management group with up to 50,000 users or computers in a single management group.

▶ **Security and administrative requirements:** Another common reason for creating multiple management groups is separating control between multiple support teams.

▶ **Separate test environment:** The authors recommend creating a completely separate test environment for Service Manager to test your changes or test new process management packs before deploying them into a production environment.

▶ **Disaster recovery functionality:** You can have a standby management group with just one management server and one Service Manager database. The active SQL Server can send the transactional logs to the standby SQL Server via log shipping.

To determine the technical physical requirements, you must talk to the stakeholders who are responsible for the service desk, IT processes, and so on. Typically, those are the following but not limited to:

▶ Technical business decision makers

▶ Service Manager project manager

▶ Service desk owner

Questions you can ask the administrators to determine the number of management groups needed include the following:

▶ How many computers or users will you have as CIs in your CMDB?

▶ Do you have any security or administrative boundaries?

▶ Will you have a test environment?

Determine the Number of Data Warehouse Management Groups

Unlike the Service Manager management group, a Data Warehouse management group is not required. This management group is optional and may be implemented to provide reporting functionality. If you need to maintain historical data, you must install a Data Warehouse management group. In addition, some management packs require a data warehouse—one example is the IT GRC Process management pack.

Similar to the Service Manager management group, in most cases a single Data Warehouse management group is the simplest configuration to implement, support, and maintain. However, in some situations, you want to have multiple Data Warehouse management groups in an organization:

▶ **Security and administrative requirements:** In some cases, you may be legally required to store data in different Data Warehouse databases.

▶ **Exceeding Management Group Support Limits:** As mentioned in the "Determine the Number of Service Manager Management Groups" section, a Data Warehouse management group can have up to five Service Manager management group connections. This enables you to create a single report using data from multiple Service Manager management groups. If you have more than five Service Manager management groups to connect to a data warehouse, you must establish an additional Data Warehouse management group.

Questions you can ask the administrators to determine the number of data warehouse management groups needed include the following:

▶ How many Service Manager management groups do you intend to have?

▶ Do you have any legal constraints that require separate data warehouses?

Design the Service Manager Management Server Infrastructure

In the previous two sections, you determined the number of management groups necessary. Based on this, you can now start designing the Service Manager management server infrastructure. You need to determine the placement of each Service Manager component, the required hardware, and the number of Service Manager servers required.

An important part of the functional specification is the physical Functional Specification, where you document the designed configuration, including key settings. Table 5.1 is an example of such a document. This table is taken from a lab configuration. A production

implementation would likely have Exchange, Operations Manager, and Configuration
Manager installed on separate systems.

TABLE 5.1   Section of the Physical Functional Specification

Server	DC	SCOMCM	SCSM	SCSMDW	USER
Description	Domain Controller	Server hosting Operations and Configuration Manager	Server hosting the Service Manager Management Server	Server hosting the Service Manager Data Warehouse Server	Client Machine hosting the Service Manager Console
Domain	odyssey	odyssey	odyssey	odyssey	odyssey
Role	Domain Controller	Exchange, Operations Manager, Configuration Manager	Service Manager Management Server	Service Manager Data Warehouse	Service Manager Console Service Manager Authoring Tool
Operating System (OS)	Windows Server 2008 R2 x64	Windows Server 2008 R2 x64	Windows Server 2008 R2 x64	Windows Server 2008 R2 x64	Windows 7 Ultimate x64
Applications	Domain Controller Active Directory DNS Certificate Services	Exchange 2010 Operations Manager 2007 R2 Configuration Manager 2007 R3	SQL Server 2008 R2 Service Manager Server Self-Service Portal	SQL Server 2008 Reporting Services SP1 Service Manager Data Warehouse Server	Service Manager Console Service Manager Authoring Tool
RAM	2G	8G	8G	16G	2G
Disks, Size	C:\ 120GB	C:\ 120GB	C:\ 120GB D:\ 400GB	C:\ 120GB	C:\ 120GB
# Processors	2	2x4 cores	2x4 cores	2x4 cores	2
IP Address	10.10.0.10	10.10.0.11	10.10.0.12	10.10.0.13	10.10.0.14
DefGateway	10.10.0.1	10.10.0.10	10.10.0.10	10.10.0.10	10.10.0.10
PrimDNS	127.0.0.1	10.10.0.10	10.10.0.10	10.10.0.10	10.10.0.10

In addition to the values in Table 5.2, you should include additional information about software, versions, roles, features, hotfixes, and such. To check for completeness, determine whether Service Manager, built according to this specification alone, would function adequately. If someone were to use this table as a checklist to validate your installation, is it complete and detailed enough that they would take note of everything that is relevant?

TABLE 5.2   Clusterable Service Manager Components

Component	Fault-Tolerance Option
Service Manager server	Load balance
Service Manager database	SQL cluster
Service Manager Data Warehouse server	N/A
Service Manager Data Warehouse database	SQL cluster
Service Manager SSP	Load balance

Determine Placement of Each Service Manager Server Component   You need to determine the placement of each Service Manager server component. This includes the databases, SSP, Service Manager management servers, analyst consoles, Data Warehouse servers, and so on. Similar to OpsMgr, the SQL and Service Manager servers should be well connected and reside in the same network with as little latency as possible between the different Service Manager components.

The Service Manager database can be co-located with the Service Manager management server; this is perfectly valid for small or test environments. Be careful when selecting this option, though. If later you decide to relocate the database, moving databases from the Service Manager management server is not an easy task. The authors suggest separating the database from the Service Manager management server because of the performance gain you incur with role specialization. Another reason to not co-locate the database with the Service Manager management server is if you are considering database fault tolerance. The database can be clustered, but the Service Manager management server cannot. This is discussed in more detail in the "Determine the Fault Tolerance Requirements" section. If you are considering clustering your database now or in the future, separate the roles initially or you will have to move the Service Manager database to another system.

Because they will be in separate management groups, the Service Manager management server cannot be co-located on the Data Warehouse management server. The Service Manager data warehouse databases can be co-located with the Service Manager Data Warehouse management server. As discussed in Chapter 4, "Looking Inside Service Manager," the Service Manager data warehouse consists of three physical databases:

- ▶ DWStagingandConfig
- ▶ DWRepository
- ▶ DWDatamart

For high-volume environments, place the DWStagingandConfig and DWRepository databases on hardware optimized for read and write input/output (I/O), while optimizing the DWDatamart for read I/O. You can separate the DWDatamart to a different instance or server and drive from DWStagingandConfig and DWRepository. The DWStagingandConfig and DWRepository databases must reside within the same instance on the same server.

As discussed in Chapter 20, "Reports, Dashboards, and Data Analysis," data is automatically transferred by the extract, transform, and load (ETL) workflow processes from the Service Manager servers to the DWDatamart with a 30- to 60-minute delay. Because of this large amount of data transfer, the Data Warehouse management server and database should be in the same local area network (LAN), and close to the Service Manager management server and database, with no or very limited latency.

Because Service Manager resides on the same architecture as OpsMgr, you must be careful with placing your Service Manager components when OpsMgr is installed:

▶ To monitor your Service Manager server, first install the Service Manager management server and only then install the OpsMgr 2007 R2 agent. This means that if you have already installed an OpsMgr agent, you must uninstall it prior to your Service Manager installation.

▶ A Service Manager management server cannot reside on the same system as an OpsMgr management server.

Because the Service Manager SSP needs to communicate with the Service Manager management server and Service Manager database, it should be well connected via a LAN. The users are able to access the portal from the wide area network (WAN) if needed.

TIP: LOCATION OF THE SELF-SERVICE PORTAL

Although the Service Manager SSP can be installed on a Service Manager management server, it is not recommended. If you later want to uninstall the SSP, you must also uninstall the Service Manager server.

Ensure that the latency between your Analyst console and other Service Manager components is less than 150ms. If it is higher, your analysts will have a poor performance experience.

Determine the Number of Service Manager Servers   Each management group can have only one Service Manager database, but multiple Service Manager servers can connect to that database. Here are reasons to have multiple Service Manager servers:

▶ **Dedicating a Service Manager management server to run workflows:** The first Service Manager management server installed is the server that runs and manages the workflows. For performance reasons, you could dedicate this workflow server to run only workflows and let the Service Manager consoles connect to other dedicated Service Manager management servers.

▶ **Scaling of Service Manager consoles:** The authors recommend running no more than 40 concurrent consoles per management server. If you have a higher number of concurrent Analyst consoles, add an extra management server for performance reasons.

▶ **Quick recovery of the Service Manager server:** The management server running the workflows is a single point of failure. The workflow management server has no fault-tolerance options such as clustering or load balancing. Should this server go down, no workflow will run, which will greatly affect your Service Manager solution. None of the automatic processes (such as email notifications, automatic applying of templates, automated activities in a change request, and such) will run if your main Service Manager management server is unavailable. You could install an extra Service Manager management server that you can easily and quickly promote to become the primary Service Manager management server.

Similar to the Service Manager management servers, the SSP servers are tied to one and only management group. You can install the SSP server separately or on another Service Manager server. Although the other Service Manager components consume more resources than the SSP, it is suggested you separate the portal if you suspect you will have many user transactions and custom workflows. You can add more than one SSP in a load-balancing configuration for scaling.

TIP: WHEN TO ADD ADDITIONAL SELF-SERVICE PORTAL SERVERS

The Service Manager product team recommends that you add an extra SSP server for each 200 simultaneously connected users.

When determining the number of Service Manager management servers, keep the design principles in mind; begin with one Service Manager management server and add others if needed for the reasons listed in this section.

If you will be performing a proof of concept (POC) or installing Service Manager in a lab environment, you could install the Service Manager management server and all databases on a single physical server and the Data Warehouse management server on a separate (virtual) server, as shown in Figure 5.1.

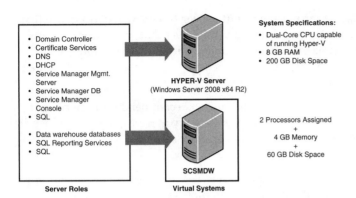

FIGURE 5.1   Small scenario, ideal for POC and demo purposes.

Although this scenario is a perfect solution for POCs and demo environments, it is not supported in a production environment, because Microsoft has not performed performance tests for this configuration. The minimum supported configuration for small environments consists of separating the CMDB from the Service Manager workflow management server. This is shown in Figure 5.2.

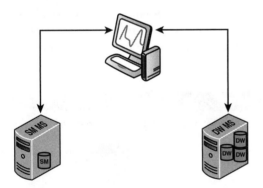

FIGURE 5.2   Medium scenario.

In a third scenario (see Figure 5.3), you can separate the SQL Server roles from the Service Manager roles. This increases performance for the Service Manager server but does not cover failover or high-availability requirements.

A fourth scenario is the most advanced one and used in large environments. In this scenario, you have load balanced both Service Manager management servers and clustered your SQL servers. This scenario, shown in Figure 5.4, not only provides you with failover capabilities but also ensures adequate performance.

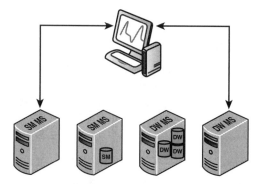

FIGURE 5.3   Large scenario.

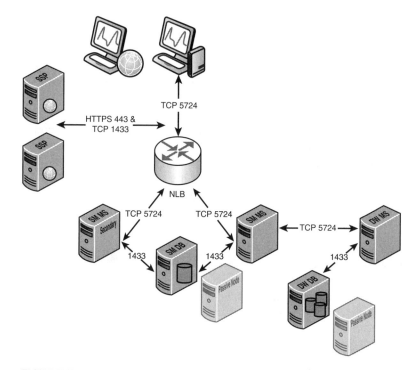

FIGURE 5.4   Advanced scenario.

Determine the Fault-Tolerance Requirements   When determining availability and fault-tolerance options for your Service Manager solution, you should first understand the significance of losing data or functionality for each Service Manager component:

▶ **SSP server:** If the SSP server is not available, end users cannot request software, request a password reset, search for knowledge articles, check the status of their work items, and so on.

▶ **Service Manager management server:** If the Service Manager management server is unavailable, the workflows will not run, and the connectors will not import data. The Service Manager server is a single point of failure and is not clusterable.

▶ **Service Manager database:** If your Service Manager database is unavailable, you cannot open the Service Manager console, because it cannot retrieve work items and such, and most important, data will not be updated in the Service Manager database.

▶ **Service Manager Data Warehouse management server:** If the Service Manager Data Warehouse management server is not available, data is not updated in the data warehouse, and you cannot run reports through the Service Manager console.

▶ **Service Manager data warehouse databases:** If your data warehouse databases are unavailable, you cannot run Service Manager reports through the console or through the SQL Reporting Server, and most important, data will not be updated in the data warehouse databases.

Determine the significance of each Service Manager component and decide which fault-tolerance features you want to apply, based on the information in Table 5.2.

See Chapter 6 for additional information about fault tolerance and high availability for Service Manager.

Determine the Required Hardware   Based on the business and technical requirements you have collected, you can now determine the hardware required to install Service Manager. Similar to Operations Manager, Service Manager is a three-tiered application with databases, the data access module, and consoles. When determining the hardware needed for your Service Manager servers, keep performance and scalability in mind for all components in your three-tiered application.

TIP: SIZING HELPER TOOL AVAILABLE

The Service Manager product team provides a Service Manager Sizing Helper tool. This utility helps you determine the required hardware based on specific scenarios. The tool is available in the Service Manager Job Aids documentation set, available at http://go.microsoft.com/fwlink/?LinkId=186291.

Here are the Service Manager components that poorly performing resources negatively impact:

▶ **Connector performance:** There will be a negative impact on the time it takes a connector to synchronize and insert data. When you first configure a connector, the initial synchronization can take a significant amount of time. When working in several large Configuration Manager and AD environments, the authors have seen the connectors' initial synchronization take up to 10 hours. During this initial synchronization, you can expect performance issues on all Service Manager server roles. This results from SQL Server inserting the data sequentially into the Service Manager database, which can take a long time. The authors recommend planning your initial connector synchronization and ensuring the synchronization process runs successfully before placing Service Manager into production.

▶ **Console performance:** Your console responsiveness will be heavily impacted if you have poor performance.

▶ **Workflow performance:** The length of time it takes for a workflow to apply some type of action will also be impacted by performance issues. Typically, workflows, such as notification subscription and applying templates, run within 1 minute of when the work item is generated.

When determining required hardware, there will be differences in requirements for the various Service Manager roles:

▶ **Service Manager management server:** CPU and memory are critical factors for this server. Each core on a processor within the Service Manager management server can support up to 10 concurrent consoles. Memory capacity is even more important because of the high memory-intensive operations on a Service Manager management server. Using 64-bit hardware enables you to increase memory beyond 4GB. Even if your deployment does not currently require more than 4GB, 64-bit hardware provides room for growth should memory requirements later change. You should have at a minimum 8GB of RAM and one CPU core for each 10 concurrent consoles.

▶ **Service Manager database:** For this server, memory and disk I/O are critical factors. Performance of the Service Manager database is primarily impacted by the number of concurrent console connections retrieving or writing data and data inserted by the connectors. For your database environment, 64-bit hardware and a 64-bit operating system are required by Service Manager. For SQL hardware best practices, see the "SQL Hardware Best Practices" section, later in this chapter. You should have a minimum of 8GB of RAM.

▶ **Service Manager SSP:** The SSP is more stateless without many I/O operations; performance is merely impacted by the number of concurrent users creating a work item or requesting software.

▶ **Service Manager console:** The console caches information such as forms in memory. Performance of the console is primarily impacted by the number of forms you open and the number of items retrieved. You should have at a minimum 2GB of RAM and a dual core for the system where the Service Manager console is installed. The cache is located at C:\Users\%*user*%\AppData\Local\Microsoft\System Center Service Manager 2010.

▶ **Service Manager Data Warehouse management server:** The Data Warehouse management server is more stateless than any other Service Manager server, even without a considerable number of I/O operations. The number of Service Manager management servers registered with the Data Warehouse management server has a direct impact on its performance. The more Service Manager management servers registered, the more RAM you need to add. You should have a minimum of 4GB of RAM for the Data Warehouse management server.

▶ **Service Manager Data Warehouse database server:** Similar to the server running the Service Manager database, RAM and disk I/O are critical factors. Performance of the Data Warehouse database server is directly impacted by the frequency of the ETL process workflows, data-retention period, number of Service Manager servers sending data, the rate of data change, and so on. The "SQL Hardware Best Practices" section discusses additional SQL hardware best practices. You should have a minimum of 4GB of RAM for the Data Warehouse database server and 8GB of RAM if you have more than 4,000 computers.

Table 5.3 lists the minimum recommended hardware requirements for the Service Manager components.

TABLE 5.3   Minimum Recommended Hardware Requirements

Component	Memory	Disk
Service Manager management server	8GB	64GB RAID 5.
Service Manager database	8GB	RAID 1. Chapter 6 discusses how to estimate the database size.
Service Manager Data Warehouse management server	4GB	64GB RAID 5.
Service Manager Data Warehouse database	4GB	RAID 1. Chapter 6 discusses how to estimate the database size.
Service Manager SSP	4GB	64GB RAID 5.

NOTE: PERFORMANCE AND CAPACITY PLANNING

You can find more information about performance and capacity planning for the Service Manager databases in Chapter 6.

SQL Hardware Best Practices

The Service Manager database is often a performance bottleneck. All Service Manager data either comes from or goes to SQL Server, which is why you need to size and configure your SQL disks appropriately; the faster the disks, the better the performance. This section discusses database hardware recommendations specific for a Service Manager environment. These guidelines are based on observations by the authors during multiple Service Manager deployments.

As mentioned previously, for your database environment, 64-bit hardware and a 64-bit operating system are required by Service Manager.

Here are some considerations for disk and SQL database file placement (and the ideal configuration):

▶ If there are many concurrent reporting users, place the Service Manager reporting server on a different system from the data warehouse. Doing so increases performance, because running reports that query large data ranges or targeting many objects demands additional resources.

▶ Configure the database server with one disk for the OS, one disk for SQL, one disk for Tempdb, and one disk for transaction logs.

▶ Use multiple physical files for your databases to increase physical I/O operations. The more I/O SQL Server performs at a disk level, the better your database performance. If you use separate database physical files, verify that the files have the same initial size and growth settings. If they are of different sizes, SQL Server tries to fill the physical file with the most free space first to maintain an equal amount of free space within all the files. If the files are of identical size, writes are distributed across the various database files, improving performance.

Here is a preferred drive configuration:

▶ Do not place database data files on the same drive as the operating system.

▶ Place transaction logs and database data files on separate drives. The transaction log workload consists of mostly sequential writes; putting the transaction logs on a separate volume allows that volume to perform I/O more efficiently. A single two-spindle RAID 1 volume is sufficient for most environments when handling very high volumes of sequential writes.

▶ Place the Tempdb database on its own drive.

▶ Resize Tempdb and its transaction log to be 20% of the total size of the Service Manager database and data warehouse.

▶ As a best practice, Microsoft suggests a battery-backed write-caching disk controller for the Service Manager database and the data warehouse. Testing has shown that the workload on these databases benefit from write caching on disk controllers. When configuring read caching versus write caching on disk controllers, allocate 25% to read caching and 75% of the cache to write caching. When using write-caching disk controllers with any database system, a proper battery backup system can prevent data loss in the event of an outage.

TIP: MOVING TEMPDB TO ITS OWN DRIVE TO INCREASE PERFORMANCE

During a typical SQL Server installation, the Tempdb and Tempdb transaction log files are installed on the same disk drive as the other databases. Here is a query to move these files to another drive (D:\data\MSSQLserver\ in this example):

```
USE MASTER

GO

ALTER DATABASE TEMPDB

MODIFY FILE (NAME = TEMPDEV, FILENAME = 'D:\DATA\MSSQLSERVER\TEMPDB.MDF')

GO

ALTER DATABASE TEMPDB

 MODIFY FILE (NAME = TEMPDEV, FILENAME = 'D:\DATA\MSSQLSERVER\TEMPLOG.LDF')

GO
```

Restarting the SQL Server instance applies the changes.

Functional Specification: Logical Design

Logical design produces a specification documenting decisions about configuration settings and drop-down (enumeration) list value settings. Ideally, the specification includes the default or required values where applicable, documented next to the customer-chosen values and best practice notes, with annotations wherever the customer is varying from these values. The intent is to plainly show where chosen values vary from or align with both default and best practice values. Here are some list and setting values to capture in the logical design:

▶ Settings (Incident, Problem, Change, Knowledge, Data Retention, and Activity) Enumeration (drop-down) list values

▶ Requirements for custom forms (such as hidden or added custom fields or layout changes), views, templates, workflows, subscriptions, and notifications

▶ Reporting specification (who will produce what report, at what interval, for what audience, to what end; custom reports, if required)

▶ Product licensing

You must speak with a different set of key stakeholders to drive decisions and specifications. Usually these include IT management from IT support groups, process owners, service owners, IT administrators, and project managers. Here are some of the questions you want answered:

▶ What process requirements exist beyond the out-of-the-box defaults?

▶ Are default settings and drop-down (enumeration list) values adequate, or is something more needed?

▶ What customizations of workflows, forms, views, notifications, and subscriptions are required? What effort do they require to complete? What value do they provide? What is their resultant priority? What then is in and out of scope, given limited resources?

Figure 5.5 outlines the authors' recommended approach to deciding on taking defaults, configuring (low effort), or customizing (high effort).

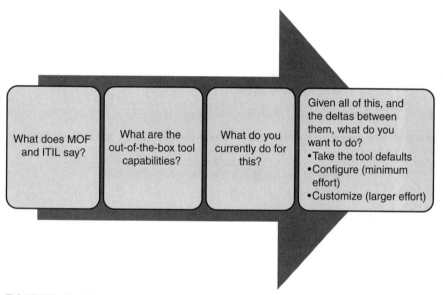

FIGURE 5.5   A logical approach to keeping your solution as simple, standards-aligned, and out-of-the-box as possible.

Settings

There is a basic list of settings for incidents, problems, changes, knowledge, data retention, and activities. Specific considerations on how to arrive at value for these beyond the defaults are covered in Chapters 10, 11, and 12. The work to be accomplished in the design stage is to ensure that you capture specifications for these parameters as a part of the design.

For example, incident settings include the following:

▶ General settings

▶ Priority Calculation

▶ Resolution Time

▶ Operations Management

▶ Incoming E-Mail

The specific considerations for choosing these settings are covered in Chapter 10, which discusses Incident Management. In the design stage, you need to ensure you have identified all areas such as these that require parameters to be decided and recorded, to be clear about who you need to talk with to do so, and the best way to drive these decisions.

A typical approach to determining these settings is to create a worksheet with default and recommended values, along with a place to record the values you have chosen and any rationale you want to include. Table 5.4 shows an excerpt from such a worksheet.

TABLE 5.4   Excerpt from a Settings Worksheet

Setting	Description	Default Value
Incident Prefix	Primary user affected by the incident	IR
Maximum Number of Files Attached	Specifies the maximum number of files that can be attached to a single incident record	5 files
Maximum Size	Maximum size of each file attachment	2048KB
Default Support Group	Specifies the default selection for the support group	No value
Incident Retention Time	Specifies the amount of time a closed incident record will remain in the database (after which it is available only for reporting)	90 days
Setting	Description	Default value
Incident Prefix	Primary user affected by the incident	IR

This approach allows you to juxtapose the out-of-the-box values with any variations chosen, along with why they were chosen, which aids greatly in driving decisions. A recommended approach is to take an initial pass at the spreadsheet with a smaller group, typically the project sponsor and Service Manager administrators, and then open it up to a larger group to review. It is better to start with a draft the group can discuss and revise than with a blank sheet of paper. A good draft will help the group stay on track and channel the decision-making process, thus preventing tangential discussions.

Enumeration (Drop-Down) List Values

The Library workspace contains lists. Use lists to customize values in drop-down boxes in forms.

Similar to settings, your challenge here is to find a way to efficiently drive decisions on which defaults you will accept and which will require modifications and why. Service Manager 2010 includes many default lists. As with settings, a recommended best practice is developing and filling in a list table for each process area, like the one shown in Table 5.5. In addition to the columns shown, include columns for the values you chose and the rationale for choosing them.

TABLE 5.5   Incident Management Lists and Default Values

List	Purpose	Default Value
Classification Category	Classifies the overall incident.	Configuration data problems Email problems Enterprise application problems Hardware problems Networking problems Printing problems Software problems Other problems
Source	Specifies the source of the incident. (Some values are locked.)	Console Configuration Manager Email Phone Portal Operations Manager System
Impact	Specifies the incident's impact or scope; used in conjunction with urgency to calculate priority.	Low Medium High
Urgency	Specifies how quickly the incident needs to be resolved; used in conjunction with impact to calculate priority.	Low Medium High
Support Group	Specifies the team responsible for resolving the incident.	Tier 1 Tier 2 Tier 3
Resolution Category	Classifies how the incident was resolved.	Auto-resolved by problem Canceled Fixed by analyst Fixed by higher tier support Walk through knowledge article

5

Requirements for Customizations

Are specific customizations required for forms, views, templates, workflows, subscriptions, and notifications? If so, you need to capture what they are in your logical Functional Specification. Often, there are more desired customizations than will fit into the budget for the project. A best practice is to prioritize the list of desired customizations based on the effort they require and the expected return on that investment, taking the highest-priority customizations and including them in scope. It is also worth considering and flagging those that are just not feasible, those that should wait for a later stage, and those that should wait for the next version of the product, should the desired custom functionality be planned for the next version.

Reporting Specification

Your goal here is to develop a written agreed specification for the set of reports required for informed decision making and effective communication, including for each report its purpose, audience, and frequency of distribution. Typically, you want to involve managers of IT support groups, process owners, and Service Manager, Configuration Manager, and Operations Manager administrators in reporting specifications.

Service Manager comes with a set of basic canned reports that cover Change, Configuration, Incident, and Problem Management, in addition to activities that span all workflows.

Table 5.6 lists the full set of out-of-the-box reports in Service Manager. Your objective in design is to determine the scope of reporting for the implementation. A table such as Table 5.6 can help you determine and document this scope. The table lists all the canned reports in Service Manager and leaves room for adding custom reports. A column is included for you to indicate whether the report is included in the scope of the implementation. Note that the report will be installed regardless; the key here for "in-scope" reports is that a decision must be driven as to who will generate the report, when, for whom, and to what end or purpose. This last item is essential: What will the recipients do as a result of receiving the report? What "next action" will they take? If you cannot define this, there is probably no reason for distributing the report to them!

TABLE 5.6   Report Specifications

Report	In Scope? (Y/N)	Who Will Generate?	At What Interval? Daily, Weekly, Monthly, Ad Hoc, Other (Specify)	How Will Reports Be Distributed?	Distribution List	Purpose
Activity Reports						
Activities Distribution						
List of Activities						

TABLE 5.6   Report Specifications

Report	In Scope? (Y/N)	Who Will Generate?	At What Interval? Daily, Weekly, Monthly, Ad Hoc, Other (Specify)	How Will Reports Be Distributed?	Distribution List	Purpose
List of Review Activities						
List of Manual Activities						
Manual Activity Details						
Review Activity Details						
Change Request Reports						
Change Management KPI Trend						
List of Change Requests						
Change Request Details						
CI Reports						
List of Computers						
Computer Details						
Incident Reports						
Incident KPI Trend						
Incident Analyst						

TABLE 5.6   Report Specifications

Report	In Scope? (Y/N)	Who Will Generate?	At What Interval? Daily, Weekly, Monthly, Ad Hoc, Other (Specify)	How Will Reports Be Distributed?	Distribution List	Purpose
Incident Resolution						
List of Incidents						
Incident Detail						
Problem Reports						
List of Problems						
Problem Details						
CIs to Incidents						
Custom Report1						
Custom Report2						
Custom Report3						

...

USE REPORT SPECIFICATIONS TO DRIVE CONFIGURATION PARAMETERS AND CONFIRM YOUR DESIGN

Your design may call for a "Phase One," which is simply a production stand up of Service Manager taking many defaults, including default reports. Although this approach is valid, you will want to be wary of such an approach. The value of Service Manager as seen by management will most readily come through in reporting. Through reports, they can see the information they need to manage (presuming the reports produce that information).

This area is where issues can arise in design, and why many experienced tooling professionals say, "Start with the reports and work your way back to configuration settings and values." For example, if six months into the operation of Service Manager, a manager asks to see all incidents associated with a specific area, and that area was not defined up front as part of the design, either the report will not be able to be produced or it will (with a considerable amount of manual effort). Multiply that by several reports, and you can quickly see why starting with reporting is a good idea; reports should drive configuration settings.

It is essential to get these canned reports in front of key stakeholders in the design stage so they fully understand the information the reports do and do not provide. If there truly is a need for different information, it means customization is required to the data source, reports, or both (which in every case means a larger scope for the design and implementation). In addition, if custom reports are required, additional physical design components (for example, Report Builder, Business Intelligence Development Studio, the Service Manager Dashboard, or a partner solution such as Bay Dynamics reporting for Service Manager) may be required.

Product Licensing

Part of your decision about Service Manager includes evaluating licensing options for the product. System Center is licensed as individual products or can be obtained as a suite with several System Center components bundled together. The ultimate source of information for System Center licensing is Microsoft's website, at http://www.microsoft.com/ systemcenter/en/us/pricing-licensing.aspx. Microsoft has several discount levels for licensing. Be sure to discuss licensing requirements and specific license pricing with a reseller that can assess the licensing pricing level for your organization. This section provides information that serves as a guide.

Here is some terminology to be aware of prior to any licensing discussion:

▶ **Operating system environment (OSE):** The operating system of a given device such as a computer, switch, or other computing device, either physical or virtual. The device does not actually have to be running a Microsoft operating system! Printers and smart phones are additional examples of devices considered to have an OSE.

   In many cases, Microsoft has transitioned from per-device licensing to per-OSE licensing.

▶ **Management license (ML):** A management license is required for each managed system, regardless of System Center product. There are different classes of MLs for each product: server and client. An ML is often required for each OSE you intend to manage.

Service Manager differs from other System Center products in that licensing is not based on a deployed agent on a computer, but rather on the number of computers and servers that are under management and stored within the CMDB.

Service Manager is available as part of the System Center suite of products that Microsoft offers and as such is part of the following options for licensing System Center as a suite:

- ▶ Server Management Suite / Enterprise (SMSE)

- ▶ Server Management Suite / Datacenter (SMSD)

- ▶ Enrollment for Core Infrastructure (ECI)

- ▶ Enterprise Client Access Licenses (eCAL)

Prices listed in Table 5.7 include the license and two years of Software Assurance (SA), which is required for licensing SMSE and SMSD.

TABLE 5.7   System Center Suite Licensing Options

Suite Package	Description	Starting List Price (USD)
SMSE	System Center Server Management Suite Enterprise is licensed per physical host, allowing a customer to manage up to four virtual OSEs plus the host OSE.	$1,569
SMSD	System Center Server Management Suite Datacenter is licensed on a per-host processor (socket) basis with a two-processor minimum quantity. Using SMSD, customers can manage an unlimited number of OSEs.	$2,620 (minimum two licenses)
ECI	ECI is a Microsoft Enterprise Agreement (EA) enrollment for customers who want to simplify licensing, help reduce costs, and manage their core infrastructure more efficiently by providing simplified licensing, lower costs, and greater flexibility.	10% to 34% surcharge on top of Standalone Windows Server License depending on server edition (Datacenter, Enterprise, or Standard)

The prices listed in Table 5.7 are estimated prices and reflect the starting prices available in Volume Licensing programs; reseller pricing may vary. Ultimately, licensing is based on a number of factors to be reviewed and confirmed with your Microsoft account representative or software reseller.

Service Manager has both server and client licensing requirements. Service Manager has a number of components to be taken into account for licensing: the core infrastructure, the clients that are managed and stored within the Service Manager CMDB, and the servers that are stored within the Service Manager CMDB.

Server licenses pertain to the physical infrastructure that is required to establish the Service Manager environment, whereas client licenses pertain to any OSE monitored or managed under Service Manager. Service Manager includes client and server MLs.

Table 5.8 provides a breakdown of the components described to be licensed (and described earlier), their description, and associated estimated licensing costs. These

prices are based on the information at http://www.microsoft.com/systemcenter/en/us/
service-manager/sm-pricing-licensing.aspx.

TABLE 5.8   Individual Component Licensing Options

Component	Description	Starting List Price
Service Manager Management Server Software License	This is the server license for the full application, server, and client management capabilities.	$602 per server
Service Manager Management Server Software License with SQL 2008 Technology	This is the full server license as above for the full application, server, and client management capabilities and includes a runtime-restricted version of SQL Server 2008 Standard Edition.	$1,373 per server
Service Manager Server Management License (SML)	Includes the ML for the management of a server OSE that is stored within the Service Manager CMDB.	$259 per server OSE (physical or virtual)
Service Manager Client Management License (CML)	Includes the ML of the client OSE that is stored within the Service Manager CMDB.	$46 per client OSE (physical or virtual)

An ML must be assigned to a device for each OSE on that device that is managed by
Service Manager 2010, except for OSEs on devices functioning only as network infrastructure devices (Open Systems Interconnection [OSI] Layer 3 or below). A device can be a
single server, single personal computer, workstation, terminal, handheld computer, pager,
telephone, personal digital assistant, or other electronic device. An OSE is all or part of an
operating system instance, or all or part of a virtual (or otherwise emulated) operating
system instance that enables separate machine identity (primary computer name or
similar unique identifier) or separate administrative rights, and instances of applications, if
any, configured to run on the operating system instance or parts identified previously.

There are two types of OSEs, physical and virtual:

▶ A physical OSE is configured to run directly on a physical hardware system.

▶ A virtual OSE is configured to run on a virtual (or otherwise emulated) hardware
  system.

A physical hardware system can have either or both of the following: one physical OSE
and one or more virtual OSEs.

The decision matrix in Figure 5.6 can help with determining whether a device stored in
the CMDB is to have a client ML or server ML applied to it.

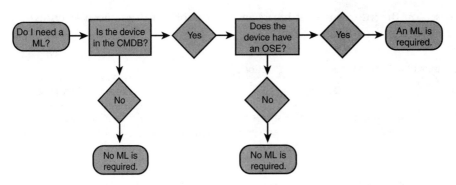

FIGURE 5.6   Decision matrix for determining if a device requires a client or server ML.

Summary

This chapter covered how to create a Vision / Scope document and a Functional Specification that document the business drivers for the solution, along with the physical and logical specifications that fulfill them. Taking this step provides a sound foundation for the build-out, deployment, and operation of Service Manager. This chapter covered the various approaches to capturing scope and specification, driving decisions, and gaining agreement.

Physical design specifications for hardware, software, OS, network, database, and virtualization were discussed, as was logical design specification, including configuration settings and drop-down (enumeration) list values, reporting, and customizations. These explicit statements of requirements are meant to capture requirements well enough to drive a successful build, test, and ultimately, deployment into production.

The chapters that follow build on these specifications and cover implementation considerations for the specifications set out in the design stage.

CHAPTER 6

Planning Complex Configurations

This chapter discusses information to consider when planning complex configurations of Service Manager 2010. Service Manager can provide solutions when running on a single server or can scale to multiple servers, depending on the specific requirements of your organization as determined in Chapter 5, "Designing Service Manager." This chapter offers insight for deploying Service Manager in environments that require redundancy, virtualization, and capacity planning. The chapter also provides performance recommendations to consider when implementing complex configurations of Service Manager.

Planning for High Availability

If you require a highly available Service Manager environment, you will want to assess each Service Manager component to determine the best approach to make it highly available for your environment. This section reviews each of the Service Manager components, discusses the impact of an outage for each component, looks at high availability solutions for the component, and provides best practices around high availability for Service Manager.

With the current architecture of Service Manager 2010, the database and the first installed Service Manager management server are single points of failure. Should one of these components fail, all functionality will stop until the failing component is recovered. If your organization requires high availability and cannot tolerate failures, you want to ensure that your Service Manager environment can tolerate a simultaneous failure of different Service Manager components, such as the management server, data warehouse servers, and databases.

The requirement for a high-availability Service Manager environment should have been identified during your Assessment stage and integrated in the Service Manager design document, as discussed in Chapter 5.

The key to designing a highly available Service Manager configuration is to understand its components and the different options available for redundancy. Table 6.1 presents a high-level overview of redundancy options for the Service Manager components.

TABLE 6.1   Components and Redundancy Options Available

Component Name	Redundancy Option	Microsoft Supported?	Details
Workflow management server	Standby management server	Yes	—
Additional management server	Network Load Balancing (NLB) Configuration for OMSDK Service	Yes	You can find a discussion about NLB configuration in the "Service Manager Server High Availability" section.
Self-Service portal server	NLB Configuration	Yes	See the "Self-Service Portal High Availability" section for a discussion about NLB configuration.
Data Warehouse management server	None	No support	—
Service Manager CMDB database	SQL clustering SQL log shipping	Yes	You can find additional information about active/passive clusters in the "Service Manager Databases High Availability" section.
Data Warehouse DWDataMart database	SQL clustering SQL log shipping	Yes	The "Service Manager Databases High Availability" section provides details on clustering.
Data Warehouse DWRepository database	SQL clustering SQL log shipping	Yes	You can find information about clusters in the "Service Manager Databases High Availability"
Data Warehouse StagingAndConfig database	SQL clustering SQL log shipping	Yes	You can find information about clusters in the "Service Manager Databases High Availability" section.

High availability within Service Manager is not an all-or-nothing situation. If during assessment it was determined that high availability is a business requirement, this may not necessarily apply to all components. For example, if there is a requirement to provide high availability for the Service Manager management server (MS) and Self-Service portal (SSP), it might not be necessary to provide high availability for the data warehouse components.

After determining your availability requirements, you want to test the available configurations in a proof of concept (POC), deploy them as part of the pilot stage, and ultimately implement them into your production environment.

Table 6.1 shows a high-level overview of the components and redundancy options that are available. The following sections look at each component individually.

Service Manager Management Server High Availability

As discussed in Chapter 4, "Looking Inside Service Manager," the Service Manager MS is where the primary software portion of Service Manager is installed and running. The Service Manager console connects to this server role. This server is also the server hosting the System Center Management (HealthService) service, which runs all workflows, and the Configuration service.

The Service Manager MS is the first MS you install, and it handles all workflows in your Service Manager 2010 environment. Any additional Service Manager 2010 management servers deployed are used to load balance Service Manager 2010 console connections. Because workflows run only on the first installed MS, should the first Service Manager server fail, no workflows will run, connectors will not import data, and so on.

Workflow Management Server

The first Service Manager MS installed is also known as the *workflow management server*. This server is a single point of failure because there are no high-availability solutions that are workflow aware. No clustering or load-balancing solution exists to move, migrate, or fail over running workflows.

If the workflow MS fails, perhaps because of a hardware failure, you must promote another MS to handle the workflows. Both the Service Manager database and an MS should be continuously available to provide uninterrupted continuity of management functions. This requirement makes clustering the Service Manager database and load balancing the MS key considerations when designing a highly available management solution for your organization.

Additional Management Servers

Additional Service Manager 2010 servers load balance Service Manager console connections. Windows Server NLB uses a distributed algorithm to load balance network traffic to enhance the scalability and availability of applications. In addition to performance-scaling capabilities, NLB has fault-tolerance capabilities. If a host in an NLB cluster dies, NLB pulls out the host and redistributes traffic to the surviving hosts. A common use of NLB is to load balance mission-critical websites. Figure 6.1 illustrates using load balancing with Service Manager. The initials SM in the figure stand for Service Manager.

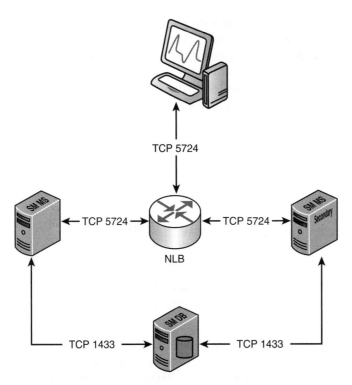

FIGURE 6.1   Service Manager load balancing.

TIP: WHEN TO ADD AN ADDITIONAL MS

The authors recommend installing an extra additional Service Manager server for every 50 concurrent Service Manager console connections or if high availability is a requirement.

In addition to load balancing the Service Manager consoles, you can use an additional Service Manager MS as a standby server. If the first Service Manager server that runs the workflows is no longer available, you can promote this additional Service Manager server to run the workflows.

NOTE: INFORMATION ON NETWORK LOAD BALANCING

For more information about Windows Server Load Balancing, see the "Network Load Balancing Deployment Guide" at http://technet.microsoft.com/en-us/library/cc754833(WS.10).aspx.

The System Center Data Access Service (OMSDK) can be considered the core service for Service Manager 2010. Although this service is installed on all management servers, it runs only on the workflow MS. All data flowing to and from the database is transported via the

System Center Data Access Service. If the server running this service is unavailable or the OMSDK cannot connect to the SQL Server, you will be unable to connect with the Service Manager console through TCP port 5724 (this is the same port as the Operations Manager console port) and connect to the Service Manager server. You will get a "failed to connect to server" message if you try to open the console, as shown in Figure 6.2, where Hurricane is the workflow MS.

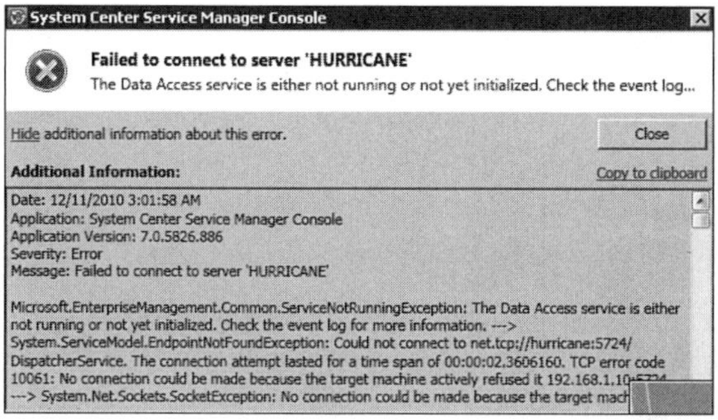

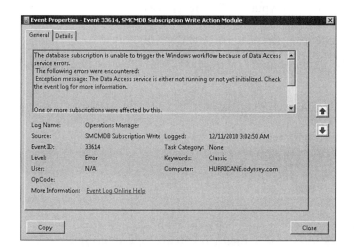

FIGURE 6.2   Service Manager server unavailable error.

If the Service Manager workflow server is not available, you also get alerts in the Operations Manager event log. (Service Manager uses the Operations Manager event log, which hosts the Service Manager events.) Figure 6.3 shows error 33614 generated in the event log when the workflow server is unavailable.

FIGURE 6.3   Workflow Server unavailable generates error 33614.

The Service Manager event IDs and event descriptions generated if there is a failure are exactly the same errors you would receive if your Operations Manager root management server (RMS) were not available. As discussed in Chapter 4, "Looking Inside Service Manager," both products utilize the common System Center architecture. Figure 6.4 provides an example of this alert on the Service Manager workflow server.

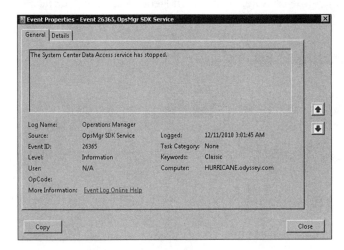

FIGURE 6.4   System Center Operations Manager alerts.

This is expected behavior, because Service Manager uses the same services as Operations Manager (although it can be somewhat confusing the first time you see these alerts).

You have two possible scenarios in the event your Service Manager workflow server is down:

▶ Promote an existing Service Manager server to become the workflow MS.

▶ Install a new server with the same computer name and restore the encryption key.

Self-Service Portal Server High Availability

The Self-Service portal is a web-based portal divided into two major areas:

▶ An end-user portion

▶ An analyst section

If the SSP is not available, end users cannot request software, request a password reset, search for knowledge articles, check the status of their work items, and so on. Figure 6.5 shows the error received when the SSP is not available. This is the standard error generated when Internet Explorer cannot access a website.

The Service Manager SSP server is not cluster aware. However, similar to the approach suggested for the Service Manager MS, you can deploy multiple SSP servers in a load-balancing configuration. If an SSP server in an NLB cluster dies, NLB pulls out the server from the cluster and redistributes traffic to the surviving SSP servers. In Figure 6.6, the SSP server is added to the load-balanced configuration introduced in Figure 6.1.

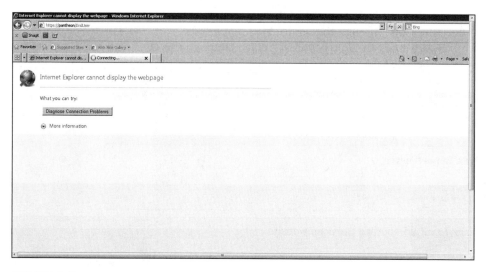

FIGURE 6.5   Self-Service portal server unavailable.

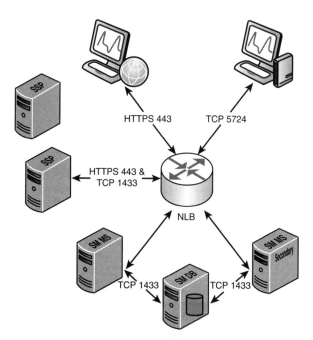

FIGURE 6.6   Self-Service portal server in load balancing.

Service Manager Data Warehouse Server High Availability

The Data Warehouse MS controls the workflow processes associated with the data warehouse.

If the Data Warehouse MS is unavailable, data is not updated in the data warehouse, and you cannot run reports through the Service Manager console. However, you would still be able to run reports using the SQL Reporting server, although this console is not as user-friendly as the Service Manager console. Figure 6.7 shows the SQL Reporting server interface.

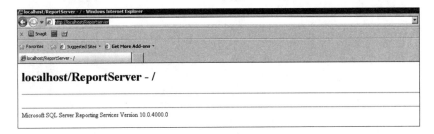

FIGURE 6.7   SQL Reporting Services website.

Figure 6.8 shows the error you receive when opening the Service Manager console in the event the Data Warehouse MS is not available. You will be able to open the console, but the Reporting button will not be visible.

FIGURE 6.8   Data warehouse server unavailable.

There is no redundant solution for the Service Manager Data Warehouse MS. You cannot promote another server to become a Data Warehouse MS. The only scenario is to install a new Data Warehouse management server with the same name as the old server.

Service Manager Databases High Availability

When you implement Service Manager with the Reporting feature, you have four SQL Server databases: one for Service Manager and three as part of the Reporting implementation. Here is information about these databases:

▶ **Service Manager CMDB:** The ServiceManager database (default installation name) contains all configuration and operating data for the management group and installation of Service Manager 2010. This database is also the Service Manager 2010 implementation of the CMDB (configuration management database). The CMDB contains Service Manager configuration items such as computers and printers. It also contains all work items, such as incidents and change requests.

▶ **Data warehouse databases:** Service Manager uses the data warehouse for long-term storage of data, such as incidents. The database is used as the data source when running reports in Service Manager 2010. The data warehouse database actually consists of three databases with different roles within the data warehouse:

  ▶ DWStagingAndConfig

  ▶ DWRepository

  ▶ DWDataMart

If your data warehouse databases are unavailable, you will not be able to run Service Manager reports through the console or the SQL Reporting Server, and most important, data will not be updated in the data warehouse databases.

The three data warehouse databases can use the same SQL Server or SQL cluster as the Service Manager database, and doing so reduces the number of required SQL licenses. However, using a single server requires watching the growth of the data warehouse and ensuring that there are adequate resources to host the four databases on this system. If you will be installing the four databases on one SQL Server, consider using two SQL instances:

▶ One instance for the Service Manager database

▶ The other instance for the data warehouse databases

Using separate instances enables you to configure different settings for each instance, such as performance settings. The "SQL Post-Installation Steps" section of this chapter provides information about how to configure different memory limits for multiple instances. This also allows you to run an active/active clustering scenario, where one instance is running on each node in the cluster.

A common question in the support forums is whether a difference exists between SQL Server Standard Edition and SQL Server Enterprise Edition for high availability. From a high-availability perspective, both SQL Standard and SQL Enterprise editions support failover clustering. However, there are several differences:

▶ SQL Server Standard Edition supports up to two clustered nodes. For the Service Manager databases, those can be configured as active/passive or active/active.

▶ SQL Server Enterprise Edition supports up to 16 clustered nodes. Enterprise Edition also supports online indexing, support for hot-add memory and CPU, database snapshots, and online page and file restore.

NOTE: OPERATING SYSTEM REQUIREMENTS WHEN CLUSTERING SQL SERVER

When clustering SQL Server, the operating system (OS) must be running Windows Server Enterprise or Datacenter Edition.

Figure 6.9 shows a perfectly viable fault-tolerance solution using an active/passive SQL configuration.

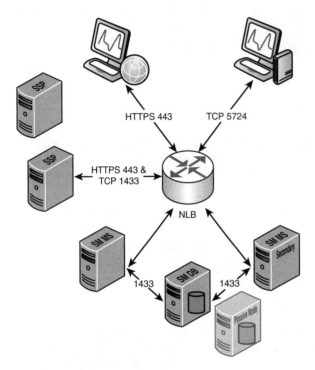

FIGURE 6.9   Service Manager database configured for fault tolerance with active/passive clustering.

SQL clustering is not the only fault-tolerance option available. Here are some implementations of SQL Server to consider if you require fault tolerance for your SQL database:

▶ **SQL clustering:** SQL clustering is the only failover mechanism that provides high availability on the instance level, which is the level at which Service Manager connects to the SQL databases. An advantage of clustering is automatic detection failover in case of failure; manual failover is also possible and is completely transparent for Service Manager. Both active/passive and active/active clustering are fully supported for Service Manager 2010.

▶ **SQL log shipping:** SQL log shipping sends transaction logs to one or more secondary databases on separate SQL Server instances where the transaction logs will be applied to each secondary database. See the sidebar "Redundancy Using Log Shipping" for more information about log shipping. This is also a supported option for Service Manager 2010.

▶ **SQL mirroring:** SQL mirroring maintains two copies of a single database. Those copies need to reside on different SQL Server instances. Service Manager connects through the principal instance with a mirror instance acting as a standby server. Database mirroring provides you with rapid failover without data loss because the two databases are always synchronized. The Service Manager team has performed some limited testing of SQL mirroring for the Service Manager databases, but it is not officially supported.

REDUNDANCY USING LOG SHIPPING

Service Manager 2010 supports log shipping for redundancy (and geo-redundancy) on the Service Manager database and the three data warehouse databases.

Log shipping is essentially the process of automating the backup of databases and transaction log files on a production SQL Server and then restoring them to a standby server. A key feature of log shipping is that it automatically performs backups of transaction logs at an interval you specify, automatically restoring them to the standby server. This essentially keeps the two SQL Server systems in sync. If the production server fails, all you have to do is point your users to the new server and "go."

Log shipping requires the database to be set to Full Recovery mode. You can change the recovery mode using the ALTER DATABASE statement with T-SQL or using SQL Management Studio. Open SQL Management studio, select **<Databases >** *<database name>*, and then right-click to select **Properties**. On the Options page, select the drop-down for recovery model to change from Simple to Full, as displayed in Figure 6.10 for the Service Manager database.

The authors recommend SQL log shipping for off-site redundancy scenarios.

Service Manager and Virtualization

Hardware virtualization enables running multiple operating systems at the same time on a single physical computer. Because virtualization can save significant amounts of money and time, more and more organizations are virtualizing their server workloads, particularly as cloud computing becomes more prevalent.

An often-asked question is whether one can virtualize the various Service Manager components. As with many things in Information Technology (IT), the answer is *it depends*. Before looking at whether you can virtualize your Service Manager components, let's look at the benefits of virtualization:

▶ Using a single hardware server to run multiple operating systems reduces IT costs. You can run more servers per square foot/meter and thus reduce the cost of space, power, and cooling.

▶ Because a virtual machine is not tied to a particular type of hardware, virtualization enables you to move virtual machines between physical machines easily.

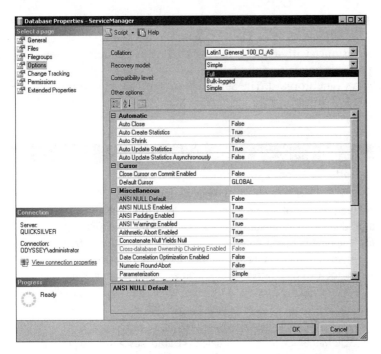

FIGURE 6.10   Changing the recovery model for the Service Manager database.

▶ Leveraging high-availability features of the host, such as Microsoft Hyper-V failover clustering, helps increase uptime of the virtual machines, particularly those without redundant Service Manager components such as the first installed Service Manager server that runs the workflows.

▶ Virtualization enables you to dynamically respond to changing business needs; you can easily increase or decrease your management group capacity using the features available from virtualizing your environment (such as cloning, storing, and deploying management servers as virtual machines).

From a Service Manager support perspective, Microsoft officially supports virtualization of the following components:

▶ Service Manager server

▶ Service Manager database

▶ Service Manager console

▶ Data Warehouse server

▶ Data Warehouse databases

▶ Self-Service portal

This support presumes the component is running on a Microsoft hypervisor such as Windows Server 2008 or later, using Hyper-V or Microsoft Hyper-V Server 2008 or later or any other hardware virtualization software that is part of the Server Virtualization Program (SVP) such as VMware. For more information about the SVP, see http://www. windowsservercatalog.com/svvp.aspx?svvppage=svvp.htm.

Small and test environments are perfect candidates for complete virtualization. The smaller test environments will most likely never reach the performance limits of virtualized operating systems, and performance in lab and demo environments is not as critical as in a production environment.

Based on the authors' experiences, the suggestion is to not virtualize any of the database components (Service Manager database and data warehouse databases) because these are disk and memory intensive:

▶ Service Manager database performance is impacted primarily by the number of concurrent console connections that are retrieving or writing data, and the data inserted by the connectors.

▶ Performance of the Service Manager data warehouse database server is directly impacted by the frequency of the Extract, Transform, and Load (ETL) workflows, data retention period, number of Service Manager servers sending data, rate of data change, and such.

A good document on SQL Server 2008 virtualization is at http://download.microsoft.com/ download/d/9/4/d948f981-926e-40fa-a026-5bfcf076d9b9/SQL2008inHyperV2008.docx.

Here are the Service Manager components recommended as candidates for virtualization:

▶ **Data Warehouse management server:** The Service Manager Data Warehouse server is more stateless than the other Service Manager servers without as many input/output (I/O) operations. However, the number of Service Manager servers registered with this server has a direct impact on its performance. The more Service Manager servers registered to the Data Warehouse MS, the more RAM that is necessary.

▶ **Self-Service portal server:** The Self-Service portal is a perfect candidate for virtualization because it does not have not many I/O operations. Should you encounter any latency when running a virtual SSP, you should increase the amount of RAM available or install a second SSP and load balance the Self-Service portal.

▶ **Additional Service Manager servers:** Because the additional Service Manager servers are not running any workflows but are just used to load balance the console connections or used as standby servers, these are excellent candidates for virtualization.

Table 6.2 provides an overview of the different Service Manager components and their suitability for virtualization.

Figure 6.11 shows an example of a virtualized Service Manager environment. In this example, the Self-Service portal, an additional Service Manager server, and the Data Warehouse MS are running as virtual machines. For optimal performance, the first Service Manager server and the SQL Server are kept on physical servers because of the workload.

TABLE 6.2   Service Manager Virtualization Suitability

Component	Okay as VM?	Notes
CMDB	Generally no	Only virtualize the CMDB in lab/test.
Data Warehouse Databases	Generally no	Only virtualize the data warehouse in lab/test.
Workflow MS	Generally no	—
Additional MS	Yes	—
Self-Service portal	Generally yes	Eventually scale out with NLB.
Data Warehouse MS	Yes	—

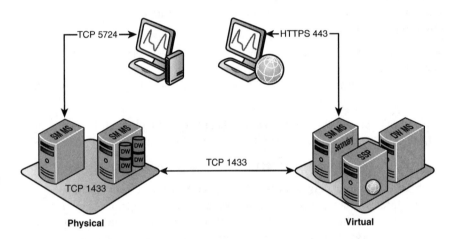

FIGURE 6.11   Service Manager virtualization.

Here are some recommendations for virtualizing:

▶ Use pass-through disks or fixed virtual hard drives (VHDs). Dynamic VHDs are not recommended (due to performance reasons). Pass-through disks and fixed VHDs give you the best results for SQL Server workloads, such as your Service Manager databases.

▶ Allocate at least two virtual CPUs for the instance of your SQL Server.

In general, when considering virtualization, you should strongly consider using System Center Virtual Machine Manager (VMM) combined with System Center Operations Manager (OpsMgr) to monitor and manage your virtual workload. See *System Center Operations Manager 2007 R2 Unleashed* (Sams, 2010) for additional information on monitoring virtual environments using Operations Manager. The book includes a discussion on how to deploy VMM and integrate it with OpsMgr. This integration enables you to manage and monitor your entire virtual environment.

Performance and Capacity Planning

This section describes capacity guidance planning for your Service Manager environment. Service Manager has multiple mechanisms and scenarios enabling you to scale to very large environments, although there may be design limitations depending on your particular Service Manager implementation.

Inadequate or improper performance and capacity planning for Service Manager will negatively affect your Service Manager performance. Negatively impacted performance is most noticeable in the following areas:

- **Service Manager console responsiveness:** This is the length of time it takes to complete a request from the moment you take an action in the console.

- **Workflow completion time:** Workflow completion time is the time it takes to apply a workflow. Automatic internal jobs such as calculating Target Resolution Time for an incident take longer to complete, as do executing user-defined workflows such as for automating a change request. Typically, workflows such as notification subscription and applying templates run within 1 minute of each work item being generated.

- **Time for data insertion with the connectors:** Performance issues result in Service Manager taking longer than usual to synchronize data from the connectors.

During an initial synchronization, expect performance issues on all Service Manager Server roles. This is primarily due to SQL Server and the fact that data is being inserted sequentially into the Service Manager database, which can take a long time. The authors recommend scheduling the initial connector synchronization appropriately and ensuring the synchronization process runs completely and successfully before putting Service Manager in production.

There are four key areas to consider for providing an optimally performing configuration when you create a Service Manager 2010 environment:

- Memory
- Disk
- Processor
- Network Performance

The next sections of the chapter discuss these areas.

Service Manager Performance

CPU and memory are critical factors for the Server Manager MS. Each core on a processor within the Service Manager server can support up to 10 concurrent consoles. Memory capacity is even more important because of the highly memory-intensive operations on a Service Manager server.

TIP: USE OPSMGR TO MONITOR SERVICE MANAGER PERFORMANCE

If you have Operations Manager installed, use it to monitor your Service Manager and SQL Server systems for performance issues.

Processor Performance

Pay attention to the number of concurrent Service Manager consoles connecting to the Service Manager server. Each core on a processor on the Service Manager server can support up to 10 concurrent consoles. Although processor performance is important in Service Manager, Service Manager bottlenecks are most likely memory or disk and not processor related.

Network Performance

The logic applying to processor performance also applies from a networking perspective. For high-usage environments, consider a gigabit network connection for the various Service Manager components to communicate with each other; bottlenecks on the network adapter are not that likely, from what the authors have observed. Just ensure that your Service Manager components are well connected to each other with nearly no network latency. Network latency between the different components may lead to Service Manager performance degradation. If your network latency is between 150 and 200 milliseconds, there is a 40% degradation in response time, particularly when expanding the service maps in the Service Manager console. If your network latency is more than 200 milliseconds, you can expect serious console response time issues and should consider remote desktop scenarios.

Service Manager Database Performance

The Service Manager database contains all configuration and operating data for the management group and Service Manager 2010 installation. The Service Manager 2010 implementation of the CMDB also has this database containing Service Manager configuration items, such as computers and printers. In addition, it contains all work items, such as incidents and change requests.

Memory and disk I/O are critical factors for the server on which this database resides. Performance of the Service Manager databases is primarily affected by the number of concurrent consoles connections retrieving or writing data and data inserted by the connectors.

A primary reason for poor Service Manager console performance is poor SQL performance. Chapter 5 includes a section on SQL hardware recommendations. The next sections discuss how to troubleshoot poor SQL performance.

Disk Performance

Here are counters you can check to determine whether your disks are experiencing performance issues:

▶ **Physical Disk/Avg Disk Sec/Transfer:** This is the number of seconds it takes to complete disk I/O. This number should never spike over .50 and should be around .20 seconds.

▶ **Physical Disk/%Idle Time:** This is the idle time of the disk, and should be below 20%. Everything below 20% is considered 0%.

▶ **Physical Disk/Disk Bytes/Sec:** This gives you a rough estimate on how much data you can push to the disks. Use it when your %Idle time is below 20%.

▶ **Physical Disk/Average Queue Length:** Make sure this queue length never spikes above 50.

If these performance counters do not look optimal, the next thing to check is memory performance.

Memory Performance

The most direct impact on Service Manager's performance is the amount of memory available to the servers. Here are the counters to check to verify memory is not the cause of performance issues:

▶ **Memory/Available Mbytes:** The operating system tries to keep a certain amount of RAM available for immediate use by copying those virtual memory pages not in active use to the pagefile.

▶ **Memory/CommitedBytes:** Paging increases as Committed Bytes grows above the available RAM. The amount of the pagefile in use also increases; this can significantly impact performance.

▶ **Paging File, %pagefile in use:** Proper utilization of the pagefile is one of the most unused performance boosts available within Windows. The pagefile takes memory and uses it to store data accessed from the drive into memory. You can measure how much of the pagefile is actually being used with the Paging File, %pagefile counter. If this counter reaches 100, the pagefile is completely full and operations stop. You will want to set the pagefile size high enough that no more than 50% to 75% of it is used.

Service Manager Data Warehouse Performance

The data warehouse database is the long-term data repository for Service Manager reporting. As mentioned in the "Server Manager Databases High Availability" section, the data warehouse database actually consists of three databases with different roles within the data warehouse, as follows:

▶ DWStagingAndConfig

▶ DWRepository

▶ DWDataMart

The primary reason Service Manager was designed using three physical databases for the data warehouse was to enable organizations to more easily optimize their hardware environments. In high-volume environments, the DWStagingAndConfig and DWRepository databases should be on hardware optimized for read and write I/O, whereas you want to optimize the DWDataMart for read I/O only. By using separate databases, organizations can locate the DWDataMart on a different server and disk from the DWStagingAndConfig and DWRepository. The DWStagingAndConfig and DWRepository databases must be on the same server.

Service Manager Capacity and Sizing Planning

Inadequate or improper performance and capacity planning for Service Manager will negatively affect your Service Manager performance and limit the growth of your environment. The "Performance and Capacity Planning" section of this chapter discussed how to scale and optimize the performance of your Service Manager environment and how to assess and measure the performance of your servers. In addition to performance, you need to ensure that your environment is scalable and your databases are sized properly.

TIP: USE THE SERVICE MANAGER SIZING HELPER TOOL

The Service Manager Sizing Helper tool can help establish the number of Service Manager servers you need and assist in determining the correct sizing for your databases. You can download the tool from http://go.microsoft.com/fwlink/?LinkId=186291.

Service Manager Database Sizing

The ServiceManager database, which is the Service Manager 2010 implementation of the CMDB, contains all configuration and operating data for the management group and Service Manager 2010 installation. When planning the size of your database, make sure it will scale enough for future business requirements. Sizing this database is a very complex undertaking. You must consider many factors, including the number of users creating incidents, the number of computers, the number of days you want to keep the data (retention period), and so on. If space limitation is an issue, you can decrease the retention period for the CMDB and the data warehouse. For information about grooming and data retention, see Chapter 7, "Installing Service Manager 2010."

Based on the Service Manager Sizing Helper tool, the authors developed the following formula to determine the size of the Service Manager CMDB:

```
(500 + 5 * retention days) * (((number of computers in the Service Manager database *
number of new incidents per month for each computer) + number of new change
requests per month)) / 1000000
```

The authors analyzed the sizing formula the Service Manager product team uses to determine the size of the CMDB and determined that four main components impact the size of the CMDB, as follows:

▶ Retention period

▶ Number of computers

▸ Number of incidents per month for each computer

▸ Number of change requests per month

Obviously, the more computers you have in your environment and the CMDB, the more work items will be created, such as incidents, change requests, and so on. Notice that the size of the CMDB is calculated based on one incident per computer/user per month. Based on the authors' experience, you will end up with more than just one incident per month per computer.

Figure 6.12 displays a graph showing the size of the CMDB based on the number of computers in your environment.

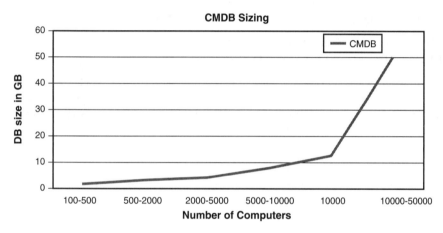

FIGURE 6.12   Service Manager (CMDB) database sizing.

Service Manager lets you adjust the CMDB's data retention period. Figure 6.13 shows the impact on the size of the CMDB based on different retention periods. The retention period was set to 10, 30, 50, 70, and 90 (default) days to see the impact it has on the CMDB size. Notice that varying the retention period does not significantly affect the size of the CMDB database.

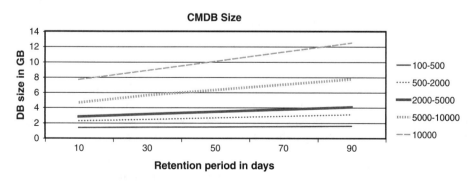

FIGURE 6.13   Service Manager database sizing, depending on the retention period.

Service Manager Data Warehouse Database Sizing

The data warehouse databases are the long-term data repository for Service Manager reporting. Data from the Service Manager database is transferred to the data warehouse through three SQL jobs, which run on a recurring schedule for archiving. As discussed in Chapter 4, one of the SQL jobs populating the data warehouse is the Transform job. This job takes the raw data from the staging area and does any cleansing, reformatting, and aggregation required to get it into a final format for reporting. This transformed data is written into the DWRepository database. Using this approach has the potential to provide longer-term reports for a large number of work items and computers while using a smaller data warehouse database.

When estimating the size of the three data warehouse databases, it is important to consider the amount of data inserted daily and how long you intend to keep that data in the data warehouse, as this affects the required amount of storage.

Based on the Service Manager Sizing Helper tool, the authors developed the following formula to determine the size of the three data warehouse databases:

```
3 * total size of CMDB + 2 *(retention period / 365) + total size of cmdb
```

Figure 6.14 displays a graph showing the size of the three data warehouse databases combined based on the number of computers in your environment.

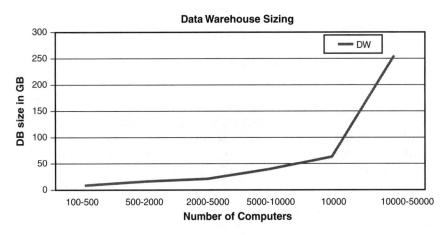

FIGURE 6.14   Service Manager data warehouse database sizing.

Similar to the options available with the CMDB, you can reduce the data retention period. Figure 6.15 shows the impact on the size of the data warehouse databases based on different retention periods. The retention period was set to 90, 150, 365 (default), and 500 days to see the impact it had on the data warehouse size.

Varying the retention period for the data warehouse has more of an impact on the size of the database than doing so for the CMDB, particularly in larger environments of more than 5,000 computers.

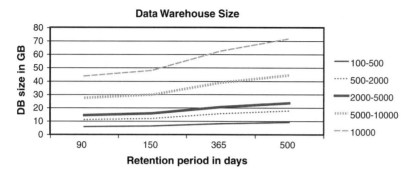

FIGURE 6.15   Service Manager data warehouse database sizing depending on the retention period.

If reducing the data retention period is not an option, you have several other solutions for managing the volume of data:

▶ **Reduce the time interval:** By default, data is kept for a year, but based on your business requirements it might be sufficient to keep data only for a quarter or so. If this is the case, you might change the grooming settings.

▶ **Create archive snapshots:** Another approach to deal with storage requirements is to create a snapshot of the databases on a regular basis. You can archive and restore these database backups to a temporary database when needed.

▶ **Extract the data to reports:** The last approach to resolve the huge amount of storage required is to generate monthly reports of the data and archive the reports. This provides a quick method to summarize the data and retain it for a long period. The downside is you cannot generate new reports from the data or change the generated reports.

You can easily implement these potential workarounds to resolve your storage issues individually or together. For example, you might create quarterly archive snapshots to review the historical data up to 1 year old and use archived monthly reports to view historical data up to 5 years old.

It is important to note that the formula to determine the sizing of the CMDB and the data warehouse databases takes into account only user-based created work items and not automated work items created by connectors such as the OpsMgr and ConfigMgr connectors. Although those connectors can generate many work items (particularly incidents), it is impossible to consider them in the equation.

Configuring the OpsMgr alert connector to forward alerts to Service Manager will affect your sizing. Although a correlation exists between the number of management packs and the size of your CMDB, the size of the CMDB depends on the configuration settings of your connector, the alerts that are forwarded, and those that are not. If you have not configured your connectors and subscriptions correctly and are forwarding everything to Service Manager, it will have tremendous effect on your CMDB size and create a huge overhead in managing the incidents that are created.

SQL Server Complex Planning

In the "Service Manager Capacity and Sizing Planning" section of this chapter, you read how to scale and optimize the performance of your Service Manager environment and how to assess and measure the performance of your servers. Let's now take a more in-depth look at SQL Server performance planning and several SQL post-installation steps for Service Manager.

SQL Server Performance Planning

Because the main function of SQL Server is to store and manipulate data and that data resides either in memory or on disk, any database server performance issues can have a massive impact on the performance of your Service Manager installation.

IOPS and Throughput Required

Disk performance is measured by disk throughput. Disk throughput is a performance measure of the data transfer rate through an I/O disk subsystem. The performance of Service Manager, particularly in virtual environments, depends on a combination of the following:

▶ Read IOPS (Input/Output Operations Per Second)

▶ Write IOPS

▶ Available memory

If you have a user-acceptance environment, the authors recommend that you assess the read and write IOPS to estimate whether the performance is adequate to handle the extra load of virtualization in a production environment.

You can check the following performance counters:

▶ **LogicalDisk(*)\\% Idle Time:** This counter reports the percentage of time that the disk system was not processing requests and no work was queued. This should be around 100%.

▶ **LogicalDisk(*)\Avg. Disk Queue Length:** The counter tracks the number of requests that are queued and waiting for a disk during the sample interval, as well as requests in service. This counter should be less then 2 (for each physical disk in a redundant array of independent disks (RAID) 0+1 configuration).

▶ **LogicalDisk(*)\Avg Disk sec/Read:** This counter measures the average time of each data transfer, regardless of the number of bytes that are read. The counter shows the total time of the read operation, from the moment it leaves the diskperf.sys driver to the moment it completes. This time should be less then 20ms and preferably around 10ms.

▶ **LogicalDisk(*)\Avg Disk sec/Write:** This counter measures the average time of each data transfer, regardless of the number of bytes that are written. The counter shows the total time of the write operation, from the moment it leaves the diskperf.sys driver to when it completes. The time shown by the counter should be less then 20ms and preferably around 10ms.

Figure 6.16 shows these performance counters using the Performance Monitor.

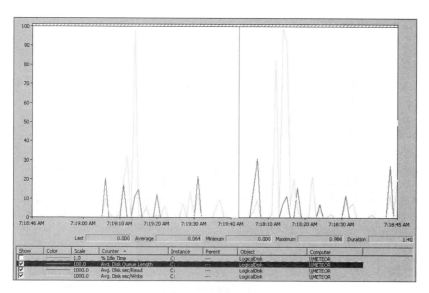

FIGURE 6.16   SQL IOPS performance counters.

If any of those counters do not meet your performance requirements, add more disk spindles to handle the required read and write IOPS.

In addition to disk IOPS, ensure that the SQL Server hosting the Service Manager database has enough memory. You can check this with the MSSQL:Buffer Manager\Buffer cache hit ratio counter:

▶ The counter should be as close as possible to 100%. If lower than 80%, your server needs additional memory.

▶ If the performance counters fall well within range, you have a management group that can meet the required performance.

Disk Storage Required

Storage planning can be divided into two areas:

▶ Capacity requirements (the amount of disk space needed to store data)

▶ Disk performance

It is relatively easy to determine the amount of disk space required; the "Service Manager Capacity and Sizing Planning" section provides information about disk space calculation. The necessary performance and fault tolerance needed for the disk and server will affect your choice of implementation for disk storage. For example, a single 1TB (terabyte) could be enough to store the required data, but one large disk will probably not be enough to meet the required performance and availability.

TIP: DISK SPINDLES

The more spindles on a drive, the better its performance. For example, a RAID 10 array with four drives outperforms a RAID 10 array with only two drives.

SQL Server Post-Installation

You can have different SQL instances running on a single SQL Server. Each instance has its own unique name, its own sqlservr.exe process running in memory, its own copies of the system databases, and its own set of user databases. A default instance is identified by the name of the computer. All other instances have a unique name and are identified by the instance name specified during installation. Applications such as Service Manager connect to a named instance by specifying the computer name and the instance in the format of *<computername>\<instancename>*. A single instance can have up to 32,767 databases; the number of instances per server depends on the version of SQL Server you are using. SQL Server 2008 Enterprise Edition supports up to 50 instances, and SQL Server 2008 Standard Edition supports up to 16 instances.

CAUTION: CASE SENSITIVITY NOT SUPPORTED

Service Manager does not support case-sensitive instances. Setup fails if you try to install Service Manager on a case-sensitive SQL instance.

Here are some advantages of using separate SQL instances:

▶ Memory isolation is set at the instance level. You can give the instance hosting the Service Manager database more memory and limit the memory available for the instance hosting the data warehouse server.

▶ Regulatory requirements may demand that a database must run in an isolated environment without any other database or other users accessing it.

▶ Authentication is set at the instance level. This means you can give different permissions (such as administrator permissions) on a per-instance level.

▶ You might have a database that needs to run on a SQL instance without service packs. For example, you can have an application database that will not support SQL 2008 Service Pack (SP) 1 but only the SQL 2008 base release (known as RTM or Released to Manufacturing). You can install that database in the RTM instance and create a secondary instance to update to SP 1.

Fault tolerance is set at the instance level.

With its default configuration, SQL Server uses as much memory as possible. The authors have worked in small environments and combined the four Service Manager databases on one SQL Server where the SQL database instance consumed more than 11GB of the 16GB available on the server. You want to configure the SQL maximum memory limit such that the OS and other applications have at least 2GB RAM available. Ideally, allocate as much memory as possible to SQL Server without causing the OS to swap. Here is a formula to calculate the amount of memory to allocate to your SQL Server instance:

```
Maximum SQL Server memory = amount of memory in server - 2GB for operating system -
memory required for other applications
```

For instance, if SQL Server is installed on a system with 16GB of memory and no other applications, you can configure the SQL maximum memory limit to 14GB. By design, SQL Server continually uses more and more memory. The SQL Server buffer pool is a caching feature that caches pages in RAM rather than disk, which is slower. The buffer pool uses all available memory allocated to SQL Server. If SQL Server consumes *all* available RAM, the operating system will have inadequate memory, and SQL Server will run as if it is memory constrained. This causes CPU usage to go up, disk I/O to rise as Windows begins paging, and query response time to increase drastically.

To prevent the SQL Server buffer pool from consuming more than the specified allowed amount of memory, configure the SQL max server memory usage by instance parameter using the sp_configure system stored procedure or with SQL Management Studio. In SQL Management Studio, you can configure the maximum server memory option by opening the Server Properties page and specifying an amount for Maximum server memory (in MB), as shown in Figure 6.17.

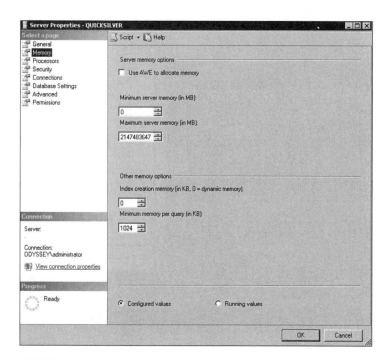

FIGURE 6.17   Configuring maximum server memory for a SQL Server instance on the Quicksilver database server.

Summary

This chapter discussed complex Service Manager 2010 configurations along with considerations to keep in mind when virtualizing your environment. With all the different components available within Service Manager, providing a Service Manager environment that is fully redundant and highly available can be a complex undertaking.

The next chapter discusses the steps to install Service Manager, including optional components discussed in this chapter.

CHAPTER 7

Installing Service Manager

This chapter discusses the procedures to install a new Service Manager 2010 environment. The discussion focuses on installation prerequisites and the steps for installing the various Service Manager components. These steps are the same for the RTM (released to manufacturing) and Service Pack (SP) 1 versions of Service Manager 2010, provided you have the slipstreamed SP 1 version of the product.

By this point in the book, you should have a good understanding of the different Service Manager components (as discussed in Chapter 4, "Looking Inside Service Manager") and be very familiar with the planning and sizing of Service Manager environment and the different complex configurations, as discussed in Chapter 5, "Designing Service Manager," and Chapter 6, "Planning Complex Configurations."

Planning Your Installation

Before actually running the setup program and launching your Service Manager installation, determine what your Service Manager environment will look like. As part of the planning and design discussion in Chapters 5 and 6, you should have considered the following questions:

▶ Which server will run the workflows?

▶ Which servers will host the configuration management database (CMDB)?

▶ Will you install the reporting components? Which system will host the different data warehouse databases?

▶ Do you need a highly available Service Manager environment?

Prior to installation, be sure you have worked through the planning and design discussions in Chapter 5 and 6. Use the design document you created in these chapters as you begin the installation.

Installation Prerequisites

Specific installation prerequisites will vary based on the Service Manager component you are installing. A number of prerequisites are common to all Service Manager components; these should be installed or verified prior to the installation. These minimum prerequisites needed for all components include

▶ Minimum hardware requirements

▶ Domain requirements

▶ Operating system requirements

▶ Order of installation

▶ Several hotfixes, including the Authorization Manager (AzMan) hotfix and the Microsoft Report Viewer redistributable, used with reporting

When you start the Setup wizard, the Prerequisite Checker is automatically launched to check for missing prerequisites. Figure 7.1 is an example of missing prerequisites identified by the Prerequisite Checker. Verify that you do not have any critical (red) alerts; otherwise, you will be unable to continue with the installation.

TIP: INSTALLATION PREREQUISITES

As a best practice, go for "green" on your prerequisites for the Service Manager components. To install the product, technically you need to fix only the red or critical issues. Service Manager can be installed with yellow warnings; however, the installation will not be a recommended installation and can result in a solution that performs poorly.

Figure 7.1 shows the Authorization Manager hotfix and Microsoft Report Viewer Redistributable are missing. The Authorization Manager hotfix resolves an issue where the Service Manager management server, date warehouse server, or Self-Service portal (SSP) connections to the SQL databases are broken and cannot be reestablished. Additional information about the Authorization Manager hotfix is available at http://support.microsoft.com/kb/975332.

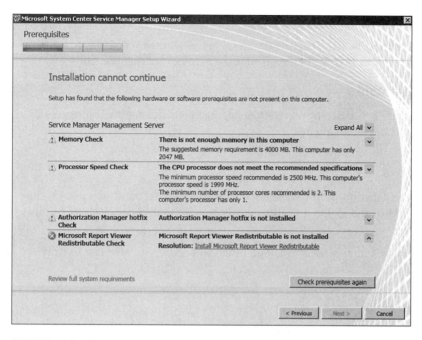

FIGURE 7.1   Example of common Service Manager missing prerequisites.

Without installing this hotfix, you will get alerts as shown in Figure 7.2 in the Operations Manager Event log on your Service Manager management server, SSP server, and Data Warehouse management server.

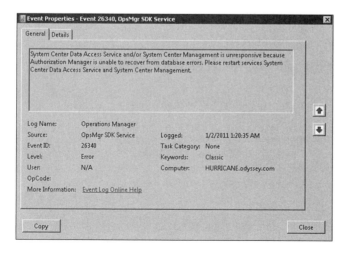

FIGURE 7.2   Authorization Manager alerts.

Windows Domain Prerequisites

Service Manager 2010 must be installed in a Windows Active Directory domain, which must be at Windows 2003 level or higher. All servers must be members of that domain.

Software Requirements

Obtain all software required to deploy Service Manager before installing the components. Table 7.1 lists the software requirements.

Security Accounts

Prior to starting the installation process, create the Windows user accounts required for the installation. Table 7.2 lists the required security accounts and the necessary level of permissions.

See Chapter 15, "Service Manager Security," for a discussion on Service Manager security.

Order of Installation

You cannot install certain components before others. For example, you cannot install a Service Manager management server without first installing the Service Manager database. The following list is a recommended order of installation, which focuses on installing the core components first (CMDB, Service Manager management server, Service Manager console, SSP), followed by optional components such as the reporting components. Install the Service Manager components as follows:

- ▶ Service Manager database
- ▶ Service Manager management server (this will be the Workflow management server)
- ▶ Additional Service Manager management servers
- ▶ Service Manager console (automatically installed on all management servers)
- ▶ Self-Service Portal server
- ▶ Data warehouse databases
- ▶ Service Manager Data Warehouse management server
- ▶ Service Manager Authoring Tool

TABLE 7.1   Software Requirements

Component	Operating System	.NET	SQL	IIS
Management Server	Windows 2008 64-bit or higher	.NET 3.5 with SP 1		
CMDB OS	Windows 2008 64-bit or higher			
CMDB SQL Instance			SQL 2008 64 bit with SP 1 Full text search enabled, or SQL 2008 R2	
Console	Windows 32 or 64-bit Windows XP SP 3 or higher, Windows Server 2003 SP 1 or higher	.NET 3.5 with SP 1		
SSP	Windows 2008 64-bit or higher	ASP.NET 2.0		IIS 7.0 with IIS 6.0 compatibility SSL certificate Basic Authentication Windows Authentication
Data Warehouse management server	Windows 2008 64-bit or higher	.NET 3.5 with SP 1		
Data Warehouse SQL instance			SQL 2008 64-bit with SP 1 or SQL 2008 R2	
SQL Server Reporting Services	Windows 2008 64-bit or higher		SQL 2008 Reporting 64-bit with SP 1 or SQL 2008 R2	

7

TABLE 7.2   Service Manager Required Security Accounts

Component	Services Account (SDK Account)	Reporting Account	Workflow Account	Account Required to Install
Management server	Local Admin Assigned to ServiceManager Config account Assigned to ServiceManager SDK Service account		Made member of the Service manager admin group	Local admin
CMDB OS				Local admin
CMDB SQL Instance	Becomes a member of the sdk_users and configsvc_users database roles for Service Manager database			SysAdmin
Console				Local admin
SSP	Must run under the SDK account			Local admin
Data Warehouse management server	Local admin			Local admin
Registering with the data warehouse				SysAdmin Member of the Service Manager Admin role

TABLE 7.2 Service Manager Required Security Accounts

Component	Services Account (SDK Account)	Reporting Account	Workflow Account	Account Required to Install
Data Warehouse SQL instance	Becomes a member of the db_datareader database role for DWRepository database Becomes a member of the sdk_users and configsvc_users database roles for DWDataMart database	Becomes a member of the db_datareader database role for DWDataMart database Becomes a member of the reportuser database role for DWDataMart database		SysAdmin
SQL Server Reporting Services				SysAdmin

7

Single Service Manager Server Deployment

You cannot install all Service Manager components on a single system. If you want to deploy Service Manager in a minimal environment with one physical machine, install Hyper-V and run a virtual machine to install the additional components. It is also possible to run both the management server and data warehouse on two virtual servers on one physical box.

The data warehouse solution delivered with Service Manager is ultimately intended to be the data warehouse for multiple System Center products. The Service Manager data warehouse is built using the same platform as the rest of Service Manager, which makes it impossible to host all Service Manager roles on the same machine—because the Data Warehouse management server and the Service Manager management server utilize the same Windows services.

NOTE: SINGLE SERVICE MANAGER SERVER IS NOT FULLY SUPPORTED

The single Service Manager server deployment, with all the Service Manager components on one machine other than the Data Warehouse management server, is not a fully supported configuration because Microsoft does not provide scalability and performance estimates. This deployment solution is not appropriate for a production environment, although you can use it in a lab or demo environment.

When installing the single server deployment, begin by selecting the option **Install a Service manager management server** as shown in Figure 7.3, and install the Service Manager database and Service Manager management server on the Hyper-V physical host.

After you have installed the Service Manager management server on the physical host, install the Service Manager data warehouse management server on a virtual machine.

Multiple Service Manager Server Deployments

This section discusses the process of installing Service Manager 2010 in a multiple-server configuration. Table 7.3 lists the servers used in the Odyssey organization and their roles, and Figure 7.4 displays the server topology installed, for reference throughout this book.

NOTE: INSTALLING SERVICE MANAGER MANAGEMENT SERVER IN A NLB TOPOLOGY

As discussed in Chapter 6, you can install Service Manager in a Network Load Balancing (NLB) configuration to provide load balancing of the Service Manager consoles and failover of the Service Manager management server that is running the workflows. The blog posting at http://scug.be/blogs/scsm/archive/2011/06/13/ service-manager-management-servers-in-nlb.aspx discusses how to install and configure NLB with multiple Service Manager management servers.

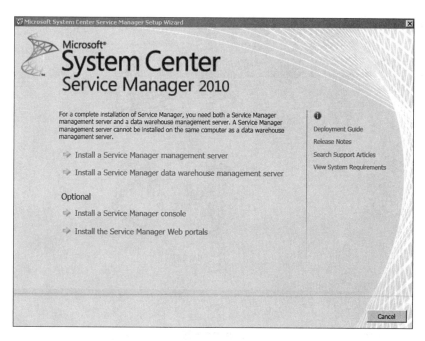

FIGURE 7.3   Setup splash screen.

TABLE 7.3   Service Manager Servers and Roles

Server Name	Service Manager Component
Hurricane	Service Manager management server
Meteor	Reporting server
Quicksilver	Service Manager database
Pantheon	Service Manager data warehouse server and SSP
Pioneer	Exchange and domain controller
Tabor	Service Manager console and Authoring Tool
Wildflower	System Center Configuration Manager site server and database
Hydra	System Center Operations Manager RMS and database

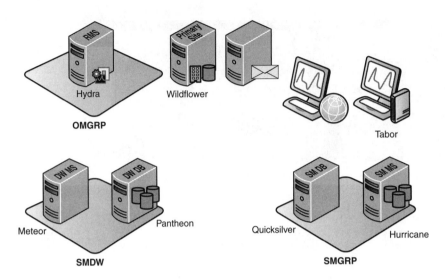

FIGURE 7.4   Service Manager topology.

Installing the Service Manager Database and Service Manager Management Server

The first step in implementing a Service Manager 2010 environment is to install the Service Manager database and Service Manager management server. To install Service Manager follow these steps:

1. After you launch the Setup splash screen from the Service Manager server (Figure 7.3), the installation process invokes the standard System Center Service Manager Setup wizard. The first screen is a welcome screen, where you select the component you want to install. Select **Install a Service Manager management server**.

2. The next screen shows the End User License Agreement, which must be accepted to proceed. Select **I have read, understood, and agree with the terms of the license agreement** and click **Next**. Note that if you install an evaluation version of Service Manager 2007, it is not upgradeable.

3. At the Installation Location screen (see Figure 7.5), specify the location where you will install System Center Service Manager 2010. Service Manager needs about 1 gigabyte (GB) of disk space; the wizard automatically verifies whether there is enough space on the selected drive to perform the installation.

4. The Prerequisite Checker is launched, as shown in Figure 7.6. The Prerequisite Checker checks for missing prerequisites; ensure you do not have any critical (red) alerts or you will be unable to continue with the installation. If you have a failed prerequisite check, perhaps due to a missing hotfix, you can easily click the **Check prerequisites again** button after installing the hotfix.

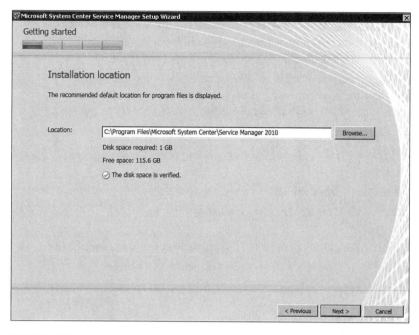

FIGURE 7.5   Installation Location screen.

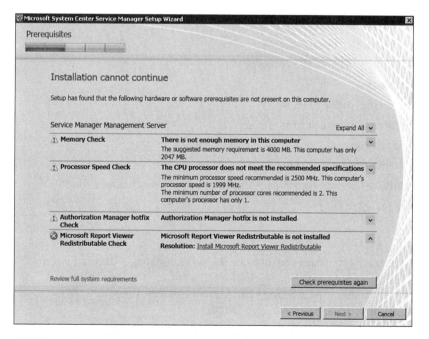

FIGURE 7.6   Prerequisite Checker.

NOTE: PREREQUISITEINPUTEFILE.XML

The Prerequisite Checker reads the PreRequisiteInputeFile.xml file in the setup folder, and based on the component selected, checks the prerequisites listed in the XML file.

PreRequisiteInputFile.xml, a portion of which is included here, shows the Prerequisite Checker looks at the Registry to determine items such as processor speed, whether ASP.NET is installed, and so on. Microsoft does not support making changes to this file.

```xml
<?xml version="1.0" encoding="utf-8"?>

<Prerequisites>

    <ComponentTitles>

        <ComponentTitle Id="CONSOLE">Service Manager Console</ComponentTitle>

        <ComponentTitle Id="SERVER">Service Manager Management
Server</ComponentTitle>

        <ComponentTitle Id="DATAWAREHOUSE">Data Warehouse</ComponentTitle>

        <ComponentTitle Id="PORTAL">Service Manager Self-Service
Portal</ComponentTitle>

    </ComponentTitles>


    <Check Order="01">

        <Id>6C213FEF-2ACA-4f82-852F-67D29ECAA019</Id>

        <Components>

            <Component>SERVER</Component>

            <Component>PORTAL</Component>

        </Components>

        <Title>Memory Check</Title>

        <PassedDescription>Requires at least 4 GB of memory</PassedDescription>

        <FailedDescription>There is not enough memory in this
computer&#xA;</FailedDescription>

        <Resolution>To ensure good performance, install more memory in this
computer.</Resolution>
```

5. Now, identify the SQL Server database instance the Service Manager database will run in. Type in the name of your SQL Server and press any key to continue. The Setup wizard connects to the specified SQL Server and retrieves a list of supported SQL instances that can host the Service Manager CMDB.

If a SQL instance is not listed in the Setup screen, it means that particular instance does not meet the prerequisites. Service Manager 2010 requires SQL Server 2008

Service Pack 1 64-bit or higher or SQL Server 2008 R2. SQL Server 2005, SQL Server 2008 without SP 1, and 32-bit versions of SQL Server are not supported.

If you installed SQL Server using the default collation settings (SQL_Latin1_General_ CP1_CI_AS), you will receive a warning message as shown in Figure 7.7. This message warns that support for multiple languages in Service Manager is not supported if using SQL_Latin1_General_CP1_CI_AS.

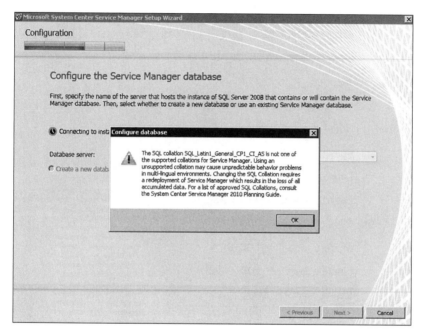

FIGURE 7.7   Warning for SQL collation settings.

You can only configure the collation setting of a SQL instance during installation. You can ignore this warning and continue the installation, but changing the SQL collation later will require reinstalling Service Manager. Table 7.4 presents a list of supported SQL collation settings.

TABLE 7.4   Supported SQL Collation Settings

Windows Local	SQL Collation
English	Latin1_General_100_CI_AS
Chinese_PRC	Chinese_Simplified_Pinyin_100_CI_AS
Chinese_Taiwan	Chinese_Traditional_Stroke_Count_100_CI_AS
Czech (Czech Republic)	Czech_100_CI_AS
Danish (Denmark)	Danish_Norwegian_CI_AS

TABLE 7.4   Supported SQL Collation Settings

Windows Local	SQL Collation
Dutch (Netherlands)	Latin1_General_100_CI_AS
Finnish (Finland)	Finnish_Swedish_100_CI_AS
French	French_100_CI_AS
German_Standard	Latin1_General_100_CI_AS
Greek (Greece)	Greek_100_CI_AS
Italian_Standard	Latin1_General_100_CI_AS
Japanese	Japanese_XJIS_100_CI_AS
Korean	Korean_100_CI_AS
Norwegian (Bokmål, Norway)	Norwegian_100_CI_AS
Polish (Poland)	Polish_100_CI_AS
Portuguese (Portugal)	Latin1_100_CI_AS
Portuguese (Brazil)	Latin1_General_100_CI_AS
Russian	Cyrillic_General_100_CI_AS
Spanish_Modern_Sort	Modern_Spanish_100_CI_AS
Swedish (Sweden)	Finnish_Swedish_100_CI_AS
Turkish (Turkey)	Latin1_General_100_CI_AS

6. After identifying the instance into which the Service Manager database will install, select **Create a new database**. This allows you to create a new database on the selected SQL Server, and to specify the database and log file options. This is shown in Figure 7.8.

The default name of the Service Manager database is ServiceManager, and is customizable. The default database size is 2GB, but you should specify a size as close as possible to the estimated final size of the Service Manager database to limit the usage of SQL Server's autogrow functionality, which has a performance impact. Chapter 6 discusses SQL performance and the autogrow functionality.

NOTE: DATABASE SIZE ESTIMATES

Chapter 6 discusses approaches to providing estimated sizes for the CMDB and data warehouse databases.

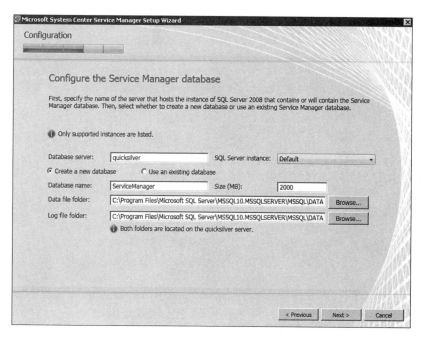

FIGURE 7.8   Specify the database and log file options.

7. On the next screen of the wizard, specify the management group name for your Service Manager 2010 environment. The management group name should be unique and easy to identify.

   For the environment used in this book, the management group name "smgrp" is used, as shown in Figure 7.9. Note that once specified, you cannot change the management group name without reinstalling the whole management group!

NOTE: ABOUT MANAGEMENT GROUP NAMES

Management group names must be unique. Do not use the same management group name when deploying a Service Manager management server and a Service Manager Data Warehouse management server. Furthermore, do not use the management group name you are using for your Operations Manager installation. Note that management group names are also case sensitive.

8. The next screen prompts you to identify the account for the Service Manager services. As discussed in the "Security Accounts" section, you should already have identified and configured the required service accounts prior to this step in the installation process. The account must be at least a member of the local Administrators group.

   The Odyssey domain uses the SVC_SM account, as shown in Figure 7.10.

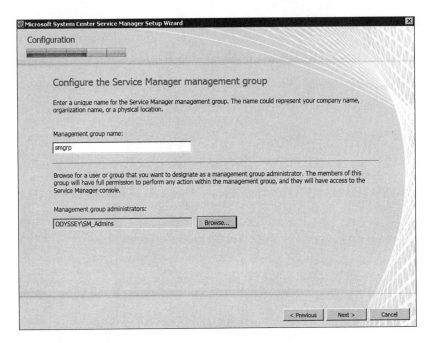

FIGURE 7.9   Configure the Service Manager management group.

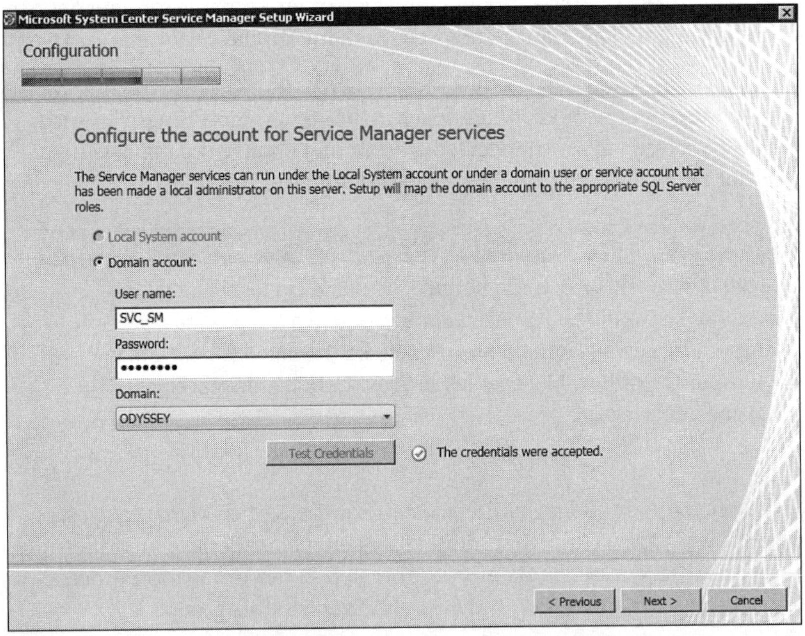

FIGURE 7.10   Configure the Service Manager service account.

9. Specify the Service Manager Workflow account. The account needs at least the following privileges:

   ▸ Permissions to send email and have a mailbox on the SMTP server

   ▸ Member of the Service Manager Administrator member group in Active Directory

   ▸ Member of the local Users security group

   The Odyssey domain uses the SVC_SM account, as shown in Figure 7.11.

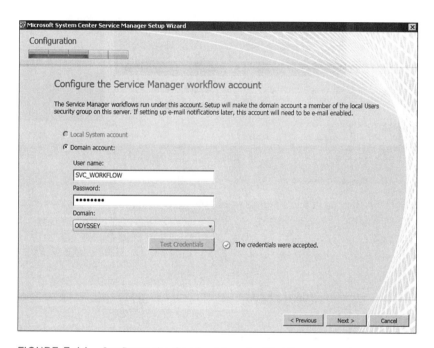

FIGURE 7.11   Configure the Service Manager Workflow account.

The Workflow account is only used for the Workflow Run As Account. This account is added to the Workflows user role so that workflows running under this security context will have the permissions necessary to query and update Service Manager.

10. The next screen asks whether you want to join the Service Manager Customer Experience Improvement Program. Make your selection and click **Next** to continue.

NOTE: PARTICIPATING IN THE CUSTOMER IMPROVEMENT PROGRAM

Marnix Wolf, Operations Manager (OpsMgr) MVP, has a great series of blog posts on the Customer Improvement Program at http://thoughtsonopsmgr.blogspot.com/2010/02/ceip-odr-and-lot-what-are-they-and-why.html.

11. Specify if you want to use Microsoft Update to keep the system current with various security patches and other updates. If you do not currently have a method or solution (such as System Center Configuration Manager) to provide patch management to the servers in your environment and your servers can access the Internet, you should check the option to use Microsoft Update.

12. Following the Microsoft Update screen, the next screen (see Figure 7.12) gives an overview of the Service Manager components that will be installed and the configuration settings. Click **Install** to continue with the installation process.

   During installation, the wizard shows you the particular stage of the installation process.

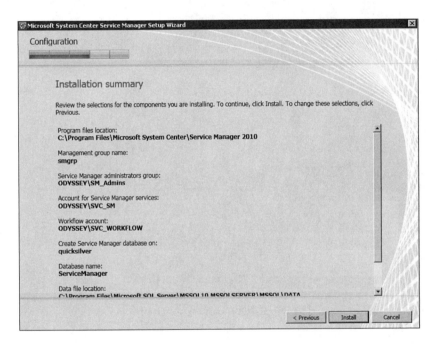

FIGURE 7.12   Installation Summary screen.

13. When the installation completes, the wizard displays the Setup Completed Successfully screen, shown in Figure 7.13. Notice the option to open the Encryption Backup or Restore wizard after setup is complete; run this wizard to back up the encryption key, as discussed in the next section.

   Closing this screen completes the installation of the Service Manager database and Service Manager management server.

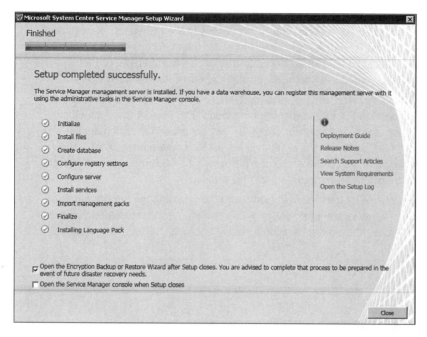

FIGURE 7.13   Setup completed successfully.

Backing Up the Encryption Key

When you complete installing your first Service Manager server, you will want to back up your encryption key. This encryption key, created during installation, is used to encrypt the data between the Service Manager components. If you need to restore your Service Manager environment, perhaps due to a hardware failure, you must restore the encryption key, as well, so that the data can be decrypted again. Follow these steps:

1. Once the Encryption Key Backup or Restore wizard is launched, click **Next**, as shown in Figure 7.14.

2. Select the option to **Backup the Encryption Key**, as shown in Figure 7.15.

HOW THE ENCRYPTION KEYS WORK

The encryption keys are a unique public/private key pair used to send and transmit sensitive data between the database server and the management server in encrypted form using a symmetric key encryption scheme. They are also used to encrypt Run As Account information within the Service Manager database and the DWStagingAndConfig database for the Data Warehouse management server.

This key pair is required to successfully restore the Service Manager server should it need to be rebuilt. The encryption key provides the server access to the encrypted content in the database, such as the Run As Accounts used to perform specific operations. If you have just a single management server and need to restore Service Manager on that server and lose your encryption key, you must reinstall the entire management group.

Each time an additional management server or portal server is installed, it receives a copy of the symmetric encryption key for the management group. This copy of the symmetric encryption key is encrypted using a private encryption key generated for each management server or portal server. There is a symmetric key for the entire management group, used to actually encrypt all the passwords, and a private key for each management server or portal server to encrypt the symmetric key for that server.

The encryption keys should be backed up immediately after installing the Service Manager server, Data Warehouse management server, and SSP using the securestoragebackup.exe tool, found on the Service Manager installation media in the Tools\SecureStorageBackup folder.

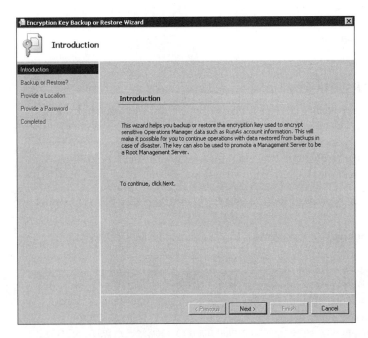

FIGURE 7.14   The first screen of the Encryption Key Backup/Restore wizard.

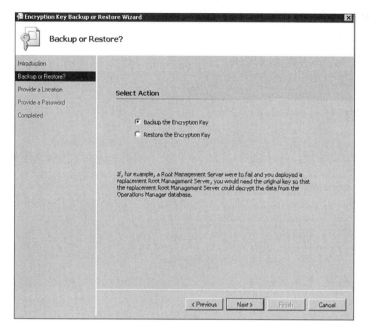

FIGURE 7.15   Choose the Backup the Encryption Key option.

NOTE: BACKING UP THE ENCRYPTION KEY FROM THE COMMAND PROMPT

You can also back up the encryption key from the command prompt. Type in the following syntax and press Enter:

```
securestoragebackup backup c:\UnleashedSCSM\SMkey.bin
```

where **c:\UnleashedSCSM\SMkey.bin** is the location to store the key

3. Specify the location to store the encryption key as shown in Figure 7.16. This should be a safe location and easily accessible should you need to restore the key.

4. The following screen (see Figure 7.17) requires that you specify a password to protect the encryption key. Store the password to the private encryption key file in a secure location with redundancy, ideally in a separate location from the encryption key backup file. Because there is no way to recover a lost password, be careful how you store it so that you can retrieve it if necessary. When restoring the encryption key, you will have to specify the password.

5. Figure 7.18 shows the final page of the Encryption Key Backup or Restore wizard.

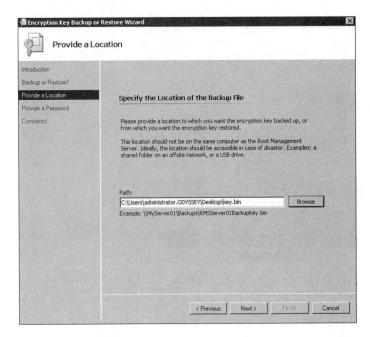

FIGURE 7.16   Specify the location of the encryption key backup file.

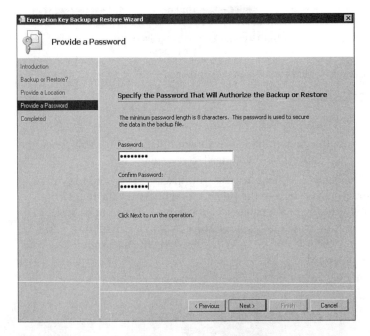

FIGURE 7.17   Specify a password for storing the encryption key.

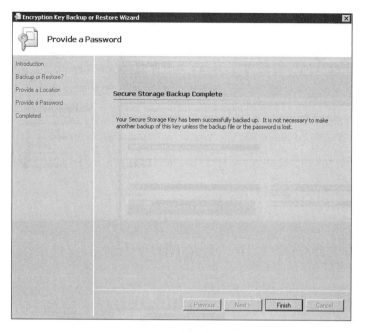

FIGURE 7.18   Encryption key backup complete.

TIP: MORE ON RECOVERING A MANAGEMENT SERVER

Should you lose the encryption key or forget the password and your management server is down, you can back up a new encryption key from the secondary management server and use it to restore the management server that went down.

Installing the Data Warehouse Management Server

As described in Table 7.3, the Service Manager Data Warehouse management server in the Odyssey environment is installed on Pantheon and uses SQL Reporting Services installed on Meteor.

Prior to installing the Data Warehouse management server and reporting functionality, validate that SQL Reporting Services (SRS) is working correctly. Do this by opening Internet Explorer and browsing to both http://localhost/reports and http://localhost/reportserver from the SRS server.

REAL WORLD: TROUBLESHOOTING SQL REPORTING SERVICES

Installing SRS is straightforward, but sometimes a supposedly successful installation will have issues when you try to verify the installation. Here's an error the authors encountered recently while checking whether SQL Reporting was up and running:

```
SQL Reporting: The underlying connection was closed: Could not establish trust
relationship for the SSL/TLS secure channel.
```

Trying to remove the SSL bindings using the SQL Reporting Configuration did not resolve the issue.

The next step was to look at the RSReportServer.config, the reporting server configuration file. This file stores settings used by the Report Manager, the Report Server Web service, and background processing. All Reporting Services applications run within a single process that reads configuration settings stored in RSReportServer.config.

Resolving the issue required editing the file to disable Secure Sockets Layer (SSL) and configuring it to use the non-SSL URL to the reporting server virtual directories. To accomplish this, follow these steps:

1. Change

   Add Key="SecureConnectionLevel" Value="2"

   to

   Add Key="SecureConnectionLevel" Value="0"

2. Delete any URLs under the <Configuration> section that pertain to SSL.

3. Restart SRS.

Before beginning the data warehouse installation, you should identify the SQL instance, management group name you want to use, and any AD user accounts you might need to provide to the wizard—such as the reporting account. This information should be identified during the design process, as discussed in Chapter 5, "Designing Service Manager." To avoid potential installation issues, you will also want to verify SRS is functioning correctly. Now follow these steps to install the data warehouse:

1. Choose the option to install a Service Manager Data Warehouse management server from the Setup splash screen shown previously in Figure 7.3. The wizard will display the start screen, the license agreement, and product registration.

2. You specify where to install the Service Manager data warehouse server. Setup installs everything by default in the *%ProgramFiles%* Microsoft System Center\Service Manager 2010 folder, but this is customizable by browsing to a folder of your choice. The wizard also automatically checks whether you have enough free space available on the specified disk.

3. The wizard then launches the Prerequisite Checker. Ensure that all prerequisites are met before proceeding.

4. At the next screen, specify the SQL Server database instance on which to install the data warehouse databases. You may install the DWDataMart database on another SQL Server system if desired. Organizations can separate the DWDataMart to a different server and disk drive from DWStagingAndConfig and DWRepository for performance reasons. The DWStagingAndConfig and DWRepository databases must be co-located on the same server.

Now, identify the SQL Server database instance of the Service Manager database. Type in the name of your SQL Server and press any key to continue. Setup connects to the specified SQL Server and retrieves a list of supported SQL instances that can host the Service Manager data warehouse databases.

If your SQL instance is not listed in the Setup screen, it means that instance does not meet the prerequisites. You will need at least SQL Server 2008 SP 1 64-bit; SQL Server 2005, SQL Server 2008 without SP 1, and 32-bit versions of SQL Server are not supported.

You can also specify the name of the databases and their sizes and location, as shown in Figure 7.19.

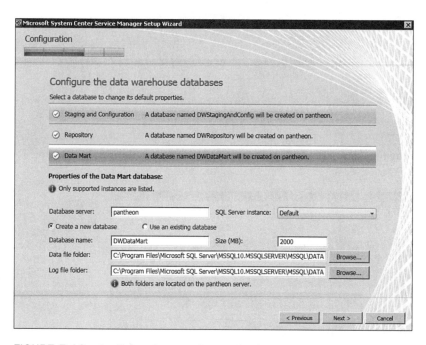

FIGURE 7.19   Configure data warehouse databases.

5. Now, configure the Data Warehouse management group as shown in Figure 7.20 by specifying a management group name. Remember that this name must be unique and is case sensitive.

6. Specify a group for the management group administrators; best practice is to use the same security group used when installing the Service Manager server.

7. Specify the reporting server to use and its configuration, including the Reporting instance to use, as shown in Figure 7.21.

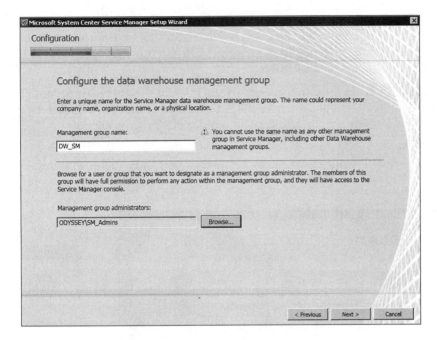

FIGURE 7.20   Specify the management group name.

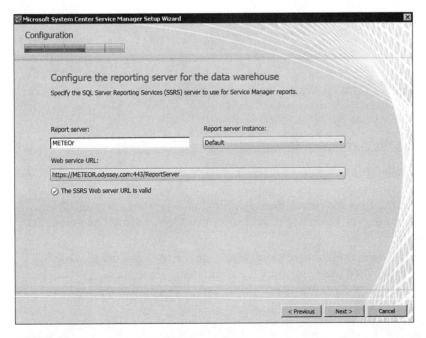

FIGURE 7.21   Specify the reporting server to be used for the data warehouse.

MANUAL STEPS TO CONFIGURE REMOTE SQL REPORTING SERVICES

When configuring which SQL reporting server to use, the wizard chooses the local SRS installation by default. If for performance reasons you decide to implement a dedicated SQL reporting server, you must manually configure the remote server before continuing with the installation. Follow these steps:

1. Copy the Microsoft.EnterpriseManagement.Reporting.Code.dll file from the Service Manager media in the Prerequisite folder to the computer that is hosting SRS in the folder %*ProgramFiles%*\Microsoft SQL Server\MSRS10.MSSQLSERVER\ Reporting Services\ReportServer\Bin.

2. Add the following code to the RSSrvpolicy.config file you will find in the %*ProgramFiles%*\Microsoft SQL Server\MSRS10.MSSQLSERVER\Reporting Services\ReportServer folder:

```
<CodeGroup  class="UnionCodeGroup"     version="1"
PermissionSetName="FullTrust"

Name="Microsoft System Center Service Manager Reporting Code Assembly"

Description="Grants the SCSM Reporting Code assembly full trust permission.">

    <IMembershipCondition     class="StrongNameMembershipCondition"

version="1"

PublicKeyBlob="0024000004800000940000000602000000240000525341310004000001000100010
0B5FC

90E7027F67871E773A8FDE8938C81DD402BA65B9201D60593E96C492651E889CC13F1415EBB53F
AC11

31AE0BD333C5EE6021672D9718EA31A8AEBD0DA0072F25D87DBA6FC90FFD598ED4DA35E44C398C
4543

07E8E33B8426143DAEC9F596836F97C8F74750E5975C64E2189F45DEF46B2A2B1247ADC3652BF5
C308

055DA9" />

</CodeGroup>
```

This code is available on the Microsoft TechNet site at http://technet.microsoft.com/en-us/ library/ff461215.aspx.

3. Close the RSSrvpolicy.config file and continue the installation.

8. On the following screen, specify the Server Manager services account, as shown in Figure 7.22.

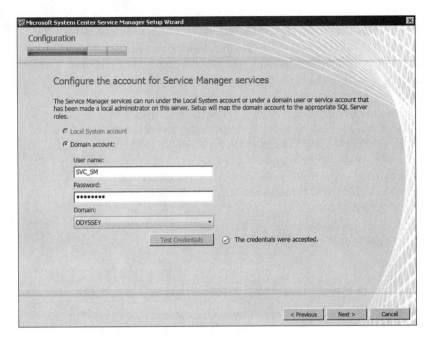

FIGURE 7.22   Specify the Service Manager services account.

As discussed earlier in the "Security Accounts" section, you should already have identified and configured the required service account prior to this step in the installation process. The account must be at least a member of the local Administrators group.

9. Specify the Reporting account, as shown in Figure 7.23. This account is used to read data from the data warehouse and generate reports.

You should have previously identified and configured the account prior to this step in the installation process. The account must be at least a member of the local Administrators group.

10. The following screen is an installation summary as shown in Figure 7.24. Verify that everything is correct and click **Next** to begin the installation.

11. During the installation, you can follow the installation progress, as shown in Figure 7.25.

12. After everything has installed successfully, you will see the screen shown in Figure 7.26.

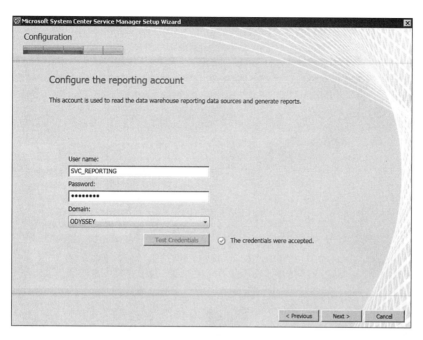

FIGURE 7.23   Specify the reporting account to use.

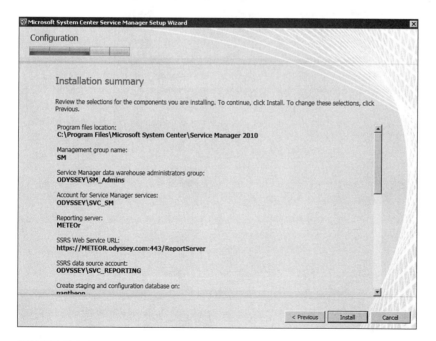

FIGURE 7.24   Installation summary.

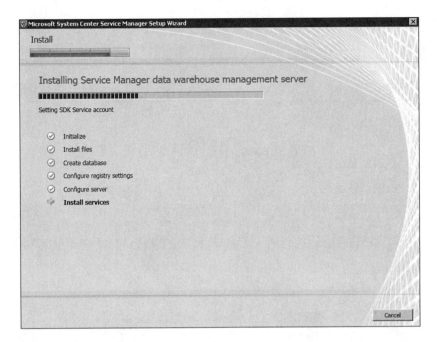

FIGURE 7.25   Installation progress.

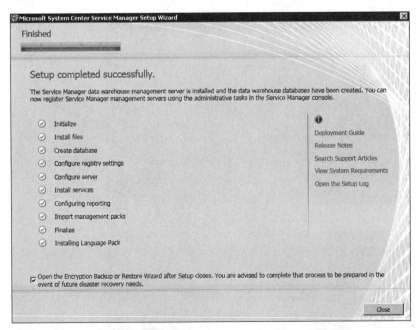

FIGURE 7.26   Setup completed successfully.

Installing the Self-Service Portal

With the Service Manager server and Data Warehouse server successfully installed, now it is time to install the SSP. Before starting this installation, verify that you have the correct security accounts in place (see Table 7.3) and an SSL certificate to secure the SSP website. During the installation, you need to provide a certificate; http://technet.microsoft.com/en-us/library/cc732906(WS.10).aspx discusses how to request a new certificate. Follow these steps:

1. Choose the option to install the Service Manager Web portals from the Setup splash screen shown in Figure 7.3. The wizard displays the starting screen, the license agreement, and product registration screen.

2. In the next screen, specify where to install the virtual website. As shown in Figure 7.27, Setup installs everything in the C:\inetpub\wwwroot\System Center Service Manager Portal folder by default, but you can customizable this by browsing to a folder of your choice. The wizard also automatically verifies that you have enough free space available on the chosen disk drive.

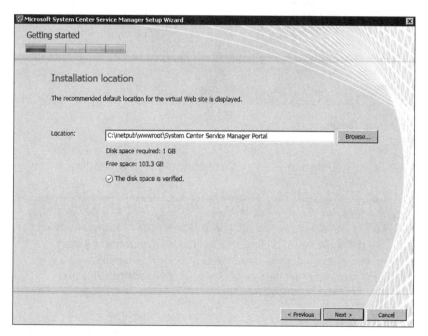

FIGURE 7.27   Specify the installation location.

3. The Prerequisite Checker is launched, as shown in Figure 7.28. The Prerequisite Checker checks for missing prerequisites; ensure that you do not have any critical alerts

or you will be unable to continue with the installation. If you have a failed prerequisite check, perhaps due to a missing hotfix, you can easily click the **Check prerequisites again** button after installing the hotfix.

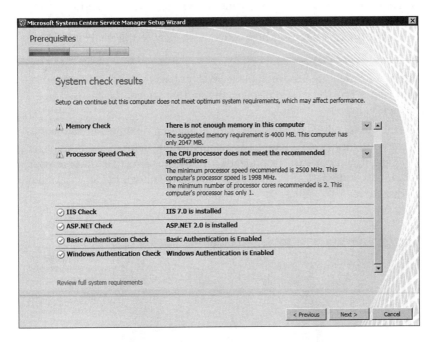

FIGURE 7.28   Prerequisite Checker results.

4. Specify the name of the website and select an SSL certificate, as shown in Figure 7.29.

CAUTION: SSP AND DATA WAREHOUSE MANAGEMENT SERVER MUST BE SEPARATE

Do not install the SSP on the same server as the Data Warehouse management server; otherwise, reports might be deleted when you install the SSP. Guidelines for deploying the SSP are available online at http://technet.microsoft.com/en-us/library/ff461125.aspx.

---

5. Now, specify the name of the Service Manager database server as shown in Figure 7.30. Prior to installing the SSP, verify that you are a member of the Service Manager Administrators user group or the setup process will fail.

6. In the next screen, specify the account previously specified when you installed your first Service Manager management server, as shown in Figure 7.31. In the example used in this chapter, the account used is SVC_SM, which is the Data Access SDK account used in the Odyssey environment.

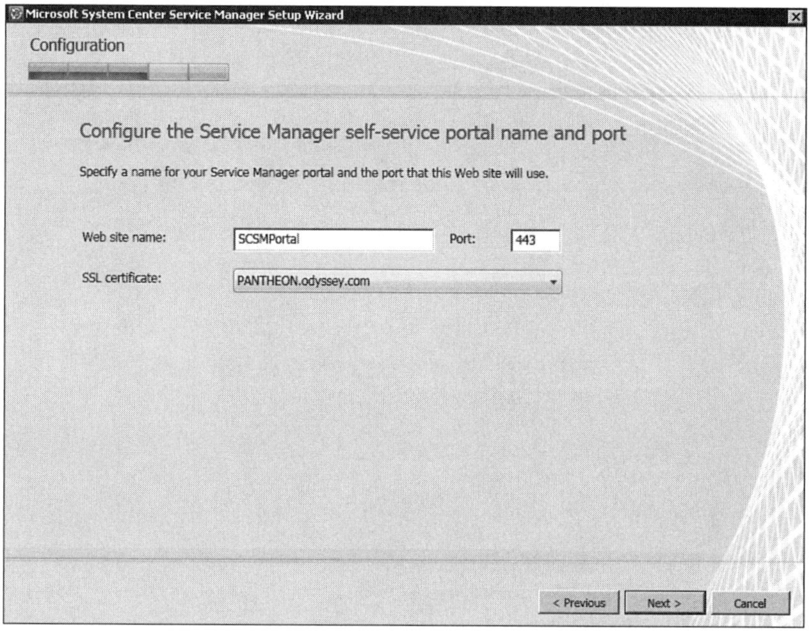

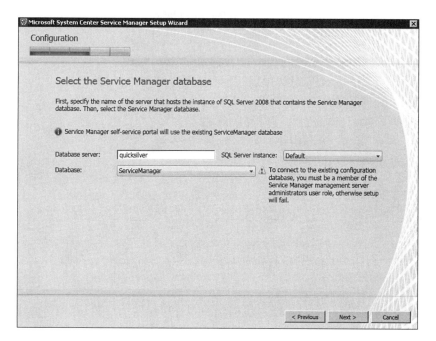

FIGURE 7.29   Specifying the SSP name, port, and certificate.

FIGURE 7.30   Select the Service Manager database.

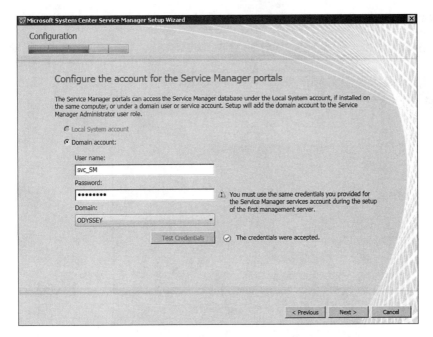

FIGURE 7.31   Configure the account used for the Service Manager portals.

7. Review the configuration information shown in the Installation summary screen and click Install, as shown in Figure 7.32.

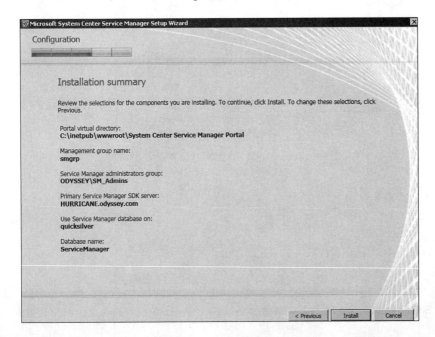

FIGURE 7.32   Installation summary.

8. Verify that all the components are successfully installed (see Figure 7.33), and click **Close** to launch the Encryption Backup or Restore wizard.

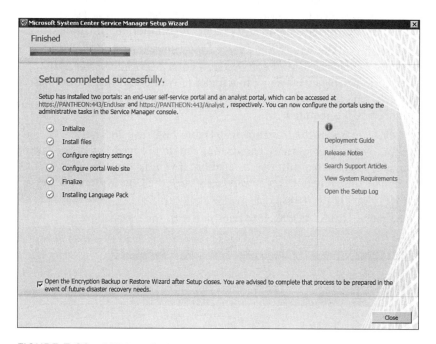

FIGURE 7.33   SSP installed successfully.

TIP: CUSTOMIZING THE PORTAL

The product team has provided two SharePoint web parts, enabling you to integrate the SSP and Analyst portal into SharePoint. See the article at http://blogs.technet.com/b/servicemanager/archive/2010/04/26/deploying-the-service-manager-self-service-portal-web-parts-with-sharepoint-services-3-0.aspx for detailed steps on how to accomplish this.

The current Self-Service portal lacks customization capabilities. Many installations have asked to be able to hide buttons or web parts, change colors and styles, show more or less information, and so on. To enable this level of customization, the product team has released the source code so you can customize the portal to your own needs. You can download the Self-Service portal source code from http://www.microsoft.com/downloads/en/details.aspx?FamilyID=65fbe0a3-1928-469f-b941-146d27aa6bac.

Installing the Service Manager Console

In addition to the console initially installed by default on the Service Manager management server, you can install additional Service Manager consoles. The authors highly recommend installing additional consoles and placing them on workstations to reduce the load on the management server. Follow these steps:

1. To install additional Service Manager consoles, select **Install a Service Manager Console** from the Splash screen previously shown in Figure 7.3. The wizard displays the starting screen, the license agreement, and product registration information.

2. Choose the folder to install the Service Manager console. By default, Setup installs everything in the *%ProgramFiles%*\Microsoft System Center\Service Manager 2010 folder, but this is customizable by browsing to a folder of your choice. The wizard also automatically checks whether you have enough free space available on the chosen drive. A minimum of 1GB is required.

3. The Prerequisite Checker is launched, as shown in Figure 7.34. The Prerequisite Checker checks for missing prerequisites; ensure that you do not have any critical alerts or you will be unable to continue with the installation. If you have a failed prerequisite check, perhaps due to a missing hotfix, you can easily click the **Check prerequisites again** button after resolving the issue.

4. After meeting the prerequisites, click **Next** to continue with the installation.

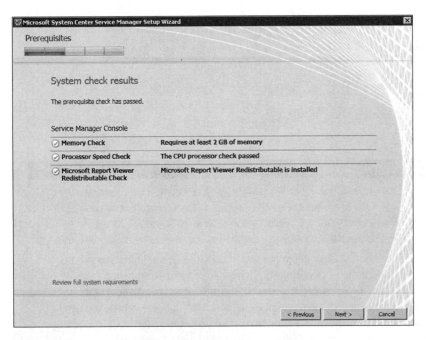

FIGURE 7.34   Prerequisite Checker.

Installing the Service Manager Authoring Tool

In addition to using the Service Manager console, if you want to customize Service Manager or extend the database schema you can install the Service Manager Authoring Tool. The

Service Manager Authoring Tool is not on the Service Manager media, download the SP 1 version of the Authoring Tool from http://www.microsoft.com/downloads/ en/details.aspx?FamilyID=78dcb15b-8744-4a93-b3fa-6a7a40ffeaae&displaylang=en. (This link is also available as a live link in Appendix A, "Reference URLs.") After downloading it, launch the splash screen. Follow these steps:

1. To install the Service Manager Authoring Tool, select **Install a Service Manager Authoring Tool** on the splash screen. The wizard displays the starting screen, the license agreement, and product registration information.

2. Choose the folder to install the Service Manager Authoring Tool. By default, Setup installs everything in the *%ProgramFiles(x86)%*\Microsoft System Center\Service Manager 2010 Authoring folder, but this is customizable by browsing to a folder of your choice. The wizard also automatically checks whether you have enough free space available on the chosen drive. A minimum of 1GB is required.

3. The Prerequisite Checker is launched, as shown in Figure 7.35. The Prerequisite Checker checks for missing prerequisites; ensure that you do not have any critical alerts or you will be unable to continue with the installation. If you have a failed prerequisite check, perhaps due to a missing hotfix, you can easily click the **Check prerequisites again** button after installing the hotfix.

4. After meeting prerequisites, click **Next** to continue with the installation.

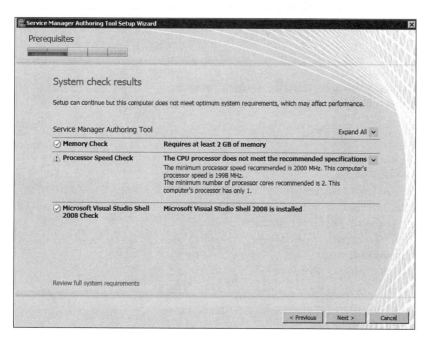

FIGURE 7.35   Prerequisite Checker for Authoring Tool.

For additional information about the Authoring Tool, see Chapter 17, "Management Packs," and Chapter 18, "Customizing Service Manager."

Installing Service Manager from the Command Prompt

Command-line parameters enable automating your Service Manager installation. Using the command-line installation, you can easily create a script that installs your entire Service Manager environment. This section shows the setup options to install various components.

Here is the script to install the Service Manager management server:

```
setup.exe /silent /install:ServerName
/AdminRoleGroup:<Domain>\<Account>
/CreateNewDatabase: /SqlServerInstance:<SQLServerInstance>
/ServiceRunUnderAccount:<Domain>\<Account>\<AccountPassword>
/WorkflowAccount:<Domain>\<Account>\<AccountPassword>
/ManagementGroupName:<ManagementGroupName>
/EnableErrorReporting:No
/CustomerExperienceImprovementProgram:No
```

The following script enables you to restore a Service Manager management server using an existing database:

```
Setup.exe /Silent /Install:Server
/UseExistingDatabase:<SqlServerInstance>:<ExistingServiceManagerDBName>
/ServiceRunUnderAccount:<Domain>\<Account>\<AccountPassword>
/CustomerExperienceImprovementProgram:No /EnableErrorReporting:No
```

Use the following script to install the Data Warehouse server:

```
Setup.exe /silent /install:Datawarehouse
/AdminRoleGroup:<Domain>\<Account>
/CreateNewDatabase: /SqlServerInstance:<SQLServerInstance>
/ServiceRunUnderAccount:<Domain>\<Account>\<AccountPassword>
/DatasourceAccount:<Domain>\<Account>\<AccountPassword>
/ManagementGroupName:<ManagementGroupName>
/ReportingServer:<ServerName>
/ReportingWebServiceURL:<Virtual Dir Name>
/EnableErrorReporting:No /CustomerExperienceImprovementProgram:No
```

The next script enables you to install the Service Manager console:

```
Setup.exe /silent /install:Console /EnableErrorReporting:No
/CustomerExperienceImprovementProgram:No
```

TIP: AUTOMATICALLY POINT THE SERVICE MANAGER CONSOLE TO THE MANAGEMENT SERVER

If you install the Service Manager console from a script, you can also point it automatically to your Service Manager management server by including a step to add a Registry key:

```
reg add "HKEY_CURRENT_USER\Software\Microsoft\System Center\2010\Service
Manager\Console\User Settings" /v SDKServiceMachine /t REG_SZ
/d"ManagementServerName"
```

Just replace *ManagementServerName* with the name of your Service Manager management server.

With the following script, you can install the Service Manager portal:

```
Setup.exe /Silent /Install:Portal
/UseExistingDatabase:<SqlServerInstance>:<ExistingServiceManagerDBName>
/PortalWebSiteName:<PortalWebSiteName> /PortalWebSitePort:<PortNumber>
/PortalAccount:<domain\username\password>
/CustomerExperienceImprovementProgram:No /EnableErrorReporting:No
```

If you previously installed the RTM version of Service Manager 2010 and want to upgrade Service Manager to Service Pack 1, use this command:

```
Setup.exe /silent /upgrade
```

You can find additional command-line parameters by running `setup.exe /?` from the command prompt. This gives you an overview of all the command-line parameters, as shown in Figure 7.36.

Removing a Service Manager Installation

If you need to remove Service Manger from your environment, the recommended process is by reversing the order in which you installed the various components. Service Manager was installed in the following order:

- ▶ Service Manager database
- ▶ Service Manager management server (this will be the Workflow management server)
- ▶ Additional Service Manager management servers
- ▶ Service Manager console
- ▶ SSP server
- ▶ Data warehouse databases
- ▶ Service Manager Data Warehouse management server
- ▶ Service Manager Authoring Tool

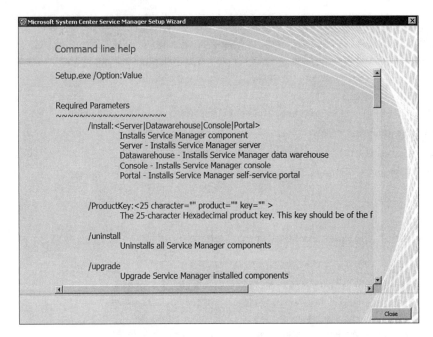

FIGURE 7.36   Command-line parameters.

To remove Service Manager, reverse the order of this process by starting with the Authoring Tool, the data warehouse databases, then the Data Warehouse management server, and the data warehouse databases.

After successfully uninstalling the consoles and data warehouse components, you can uninstall the SSP, any additional Service Manager servers, and then lastly uninstall your first installed Service Manager server and only then your Service Manager database. Use the SQL Server 2008 tools to archive or delete the databases from the SQL Server as well as SQL Reporting.

Troubleshooting Tips

Following the installation steps described in this chapter and using the prerequisite checker will help avoid many installation issues. However, you may encounter some common problems when installing Service Manager. These are listed in this section.

Table 7.5 describes some of the potential errors that might occur when installing Service Manager.

As part of setup, an installation log file is generated during installation of any Service Manager component and can be found in the *%temp%* folder. If you have any issues during the installation process, open the log file and search for **Value 3** in the log file, which will give you a good indication of what went wrong.

TABLE 7.5   Potential Installation Errors and Their Resolutions

Process Erroring	Error Message	Potential Cause	KB Article
Disjointed NameSpace	Setup might fail when installing the Service Manager components in a disjoint namespace.		http://technet.microsoft.com/en-us/library/ff625834.aspx.
Install	Finalize An Error occurred while executing a custom action:RollbackCleanup.	Characters in password may cause issues, especially the pipe, | (which is used to separate the usernames from domains).	
Indexing non-English Knowledge Articles	If you have non-English knowledge articles, the indexing in SQL 2008 SP 1 may cause an issue.		http://technet.microsoft.com/en-us/library/ff625833.aspx.

Post-Deployment Steps

After successfully installing the Service Manager components, there are several post deployment steps to follow to have a functional Service Manager environment. The next sections discuss these procedures.

Configure the Self-Service Portal

After you deploy the SSP, you must configure the password reset link, software provisioning, and other items, as discussed in depth in Chapter 8, "Using Service Manager."

Import Management Packs

Management packs (MPs) are eXtended Markup Language (XML) files used to extend Service Manager. An MP contains views, workflows, work items, classes, and so on, and can add additional functionality to Service Manager.

ABOUT MANAGEMENT PACKS

MPs contain definitions that define not only data models but also objects such as views for the Service Manager console, workflows, groups, queues, tasks, connectors, and so on. For additional information and details on how to define such objects, see Chapter 17, Chapter 18, and Chapter 19, "Advanced Customization Scenarios."

For example, if you want to use the Operations Manager Configuration Item connector, you must import the related Operations Manager MPs. This is discussed in Chapter 8.

MPs can be imported through the console or by using PowerShell cmdlets. Here is an example of the syntax to import an MP:

```
C:\PS>Import-SCSMManagementPack -Fullname
```

If you are importing many MPs, it is suggested you use PowerShell, because this will be faster.

Register with a Data Warehouse Management Server

After installing the Service Manager management server and the Data Warehouse management server, you need to run the Data Warehouse Registration wizard to register your Service Manager server to the Data Warehouse server to enable the Service Manager reports. This wizard registers the Data Warehouse management group to the Service Manager management group and deploys the MPs to the data warehouse.

> **NUMBER OF MANAGEMENT GROUPS YOU CAN REGISTER TO A DATA WAREHOUSE**
>
> You can register up to five Service Manager management groups to one Data Warehouse management group if you want to consolidate reports to a single data warehouse.

Follow these steps to register the data warehouse:

1. Open the Service Manager console and select the **Administration** space. In the Administration Overview screen, select the option to **Register with Service Manager Data Warehouse**, shown in Figure 7.37.

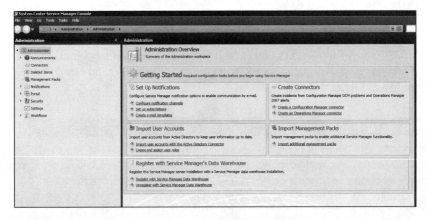

FIGURE 7.37   Service Manager Administration Overview.

2. The Data Warehouse Registration wizard opens, as shown in Figure 7.38. Click **Next** to continue.

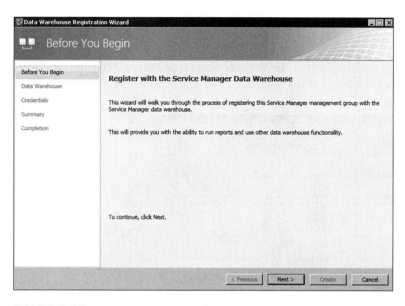

FIGURE 7.38   Registering with the Service Manager data warehouse.

3. In the following screen, specify the name of the Data Warehouse management server, as shown in Figure 7.39.

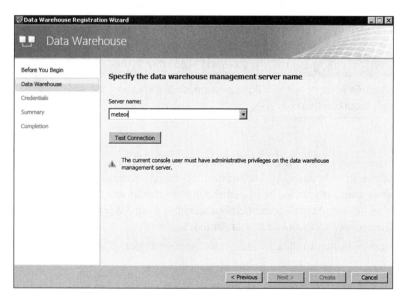

FIGURE 7.39   Specify the Data Warehouse management server name.

NOTE: ADMINISTRATOR PRIVILEGES REQUIRED TO REGISTER

You should have administrator privileges on the Data Warehouse management server to register it correctly.

4. You are asked to provide credentials for the data warehouse Run As Account (see Figure 7.40). You can click the **New** button to create a new Run As Account.

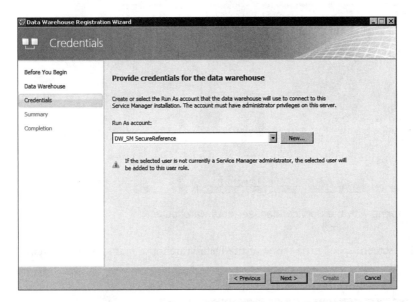

FIGURE 7.40   Provide credentials for the data warehouse.

NOTE: DATA WAREHOUSE RUN AS ACCOUNT WILL BE AN ADMINISTRATOR

Notice if the selected Run As Account is not a Service Manager administrator, the wizard adds the selected user account to this user role.

5. When creating a new Run As Account (see Figure 7.41), you associate an Active Directory account to a Run As Account. The account specified becomes a Service Manager administrator and is granted Read permissions on the Service Manager database. The authors recommend that you associate a service account with the Run As Account, rather than a user account used by an individual user.

6. In the Summary screen shown in Figure 7.42, verify your settings and click **Create**.

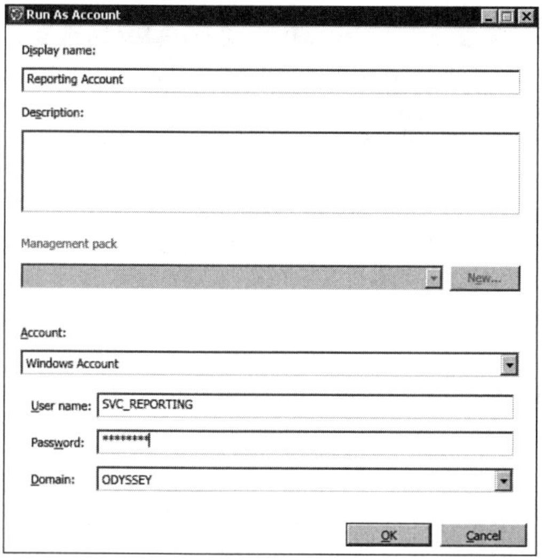

FIGURE 7.41   Create a new Run As Account.

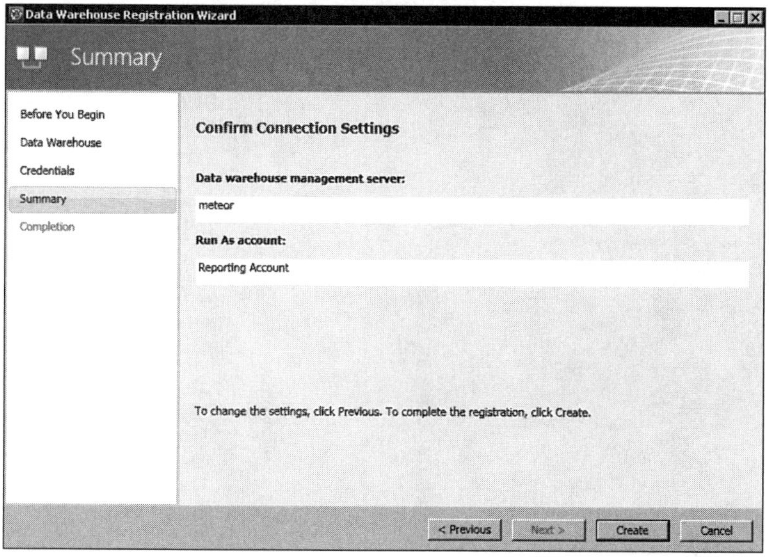

FIGURE 7.42   Summary screen for registering with a data warehouse.

TIP: CONNECTION FAILURES

If the connection does not succeed, verify that the Windows firewall on your data ware-house server is configured to allow communication from your Service Manager manage-ment server. For example, if you intend to eventually import information from your Active Directory, you must allow incoming traffic from your Service Manager system on port 389. For additional information about troubleshooting the data warehouse, read the blog post-ing at http://blogs.msdn.com/b/scplat/archive/2010/06/07/troubleshooting-the-data-warehouse-an-overview.aspx.

If you look in the Event Viewer in the OperationsManager log on the Data Warehouse management server, there are events related to registering the data warehouse to the Service Manager server:

▶ MPs are deployed automatically when you register the data warehouse. The event showing this is shown in Figure 7.43.

▶ Figure 7.44 shows events generated indicating the data warehouse jobs are created.

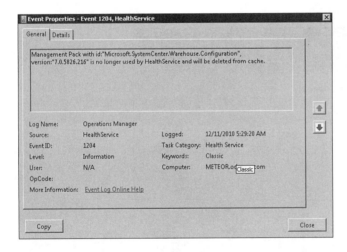

FIGURE 7.43   Deploying MPs.

You can verify completion of the MP deployment in the Service Manager console, as shown in Figure 7.45. Open the MPSync job and verify the deployment status of the MPs in the Status column. If the status is Associated or Imported for all MPs, the deployment is complete. This can take up to two hours in some environments, and will only be complete once five jobs are created and showing under the jobs list in the Data Warehouse wunderbar. For information about the specific data warehouse jobs, see Chapter 4.

Close the Service Manager console and reopen it so that the Reporting workspace is visible.

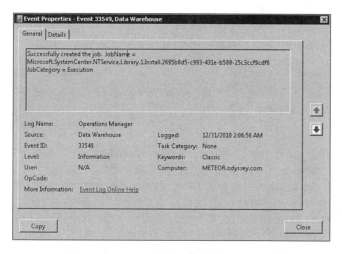

FIGURE 7.44   Data warehouse jobs created.

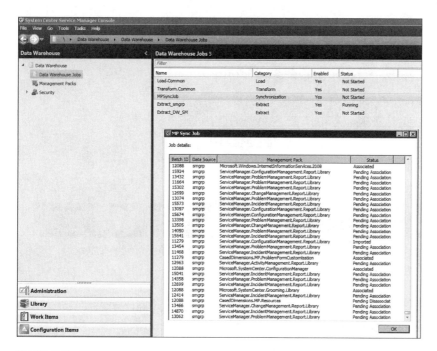

FIGURE 7.45   Verify MP deployment.

Connectors

After installing your Service Manager environment, you may want to connect it to other systems such Active Directory, Operations Manager, Configuration Manager, and others. Chapter 8 discusses this process.

Grooming

Grooming is the process that cleans out orphaned objects in your Service Manager databases. Service Manager includes two types of grooming, discussed in the next sections:

▶ Manual grooming, used for configuration items

▶ Automatic grooming, used for work items

Manual Grooming

When you delete a configuration item (CI), the CI is not actually deleted from the database. What happens instead is the state of the CI is changed from Active to Pending delete. When the CI is in Pending delete state, it is not shown in the user interface (UI). Only an administrator can permanently remove the object from the Deleted Items view in the Administration workspace. When the administrator removes the CI, the object is removed from the Deleted Items view and the Isdeleted value in the BasedManagedEntity table in the Service Manager database is changed from 0 to 1, as shown in Figure 7.46. When the Isdeleted value of the CI is 1, the purging workflow removes it from the database.

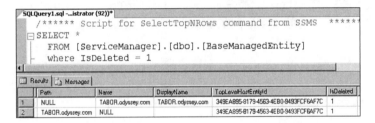

FIGURE 7.46   Removed CIs in the database.

TIP: AUTOMATICALLY DELETE CONFIGURATION ITEMS WITH THE STATUS PENDING DELETE

You can automatically remove CIs that are in the Pending delete state by running the following PowerShell script:

```
import-smlets

$class = Get-SCSMClass | where{$_.name -match "system.configitem"}

$deletedobjects = Get-SCSMObject -class $class |

where{$_.objectstatus -match "Pending"}

$deletedobjects | set-scsmobject -property objectstatus -value deleted
```

The script gets all the CIs that have the Pending status and updates them with the Deleted value. For more information, check the blog post at http://blog.scsmfaq.ch/2011/03/16/automatically-delete-objects-in-status-pending-delete/. Although this is not supported by the Service Manager product team, if you use Opalis Integration Server with this script you can automate the removal of CIs.

Automatic Grooming

Here is the default retention period for work items:

- **Incidents:**90 days

- **Change requests:**365 days

- **Problems:**365 days

Work items are groomed only if they meet the following criteria:

```
Is Deleted = False AND Last Modified < Now() - retention period AND Status = Closed
```

If a work item meets this criteria, similar to the behavior of a CI, the `Isdeleted` value is changed to 1 and the purging workflow removes or purges this work item from the database the next time it runs.

Work items that are hosted by another work item will automatically also be deleted if the host work item is deleted. Similar to Operations Manager, objects have relationships with each other. There are three types of relationships:

- Reference relationships

- Containment relationships

- Hosted relationships

Objects with hosted relationships are deleted automatically; objects with a reference or containment relationship are not deleted automatically. To better understand the hosted relationship, consider an example with two objects: a building and a room. These two objects have a hosting relationship with the following characteristics:

- The hosted object can be hosted by only one other object; it has an exclusive relationship with the host. That is, a room can be hosted by exactly one building. A room never "belongs" to more than one building.

- The hosted object cannot host the hosting object. That is, a room can never host a building.

- The hosting object can host multiple other objects. For example, a building can have multiple rooms in it or a building can host both rooms and corridors.

Replacing the words *building* and *room* in these examples with *activity* and *change request* shows another hosting relationship. An activity has a hosted relationship with a change request, because an activity cannot exist without a change request and a change request can contain multiple activities.

This means that if you delete a change request, the activities of that change request are also deleted. However, if you delete an incident, the related computer is not deleted because an incident has no hosting relationship with the computer.

For more information about grooming, see an article by Travis Wright at http://blogs.technet. com/b/servicemanager/archive/2009/09/18/data-retention-policies-aka-grooming-in-the-servicemanager-database.aspx.

Indexing Non-English Knowledge Articles

Service Manager uses SQL full-text search to search for keywords across knowledge articles. SQL full-text search allows you to search quickly and efficiently across a large amount of unstructured stored data, such as knowledge articles, by using the out-of-the-box RTF iFilter that is provided with SQL server. You can determine the iFilter used by Service Manager by launching the following query on your Service Manager database, seen in Figure 7.47:

```
select * from sys.fulltext_document_types where document_type = '.rtf' or
document_type = '.txt'
```

The default SQL iFilter doesn't allow indexing of non-English knowledge articles. The product team has provided a workaround for you to index non-English knowledge articles, described at http://technet.microsoft.com/en-us/library/ff625833.aspx.

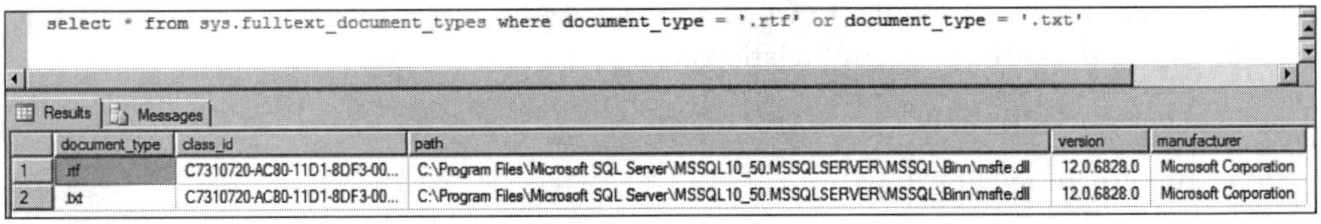

FIGURE 7.47   SQL default iFilter

Summary

This chapter discussed the steps involved in deploying a multiple-server Service Manager 2010 environment. It discussed the installation steps, provided some troubleshooting tips, and explained the post-deployment steps to have a fully functional Service Manager environment.

PART III

Service Manager Operations

IN THIS PART

CHAPTER 8

Using Service Manager

This chapter discusses the various Service Manager consoles used to access the tool. You will find that Service Manager 2010 is used within many different levels in your organization:

▶ Tier 1 Analysts

▶ Tier 2-3 Advanced Operators

▶ Managers

▶ End Users

▶ Administrators

▶ Developers

▶ Change Managers

The extent of usage makes it important to have a good understanding of the different consoles and know what console to use for each set of individuals. Service Manager 2010 has five different consoles, each with their own specific purpose and used by the different levels in the organization:

▶ Service Manager Console

▶ Service Manager Authoring Tool

▶ Service Manager Self-Service Portal

▶ Service Manager Analyst Portal

▶ Service Manager PowerShell

Table 8.1 matches the different consoles to the groups that will use them.

TABLE 8.1   Usage of Service Manager Consoles

Console	Users
Service Manager PowerShell console	Administrators
Self -Service portal	Managers
	End Users
Analyst portal	Tier 1 Analysts
	Tier 2-3 Advanced Operators
	Change Managers
Service Manager console	Tier 1 Analysts
	Tier 2-3 Advanced Operators
	Managers
	End Users
	Administrators
	Developers
	Change Managers
Service Manager Authoring Tool	Developers

This chapter discusses use of each of these consoles.

The Service Manager Console

The Service Manager 2010 console is used by all different areas within your environment. The console experience is controlled by role-based security, which gives each security role a common set of views, tasks, templates, and objects. Those things you are able to see and do in the console are controlled by these security roles, configured by Service Manager administrators. If you are a service desk analyst, you may only need to see those incidents assigned to you or your team. If you are the service desk manager, you might need to see all active incidents for all levels of support, and want to run reports to ensure the support unit is working as it should. For information regarding the role-based security used in Service Manager, see Chapter 15, "Service Manager Security." Figure 8.1 shows the Service Manager console.

When you log on as an end user, you will notice there is a different user experience from that of an administrator, as shown in Figure 8.2. In this figure, the end user cannot see the Administration, Reports, or Data Warehouse workspaces—they are limited to the Library, Work Items, and Configuration Items workspaces.

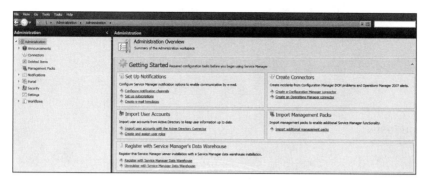

FIGURE 8.1   Service Manager console.

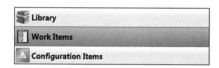

FIGURE 8.2   Workspace buttons visible to the end user.

A non-administrator will use the Library workspace to look into knowledge articles, tasks, templates, and such. The Work Items workspace groups all service desk-like items such as incidents, problems, changes, activities, and so on. The Configuration Item workspace shows all configuration items (CIs) that have been imported or synced in the configuration manager database (CMDB). Figure 8.3 shows the different workspaces as seen by a non-administrator.

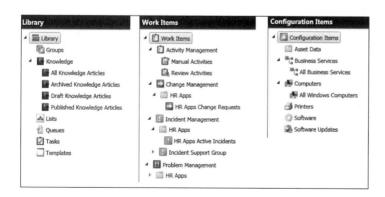

FIGURE 8.3   Workspace views seen by a non-administrator

By default, the Service Manager console contains six different workspaces, as shown in Figure 8.4, each with its own specific function:

▶ Administration

▶ Library

▶ Work Items

▶ Configuration Items

▶ Data Warehouse

▶ Reporting

FIGURE 8.4   The six Service Manager workspaces.

If you install additional Service Manager management packs (MPs), you may have more workspaces. For example, if you install the SLA Management pack, you will have an additional workspace that will let you configure service level agreements (SLAs), as shown in Figure 8.5.

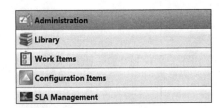

FIGURE 8.5   SLA Management workspace is added by the SLA MP.

Table 8.2 matches the workspaces in the Service Manager console with those individuals most likely to use them.

TABLE 8.2   Usage of the Service Manager Console

Workspace	Users
Administration	Administrators
Work Items	Tier 1 Analysts
	Tier 2-3 Advanced Operators
	Managers
	End Users
	Administrators
	Developers
	Change Managers
Library	Tier 1 Analysts
	Tier 2-3 Advanced Operators
	Change Managers
Configuration Items	Tier 1 Analysts
	Tier 2-3 Advanced Operators
	Managers
	Administrators
	Change Managers
Data Warehouse	Administrators
Reporting	Tier 1 Analysts
	Tier 2-3 Advanced Operators
	Managers

Managing Service Manager with the Service Manager Console

You will sometimes need to perform administration and maintenance on your Service Manager environment. This could be importing new MPs, setting up notifications, or changing security restrictions. To perform these actions, you use the Administration workspace of the Service Manager console, displayed in Figure 8.6, and must be a Service Manager administrator.

Administration Workspace

The Administration workspace is used to configure high-level settings of the Service Manager 2010 management group. Examples of tasks you can perform in this workspace are configuring notifications, working with MPs, working with accounts, and configuring connectors. Only Service Manager administrators have access to the Administration workspace. The following sections describe areas in this workspace.

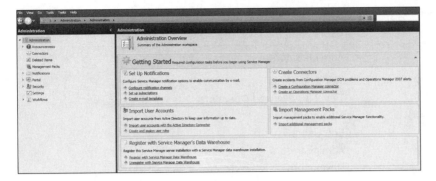

FIGURE 8.6   The Service Manager Administration workspace.

Deleted Items Node

The Deleted Items node shows CIs that have been marked as deleted. When you delete a CI from the console, it does not actually delete the CI; instead, the priority of the property of the instance you want to delete changes from Active to Pending Delete. The Deleted Items node in the Service Manager console is scoped to show only those items with a state of Pending Delete. A Service Manager administrator can then complete the deletion process. Only members of the Advanced Operators, Authors, and Administrators roles can initiate the deletion process; and only Service Manager administrators can confirm the deletion.

Management Packs Node

In the Management Pack node, you import new MPs into Service Manager. Importing new MPs enables you to add new models describing your own CIs or work items to track their life cycle, perform actions such as creating incidents, or importing new customized forms.

You can also delete MPs. Should you delete an MP in Service Manager, the matching database objects such as tables and relationship entries are also deleted.

Announcements Node

In the Announcements node, you can create new announcements that display in the portal and are visible to the end user. For example, if you are planning server maintenance at the end of the week, you could make an announcement to notify the end users that a business service will probably encounter performance issues by the end of the week.

REAL WORLD: ENABLING NON-ADMINISTRATORS TO CREATE AND EDIT ANNOUNCEMENTS

When you look at the Security Manager security matrix (described in Chapter 15), you will notice that members of the Administrators, Advanced Operators, and Authors user roles can create announcements. The caveat is the Announcement view by default is available only in the Administration workspace, which can be accessed only by Service

Manager administrators. Travis Wright describes a solution for this at http://blogs. technet.com/b/servicemanager/archive/2010/12/01/faq-how-can-i-enable-non-admins-to-create-edit-delete-announcements.aspx. The article suggests you create an announcement view in the Configuration Items node that can be viewed by other security groups.

Users will value announcements made on a regular basis regarding new changes, possible impacts on infrastructure, and so on.

TIP: TARGETING ANNOUNCEMENTS TO SPECIFIC USERS

A question often asked is if it is possible to target announcements to specific users. By default, announcements are targeted toward all users. This means any authenticated user can see the announcement you just made. To target announcements, read the blog posting on Anders Bengtsson's blog at http://contoso.se/blog/?p=1243.

Notification Node

In the Notification area, you can define and configure new notifications and subscriptions. Notifications provide the mechanism to deliver alert messages to various endpoint devices and messages to the respective owners at any place, any time. Users can also create their own personal notification subscriptions.

To create notifications, you must first configure the notification channels. A notification channel is a means to transport your message to the end user. Unlike Operations Manager (OpsMgr), where you can have various transport mechanism like Simple Mail Transport Protocol (SMTP), Short Message Service (SMS), scripts, and so on, this release of Service Manager supports only SMTP. For information about setting up notifications and notification channels, see Chapter 14, "Notification."

You need to be aware of several security boundaries when creating new notification subscriptions, including the following:

- ▶ End users cannot create their own personal subscriptions.

- ▶ Only administrators can create global notification subscriptions.

- ▶ Only administrators are allowed to change or edit the notification channels.

- ▶ Only administrators can create or edit notification templates.

TIP: NOTIFY ON UNASSIGNED INCIDENTS

The authors have been asked whether it is possible to create a notification on unassigned incidents. It may happen that incidents are created but not assigned. Most likely, unassigned incidents will take longer to be resolved.

Suppose you want to create a notification that notifies you when an incident is older than *X* hours and unassigned. Out of the box, this is difficult to achieve within the console because of the lack of relationships with unassigned incidents. However, this can be accomplished with a script, as described on Anders Bengtsson's blog, at http://contoso.se/blog/?p=1875.

Settings Node

In the General Settings pane, you can configure various general settings, including the following:

▶ Configuring the incident/problem priority to define a priority calculation based on the impact and urgency of an incident.

▶ Specifying Operations Manager settings such as the OpsMgr web URL.

▶ Modifying the incident ticket prefix (the default is IR*xxx*, where *xxx* = the sequence of numbers incremented with each new ticket); you can change this to match your company requirements.

▶ Changing the change request prefix (the default is CR*xxx*, where *xxx* = the sequence of numbers incremented with each new change request); you can change the prefix to match your company requirements.

Workflows Node

Workflows are a sequence of activities that automate a business process. Workflows can update incidents when various changes occur or automatically generate incidents from the Operations Manager and Configuration Manager connectors. You can check the status of workflows in the status folder of Workflow Items. By default, Service Manager provides workflows for the Self-Service portal (SSP), Operations Manager Alerts, and Desired Configuration Management Event Workflow.

Portal Node

The Portal area lets you define configuration settings for the Self-Service portal. This includes configuring settings for software requests, Information Technology (IT) contact settings such as Service Desk Phone Number, email, and Chat URL with their expected response times. You can also define the applications published for users of the portal (depending on the System Center Configuration Manager [SCCM] connector) and Automated Software Deployment workflow for users when they request published software (this depends on the SCCM Connector as well as Configuration Manager being configured to allow creation of deployment objects).

Security Node

In the Security section, you can define your Run As Account and User Roles.

The Run As Accounts section is where you configure and store connector and Service Manager-controlled user accounts. Examples include the workflow/system accounts, Active

Directory connector account, and so on. This will vary by environment; refer to the Service Manager documentation for best practice guidance.

The User Roles section lets you configure role-based security settings (who has access to do what and those objects to which they have access). You can find more information about User Roles in Chapter 15.

Connectors Node

Connectors enable you to import data from various different sources into Service Manager. You can create two types of connectors in Service Manager: automatic and manual.

Using manual connectors, you can import work items and CIs by importing a comma-separated value (CSV) file. To import a CSV file, you must also provide a format file. A format file is an eXtensible Markup Language (XML) file that specifies the class type or projection type of the instances you want to import into Service Manager. The format file (also known as a *parameter file*) specifies the properties of the instances and the order in which those properties appear in the CSV file. Figure 8.7 shows an example.

```
- <CSVImportFormat>
  - <Projection Type="System.WorkItem.Incident.ProjectionType">
    - <Seed>
      - <Class Type="System.WorkItem.Incident">
          <Property ID="Id" />
          <Property ID="Status" />
          <Property ID="Source" />
          <Property ID="Impact" />
          <Property ID="Urgency" />
          <Property ID="TierQueue" />
          <Property ID="CreatedDate" />
          <Property ID="ResolvedDate" />
          <Property ID="ClosedDate" />
          <Property ID="TargetResolutionTime" />
          <Property ID="Classification" />
          <Property ID="Title" />
          <Property ID="Description" />
        </Class>
      </Seed>
    - <Component Alias="AffectedConfigItems" Count="1">
      - <Seed>
        - <Class Type="Microsoft.SystemCenter.BusinessService">
            <Property ID="ServiceID" />
            <Property ID="IsBusinessService" />
            <Property ID="Classification" />
            <Property ID="DisplayName" />
          </Class>
        </Seed>
      </Component>
```

FIGURE 8.7   CSV Parameter file.

When you launch the Import instances from the CSV File wizard, you must provide the XML format file and data file, as shown in Figure 8.8. When creating an XML format file, you must provide required class properties in order to import instances of that class. Give the Parameter file the same name as the CSV file; otherwise, you cannot import the CSV file.

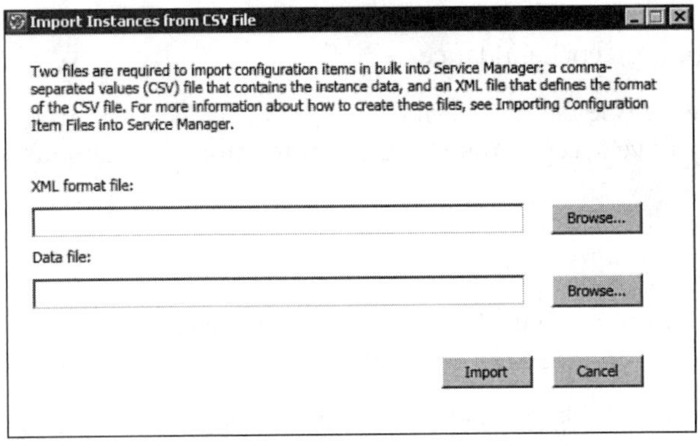

FIGURE 8.8   The Import CSV file dialog.

After the initial load, automatic connectors run periodically and update the CMDB with changes from each source system. This functionality gives Service Manager what has been called a dynamic CMDB, as it is a CMDB that is updated automatically.

Manual connectors such as the CSV import do not run periodically. If you want the CSV connector to run periodically, http://scsmcsvconnector.codeplex.com/ discusses how to accomplish this.

Here are the connectors provided for Service Manager:

▶ **Active Directory Connector:** Use the Active Directory Connector to import information about users, groups, printers, and computers.

▶ **Configuration Manager Connector:** Use the Configuration Manager Connector to import hardware and software information from Configurations Manager.

▶ **Operations Manager Alert Connector:** This connector registers incidents in Service Manager based on alerts in Operations Manager.

▶ **Operations Manager Configuration Item (CI) Connector:** The Operations Manager CI Connector imports objects into the Service Manager database that are discovered by Operations Manager. The MPs used in Operations Manager that contain the class definitions for the CIs need to be imported into Service Manager prior to importing the associated objects.

▶ **CSV Connector:** Use a CSV file to import any type of object defined in the CMDB.

▶ **Exchange Connector:** Microsoft recently released the Exchange connector out-of-band. You can download this connector from http://www.microsoft.com/downloads/en/details.aspx?FamilyID=0b48d1f1-434a-4ee6-8017-fc13f4c16785&displaylang=en. Note that Microsoft does not support the Exchange Connector.

Additional information on the connectors provided with Service Manager 2010 is available at http://scug.be/blogs/scsm/archive/2009/11/04/importing-data-into-scsm-part-1-the-scsm-ad-amp-sccm-connectors.aspx.

CAUTION: DELETING CONNECTORS

Should you delete a connector, Service Manager deletes all its imported CIs that do not belong to another connector, have active incidents or change requests associated with them, or have been updated manually. If you want to create a new connector and keep the CIs, first create the new connector and synchronize it, and only then delete the old connector.

Using Connectors

To create incidents in Service Manager based on alerts from OpsMgr, you must create a new Operations Manager Alert item connector. Perform the following steps to create a new connector:

1. Open the Service Manager console and click the Administration workspace. In the Administration workspace, open the connector space and select **Operations Manager Alert** connector.

2. Enter a name for the connector, specifying a name that represents that type of connector. Verify the Enable check box is checked.

3. In the Server Details tab, provide the name of your Operations Manager root management server (RMS) and select a Run As Account that has sufficient privileges to connect to the RMS, as displayed in Figure 8.9. If you have not created a Run As Account, you can create one by clicking **New** to open the dialog box shown in Figure 8.10.

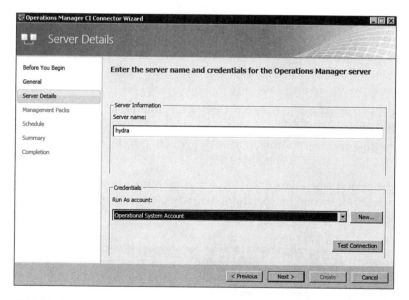

FIGURE 8.9   Details for connecting to the Operations Manager RMS.

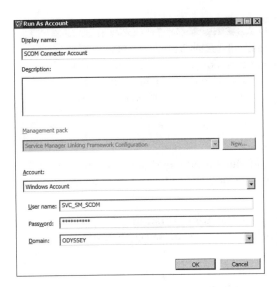

FIGURE 8.10   Creating a Run As Account.

REQUIRED PERMISSIONS FOR SCOM RUN AS ACCOUNT

When creating a Run As Account, you must use an account with the following permissions:

- ▶ User must be a domain account.
- ▶ Must be a member of the Local User Group on the Service Manager server.
- ▶ Must be a member of the Operations Manager administrator group.

4. After identifying your Run As Account, specify the alert routing rules for incoming alerts. This is displayed in Figure 8.11.

5. Specify a new alert rule and specify the template to apply to new incoming alerts, as shown in Figure 8.12.

   You can choose the default Operations Manager incident template if desired. You can also create several rules for incoming Operations Manager alerts and apply a different template based on the settings defined in the Alert Routing rule.

NOTE: INCOMING OPERATIONS MANAGER ALERTS ARE UNASSIGNED

When new incidents are created from incoming Operations Manager alerts, by default the incidents are unassigned and no affected user is specified. You can populate some of this information based on an incident template to be applied automatically to a new Operations Manager alert.

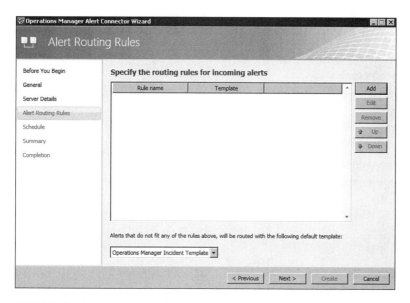

FIGURE 8.11   Add a new Alert Routing rule.

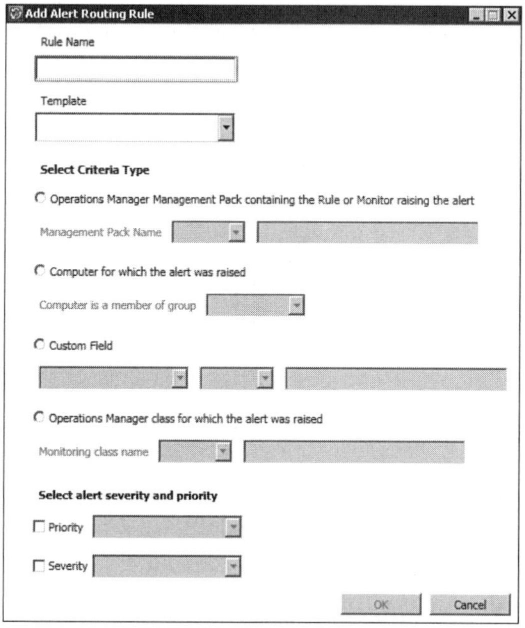

FIGURE 8.12   Specify the template to apply to new alerts.

6. Next, select the schedule interval as displayed in Figure 8.13 and specify whether you want to automate closing the incidents in Service Manager if they are resolved or closed in Operations Manager. You can also choose to close the alerts in Operations Manager when a Service Manager operator closes the incident in Service Manager.

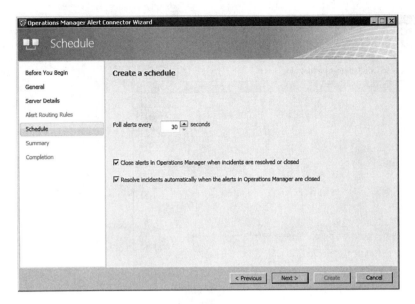

FIGURE 8.13   Schedule the interval.

7. Review the settings in Figure 8.14, and then select **Create** to create the connector.

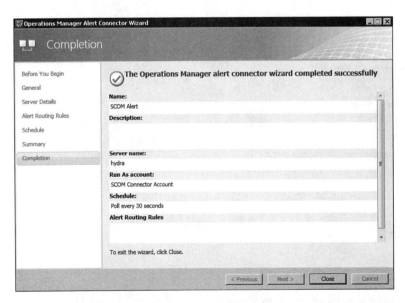

FIGURE 8.14   Summary screen for the OpsMgr Alert Connector Wizard.

Creating and Managing Subscriptions

With the Operations Manager alert connector created in Service Manager, you must also create an alert subscription in Operations Manager. This Operations Manager alert subscription determines which alerts to forward to Service Manager. Event ID 34085 will appear in the Operations Manager event log (see Figure 8.15), indicating an alert subscription should be initialized.

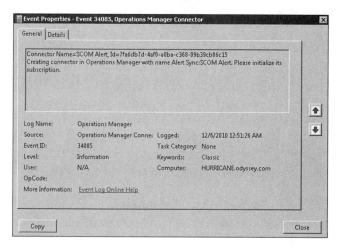

FIGURE 8.15   Event ID 34085 indicates a subscription should be initialized.

REAL WORLD: DETERMINING WHAT TO FORWARD TO SERVICE MANAGER

The authors suggest caution when creating alert subscriptions in Operations Manager. If you create an alert subscription that forwards all alerts, you will have a large number of incidents in Service Manager that are not relevant. It is critical you have a very fine-tuned OpsMgr environment before forwarding OpsMgr alerts to Service Manager. The OpsMgr alert-to-incident ratio can be a good indicator of how well OpsMgr is tuned. If you have considerably more alerts in OpsMgr than incidents, you can conclude your OpsMgr environment needs more fine-tuning because it is generating non-relevant alerts. Speak with the different stakeholders in your organization and decide what to forward to Service Manager and when to create a new incident.

For example, determine whether to create an incident when a logical disk is full or only when alerts occur that are more urgent. To assist with this process, see Chapter 10, "Incident Management."

Perform the following steps to create a subscription in Operations Manager:

1. Open the Operations Manager console and click the Administration workspace. In the Administration workspace, open the Internal connector space as displayed in Figure 8.16. Typically, you see a new connector that has been created for you with the name specified in step 2 of the previous procedure in this section. Open the Properties page of this connector.

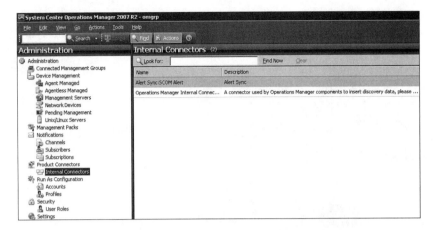

FIGURE 8.16   Internal connectors in the Operations Manager console.

2. After opening the properties of the connector, add a subscription to it. A connector without a subscription will not forward any alerts to Service Manager. Click **Add** to create a new subscription.

3. In the General properties view, give your new subscription a name.

4. In the next screen, specify the Operations Manager groups allowed to forward alerts. This is shown in Figure 8.17. Click **Next**.

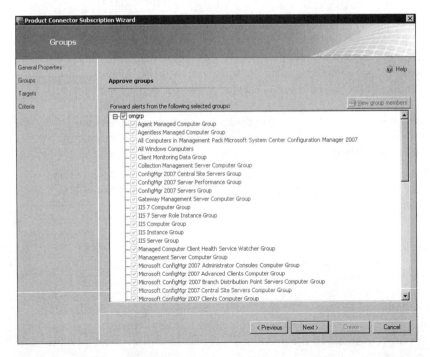

FIGURE 8.17   Specify groups to forward alerts.

5. If you need more granularly and control over the targets that can forward alerts, tick the selection to only forward alerts with targets explicitly added to the Approved Target grid in Figure 8.18.

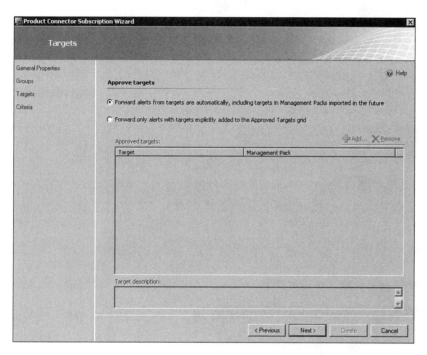

FIGURE 8.18   Approving targets.

6. In the Criteria screen shown in Figure 8.19, define the type of alerts to forward to Service Manager. As discussed in the sidebar "Real World: Determining What to Forward to Service Manager," be careful what you select.

Based on new alerts from Operations Manager (Figure 8.20), a new incident will be created in Service Manager under the All Open Operations Manager Incidents view in the Service Manager console, as shown in Figure 8.21.

You can also right-click in the Operations Manager console to forward a specific alert to Service Manager. This is displayed in Figure 8.22.

8

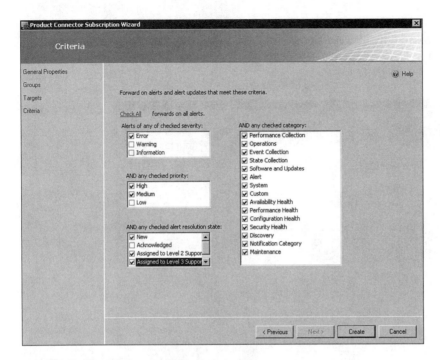

FIGURE 8.19   Define criteria for the connector.

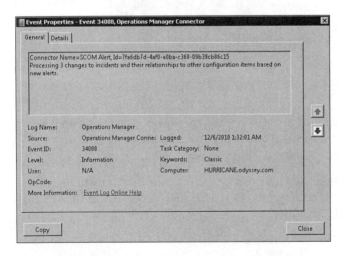

FIGURE 8.20   Alerts forwarded to Service Manager, indicated by event 34088.

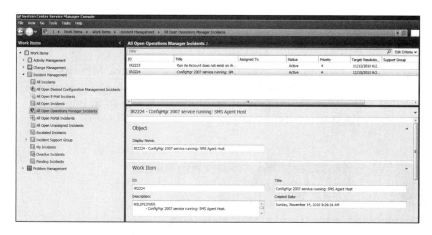

FIGURE 8.21   New incidents based on Operations Manager alerts.

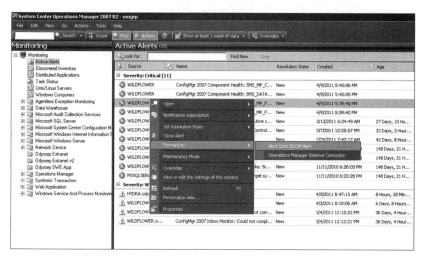

FIGURE 8.22   Forward alert to Service Manager manually.

Next, create a new Operations Manager Configuration Item connector, as follows:

1. Open the Service Manager console and click the Administration workspace. In the Administration workspace, open the Connector node and select **Operations Manager CI** connector.

2. Enter a name for the connector. Ensure you choose a name that correctly represents the type of connector. Verify that the Enable check box is checked.

3. In the Server details tab, provide the name of your Operations Manager root management server and select a Run As Account with privileges to connect to the RMS. To create a new Run As Account, click on **New**.

4. In the Management Packs screen, displayed in Figure 8.23, select the MPs that are new to Service Manager. These MPs will be synchronized with Operations Manager, with the derived classes and instances properties imported. You need to import the OpsMgr management packs into Service Manager.

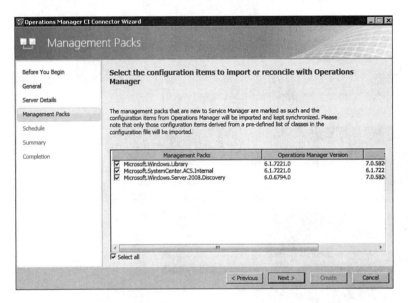

FIGURE 8.23   Select Management Packs for the connector.

5. Select a schedule for when you want to synchronize the CIs shown in Figure 8.24. During each synchronization, newly or updated discovered instances by Operations Manager are imported into Service Manager.

6. Review the settings and click **Create connector**. Once completed, the connector is successfully created, as shown in the Summary screen in Figure 8.25.

After you create the Operations Manager CI connector, synchronization occurs. Figure 8.26 indicates a successful synchronization, shown by event 34084 in the Operations Manager event log.

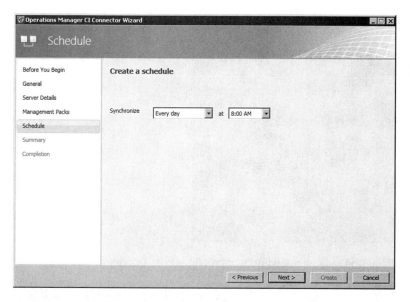

FIGURE 8.24   Schedule synchronization.

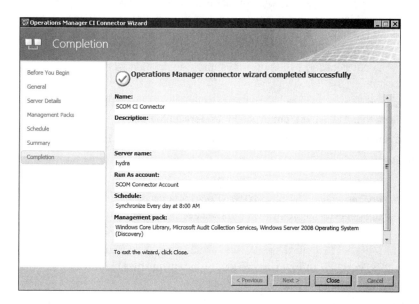

FIGURE 8.25   Summary screen for the Operations Manager CI Connector Wizard.

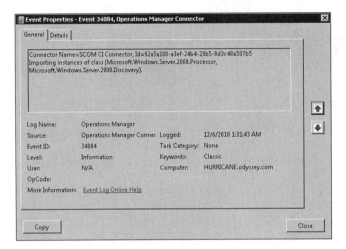

FIGURE 8.26   Event ID 34084 indicates synchronization of CIs from Operations Manager.

CONTROL WHAT IS SYNCHRONIZED THROUGH THE OPSMGR CI CONNECTOR

After setting up the Operations Manager CI Connector between Operations Manager and Service Manager, all Windows systems with an installed Operations Manager agent will be synced with Service Manager. This is because out of the box Service Manager already has the Windows MP imported. To import other items from your Operations Manager environment, you just need to import the respective MPs that contain the library and classes—it is not necessary to import MPs into Service Manager that only contain rules and monitors.

Service Manager maintains an `AllowList` to control what is put into the CMDB. Only classes that derive from this `AllowList` are synced into Service Manager.

Here is a PowerShell command to retrieve all the classes that are in the `AllowList`:

```
Get-SCSMAllowList
```

For more information about the `AllowList`, see Travis Wright's blog post at http:// blogs.technet.com/b/servicemanager/archive/2010/02/26/managing-the-allowed-list-for-the-operations-manager-ci-connector-with-powershell.aspx.

When creating connectors, you can follow the process by opening the Operations Manager event log and searching for the following events:

▶ **Event ID 34201, Source: Service Manager Console:** This message indicates that the connector has been successfully created.

▶ **Event ID 34085, Source: Operations Manager Connector:** This message states an internal Operations Manager connector was created and that its subscription should be initialized.

▶ **Event ID 34082, Source: Operations Manager Connector:** This message indicates the sync process has started.

▶ **Event ID 34087, Source: Operations Manager Connector:** This message indicates the sync process has ended.

To assist in troubleshooting, you can enable verbose logging for your connectors to see when and how synchronization happens. Perform the following steps:

1. Run regedit to open the Registry, and navigate to the following:

   ```
   HKLM\SOFTWARE\Microsoft\System Center\2010\Service Manager
   ```

2. Under the Service Manager node, create a new subkey named **OperationsManagerConnector**.

3. Under this subkey, create a new string value called **FirstRun** with a value of **FirstRun**.

You will now notice many events regarding the connectors in the event log. Because of the high level of synchronization, the event log can fill up quickly. Don't forget to remove the Registry key after troubleshooting! Also note that due to the high synchronization frequencies of the Operations Manager alert connector (every 30 seconds), you will not have an event each time synchronization occurs.

DELETING OLD CONNECTORS IN OPERATIONS MANAGER

You might have connectors in Operations Manager that are no longer in use. For example, if you install Service Manager in a test environment and then reinstall Service Manager, the connector remains in OpsMgr. Because the connector still exists, alerts will be sent via the subscription, but they are not picked up. One way to deal with this is to remove the subscription in the OpsMgr connector. This stops events from forwarding without deleting the connector. A cleaner way is to delete the OpsMgr connector. Perform the following steps to delete a connector:

1. Delete all the subscriptions assigned to this connector. Open the connector in the Operations Manager console and delete the assigned subscription. This step is very important; otherwise, you will have orphaned subscriptions with broken relationships, which can cause numerous issues in your Operations Manager environment.

2. Next, identify the ConnectorID by using SQL Management Studio to run the following SQL query against your Operations Manager database, as shown in Figure 8.27:

   ```
   select DisplayName,IsInitialized,ConnectorID from
   Connector,BaseManagedEntity
   where Connector.BaseManagedEntityID=BaseManagedEntity.BaseManagedEntityID
   ```

3. Find the corresponding ConnectorID and uninitialize the connector by launching this SQL query in SQL Management Studio:

```
EXEC p_ConnectorUpdate '5fabdf4c-a1f8-43bf-ac18-e46e20bd470b',NULL,0
```

The first parameter is the ConnectorID you found in step 2, the second is a bookmark, and the third is the initialized state, which should be 0 to uninitialize the connector.

4. Now, delete the connector by running the following SQL command:

```
EXEC p_ConnectorDelete '5fabdf4c-a1f8-43bf-ac18-e46e20bd470b',Comments,Alex
```

The first parameter is your ConnectorID found in step 2, the second is the comments you want added to the alert history when the connector is deleted, and the third is the Modified By field you want added to the alert history (Alex, in this case).

For additional information about deleting a connector, check the posting on Kevin Holman's blog: http://blogs.technet.com/b/kevinholman/archive/2009/09/10/removing-an-old-product-connector.aspx. Note that Microsoft does not support the steps described here.

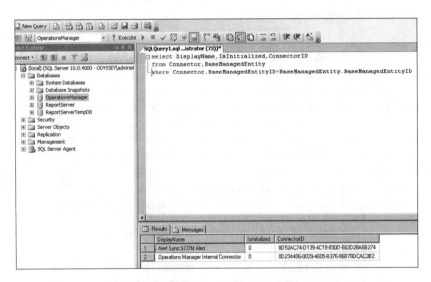

FIGURE 8.27   Find the connectorID using SQL Management Studio.

Using the Service Manager Console

The Service Manager console is used by all different levels of user roles in your environment. The "Managing Service Manager with the Service Manager Console" section discussed how to manage and administer your Service Manager environment using the Administration workspace. The next sections discuss the other workspaces of the Service Manager console. With the exception of the Data Warehouse workspace, these are 'ssed from the perspective of non-administrators.

Library Workspace

The Library workspace enables using templates, tasks, queues, groups, knowledge, and lists. In general, this is where you configure values that will be shared between a number of objects in the other workspaces. For example, you create templates here to use in change requests or incidents. You also manage your groups here, which can be used with security roles. Figure 8.28 displays the areas of the Library workspace.

FIGURE 8.28   Library workspace.

Here are some of the nodes in the Library workspace:

- ▶ **Groups:** Groups are used to manage CIs. Groups in Service Manager are identical to the groups you might already know from Operations Manager. Similar to OpsMgr, you can create dynamic or manual groups. A manually created group allows you to identify explicit group members and manually add them to the group. This can be prone to increased administration however, and is best avoided. Dynamic groups allow you to use an existing attribute or multiple attributes and build an expression that defines the membership of the group.

    Similar to OpsMgr, once you have created a group, you can use it for targeting reports, when creating new notification subscriptions, and to scope down the console. For example, you can create a dynamic group that contains all SQL Servers, so SQL administrators are only able to view information about those SQL Servers.

- ▶ **Knowledge:** You can create knowledge articles to assist operators or end users to understand and potentially solve issues. You can link knowledge articles to work items.

TIP: TARGET KNOWLEDGE ARTICLES TO SPECIFIC USERS

A question often asked is whether you can target knowledge articles to specific users. By default, knowledge articles are targeted to the users. This means any authenticated user can see the knowledge articles you just created. To target knowledge articles, read the blog post on Anders Bengtsson's blog at http://contoso.se/blog/?p=1262.

You can configure multiple knowledge base providers for a user. By default, when you search for a knowledge base article in Service Manager, only those results found in your CMDB display. However, if you want to search with one search string in multiple sources, you can add several knowledge base providers. Follow these steps to add more knowledge base providers:

1. Click **Manage Knowledge Search Providers** on the knowledge search screen.

2. Click **Add new Knowledge Search Provider**.

You can provide extra knowledge search providers such as Bing, TechNet, or even your own company SharePoint site.

On the Knowledge Search screen, you will now see the newly added providers, as shown in Figure 8.29.

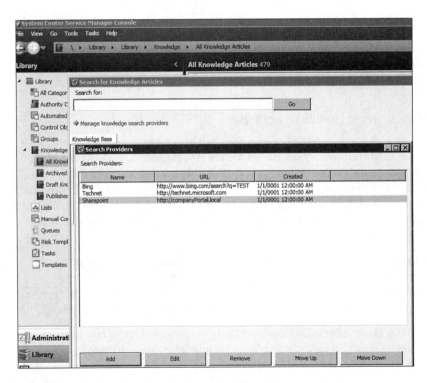

FIGURE 8.29   Extra knowledge base providers.

▶ **Lists:** Lists are used to customize forms. The Service Manager console uses lists in forms and dialog boxes to provide predefined values to the user. For example, if you want to create a new Incident, the user can select from the Classification category of the incident from a predefined list. You can create customized lists if you want, but do not delete the out-of-the-box lists, because some out-of-the-box MPs refer to or need those default lists. The same goes for the values inside a list: Do not delete them; some workflows use them. You can rename the values as necessary, as the GUID will not change. Figure 8.30 shows an example of a list in Service Manager.

FIGURE 8.30 Customize lists.

▶ **Queues:** Queues are used to manage work items. Queues are very similar to groups, because a queue is a way to group work items of the same type. You can create queues for incidents, problems, change requests, and activities. For example, you can create a queue to show only SQL incidents and scope control to the SQL administrators and use that same queue to create a notification subscription based on this queue. For more information about queues and using them for Incident, Problem, and Change Management, see Chapter 10, Chapter 11, and Chapter 12, respectively. Chapter 10 discusses how to create an incident queue.

Work Items Workspace

This area is where you create work items and work with work items such as change requests, incidents, activities, and problems, as shown in Figure 8.31. You can scope this workspace to different security roles to fit your organization's requirements. Here are some of the different sections under this workspace:

▶ **Incident Management:** You can find more information about Incident Management in Service Manager in Chapter 10.

▶ **Problem Management:** You can find more information about Problem Management in Service Manager in Chapter 11, "Problem Management."

▶ **Change Management:** You can find more information about Change Management in Service Manager in Chapter 12, "Change Management."

▶ **Activity Management:** You can find more information about Activity Management in Service Manager in Chapter 12.

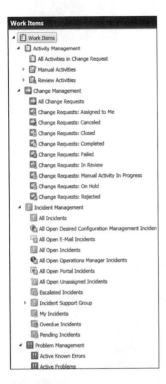

FIGURE 8.31   Work Items workspace.

Configuration Items Workspace

The Configuration Items workspace, shown in Figure 8.32, is where you can look at your CIs. This is the workspace where you can see all computers or open the properties of a specific computer to see how many CPUs it has. You can extend Service Manager 2010 with more CI classes, such as one for projects; these additional classes can be shown in this workspace.

The Configuration Items workspace includes a default set of views automatically populated based on the CIs in the CMDB. Computer objects from Active Directory, Configuration Manager, and Operations Manager are visible in the Computer view, and you will see distributed applications from OpsMgr in the Business Services view. However, you can easily customize the Configuration Items view, as shown in Figure 8.32. This shows a new folder named OdysseyCIs, which contains the custom CIs from the Odyssey company's CIs. These custom views can show you CIs imported through a CSV connector or other connector.

FIGURE 8.32   Configuration Items workspace with CustomizeCIs folder.

Let's say you are a large SharePoint shop and use Operations Manager to monitor SharePoint. Utilizing the OpsMgr CI connector between Operations Manager and Service Manager will populate the CMDB with your SharePoint websites and properties once you import the Operations Manager SharePoint MP. Service Manager, unlike Operations Manager, does not automatically create views when MPs are imported. To see imported SharePoint items in the Service Manager console, you must create a custom CI view targeted at the SharePoint class. To create a new CI view, follow these steps:

1. In the Service Manager console, open the Configuration Item workspace.
2. In the Tasks pane on the right side of the console, select **Create new folder**.
3. Once your custom folder is created, again on the right side select **Create View**.
4. In the Choose class form, browse for the SharePoint class you need.
5. On the Display tab, customize your view to show the properties of your selected class that are of interest.

Data Warehouse Workspace

The Data Warehouse workspace, displayed in Figure 8.33, is visible if you install the Service Manager Data Warehouse component. In this workspace, administrators can work with data warehouse settings and configure high-level settings of the Data Warehouse management group. The data warehouse used in Service Manager is designed to ultimately be the System Center data warehouse and not only the Service Manager data warehouse. As such, its security is separate from Service Manager. During data warehouse setup, the account or group specified during installation is placed into the Administrators role in the data warehouse management group.

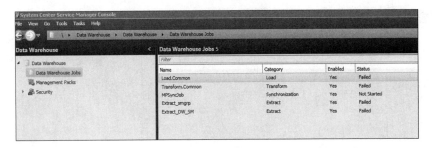

FIGURE 8.33   The Data Warehouse workspace.

To save historical data for long-term reporting, you must register your Service Manager management group with a Data Warehouse management group.

NOTE: PERMISSIONS REQUIRED TO REGISTER

To run the Data Warehouse Registration wizard successfully, you must be a member of the Service Manager Administrators security group, as well as a member of the Data Warehouse Administrators security group. The authors recommend using the same security group for the Service Manager Administrators security group and the Data Warehouse Administrators security group.

To register your server, follow these steps:

1. In the Administration workspace in the Service Manager console, select **Register with Data Warehouse Server** and click **Next**.

2. In the Specify the data warehouse management server name dialog, specify the name of your Data Warehouse server. This is shown in Figure 8.34.

3. On the next screen (see Figure 8.35), use the default credentials provided or specify your own credentials. These are used to connect to the Service Manager management server and Service Manager database. The account used here will be granted read permissions on the database and administrative permissions on the Service Manager server.

4. If, like the authors, you prefer to work as granularly as possible and keep control over the accounts used in Service Manager, create and specify a new Run As Account, as shown in Figure 8.36, which will be used only for reporting.

5. On the Summary screen, verify all the configuration settings are correct and click **Create** to register the data warehouse.

Once the data warehouse is registered, your Service Manager server will deploy MPs to the Data Warehouse management server. You should see the event shown in Figure 8.37 with Event ID 1204 in the Operations Manager event log, indicating the MP deployment process is occurring. Note that this might take several hours.

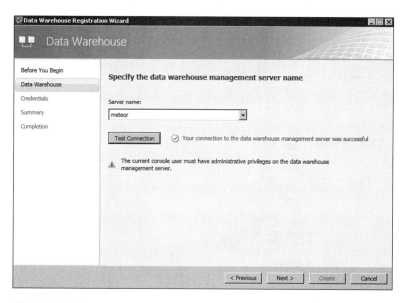

FIGURE 8.34   Specify the Data Warehouse server.

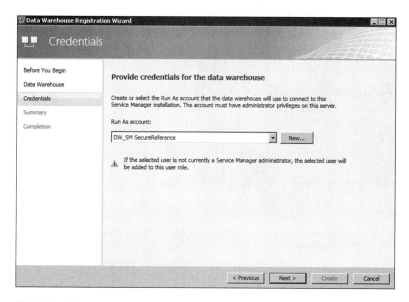

FIGURE 8.35   Specifying security credentials.

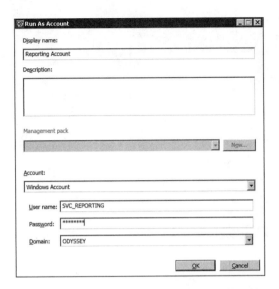

FIGURE 8.36   Creating a new Run As Account.

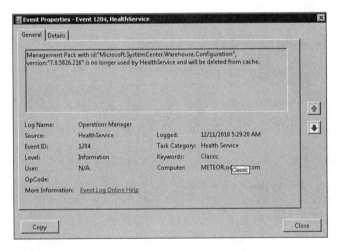

FIGURE 8.37   Outdated Management Pack server configuration will be deleted.

When the new configuration becomes active, you will see the event displayed in Figure 8.38 in the Operations Manager event log with Event ID 1210.

You can view the process of what occurs after the data warehouse is registered in the Operations Manager event log. When the new configuration becomes active, a new job is created on your Service Manager server, as shown in Figure 8.39.

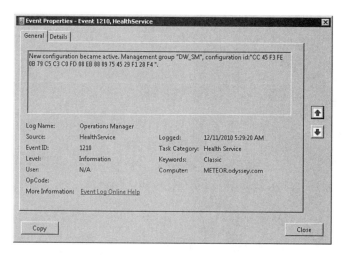

FIGURE 8.38   New Data Warehouse configuration is active.

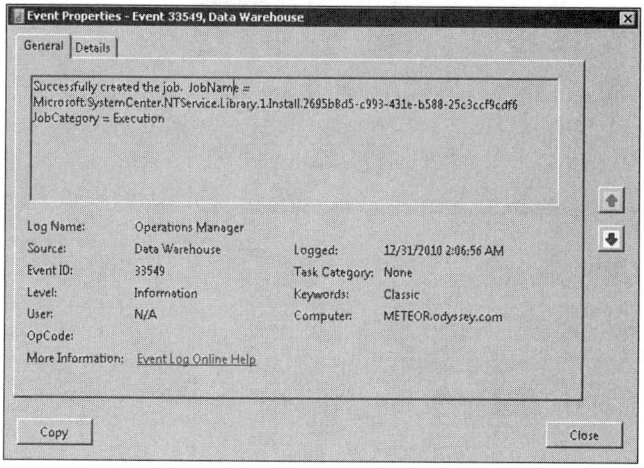

FIGURE 8.39   New MPsync job created.

With the Data Warehouse management server registered and the MPsync job created, synchronization and deployment of the MPs can begin. This is indicated in Figure 8.40.

You can also verify the status of the Data Warehouse jobs in the Service Manager console under the Data Warehouse workspace, shown in Figure 8.41.

Reporting Workspace

If you installed the Service Manager data warehouse, the Reporting workspace is visible as shown in Figure 8.42. The Reporting workspace enables you to run reports against your data warehouse, such as the number of incidents last week or the most common change category.

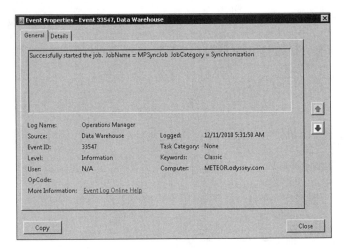

FIGURE 8.40   MPsync job started.

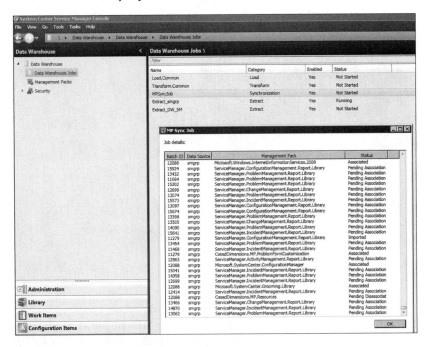

FIGURE 8.41   Viewing Data Warehouse jobs.

To be able to access reports in the Service Manager console, a user must be a member of the Report Users user role in the Data Warehouse management group. A data warehouse administrator can manage the membership of the Report Users user role from the User Roles view in the Data Warehouse workspace. The user must be granted permissions in SQL Server Reporting Services to at least some of the reports under the System Center -> Service Manager folder.

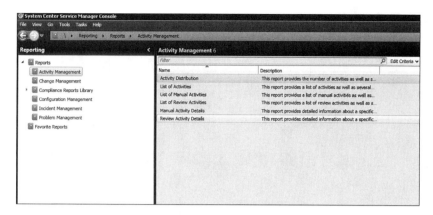

FIGURE 8.42   The Reporting workspace in the Service Manager console.

About the Service Manager PowerShell Console

PowerShell is Microsoft's next-generation scripting and shell language. Based on Microsoft's .NET framework, PowerShell runs on Windows operating systems beginning with Windows XP, and is included with Windows 2008 builds. PowerShell is part of Microsoft's Common Engineering Criteria (CEC), meaning that all Microsoft server products must provide some level of PowerShell support.

PowerShell plays a very important role in managing Service Manager. PowerShell lets you automate and enable some Service Manger administrative tasks. For example, you can easily export all your MPs using the Export-SCSMManagementPack cmdlet.

Installed with the Service Manager 2010 product are the Service Manager cmdlets for Windows PowerShell. To start using these cmdlets, follow these steps:

1. Open a PowerShell window on your Service Manager management server.

2. Type the following:

```
Add-PSSnapIn SMCmdletsSnapIn
```

For more information about the PowerShell snap-in and cmdlets, see Chapter 4, "Looking Inside Service Manager."

Using the Self-Service Portal

The end user interacts with Service Manager through the Self-Service portal. The end user portion of the console enables users to report incidents, read announcements and IT-related news, search knowledge articles, and request software. The software provisioning components require Service Manager is connected to Configuration Manager, which manages the end user computers. If you run Forefront Identity Lifecycle Management and connect it to Service Manager, end users can also reset passwords from the portal. Figure 8.43 displays the Self-Service portal.

8

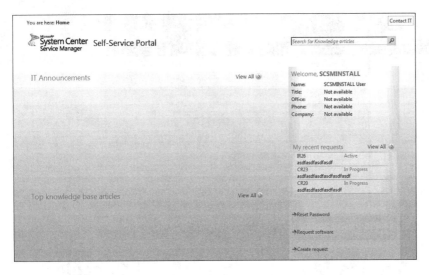

FIGURE 8.43   Self-Service portal.

CHANGING THE RECYCLE INTERVAL IN IIS TO HELP RESPONSE TIME

If you encounter slow response times from the Self-Service portal, you can change the recycle interval of the Application pool in Internet Information Services (IIS) to never recycle, as follows:

1. Open IIS Manager and go to the Application Pools section.
2. Open Advanced Settings and scroll down until you see Regular Time Interval (Minutes) and change it to **0** (never recycle), as shown in Figure 8.44.

TIP: TARGET SOFTWARE PACKAGES TO SPECIFIC USERS

A question that comes up is whether you can target software packages to specific users. Software packages are targeted toward all users by default, which means any authenticated user can see and request all software packages. To target software packages, read Anders Bengtsson's blog post at http://contoso.se/blog/?p=1269.

One of the features of the Self-Service portal is the ability for the end user to reset his password. Microsoft intends to leverage Forefront Identity Manager (FIM) in this process.

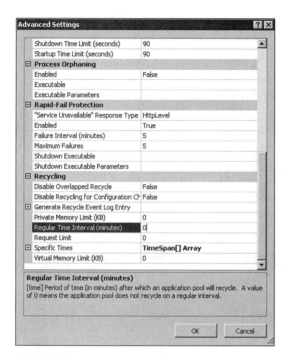

FIGURE 8.44   Change the recycle intervals in IIS.

TIP: RESET PASSWORD WITH SERVICE MANAGER

There are several ways to reset a user's password without implementing FIM. Anders Bengtsson describes an approach that sends the user a new password in an email and creates a closed incident. Creating a closed incident enables the Service Desk to track the number of password reset incidents. Read the post at http://contoso.se/blog/?p=1605.

If you don't want users to reset their passwords because you don't have the tools (such as FIM) implemented yet, you can disable the Reset password link on the website, as follows:

1. Open Windows Explorer and navigate to c:\inetpub\wwwroot\System Center Service Manager Portal\EndUser.

2. Right-click **Home.aspx** and select **Open With -> Notepad**.

3. Search for **SM_WebParts:HomePageTasks ID="HomePageTasksWebPart"**.

4. Add the following attributes to the file:

```
ShowResetPasswordLink="false"
```

The string should now look like this:

```
for <SM_WebParts:HomePageTasks ID="HomePageTasksWebPart"
Title="   "ShowResetPasswordLink="false"/>
```

5. Make the same change to these files:

- ▶ c:\inetpub\wwwroot\System Center Service Manager Portal\EndUser\MasterPages\ServiceManagerPortal.master

- ▶ c:\inetpub\wwwroot\System Center Service Manager Portal\EndUser\MasterPages\ServiceManagerCommandsMaster.master

Figure 8.45 shows the effect of this change. On the left side, you will see the original website with the reset password link visible; on the right side, the reset-password link is no longer visible.

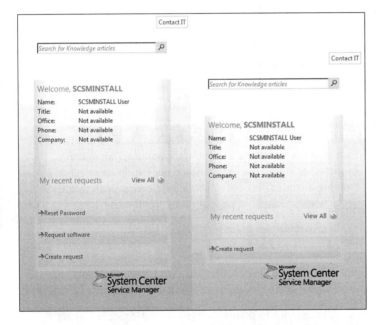

FIGURE 8.45   Results of disabling the Reset Password list.

> **TIP: SELF-SERVICE PORTAL SOURCE CODE AVAILABLE**
>
> Microsoft has made the Self-Service portal source code available, enabling you to create and customize your own portal! Microsoft also added some new features to this version, such as being able to update an incident from the portal. You can download the source code from http://www.microsoft.com/downloads/en/details.aspx?FamilyID=65fbe0a3-1928-469f-b941-146d27aa6bac&displaylang=en. For more information and a preview of how you can customize the portal, see http://blogs.technet.com/b/servicemanager/archive/2011/03/02/service-manager-portal-source-code-released.aspx.

About the Analyst Portal

Analysts can use a part of the portal to work with change requests—for example to review and approve change requests. They can also get an overview of the number of active changes and changes within their area. Figure 8.46 shows the Analyst portal.

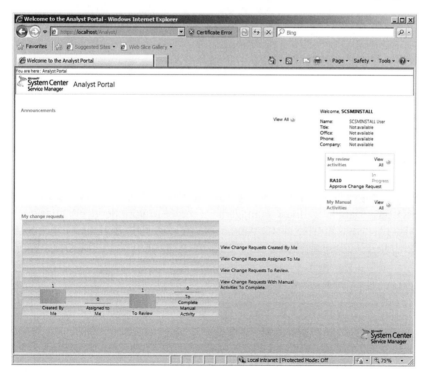

FIGURE 8.46   Analyst portal.

About the Authoring Tool

The Service Manager Authoring Tool is used by developers to create customized Service Manager MPs. Figure 8.47 shows the Authoring Tool.

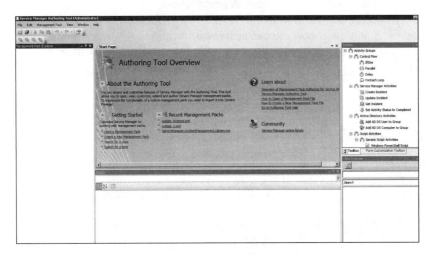

FIGURE 8.47   Service Manager Authoring Tool.

The Authoring Tool is discussed in Chapter 18, "Customizing Service Manager," and Chapter 19, "Advanced Customization Scenarios."

Summary

This chapter discussed the various Service Manager consoles and their functionalities. It covered how to register a Data Warehouse management server to your Service Manager environment. It also discussed how to create connectors to store data in the CMDB from Operations Manager, Configuration Manager, Active Directory, or even from a CSV file.

CHAPTER 9

Business Services

Operations Manager (OpsMgr) 2007 introduced the visual representation of a service, using the distributed application feature. The distributed application designer (DAD) in Operations Manager enables you to define groups of components that your service includes. You can then use the distributed application to scope security roles, reports, and views to work with your service, regardless of where the components are physically located.

Service Manager 2010 introduces business services as a virtual representation of a service from the business and user perspective, a perspective that will show dependencies, responsibilities, and settings.

Service Manager combines business services with Operation Manager's distributed applications to get a complete *service map* (introduced in Chapter 3, "MOF, ITIL, and Service Manager"), which is a logical view of the service:

▶ Service Manager provides soft properties of this map, such as affected users and the service owner.

▶ Operations Manager supplies all components and settings.

Together, the combination gives you a powerful and complete view into your services.

This chapter discusses how you can create and maintain business services, and how to use them in your daily work.

Introducing Service Manager Business Services

Business services is an approach for viewing and presenting Information Technology (IT) services from a business and user perspective. A business service or a service map is helpful in almost all areas of operations management as well in change management and when designing new infrastructures. The business service will show you relationships defined among services, and how the different services affect each other; this can help your support team in troubleshooting problems. This same relationship mapping can also proactively assist in defining dependencies when planning changes and assessing risks associated with those changes. The service ownership identified in the service map can help ensure proper problem escalation and identify approvers for a change against a business service.

An organization-wide service map shows the relationships between a single server or service to all other components in the organization. It enables the organization to easily identify how a simple change can cause a chain reaction affecting multiple other services and service areas, and the business as a whole.

Business Service Defined

A distributed application in Service Manager contains a large number of properties and attributes presented in the user interface by a number of tabs, as shown in Figure 9.1, which displays a service map for the Messaging Service. You can customize your business services to include more attributes as needed.

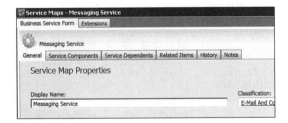

FIGURE 9.1   Tabs of a Business Service Form.

The Notes tab on the rightmost portion of Figure 9.1 enables you to insert notes about your service. You will not want to not store any important information here; important information should have its own property instead.

The History tab, also displayed in Figure 9.1, is managed by Service Manager and does not require any manual entry. As shown by the example in Figure 9.2, Service Manager keeps a record of all changes made to an object. If you update any property or edit a relationship of an object, that activity is recorded in the history.

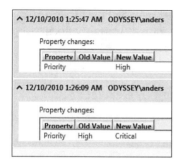

FIGURE 9.2   History record of a business service.

Here is how this information can be useful:

▶ To see what was changed, and when it was changed.

For example, you can determine when extra memory was added to a computer or when an Internet Information Services (IIS) site was removed from a web farm.

▶ To find out who changed something.

You would want to know who changed the priority of the service to Low, resulting in engineers on duty not being notified about alerts occurring in the middle of the night!

You can also use this information to see if a change was made in connection with a change made to an object. If this is not the case, there could be an audit problem when performing an audit against the configuration management database (CMDB).

The Related Items tab in Figure 9.3 shows you other objects within Service Manager related to this business service:

▶ The Work items affecting this configuration item section shows all incidents, problems, and change requests that have this business service as an affected item. These work items are directly related to this configuration item (CI). An example is change requests about upgrading this service.

▶ The Work Items area shows you all work items to which this business service is related. For example, this could be a change that has the business service as a related item, but not as the service that will be changed. For example, if you are going to change a router, it can affect a number of services, even if they are not the direct target for the change.

▶ The Configuration Items section shows you configuration items (CIs) related to this business service. Figure 9.3 shows this text box.

▶ Knowledge Articles shows you all knowledge articles related to this business service. This could be documentation or related user guides.

▶ Attached Files (not displayed in Figure 9.3) shows all files uploaded to this business service. This could be guides in a non-knowledge article format, warranty documents, or configuration files.

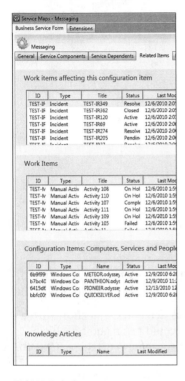

FIGURE 9.3   Related items in a business service.

Attributes of a Business Service

A significant amount of information is associated with a business service. Tables 9.1, 9.2, and 9.3 provide information about each property of a business service object and its purpose.

TABLE 9.1   The General Properties Tab of a Business Service

Property	Description
Display Name	The name of the service (Messaging Service, for example).
Classification	The type of service. For example, this could be an internal application or storage. You can use this setting to calculate how critical an incident or change is, based on the service classification and priority. You can modify this list in the Library workspace. The list name is Service Classification.
Owned By Organization	The person or organization that provides the service (for example, the messaging team).

TABLE 9.1   The General Properties Tab of a Business Service

Property	Description
Priority	The priority of the service. This setting can be used to calculate how critical an incident or change is, based on the service classification and priority. This list can be modified in the Library workspace. The list name is Service Priority.
Status	Status shows you the state in which the service is. This setting can be used to calculate how to work with change requests, incidents, and problems. For example, if there is an incident reported related to this service and the service is in maintenance, the incident will not get the priority as if the service was in service. This list can be modified in the Library workspace. The list name is Service Status.
Availability Schedule	Availability agreements describe the availability of a CI within a specified period. For example, office hours would have 100% availability. A good practice is to decide in which format you will input this value in your organization, because there is no drop-down list from which to pick. An example is 24/7/365, which means 24 hours, 7 days a week, 365 days a year.
Service Owner	The service owner is responsible for delivering the service within the service level. Most often, the service owner is the leader for the team of engineers or specialists that owns the service.
Service contacts	Individuals to contact about the service. Sometimes it is suitable to extend this field with information about the roles each service contact has. For example, if the contact is a service engineer, technical specialist, or perhaps a team leader. This is the contact for all daily questions.
Service customers	Persons using the service as one of their primary tools. Who are customers is controlled by the service contract.
Affected users	Persons affected if the service is not working. They are not using the tool as one of their primary tools.

TABLE 9.2   Properties of the Service Components Tab of a Business Service

Property	Description
Service Components	This field shows all components in the business service. Components are based on a distributed application from Operations Manager.
Properties of the selected item	This field shows you the class name and name of the selected component. You can use the Open button to open the properties of the CI. For example, if you select a site link, you can see it is an instance of the `Microsoft.Windows.Server.AD.ConnectionObject` class, but if you open the Properties, you can see transport type and all other attributes of the CI.

9

TABLE 9.2   Properties of the Service Components Tab of a Business Service

Property	Description
Related work items for the selected item	This field shows you related items. For example, if a CI in the business service is added as an affected item in an incident, that incident will be shown in this field.

TABLE 9.3   Properties of the Services Dependents Tab of a Business Service

Property	Description
Service Dependents	This shows all CIs the business service is dependent on. You should add other business services here, to minimize number of objects in the list and ensure you get an easy overview of the list of service dependents. If you add each component one by one, the list will be difficult to go through and the overview of what CIs your business service is dependent on will be difficult to see.
	This list will also show you whether the business services this service depends on is currently affected by an incident or change request. Use the drop-down menu on the right-hand side to expand business services to see subcomponents; this is a way to investigate which component is affected by a change request or incident.
Properties of the selected item	This field shows the class name and name of the selected component. You can use the Open button to open up properties of the CI. For example, if you select a Windows Computer, you can see it is an instance of the `Microsoft.Windows.Computer` class, but if you open the Properties, you can see all other attributes of the CI, such as hardware and software.
Related work items for the selected item	This field shows you related items. For example, if the CI is added as the affected item in an incident, that incident is shown in this field.

NOTE: SELECTING OBJECTS

You can select only one object at a time when working within service maps. Do not attempt to add multiple objects at the same time.

Using Operations Manager with Business Services

Operations Manager is Microsoft's software tool for solving operation management problems and is a key component in Microsoft's management strategy and System Center product suite. Operations Manager is a comprehensive operations management solution, using an agent-based centralized management model to localize data collection while centralizing collected data and agent configuration information. Operations Manager 2007 provides the following benefits:

▶ **End-to-end service management:** This is the capacity to integrate application, client, server, and synthetic transaction monitoring into a single end-to-end solution. Service-oriented views and availability reporting enables your operations team and IT management to get the information needed to quickly identify and resolve issues that affect service levels. You get end-to-end management without the day-to-day drama.

▶ **Best-of-breed for Windows:** Operations Manager expertise from the Microsoft server, client, and application teams provides you with prescriptive knowledge and automated inline tasks that improve monitoring, troubleshooting, and problem resolution for more than 60 Microsoft applications and Windows Server components. Operations Manager also includes problem management and troubleshooting of client computers to accelerate identifying and resolving end-user issues. Microsoft also provides management packs for non-Microsoft devices such as UNIX and Linux. Operations Manager also supports monitoring of network devices.

▶ **Increased efficiency and control of your IT environment:** Operations Manager automates routine and redundant tasks, providing intelligent reporting and monitoring that can help increase efficiency and control of your environment. Its scalability can support organizations with tens of thousands of managed servers and hundreds of thousands of managed clients, using multiple management servers and connected management groups for a consolidated view of your entire enterprise.

Agents operate under sophisticated sets of rules, collected in management packs (MPs). These MPs, which are models based on the Service Modeling Language (SML) schema, allow the rules to be targeted to just the systems that need them. Operations Manager uses SML to monitor not only servers, but also logical services. Using this service-centric view, Operations Manager can understand service and application structures, and monitors the overall health of services and applications by viewing the state of any object. Problems identified by these rules can be acted on by operational and system personnel; the results collected by this process can be analyzed and published using Operations Manager's dashboard and reporting capabilities.

Distributed Applications

Distributed applications are one of the most powerful features of Operations Manager. When you incorporate robust monitoring of your IT environment, you can create a distributed application that shows an overall monitoring state, as in Figure 9.4. You can use the distributed application to show all components of a service, from the end user to the hardware in a server; this is also known as *end-to-end monitoring*.

Early monitoring software focused on servers and devices. Problematic to that focus was the alerts were very isolated and narrow in scope. Today, with applications and services spanning multiple servers and locations, an isolated alert saying some Windows service is unavailable simply does not provide enough information.

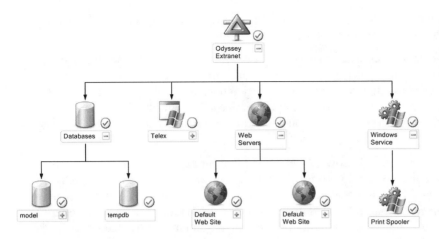

FIGURE 9.4   An Operations Manager distributed application.

Using an Operations Manager distributed application lets you monitor the service from all angles. If any service component fails or is not working as needed, the entire distributed application is indicated as unhealthy. You can then use the distributed application to drill down to see which component is the root cause. This enables you to easily identify the failing component within the monitoring solution, which in turn decreases troubleshooting reaction time. In addition to Windows components, Operations Manager supports Linux, UNIX, and network devices. You can include all types of components in a distributed application.

A distributed application is based on a number of component groups that work in conjunction with one another. A component group is a logical group of components, almost like a folder containing files. Figure 9.4 shows an example with one component group for databases and another for web servers. You can create relationships between component groups. This relationship is for display purposes only; it does not affect the health rollup or how alerts are generated.

Before you can include objects in a distributed application, Operations Manager must discover those objects. An important consideration when planning your distributed applications is that a distributed application can only have relationships between objects already known to Operations Manager. In some scenarios, it is easier to create the relationships directly in eXtensible Markup Language (XML) in an MP than to use the distributed application editor built into the Operations Manager console. An example is if you do not want to use the default component box; instead, you build your own custom structure of the application.

Distributed Application Best Practices

Some MPs, such as the Microsoft Active Directory MP and Microsoft Exchange MP, come with predefined distributed applications. In these cases, the MP automatically keeps these distributed applications up-to-date. When building custom distributed applications, it can be difficult to determine what to include. Consider an example where you want to use the distributed application for availability monitoring and run service level agreement (SLA) reports based on it.

In this case, you do not want to include every component of a service. Suppose your IT organization is responsible for maintaining a web shop that includes a number of web servers in a web farm and a SQL Server cluster. The cluster has two nodes. If you were to include both nodes and all 20 web services in your distributed application, and the passive SQL cluster node has a problem, the application will show availability is affected. However, in this particular instance, the health of the passive cluster actually does not affect the availability of the service. In this situation, you do not want the incident to roll up and affect the availability and decrease the percentage uptime in the SLA report.

Instead, you create two distributed applications:

▶ **An application used as a foundation for SLA monitoring:** This includes only components that will affect the availability of the service.

▶ **An application used by engineers:** This version includes all components. This view can be used for troubleshooting by the group that is operating and maintaining it.

Building distributed applications that will be transferred to Service Manager adds another layer of complexity. A business service or a service map is a graphical description. Here are the five component categories into which you can categorize most service map components:

▶ **Software:** All software associated with the service, including all supporting or dependent software. For example, this could be Windows Server 2008 R2 Service Pack (SP) 1 and network software.

▶ **Hardware:** All servers, network devices, and hardware devices that the service requires to function. This should also include model and configuration (for example, HP DL 380 G6).

▶ **Services:** Other services this service requires to function. Services can be divided into two subcategories:

　▶ **Upstream:** Upstream services are services that will provide this service with required input.

　▶ **Downstream:** Downstream services are services this service will provide with input. For example, Microsoft Exchange will rely on downstream services such as Active Directory and backup.

▶ **Settings:** All configuration settings that the service requires to work. This could include server roles such as database server or reporting server, and also Internet Protocol (IP) addresses.

▶ **Customers:** Information about the customer of the service, with examples being the accounts payable department and geographical regions. This category is metadata that you will add in Service Manager.

Some settings data can be synchronized from Operations Manager, but some will need to be added in Service Manager. You can document settings and related items to your business service in Service Manager. You must build the other categories' components in Operations Manager before importing the distributed application into Service Manager.

As services change over time, business services existing in Service Manager and distributed in Operations Manager need to be updated periodically to ensure they correctly represent the real world. Both the organizational structure and technical components may change over time. Organizational structure changes are generally updated in Service Manager, with technical components updated in Operations Manager. For example, the Microsoft Exchange team might be migrated into a messaging team, or new Exchange clusters are added to the service. These changes need to be updated in both the distributed application and the business service.

Maintenance of business services and distributed applications requires the following activities:

▶ An owner should be assigned to each business service and distributed application, with the responsibility for keeping them updated. The owner should be someone with knowledge about the service, perhaps the original architect who built the first version.

▶ At least once each quarter, there should be a review of the distributed application and business service. This review should also review knowledge articles in Service Manager and verify that the monitoring in Operations Manager is carried out in an optimized way. It is also recommended to include this review in the change management process. If anything changes that will affect the structure of the distributed application or the metadata of the business service, it should be updated in the same process.

You can use Microsoft Operations Framework (MOF) for guidance to build and maintain a service map. Building a service map is often a quick endeavor when you have gathered all the necessary information. The challenge can be to get everyone engaged in the project and make sure everyone understands the value of a complete service map. Here are the steps to build a service map:

1. **Identify the team:** To build a correct service map and in the prolongation a business service in Service Manager, you must have deep knowledge about the service. This step makes sure that the correct knowledge is included in the project group.

2. **Define the mapping template:** This step establishes a guideline to how a service map should look. For example, a service map might include naming standards and software to use.

3. **Determine the appropriate level of resolution:** How many details will be included? Maps with more details are often better to use and provide more value to the organization. On the other hand, more details make maps much more complex to maintain and build.

4. **Select services for mapping:** This step will help you identify which services to map. A good rule could be to start with the top most customer-facing services.

5. **Gather data and draw the service maps:** Collect all data needed and draw the first version of the map.

6. **Establish service relationships:** Investigate and add to your map all relationships between your service and other services.

7. **Maintain the service maps:** Establish a plan for how to maintain and update the map.

Creating a Business Service

The following example creates a distributed application in Operations Manager and synchronizes it to Service Manager 2010 as a business service. The application is called Odyssey Extranet and contains several databases and websites. It also includes one Windows service. The procedure first builds the distributed application with the Operations Manager console, and then exports the MP and imports it into Service Manager. When you are building business services, you often use components from a number of MPs, meaning your business service will depend on a number of other MPs. All dependent MPs must also be imported into Service Manager 2010. To create a distributed application in Operations Manager, perform these steps:

1. In the Operations Manager console, navigate to the Authoring workspace and the distributed application node.

2. In the Actions pane, select **Create a New Distributed Application**.

3. In the Distributed Application Designed window, click **New** to create a new MP.

4. In the Create a Management Pack window, input the following information and then click **Next**:

   ▸ Name: **Odyssey Extranet**

   ▸ Description: **Management Pack for Odyssey Extranet**

5. In the Knowledge window, click **Create** to create the MP. You have now created an unsealed MP in which to store your distributed application. The associated monitors and rules become part of that MP.

6. In the Distributed Application Designer window, input the following information:

   ▸ Name: **Odyssey Extranet**

   ▸ Description: **Odyssey Extranet for customers**

   ▸ Template: **Blank (Advanced)**

7. Click **OK** in the Distributed Application Designer window. The distributed application designer will now open, as shown in Figure 9.5.

FIGURE 9.5   The panes of the Operations Manager distributed application designer.

The Distributed Application Designer window shown in Figure 9.5 is divided into a number of panes:

▶ The Diagram pane (1) is the distributed application designer drawing board. This is where you draw your distributed application, which will become the structure for your business service in Service Manager 2010. You add component boxes to categorize the application components.

▶ Click **Add Component** (5) to create a component box. In the example in this section, you need one component for SQL databases, one for Internet Information Services (IIS) websites, and one for the Windows service. The Object pane (3) shows you all components that you can drag and drop to your component groups.

▶ Click **Create Relationship** (2) on the toolbar to use a cursor to draw relationships that describe the workflow between the component groups of your distributed application.

▶ Click **Save** (4) on the toolbar to save the distributed application to an unsealed MP (in this case, the Odyssey Extranet MP).

To add objects to the distributed application, follow these steps:

1. In the distributed application designer, click **Add Component**.

2. In the Create New Component Group dialog box, input **Databases** as the name for your component group. In the objects list, select **Application Component/Database/SQL Database**. Click **OK**.

   Note that on the left side of the distributed application designer, in the Object pane, you now see all databases. Because the component was configured to only accept SQL databases, you will only see this type of object.

3. In the distributed application designer, from the object list, drag and drop several databases to the Databases component group.

4. In the distributed application designer, click **Add Component**.

5. In the Create New Component Group dialog box, type **Web Servers** as the name for your component group. In the objects list, select **Application Component/Web Site/IIS Web Site**. Click **OK**.

6. In the distributed application designer, from the object list, drag and drop several IIS websites to the Web Servers component group.

7. In the distributed application designer, click **Add Component**.

8. In the Create New Component Group dialog box, input **Windows Service** as the name for your component group. In the objects list, select **Local Application/Windows Local Application/Windows Local Service/Windows Service/Windows Service**. Click **OK**.

9. In the distributed application designer, from the object list, drag and drop a Windows service to the Windows Service component group.

10. Save the distributed application and close the distributed application designer.

11. In the Operations Manager console, right-click the **Odyssey Extranet** distributed application and select **View Diagram View** from the menu. A Diagram view will open and show you the distributed application, as in Figure 9.6.

NOTE: DISTRIBUTED APPLICATION STATE CALCULATED

If you have a large deployment, a delay might occur between the time a new distributed application is created and when its state is calculated. Until rollup configuration is calculated, the state is displayed as unmonitored (white icon).

After creating the distributed application in Operations Manager, you need to export the MP. Version 1 of Service Manager (Service Manager 2010) does not include automatic synchronization of MPs between Operations Manager and Service Manager. If an MP in Operations Manager is changed, you must manually export it and import it into Service Manager. Using an administration workstation with both the Service Manager and Operations Manager consoles makes the process of exporting and importing MPs easier, because you don't need to transfer files between servers and can just perform all steps from the same desktop.

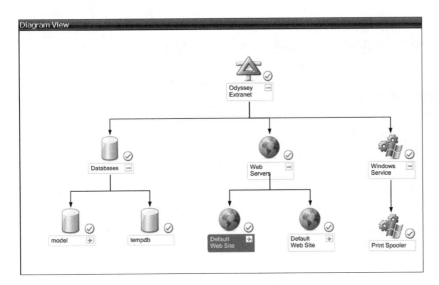

FIGURE 9.6   The Odyssey Extranet distributed application.

When exporting MPs from Operations Manager, you can use the Operations Manager Shell, which is a PowerShell snap-in, or the Operations Manager console. If you have a large number of MPs to export or need to automate the process, you might want to use a script. To export the Odyssey Extranet MP from the console, follow these steps:

1. In the Operations Manager console, navigate to the Administration workspace and the Management Packs node.

2. In the Result pane showing the list of MPs, select the **Odyssey Extranet** MP. Click **Export Management Pack** from the Actions pane.

3. In the Browse for Folder dialog box, select the target folder for the MP. Export it to (for example) **C:\MP Export**.

4. In the System Center Operations Manager pop-up window, verify that the export was successful and then click **OK**.

To achieve the same task with Operations Manager Shell, follow these steps:

1. From the Start menu, start the Operations Manager Shell.

2. In the Operations Manager Shell, type the following command:

    ```
    get-managementpack ¦ where {$_.displayname -eq "Odyssey Extranet"}
    ¦ export-managementpack -path "C:\MP Export"
    ```

If you need to determine the MPs your MP depends on, follow the steps in this next example:

1. In the Operations Manager console, navigate to the Administration workspace and the Management Packs node.

2. In the Result pane of the list of MPs, select the **Odyssey Extranet** MP, and then click **Properties** from the Actions pane.

3. In the Odyssey Extranet window, click the **Dependencies** tab. You will see a list of the MPs that depend on this MP and the MPs this MP depends on, as shown in Figure 9.7.

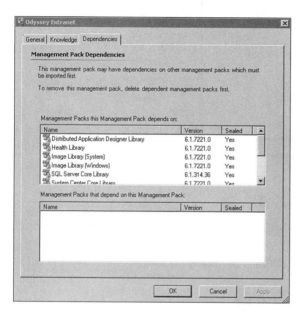

FIGURE 9.7   Dependencies of the Odyssey Extranet MP.

Next in this process is to import the Odyssey Extranet MP into Service Manager 2010. To import the MP into Service Manager using the Service Manager console, follow these steps:

1. In the Service Manager console, navigate to the Administration workspace and the Management Packs node.

2. Select **Import** in the Tasks pane.

3. In the Select Management Packs to Import window, browse and select the MP you exported (for example, the MP in C:\MP Export).

4. In the Import Management Packs window, click **Import**. The first time you do this, you will most likely get the error message shown in Figure 9.8. Service Manager is telling you that there are missing MPs that your MP depends on. You need to import these MPs first.

It is sometimes difficult to find the MPs to import or understand which MPs are required. As you can see in Figure 9.8, Service Manager displays the IDs of MPs, not the friendly name. Figure 9.9 shows the Windows Server Internet Information Services Library MP file, part of the IIS MP. In the console, the MP is displayed as Windows Service Internet Information Services Library, but behind the console, Service Manager and Operations Manager is calling it by its ID `Microsoft.Windows.InternetInformationServices.CommonLibrary`. You can use the Operations Manager Authoring console to find the internal MP name.

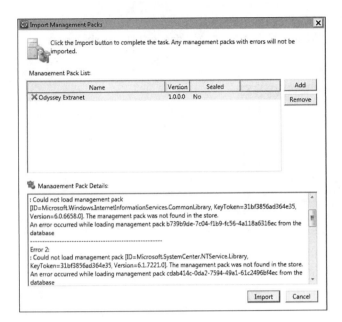

FIGURE 9.8   Error displayed when dependent MPs are not found.

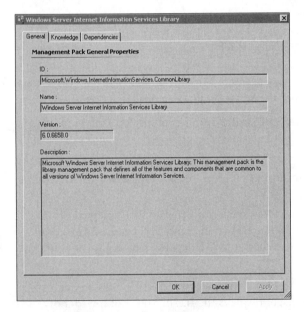

FIGURE 9.9   The MP name and its associated ID.

In some cases, you can download MPs directly from the Microsoft website, such as the SQL and IIS MPs in this example. You can often copy core Operations Manager MPs from the Operations Manager installation folder on your management server.

After importing all MPs your MP depends on and finally your own unsealed MP, verify that the import is successfully, as shown in Figure 9.10.

FIGURE 9.10   Successful import of MP into Service Manager.

If you open the Properties page of your new business service (in this example, the Odyssey Extranet business service), you will not see any service components on the service components tab. There will not be any service components until you enable synchronization. To enable synchronization for the Odyssey Extranet MP, follow these steps:

1. In the Service Manager console, navigate to the Administration workspace and the Connectors node.

2. In the Result pane, select the **Operations Manager CI** connector and click **Edit** in the Tasks pane.

3. In the Edit dialog box, select the **Management Pack** tab.

4. On the Management Packs tab, click the **Refresh** button to refresh the list of MPs to synchronize.

5. In the Management Pack list, ensure the **Odyssey Extranet** MP is selected. Click **OK**.

6. In the Result pane, select the **Operations Manager CI** connector and click **Synchronize Now** in the Tasks pane.

9

NOTE: SYNCHRONIZATION OF SERVICE COMPONENTS

The Operations CI connector transfers configuration items from Operations Manager to the Service Manager database (CMDB). These components are the components that you see in your business service as service components. This connector needs to run successfully before your service components are listed in the business service.

7. Verify that the connector status is first Running and then changes to Finished Success. Note at this point that the Operations Manager CI connector has not synchronized with Operations Manager.

8. Navigate to the Configuration Items workspace in the Service Manager console. Expand Business Services and select the **Odyssey Extranet** business service. Click **Edit** in the Tasks pane.

9. In the Service Maps - Odyssey Extranet window, click the **Service Components** tab and verify you see all the components of the service, as shown in Figure 9.11.

If you are missing any components in the Service Components view, you most likely are missing an MP or have not configured the connector to synchronize it.

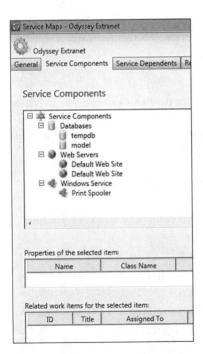

FIGURE 9.11   Components of the Odyssey Extranet.

On the right side of the Service Components field, you can expand the drop-down menu to show more or fewer components and subcomponents in the service component field.

With all the components in place and a business service object, you can now start to fill in the rest of the information for this business service, such as service owner and affected users.

Non-Operations Manager Components

In some scenarios, you will need to include components in your business service that you don't have in Operations Manager. Because all business services are built with a distributed application as a foundation, you always need to include the objects in a distributed application first. This is not a problem with normal components like SQL Server databases, logical disks, and Apache web servers. However, if you need to include a component that you do not have in Operations Manager, you can resolve this in several different ways. You can first research and see whether there is an MP to import. Often, there is an MP from a Microsoft partner or the user community for unusual services and technologies. However, if one does not exist, you must author it yourself.

In some scenarios, you don't really need to have the components in Operations Manager to be monitoring them. In these cases, there is nothing you can or need to monitor; you only need the objects in Operations Manager to include them in a distributed application. The goal with the distributed application is then to include the components in a business service. In the case where you need "fake" components, you can author an MP that discovers them based on any Registry key on any server. The discovery discovers instances of your class. Operations Manager keeps the health of these fake objects as unknown, and you will not notice them in the Operations Manager console.

The next example shows how to author a simple MP for a Telex device. The MP discovers an instance of the `Telex` class. The management performs discovery based on a Registry key on the root management server in Operations Manager. To author this MP, you use the Operations Manager Authoring console. The Authoring console is free to download from the Microsoft website as part of the Operations Manager 2007 R2 Authoring Resource Kit at http://www.microsoft.com/downloads/en/details.aspx?FamilyID=9104af8b-ff87-45a1-81cd-b73e6f6b51f0, and will help you author MPs for Operations Manager. Complete the following steps:

1. In the Operations Manager Authoring console, open the **File** menu and select **New**.

2. In the New Management Pack window, select the **Empty Management Pack** template. Input **Odyssey** as the MP identity. Click **Next**.

3. On the Name and Description page, input **Odyssey Telex** as the display name. Click **Create**.

4. In the Authoring console, navigate to Service Model, right-click **classes**, and select new **Windows Local Application**.

5. In the Windows Local Application, input `Odyssey.Telex` as the ID and **Odyssey Telex Discovery** as the display name. Click **Next**.

6. On the Key Properties page, click **Finish**.

7. In the Authoring console, navigate to the Health Model workspace. Right-click **Discoveries** and select **New > Registry (Filtered)**.

8. On the General page, input `Odyssey.Telex.Discovery` as the ID and **Odyssey Telex** for the display name. Configure Target to `Microsoft.SystemCenter.RootManagementServer`. Click **Next**.

9. On the Schedule page, input **24** hours. Because this discovery will discover a fake object, it does not need to be run very often; most likely, only once is enough. Click **Next**.

10. On the Computer page, click **Next**.

11. On the Registry Probe Configuration page, click **Add**.

12. Configure the Edit Attribute Properties window, as shown in Figure 9.12. Input **Telex** as the name. Input **SOFTWARE** in the path text field and change the attribute type to **Check if exists**. Click **OK**.

FIGURE 9.12   Attribute properties of the Odyssey Telex MP.

13. In the Edit Attribute Properties window, click **Next**.

14. On the Expression Filter page, click **Insert**.

15. Configure the expression filter, as shown in Figure 9.13. Input **Values/Telex** as the parameter name. Input **Equals** as Operator and **true** as value. Click **Next**.

16. On the Discovery Mapper page, select **Windows Computer Display Name (Entity)** as the non-key property value. Select **Windows Computer Principal Name (Windows Computer)** as the value for the key property. Click **Finish**.

17. From the File menu, select to save your MP. The MP will be saved in unsealed format as an XML file.

The next step is to import the MP into Operations Manager. You can open the Operations Manager console and import the MP from the Administration workspace. You can also export the management directly from the Operations Manager Authoring console. To export the management from the Authoring console to the management group, use the **Export to Management Group** option in the Tools menu of the Authoring console.

FIGURE 9.13   The expression filter in the Odyssey Telex MP.

To verify your Odyssey Telex discovery works, you can use the Discovered Inventory view in the Monitoring workspace in the Operations Manager console. The Discovered Inventory view lets you choose a target class and then list all instances of that class. It also shows you the properties of that class. Figure 9.14 shows you the view targeted to the Odyssey Telex class. As you can see, the instance of the class has an unknown health state. This is because there aren't any monitors rolling up to this class, so nothing can affect the health of the class, as shown in Figure 9.15.

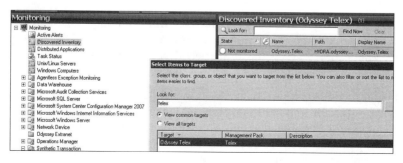

FIGURE 9.14   Use the discovered inventory view to see the discovery result.

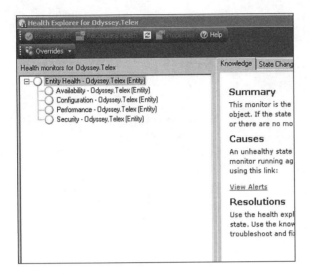

FIGURE 9.15   The health of the Odyssey Telex class, displayed in the Operations Manager Health Explorer.

To force the state of the Odyssey Telex class to be healthy, you can create any monitor targeting the Odyssey Telex class. You don't need to monitor anything with the monitor; you can simple reset the health of it to healthy in the Health Explorer.

You now have a new object type in Operations Manager—in this example, Odyssey Telex—that you can use in distributed applications. For this example, you created a new unsealed MP for the Odyssey Telex discovery and class. If you want to include this into a distributed application in another MP, you must seal the Odyssey Telex MP first. An MP cannot reference or depend on an unsealed MP. Sealing an MP is performed from the Authoring console or with the MPSeal tool that is available on the Operations Manager installation media.

Updating a Business Service

This section shows you how to include the Odyssey Telex object in the Odyssey Extranet business service:

▶ The first operation is to update the Odyssey Extranet distributed application, and then import the updated MP into Service Manager. As you change the class structure of the distributed application when you add the new Odyssey Telex object type, you need to import the MP in Service Manager also, to reflect the structure change.

▶ The second example adds the Odyssey Telex object, which is from another MP. The Odyssey Telex MP needs to be imported into Service Manager, as well. The Odyssey Extranet MPs including the distributed application will reference to the Odyssey Telex MP; therefore, you must seal the Odyssey Telex MP first. Remember, an unsealed MP cannot reference another unsealed MP.

To update the distributed application and import the MP into Service Manager, follow these steps:

1. In the Operations Manager console, navigate to the Authoring workspace and the Distributed Application node.

2. In the Distributed Applications pane, select the **Odyssey Extranet** distributed application and click **Edit** in the Actions pane.

3. In the distributed application designer, click **Add Component**.

4. In the Create New Component Group dialog box, input **Telex** as the name for your component group. In the Objects list, select **Local Application/Windows Local Application/Telex**. Click **OK**.

5. In the distributed application designer, from the Object list, drag and drop a Telex instance to the Telex component group.

6. Save the distributed application and close the distributed application designer.

7. In the Operations Manager console, right-click the **Odyssey Extranet** distributed application and select **View Diagram View** from the menu. A Diagram view will now open and show you the distributed application, as in Figure 9.16.

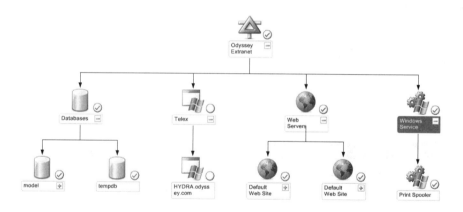

FIGURE 9.16   Components of the updated Odyssey Extranet.

You now need to update the Service Manager side. The following steps describe the actions you need to complete to update Service Manager:

1. In the Operations Manager console, export the Odyssey Extranet MP. You need to export this MP to Service Manager because the structure of the service has changed. Do not forget to add 1 to the version number of the MP; otherwise, you can't upgrade the MP in Service Manager.

2. In the Service Manager console, import the sealed version of the Odyssey Telex MP.

3. In the Service Manager console, import the updated version of the Odyssey Extranet MP.

4. In the Service Manager console, verify that the Operations Manager CI connector includes the Odyssey Extranet MP.

5. In the Service Manager console, verify that the service map includes all new components, as shown in Figure 9.17.

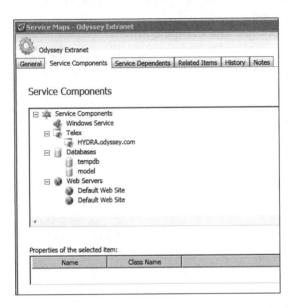

FIGURE 9.17   Updated service map in the Service Manager console.

NOTE: BUSINESS SERVICE MANAGEMENT PACK UPDATE

When you update an MP in Service Manager with a new version, all customization and configuration information is kept. If you delete an MP with a distributed application, all customization is deleted as well.

For example, consider if you have configured service customers on a service and upgrade the MP with the distributed application to version 2. All customization is kept. However, if you delete version 1 and import version 2 of the MP, all your customizations from version 1, such as service customers, are deleted.

There is a known issue when updating business services with a new MP from Operations Manager. The symptom is the business service is not updated in Service Manager according to the new version in the newly imported MP from Operations Manager. This will be fixed in a future release of Service Manager. The current workaround is to delete the MP in Service Manager and then import the updated MP. In other words, this is a new import, not an upgrade or update of the MP.

Connector Allowed List

The Operations Manager CI Connector synchronizes discovered managed objects from Operations Manager to the Service Manager CMDB. If you need data in your Service Manager CMDB from Operations Manager classes (for example, IIS web servers and SQL servers) to be automatically be synchronized by the Operations Manager CI connector, you can import these MPs into Service Manager. You need to import only the MP that contains the model (in other words, classes, relationships, and properties). If you are not certain which MP that is, it is harmless to import, for example, all the files that come with the Exchange MP for Operations Manager. You can import only Operations Manager MPs that have a class definition built into them. Otherwise, they will appear with a red sign in Service Manager when trying to import.

To keep the Service Manager CMDB healthy, the Operations Manager CI connector does not synchronize all classes from Operations Manager. Instead, Service Manager uses an Allowed List to control what to synchronize; only objects of classes that derive from classes in the Allowed List are synchronized. The example in the "Non-Operations Manager Components" section derives from the local application class. By default, Local Application is not on the Allowed List.

Modifying the Connector Allowed List

The following steps describe the actions you need to perform to allow classes derived from Local Application to be synchronized by the Operations Manager CI connector:

1. On a Service Manager server, start Windows PowerShell.
2. In PowerShell, run add-pssnapin smcmdletsnapin. This loads the Service Manager PowerShell snap-in.
3. In PowerShell, run get-SCSMAllowList. This shows you the default list of classes in the Allowed List.
4. In PowerShell, run add-SCSMAllowListClass -Classname Microsoft.Windows. LocalApplication. This adds the Local Application class to the Allowed List.
5. In PowerShell, run get-SCSMAllowList. Verify that the new class is in the list, as in Figure 9.18. Close PowerShell.

Mapping Operations Manager Incidents to a Business Service Automatically

What if you want alerts from Operations Manager to display as related incidents for your business service in Service Manager? Service Manager will not connect related incidents and services to each other by default. For example, there is an alert about C:\ on a logical disk in your service component list; the incident will not show up as a related item on your service. The service also will not show up as a related item on the incident. To get this to work, you must generate an alert with the same source as the service name. The examples in this chapter use the alert source of Odyssey Extranet. You can accomplish this using an extra dependency rollup monitor in Operations Manager.

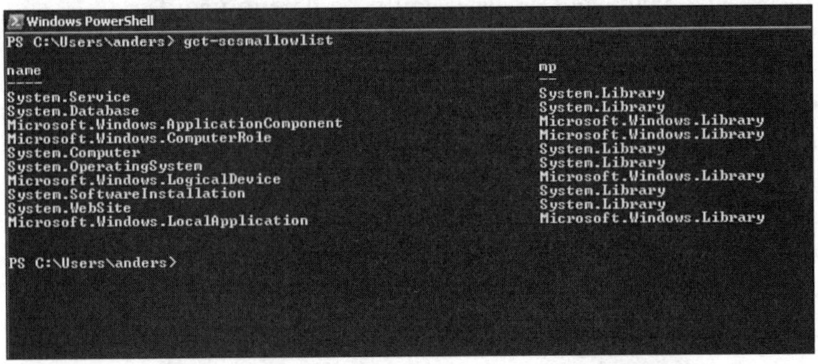

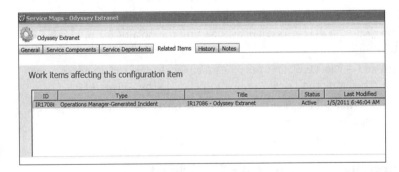

FIGURE 9.18   Service Manager Allowed List for the Operations Manager CI connector.

The following procedure describes the actions to perform to generate an alert when the Windows Service in the Odyssey Extranet services changes state and have the alert generated using Odyssey Extranet as the source. See Figure 9.15 for the layout of the Odyssey Extranet service. The procedure creates a dependency rollup monitor between the Windows Service component group and the availability monitor. When the Windows Service component group changes state, the dependency rollup monitor will also change state. When the source of the alert is the same as the business service name, the incident will be automatically related to the service, as shown in Figure 9.19.

FIGURE 9.19   Operations Manager-generated incident related to a business service.

Perform the following steps to create a dependency rollup monitor for the windows service in the Odyssey Extranet service. This monitor will generate an alert as Odyssey Extranet:

1. In the Operations Manager console, navigate to the Authoring workspace.

2. Right-click **Monitors** and choose **Create a Monitor**; then choose **Dependency Rollup Monitor**. Configure the General properties, as shown in Figure 9.20.

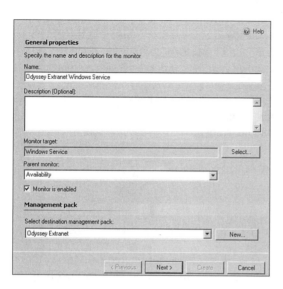

FIGURE 9.20   General configuration of the dependency rollup monitor.

3. In the Create a Dependency Monitor Wizard, General properties page, input **Odyssey Extranet Windows Service rollup** as the name.

4. In the Create a Dependency Monitor Wizard General properties page, input **Windows Service** as the monitor target. You may have multiple targets named Windows Service; select the one in the Odyssey Extranet MP.

5. In the Create a Dependency Monitor Wizard, General properties page, select **Odyssey Extranet** as the MP. Then click **Next**.

6. In the Create a Dependency Monitor Wizard, on the Monitor Dependency page, select **Windows Service/Entity Health** as the monitor to depend on. Click **Next**.

7. Click **Next** in the Create a Dependency Monitor Wizard on the Health Rollup Policy page.

8. In the Create a Dependency Monitor Wizard, on the Configure Alerts page, check the **Generate alerts for this monitor** check box. In the Alert Description, input a short message that describes that the windows service is down (for example, **Telex Service down, please investigate**). Click **Create**.

Note that in this example, you will still get the original alert about the Windows service. When planning mapping between incidents and business services, it is important to consider this.

You could also enable one of the default aggregate rollup monitors in the Odyssey Extranet distributed application health model to generate an alert. A disadvantage of this is that you cannot control the alert description.

> **NOTE: TROUBLESHOOTING WITH BUSINESS SERVICES**
>
> A business service includes a visual representation of your service from the business and user perspective. The business service shows your critical dependencies, settings, components, and areas of responsibility. Because a business service can show you the relationship between incidents and configuration items, it can be very useful when troubleshooting issues in your IT environment. If the issue affects multiple incidents and configuration items, you can see the relationship between these within your business service.

Summary

This chapter covered a significant amount of Operations Manager-related content, with a focus on business services and on building those services. In addition, you learned how to plan and design your distributed applications in Operations Manager, because they will be the foundation of your service maps (Business Services) in Service Manager.

The chapter started with the root of the service map, explained what a service map is, and explained what a distributed application is. It looked at all the different properties of a business service. The chapter discussed how to create a distributed application in Operations Manager and export it to Service Manager. You read about handling components that are not in Operations Manager, using the Telex example. You also read about the Operations Manager CI connector and modifying the allow list. The chapter stepped through the process of updating a service map and looked at how to connect Operations Manager alerts with business services as related incidents.

In this chapter, you stepped through the process of creating a distributed application, exporting it to Service Manager as a service map, and keeping it updated.

CHAPTER 10

Incident Management

Service Manager 2010 (also known as SvcMgr or SCSM) enables the Incident Management process by implementing and automating ticketing best practices in compliance with Microsoft Operations Framework (MOF) and Information Technology Infrastructure Library (ITIL). Compliance with MOF and ITIL best practices provides your organization with the confidence that the necessary building blocks are available in the System Center Service Manager tool to underpin configuring your own Incident Management process in accordance with industry-accepted standards.

Chapter 3, "MOF, ITIL, and Service Manager," explains the value of using ITIL and MOF management frameworks. In this chapter, the rubber meets the road. The chapter discusses how to configure the Incident Management process in Service Manager to create that value for your organization. It examines the activities of this process to see which components in Service Manager—such as workflows or templates—can help in enabling and automating the Incident process. This lets you know what to configure for each process activity; with the information documented, you have your Incident Management detailed configuration list for Service Manager, and can proceed with configuring Incident settings in Service Manager 2010.

Understanding the Incident Process

A starting point for planning your Incident Management configuration in Service Manager is that the Incident Management process is defined, agreed upon, and described—in writing—such that you, as a Service Manager administrator, can determine necessary customizations and determine the process steps to automate. This doesn't have to be that complicated; a commented Visio diagram along with a description and definition of the process in a Word document should get you started. By defining the Incident process, you can translate the process definition into a list of configuration tasks to enable that process in Service Manager.

To assist with this process definition, here are some terms used with Incident Management (more detailed information was discussed in Chapter 3):

▶ **Incident:** An incident is any event not part of the standard operation of a service. An incident causes, or may cause, an interruption or reduction in the quality of that service. Examples include service not available or system down or function not working.

▶ **Service request:** A service request is an incident that is not a failure in the IT infrastructure. An example is a login reset request.

▶ **Problem:** This is an unknown error, the underlying cause of one or more incidents.

▶ **Known error:** A known error is a problem for which a root cause and permanent fix or workaround are identified but the fix is not yet implemented.

▶ **Workaround:** This is a temporary fix or technique that eliminates the end user's reliance on the faulty service component.

You can build an Incident Management process with different tasks, resulting in a configuration enabling this process in Service Manager 2010. In general, here is how you can categorize the Service Manager configuration tasks:

▶ **General Incident Management Service Manager Configuration Settings:** These are overall configuration settings to enable Incident Management functionality. This includes settings in the Incident settings section of the Administration space of the console, which houses the basic settings for each process.

▶ **Enumeration (drop-down) lists in the Service Manager console and the "lists" section of the console:** These are a list of properties that show up in drop-down lists on forms and dialog boxes. Incident Classification is an example of such a list that contains a default set of list items and can be adjusted with specific values for your organization.

▶ **Incident Management Automation Configuration:** These are template and workflow configuration for process automation.

▶ **Incident Management Customization:** Customization goes beyond settings and requires the Authoring Tool or custom development; this includes adding or hiding fields and drop-down lists and check boxes.

▶ **Incident Management Extension:** This is where you create or acquire and implement solutions that extend Incident Management capabilities beyond what is out of the box (for example, implementing the Service Manager Dashboard Solution Accelerator and configuring it to provide required Incident Dashboard elements).

Incident Management in Service Manager

The Incident Management process is responsible for managing the life cycle of all incidents. The goal of this process is to restore to a normal service operation as quickly as possible and minimize the business impact. Solving incidents is a basic technical task. Providing an interface to log incidents and/or route incidents to the correct support group will assist with incident resolution. In addition, organizations with well-tuned incident processes can use the tool to resolve incidents quickly. Service Manager orchestrates these basic tasks and provides a platform to automate the different elements in the process. Here's how:

- ▶ Multiple sources are possible to create incident work items, and incident workflows can further route incidents.

- ▶ Service Manager automates populating the configuration management database (CMDB) with information and keeping it current. CMDB information is used as context for incident forms, dialog boxes, and tasks. When handling an incident, an IT support analyst can view the user's computer details and ping or remote control that computer directly from the console. This integrated environment brings the context into the action; the support analyst does not have to step outside of the tool to do such tasks and reenter context data, saving much-needed work cycles in IT and speeding incident resolution.

- ▶ The Incident process can be automated with incident templates and workflows.

- ▶ Knowledge articles can help service desk analysts and end users understand and solve incidents and provide workarounds for incidents when no resolution is available.

- ▶ Incident Management is linked to other management functions in Service Manager such as Change, Problem, and Knowledge Management. This means you can look at an incident and see related changes, or look at a problem and see related incidents, and so on.

- ▶ Incident information is stored in the Service Manager data warehouse for further reporting.

Figure 10.1 illustrates an overview of Incident Management in Service Manager 2010.

Interaction between the elements in Figure 10.1 for Service Manager Incident Management functionality should become clearer as this chapter goes deeper into the process activities. To understand the interactions and define the Incident Management functionality in Service Manager, it is important you know the Service Manager components you can configure as building blocks to enable the Incident process.

By default, Service Manager contains the preimported sealed Incident management pack (MP) that enables core Incident Management functionality. This MP contains required classes, workflows, views, forms, and reports for configuring your Incident process in Service Manager. Those items configured for your environment such as groups, queues, tasks, templates, connectors, and list items are stored in your own custom unsealed MP.

10

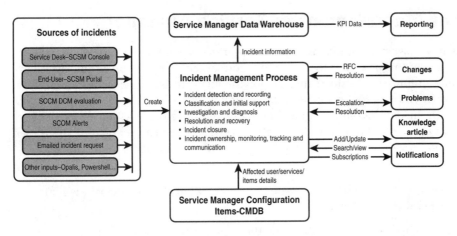

FIGURE 10.1   Incident Management in Service Manager.

These MP settings are applied on all incident work items, and are considered part of general Incident Management configuration.

The configuration of Incident Management in Service Manager takes place in different areas of the console, with the primary area being the Incident Settings section in the Administrative space of the console. Here are some of those settings:

▶ **Configuring Incident Work Item Prefix:** In Service Manager 2010, all incident numbers start with IR. However, you can change the prefix that is used for your incident numbering.

▶ **Incident File Attachment Policy:** Your company policy may limit the number of files you can attach to each incident to no more than five and limit the maximum file size for each file at 500 kilobytes (KB). The maximum number of attached files and maximum file size settings specified also apply to the attached files in the Related Items tab for configuration items. Give this some thought; certain tickets may require a number of attachments/screenshots to resolve.

   To keep storage at a reasonable size, you might want to establish policies and provide training to support analysts regarding screenshot resolutions and storing commonly used documents on a support analyst SharePoint site with a link from Service Manager (providing the added benefit of version control).

▶ **Incident Default Support Group:** Without a default support group defined for incidents, support personnel may have to search the All open incidents view to find their incidents. These orphan incidents can cause consternation as no one is picking them up and they are not being resolved. This configuration setting can be the first step in the incident routing policy for your environment. Typically, this setting is set to the first-tier support group: the service desk or help desk.

▶ **Incident Priority Calculation:** Incident priority calculation is rated on a scale from 1 to 9, with 1 being the highest priority. Priority is based on a combination of impact and urgency, with impact and urgency settings defined by default as High, Medium, or Low, and configured when the incident is created.

▶ **Resolution Time Configuration:** The resolution time defines how much time it should take to resolve an incident. Resolution time is based on priority. You should usually set resolution times for higher-priority incidents.

▶ **Operations Manager Web Site:** If you use Operations Manager (OpsMgr) for monitoring, you can integrate web portal functionality into Service Manager incident tasks. This would enable support personnel to check the OpsMgr configuration item (CI) health status out of the Service Manager console. Port 51908 is the default port used when OpsMgr is configured for Windows authentication with the OpsMgr web console. If Forms authentication is enabled, an HTTPS port (default 443) is used for OpsMgr web console connectivity.

▶ **Incoming Email Support:** Configuring incoming email support enables users to send incident support request by email.

▶ **Service Manager Notifications:** Communication is an important component in the Incident Management process. Affected users, support personnel, or managers may want to be notified when incidents or other changes occur. Service Manager lets you generate notifications for almost any type of change.

▶ **Service Manager Incident Management Workflows:** A workflow is a sequence of activities that automates a business process, in this case the Incident Management process. Workflows in Service Manager can update incidents when various changes occur or automatically generate incidents out of the Operations Manager and Configuration Manager connectors. You create a workflow that defines when and under what circumstances it will run. For example, a workflow can automatically change the support tier from a setting of 1 to 2 when a low-priority incident is changed to a higher priority. Workflow activities function by applying templates and send notifications. By default, Service Manager provides workflows for the Self-Service portal (SSP), Operations Manager alerts, and Desired Configuration Management (DCM) event workflow.

In the Library workspace of the console, you can configure groups, knowledge, queues, incident lists, tasks, and templates. Here is a definition of these items:

▶ **Groups:** Groups are a collection of CIs. You can use them in Incident Management to assign incident work items to a specific support team.

▶ **Service Manager Knowledge:** Knowledge articles can help service desk analysts and end users understand and resolve the incident. You can add knowledge to the incident work item as an additional source of information to resolve the incident.

▶ **Incident Management Lists:** An incident work item is an object in Service Manager that has a set of properties. A list represents a property of an object, and it includes one or more list items. Each list item represents a possible value that can be selected in the incident work item. Service Manager includes some default incident lists you can use in your incident forms.

▶ **Incident Queues:** Queues are used to group similar work items that meet specified criteria. For example, you can group all incident work items of the classification Email problems in a single queue monitored by the service desk. You can define what rights a user has to a queue and control what actions a user can perform on the content in the queue; this is not possible for objects in a group.

▶ **Tasks:** Tasks are the actions listed on the right side of the incident work item. These automate repetitive actions a support analyst has to perform. IT support analysts typically use tasks to help troubleshoot user incidents. Service Manager includes a set of tasks, such as ping the affected computer or create a remote desktop connection. You can create your own tasks in the Service Manager console.

▶ **Service Manager Incident Management Templates:** You can create an incident template to populate certain fields for a specified incident type. Support personnel use templates when creating incidents; they can also be used in incident workflows to automate the process. The template can prepopulate certain property fields in the incident work item, such as the name of the support group or assigned analyst for the incident work item. Here are the default Incident Management templates provided by Service Manager:

  ▶ Default Incident

  ▶ Software Issue Incident

  ▶ Networking Issue

  ▶ Printing Issue Incident

  ▶ High Priority Incident

  ▶ Hardware Issue

  ▶ Operations Manager Incident

You can also use the Service Manager Authoring Tool to configure or automate Incident Management with MPs. The Authoring Tool is discussed in Chapter 17, "Management Packs," and Chapter 18, "Customizing Service Manager."

Service Manager is tightly integrated with other System Center products, such as Operations Manager and Configuration Manager. Incident Management integration is implemented by configuring connectors. The "Incident Management Automation" section discusses configuring the connectors for Incident Management. You can configure the connectors to automate the following functionality in Service Manager:

▶ **Operations Manager alerts connector:** Use the alert connector to automatically generate incidents that are based on Operations Manager alerts. In addition to the alert-incident creation, support analysts can have access to detailed alert information by the incident work item tasks.

▶ **Configuration Manager connector:** In Service Manager, you must create a Configuration Manager connector to import baselines, and configure Incident Management to automatically generate incidents based on desired configuration management in ConfigMgr.

The next section maps incident process activities to Service Manager functionality.

Incident Management Process Activities

This section of the chapter assesses each critical process activity and examines how to apply Service Manager to optimize every stage of the process. It highlights the elements of the Incident Management process and indicates where Service Manager can help configure and automate that process. Making the association between the Incident process activities and the Service Manager components should provide the capability to translate your company's Incident process and configure the Service Manager incident environment. This provides cohesion between how you work in your processes and takes advantage of the functionality provided by the tool. The "Configuring Incident Management" section discusses configuring this functionality in Service Manager.

Here is the Incident Management process, illustrated in Figure 10.2 and discussed in the following sections:

▶ **Incident detection and recording:** This is one of the primary jobs of support personnel, which can be automated with Service Manager connectors.

▶ **Classification and initial support:** An important task of first line support is to populate the incident form, categorize it, and assign it to an appropriate queue or assignment group, in case it cannot be resolved in the initial call.

▶ **Investigation and diagnosis:** This technical activity is logical in the overall Incident process.

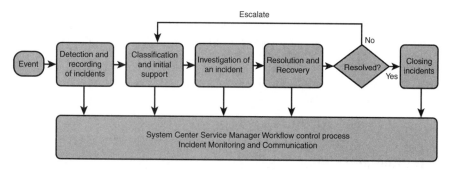

FIGURE 10.2   Activities in Incident Management.

▶ **Resolution and recovery:** An incident can be resolved when the service is restored to its standard operation mode.

▶ **Incident closure:** A very good ITIL recommendation is this two-step incident closure. After resolution, the affected user is notified, and only upon confirmation is an incident closed. It is also a best practice not to open a closed incident but to create a new one and reference to the closed incident.

▶ **Incident ownership, monitoring, tracking, and communication:** Wherever the incident is created, someone in Incident Management owns it and takes care of it. Incidents do not go to an unmonitored queue.

Events

Events occur and cause the affected user to call or email the service desk. In other scenarios, an event can trigger a system for a certain action and Service Manager captures this event using a connector. In all cases, you need to ensure the end user has the ability to request support and the service desk can log the needed information.

Here are the Service Manager components involved in the Incident Management process that can generate events:

▶ **Default incident form in the Service Manager console:** A default incident form is provided in the Incident MP, which can be customized to your company's needs. If additional properties are configured for the incident class, you can integrate them into the default incident form.

▶ **SSP:** The SSP is used by end users to contact support analysts for support requests. Users can also use the SSP to view announcements, search the knowledge base, perform tasks, and manage their support requests.

▶ **Operations Manager alert connector:** The connector provides automatic incident creation based on alert subscriptions in Operation Manager.

▶ **Configuration Manager DCM compliance incidents:** This connector automatically creates incidents based on alert subscription on ConfigMgr DCM CIs compliancy.

▶ **Incoming email support:** Configure this functionality if you want to enable end users to email support requests.

Incident Detection and Recording

In a classical Incident Management process, detecting an event is related to something occurring on an end user's system. Service Manager 2010 extends this functionality by integrating infrastructure events into the detection and recording activity of the Incident process. The recording is dependent on the different detection methods that Service Manager 2010 provides for creating incidents:

- ▶ **User-related incidents:** Manual incident creation by help desk personnel or end users using the Service Manager console, portal, or email.

- ▶ **Infrastructure-related incidents:** Automated incident creation with the OpsMgr alerts connector, ConfigMgr DCM functionality, or other sources such as Opalis or CSV import.

Service Manager ensures that all incidents are tracked and provides information to help solve the problem. How "rich" the incident form is populated with information depends on the support people logging the incident; automatically created incidents have a strong dependency on the CI details available in Service Manager. For example, details of the affected user are CI information. These can be created manually or with the Active Directory connector. The same goes for the affected service; this information depends on the business services defined in Service Manager, and this relationship is made when it is defined. There is a strong dependency on CI information to populate the incident work item with the information to solve the problem.

TIP: CHECK DATA SOURCES OF THE SERVICE MANAGER CONNECTORS

The connectors can highlight weaknesses in your Active Directory (AD), OpsMgr, and ConfigMgr data and configuration. It is a best practice to clean up the source before configuring the Service Manager connectors or importing the data via CSV. This ensures that only valid data is imported in Service Manager using the connector framework and you can trust it for further process automation.

You can easily add and remove CIs imported by the connectors. You can flush imported CIs by removing the connectors, updating the data source, and re-creating the connector to reimport the CIs into Service Manager (with the caveat that this is possible only if the CI has not been updated by another connector or manually by a support analyst).

Here are the Service Manager components involved in this process:

- ▶ **Default incident form:** Service Manager provides a default incident form based on incident class properties and relationships. This form can be extended. For more information, see Chapter 18.

- ▶ **Incident event templates:** Incident templates can be used to achieve Incident Management flexibility.

  Incident templates include common settings for different types of incidents. For example, when a service desk receives a call from a user who cannot access email, the service desk operator can apply the email issue incident template and verify all necessary information is collected from the user reporting the incident. The templates also guarantee that incidents are configured with correct owner information, category, priority, and other related items.

Service Manager provides a set of templates to log incidents from various sources and classifications. You can use these templates as is or adjust them to support your own process. Applying your own incident templates can be accomplished with the Service Manager console, such as the SSP configuration or Operations Manager connector configuration, or with workflows.

▶ **Incident event workflows:** Workflows are important in detecting and recording activity. Using workflows, you can route the incidents to the correct incident queue or assign it directly to the correct support group. This will be particularly important for automatically created incidents.

You can use workflows to prepopulate common settings on the incident work items and for incident routing. Incidents created using the portal can be routed to a dedicated queue. Alternatively, if the OpsMgr Alert connector is configured, you can apply templates based on the MP that raised the alert.

▶ Notifications may be sent, depending on the defined Incident process and the criteria configured in workflows.

Incident Classification and Initial Support

The classification activity categorizes the incident by assigning an incident classification and priority to the work item. The initial support activity can provide a first-line resolution for incidents by checking the incident symptoms against documented workarounds in knowledge articles or similar incidents. An important task of the support analysts in this activity is to collect adequate information for the incident, such as categorizing it properly or providing enough details about the event. This information is valuable for later resolution of the incident or information lookups by support analysts.

Service Manager provides a default incident classification and allows customizations such as adding or removing categories, and dynamically creates different depths of classification based on the type or category. Keep in mind when creating your own incident classification that IT support and management understand your categories, although these are usually technical.

Here are the three primary reasons to classify incidents:

▶ **Assignment and escalation:** If not solved on first call, it is an operator's task to assign the incident to a proper priority (urgency/impact), category, and support group.

▶ **Problem analysis:** Classifying incident makes it possible to easily look up similar closed incidents for documented solutions.

▶ **Reporting:** Reporting is important because it provides inputs to other Information Technology service management (ITSM) processes (Problem, Change, and so on), and it is the primary tool of service managers in the IT environment.

When defining your own incident classification list, it is best to not create too deep a classification schema.

CLASSIFICATION LIST STRATEGY INFORMATION

There is a tradeoff regarding the levels in a classification list:

▶ When classification lists are not deep enough, reporting is not granular enough.

▶ If lists are too deep, support analysts struggle with the number of options, and the quality of ticket classification may suffer. (They end up choosing the easiest option; especially beware of categories such as Miscellaneous or Other.)

Striking a balance between ease of use for analysts and reporting granularity is a bit of an art. In most cases, a two-tier or at most a three-tier classification schema should fit your needs.

Priority assigned on the incident work item is calculated based on the urgency and impact associated to the work item. The calculation of incident priority is based on a matrix that can be configured directly in the incident event management settings of the console. By default, Title, Classification category, Urgency, and Impact are mandatory fields for the incident work item.

Here are the Service Manager components involved in this process:

▶ **Incident Priority Calculation:** This is a general setting that is placed on the incident settings. It is valid for incident work items.

▶ **Service Manager Knowledge:** Internal Service Manager knowledge is an important source for solving incidents on first call. Service Manager provides the possibility to configure other search providers such as your own SharePoint Knowledge site, Microsoft TechNet, and other search engines.

▶ **Incident Event Templates:** Incident templates can be used to achieve Incident Management flexibility. Service Manager 2010 includes a number of default templates you can use to create incident work items. Depending on your Incident process, you might need to create additional templates for incident work items or to use in Incident Management workflows.

▶ **Incident Event Workflows:** Based on classification, the appropriate support group can be assigned via workflows to solve the issue. Another example of incident event workflow usage is that the calculated priority (urgency/impact settings) on the incident can trigger a workflow to assign the incident to a specialized support group.

▶ **Operations Manager Connector:** Infrastructure-related incidents are created via the Operations Manager connector. Using the connector settings in the console, you can configure alert routing rules to apply an incident template. This can help categorizing automatically created incidents via Operations Manager connector. The Operations Manager Incident template is applied if no filters are configured.

▶ **Desired Configuration Manager:** Desired Configuration Manager event workflow configuration lets you create incidents based on Configuration Manager configuration items compliancy and apply a template accordingly. Category, urgency, and impact of the incident are defined in the process.

▶ **Incident Event Management Workflows:** Using the Incident Event Management Workflows Configuration, you can create workflows for other automatically created incidents.

Incident Investigation and Diagnosis

Service Manager 2010 provides a set of information sources for investigating incidents in the Incident process. Here are the sources for investigating incident work items:

▶ The information included in the incident work item is the initial source of information that can be used to solve the issue.

▶ The knowledge base can help resolve incidents. Your own documented solution can be associated and is accessible from the incident form.

▶ Service Manager tasks can help find a solution for the incident. The Service Manager console provides some predefined tasks, and you can create your own tasks for actions frequently used by the support team. For example, select the incident work item, and you can run the ping-related computer task.

▶ Business service definition can help resolve incidents. Once an incident is created for an affected CI that is a member of a business service, the service reference is added to the incident work item.

▶ Service Manager announcements can be used to announce service outages.

Support analysts will collect updated incident details and analyze all related information, particularly configuration details from a CMDB linked to the service desk. First-line support or the affected user provides the information for creating incidents, be that through the Service Manager console, SSP, or email. The incident creator must ensure that enough information is included to resolve the issue. For incidents created through the connectors, this information is automatically added to the incident work item.

TIP: IMPORT OPSMGR MPS FOR ADDITIONAL CLASSES

Operations Manager collects information about many different types of objects, such as hard disk drives and websites. Service Manager requires a list of class definitions for these objects; this list of definitions is provided by the Operations Manager MPs. For this information to be available in the incident work item, you must import the associated Operations Manager MPs into Service Manager.

Here are the Service Manager components involved:

▶ **Service Manager Knowledge:** Same functionality as in the initial support activity. Support personnel can search for documented solutions using different search providers.

▶ **Service Manager Tasks:** Tasks can be created in the management console and associated to the Incident Management folder. You can configure tasks for frequently used actions such as executables to launch from the command line while investigating. Incident properties can be added as arguments to the command to execute.

▶ **Business Services:** Defining business services in Service Manager has many advantages. It enables the support people to see the service relationship on a configuration item. When investigating problems, all related information around the service, such as other open incidents or CIs that enable the service, is available in the incident work item.

▶ **Configuration Items:** CIs in Service Manager are the main source of information. The support team will suffer and lose time if this information is outdated or incomplete.

Escalating Incidents

Critical to escalation is the ability to escalate incidents rapidly according to agreed service levels or to allocate more or specialized support resources if necessary. Escalation can follow two paths:

▶ **Functional escalation** (a handoff to the organizational unit or function owning the technology stream) is required when the incident needs to be escalated to support groups better able to resolve the incident or if the support group is unable to resolve the incident within agreed target times. In Service Manager, this is a reassignment of the support group with the escalated class property selection or using workflow automation.

▶ **Hierarchic escalation** (escalation up the management chain) occurs when the incident needs to gain higher levels of priority. When the urgency or impact of an incident rises, its priority changes, and this can trigger Service Manager workflow automation.

For each resolution attempt, data is attached to the incident work item to save repeating recovery procedures, which can lengthen overall resolution times. Here, Service Manager 2010 can play yet another key role by automating the escalation process itself and pinpointing the exact source of errors.

Here are the Service Manager components involved:

▶ **Incident Event Workflows:** Incident event workflows can be configured to automate both escalation paths. For example, the escalation property is set on the work item as soon as the incident support group is changed from first-level support to second-level support in the work item. This can also be applicable for priority changes.

▶ **Incident Notifications:** The service desk should keep the user, incident primary owner, or assigned analyst informed of any escalation occurring and ensure the

10

incident work item is updated accordingly to maintain a full history of actions. Configuring accurate notifications and subscriptions in Service Manager is required to support this process.

Incident Resolution and Recovery

An incident is resolved when the service is restored to its standard operation mode. Potential resolutions should be applied and tested. The specific actions to undertake and the people involved in taking the recovery actions may vary, depending on the nature of the incident:

▸ The service desk can ask the affected user to undertake activities on his own desktop or remote equipment. As in all activities of the process, incident work item information must be current to be able to contact the affected user or apply the resolution on the affected CI.

▸ The service desk implementing the resolution either centrally (say, apply a hotfix with ConfigMgr) or remotely using software to take control of the user's desktop to diagnose and implement a resolution.

▸ Specialist support groups may be asked to implement specific recovery actions (such as the Network Support group reconfiguring a router).

▸ A third-party supplier asked to resolve the incident.

Here are the Service Manager components involved:

▸ **Incident Event Templates:** Service Manager includes a list of default incident resolution items. You can adjust this list to your needs to support reporting requirements. The default incident resolution items are Auto Resolved by Problem, Cancelled, Fixed by analyst, Fixed by higher tier support, and Walk through knowledge article.

▸ **Incident Notifications:** Notifications and subscriptions in Service Manager can notify the necessary individuals for closure of the incident.

Closing Incidents

The support team should verify that the incident is fully resolved and the users are satisfied and willing to agree the incident can be closed. A distinction exists between a resolved and closed incident work item: A resolved incident work item is when the support analyst believes it is solved to the satisfaction of the user, and closed is when the solution is confirmed by the user.

A closed incident work item cannot be reopened. (Although this can be scripted in Service Manager, it is considered a "no can do" in ITIL/MOF-compliant tools.) The support analyst can reopen resolved incident work items if the event is not resolved or the affected user does not accept the solution. It is a best practice to leave incident work items in a resolved status for some time. This allows the affected user to react to the proposed solution. You then create incident closure workflows to automate closure of incident work items.

Here are the Service Manager components involved:

▶ **Incident Event Workflows:** As specified in the "Incident Management in Service Manager" section, you can create incident event workflows to automate closing incidents. For example, if the incident is in a resolved status for two days, a workflow automatically closes the incident work item.

▶ **Incident Notifications:** Notifications and subscriptions in Service Manager can notify the needed persons for closure of the incident.

Configuring Incident Management

The "Incident Management Process Activities" section of this chapter provides an overview of the Incident Management activities from a Service Manager 2010 perspective. The section describes information about the tasks in the activities and the mapping to functionality in Service Manager. This section presents an overview of configuration options for Incident Management in Service Manager 2010.

The primary goal of Incident Management is to ensure users can get back to work as quickly as possible. Therefore, activities of the Incident Management process should be supported by technology—not only to enable the Incident Management process, but also to enhance (automate), measure, and support the constant improvement activity of that process. The configuration required for Service Manager depends on the defined Incident process in your organization. Settings such as prefix, priority calculation, security settings, and notifications are global settings. Other configurations depend on the service you want to provide to the end user. Here are some examples:

▶ If you plan to provide user functionality to send an email to report an incident, you must configure Service Manager to support emailed incident requests.

▶ Determine whether you want to integrate your infrastructure in the Incident Management process. Service Manager 2010 provides automatic incident work item creation for Operations Manager alerts and Configuration Manager DCM evaluations.

A process breakdown can help define the configuration necessary for Service Manager. The next sections guide you through configuring the Incident Management settings.

Incident User Roles, Groups, Queues, and Lists

The starting point of incident management configuration is ensuring the support team has access to the required work items, views, tasks, and templates. By default, a single Incident Resolvers user role is defined with access to all incident work items, views, and so on. This is very important in Incident Management. Access, as well as routing incident work items, is provided to the support team by configuring the Service Manager 2010 user roles. You can use the Incident Resolvers user role if you do not need to limit access to the incident work items in the console. This user role has access to all incident work items; routing of the incident work items can then be based on AD security groups and incident queues. If you plan to limit console access, you must configure the underlying components before defining user roles. You can find detailed information about how to create user roles in Service Manager in Chapter 15, "Service Manager Security."

Creating Groups for Incident Management

Service Manager groups contain objects, which typically are CIs and can be used to scope views, run reports, and scope Service Manager user roles. (Groups are for configuration items, such as computers; queues are for work items, such as incidents.) Groups can include collections of objects of the same class or different classes. You can create a static group, a dynamic group, or a combination of static and dynamic. The following procedure guides you through the process of creating a group in the Service Manager console:

1. In the Service Manager console, navigate to **Library -> Groups**. Initially, there are no groups; the console displays an empty Result pane. To create Incident Management groups, go to the Tasks pane, under Groups, and click **Create Group**.

2. The Create Group wizard starts. On the Before You Begin page, click **Next**.

3. On the General page, provide a name and description for the group, such as **Tier 1 Configuration items**. Under Management pack, make sure you have selected an unsealed MP. Click **Next**.

4. On the Included Members page, click **Add** to select the configuration items:

   ▶ In the Select Objects dialog box, in the Filter by class list, select a class, such as Windows Computer.

   ▶ In the Search by name box, type the search criteria you want to use to locate an object, and then click the filter (magnifying glass) button.

   ▶ Select one or more items in the Available Objects list and then click **Add**. For example, a set of clients in a specific location can be added as configuration items for Tier 1 support.

   ▶ Verify the objects you selected in the Available Objects list appear in the selected objects list displayed in Figure 10.3, and then click **OK**.

5. On the Included Members page displayed in Figure 10.4, click **Next**:

   ▶ Choose the property you want to build your criteria. For example, after specifying the Windows Computer type, select the **Active Directory Site** property, and then click **Add**.

   ▶ In the related text box, enter the AD site name so that all the computers located in that site are included, and then click **Next**. Figure 10.5 displays the Dynamic Members page.

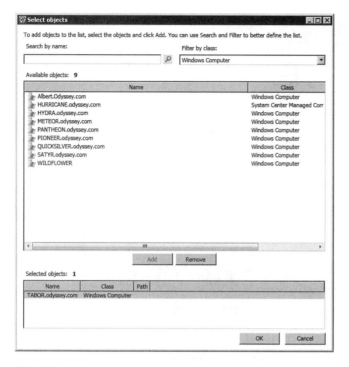

FIGURE 10.3   Group member object selection when creating a CI group.

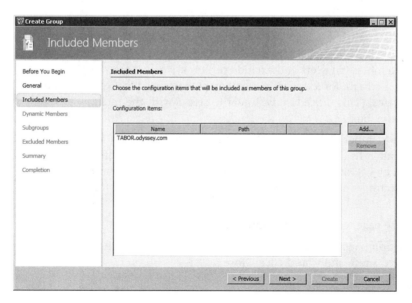

FIGURE 10.4   Included Members when creating a CI group.

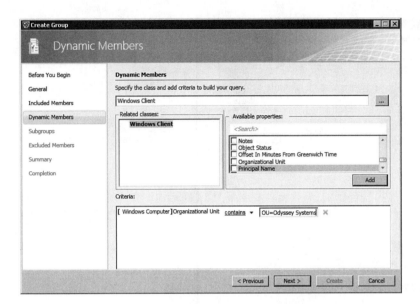

FIGURE 10.5   Adding dynamic members when creating a CI group.

6. Optionally, use the Subgroups page to select subgroups of the groups you create. For example, if you have organized your configuration items in groups and you need a Master – all including group, you can create a group that includes all other Incident Management-related groups.

   On the Subgroups page, click **Modify**, and then select the specific groups you want as subgroups of this group. Click **OK**, and then click **Next**.

7. The Excluded Members page lets you exclude certain systems. For example, suppose you have defined criteria for a dynamic membership and need to exclude certain configuration items. (This procedure is similar to step 5 with the Include Membership dialog box.)

   In the Excluded Member dialog box, in the Filter by class list, select a class such, as Windows Computer. In the Search by name box, type the search criteria you want to use to locate an object, and then click the filter (magnifying glass) button. Click **Modify** and select the specific configuration items to exclude from this group. Click **OK**, and then click **Next**.

8. On the Summary page, confirm the group settings that you made. Click **Create**.

9. On the Completion page, verify you receive a confirmation message that the new group was created successfully, and click **Close**.

> **TIP: VALIDATE THE CREATION OF THE SERVICE MANAGER GROUP**
>
> Here's how to directly validate creation of the group in the console: Verify that the group appears in the Groups pane. If necessary, press the **F5** key to refresh the Service Manager console view. In the Tasks pane, under the name of the group, click **View Group Members** to make sure that the CIs are displayed in the Group Members window.

Create an Incident Queue

The word *queue* is used differently in Service Manager than most other service management tools. Typically, a queue is a screen you go into to view your tickets; in Service Manager, this is a view. A Service Manager queue is a container of related work items (for example, incidents). This is related to a view, or what is typically understood as a queue, but it is not the same. Service Manager 2010 includes several predefined queues. You can also create queues if your organization requires custom queues. For example, you can create a queue for all incident work items for the Tier 1 support team. This queue can be used to route that incident type to the queue, create a console view, or scope the Service Manager user role. To create an incident queue, follow these steps:

1. In the Service Manager console, click **Library**. In the Library pane, expand Library, and then click **Queues**. In the Tasks pane, click **Create Queue**.

2. Click **Next** on the Before You Begin page.

3. On the General page, type a name in the Queue name box. In this example, type **All Odyssey Tier 1 incidents**.

   Next to the work item type box, click the ellipsis button (...). In the Select a Class dialog box, select a class, such as Incident, and then click **OK**.

   In the Management Pack list, select the unsealed MP you will use to store the new queue definition. Click **Next**.

4. On the Criteria page, build the criteria you want to use to filter work items for the queue, and then click **Next**. The example used here is building a Tier 1 incident queue, with an objective of keeping System Center Operations Manager and System-created incidents out of this queue. Figure 10.6 shows two exclusions made to not include system- and OpsMgr-created incidents. Only work items that meet the specified criteria are added to that queue. Click **Next** to proceed.

5. On the Summary page, click **Create** to create the queue.

6. On the Completion page, click **Close**.

   Here's how to validate creation of a queue: In the Service Manager console, verify that the new queue appears in the Queues pane. In the Tasks pane, click **Properties**, and then confirm that the queue appears as you defined it.

10

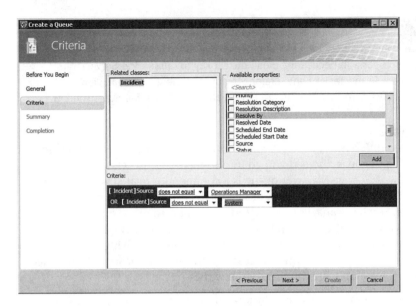

FIGURE 10.6   Create Tier 1 queue.

Incident Lists Library

An incident work item includes different fields with useful information to help solve the incident. Although the primary goal of Incident Management is solving incidents, routing incident work items and key performance indicator (KPI) reporting are also key. Service Manager lists represent a property of an object and include one or more list items. Each list item represents a possible value for the property the support team can select on the incident forms and dialog boxes. Using lists lets you classify different objects such as incidents, change requests, activities, and CIs. This classification can be used to route the incident work item or with KPI reporting.

Service Manager 2010 has several default list items for Incident Management. The default lists and list items represent a predefined list of values for the incident work item creator to select. You can customize the Incident Lists library to reflect the business practices and requirements of your organization. Table 10.1 provides an overview of the default incident lists.

TABLE 10.1   Incident Management Lists

List Name	Description	Management Pack
Incident Tier Queue	Incident Tier Queue List	Incident Management Library
Incident Status	Incident Status List	Incident Management Library
Incident Source	Incident Source List	Incident Management Library
Incident Classification	Incident Classification List	Incident Management Library
Incident Resolution	Incident Resolution List	Incident Management Library

When creating an incident, the Classification category is mandatory; you must select a list item. The default list items included for incident classification are a first-level categorization; your organization may require additional levels. Consider, for example, the Enterprise Application Problems list item, which may be required to create a set of child list items reflecting applications in your organization. You can use these child list items to route the incident work item to the correct support team and for reporting.

To configure the Incident Classification List for Incident Management in the Odyssey Service Manager environment, follow these steps:

1. In the Service Manager console, click **Library**. In the Library space, click **Lists**. The Lists pane displays all existing lists. You can organize the Result pane information by clicking the column titles; this makes it easy to find the list you want to edit.

2. Select the list to which you want to add a list item. (So, in this case, select the **Incident Classification** list.) In the Tasks pane, under Incident Classification, click **Properties**.

3. In the List Properties dialog box, click **Enterprise Application Problems**, and then click **Add Child**. Notice a new List Value list item is added. You can change the name of the new list item by clicking the item and then entering the new list item name in the name fields of the dialog box.

4. Click the new **List Value** list item. In the Name box, type a name for the new list item. You can type an optional description in the Description box. Figure 10.7 specifies the Company Web Application as a child item of the Enterprise Application Problems List item.

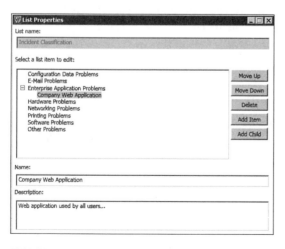

FIGURE 10.7   Edit List properties.

5. Repeat steps 2 to 4 to create additional list items in the Incident Classification List properties. Click **OK** to save your changes.

TIP: SERVICE MANAGER MANAGEMENT PACK GUIDELINES

When you click Add Item or Add Child, a Select MP dialog box may appear. Here are some MP guidelines:

▶ Do not save the configuration in the Default MP.

▶ Watch out for unsealed MPs. List items are in many cases referenced in other forms, workflows, and reports; it is not possible to reference objects from an unsealed MP.

Because incident classification is an important part of the Incident Management process, you want to be clear about the required classifications for your organization. As specified in the "Incident Management in Service Manager" section, routing and reporting requirements for Incident Management are the primary sources of information to build up your incident classification list items. It is best that you not have a deep classification list (more than three levels). The support team can lose time scrolling down the classification menu, the list becomes too complex, and incidents can end up with wrong incident classification.

Having a good incident classification list that reflects your organization's requirements and is known by the support team avoids incident work items being classified as "other problems." This is a very weak classification and should be avoided, although you can use it for certain incidents if necessary.

TIP: DO NOT DELETE THE DEFAULT LIST ITEMS

Do not delete the default list items included in Service Manager 2010, because each default list item is defined by a globally unique identifier (GUID). It is recommended that you change the display name of the existing item instead of deleting the default list items.

Configuring the General Incident Settings

General Incident Settings is a globally scoped incident configuration. This part of the chapter discusses customizations for Incident Management in Service Manager 2010.

The Incident Management settings are configured in the Administration space of the management console. To access these settings, follow these steps:

1. In the Service Manager console, navigate to **Administration -> Settings**.

2. In the Settings folder, click **Incident Settings** in the Results pane.

3. In the Tasks pane, under Incident Settings, click **Properties** to open the Incident Settings dialog box.

The ticket prefix setting, displayed in Figure 10.8, is the first configuration option of the General incident settings configuration.

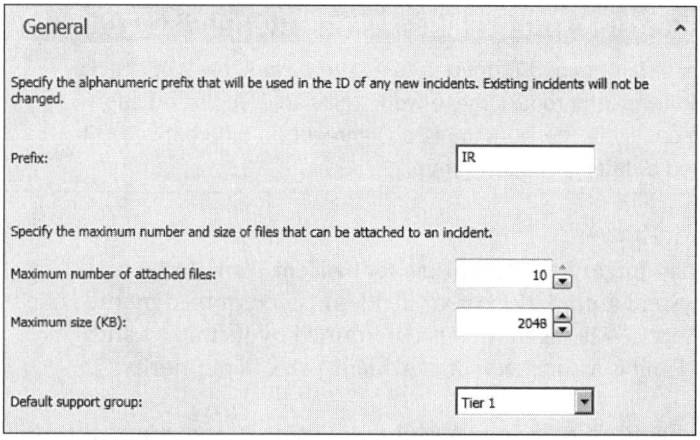

FIGURE 10.8   General incident settings.

NOTE: INCIDENT WORK ITEM PREFIX SETTINGS

You can specify alphanumeric and numeric characters as a prefix for incident work items. In general, do not specify a numeric prefix to distinguish work items; this could be confusing when the number of the work item is added. The prefix specification is limited to 15 characters.

Attached File Policy Configuration

Files associated with an event can be added to the incident work item. You can configure the number of files you can add and maximum file size in the General incident settings. Default settings are a maximum of 10 files and file size of 2048KB. Find a configuration that fits your needs; ensure you do not block the support team from adding important information while preventing bulk uploads of files in the work item.

TIP: IMPACT OF THE ATTACHED FILE POLICY CONFIGURATION

The maximum number of attached files and maximum file size settings you configure will also apply to the attached files in the Related Items tab for CIs.

Default Support Group Configuration

Incident work items not assigned to a support group could negatively affect your KPIs. The work items end up in the overall Open Incidents queue; it is possible no one is watching this queue or the work items are handled with low priority. Service Manager 2010 will let you specify a default support group. In the event an incident work item is created and no workflow routes the work item to a support group, the incident tier queue configured as the default support group is automatically added to the work item.

TIP: ALTERNATE CONFIGURATION FOR DEFAULT SUPPORT GROUP SETTINGS

An alternative to specifying a default support group is to create a workflow that checks for unassigned incident work items and routes these work items to a dedicated support team. Although you can configure the work items assignment on different ways, it is always best to have defined a default support group.

Configure Priority Calculation and Target Resolution Time for Incident Work Items

The routing, assigning, and system automation of an incident is determined by the issue's priority. Incident priority in Service Manager 2010 is determined by its impact and urgency. A Target Resolution Time is associated with incident work item priority:

▶ *Impact of the incident* is the measure of how business critical it is. Sometimes this is difficult to determine for a service desk operator, but impact is usually directly proportional to a number of users influenced by the incident or how critical an impacted service is to the business or business function.

▶ *Urgency* is the required time of resolving an incident. Incident urgency is not an exact property of an event. This may vary in time for particular users or business services. (Examples include VIP users or an event on the HR application during payroll calculation.)

▶ *Resolution time* is the time to resolve an incident. The Target Resolution Time is the total time from incident work item creation to incident resolution and restoring the service to the user.

Impact and urgency settings are defined as High, Medium, or Low, and are mandatory fields when the incident is created. You can configure the priority on an incident work item with a priority calculation table, as illustrated in Figure 10.9. Figure 10.10 illustrates the settings you can make for incident work item impact and urgency.

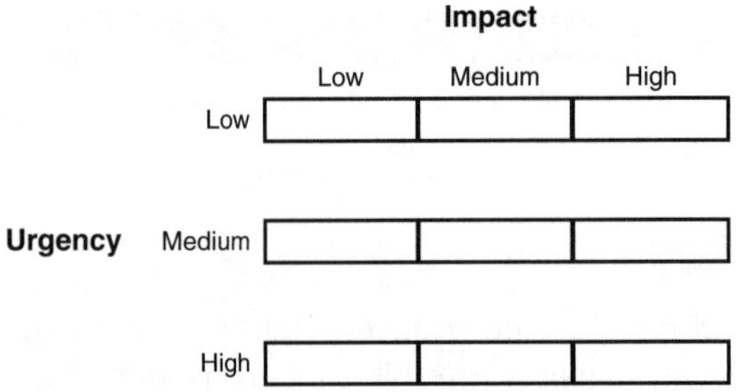

FIGURE 10.9   Priority configuration table.

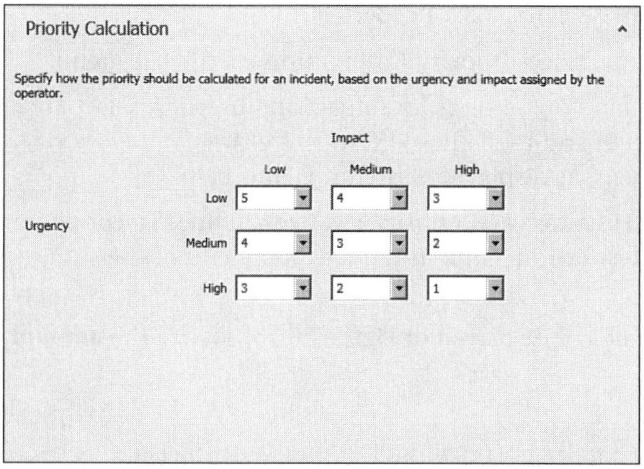

FIGURE 10.10   Example priority calculation.

NOTE: ADJUSTING THE IMPACT AND URGENCY LIST ITEMS

You can adjust the impact and urgency settings of High, Medium, or Low, or define additional options via the Urgency and Impact List configuration in the Lists folder of the Library console pane. Be careful with adjusting the values of these list items; they are applied in all work items' priority matrixes.

Before configuring priority, it is important to first define the terms impact and urgency for your organization. You can raise service desk awareness on these definitions by educating service desk operators on a regular basis.

Although the configuration matrix lets you define priority levels from 1 to 9 (with corresponding resolution time), this is not mandatory. Define the priority levels based on your particular Incident Management process requirements. For most scenarios, a priority level configuration of four or five different levels is recommended. It is also worth considering a VIP impact category, elevating the resulting priority of the issue.

TIP: PRIORITY-LEVEL CONFIGURATION FOR INCIDENT WORK ITEMS

Take care when configuring priority levels for Incident Management work items:

▶ Priority levels correspond with a Target Resolution Time.
▶ Correct and timely handling of incidents work items depend on these values.

You can configure the urgency, impact, and Target Resolution Time settings for Incident Management in the Service Manager console by following these steps:

1. In the Administration space, expand **Administration -> Settings**. In the Settings pane, click **Incident Settings**.

10

2. In the Tasks pane, under Incident Settings, click **Properties**.

3. In the Incident Settings dialog box, select **Priority Calculation** on the left menu.

4. For each of the High, Medium, and Low settings for impact and urgency, select an incident priority value from 1 to 9, and then click **OK**. In this example, the priority configurations consist of five levels, as displayed earlier in Figure 10.10.

5. You must set Target Resolution Time for each priority level you define. To configure Target Resolution Time, select **Resolution Time** in the left-side menu of the Incident Settings.

6. For each of the priority settings of 1–9 displayed in Figure 10.11, specify the amount of time for incident resolution.

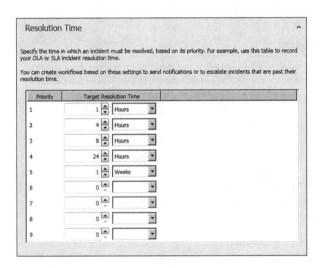

FIGURE 10.11   Example target resolution time configuration.

7. Click **OK** to close the Incident Settings wizard.

Configuring Incoming Emailed Incidents

The service desk can use the console to create incidents. Consider a scenario where a user calls the service desk and the issue is not immediately resolved, so the service desk creates an incident work item in the Service Manager console. Service Manager extends this functionality with support for emailed support requests. End users can submit incidents by sending an email to a dedicated email address; Service Manager picks up this email and creates an incident. You can use several email addresses, such as one for enterprise applications, another for hardware, and one for printer events.

One way to configure this functionality in Service Manager is using a Simple Mail Transfer Protocol (SMTP) server for emailed incident "pickup." Another option for emailed incidents is the Exchange connector. Both configuration options are further explained in the following sections.

Incoming Emailed Incidents via an SMTP Server

When the end user sends an email to log a support request, Microsoft Exchange routes the message to a drop folder on the computer hosting an SMTP server service. Service Manager monitors this share and processes the message into an incident. Service Manager parses the From address and attempts to match the user in the Service Manager database. If Service Manager cannot find the user in the Service Manager database, the message moves to a Badmail folder, and an incident is not created.

The infrastructure required to handle incoming emailed incidents includes an existing server running Microsoft Exchange or mail server that supports the SMTP protocol, and a server that runs the SMTP service for Service Manager. The SMTP service role uses Internet Information Services (IIS) 6.0 SMTP services and can be installed on the server hosting the Service Manager management server component or a separate remote server (requires remote folder access between the SMTP server and Service Manager server). Figure 10.12 presents an overview of mail flow.

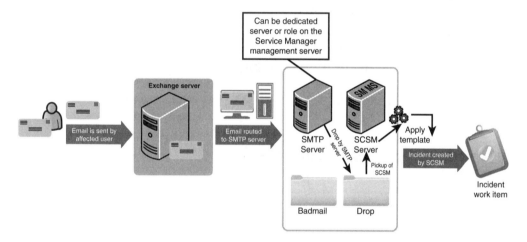

FIGURE 10.12   Emailed incidents flow.

Here is what configuring the functionality includes:

▶ Configuring the mail server to route emails to the Service Manager SMTP server.

▶ Setting up and configuring the Service Manager SMTP server.

▶ Configuring the inbound email settings in Service Manager.

These are discussed in the next sections.

Configure the Mail Server to Route Emails

A detailed overview of the Exchange server routing configuration is beyond the scope of this book, but a walkthrough of the required configuration for your Exchange server is

10

included for completeness. The goal is to define the email addresses as an accepted email domain on the server and route email for that domain to the SMTP server. Perform the following steps:

1. Open the Exchange Management console. Expand **Organization Configuration -> Hub Transports**.

2. In the Hub Transport pane, click **Accepted Domain**. In the Actions pane, click **New Accepted Domains**.

   In the New Accepted Domains dialog box, create a new accepted domain of the type Internal Relay (for example, ***.support.Odyssey.com**).

3. In the Hub Transports pane, click **Send Connectors**. In the Actions pane, click **New Send Connector**.

4. In the New SMTP Send Connector wizard, create a new send connector by using the following information:

   Address space = *.support.Odyssey.com

   Add Smart Host by using the IP Address of the computer that will host the SMTP Server service defined in the next section.

   Set smart host authentication settings to **None**.

After you create the routing transport on your Exchange server, the settings should look like Figure 10.13.

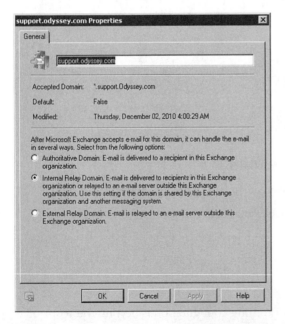

FIGURE 10.13   Accepted domain configuration for the Exchange Hub transport.

Set Up and Configure the Service Manager SMTP Server

The SMTP server is a capability on Windows Server and configurable using Internet Information Services Manager. Service Manager uses the SMTP server to pick up routed email from your production mail environment and drop it into its mail folder. Service Manager monitors the folder and creates incidents from these emails. You can place this role on the management server if the Web Server role is installed, or use another server. To configure the SMTP server service, follow these steps:

1. On the computer that will host the SMTP server service, select **Programs -> Administrative Tools**, and then **Internet Information Services (IIS) 6.0 Manager**.

2. Right-click the local computer node, select **New**, and then click **SMTP Virtual Server**.

3. In the New SMTP Virtual Server wizard, in the Name field, type the name for the SMTP server, and then click **Next**. The example displayed in Figure 10.14 uses support.Odyssey.com as the name of the SMTP server.

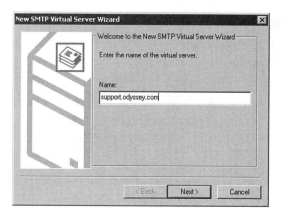

FIGURE 10.14   Naming the Service Manager SMTP server.

4. On the Select IP Address page, click the drop-down list and select the IP address of the computer hosting the SMTP server, and then click **Next**.

5. On the Select Home Directory page, click **Browse** and click to the folder for your home directory. For example, select **C:\inetpub\mailroot**, as shown in Figure 10.15. In step 8 of this procedure, you need to share this folder to enable Service Manager 2010 to pick up email from this SMTP server.

6. On the Default Domain page, type the domain name for this virtual SMTP server (see Figure 10.16), and then click **Finish**. The domain name you enter must match the domain name from step 3. Here the domain name is **support.Odyssey.com**.

7. Click **Close** on the New SMTP Virtual Server wizard to complete your changes. If you navigate to the configured Home folder for the SMTP server, you will notice a folder structure created to handle email, as shown in Figure 10.17.

10

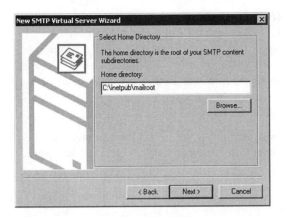

FIGURE 10.15   Service Manager SMTP server.

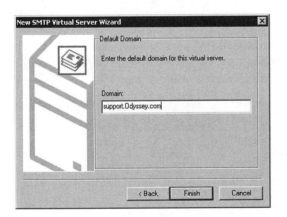

FIGURE 10.16   SMTP server default domain.

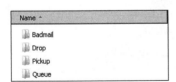

FIGURE 10.17   SMTP server folders.

8. Next, create a share for the mail root folder. On your desktop, right-click the **Start** button, and then select **Explore**. In Windows Explorer, drill down to the folder that you specified as the home directory in step 5 (C:\inetpub\mailroot). If needed, create two subfolders: **Badmail** and **Drop**.

9. Right-click the home folder and select **Share**.

   In the File Sharing dialog box, select the domain user specified as the Service Manager Operational System account, click **Contributor**, click **Share**, and then click **Done**.

To double-check the Operational System account, open the Service Manager console. Select **Administration -> Security**, and then select **Run As Accounts**. You should also verify the SMTP service on the server is set to Automatic and is started.

Configure the SMTP Server for Service Manager

Last in configuring support for incoming emailed incidents is to configure Service Manager 2010 with the correct SMTP server and drop folder you configured on the SMTP server. Perform the following steps:

1. In the Service Manager console, select **Administration -> Settings**.

2. In the Settings space, double-click **General Incident Settings**.

3. In the General Incident Settings dialog box, select **Inbound E-mail**.

    a. In the SMTP Service Drop Folder Location field, type the path, share, and folder to the drop folder. For this case, type \\<*computername*>**mailroot****Drop** where *computername* is the name of the computer hosting the SMTP Server service displayed in Figure 10.18, mailroot is the share name, and Drop is the subfolder. For this example, METEOR is the SMTP server and default path to the folders.

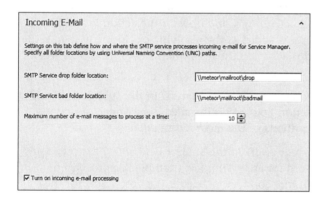

FIGURE 10.18   Incoming E-Mail sample configuration.

    b. In the SMTP Service Bad Folder Location field, type the path, share, and folder to the bad mail folder. Type \\<*computername*>**mailroot****Badmail**, where <*computername*> is the computer hosting the SMTP Server service, mailroot is the share name, and Badmail is the subfolder.

    c. In the Maximum number of e-mail messages to process at a time field, enter the number of emails you want Service Manager to process during an email processing cycle.

    d. Tick the box to Turn on inbound email processing.

    Figure 10.18 shows the Incoming E-Mail screen.

4. Click **OK** to save your changes.

10

TIP: VERIFY THE SMTP MAIL FLOW

If Service Manager is not receiving and SMTP is on a remote server, try logging in using the Workflow account. You can open Explorer, type in the UNC path (*computername*\ *folder*\), and verify the Workflow account has access to the SMTP folders.

Incoming Emailed Incidents via Exchange Connector

The Exchange connector connects Service Manager to Exchange for processing incoming email related to incidents and change requests. The following functionality is available when the Exchange connector is configured:

▶ When a new email is sent to the monitored Exchange mailbox and no work item ID is present in the Subject field of the email, the Service Manager Exchange connector processes the incoming email and creates a new incident work item.

▶ When an email is sent in reply to an email sent from the Service Manager system regarding an existing incident with the incident ID in the Subject field (for example, "Subject" - [IR0012]), the connector appends the email message to the action log of the incident identified in the subject by the ID.

▶ When an email with an incident ID (for example, [IR0012]) in the Subject field also contains the keyword for resolving or closing the incident work item, the connector changes the status of the incident accordingly and updates the action log and attaches any files. The sending user is added as the resolving or closing user, and the content of the most recent email is added to the Resolution Description field when the resolved keyword is sent.

▶ When an email is sent with a change request work item ID in the Subject field and the included Change Request "Action Log" MP is installed, the connector updates the Action Log field to add the contents of the most recent email.

▶ If an email is sent with a change request ID in the Subject field and the most recent message body contains the keyword for approving (for example, [Approved]) or rejecting (for example, [Rejected]), the connector changes the vote status for the sending user in the review activity in the change request work item. This approach cannot be used to change the vote status of a reviewer's group.

▶ If an email is sent with a manual activity ID in the Subject field, the connector appends the Notes field with the contents of the latest message body (up to 4,000 characters). If the keyword for completion of the activity (for example, [Completed]) is present, the connector changes the status of the activity to Completed.

Additional information about the work item is populated with the email content by the Exchange connector. For example, the email subject becomes the incident title, the email body becomes the incident description, and email attachments are added to the incident work item as file attachments.

Each email sent from the Service Manager system must contain the work item ID enclosed in square brackets in the subject so that when people reply the work item ID will be in the

Subject field and can be processed by the connector. If the work item ID is not present in the Subject field, the connector assumes the email should be a new incident!

Perform the following steps to configure the Exchange connector in your Exchange environment:

NOTE: EXCHANGE CONNECTOR VERSION

The Exchange connector version 1.0 is used in this procedure. As Microsoft releases newer versions, review the installation guidelines for that version and review the specified file versions before starting the installation. For this release only, the workflow account's email inbox can be used. In addition, the mailbox of the workflow account itself is the only mailbox that can be monitored. The connector relies on the Exchange Auto Discover service being configured in AD/DNS.

1. Navigate to the folder where you have extracted the Exchange connector binaries. You must download and install the 64-bit Exchange Web Services Managed API Client DLL (Microsoft.Exchange.WebServices.dll), which you can find on Microsoft's download site. (The minimum required version is 14.0.650.7.)

2. Copy the Microsoft.SystemCenter.ExchangeConnector.dll (from the Exchange connector folder) and Microsoft.Exchange.WebServices.dll (from the Exchange Web Services program folder) files to the installation directory on the Service Manager management server where you are running workflows and wherever you plan to use a console to configure the Exchange connector.

3. In the Service Manager console, select **Administration**. Right-click the **Management Pack** folder, and then select **Import the management pack**. Navigate to the Microsoft.SystemCenter.ExchangeConnector.xml file of the folder where you extracted the Exchange connector binaries, and import into Service Manager. Figure 10.19 provides an overview of the Exchange connector MP import page.

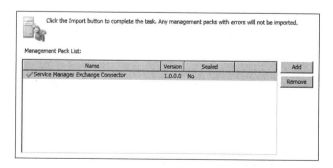

FIGURE 10.19   Import the Exchange connector MP.

4. After importing the MP, it is suggested you close and then reopen the console, and then navigate to the Administration pane and select the **Connectors** folder. Click

Create Connector -> Exchange Connector (as illustrated in Figure 10.20) in the Tasks pane.

Active Directory Connector
Configuration Manager Connector
Exchange Connector
Operations Manager Alert Connector
Operations Manager CI Connector

FIGURE 10.20   The Exchange connector menu item.

5. The Create Exchange Connector wizard starts. Click **Next** on the welcome page. On the General page, provide a name and description, as shown in Figure 10.21, and then click **Next**.

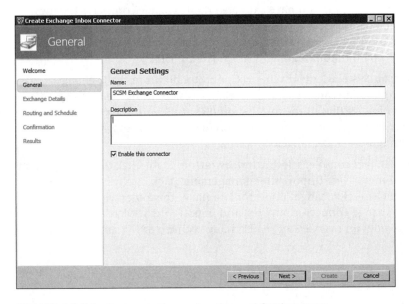

FIGURE 10.21   Exchange Connector: General Settings page.

6. On the Exchange Details configuration page, provide the following information and then click **Next**:

   ▶ The email address alias to monitor for incoming emails (for example, support@Odyssey.com).

   ▶ The keyword, which is how the email messages are parsed to determine the content of just the most recent message (for example, From:).

Additional fields in the wizard are configuration fields to configure the word to use to look in Outlook at an email thread and use the word in this position:

▶ Manual Activity completed (for example, [Completed])

▶ Incident resolved (for example, [Resolved])

▶ Incident closed (for example, [Closed])

▶ Incident resolved (for example, [Resolved])

▶ Review Activity rejected (for example, [Rejected])

You can use whatever words/phrases you prefer, but make sure you choose a string that would not normally occur in regular email conversation; this is best achieved by enclosing the text in square brackets.

The AD forests to search for users in are for the Exchange auto-discover functionality on which this connector is depending. If there is more than one, you can delimit them with a semicolon.

The Configuration page asks you to specify whether to move the email items to the Deleted Items folder after processing, and whether to append the whole body of the email message (up to 4,000 characters) to the incident action log.

Figure 10.22 illustrates the configuration of the Exchange Details page.

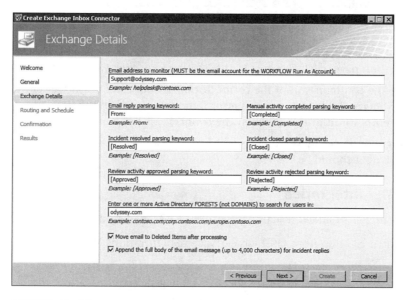

FIGURE 10.22   Exchange Connector: Exchange Details page.

7. On the Schedule and Routing page, provide the following information and click **Next**.

You can configure the template to apply when updating or creating new incidents via the Exchange connector. This template can specify the initial impact, urgency, and support group property values. The frequency to check for new emailed support requests can be configured in minutes.

Figure 10.23 provides an overview of the routing and schedule configuration.

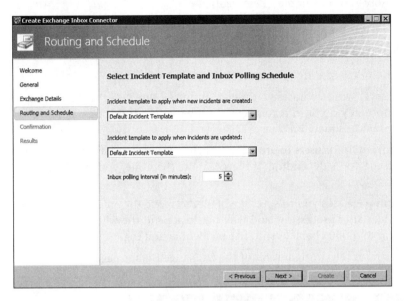

FIGURE 10.23   Exchange Connector: Routing and Schedule page.

1. On the Confirmation page, click **Create**. On the Results page, click **Close**.

2. You can validate the configuration of the connector using the server event viewer in the Operations Manager folder. Success and error information is found there, and this is your first entry for information when the connector is not working.

3. Test the Exchange connector by sending an email to the monitored email address. An incident work item should be created.

Configuring OpsMgr Integration

Operations Manager can deliver added functionality in Service Manager on two levels:

▶ Automated incident creation from OpsMgr alerts via the Operations Manager Alert connector.

▶ Support group analysts responsible for the OpsMgr-managed server can check the health state of a CI using a Service Manager console task.

Configuring Operations Manager alert incidents in Service Manager 2010 consists of configuring the OpsMgr Alert connector in the Administration space of the Service Manager console and configuring the Operations Manager Web Setting on the Incident settings. This enables support analysts to view incident alert detailed information from OpsMgr by using two additional tasks from the work items folder:

▶ View Alert details

▶ View CI Health State

For the Odyssey environment used in this book, HYDRA is the OpsMgr server and specified in the Incident Settings. Figure 10.24 shows the Operations Manager web settings.

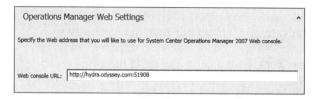

FIGURE 10.24   Operations Manager Web Settings.

In addition to the connector and web settings, you can automate routing and assignment of incidents that are created via the connector. OpsMgr incident routing configuration is described in the "Incident Management Automation" section of this chapter.

ABOUT ENABLING AUTOMATED INCIDENT CREATION WITH OPSMGR ALERTS

Enabling automated incident creation from OpsMgr alerts introduces infrastructure incidents into your Incident Management process. This is a completely different concept; normally, an incident is created when a user calls the service desk, and creation is "controlled" by the incident creators. Because OpsMgr alerts are automatically generated, the only way to control incident creation is to ensure the source is under control. Given that useless OpsMgr-generated alerts generate incident work items, you should perform any necessary noise canceling in your OpsMgr environment before introducing automated incident creation from OpsMgr.

It is not mandatory to enable incident creation for all OpsMgr-created alerts. Setup of the OpsMgr connector includes two steps:

▶ Configuring your connector in Service Manager. Here you can automate the incident routing (more in the "Incident Management Automation" section).

▶ Managing the connector subscriptions in the OpsMgr console, where you can subscribe particular OpsMgr groups (generally associated with the imported MPs). In this manner, you can gradually introduce infrastructure incident into your Service Manager environment.

You can also forward OpsMgr alerts in a semi-automated way to Service Manager. In the OpsMgr console, you can select an alert and "forward" it manually to Service Manager.

Configuring ConfigMgr Desired Configuration Management Integration

DCM in Configuration Manager enables monitoring ConfigMgr clients to ensure they are compliant with defined values. This lets you monitor software versions, security settings,

10

and software updates. Service Manager lets you import configuration baselines from ConfigMgr with the Configuration Manager connector. You can then configure Service Manager to create incidents for each Service Manager CI reporting as noncompliant against the defined values.

To configure Configuration Manager DCM in Service Manager 2010, start by creating Desired Configuration baselines in ConfigMgr. In Service Manager, define a workflow for each ConfigMgr DCM baseline or include them all in one workflow. The DCM workflow lets you apply an incident template and notify the support team of non-compliant computers. In this way, Service Manager extends ConfigMgr's DCM functionality to include proactive configuration management functionality. Service Manager creates an incident work item for CIs reporting non-compliant against the DCM baseline in ConfigMgr. The service desk can then be notified, or the incident work item routed to a queue where the proper actions can be taken. This functionality enables you to keep your systems healthy. A complete ConfigMgr DCM workflow configuration is described in the "Incident Management Automation" section of this chapter.

Configuring Incident Notifications

Notifications can be sent through Service Manager when an incident work item is created or updated. Based on the defined criteria, almost any type of change can be triggered to send out notifications. Although notification functionality is explained in Chapter 14, "Notifications," here is a high-level listing of the steps required to set up your incident notification plan:

1. Enable email notifications and establish a notification channel with your SMTP mail server.

2. A notification template is used as the basis for your notification message. You can create your own HTML-based template (say in Microsoft Word) and paste it into Service Manager as your notification template. You can extend the incident notification template to include properties of the incident work item.

3. Specify the criteria to send notifications. The criteria to send the notification are specified on the subscription configuration. In the Subscription Configuration wizard, you can specify sending notifications whether an incident work item is created or updated. This condition can be extended by querying the incident work item properties for changes and using this as a trigger for sending notifications. When the criteria are met, an incident template is applied and a notification message sent.

Incident Management Automation

You now have seen how to configure Incident Management in Service Manager. Configuring Incident Management provides the building blocks for further automation. The "Incident Management Process Activities" section discusses automation opportunities in Service Manager Incident Management, applying a mapping between Service Manager functionality and the Incident Management process activities. Consider the categorization and assignment of an incident work item: You can create a workflow that triggers on certain criteria and applies a template to categorize the incident work item and assign it to a support group, letting you define workflows for different types of process steps that are unlikely to change often.

Incident Management automation is accomplished using workflows. This part of the chapter explains and creates incident event workflows for different scenarios. Here are the three primary scenarios for creating a workflow:

▶ Incident event workflow classification, routing, and customizing the incident work item.

▶ Automating incoming OpsMgr alerts

▶ DCM event workflow

NOTE: ABOUT ENABLING INCIDENT AUTOMATION

You can import information from AD, OpsMgr, ConfigMgr, or CSV, enabling you to keep your Service Manager CIs automatically in sync with their source. This is a very nice functionality of Service Manager and a real added value, but be aware that when you create workflows in Service Manager, you must ensure all involved CIs have the attribute information available that triggers the workflow. If certain attribute information is not available for a subset of CIs or the information is not up-to-date, this could break your automation, and you could end up with, for example, incidents in the wrong queue or having the wrong priority assigned. This could negatively affect your KPI reporting.

To begin, you need to have a clear view of what happens in an incident event workflow. Figure 10.25 is a graphical overview of the steps in an incident event workflow.

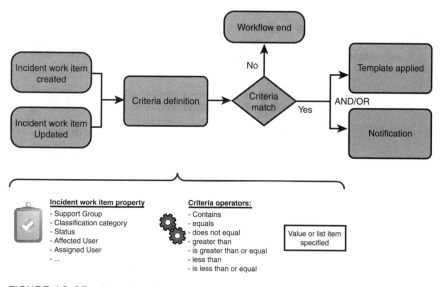

FIGURE 10.25 Overview of workflow automation.

Here is what Figure 10.25 shows:

1. The first trigger in an incident event workflow is an action (input) on the work item. An incident work item is created or updated.

2. The criteria definition checks the incident work item property for a certain value. Different operators can be used to evaluate the incident work item property.

3. Once there is a match, you can apply a template or send out a notification (action). You can create workflows only for applying templates or to send out notification based on the defined criteria, or you can combine the two.

Let's see what is required before the different workflows can be created. Table 10.2 lists the necessary templates required for the Company Web application that is used as an example in this chapter. As illustrated in Figure 10.25, configuring automation in the Incident process requires a trigger (see Table 10.2), notification requirements (shown in Table 10.3), and settings you want to apply (see Table 10.4).

TABLE 10.2   Incident Automation: Templates Overview

Workflows	Incident Work Item Template
Company Web Application	Urgency, impact incident properties must be set to High. Support group needs to be assigned—Tier 2. Need to be assigned directly to an AD security group.
OpsMgr incoming Alerts	SQL alerts need to be assigned to Tier 2 support group. Classification category must be set.
ConfigMgr DCM Event	DCM events urgency, impact incident properties need to be set to Medium. Classification category must be set.

TABLE 10.3   Incident Automation: Notification Templates Overview

Workflows	Notification Template
Company Web Application	Notification to assigned support analyst
OpsMgr incoming Alerts	Notification to assigned support analyst
ConfigMgr DCM Event	No notification required

TABLE 10.4   Incident Automation: Workflow Criteria Overview

Workflows	Workflow Criteria
Company Web Application	Incident work item created Classification category = Company Web Application
OpsMgr incoming Alerts	Alert generated by the OpsMgr SQL MP
SCCM DCM Event	DCM noncompliancy event from ConfigMgr

Table 10.3 reviews the required notification templates for the different scenarios. For the Company Web application notification template, you can use the template created in the "Notification" section of this chapter. The OpsMgr Alert notification template is a new template and must be created.

Table 10.4 lists the different criteria for the workflows.

Now you can start preparing the environment for the workflow creation. This is just one example of an automation, but it shows you should document some information before beginning to automate the Incident process. Taking this approach, you can create an overview of your automation configuration. The individuals who must validate the automation process can understand the information, and you have documented the workflows for later troubleshooting.

Incident Management Templates

As specified in the "Incident Management in Service Manager" section of this chapter, templates are used to preconfigure certain work item properties or apply properties on work items using a workflow. The next example creates an incident template for the Company Web application. Table 10.2 provided input for this configuration, which defined the requirements for the template. Perform the following steps:

1. In the Service Manager console, click **Library**. Now expand **Library -> Templates**. In the Tasks pane, click **Create Template**.

2. In the Create Template dialog box (see Figure 10.26), specify name, class, and MP.

FIGURE 10.26   Create template.

This example creates a template for Company Web application incidents; the name of the template is **Company Web App incidents template**. In the Description box, type a description for the incident template.

Click **Browse** to choose a class. In the Choose Class dialog box, click **Incident**, and then click **OK**.

3. On the Incident Information screen (see Figure 10.27), perform these steps:

In the Classification Category box, select the category that reflects the problem to report. For this example, select **Company Web app** and set the Impact and Urgency boxes to **High**.

In the Support Group box, select a tier. For example, if all Company Web application issues are assigned to the Tier 2 support group, select Tier 2. The Assigned to property is populated with the AD security group.

4. Click **OK** to save the template.

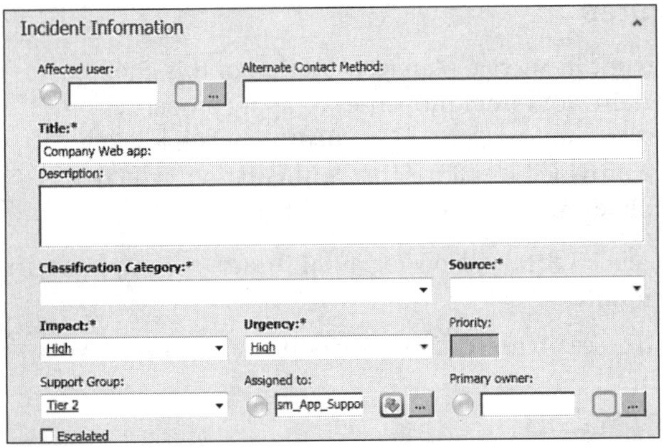

FIGURE 10.27   Specifying incident properties.

This procedure created an incident template you can use to create templates for OpsMgr Alert incident events and ConfigMgr DCM events. The only differences on the template creation for these templates are the incident properties you need to select. Table 10.2 provides input to create these events.

Incident Management Workflows

A workflow is a sequence of activities that automate a process. The following steps create an incident event workflow configuration for the Company Web application. Tables 10.3, 10.4, and 10.5 provide input for the workflow configuration.

1. In the Service Manager console, click **Administration**. Expand **Workflows**, and click **Configuration**.

2. In the Configuration pane, double-click **Incident Event Workflow Configuration**.

3. In the Configure Incident Event Workflows dialog box, click **Add**.

Follow these steps in the Add Incident Event Workflow dialog box, shown as Figure 10.28:

a. On the Before You Begin page, click **Next**.

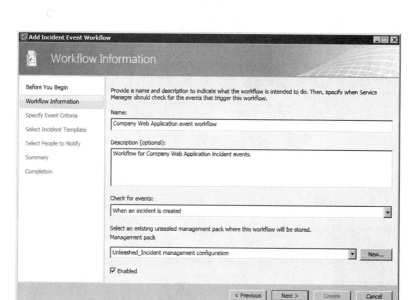

FIGURE 10.28   Workflow Information page.

b. On the Workflow Information page, in the Name box, type a name for the workflow, such as **Company Web application event workflow**. In the Check for
events list, select **When an incident is created**, make sure that the Enabled check
box is checked, and then click **Next**.

c. On the Specify Event Criteria page shown in Figure 10.29, click the **Changed to**
tab. In the Available Properties list, select **Incident Classification**, and then click
Add. In the Criteria box, select **equals**. In the list, select **Company Web application**. Then, click **Next**.

d. On the Select Incident Template page (see Figure 10.30), click **Apply the following template**, and select the **Company Web App Incidents** template. This
template sets the support group to Tier 2, Urgency to High, Impact to High, and
provides a Title start text. Click **Next**.

e. On the Select People to Notify page displayed in Figure 10.31, optionally check
the Enable notification check box, select the user to notify, and then click **Next**.

4. On the Summary page, review your settings and click **Create**. Click **Close** on the
Completion page, and OK in the Configure Incident Event Workflows dialog box.

A workflow is now triggered whenever an incident is created with the classification category Company Web application. You can review the workflow runtime in the space pane
of the console, in the Status folder under Workflows.

10

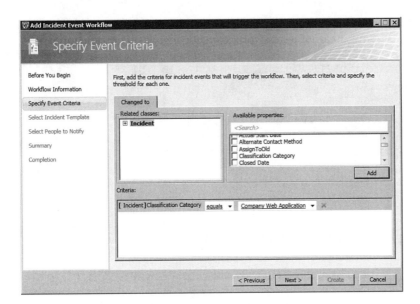

FIGURE 10.29 Specifying criteria.

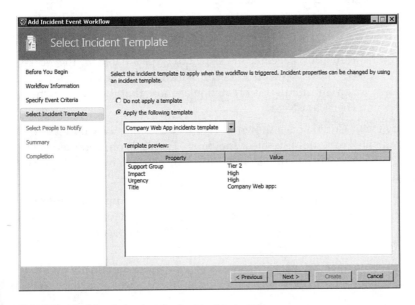

FIGURE 10.30 Selecting the incident template.

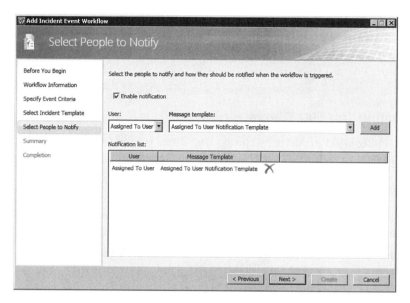

FIGURE 10.31   Specifying notifications.

Two views are available, one with all instances and another with the runtime instance that needs attention. The All Instance view consists of all success and failure instances, and the Need Attention view displays only those instances when a workflow failed. In the All Instance view, you can view the log, view the related object, retry the workflow, and ignore the status instance. Watch out for the Retry and Ignore options in the Status result pane; both options remove the workflow status instance entry.

TIP: CRITERIA DEFINITION FOR WORKFLOWS

In most cases, it is a best practice to use both from and to selection criteria for updated work items. If the criteria definition is not precise enough, the workflow might be triggered unintentionally.

To view the workflow runtime successes and failures in the Service Manager console, follow these steps:

1. In the Service Manager console, click **Administration**. Expand **Administration**, expand **Workflows**, and select **Status**.

2. In the Status pane, click the workflow that you want to view (for example, Company Web Application event workflow).

10

The Need attention view in the Status results pane lets you see the failing run-times. Click **All Instances** and **View log** to view the list of events that occurred when the workflow ran. Click **View related object** to view the form used when the workflow ran.

Automating Incoming OpsMgr Alerts

You can automate incoming OpsMgr Alerts by configuring filters on the Operations Manager connector or using workflows where the criteria are adjusted to capture the specific alerts. To use the OpsMgr connector filter configuration to apply templates on incidents created by the SQL MP, follow these steps:

1. In the Service Manager console, click **Administration**. In the Administration space, expand **Administration**, and then click **Connectors**.

2. In the Tasks pane, under Connectors, click **Operations Manager Alert Connector** and select **Properties** from the Tasks pane. When the Edit Connector wizard opens, navigate to the Alert Routing Rules configuration.

   Click **Add** to create an alert routing rule. The alert routing rule has several options to filter out the specific alerts. You can define rules that filter out alerts from a specific MP, a specific computer, or a custom field specification on the alert. Based on the defined rule, you can apply a specific incident template. Click **OK** to create the routing rule.

   If you have a complete overview of the routing rules for your organization, you can specify multiple routing rules on the Operations Manager connector. Figure 10.32 shows an alert routing rule configuration that filters out the alerts raised by the OpsMgr MPs that start with **Microsoft.SQLServer** and applies the SQL alerts using the OpsMgr template. (This template is listed in Table 10.2 and was created using the procedure in the "Incident Management Templates" section.)

3. Click **OK** to finalize the configuration of the Operations Manager connector.

You cannot configure notifications when defining an alert routing rule on the OpsMgr connector. When notifications are required for an incident work item created with the connector, you need to create an additional incident event workflow with a notification rule. Refer to the procedure detailed in the "Incident Management Workflows" section to create this additional workflow.

TIP: GENERIC APPROACH FOR FORWARDING ALERTS TO SERVICE MANAGER

If you need a generic way to forward alerts to Service Manager, create a generic override in Operations Manager, and Service Manager can then filter on this. For example, you can set the priority field of an event in OpsMgr to High, which is a general override; this forwards the alerts to Service Manager. Very few Operations Manager alerts have the priority set to High.

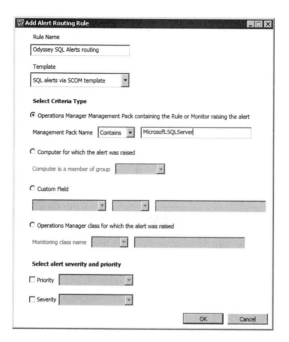

FIGURE 10.32   OpsMgr alert routing filter rule.

Creating a Desired Configuration Management Workflow

If a DCM workflow is created, Service Manager automatically generates incidents when computers fall out of compliance from DCM in ConfigMgr. DCM baselines are synchronized via the Configuration Manager connector and are a selection option when creating a DCM event workflow. This means you can create a workflow for a single baseline or select multiple baselines in a single workflow.

DCM event workflows are created in the Administration space of the Service Manager console. You configure DCM baseline rules in the ConfigMgr console and apply them to a ConfigMgr collection. Before configuring the DCM event workflow, you must install the Configuration Manager connector and configure ConfigMgr DCM baselines.

The next example imports the Windows 7 Enterprise Client DCM baseline from the Microsoft Security Compliance Manager tool. This baseline evaluates the ConfigMgr client on different security settings. Perform the following steps:

1. In the Service Manager console, click **Administration**. In the Administration space, expand **Administration**, expand **Workflows**, and then click **Configuration**.

2. In the Configuration pane, double-click **Desired Configuration Management Event Workflow Configuration**.

3. In the Configure Desired Configuration Management Workflows dialog box, click **Add** to create a new DCM event workflow.

4. In the Add Incident Event Workflow dialog box, follow the wizard to provide the necessary information. For this example, the Win7-EC-Desktop baselines are imported in Configuration Manager and available in the DCM event workflow wizard after synchronizing the connector:

   ▶ On the Before You Begin page, click **Next**.

   ▶ On the Workflow Information page displayed in Figure 10.33, in the Name box, type a name of the workflow.

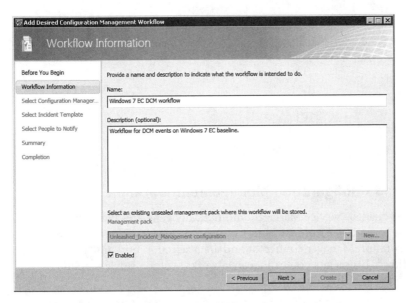

FIGURE 10.33   Information overview of the DCM workflow.

   ▶ On the Select System Center Configuration Manager Configuration Items page, expand all the configuration baselines listed, select the Configuration Manager CIs that you want to include in the rule, and then click **Next**. You can see in Figure 10.34 that the Win7-EC-Desktop security consists of different baselines; all these baselines are included in the workflow.

   ▶ On the Select Incident Template page, click **Apply the following template**, and then select the template you want to apply for the DCM-created incident work items. Figure 10.35 shows a sample configuration where the SCCM DCM template is applied. This template was created in the "Incident Management Templates" section and sets the support group property to Tier 2. Click **Next**, and then proceed with DCM event workflow creation.

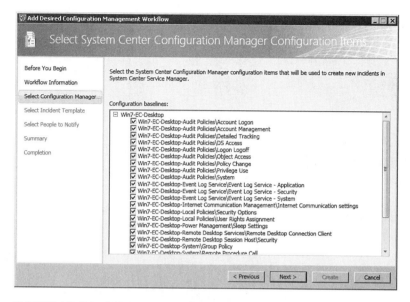

FIGURE 10.34   DCM baseline selection.

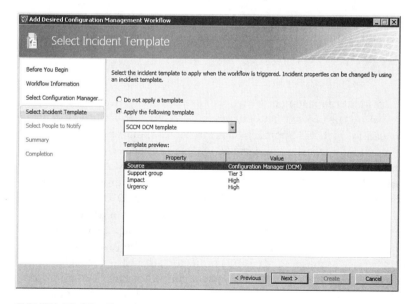

FIGURE 10.35   Template selection.

► On the Select People to Notify page (see Figure 10.36), check the Enable notification check box. Select the users to be notified when this rule creates an incident. For each user, specify the notification method and a template, and then click **Add**. Click **Next**.

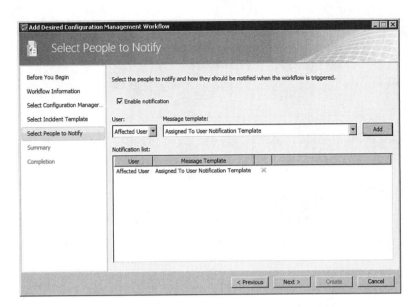

FIGURE 10.36   Specifying notification for the DCM Workflow.

5. On the Summary page, review your settings and click **Create**. Click **Close** on the Completion page, and **OK** in the Configure Incident Event Workflows dialog box.

Summary

This chapter discussed Incident Management in Service Manager 2010, from the components involved to automating the process. This chapter covered the Service Manager console with a "Where can I do what?" approach. The "Incident Management Process Activities" section of this chapter translates process activities to Service Manager Incident Management elements. Each process activity is associated with Service Manager functionality that can help enable the process in the tool. This chapter used examples to explain the actual configuration of Incident Management in Service Manager 2010, providing you with a complete Incident Management model. With this information, you should be able to translate your own process to Service Manager configuration and map it to Service Manager settings, templates, workflows, and so on. You can extend the Incident Management process in Service Manager 2010 using connectors. Infrastructure-related events can be introduced through the Operations Manager connector and Configuration Manager connector (DCM). An example workflow configuration for both extensions on the Incident process is provided in the "Incident Management Automation" section of this chapter.

Your own Incident process may require additional customization of Incident Management in Service Manager. You can find information about extending the incident form and creating custom workflows and notifications in Chapter 18. Reporting requirements can have an impact on customizing your Incident Management environment. For more information about that topic, see Chapter 20, "Reports, Dashboards, and Data Analysis."

CHAPTER 11

Problem Management

Service Manager 2010 (also known as SvcMgr) enables the Problem Management process by implementing and automating Problem Management in compliance with Microsoft Operations Framework (MOF) and the Information Technology Infrastructure Library (ITIL). By complying with MOF and ITIL best practices, your organization can be confident the necessary building blocks are available in the System Center Service Manager tool to configure your own Problem Management process in accordance with industry-accepted standards.

Chapter 3, "MOF, ITIL, and Service Manager," describes in detail the value of using ITIL and MOF with Service Manager 2010. This chapter explains how to configure Problem Management in Service Manager. The main objectives of Problem Management are to identify the root cause of problems and initiate activity to create workarounds or permanent solutions to identified problems. The primary activity in the process is a technical activity performed outside service management tooling. Service Manager 2010 provides the interface to manage the life cycle of problems with the different interfaces to other management functions, such as Incident and Change Management.

This chapter discusses how to configure Problem Management in Service Manager 2010. As with any tool, it is better to first define what you need to configure instead of just jumping into the tool. In an attempt to provide a full understanding, this chapter begins with a discussion about the process. It then explains your various Problem Management configuration options for Service Manager 2010, and then describes an actual configuration of the Problem Management functionality in Service Manager.

Understanding the Problem Process

According to ITIL, *a problem is the unknown cause of one or more incidents*. When you look at the role of Problem Management in your Information Technology (IT) environment, you can see Problem Management as the management function that removes those errors from the IT infrastructure that lead to incidents. Problem Management is closely related to Incident Management, as one or more incidents may be caused by a single problem. However, it is important to understand that an incident and the Incident Management process are distinct from a problem and the Problem Management process, respectively.

You can think of an incident as a single instance of a user being unable to work or a server or other IT component being down. The imperative of the Incident Management process is to get that incident resolved, whatever it takes, through a workaround if necessary. The point of the process is not to get to the root cause of multiple related incidents, and for good reason—focus is necessary to make sure incidents are resolved in a timely manner. With that said, someone, following some process, must have the imperative to get to the root cause of multiple incidents to help prevent reoccurrence; this is the job of Problem Management.

Problem analysts look for the root cause of problems or provide workarounds for the Incident Management function, to minimize the impact of the problem until necessary changes can be made to definitively resolve the problem. Problem analysts work to be able to answer these questions: What are the top *N* problems, what has been done so far to minimize their impact or eliminate them, and what is being done next? The outcome of Problem Management can be an RFC (request for change), the problem defined as a known error with a workaround, or an update on the problem work items (problem solved). The goal of Problem Management is to minimize the negative impact of incidents and problems on the business services caused by errors in the IT infrastructure and prevent the recurrence of incidents related to these errors. Problem Management includes activities that are required to investigate the root cause of incidents and to determine the resolution for these problems. A resolution for the problem must be implemented through the appropriate control procedures, in particular Change and Release Management.

Service Manager 2010 provides an interface to manage the life cycle of all problems. The default Problem management pack (MP) includes knowledge to link problem work items with one or more incident work items or change work items that may be required to resolve a problem. The Problem MP comes without Problem Management workflows, but you can extend the default functionality where needed. If you have configured the Operations Manager (OpsMgr) connector in your Service Manager environment, you can extend the Problem Management functionality in a similar manner to how you extended the functionality for Incident Management. Problem work items include incidents with a rich set of information about the event (defined by the MP in OpsMgr). This information can prove very useful during diagnostic activities of the process. Service Manager Problem Management will also maintain the problem information with appropriate workarounds and resolutions, enabling your organization to reduce the number and impact of incidents over time. Therefore, Problem Management has a strong interface with Knowledge Management.

Starting your Problem Management process does not have to be complicated. You can begin by selecting the top 5 or 10 incidents in your business-critical services. Start to analyze the information so that you can define a problem work item and find the root cause of the error. Effective Problem Management requires a clear definition of the people, their role in each process activity, and an effective Incident Management process. Initially, by default, only the Problem Analyst role exists in the Service Manager environment. You must configure those user roles necessary for your own Problem Management process. It is important to have defined all these items before beginning to configure Problem Management in Service Manager.

To assist with this process definition, here are some terms used with Problem Management. You can find more detailed information in Chapter 3:

▶ **Problem:** This is an unknown error, the underlying cause of one or more incidents.

▶ **Error:** A fault, bug, or behavior issue in an IT service or system.

▶ **Root cause:** The specific reason that most directly contributes to the occurrence of an error.

▶ **Known error:** A known error is a problem for which a root cause and permanent fix (or workaround) are identified, but the fix is not yet implemented. This is an error that has been observed and documented.

▶ **Workaround:** This is a temporary fix or technique that eliminates the end user's reliance on the faulty service component.

You can build a Problem Management process with different activities, resulting in a configuration enabling this process in Service Manager 2010. In general, here is how to split the Service Manager configuration tasks:

▶ **General Problem Management Service Manager configuration settings:** These are overall configuration settings to enable Problem Management functionality. This includes settings in the Problem Management settings section of the Administration space of the console, which houses the basic settings for the process. In addition to configuring the Problem Management settings, user roles must be configured to provide access to the Service Manager console.

▶ **Configuring the Problem Management user roles:** By default, the Problem Analyst role is the only role for Problem Management. This user role has access to all work items, view, queues, and tasks from the Problem MP. More granular role configuration and creation of additional user roles may be necessary to define the roles of your process in Service Manager.

▶ **Enumeration (drop-down) lists in the Service Manager console:** Drop-down selection options in the Problem Management form and dialog boxes are populated with default values that can be adjusted with specific values for your organization. Drop-downs are lists in the library pane of the Service Manager console, and drop-down selection options are list items. Problem classification, status, and source are lists you can configure in the Library pane of the console.

▶ **Problem Management customization:** Customization goes beyond settings and requires the Service Manager Authoring Tool or custom development. Customizing Problem Management functionality in Service Manager includes adding or hiding fields and drop-down lists and check boxes, or creating custom workflows to enable your Problem Management process.

Problem Management in Service Manager

Problem Management becomes truly optimized when integrated with other processes, such as Incident Management, Change Management, and Configuration Management, and when it incorporates Knowledge Management.

Service Manager 2010 orchestrates the interactions between the management functions and provides an interface to manage problems using the Service Manager console. For example, Problem Management must gather data from Incident Management and configuration items (CIs) such as business services, computers, or software. Essential incident information is required for problem detection and diagnosis, where the information about CIs extends this information bundle and helps in defining the priority of the problem. Connectors are used to automatically update the CI information in Service Manager; the information in the incident work item depends on the support staff responsible for including the required information in the incident work item. The problem analyst has access to all this information in Service Manager to investigate the root cause of the problem.

An important component in the investigation activity for the problem analyst is the availability of required information about the incidents or problems. Service Manager excels here in four ways:

▶ With the rich set of data on configurations items provided by the Active Directory (AD), Operations Manager, and Configuration Manager CI connectors

▶ Using the event information provided by the Operations Manager Alert connectors

▶ Through its built-in Knowledge Management capabilities

▶ Using Service Manager's built-in capability to relate for cross-referencing CIs, knowledge articles, known errors, problems, incidents, and changes

Service Manager 2010 provides extended functionality: While a large number of incidents are logged by the service desk in Incident Management, another set of incidents can be generated using the Operations Manager connector. This extends the proactive alerting of Operations Manager to Service Manager such that events detected by Operations Manager become incident work items created in Service Manager (and an infrastructure problem work item is created, as well, if required). This is known as *auto-ticketing*. What comes across the Operations Manager connector is all the knowledge information that is available from the Operations Manager MP included in the incident and problem work items. When a permanent fix or workaround is found, the problem analyst can raise a RFC to remove the problem, thus resulting in fewer recurring incidents against the relevant CIs.

The Service Manager Problem MP includes knowledge for managing the basic interactions between involved processes, and the Service Manager console is the platform for managing the life cycle of all different elements in the Problem process. Here's how:

▶ Problems can be created from the Incident Management view based on information from an incident form. A direct link can be created between a problem and the change request that is sometimes required to resolve the problem.

▶ Problems can result in known error status and have a temporary (or final) workaround defined. These work items are stored in the same database and can be differentiated from other problem work items. A known error in Service Manager is a property of a problem work item.

▶ Service Manager automates populating the configuration management database (CMDB) with information and keeping the CMDB current. CMDB information is used as context for problem forms, dialog boxes, and tasks. When handling a problem, an IT support analyst can view the problem details and details of related and affected items directly from the console; all this integrated information is available to provide input for resolving problems.

▶ Knowledge articles can help problem analysts to understand and solve problems, and provide workaround knowledge articles for problems when no resolution is available.

▶ Problem Management is linked to other management functions in Service Manager such as Change, Incident, Configuration, and Knowledge Management. This means you can look at a problem and see related incidents, services, CIs, and so on.

▶ Problem information is stored in the Service Manager data warehouse for further reporting.

▶ The Problem process can be extended using the Authoring Tool.

Figure 11.1 illustrates an overview of Problem Management in Service Manager 2010.

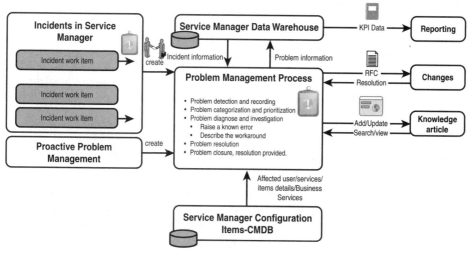

FIGURE 11.1   Problem Management in Server Manager 2010.

Building a Problem Management support team is a first aspect in configuring the management function for your environment. Configuration in Service Manager is associated with the support team roles. Configuring Problem Management in Service Manager occurs in different areas of the console, with the primary area being the Problem Settings configuration in the Administrative space of the console. Here are some of those settings:

▶ **Configuring Problem Work Item Prefix:** In Service Manager 2010, all problem numbers start with the letters PR. However, you can change the prefix used for your problem numbering.

▶ **Problem File Attachment Policy:** The policy at your company might limit the number of files that can be attached to each problem to no more than five and limit the maximum file size for each file to 500 kilobytes (KB). The maximum number of attached files and maximum file size settings that you specify also apply to the attached files in the Related Items tab for CIs. Give this some thought: certain tickets may require a number of attachments/screenshots to resolve.

To keep storage at a reasonable size, you might want to establish a policy and provide training to problem analysts regarding screenshot resolutions and storing commonly used documents on a support analyst SharePoint site with a link from Service Manager (which would provide the added benefit of version control).

▶ **Problem Priority Calculation:** Problem priority calculation is rated the same way as Incident Management, on a scale from 1 to 9, where 1 is the highest priority. Priority is based on a combination of impact and urgency, with impact and urgency settings defined as High, Medium, or Low, and configured when the problem is created.

▶ **Problem Notifications:** Notifications can be created for problems as they can created for other management functions. The notifications channel, your created problem notification templates, and subscriptions are components for building your notification plan for Problem Management.

In the Library space of the console, you can configure groups, knowledge, Problem Management lists, problem queues, and tasks:

▶ **Groups:** Groups are a collection of CIs. You can use groups in Problem Management to assign problem work items to a specific support team.

▶ **Knowledge Queues:** Knowledge articles can help service desk analysts and end users understand and apply workarounds for existing problems when new events occur. You can add knowledge to the problem work item as an additional source of information to resolve the problem.

▶ **Problem Management Lists:** A problem work item is an object in Service Manager with a set of properties. A list represents a property of an object, and it includes one or more list items. Each list item represents a possible value you can select in the problem work item form. Service Manager includes some default problem lists to use in your problem forms.

- ▶ **Problem Queues:** Queues are used to group similar work items meeting specified criteria.

- ▶ **Tasks:** Tasks are the actions listed on the right-hand side of the problem work item. These automate repetitive actions that a support analyst has to perform. The Problem Management team typically uses tasks to help manage problems.

Using the Service Manager Authoring tool is another way to configure or automate the Problem Management process using your own MPs. See Chapter 17, "Management Packs," and Chapter 18, "Customizing Service Manager," for a discussion of the Authoring Tool. Chapter 19, "Advanced Customization Scenarios," includes additional information.

The next section maps Problem process activities to Service Manager functionality.

Problem Management Process Activities

This section assesses each critical process activity and examines how you can configure Service Manager to optimize every stage of the process. Some incidents are unavoidable. Service components do fail occasionally, although many incidents are caused not by random failures but by errors somewhere in your environment. The goal of Problem Management activities is to define the different steps necessary to find the root causes of incidents so as to minimize their impact on the business services of your organization. As described in Chapter 3 and the "Understanding Problem Management" section in this chapter, Problem Management has a strong dependency on Incident Management. In addition, Change Management may be necessary to implement the fix or workaround.

Making the association between the Problem process activities and the Service Manager components should enable you to translate your company's Problem process and configure the Service Manager Problem MP. This association provides cohesion between how you work in your processes and takes advantage of the functionality provided by the tool. The "Configuring Problem Management" section takes this a bit further and discusses configuring this functionality in Service Manager.

First, let's define a couple more important Problem Management terms. Problem Management processes can be described as either *reactive* or *proactive*:

- ▶ **Reactive Problem Management:** Reactive Problem Management responds to reports of incident work items that have already occurred. You can look at the reactive approach in this way:

  - ▶ The support analyst consults the reports from the Incident Management process.

  - ▶ Members of the Problem Management team analyze this information for similarities in the description of the work items.

  - ▶ If no previously identified problem can explain the symptoms, a new problem work item is created.

- ▶ **Proactive Problem Management:** Proactive Problem Management is about taking preemptive steps to eliminate problems once and for all. As part of that goal, it includes performing a trend analysis on the existing problem and incident work items. Proactive Problem Management is a responsibility of other management functions and not within the scope of this book.

With Service Manager 2010 and the Operations Manager connector in place, you can extend the reactive problem detection with incidents (alerts from OpsMgr) that are raised before the event affects the business service. You can take advantage of the proactive monitoring in OpsMgr and take a closer look at errors on the back-end infrastructure of your business service.

> **NOTE: ACTIVITIES IN PROBLEM MANAGEMENT**
>
> Activities in Problem Management take place outside Service Manager; the result of the activity is logged in a Service Manager problem work item. In this way, each activity in Problem Management consumes information that is logged in the problem work item. Service Manager orchestrates the management around the Problem Management process.

Here is a description of the process activities illustrated in Figure 11.2:

▶ **Problem detection:** This activity involves the identification of problems in your environment via analysis of Incident Management reports. This is not the only input for this activity; problems can be raised by the service desk or the vendor.

▶ **Problem recording, classification, and prioritization:** Information provided in the incident work items is used as input for the problem definition. When a problem is identified, the amount of effort required to diagnose and investigate the problem is estimated in this activity.

▶ **Diagnose and investigation:** An investigation should be conducted to try to diagnose the root cause of the problem.

▶ **Known error status:** When the diagnosis is complete, and particularly where a workaround has been found, a known error status must be assigned and the workaround described or requested via Change Management.

▶ **Problem resolution:** A problem can be resolved when the root cause of the problem is found and a permanent fix can be recommended.

▶ **Problem closure:** When any change has been completed (and successfully reviewed) or a permanent workaround defined, the problem work item and related incident work items should be formally closed.

Problem Detection

The Problem Management detection activity focuses on the recurring business service affecting incidents where the root cause is not found or there is no permanent fix. This is one approach; Problems can come from any point in the environment and can be identified using various methods:

▶ The service desk can identify problems that are suspicious or detected as the cause of one or more incident work items. For example, the service desk engineer may have resolved the incident but has not determined a definitive cause and suspects that it is likely to recur, so will raise a problem work item to allow the underlying cause to be resolved.

▶ The analysis of an incident by a technical support group can reveal that an underlying problem exists, or is likely to exist and needs to be investigated.

▶ A problem can be detected by analyzing the infrastructure or application-related incident work items that are created from the Operations Manager connector, which may reveal the need for a problem work item.

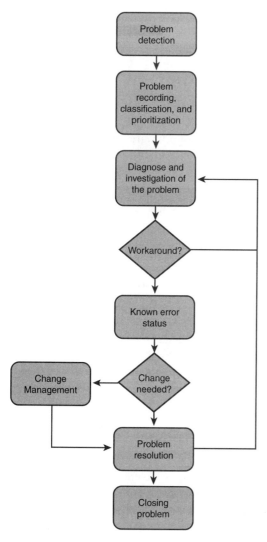

FIGURE 11.2   Activities in Problem Management.

▶ A notification from a supplier or contractor that a problem exists can be the start point for creating a problem work item.

▶ Frequent and regular analysis of incident and problem data must be performed to identify any trends as they become discernible. This requires meaningful and detailed categorization of incidents/problems and regular reporting of patterns in areas of high occurrence.

Although the service desk can detect a problem, you must evaluate the detected problem against recorded known errors and problem work items. Known errors and problem work item information can be accessed via the Problem Management folder in the Work Items pane of the console. Ideally, for those known errors in your environment, a knowledge article should be created to describe the workaround. This may already be a first filter for the service desk to detect and define problems.

The Service Manager console includes different work items, views, and queues that can help detect problems in the environment. It is important to configure the console to provide required access for the different service management roles. The specifics depend on the size of your support environment (whether you have dedicated people assigned to Problem Management roles, or if you have a smaller-size support environment where the Problem Management roles are combined with other service management roles).

The following Service Manager components are involved:

▶ **Service Manager Reporting:** Reporting in Service Manager provides access to incident information and can be used to analyze incident recurrence or trend analysis.

▶ **Operations Manager Alert Connector:** The connector provides automatic incident creation based on alert subscriptions in Operation Manager. Additional information that is included by the alert from the Operations Manager environment is included in the incident work item. This information can prove very useful in root-cause analysis.

▶ **Incident Management:** Service Manager Incident Management information can be analyzed. Information provided in the incident work item is important information for investigating the error. One or more incident work items can be integrated in the problem work item as a related item.

Problem Recording, Classification, and Prioritization

As described in the previous section, problems can be detected in various ways. The next activity in the Problem Management process is recording the problem. You do so to facilitate prioritization of problem resolutions and to link the problem to existing incidents' work items. After you record a problem, you assess the impact on the business services and determine the urgency of the resolution. This activity also determines the problem classification of the problem in the work item.

TIP: CONSIDER SEVERITY WHEN PRIORITIZING PROBLEMS

Problem prioritization that is made during the recording activity should also take into account the severity of the problems. *Severity*, in this context, refers to how serious the problem is from a business service perspective.

11

In the Service Manager console, the Create Problem work item task is available in different work item forms and tasks menus to facilitate the integration of Problem Management in other management functions. Figure 11.3 shows the default Problem Management form. When you select the Create Problem task from a single incident work item or CI, the problem work item form is already populated with information from that selected incident work item or CI. You can select multiple items in the Service Manager console to define the related items in the problem work item form.

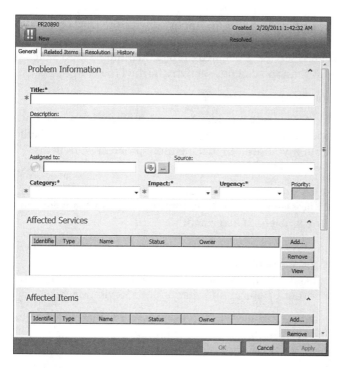

FIGURE 11.3   Default Problem Management form in Service Manager.

Similar to Incident Management and Change Management in Service Manager, every problem work item has an impact on the business services and an urgency. The impact describes the potential to which the business stands vulnerable, and its urgency illustrates the time that is available to avert, or at least reduce, this impact on the business service. Both parameters define the priority of a problem work item in Service Manager.

Information available on the affected CI or business service is an important source of input in defining the problem work item. The advantage with Service Manager is you can automate this information source using connectors. As with the other management functions in Service Manager, data source information must be current and include valid information. Otherwise, information about the affected CIs is outdated or invalid and wrong decisions might be made based on that information.

NOTE: DEFINING PROBLEM CLASSIFICATION AND PRIORITIZATION

Both Incident Management and Problem Management settings in Service Manager have classification lists and a prioritization matrix. Keeping these two configuration settings consistent between both functions will ensure effective communication when dealing with related incidents and problems.

Having business services defined in Service Manager (or imported with the OpsMgr MPs) can be important in this activity. With a clear look at the involved CIs, incident history, and other items related to the business service, a detailed problem definition is possible that will probably create more input than the diagnose activity in the Problem process.

The following Service Manager components are involved:

▶ **Default problem form:** Service Manager provides a default problem form based on problem work item class properties and relationships. (Figure 11.3 shows the default form.) You can extend this form if you need to include more problem work items. For additional information, see Chapter 18.

▶ **Incident Management:** An important input for Problem Management is the information gathered in Incident Management. A well-performing Incident Management process is a requirement for the Problem Management process.

▶ **Configuration items:** CIs in Service Manager are the main source of information. The Problem Management team makes decisions based on this information and loses time or makes incorrect decisions if this information is outdated or incomplete. Connectors automate the import of CI object information into Service Manager.

▶ **Business services:** Defining business services in Service Manager has an added value for Problem Management. The Problem Management team can easily categorize and prioritize problem work items based on the affected business service. Then, when they investigate problems, all related information about the service, such as other open incidents or CIs that enable the service, is available in the problem work item.

Problem Investigation and Diagnosis

The activity of problem investigation is similar to that of incident investigation (see Chapter 10, "Incident Management"), but the primary objective of each activity in each process differs significantly. The Problem process activity deals with the investigation of the problem and diagnosis of the root cause of one or more incidents. In contrast, incident investigation focuses on service recovery, and the root cause of an incident might not be found even if the incident shows as closed. During this activity, it is often valuable to try to re-create the failure in a lab environment. Doing so enables you to understand what has gone wrong and then try to find the most appropriate and cost-effective resolution to the problem. You can add the results of this technical investigation work to the problem work item.

In some cases, you might be able to find a workaround to the incidents caused by the problem. This can be a temporary way to overcome the service difficulties, or a permanent workaround if the indicated change to the infrastructure is too expensive. After a workaround is found, it is important that the problem record remains open and details of the workaround are always documented within the problem work item. In Service Manager 2010, you can mark the problem work item with a known error status when a workaround is found. (You can find more information about this topic in the next section, "Known Error Control in Service Manager.")

Following ITIL definitions of Problem Management, the Problem process includes dealing with major problems that require additional planning, coordination, resources, and communication, and which may result in a formal project being initiated. You can associate the major problem in Service Manager with a priority status on the problem work item.

The following Service Manager components are involved:

- **Incident Management:** Information that is included in the related incident work item is important information during the investigation and diagnosis activities of the Problem process. Additional MP information that is added via the Operations Manager connector-created incidents is an added value for Problem Management diagnosis and investigation.

- **Service Manager knowledge:** With the same functionality available as in the initial support activity and for other management functions, the Problem Management team can search for documented solutions or workarounds using different search providers. Knowledge articles can be created to document workarounds / known errors.

- **Configuration items:** CIs in Service Manager are a main source of information. The Problem Management team uses this information during the execution of this activity.

- **Business services:** Defining business services in Service Manager has many advantages. It enables the support people to see the service relationship on a CI. When they are investigating problems, all related information about the service, such as other open incidents or CIs that enable the service, is available in the problem work item.

Known Error Control in Service Manager

The known error control process addresses successful correction of known errors. You can think of known error control as bug tracking for the live production environment. In fact, development teams can use it as such, and should transfer any problems and known errors into the system as they release their services, applications, or infrastructure solutions. The objective is to change components or procedures to remove known errors affecting the infrastructure and in this way prevent any recurrence of incidents.

Known error control in the Service Manager console is part of the resolution information of a problem work item (see Figure 11.4). A problem work item in Service Manager can be marked as a known error when the root cause of the problem is found and a workaround identified. You can specify the error description and the workaround's description for the known error on the Resolution tab of the Problem form. Although the process flowchart in Figure 11.2 indicates that this is a mandatory step, for Service Manager this is not a mandatory field in the problem form or a property that must defined before closing a problem work item.

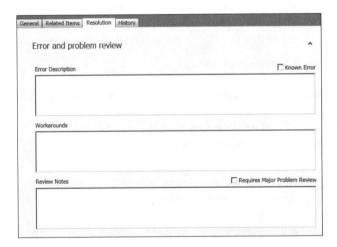

FIGURE 11.4   Known error in the default problem form.

In many cases, it might prove useful to raise a known error record, describe the workaround, and create a company knowledge base article even earlier in the overall problem process. Informing the support team of a workaround enables them to use it immediately in daily operations. For example, although the diagnosis may not be complete or a workaround identified, it is inadvisable to set a concrete procedural point in the process to raise the problem work item as a known error; you will want to do so as soon as it becomes useful. In this manner, the support team can search in Service Manager and find this information, eventually associating new incidents with the existing problem.

Service Manager enables you to mark the problem work item as known error and initiate a change request to implement the fix or workaround. The steps for this activity are defined in your Problem Management process. For example, notification of the known error status is important because it means some progress has occurred toward fixing the problem and the support team can be notified. Service Manager's notification functionality lets you notify a support group when a problem work item is marked as a known error. The team can review the workaround and consider it when handling incident work items.

> **NOTE: NOT ALL KNOWN ERRORS NEED TO BE RESOLVED**
>
> Your organization can decide to allow known errors to remain. This may occur when the resolution to fix the error is too expensive, technically impossible, is resolved in a next version of the application, or requires too much time to resolve.

The following Service Manager components are involved:

- ▶ **Default problem form:** Service Manager provides known error information in the resolution tab of the problem form. A description of the workaround is associated with the known error status of a problem work item.

- ▶ **Service Manager knowledge:** A workaround can be a temporary solution for a problem, with the final solution implemented at a later stage. In any case, the support team needs to be informed, and this can be accomplished using information in the problem form or knowledge article that describes the procedure. Company knowledge articles can help to manage this information in Service Manager.

- ▶ **Service Manager notification:** The Problem Management process should include the required steps/workflows to keep the support team informed of any progress in fixing the problem. Configuring accurate notifications and subscriptions in Service Manager is necessary to support this requirement of the process.

- ▶ **Change Management:** If any change in functionality is required, an RFC must be created and approved before applying the resolution. The RFC should follow the established Change Management process in Service Manager and the resolution applied only when the change has been approved and scheduled for release.

Problem Resolution

The resolution activity information for each known error should be recorded in the problem work item of Service Manager. Information about the CIs, symptoms, and resolution description *must be* well documented. This information is then available for incident matching and provides guidance during future investigations to resolve and circumvent Incidents.

When setting the problem work item status to Resolved, you have the possibility to auto-resolve all problem work item related incidents. This setting is on a problem work item basis in Service Manager and not a global workflow applied to all resolution state changes for problems.

The following Service Manager components are involved:

▸ **Default Problem Form:** Resolution information of a problem is set in the resolution tab of the problem work item form. Known error, workaround, and resolution description information are some examples of information that can be specified on the resolution tab of the problem form. The Service Manager problem work item form bundles this information for further handling of the problem.

▸ **Service Manager Notification:** The Problem Management process should include the required steps/workflows to keep the support team informed of any progress in fixing the problem. Configuring accurate notifications and subscriptions in Service Manager is necessary to support this requirement of the process.

Problem Closure

When a change is completed (and successfully reviewed) and the resolution applied, the problem work item should be formally closed. This is the same for any related incident work items still open; these should be closed at problem closure. The problem closure process outlines the need to record fully the details of all errors. You should perform a check at this time to ensure that the record contains a full historical description of all events. If it does not, the record should be updated. Again, it is vital to save all information related to the CIs, symptoms, and resolution or circumvention actions related to the problem. You can create company knowledge articles and make them available to the support team. Doing so helps build your organization's knowledge base.

Closing a problem work item is a status that can be adjusted after some time in Service Manager. For example, if the provided workaround or fix doesn't actually solve the problem, the work item can be reopened. In Service Manager 2010, you can reactivate a closed problem work item using a built-in task.

Major Problem Review can be seen as part of the closure activity or defined as a dedicated activity in your Problem Management process. After every major problem, while memories are still fresh, conduct a review to learn any lessons for the future. This review could examine those things done right, wrong, and what can be done better in the future. The review could check how to prevent recurrence of the major problem, whether there is any third-party responsibility, and follow-up actions needed (such as how to monitor for early warning for the error). In Service Manager, a problem work item can be marked with the Requires Major Problem Review check mark. Review information can be added to the problem work item after the review meeting.

The following Service Manager components are involved:

▸ **Default problem form:** Closing a problem in Service Manager is a problem work item status change. Your Problem process describes when this can be done and depends on the resolution execution of the problem.

▶ **Service Manager notification:** The Problem Management process should include the required steps/workflows to keep the support team informed of any progress in fixing the problem. Configuring accurate notifications and subscriptions in Service Manager is necessary to support this requirement.

Configuring Problem Management

The "Problem Management Process Activities" section provides an overview of the Problem Management activities from a Service Manager 2010 perspective. This section presents an overview of configuration options for Problem Management in Service Manager 2010.

The configuration required for Service Manager is minor and depends on the Problem process of your organization. Settings such as prefix, priority calculation, Problem Management user roles, and notification configuration are global settings for the Problem Management process in Service Manager 2010. Service Manager provides the platform for managing the problem work item life cycle. During the different activities in the process, the Problem Management team can record the proper information in the problem work item form and retrieve information out of different work items and CIs. The actual activity to find the root cause of a problem is something outside Service Manager; this is the technical part of the process. To configure Problem Management in Service Manager 2010, you should think about providing access to the different user roles, configuring the Problem Management settings in Service Manager, and defining the problem list items for your environment. All other requirements to enable Problem Management in Service Manager are provided by other management functions or are outside the tool.

As with other customizations you will make in Service Manager to enable functionality, first define what you need to configure in Service Manager before actually starting to apply that functionality. The "Problem Management Process Activities" section can help define the configuration necessary for Service Manager. The next sections cover Problem Management configuration, including Problem Management console tasks, Problem Management user roles, groups, queues, and lists, general Problem Management settings, and notification.

Problem Management Console Tasks

Problem work items can be created from multiple locations in Service Manager console. The Create Problem console task can be executed from the Problem Management folder of the Work Items pane to create a new problem or from an incident work item to create a new problem work item that automatically adds the incident information to the work item. Incidents work items can be linked afterward to a problem work item via the Link Problem console task.

From the Problem Management folder, an empty work item form is presented. From here, the Problem Management team can input additional information to describe the problem.

Figure 11.5 shows an example of a new empty problem work item. On the General page, the Problem Management team can specify the work item general settings, such as Title, urgency/impact, affected CIs, and services. Additional problem-related information can be specified on the Related Items tab of the form. Resolution information is specified on the Resolution tab. All actions taken on the problem work item are logged on the History tab of the work item.

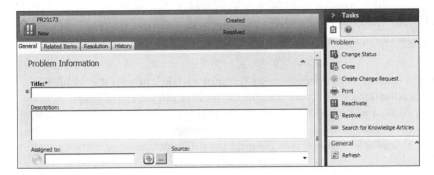

FIGURE 11.5   New Problem work item form.

The Tasks pane to the right of the Problem work item form in Figure 11.5 lists default tasks you can perform on a problem work item (for example, changing the status, closing, resolving, and reactivating). The Create Change Request task creates an RFC for actions that need to be made to the infrastructure to fix the error.

When a problem work item is created via an incident work item, the title, affected CIs, and related items are automatically filled in on the new problem work item form. In addition to creating a new problem work item from an incident work item, you can link the incident directly to an existing problem using a task in the Tasks pane.

Problem Management User Roles, Groups, Queues, and Lists

The starting point of Problem Management configuration is ensuring the Problem Management team has access to the required work items, CIs, views, and tasks. By default, the Problem Analyst user role is defined with access to all problem work items, views, and so on. Configuring user roles for Problem Management is a rather difficult task and depends on your Problem Management team setup. If you have team members who combine different roles in the overall Service Management, you need to be careful that the required access on the different objects in the Service Manager console is provided.

The procedure to create the Problem Management user roles is not different from the procedure to create user roles for Incident Management. Therefore, see the detailed procedure in Chapter 10 to create user roles in Service Manager. Chapter 15, "Service Manager Security," also provides relevant information.

The problem work item form includes different fields to classify and categorize problem work items. The values presented in the form are Service Manager lists item values. Service Manager lists represent properties of an object and include one or more list items. Each list item represents a possible value for the property that the Problem Management team can select on the problem forms and dialog boxes. Several default list items in Service Manager 2010 exist for Problem Management and can be adjusted to the needs of your environment. Table 11.1 provides an overview of the default problem lists provided by the Problem MP.

TABLE 11.1   Problem Management Lists

List Name	Description	Management Pack
Problem Status	Problem Status List	Problem Management Library
Problem Source	Problem Source List	Problem Management Library
Problem Classification	Problem Classification List	Problem Management Library
Incident Resolution	Problem Resolution List	Problem Management Library

A best practice for Problem Management is to align the problem classification lists with your Incident Management classification. By so doing, you create a clear communication path of the classification specification for both management functions in your support environment. You can address the urgency and impact configuration in a similar fashion, as described later in this section.

In the following configuration example, the Odyssey Service Manager environment has Operations Manager installed with incident work items created with the Operations Manager alert connector. The Operations Manager Connector Source in the Problem Source List must be added as an additional source for the Odyssey Problem Management configuration. To adjust this list in the Odyssey Service Manager environment, follow these steps:

1. In the Service Manager console, click **Library**. In the Library pane, click **Lists**. The Lists pane displays all the existing lists. You can organize the Results pane information by clicking the column titles; this makes it easy to find the list you want to edit.

2. Select the list to which you want to add a list item. (So, in this case, select the **Problem Source** list.) In the Tasks pane, under Problem Source, click **Properties**.

3. In the List Properties dialog box, click **Add Item**. Notice a new List Value list item is added. You can change the name of the new list item by clicking the item and then entering the new list item name in the Name field of the dialog box. If you want, you can type an optional description in the Description box. Figure 11.6 specifies the OpsMgr source as an item of the Problems Source list item.

4. Click **OK** to save your changes.

FIGURE 11.6   Edit Problem Source List properties.

Configuring the General Problem Management Settings

General Problem Settings is a globally scoped configuration for Problem Management in Service Manager. This section describes the configuration of the Problem Management settings in Service Manager 2010.

The Problem Management settings are configured in the Administration space of the Service Manager console, as follows:

1. In the Service Manager console, navigate to **Administration -> Settings**.
2. In the Settings folder, click **Problem Settings** in the Results pane.
3. In the Tasks pane, under Problem Settings, click **Properties** to open the Problem Settings dialog box.

The Problem ID prefix setting, shown in Figure 11.7, is the first configuration option of the General Problem Settings configuration.

NOTE: PROBLEM WORK ITEMS PREFIX SETTING

You can specify alphanumeric and numeric characters as a prefix for the problem work items. In general, you should not specify a numeric prefix to distinguish work items; this could be confusing when the number of the work item is added. The prefix specification is limited to 15 characters.

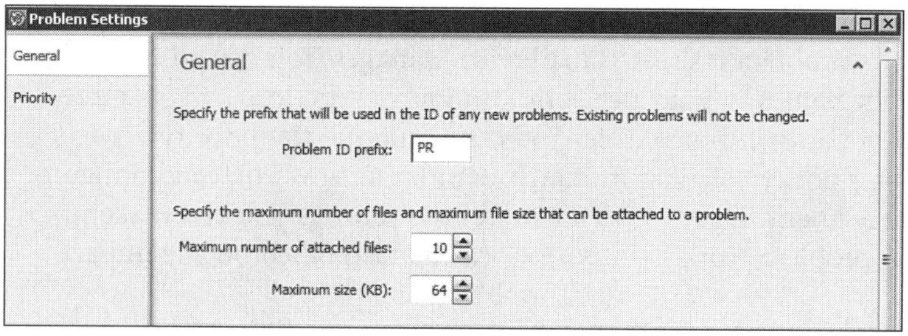

FIGURE 11.7   General Problem Settings.

Attached File Policy Configuration

You can add files associated with a problem to the problem work item, similar to how this is done with Incident Management in Service Manager 2010. The number of files that can be added to a problem work item and the maximum file size of the attached files can be specified in the General section of the Problem Settings dialog box. Default settings are a maximum of 10 files and file size of 64KB. When defining your Problem Management file attachment policy, consider the information you actually want to have directly available in the problem work item. Much of the information can be located on a document management system such as SharePoint, and you can include just the links to these documents. Similar to the process for Incident Management file policy configuration, find a setting that fits your needs. Verify that you do not block the Problem Management team from adding important information while avoiding bulk uploading of files in the work item.

The Attached File Policy Configuration setting, also shown in Figure 11.7, is a configuration option of the General Problem settings configuration.

Configure Priority Calculation and Target Resolution Time for Problem Work Items

Before configuring priority, it is important to first define the impact and urgency for your organization. Here is how you can define these terms:

▶ *Impact of the problem* is the measure of how business critical it is. A good best practice for priority settings in Problem Management is to align this configuration with the configuration you make for Incident Management.

▶ *Urgency* is the time required to resolve a problem. Urgency is the extent to which resolution of a problem or error can bear delay. As with the impact specification, align the urgency configuration with your settings for Incident Management.

Look at the work you performed to define priority settings for Incident Management (see Chapter 10) and align the Problem Management priority settings. You can take advantage of the priority levels defined for the Incident Management process and current defined business services in Service Manager. Priority-level configuration of four or five different levels is recommended for most scenarios. Ensure that you have a priority defined for major problems; you want to treat these differently from other more normal operations problems.

By default, impact and urgency settings are defined as High, Medium, or Low, and are mandatory fields when the problem is created in Service Manager. You can adjust the default impact and urgency values to your needs by configuring the Impact List and Urgency List in the Library pane of the console. You can configure the priority on a problem work item with a priority calculation matrix, similar to how you can configure priority for Incident Management. Figure 11.8 illustrates the settings you can make in Service Manager 2010 for problem work item priority calculation based on the impact and urgency.

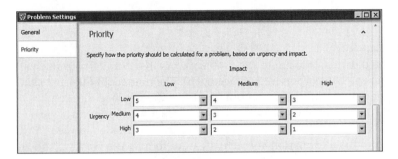

FIGURE 11.8   Sample priority calculation.

You can configure the urgency impact settings for Problem Management in the Service Manager console as follows:

1. In the Administration pane, expand **Administration -> Settings**. In the Settings pane, click **Problem Settings**.

2. In the Tasks pane, under Problem Settings, click **Properties**.

3. In the Problem Settings dialog box, select **Priority** on the left menu.

4. For each of the High, Medium, and Low settings for impact and urgency, select a priority value from 1 to 9, and then click **OK**. In this example, the priority configurations consist of five levels, similar to the Odyssey Incident Management priority configuration. Figure 11.8 displays these settings.

5. Click **OK** to close the Problem Settings wizard.

NOTE: ADJUSTING THE IMPACT AND URGENCY LIST ITEMS

As specified in this section, impact and urgency settings are defined as High, Medium, or Low. These values can be adjusted or additional levels can be defined via the Urgency and Impact List configuration in the Lists folder of the Library console pane. Be careful when adjusting the values of these list items; they are applied in all work items' priority matrixes.

Configuring Notification

Notification is an important configuration for your Problem Management process. Team members may want to be notified when problem status changes occur. In other cases, such as when major problems occur, you need to notify the complete support team that a specific business service is impacted. In Service Manager, you can ensure that notifications are generated for almost any type of change. You can configure notifications to be sent on creation or update and build a criteria list on the problem work item properties. For example, a notification subscription can be created to send an email to the service desk when a problem is marked as known error and a workaround is provided. The service desk can directly apply the workaround on upcoming similar incidents.

The following procedure steps through the creation of this notification subscription in the Odyssey Service Manager environment.

NOTE: NOTIFICATION FOR PROBLEM MANAGEMENT

Notifications can be sent through Service Manager when a problem work item is created or updated. Before you can create a notification subscription, you must complete several steps in Service Manager to send out notifications:

▶ Enable email notifications

▶ Establish a notification channel with your SMTP mail server

▶ Create a notification template for use with your notification messages

Chapter 10 describes this process.

---

1. In the Service Manager console, click **Administration**. In the Administration space, expand Notification, and then click **Subscriptions**. In the Tasks pane, click **Create Subscription**.

2. On the Before You Begin page of the Create E-mail Notification Subscription wizard, click **Next**.

3. On the General page, type a name in the Notification subscription name box. For example, type **Known Error status subscription**. Optionally, in the Description box, you can type a description for the subscription you are creating.

   Next to the Targeted class box, click **Browse**. In the Choose Class dialog box, choose a class (Problem in Figure 11.9). In the When to notify box, select **When an object of the selected class is updated**. Click **OK**.

4. If you have groups or queues defined to scope the management console for user roles, you can limit the objects tracked for notifications by selecting the appropriate groups and queues on the Group/Queue Selection page of the wizard. Click **Next** to proceed.

5. On the Additional Criteria page, select **Problem**. In the Available Properties list, select **Known Error**, and then click **Add**.

   On the Additional Criteria page displayed in Figure 11.10, click in the Criteria tab from the Changed From criteria list. In the Criteria area, next to [Problem] Known Error, select **equals**. In the list, select **False**, and then click the **Changed to** criteria tab on this page.

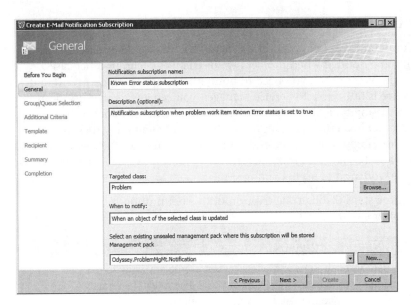

FIGURE 11.9   General Settings for the Create E-Mail Notification Subscription Wizard.

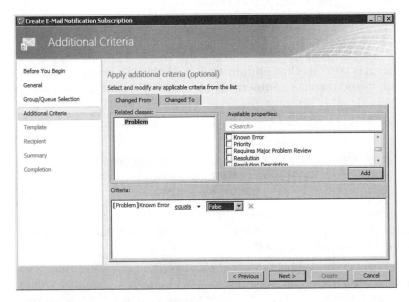

FIGURE 11.10   Specifying Changed From criteria.

The Changed To criteria information is displayed in Figure 11.11. You can follow the same procedure to specify the criteria (selecting an available property and building the criteria for your notification). In this example, the Known Error status to True is specified as the Changed To criteria. Click **Next**.

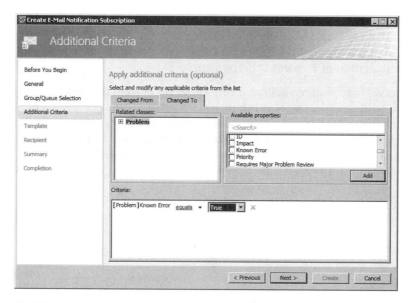

FIGURE 11.11   Specifying Changed To criteria.

6. On the Template page, click the **Select** button next to the E-mail template box. In the Select Objects dialog box, in the Templates list, select the appropriate notification template you want to apply. Click **Next** to continue. Alternatively, you can start the creation of a new notification template from out the Subscription Wizard.

7. On the Recipient page, click **Add**. In the Select Objects dialog box, search for and select the appropriate user or group. Click **Add**, **OK**, and then **Next**.

8. On the Summary page, review the settings you have selected for the notification subscription, and then click **Create**.

9. On the Completion page, click **Close**.

Problem Management Automation

The default Problem MP does not include workflows or additional templates for this management function. Should your Problem Management process require certain adjustments to the default problem work item template or you need to create workflows for your Problem Management process in Service Manager, you must do this in the Service Manager Authoring Tool and create your own MP. You can find additional information about creating MPs in Chapter 17 and Chapter 18.

Summary

This chapter discussed Problem Management in Service Manager 2010. You learned about the overall process and about how Service Manager can help you manage the problem life cycle in your environment. In this chapter, process activities were mapped to Service

Manager Problem Management elements, and so you should now be able to analyze your own process and map that to Service Manager settings. This chapter also walked through an actual configuration in the Service Manager console, using examples in procedures to explain the actual configuration of Problem Management.

Your own Problem process may require additional customization beyond the default Problem MP in Service Manager. You can find information about extending the problem form template and creating custom workflows and notifications in Chapter 18 and Chapter 19. Reporting requirements can have an impact on customizing your Problem Management environment. See Chapter 20, "Reports, Dashboards, and Data Analysis," for additional information about this topic.

CHAPTER 12

Change Management

Service Manager 2010 (also known as SvcMgr) enables the Change Management process by implementing and automating Change Management in compliance with Microsoft Operations Framework (MOF) and IT Infrastructure Library (ITIL). Complying with MOF and ITIL best practices assures your organization that the necessary building blocks in the Service Manager tool are used to configure your own Change Management process in accordance with industry-accepted standards.

Chapter 3, "MOF, ITIL, and Service Manager," discusses the benefits of using ITIL and MOF with Service Manager. This chapter gives guidance on configuring Change Management in Service Manager. Change Management is the process responsible for controlling the life cycle of all changes. ITIL defines a change as any *addition, modification, or removal of authorized, planned, or supported service or service component and its associated documentation.* Service Manager provides the capability to manage the life cycle of changes with interfaces to other management functions such as Incident, Configuration, and Problem Management.

The chapter provides information for configuring Change Management in Service Manager 2010. It also describes Activity Management. The steps defined in your Change process are activities in Service Manager that you can add to the change request work item; thus, both functions are closely related in Service Manager. The chapter clearly explains the process, which should provide the understanding to translate your Change processes to configurations in Service Manager. The functionality of the different components that build a Change process in Service Manager are described in the "Change Management Process Activities" section of this chapter. The initial configuration of Change Management in Service Manager is minimal; the actual process is created with Service Manager activities. Information about change request configuration is found in the "Change Management Automation" section.

Understanding the Change Management Process

To remain competitive, your Information Technology (IT) environment must be aligned with your organization's strategy; this means IT should share responsibility in delivering value to the business. Changes in your IT environment must not disrupt the business service delivered to the users, because IT must maintain stability even during change.

Understanding the Change Management process requires you first understand some definitions. The word *change* can be defined in many ways; however, when thinking about the term in your service delivery IT environment, the definition of a *service change* is very specific. The ITIL definition is *the addition, modification, or removal of an authorized, planned, or supported service or service component.* The management around the change has the objective to ensure that standardized methods and procedures are used for controlling the change and prompt handling of all changes. This helps minimize the impact of change-related incidents on the service quality and consequently improve the daily operations of the services.

The Information Technology service delivery environment is often affected when business requirements change or other management functions demand changes that have an impact on configuration items and/or business services. Changes can be requested from many different sources. Here are some examples of a change request:

▶ A request for change (RFC) can be required to solve a problem

▶ End users can demand greater levels of service to meet their objectives

▶ An updated version can be required on the software of a service component

For Change Management, the process starts with an RFC. This is the formal request for a change and can be issued by anyone involved in the service. Efficient Change Management is linked to Configuration Management; Configuration Management assists Change Management by tracking changes on configuration items (CIs) and controlling their status throughout the entire CI life cycle. In the beginning of the Change Management process, it is important to define the configuration as-is for those CIs in scope for the change. When the change is implemented successfully, the CI information should be reevaluated to verify that the required change is actually implemented.

NOTE: USING A CHANGE PROPOSAL

For those cases where a change has significant organization/financial implications, an RFC may not be sufficient and a change proposal can be required. This scenario can require a completely different process and templates. For example, a change proposal requires a full description of the change with business/financial justification. The form used to submit a change proposal should include space to provide this information, perhaps with limited access such that not everyone can submit this type of request, and initiate a special approval process when the proposal is submitted.

Each RFC that is created and enters the Change Management process must be evaluated. Once the RFC is submitted, there should be a preliminary assessment of the completeness of the RFC and its validity. If the change is not justified, the RFC may be rejected, or the originator of the RFC may be asked for additional information. When it is accepted, the RFC should be assigned a priority and category:

▶ *Priority* determines the relative importance of the RFC in relation to other outstanding RFCs, and is the primary data item against which pending changes are scheduled.

▶ The *category* determines the difficulty and impact of the RFC and is the main parameter used to determine the resources to be allocated, projected deadlines, and level of authorization needed before the change can be implemented.

After the RFC is accepted and categorized, the change can be approved and planned. Formal approval for the change is obtained from the Change Authority Board (CAB); this can be a role, manager, or group of individuals. Once approved, the change should be assessed as to whether it should be implemented in isolation or as part of a package of changes that would be functionally equivalent to a single change. Although Change Management is not responsible for implementing the change (typically this is the responsibility of Release Management), it is responsible for supervising and coordinating the process as a whole.

Before closing the change, it is necessary that you perform an evaluation. This allows assessment of the impact of the change on the organization's quality of service and productivity. It is essential to define reports that allow performance evaluations of the Change Management process. For these reports to provide precise information, you should develop a series of reference metrics that are important for your organization.

To assist with this process definition, here are some terms used with Change Management, taken from the ITIL Glossary. Chapter 3 provides more detailed information:

▶ **Service change:** The addition, modification, or removal of anything that could have an effect on IT services.

▶ **RFC acceptance:** Formal agreement that the change request is complete, accurate, reliable, and meets its specified requirements as specified in your Change process.

▶ **RFC approval:** A change request process typically incorporates at least one approval before carrying out the change. This is the agreement to proceed with the defined activities of the change implementation.

▶ **Change Advisory Board:** A group of individuals that advise the change manager in the assessment, prioritization, and scheduling of changes. This board typically consists of representatives from all areas within the IT service provider, the business, and third parties such as suppliers. The Emergency Change Advisory Board (ECAB) is a subset of the CAB that makes decisions about high-impact emergency changes.

▶ **Activity:** Worth mentioning for Service Manager, processes include activities. With Service Manager 2010, an activity is a step in the Change process defined in Service Manager that is added to the change request work item.

The Change settings configuration in Service Manager is limited to configuring the prefix and the attachment policy. Change request work items contain predefined values that can be adjusted in the Library workspace. You can build a Change Management process with different activities, resulting in a configuration that enables your Change process in Service Manager 2010. In general, here is how you can categorize the Service Manager configuration tasks:

▶ **Change Management Process Activities:** Process activities require Service Manager components to be configured in a specific way. In this translation exercise, you have a defined process as input; as output, you have the required configuration in Service Manager for Change Request and Activity Management.

▶ **General Change Management Service Manager Configuration Enumeration Lists and Settings:** The change request settings in Service Manager are global settings for the Change process; this is also the case for Activity Management in Service Manager. Determining change and activity list item values that are predefined selectable values in the request form and defining the user roles in the Change process will complete the configuration that is required before you begin to implement change processes.

▶ **Change Management Automation:** Templates and workflows can automate the Change process. Service Manager includes the ability to create automated activities you can use for minor changes. The process activity translation exercise provides input as to how much you can or need to automate your Change process in Service Manager.

Change Management in Service Manager

Service Manager 2010 includes an interface to manage the Change Management process. The default Change management pack (MP) included in Service Manager provides templates, manual and review activities, and the functionality to create workflows.

Change Management integrates with other management functions, such that it can provide a complete overview for impact analysis and post-review activities. Service Manager enables and manages change requests on different activities in the overall Change process:

▶ Change Management requests in Service Manager are work items that derive from a default change request form and include all required details such as the reason, priority, and impact of the change as well as links to configuration items that are impacted by the change.

▶ A change request can be initiated directly from the CI or other work items using predefined templates to ensure accurate and consistent recording.

▶ The Change MP provides the flexibility to easily adapt and change review stages in accordance with an organization's guidelines and policies.

▶ Change process steps are activities in the change request template. The Change MP provides manual and review activity templates. You can establish automated activities in the Change Request template for similar change requests; these activities automate deployment of the change.

▶ Communication is important in the Change process. Service Manager notification functionality is integrated with Change Management and can send out notifications based on a criteria list with predefined email templates.

▶ Change request event workflows can be used to apply templates and send out notifications. You can also use workflows to automate evaluating the request. For example, by checking the required fields for values you quickly verify whether a valid change request is submitted.

The basis of Change Management is the configuration baseline. The current configuration is retrieved from the configuration baseline; it is later updated to reflect the implemented change. To define the scope of the change or review its impact, you must have current CI information and information available about their relationships. Service Manager 2010 includes connectors to automate this information.

The change request in Service Manager starts with creating the change work item in the console. First, you must select a change category. This ensures that the defined path is followed for the required change. By default, there are five Change Management templates, which you can adjust to your needs. Table 12.1 provides a list of the default change request types in Service Manager.

TABLE 12.1   Change Request Types

Type of Change	Description	Example
Standard Change Request	Standard change requests are preapproved and used for low-risk pretested change operations	Installation of an approved standard software package
Minor Change Request	Minor change requests can be approved by a change manager. Use them for low-risk and low-impact changes according to the change policies of your organization	The weekly update of a virus identification file
Major Change Request	Major change requests should be screened by the change manager. The CAB approves the initial request and approves change deployment in two separate review activities. This type of change request also has post-implementation review as a last step in the process. Use the Major Change Request template for high-risk/impact changes according to the change policies of your organization.	Implementing/ upgrading company-wide software
Emergency Change Request	Emergency change requests are used for urgent changes that should be implemented in less than, say, 24 hours, and cannot follow the normal Change process. They should be approved by ECAB and contain mandatory post-implementation review. Use them for urgent changes according to the change policies of your organization	The purchase and install of a new server within the organization
Security Release	Use the Security Release template for security patch scenarios. It includes typical steps for planning, developing, testing, and rolling out security patches in the IT environment.	Monthly patching of the environment with new release security patches.

You can select change request templates from the Server Manager console or apply them using workflows. Service Manager provides default templates for review and manual activities. In addition to the manual activities, you can extend Service Manager to include your own developed automated activities. An example of an automated activity is the portal software deployment activity, which instructs Configuration Manager to deploy the requested software.

You can create Change Management workflows to apply a change template or send a notification when certain criterion on the work item is fulfilled. Activity workflows can be used similarly to the other workflows. These workflows can apply an activity template and can send out notifications. An example of using an activity workflow is to check whether the activity implementer is provided; and if not, apply the template to assign this activity to a default group. Having unassigned activities in the process can delay change implementation and negatively affect the change.

Service Manager 2010 orchestrates the interactions between the processes and provides an interface to manage change requests with the Service Manager console. While the actual implementation of the change is outside Service Manager, it is enforced with the activities in the change request template. Connectors are used to automatically update the CI information in Service Manager; the change request work item form provides the fields necessary to document all required information to implement the change.

Change Management reporting in Service Manager includes default reports providing precise information that makes it easy to evaluate your change processes. Out-of-the box reports include Change Management KPI Trend, Change Request Details, and List of Change Requests.

Figure 12.1 illustrates an overview of Change Management in Service Manager 2010 and summarizes the process.

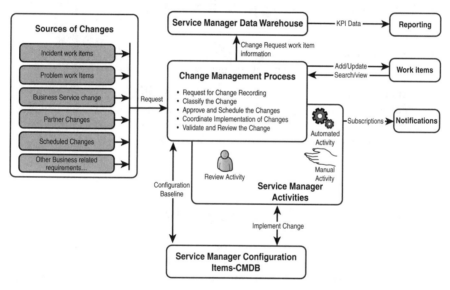

FIGURE 12.1   Change Management in Server Manager 2010.

Configuring Change Management in Service Manager occurs in different areas of the console, the primary area being the change request settings configuration in the Administrative workspace of the console. Here are some of those settings:

▶ **Configuring Change Request Work Item Prefix:** In Service Manager 2010, all change request work items numbers start with CR. Activities in the Change process have the AC prefix for activity, MA for manual activity, and RA for review activity. However, you can change the prefix used for your change and activity work item numbering.

▶ **Change Request File Attachment Policy:** The policy at your company may limit the number of files that can be attached to each change request, perhaps to no more than 10, and the maximum file size for each file to 64 kilobytes (KB). The maximum number of attached files and maximum file size settings that you specify also apply to the attached files in the Related Items tab on the change request form. Give this some thought: Certain tickets may require a number of attachments/screenshots to resolve.

To keep storage at a reasonable size, you might want to establish a policy and provide training to people involved in the Change process concerning storing commonly used documents, such as design or project management, on a Change Management SharePoint site accessible with a link from Service Manager. This approach adds the benefit of version control on the change document library and is accessible outside the Service Manager console.

▶ **Change Request Notifications:** Notifications can be created as they are for other management functions. The notifications channel, your created change and activity notification templates, and subscriptions are components used to build your notification plan for Change Management.

In the Library space of the console, you can configure groups, knowledge, queues, Change and Activity Management lists, change request queues, and tasks.

Using the Service Manager Authoring Tool is another way to configure or automate the Change Management process using your own activities or custom workflows. See Chapter 17, "Management Packs," Chapter 18, "Customizing Service Manager," and Chapter 19, "Advanced Customization Scenarios," for information on the Authoring Tool.

The next section maps Change Request process activities to Service Manager functionality.

Change Management Process Activities

Change Management process activities define the roadmap of the change needing to be implemented. You should create a change request work item even for the smallest change; because there is always the potential of a large impact from an undocumented implemented change that no one knew occurred. For trivial changes or those repeated at intervals, you might establish standard procedures that do not require Change Management approval on a case-by-case basis. You can simplify the Change process for these types of changes, using predefined templates simplifying creation of the change request work item, change request event workflows, and the appropriate notification subscriptions for the requested change.

Service Manager 2010's integration with other System Center products optimizes several activities in the process. By implementing the Operations Manager (OpsMgr) and Configuration Manager (ConfigMgr) connectors, you can review the impact of the change on the CIs in scope for the change and see the result of the implemented change via OpsMgr monitoring and alert forwarding.

The Change Management process activities illustrated in Figure 12.2 provide an overview of the process to determine the required changes and implement them with minimum adverse impact to the business service. It is essential to evaluate and examine each activity as to how you can apply Service Manager technology to optimize those activities.

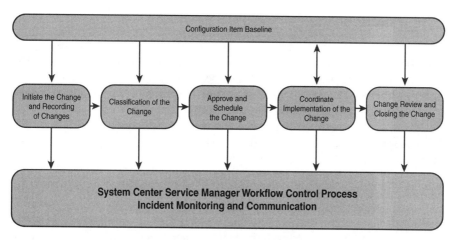

FIGURE 12.2   Activities in Change Request Management.

Figure 12.2 displays the process activities, which are described here:

▶ **Configuration item baseline:** This is the baseline of a configuration that has been formally agreed upon and is managed through the Change Management process. A configuration baseline is used as a basis for future changes and can be used to enable the IT infrastructure to restore the baseline to a known configuration if a change fails.

▶ **Initiate and recording of the change:** Information that is provided in the change request work items is used as input in upcoming activities of the process. At a minimum, the following data is required: date received, unique identifier of the RFC, and description of the proposed change.

▶ **Classification of the change:** Once the RFC is recorded, a preliminary assessment should be made of its validity and importance. After the RFC is accepted, it should be assigned a priority and category depending on its urgency and impact.

▶ **Approve and schedule the change:** In this activity, the CAB must meet at intervals to analyze and, where appropriate, approve the pending RFCs and prepare the schedule of changes. Effective Change Management requires planning. Information on CIs and other work items can provide input for appropriate change implementation planning.

▶ **Coordinate implementation of the change:** Although the Change Management function is not responsible for implementing the change, it is responsible for supervising and coordinating the process from the beginning to end. Implementation steps are Service Manager activities; the configured Service Manager activities should reflect the designed implementation roadmap.

▶ **Change review and closing the change:** Before closing the change request work item, you should evaluate its implementation. This allows the real impact of the change on the organization's business service to be assessed.

Configuration Item Baseline

This Change Management process activity is described in the Microsoft Operations Framework Solution Accelerator guidance and is important because Service Manager 2010 can be very helpful in creating this baseline. CIs can be automatically created, updated, and deleted using connectors; this automated process can be scheduled to have accurate information on the CIs. During the Change process, each activity has information that is required from CIs. Service Manager Configuration Management provides information about the relationships of CIs through the CMDB. This CI information, together with the CI relationships, is used in the Change process:

▶ The request for change work item form is populated with information from CIs and the relationship with a business service (if there is one).

▶ Accurate CI information and the relationship between the CIs will provide Change Management with a better understanding of the impact, priority, and risk of changes.

▶ A history of previous states to support efforts to analyze change requests and is important information if a rollback is required.

Keeping the Service Manager configuration management database (CMDB) up-to-date is important to successfully manage changes. Service Manager connectors automate creation of CIs and update this CI information based on a schedule defined on the connector. Relationships between the different CIs are created when defining business services or can be imported by OpsMgr MPs. This enables a rich set of information to be available for use in making decisions during the different activities of the Change process.

TIP: TAKE CONTROL ON DATA SOURCE OF THE CONNECTORS

In Service Manager 2010, the connectors create or update information from a data source, such as Active Directory or ConfigMgr, into the Service Manager database. You should define your own process so that only valid CIs are imported into Service Manager. As an example of such a process, create user and computer objects in a temporary OU in Active Directory; once they become active, move them to an OU monitored by the Service Manager connector. If you have ConfigMgr available, you can use a dedicated collection to import and update CIs. When the CIs are retired, they are removed from the monitored OU and collection. Using this type of connector configuration, you could say that only "managed" CIs are present in the Service Manager database.

Let's say an update needs to be made to a production application to introduce new required functionality. Based on the business service defined for this production application in the Configuration Items pane of the Service Manager console, you can determine the type, risk, and impact of the change request. CI information can be added in the relevant fields of the change request form; this enables a complete bundle of information to be submitted for approval and scheduling. The actual implementation changes the configuration of the CI, and the configuration baseline is updated in Service Manager via the connectors. In addition, all activity history in the Change process is logged on the change work item. As with the other management functions, it is important you have accurate data in the console and an overview of the relationship between the different CIs. By importing OpsMgr MPs into Service Manager, Operations Manager can introduce new CI classes and help define the relationships between CIs.

Here are the Service Manager components involved:

- ▶ **Service Manager connectors:** Importing and updating CI information provides accurate CI information used during different activities of the process.

- ▶ **Configuration Management:** The Configuration Management process is responsible for maintaining information about CIs required to deliver an IT service, including their relationships. Even with the connectors that are configured in the tool, you must define a process to control CI data in Service Manager.

Initiate the Change and Recording of the Change

The initiate and recording activity is performed to initiate a RFC by opening a change request form and entering the information about the requested change. Initiating an RFC starts with selecting the type of change. For Service Manager 2010, this corresponds with selecting a change request template; Figure 12.3 is the selection dialog displayed when you create a new change request. Templates created for the Change Management class will appear in the list of available change request templates. You can limit this list of change request templates by using Change Management user roles. The Change Initiators role can be scoped on groups, queues, tasks, and templates; they will see only those templates to which they have rights.

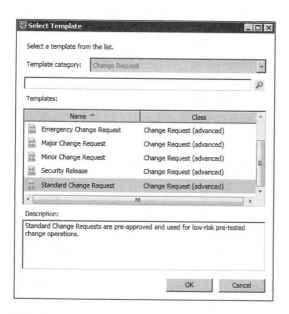

FIGURE 12.3   The change request template selection.

NOTE: CHANGE REQUEST TEMPLATES

Be aware that once you select a template, you can't "go back" and select another template. For example, should you select a standard change, enter it, and later decide it is a minor change, you have to reenter the change as a minor change. This makes it important to train IT analysts from the start as to which types of changes qualify in each type (emergency, major, and so on).

Templates have predefined fields and change work item activities to simplify creating the RFC and ensure that the appropriate procedures are followed. Service Manager includes five change request templates you can adjust to your organization's needs, or you can create additional change request templates for specific recurring changes.

You can initiate change requests in Service Manager from any CI or work item in the console. This opens a new change request form and automatically associates the selected item with the new change request (Figure 12.4 shows the default change request). Linked CIs, such as services, computers, printers, software, knowledge articles, and other custom imported classes, can be logged as CIs to change (visible in Figure 12.5). Work items such as incidents, other change requests, and problem work items, are related items to the change request in the Service Manager console and can be linked to the work item using the Related Items tab shown in Figure 12.6.

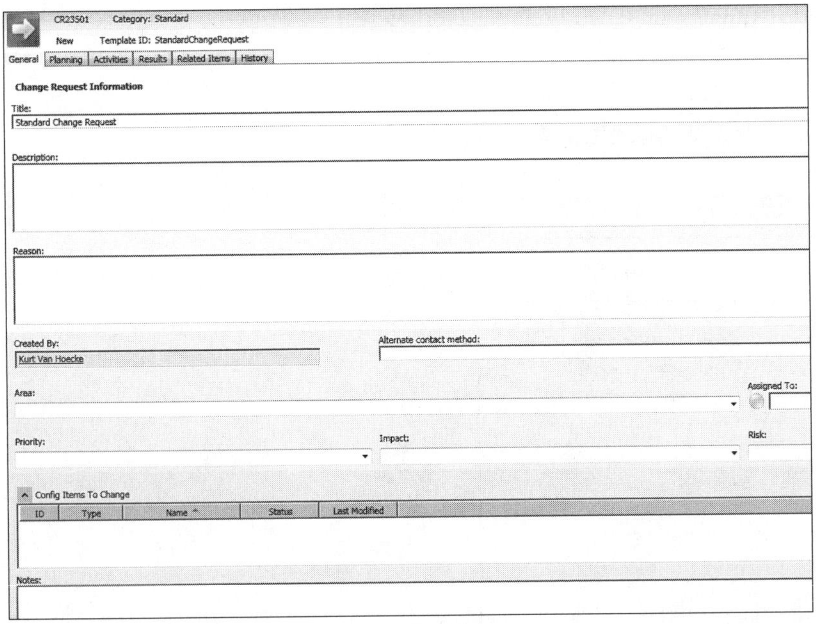

FIGURE 12.4   The default change request form.

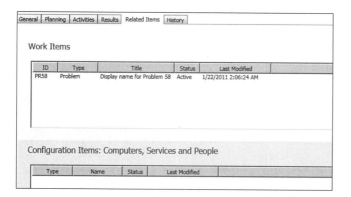

FIGURE 12.5   The Config Items To Change section in the change request form.

| General | Planning | Activities | Results | Related Items | History |

Work Items

ID	Type	Title	Status	Last Modified
PR58	Problem	Display name for Problem 58	Active	1/22/2011 2:06:24 AM

Configuration Items: Computers, Services and People

Type	Name	Status	Last Modified

FIGURE 12.6   The change request form: Related Items tab.

The Service Manager 2010 Change MP provides a platform for Change Management that you will need to adjust for your organization. You must evaluate that the necessary change request templates for your organization are available, that the default change request form includes all required fields, and that the Change Management user roles are defined such that change requests can be created and coordinated. The MP creates the Change Initiators and the Change Managers roles. Similar to with other management functions in Service Manager, these roles are globally scoped and cannot be deleted; you can only associate users or groups with these roles. You can create those additional Change Management user roles required for your organization with defined access specified to queues, groups, tasks, views, and templates.

Different types of change requests in the Change process can require that different sets of information be provided for the request to be approved. For minor changes, a simple indication of what the change involves can be added in the Planning tab of the Service Manager change request form. For other types of requests, it may be necessary to create an implementation, risk assessment, test, and back-out plan for the change. An URL to your document library system, such as SharePoint, can be added as a related item in the change request form. Figure 12.7 shows the location in the form where you can add this type of information.

It is important that the appropriate individuals are notified of the request. Using subscriptions in the Service Manager notification functionality, you can trigger a notification when a change request work item is properly created or changed. For detailed information about the notification functionality, see Chapter 14, "Notification."

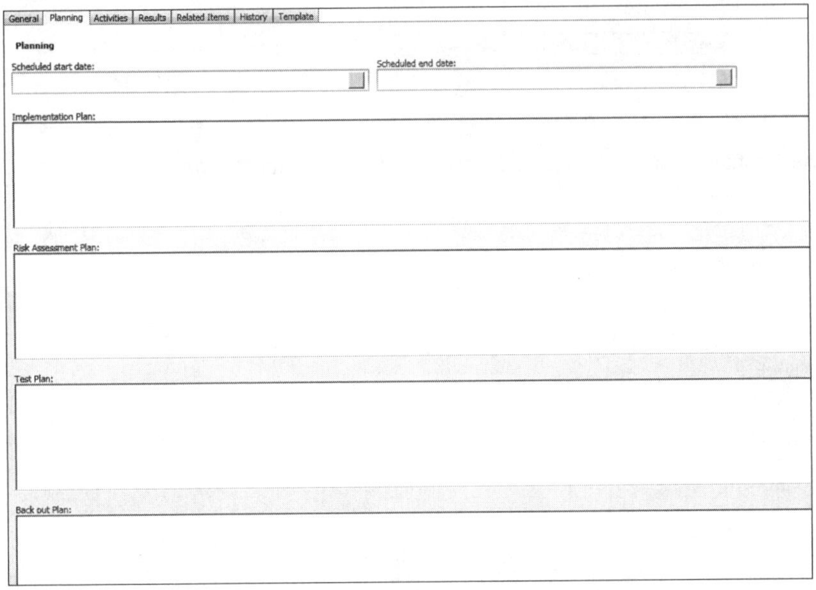

FIGURE 12.7   The Change Request Planning tab.

The following Service Manager components are involved:

▶ **Default Change Request Form:** A default change request form is provided with the Change MP. The form provides tabs and fields to include the necessary information to request the change.

▶ **Change Event Templates:** Change request templates are useful in this activity when you create a change request for a recurring type of issue; you can set an issue category and define a standard priority, effect, and risk level for it in the template. Service Manager 2010 includes a number of default templates you can use to create change request work items. Depending on your Request process, you may need to create additional templates for change request work items or to use in change request event workflows.

▶ **Change Event Notification:** The Change Management team should keep the user informed of any changes that could affect the production business services. Configuring accurate notifications and subscriptions in Service Manager is required to support this process.

▶ **Configuration Items:** CIs in Service Manager are the main source of information during the Change process. The Change process and implementation team make decisions based on this information and might lose time or make incorrect decisions if this information is outdated or incomplete. Connectors automate importing CI object information into Service Manager.

▶ **Change Request Event Workflows:** Change request event workflows can evaluate the change request at creation time. Using a set of criteria, a change template can be applied and notifications sent.

Classification of the Change

Requests for changes need to be reviewed by the change manager. Some requests simply are not practical or feasible, other requests may be a duplication of efforts. After the RFC is recorded, a preliminary assessment must be made of the validity of the request and its importance. Classification of the change request involves setting its priority, impact, and risk. This can indicate that the change request can go further in the process for approval, or if a different process needs to be followed (different RFC type). Within ITIL, the "seven R's" of Change Management is a quick checklist that is a good starting point for evaluating a request for change. This list is a practical and common sense way to minimize change rejection at the first point of change logging:

- Who *raised* the change?

- What is the *reason* for the change?

- What is the *return* required from the change?

- What *risks* are there if you do or do not carry out the change?

- What *resources* are required to perform this change?

- Who is *responsible* for the build, test, and implementation of the change?

- What *relationships* are there between this and other changes?

The classification categories (area, priority, impact, and risk) in the Service Manager change requests are predefined values (list items) that can be selected in the change request form. These Change Management lists can be adjusted to comply with your organization's needs. Change request templates can predefine classification fields and change activities. As discussed in the "Configuration Item Baseline" section of this chapter, CI information available in the Service Manager console is an important source of information for classifying change requests. Change request event workflows will help you apply templates and notify when certain criteria on the work item is fulfilled. For example, you have a minor change request that is acceptable for most cases, but when a specific area in the change request form is selected, you want to apply a specific template that sets the risk to high and applies a different change review path.

The following Service Manager components are involved:

- **Default Change Request Form:** A default change request form is provided with the Change MP. You can review the change request information and use a console task to update the status.

- **Change Management Lists:** These are lists of properties that display in drop-down lists on forms and dialog boxes. An example is change priority; the list contains a default set of list items and can be adjusted with specific values for your organization.

- **Configuration Items:** CIs in Service Manager are a main source of information. The change manager uses this information during execution of this activity.

▶ **Change Request Event Workflows:** Based on classification, the appropriate templates can be assigned via workflows in order to automate the Change process.

Approve and Schedule the Change

Approval of a change request is driven by its change request category. The approval process for a major or emergency change request can begin by presenting the change to the appropriate change reviewers. These are key people who represent many perspectives and will be held accountable for the results of the change. When referring back to the seven R's from the change classification activity, the CAB evaluates the change request for approval in a different perspective:

▶ What are the expected benefits of the proposed change?

▶ Do these benefits justify the costs entailed by the Change process?

▶ What are the associated risks?

▶ Are the necessary resources available to make the change with certainty of success?

▶ Can the change be postponed?

▶ What will the general impact be on the IT infrastructure and quality of service?

▶ Could the change affect the established IT security levels?

With Service Manager, you can use user and group CIs mapped to Active Directory Users and Groups to identify change reviewers. Individual reviewers represent and vote for themselves. Group reviewers contain multiple users, and any member of the group can vote on behalf of the whole group. Service Manager review activities can use one of the following voting logic types by default; additional approval conditions can be created via the approval list in the Library workspace:

▶ **Unanimous:** All reviewers must vote at this review activity.

▶ **Percentage:** Defines a minimum percent of reviewers that must vote for approval.

▶ **Automatic:** This can be used for the auto-approved review activities.

The default review activity form is illustrated in Figure 12.8.

You may also use the Active Directory Manager property on a user object with the Line Manager Should Review check box in this figure. When the check box is selected, the manager of the user creating the change request is added as one of the reviewers. When adding reviewers to the review activity form, you have two review modifiers that allow enforcement of the review logic:

▶ The Must vote flag indicates that the reviewer cannot skip the review activity.

▶ The Has veto flag indicates that the identified reviewer can reject the review, regardless of how other reviewers vote.

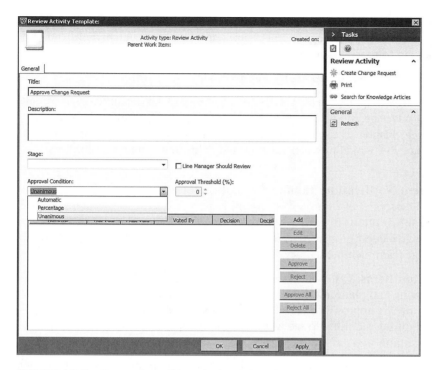

FIGURE 12.8   Approval conditions in the default Review Activity Form.

Figure 12.9 shows the dialog to select a user or group as reviewer and the two check boxes used to enforce your review logic.

FIGURE 12.9   Specify if the reviewer is required to review the activity.

Planning change implementation activities is essential for good Change Management. You can review CI and work item information in the Service Manager console to help in planning the change. The relationships between all the CIs involved or changes already planned to CIs can affect the planning of approved change requests. Because business services in Service Manager define the relationships between different CIs, it is important to have this information available in different activities of the Change process. You can create a change calendar using a custom task in the console, and create a task that is available in the change work item form to publish the change request information to a shared calendar, perhaps on a SharePoint portal. For additional information, check Vladimir Bakhmetyev's blog post at http://blogs.technet.com/b/servicemanager/archive/2010/07/02/publishing-work-item-to-part-1-sharepoint-calendar.aspx.

The following Service Manager components are involved:

- **Default Change Request Form:** Service Manager provides a default change request form based on Change and Activity class properties and relationships. This form is extensible; see Chapter 18 for more information. The form includes a Planning tab and review activity, which provides the required fields to document the process activities.

- **Change Event Notification:** Notification in this process activity is useful to inform the required personnel of an approved change request. Configuring accurate notifications and subscriptions in Service Manager is required to support this process. You can use change request properties as the trigger to send out notification to different sets of change team members.

- **Configuration Items:** CIs in Service Manager are a main source of information when approving and planning the change request. The change manager uses this information during approval to reevaluate the impact, risk, and priority of the request, and during planning to see whether other work items may influence the indicated planning.

- **Work Items:** Other work items can have a vast impact on approving and planning a change request. If the change request is initiated from another work item, it is a related item. On the other hand, change planning can be influenced when a change is requested on a business service, and while planning, you determine another change request already affects one of the components. In this case, you should plan to implement the change after implementing the previously planned change.

Coordinate Implementation of the Change

Although Change Management is not responsible for implementing the change, which is typically the responsibility of Release Management, it is responsible for supervising and coordinating implementation of the change. During the change development phase, the process should be monitored to ensure that the change is implemented as described. Different System Center products can assist in the implementation or review activity. Configuration Manager can be used for operating system (OS) rollout, software installation, software updates, and so on; Operations Manager can start monitoring the implemented change once as it is in production. The Desired Configuration Management functionality in Configuration Manager can be part of the Change process, where different components of a CI are evaluated against a baseline and compliancy reported to Service Manager using the Configuration Manager connector.

Most change implementation activities equate to manual activities in Service Manager; this can be similar to a checklist or milestones in the project plan. Activities defined in the change template that are not started have a status of Active. As the change is developed

3. In the Tasks pane, under Activity Settings, click **Properties** to open the Activity Settings dialog box.

The Activity prefix settings for the different activities in Service Manager, shown in Figure 12.14, are the general Activity Settings configuration.

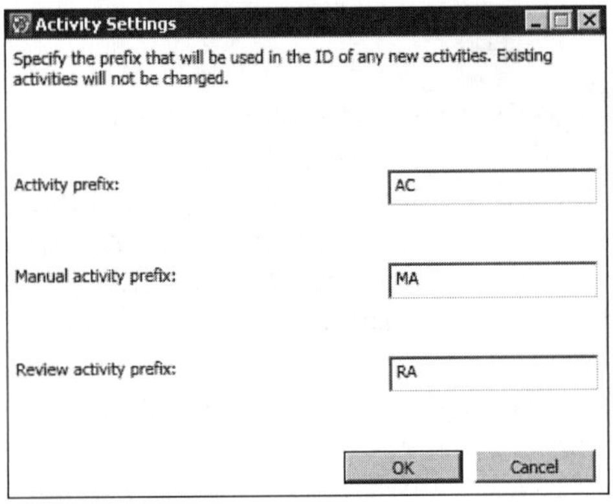

FIGURE 12.14   General Activity settings.

Configure Notification

Service Manager can send notifications when a change request work item is created or updated. Before you can create notification subscriptions, there are several steps to take for Service Manager to send out notifications: enabling email notifications, establishing a notification channel with your Simple Mail Transfer Protocol (SMTP) mail server, and creating a notification template to use as the basis for your notification message. This process is described in Chapter 14.

Communication and the associated notification to the involved individuals in a change request is an important configuration area for an efficient Change Management process. Team members may want to be notified when a change request is created or when change request work item property changes occur. In addition to the email notification functionality in Service Manager, you can use announcements to communicate major change to larger group of users.

The following procedure steps through the creation of this notification subscription in the Odyssey Service Manager environment:

1. In the Service Manager console, click **Administration**. In the Administration space, expand **Notification**, and then click **Subscriptions**. In the Tasks pane, click **Create Subscription**.

2. On the Before You Begin page of the Create E-Mail Notification Subscription wizard, click **Next**.

3. On the General page, type a name in the Notification subscription name box. For example, type **Odyssey - Major Change Request created**. Optionally, in the Description box, you can type a description for the subscription you are creating.

and tested, the change coordinator can mark each step in the process with an Updated status. To make this clearer, the following example describes an implementation flow for a major change:

- ▶ **Approval of the change request:** Approval of the change request is part of previous activity of the Change process and a requirement for implementation of the change.

- ▶ **Change development:** This is the actual design of the change. During this manual activity, it is required that all design information gathered is recorded on the change request Planning tab in the form. This information includes the change implementation plan, risk assessment plan, test plan, and backout plan if necessary. Recorded information should ensure that any usage scenarios, operational requirements, and design information satisfy the design of the change to build and test the change. When complete, the status of the Change Development implementation activity can be marked as Complete.

- ▶ **Change testing:** During this manual implementation activity, the change is implemented in a test environment. Change design information created in the Change Development activity, such as the captured implementation, risk assessment, test, and backout plans, is input for testing the change in a lab or test environment, as necessary. When complete and satisfactory results are met, the Change Testing manual activity status can be set to Completed.

- ▶ **Approval of the change for deployment:** This manual review activity of approving the change request after development and testing is a review, or voting, activity. This is the go or no-go decision for implementing the change in production environment.

- ▶ **Change deployment:** This manual implementation activity is the introduction of the change in the production environment. The updated information from testing is used for implementing the change in production.

- ▶ **Post-implementation review:** This manual activity reviews the implementation to ensure that the change is implemented as required and delivers the expected result. This implementation activity is described in the next section, "Change Review and Closing the Change." Similar to the other manual activities, the status can be set to completed, and if all are successful, the change is ready for closure.

Although change reviewers and owners update the change request throughout its life cycle, it is particularly important to ensure that up-to-date status of each manual and review activity is recorded during the development and testing process. Different status levels of the implementation activities can be configured in the Lists folder of the Library pane in the Service Manager console. The Activity Status list has default values that can be adjusted to your organization's needs to follow the different activities during the process. It is a best practice to rename the default list items in the Activity Status list.

TIP: MAINTAIN CONTROL OF THE CHANGE INFORMATION

You can use change request event workflows to apply templates and send notifications. You can also define workflows with criteria that check whether the change requester has added all required information for the type of change.

For example, when a major change is created and requires an implementation, risk, test, and backout plan added to this type of request, you could specify a workflow criterion to notify the requester of a noncompliant request, and the approval activity could be set on hold until the request is compliant. A compliancy check could be to create a change request workflow that

- ▶ Checks the change category if it is a major change request.
- ▶ Uses other criteria to check the planning fields in the form if there are no empty fields.
- ▶ When the defined criteria are evaluated (equals a noncompliant change request), the workflow applies a template to set the change request on hold.
- ▶ Sends a notification to the requester to automatically validate and update the request in order to submit a compliant request.

This is just an example; think about those fields required to define a request compliant for your own organization.

Service Manager 2010 provides additional functionality; you can configure automated implementation activities for recurring similar changes in the environment. The portal software deployment activity is an example of an automated implementation activity. With this type of automated activity, you can standardize and automate the implementation of minor changes. Using the example of the portal software deployment activity, here's what occurs:

- ▶ A request is submitted for software via the Service Manager SSP.
- ▶ A change reviewer (or the line manager) approves the software request.
- ▶ Review activity is set to approved/completed.
- ▶ The automated activity is started.
- ▶ Service Manager checks the All Service Manager Software Deployment Collections (created by Service Manager) to determine whether the collection already exists in ConfigMgr; if not, it creates a collection to deploy the software and a membership rule for the computer.
- ▶ At the next Configuration Manager client agent policy update, the software is installed by ConfigMgr.
- ▶ Automated activity status is set to complete after the computer is added to the collection.

Detailed software deployment details can be retrieved from ConfigMgr reporting. (Note that it can take up to 24 hours before the status is set to complete; this status is updated after a Configuration Manager connector sync.)

Activities in the Change process can be assigned to different individuals involved in the Change process. The Work Items pane of the Service Manager console provides views for the follow-up of the different active manual and review activities. You can create your own views, queues, and groups as with the other management functions in Service Manager. In this manner, you can personalize the management console for those users with work items assigned to them.

The following Service Manager components are involved:

- ▶ **Default Change Request Form:** Activity recording and follow-up is performed in the Activities tab of the change request work item.

- ▶ **Service Manager Activity Management:** Default review and manual activities are available that define the different steps of your Change process.

- ▶ **Service Manager Notification:** Status notification flow can be created using the Service Manager notification functionality.

- ▶ **Service Manager Activities:** Service Manager activities are defined in the change request template. Using review and manual activities, you can build your change template to ensure a predefined path is followed to implement the change. In Service Manager, you have the opportunity to create your own automated activities for similar minor changes.

- ▶ **Configuration Items:** CIs are updated, changed, or replaced during the change implementation. The technical evaluation of a successful implementation of the change is reviewing log files; service failures can be monitored with OpsMgr and reported back. The actual configuration change is updated via the Active Directory and Configuration Manager connectors or a custom-created CSV file.

Change Review and Closing the Change

When any change is released into the production environment, the next important step in the process is to validate the release and review the implementation. After this change review cycle, the change work item in Service Manager can be formally closed.

Determining whether the released change was effective and achieved the desired results requires you monitor the change in a production environment. Integrating the OpsMgr Alert connector significantly assists with this change review process activity, as after the change is applied the service is monitored with Operations Manager and any alerts are forwarded to Service Manager. For a minor change, this might be a matter of checking whether the desired functionality is still available on the changed service component. Larger changes might require monitoring network and server information, performance data, event logs, and response times. This can be a complex task that you can fully auto-mate with OpsMgr, and then report the information to Service Manager. Another scenario that can be helpful in the change review activity is the Desired Configuration Management functionality from ConfigMgr. When you have defined a desired state of a service component in ConfigMgr for the CI, as soon as the change is implemented the state can be reevaluated with compliancy reported to Service Manager. Using ConfigMgr and OpsMgr functionality and connectors configured in Service Manager provides a considerable amount of information for the change review activity.

By default, you cannot reopen closed change requests in Service Manager. It is important for post implementation change reviewers to approve a successful implementation using accurate information that is based on the results implemented by those changes. The Closed status in the change request work item in Service Manager can be set only from a Completed status of the change work item. This status is set automatically when all imple-mentation activities defined in the used template are set as *Completed*.

The following Service Manager components are involved:

▶ **Default Change Request Form:** Closure information in the change request work item is a task that finalizes the work item with a description of the closure. The Service Manager change request work item form bundles this information for further handling the change implementation.

▶ **Service Manager Notification:** Those individuals involved in the change request should be notified of the progress of the request and implementation. When the change request work item is closed, the proper notifications can be sent.

Configuring Change Management

The "Change Management Process Activities" section provided an overview of the Change Management activities from a Service Manager 2010 perspective. This section presents an overview of configuration options for Change Management in Service Manager 2010.

The configuration required for Service Manager to enable a basic platform for Change Management is minor; most of the configuration depends on the Change process defini-tions (activities) in your organization. Settings such as prefix, Change Management user roles, and notification configuration are global settings for the Change Management process in Service Manager 2010. Service Manager provides the platform for managing and automating the change work item implementation and life cycle. During the different activities in the process, the Change Management team can record the proper information in the change request work item form and retrieve information from different work items and CIs. The actual activity to implement the change in the environment is something outside Service Manager. This is the technical part of the process; minor recurring changes can be automated with custom-created automated activities.

To configure Change Management in Service Manager 2010, consider providing access for the different user roles so they can fulfill their role in the Change process. Configure the Change Request Management settings in Service Manager, and define the change list items values for your environment. Because changes include activities, this section also describes configuring Activity Management in Service Manager.

As with other modifications you will perform in Service Manager to enable functionality, define what you need to configure in Service Manager before actually starting to configure that functionality. The "Change Management Process Activities" section of this chapter can help define the configuration necessary for Service Manager. Running through this list of activities in your Change process and translating for each activity those changes necessary for the involved Service Manager components provides an overview of the required configuration. The next sections guide you through configuring the Change Management settings, specifically the following:

- ▶ Changing Management console tasks

- ▶ Changing Management user roles, groups, queues, and lists

- ▶ Configuring the general Change Management settings

- ▶ Configuring Change Management notification

Change Management Console Tasks

You can create change work items from different locations by selecting the Create Change task in the task pane of the form. Selecting Create Change Request or Create Related Change Request from different locations affects the information automatically populated in the form:

- ▶ When a request is created from the Change Management template folder, an empty work item form is presented from which the Change Request Management team can further input information to describe the change. You must add CIs and related items manually.

- ▶ If a request is created from the Configuration Item node of the console, the configuration item is directly added to the Config Items To Change field of the change request work item form.

- ▶ If a request is created from a Work Items node, the CI is directly added to the Related Items - Work Items field of the change request work item form.

The task pane of the change request form in Figure 12.10 lists default tasks you can perform on a change request work item. This includes changing the status, editing, and access to reporting in Service Manager.

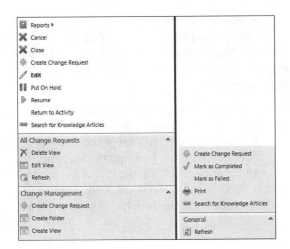

FIGURE 12.10   The change request tasks in the Service Manager console.

Service Manager activities in the change request form have their own status levels and tasks in the console. Figure 12.10 provides an overview of the tasks that are available by default in the activities. Tasks available in the activity form are status related. The status of the activity defines also the status of the change request work item; all activities must be complete before a change request can be closed.

In addition to the default tasks provided in the Service Manager console, you can create your own Change Management tasks to automate similar reoccurring tasks. Refer to Chapter 18 if you require complex tasks in the console.

Change Management User Roles, Groups, Queues, and Lists

The starting point of Change Management configuration is ensuring the Change Management team has access to the required work items, CIs, views, and tasks. By default, two user roles, the Change Initiators and Change Owner, are defined with access to all change request work items, views, and so on.

The process of creating Change Management user roles is similar to the procedure to create user roles for other management functions. Chapter 15, "Service Manager Security," explains how to create user roles in Service Manager.

The change request work item form includes different fields to categorize and prioritize change request work items. The values presented in the form are Service Manager list item values. Service Manager lists represent properties of an object, and include one or more list items. Each list item represents a possible value for the property the Change Management team can select on the change request forms and dialog boxes. Several default list items in Service Manager 2010 exist for Change and Activity Management and can be adjusted to the needs of your environment. Table 12.2 provides an overview of the default Change and Activity Management lists provided by the different Management packs.

TABLE 12.2   Change and Activity Management Lists

List Name	Description	Management Pack
Change Request Status	Change Status List	Change Request Library
Change Category	Change Category List	Change Request Library
Change Priority	Change Priority List	Change Request Library
Change Risk	Change Risk List	Change Request Library
Change Implementation Results	Change Implementation List	Change Request Library
Change Impact	Change Impact List	Change Request Library
Change Area	Change Area List	Change Request Library
Active Stage	Activity Stage list	Activity Library
Active Priority	Activity Priority list	Activity Library
Active Area	Activity Area list	Activity Library
Active Status	Activity Status list	Activity Library
Approval	Approval list	Activity Library
Decision	Decision list	Activity Library

Figure 12.11 shows the Change Priority defaults using the example of the Change Management lists. To adjust this list in the Service Manager environment, follow these steps:

1. In the Service Manager console, click **Library**. In the Library pane, click **Lists**. The Lists pane displays all the existing lists. You can organize the Results pane information by clicking the column titles; this makes it easy to find the list you want to edit.

2. Select the list to which you want to add a list item; so, select the **Change Category List**. In the Tasks pane, under Change Category, click **Properties**.

3. In the List Properties dialog box, click **Add Item**. Notice a new List Value list item is added. You can change the name of the new list item by clicking the item and then entering the name in the name fields of the dialog box. If desired, you can type an optional description in the Description box.

4. Click **OK** to save your changes.

Follow this same procedure for other change and activity lists to build a Change Management environment that is compliant with the defined Change processes in your organization.

FIGURE 12.11   Edit Change Request Source List properties.

Configure the General Change Request Management Settings

General Change and Activity Settings is a globally scoped configuration for Change Management in Service Manager. This section discusses the customizations you can make for Change Request Management and Activity Management settings in Service Manager 2010.

The Change Request Management settings are configured in the Administration workspace of the management console. Follow these steps:

1. In the Service Manager console, navigate to **Administration -> Settings**.

2. In the Settings folder, click **Change Request Settings** in the Results pane.

3. In the Tasks pane, under Change Request Settings, click **Properties** to open the Change Request Settings dialog box.

The change request ID prefix setting, shown in Figure 12.12, is the first configuration option of the General Change Request Settings configuration.

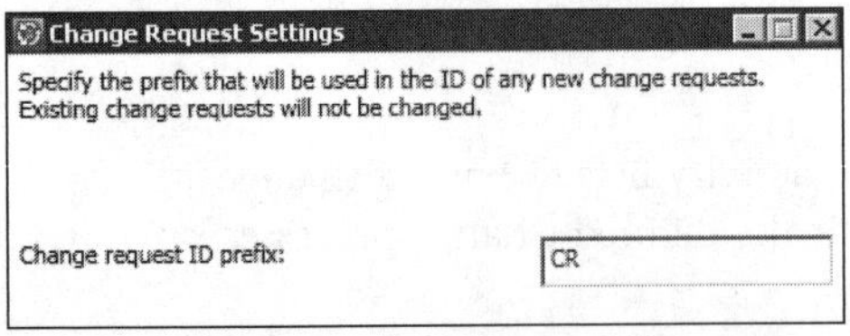

FIGURE 12.12   General Change Settings: Change request ID Prefix.

NOTE: CHANGE WORK ITEMS PREFIX SETTING

You can specify alphanumeric and numeric characters as a prefix for the change work items. In general, you should not specify a numeric prefix to distinguish work items; this could be confusing when the number of the work item is added. The prefix specification is limited to 15 characters.

You can add files associated with a change request to the change request work item. Configure the number of files and the maximum file size in the General Change Request Settings. Default settings are a maximum of 10 files and file size of 64KB. When defining your Change Request Management file attachment policy, consider the information you want to have directly available in the change request work item. Similar to the other management functions in Service Manager, much of the information can be located on a document management system, such as SharePoint, and you can just include the links to these documents. Similar to the process for Incident Management file policy configuration, find a configuration that meets your needs. Ensure that you do not block the Change Request Management team from adding important information while you avoid bulk uploading of files in the work item.

The Attached File Policy Configuration setting, shown in Figure 12.13, is a configuration option of the General Change Request Settings configuration.

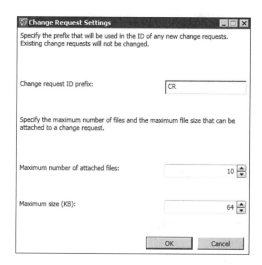

FIGURE 12.13   General Change settings.

The Activity Management settings are configured in the same location of the management console, in the Settings folder in the Administration workspace. Follow these steps to configure or adjust the Activity settings:

1. In the Service Manager console, navigate to **Administration -> Settings**.

2. In the Settings folder, click **Activity Settings** in the Results pane.

Next to the Targeted class box, click **Browse**. In the Choose Class dialog box, choose a class (Change Request, in Figure 12.15). In the When to notify box, select **When an object of the selected class is created**. Click **Next**.

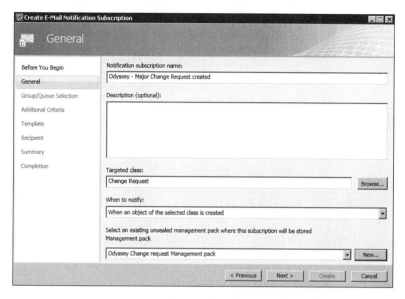

FIGURE 12.15   General settings for the Create E-Mail Notification Subscription wizard.

4. On the Additional Criteria page, select **Change Request**. In the Available Properties list, select **Category**, and then click **Add**.

   On the Additional Criteria page shown in Figure 12.16, click in the Criteria tab. In the Criteria area, next to [Change Request] Category, select **equals**. In the list, select **Major**. Click **Next**.

5. On the Template page, click the **Select** button next to the E-mail template box. In the Select Objects dialog box, in the Templates list, select the appropriate notification template you want to apply. Click **Next** to continue. Alternatively, you can create a new notification template from the Subscription wizard.

6. On the Recipient page, click **Add**. In the Select Objects dialog box, search for and select the appropriate user or group. Click **Add**, **OK**, and then **Next**.

7. On the Summary page, review the settings you have selected for the notification subscription, and then click **Create**.

8. On the Completion page, click **Close**.

Chapter 14 includes a detailed description of the notification functionality in Service Manager, and discusses procedures to create your own email templates to use in change request notification subscriptions.

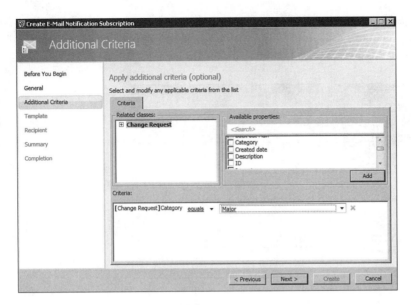

FIGURE 12.16   Specifying notification criteria.

In Service Manager 2010, you can publish announcements to all SSP users to inform them of planned changes. Most changes that need to be implemented and have an impact on a business service will be performed outside business hours. In scenarios where there is a possible impact and the users need to be notified, SSP announcements can be used to inform the users of a possible impact. Announcements are shown in the SSP until they expire or are deleted.

The following steps describe creating an announcement:

1. In the Service Manager console, click **Administration**. In the Administration space of the console, expand **Announcements**, and then click **All Announcements**. In the Tasks pane, click **Announcement**.

2. On the General tab of the form, type a name for the announcement in the Display Name box. For example, type **Business Application updated announcement**.

   In the announcement part of the form, an ID is automatically added. Figure 12.17 shows an overview of the available fields in the announcement creation. Title, body, priority, and expiration date are property fields of a new announcement. In the example, the business application is updated and SSP users are notified of the planned change and requested to schedule their training. After providing the necessary information, click **Next**.

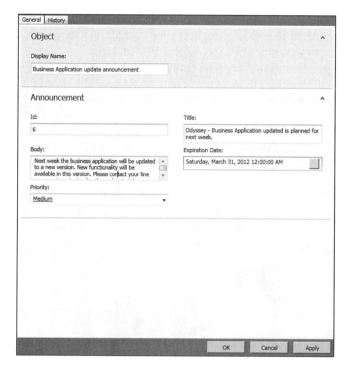

FIGURE 12.17   Specifying notification criteria.

Change Management Automation

The combination of two management packs, the Change MP and the Activity MP, enables the functionality to create workflows and additional templates for this management function. You can use templates to enforce the defined process activities for the type of change request. Activities are part of the change request form; by default, manual and review activities are provided with the exception of the post software deployment activity. You can create your own activities for recurring similar changes that can be requested. For example, a minor change needs to be performed frequently on the servers of a business service. This task involves setting the server in maintenance mode in OpsMgr, performing some manual activities, and bringing the server back out of maintenance mode. You can create an automated activity that triggers the server's maintenance mode status in OpsMgr from Service Manager to automate this process. In this way, a simplified process is executed for these types of requests and the change requestors are encouraged to apply the Change Management process because it simplifies their work.

This portion of the chapter includes information about creating templates and the configuring the automated process of requesting software using the Service Manager SSP. For detailed information about customizing the Change Management environment, refer to Chapters 18 and 19.

Another automation area in the Change Management process is using workflows. Figure 12.18 is a graphical overview of the steps in a change request event workflow. The procedure to create a workflow is similar to that described in Chapter 10, "Incident Management," although usage of event workflows can be completely different between the two management functions. For Incident Management event workflows, the criteria is built up to apply templates (and to autocomplete incident work items or route the work item to the appropriate support group). For Change Management, information about the change request must come from the change requestor. Work item properties such as priority, impact, and risk must be evaluated on a per-request basis. Workflows can be of huge benefit in your Change process; you can configure change request event workflows that check for compliancy of the request. Compliancy against your defined process and the required information is provided in the change request work item. For example, you can set different criteria in the workflow to check whether the required information is provided for the selected type of change request. If not compliant (a match criteria), the change request initiator is notified and can adjust the request.

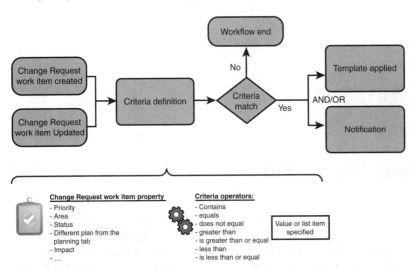

FIGURE 12.18   Overview of workflow automation in Change Management.

Here is what Figure 12.18 shows:

▶ The first trigger in a change request event workflow is an action on the work item. An incident work item is created or updated.

▶ The criteria definition checks the change request work item property for a certain value. Different operators can be used to evaluate the incident work item property.

▶ Once there is a match, you can apply a template and/or send out a notification. Here you can create workflows only for applying templates or only to send out notification based on the defined criteria, or you can combine the two.

The actual process steps of a change request are defined in a change request template. The next section describes creating a template for change request management.

Change Request Management Templates

Change request templates are generally used to define the process activities in Service Manager for a specific type of change request. Templates automate the manageability of change requests, although the actual implementation of the change is performed outside the Service Manager tooling. The next example creates a change request template for the business application in the Odyssey environment. Follow these steps to create a change request template:

1. In the Service Manager console, click **Library**. Now expand **Library -> Templates**. In the Tasks pane, click **Create Template**.

2. In the Create Template dialog box (Figure 12.19), specify name, class, and MP:

   This example creates a template for the business application change requests; the name of the template is **Business Application Change Request template**. In the Description box, type a description for the change request template.

   Click **Browse** to choose a class. In the Choose Class dialog box, click **Change Request**, and then click **OK**.

3. On the General tab of the template (Figure 12.20), provide the following information:

   In the Title box, specify the name of the change request. Area and Assignment are other fields on the form that can be predefined for this category of change requests. The Assigned to property is populated with the AD security group.

   The business application used in this example runs on the two servers and can be added in the Config Items To Change field.

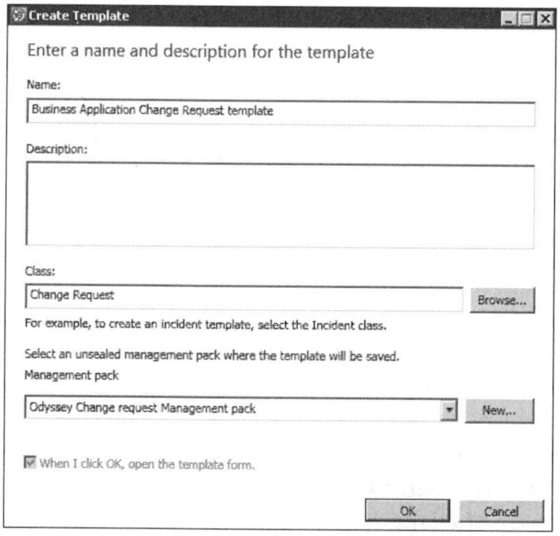

FIGURE 12.19   Specifying change request template properties.

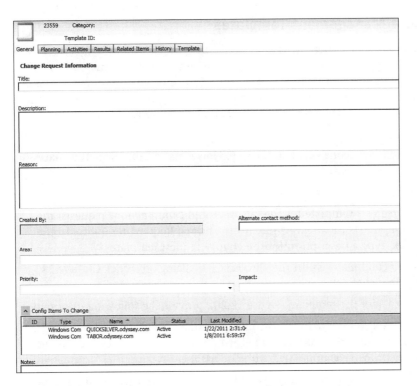

FIGURE 12.20   The General tab of the Change Request template.

4. On the Related Items tab (Figure 12.21), you can add different sets of information that is valuable for documenting the change request. For this example, the Odyssey.com business service is a related item and added as a predefined property in the template.

5. On the Activities Items tab, you can add different manual and review activities required for the category of change request. The activities are those steps necessary to implement the change in a production environment. The two types of implementation activities available by default are the manual and review activities.

Figure 12.22 illustrates a default manual activity you can add to the change request template. You can add different manual activities to orchestrate the required Change process. Examples of manual activities are the change implementation design, change testing, and the actual change implementation in the production environment. These examples are high-level descriptions of the actual activity to be performed. If your process requires a more detailed follow-up of the change implementation activities, you could drill down in defining the manual activities to the actual action that needs to be performed. For example, installing an update on a specific CI could be a manual activity in your template.

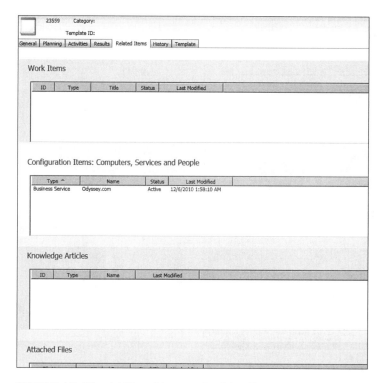

FIGURE 12.21   Additional Items tab of the Change Request template.

Figure 12.23 shows the content of the default review activity you can add to the change request template. A detailed description of the different properties and configuration options for the review activity is provided in the "Approve and Schedule the Change" section of this chapter.

6. On the Templates tab of a change request form, you can configure specific settings of the change request template that are only visible in authoring mode. The normal read-only properties of a change request work item such as status, category, and template ID can be set on the tab of the work item template.

7. When you finish configuring the change request template, click **OK** to save the template.

You can select this template when the change request task is activated or applied using the change request event workflows.

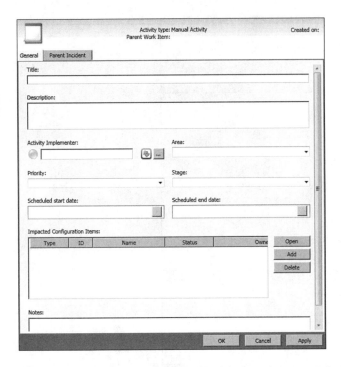

FIGURE 12.22   Specifying manual activity template properties.

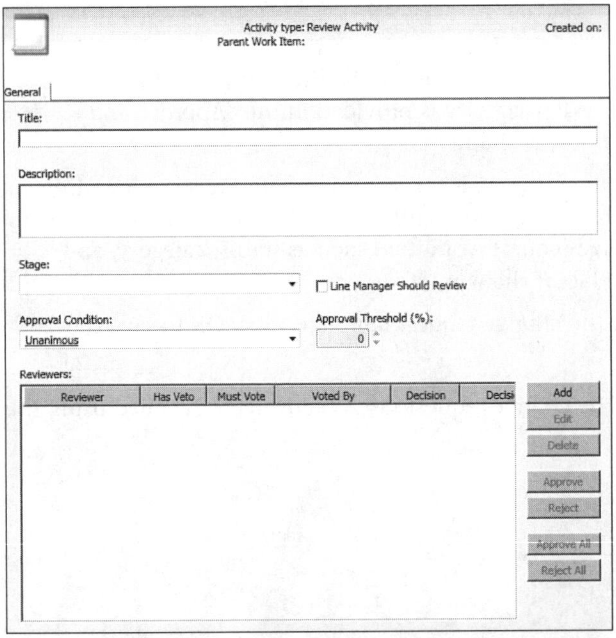

FIGURE 12.23   Specifying review activity template properties.

Configure Activity Management Workflows

You can use the procedure in this section to automatically assign all high-priority manual activities for the Odyssey business application. This example assigns the activities to a user named Travis and sends a notification to his manager to reserve the required time to implement the change.

The new change request event workflow described in the following steps applies the Business Application Change Implementer template, which assigns to Travis all activities that do not have a designated activity implementer. The New Activity Assigned Received Template sends notification to Travis and his manager Kerrie. You can follow these steps to create a template that is applicable for your environment:

1. In the Service Manager console, click **Administration**. Expand **Workflows**, and click **Configuration**.

2. In the Configuration pane, double-click **Activity Event Workflow Configuration** and select **Manual Activity** from the Select Class dialog.

3. In the Configure Activity Event Workflows dialog box, click **Add**.

4. Follow these steps in the Add Activity Event Workflow dialog box, shown in Figure 12.24:

   ▸ On the Before You Begin page, click **Next**.

   ▸ On the Workflow Information page, in the Name box, type a name for the workflow, such as **Business application Change Implementer event workflow**. In the Check for events list, select **When a Change Request is created**, make sure that the **Enabled** check box is selected, and then click **Next**.

   ▸ On the Specify Event Criteria page shown in Figure 12.25, click the **Changed to** tab. In the Available Properties list, select **Area**, and then click **Add**. In the Criteria box, select **equals**. In the list, select **Odyssey Business Application**. Select the other required property, priority, that is required for this example, and select **High** as the criteria value. Then, click **Next**.

   ▸ On the Select Incident Template page (Figure 12.26), click **Apply the Business Application Change Implementer template**. Click **Next**.

   ▸ On the Select People to Notify page, optionally check the **Enable notification** check box, select the user to notify, and then click **Next**.

5. Review your settings on the Summary page and click **Create**. Click **Close** on the Completion page, and **OK** in the Configure Incident Event Workflows dialog box.

A workflow is now triggered whenever a high-priority manual activity is created for the Odyssey business application and the activity, and Travis is automatically configured as the change implementer.

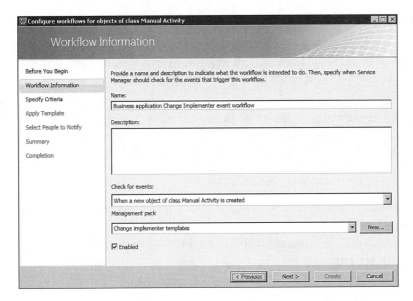

FIGURE 12.24   Change request event Workflow Information page.

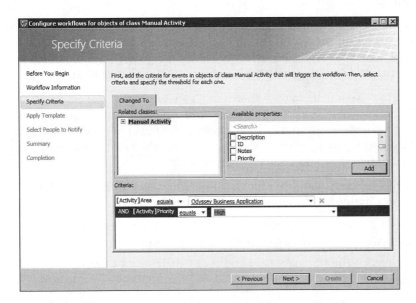

FIGURE 12.25   Activity event workflow Specify Criteria page.

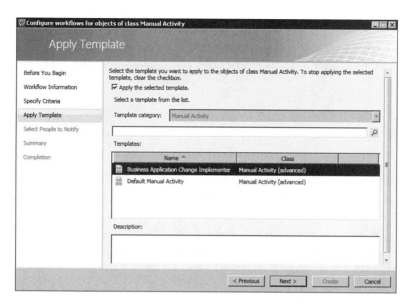

FIGURE 12.26   Selecting the activity template.

Self-Service Software Provisioning in Service Manager

This section describes a scenario used to request software through Service Manager's SSP. Based on information provided by the change requester, Service Manager creates a change request, adds automated activity for deploying software through Configuration Manager, and fulfills the request.

The line manager approves the review activity of the requested change, and Configuration Manager fulfills the request. To enable this scenario, you must have the following items configured in the two tools:

- ▶ **Configuration Manager:** Packages and programs used by Configuration Manager's software distribution feature.

- ▶ **Service Manager:** Configured Configuration Manager connector.

- ▶ **Service Manager:** Active Directory connector.

- ▶ **Service Manager:** Configuration Manager packages and programs are imported into Service Manager.

- ▶ **Service Manager:** Configuration Manager server is specified in the Service Manager portal settings.

▶ **Service Manager (optional):** New category of change requests a Request for Software template.

▶ **Service Manager:** Configuration Manager packages and programs published to the SSP.

The following steps describe configuring the self-service software provisioning functionality in Service Manager.

The first part of the procedure is to create a software deployment change category:

1. In the Service Manager console, click the **Library** workspace and select the **Lists** node.

2. In the Configuration pane, double-click **Activity Event Workflow Configuration** and select **Manual Activity** from the Select Class dialog box.

3. Select the **Change Categories** list, click **Properties**, and add a new item to the list. Replace the List Value string with **Request for Software**, move that category to the top of the list, and click **OK**. Figure 12.27 provides an overview of the list items after adding the Request for Software category.

FIGURE 12.27   Adjust the Change Category List properties.

4. Replace List Value name with **Request for Software** and click **OK**. The Request for Software category is added to the Change Category List.

You can use a Request for Software template in the self-service software deployment process. For this example, the software template contains just one review activity. The review activity is not a required activity for a software request template. For example, you can create a template without an approval for unlicensed software.

5. Open the Templates node in the Library workspace and click the **Create Template** task. The Create Template Dialog window appears.

6. On the Information page, type in **Request for Software Template** in the Name field and select **Change Request** as the class.

7. Figure 12.28 provides an overview of the configured software deployment change request template. On the General page, select the following properties:

   ▶ **Area:** Software - Installation

   ▶ **Assigned To:** Change Managers

   ▶ **Priority:** Low

   ▶ **Risk:** Normal impact

8. Switch to the Template tab and set the value of the change category to **Request for Software** (Figure 12.29).

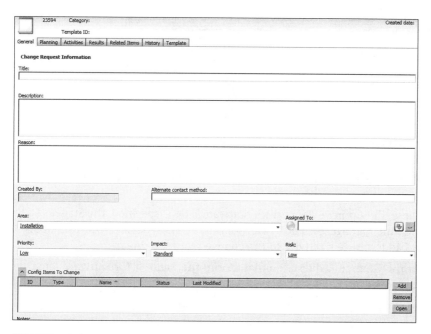

FIGURE 12.28   Software development change request template.

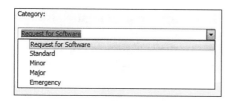

FIGURE 12.29   Selecting the Change Category on the template.

9. Select the Activities tab and add a review activity based on the Default Review Activity template.

10. Figure 12.30 provides an overview of the configuration of the default review activity.

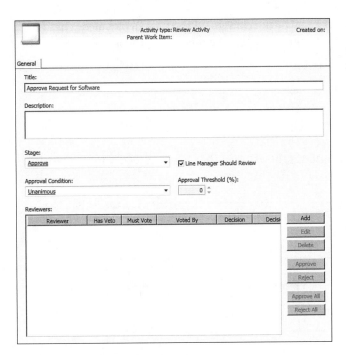

FIGURE 12.30   Creating the review activity for the request software template.

In this example, the Approve Request for Software Title is specified, the Stage is Approve, and Line Manager Should Review option is selected. Click **OK**; this closes the form and adds a review activity to the change request template.

11. Click **OK** on the Change Request Template form; the Request for Software template is ready.

The next part of the configuration is publishing the selected software package to the SSP. Follow these steps:

1. Open the Administration workspace, click the **Portal** node, and open the Software Packages view.

2. Select the software you want to publish to the SSP and select the **Configure task** from the Task view. A Package Properties page is presented to select the program to publish to the SSP. Check the **Publish this package to the Self-Service portal** check box to publish the software. Figure 12.31 illustrates the Configure page of a package in Service Manager.

3. Click **OK** on the Change Request Template Form; the Request for Software template is ready.

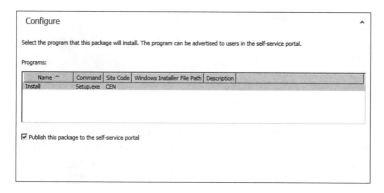

FIGURE 12.31   Configure software package for the SSP.

4. Again in the Administration workspace, click the **Portal** node, and now open the Software Deployment Processes view. Click **Create task** in the taskbar.

5. The Create New Software Deployment Process wizard appears.

6. Enter the name of the process. In this example, Microsoft Office is published to the SSP; Microsoft Office Deployment is specified in the name field.

7. Click the **Select** button to select the published software packages. In this example, the Microsoft Office software package is selected.

8. Select the **Request for Software** template in the wizard as the template to apply in the deployment process.

Figure 12.32 provides an overview of the configuration of the software deployment process.

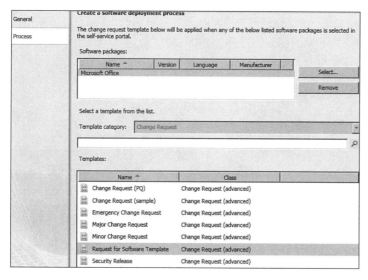

FIGURE 12.32   Configure a software package for the SSP template selection.

9. Click **OK**. The Self-Service Provisioning Feature is configured.

The functionality is now available for the SSP. Users can submit software requests using the portal, and Configuration Manager will install the software.

Summary

This chapter discussed Change Management in Service Manager 2010. It first described the Change process components and the translation toward Service Manager—a translation in the sense of how Service Manager functionality can help, where, and how in the overall Change process. This translation is necessary to discover the changes you need to make in Service Manager. Change request templates, Service Manager activities, and workflows are specific for your Change process; this information is gathered during the translation. The chapter also described the actual configuration of Change and Activity Management in Service Manager. These settings are discussed, with configuration options described. The "Change Management Automation" section included sample configurations of templates and workflows, and discussed how to use the activities in your change request template to create your change request for a specific change in your environment.

You can create custom activities to automate changes for your environment. This can be accomplished using the Service Manager Authoring Tool and is described in Chapter 16, "Planning Your Customization." Effective Change Management includes a requirement for reporting the changes in your environment; see Chapter 20, "Reports, Dashboards, and Data Analysis," for additional information on this topic.

CHAPTER 13

IT Management: Governance, Risk Management, and Compliance

The IT GRC (governance, risk, and compliance) Process management pack (MP) is an addition to Service Manager 2010 (also known as SvcMgr and SCSM). It enables Information Technology (IT) governance, risk management, and compliance by implementing and automating Compliancy Management. The IT GRC Process MP complies with Microsoft Operations Framework (MOF) and the Information Technology Infrastructure Library (ITIL). By conforming to MOF and ITIL best practices, your organization can be confident that the necessary building blocks are available in the Service Manager tool to configure your own Risk and Compliance Management process in accordance with industry-accepted standards.

This chapter provides information for configuring the Service Pack (SP) 1 release of the IT GRC MP in Service Manager 2010 SP 1. As with any process implementation, the chapter begins by discussing what makes up the risk and compliance process and those actions necessary before installation. The chapter also covers the installation of the IT GRC Process MP and discusses configuration and customization of the MP.

Understanding Governance, Risk, and the Compliance Process

What is the GRC process? Here is a definition from Wiki: *GRC is an integrated, holistic approach to organization-wide governance, risk, and compliance, ensuring that an organization acts ethically correct and in accordance with its risk appetite, internal policies and external regulations through the alignment of strategy, processes, technology, and people, thereby improving efficiency and effectiveness.* To make this more understandable, you can look at GRC as a process that delivers regulation throughout an enterprise or organization, with focus on the areas of Financial, IT, and Business Operations. These regulations can leverage how to act and present as an employee at an organization (up to regulations required by state, federal, or international law).

This chapter focuses on the IT-related part of GRC. Figure 13.1 shows the IT GRC and its components.

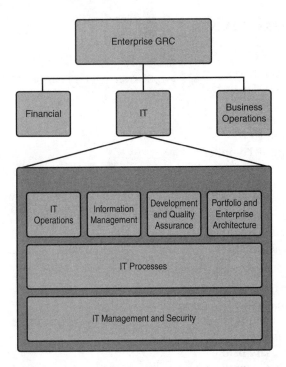

FIGURE 13.1   Governance, risk, and compliance.

So that you fully understand the process, this chapter explains each component individually. This will give you a clear understanding of the process and the key stakeholders involved in setting up IT GRC in Service Manager 2010. Here are the components:

▶ **Governance:** This is the senior executive level that sets up objectives for an organization. It is crucial for the organization that these objectives are met. Regulations are used to guide these objectives.

▶ **Risk:** This is the management level where risks are identified that may adversely affect the governance or organization objectives.

▶ **Compliance:** This is the monitoring of regulations and risks to ensure the governance or organization objectives are not adversely affected. It identifies the applicable requirements for compliance, and effective correction actions are taken if compliance is not met.

Combined, these components leverage IT standards and regulations to improve IT as an enabler to the Business.

Key Stakeholders

The key stakeholders in the process are those individuals responsible for the creation and delivery of business objectives and regulations. These can be divided into the following areas:

▶ **Executive Leadership:** The persons responsible for setting the vision of the IT organization with a goal of aligning IT to the business. For example, executive leadership is responsible for identifying applicable regulations and standards.

▶ **IT Manager:** The individual responsible for aligning IT to the business and implementing regulations and standards to achieve this. For example, the IT manager is responsible for creating policies to comply with regulations.

▶ **Auditor:** The person responsible for monitoring or auditing the organization to determine whether it meets all compliance regulations that it has to comply with. This can be an internal auditor or an independent external auditor. For example, auditors will run scheduled audits to confirm that all regulations are still being met for desktop security.

▶ **IT Compliance Manager:** The individual responsible for planning and implementing the GRC process according to the regulations or authority documents. This person functions as a translator between the IT professional and the regulations set by management. For example, this individual may create a program to assist managing the regulations in the IT organization.

▶ **IT Professional:** The person responsible for implementing and controlling the technical solution to comply with regulations. For example, this individual implements patching of servers and clients to install up-to-date security updates.

Regulations

Regulations are becoming an increasingly important standardization solution for not only IT environments but also the entire business organization. The need for regulations, particularly in the financial sector, has grown after the financial market's crash in 2007. There are numerous compliance regulations today that you must meet to run your business. These regulations can range from state, federal, up to international compliance regulations. The most common regulations that also affect IT are

▶ **Sarbanes-Oxley (SOX):** Enhanced standards and controls for all public company boards and public accounting firms

▶ **Health Insurance Portability and Accountability Act (HIPAA):** National standards for electronic healthcare transactions

▶ **Basel II (Basel III):** International standards for banks

▶ **Payment Card Industry Data Security Standard, (PCI DSS):** Standards for managing credit card information

Not being compliant with these regulations can lead to a negative reputation or even fines. Therefore, it is crucial for organizations to comply with these regulations. These regulations are not all IT based but deliver an overall compliance (with IT as part of the total regulation). Examples of these requirements are minimal password policies, data retention (backup), security logging, and so on.

TIP: REGULATION RESOURCES ON THE WEB

For additional information about regulations, both IT related and non-IT related, you can check out the following resources:

▶ **SOX:** http://www.sec.gov/spotlight/sarbanes-oxley.htm

▶ **HIPAA:** http://www.hhs.gov/ocr/privacy/hipaa/administrative/privacyrule/index.html

▶ **Basel II:** http://www.bis.org/publ/bcbsca.htm

▶ **Basel III:** http://www.bis.org/press/p100912.htm

▶ **PCI DSS:** https://www.pcisecuritystandards.org/security_standards/index.php

You can also use the authority documents, which you can access in the Service Manager console after installing the IT GRC MP (**Library** -> **Authority Documents**).

MOF 4.0 and the GRC Process

Chapter 3, "MOF, ITIL, and Service Manager," explains the value of using ITIL and MOF management frameworks. This chapter explains how GRC fit into this picture.

Microsoft Operations Framework 4.0 (MOF) is a set of publications providing both descriptive (what to do, when, and why) and prescriptive (how to do) guidance on IT Service Management. MOF 4.0 is based on the IT life cycle, which consists of three phases: Plan, Deliver, and Operate. The foundation of these three phases, as shown in Figure 13.2, is the Manage layer, which consists of three service management functions (SMFs):

▶ Governance, Risk, and Compliance

▶ Change and Configuration

▶ Team

The GRC SMFs belong to the Manage layer of MOF and consist of three processes, in the following order:

▶ **Establish IT Governance:** This is the executive level as discussed in the "Key Stakeholders" section, combined with the IT manager and IT compliance manager roles for delivering the governance and aligning it with IT.

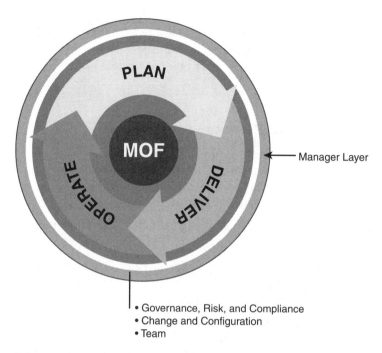

FIGURE 13.2   MOF Manage layer.

▶ **Assess, Monitor, and Control Risk:** This part is all about risk management within the IT organization and how to minimize this.

▶ **Comply with Directives:** This is the compliance part where the auditor audits the compliance of the organization to the provided regulations. The auditor reports to the executive and managers to improve risk management and compliance.

Notice the approach for implementing the IT GRC Process is the same as the organization wide implementation of the GRC Process, as discussed in the "Understanding Governance, Risk, and the Compliance Process" section of this chapter.

NOTE: MOF MANAGE LAYER

For more information about MOF 4.0 and the Manage layer, see http://technet. microsoft.com/en-us/library/cc506048.aspx.

Service Manager 2010 SP 1 and the GRC Process

You should now understand the GRC process within the IT organization. The next sections discuss how you can use Service Manager 2010 SP 1 to help implement this process, and explain how to use the System Center suite and System Center solution accelerators to help you begin the GRC process.

NOTE: IMPLEMENTATION IS TOOLS, PEOPLE, AND PROCESSES

Remember the IT GRC Process MP and System Center suite are tools to support your processes. Fully implementing the GRC processes requires other pillars, too, such as people and processes.

System Center Suite and the GRC Process

Microsoft designed the System Center suite based on the MOF and ITIL frameworks, making it perfectly aligned to use with ITIL and MOF 4.0 processes. In particular, when you look at IT GRC, System Center can make life easier. Fully automating the IT GRC process requires several products from the System Center suite.

Three phases explain the interaction between Service Manager 2010 SP 1 and the other System Center products:

▶ **Information Phase:** The GRC process requires tools to test and check compliance within your organization. The first step is to gather information about your organization. Using the System Center suite, the following products are available:

  ▶ **Configuration Manager 2007 R2 or R3:** When connected to Service Manager, Configuration Manager can deliver asset management and automated Compliance checking using Desired Configuration Management (DCM).

  ▶ **Operations Manager 2007 R2:** Connecting Operations Manager to Service Manager can deliver automated ticket creation based on health state and alerts. You can also use Operations Manager for asset registration in the Service Manager configuration management database (CMDB).

    Using Configuration Manager 2007 Release 2 (R2) or higher and Operations Manager 2007 R2 and connecting them to System Center Service Manager 2010 SP 1 enables you to import objects easily into your CMDB. You will quickly have a populated CMDB and overview of all components in your organization to use them in your GRC process. The objects are automatically populated and updated in Service Manager 2010 SP 1.

▶ **Check Compliance Phase:** After you have populated your CMDB with the correct information, the next step is to establish compliance. This is where the IT GRC Process MP comes into play. The IT GRC Process MP contains all required components. Combined with the features of Operations Manager (OpsMgr) and Configuration Manager (ConfigMgr), you can report on and audit these components for compliance. OpsMgr and ConfigMgr are used to check for compliance on your systems. Here's how:

  ▶ **Configuration Manager 2007 R2:** ConfigMgr's DCM feature is used to verify that your systems are compliant.

  ▶ **Operations Manager 2007 R2:** Operations Manager is used to check the health state of your infrastructure and whether your service level agreements (SLAs) are being met.

Using Configuration Manager 2007 R2 and Operations Manager 2007 R2 and connecting them to Service Manager 2010 SP 1 enables you to gather information to determine whether your environment is compliant. These tools monitor and track the compliance state of your current environment.

▶ **Resolve Noncompliant Phase:** The next step is to automate the remediation of the noncompliant systems. The following System Center components can leverage the automation:

> ▶ **Configuration Manager 2007 R2:** DCM can be used to force configuration settings.
>
> ▶ **Opalis Integration Server (OIS) 6.3:** This product is used to automate workflows. You can use Opalis to run a workflow to automatically resolve noncompliance issues. Service Manager logs the noncompliance and triggers a workflow in OIS to resolve it.
>
> ▶ **Operations Manager 2007 R2:** You can use OpsMgr to automate resolution of alerts and monitors. However, Opalis has more advanced capabilities in this area and is a better solution.

By using the System Center suite components together, you can achieve a fully automated GRC process within your organization. OpsMgr and ConfigMgr notify on non-compliant systems and may even resolve the systems to be compliant. The non-compliant systems are documented in Service Manager 2010 SP 1 and trigger a workflow in Opalis to automatically make the systems compliant again.

Solution Accelerators and the GRC Process

Microsoft provides solution accelerators, which are guidelines and tools to leverage the full functionality of Microsoft software usage within your organization. These are available for download at no cost at http://technet.microsoft.com/en-us/solutionaccelerators/dd229342.

There are solution accelerators specifically for GRC, known as Compliance Solution Accelerators. These contain several articles and tools to deliver GRC process guidelines.

One of the tools in the solution accelerator is the IT GRC Process MP SP1, which uses Service Manager 2010 SP 1 to deliver your compliance solution. The other tool is the IT Compliance Management Series, which is a bundle of DCM libraries and Service Manager 2010 SP 1 libraries that contain baselines to monitor the compliance of your organization. Guides accompany the libraries with information about how to install and use those libraries.

With the IT GRC MP imported into Service Manager 2010 SP 1, you have access to a massive amount of information to create your GRC process. If you combine the IT GRC Process MP with the IT Compliance Management Series, you have an even better way to comply easily with compliance regulations within your organization.

The way the libraries are set up in the IT Compliance Management Series makes it easy to determine which authority documents you should comply with according to business standards. The remainder of this chapter describes how to install and use them together.

Installing the IT GRC Process MP

The IT GRC Process MP is not part of the default installation of Service Manager 2010. The MP is part of the Compliance Solution Accelerators. After downloading the MP, verify that you have met all prerequisites before starting the installation. These are discussed in the next section.

Prerequisites

The download contains several files that are required for the installation:

- **ITGRCProcessManagementPack_amd64SP1.exe:** This is the server installation package for installation of the IT GRC Process MP on the Service Manager 2010 SP 1 server. It also includes the client installation files to install the x64 client.

- **ITGRCProcessManagementPack_DocumentationSP1.exe:** This executable contains the documentation for installing and deploying the service pack.

- **ITGRCProcessManagementPack_x86SP1 .exe:** This contains the Client installation files to install the client on the x86 platform and supports Excel 2007 and Excel 2010.

- **ITGRCProcessManagementPack_AuthoringLibrariesSP1.exe:** These are the libraries required for extending or customizing the IT GRC Process MP in the Service Manager Authoring Tool.

- **Test ID Sync Tool.exe:** This is the tool for synchronizing automated activities in Service Manager 2010 into Compliance Management Series Baselines (DCM) in System Center Configuration Manager.

In addition to the software, there are required server and client components.

Here are the components required for the server:

- **Service Manager 2010 Service Pack 1:** This version of Service Manager 2010 is required to support the IT GRC Process MP. You must have Service Pack 1 installed on all Service Manager server roles.

- **System Center Configuration Manager 2007 R2:** This software is required to support automated control activities that use the DCM feature.

- **User Account Control (UAC):** UAC must be turned off on Service Manager Servers. A reboot is required to turn off UAC; after installation, this feature can be turned on again.

Here are the components required for the client:

- **Microsoft Visual Studio Tools for the Microsoft Office System (VSTO) 3.0 and VSTO 3.0 Service Pack 1:** These need to be installed on the client.

- **Microsoft Office Excel 2007 or Microsoft Excel 2010 (32 bit):** Excel must be installed on the client.

> **NOTE: DIFFERENCES WHEN UPGRADING IT GRC PROCESS MP**
>
> The official documentation for installing the IT GRC Process MP points out differences between a new install and upgrade. Both procedures are the same, with the following exceptions:
>
> ▶ When starting setup, click **Upgrade** rather than Install IT GRC Process MP.
>
> ▶ Verify you are using Service Manager 2010 SP 1 and have the Released to Web (RTW) version of the IT GRC Process MP installed. Otherwise, you must first uninstall the beta version of the IT GRC Process MP.

Installation

You must run the IT GRC MP SP1 installation on the Service Manager management server running the System Center Data Access Service.

> **CAUTION: DATA WAREHOUSE JOBS**
>
> If you have just installed the Service Manager management server and the data warehouse, it is suggested you wait until the data warehouse jobs run successfully one time. This way, all data necessary for the Service Manager installation is transferred to the data warehouse.
>
> After the MPSync job runs, you can proceed to install the IT GRC MP. Remember that the MPSync job can take several hours to complete.
>
> For information about installing the data warehouse, see Chapter 7, "Installing Service Manager 2010."

Before beginning to install the IT GRC MP, you must suspend the extract jobs in the Data Warehouse pane of the console. To do so, follow these steps:

1. Navigate to the Data Warehouse pane in the Service Manager console and select **Data Warehouse Jobs**.

2. Navigate to extract jobs and click **Suspend**.

3. Refresh the console to verify the jobs are stopped, as shown in Figure 13.3.

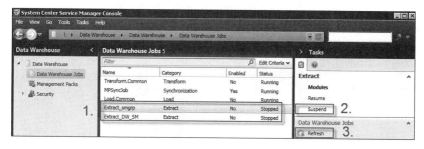

FIGURE 13.3   Data Warehouse extract jobs are stopped.

After stopping the extract jobs, you can continue with the installation.

Run ITGRCProcessManagementPack_amd64SP1.exe to extract the installation files:

1. Start setup.exe from the folder where you extracted the file ITGRCProcessManagementPack_amd64SP1.exe.

2. Select **Install IT GRC Process Management Pack SP1** to start the setup process.

3. Fill in the user information and agree to the license agreement.

4. Specify the Data Warehouse management server name and credentials with access to the data warehouse, as shown in Figure 13.4. You want to test credentials before you continue. The Test Credentials button checks whether the account has the appropriate privileges, which are as follows:

   ▶ The user should be a member of the local Administrators group on both the Service Manager management server and Data Warehouse management server.

   ▶ The user should be a member of the Data Warehouse administrator group and Service Manager administrator group.

   ▶ UAC should be disabled on the Service Manager management server.

   ▶ The user should have read and execute permissions on the GRC setup files.

5. Review the configuration settings on the screen and start setup.

6. After installation, verify the installation was successful.

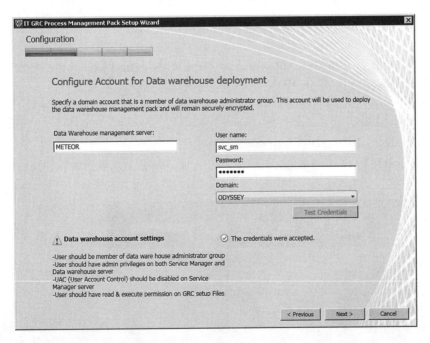

FIGURE 13.4   Configuration screen setup.

When setup completes, you need to start the data warehouse jobs again. Log on to the Service Manager console and navigate to **Data Warehouse -> Data Warehouse Jobs**. Select **MPSyncJob** and click **Resume** to resume the sync job. Refresh the Data Warehouse pane again and verify the MPSync job is running. You need to wait for the MPSync job to finish; this can take over an hour. When the MPSync job completes, you can restart the Service Manager Data Warehouse services. This will ensure all data updates are processed before starting the extract jobs again.

Restart the following services on the Data Warehouse management server:

- ▶ System Center Data Access Service
- ▶ System Center Management
- ▶ System Center Management Configuration

Next, resume the extract jobs. Follow the same procedure shown in Figure 13.3; only now resume the extract jobs. Navigate to the Data Warehouse pane in the Service Manager console and select **Data Warehouse Jobs**. Navigate to the extract jobs and click **Resume**. Now all data from the compliance MP should be transferred to the data warehouse.

TIP: RESUMING THE EXTRACT JOBS

Although the official documentation mentions resuming the extract jobs, experiences from the field and lab do not show this is necessary. The MPSync job usually starts the other jobs automatically and therefore they do not need to be started manually.

Just be sure you resume the MPSync job and watch the results of the jobs; verify that they are running.

If necessary, you can resume the extract jobs as stated.

When all data is transferred—meaning the data warehouse jobs ran successfully—you can check the status of the IT GRC Process MP installation. Navigate to the Reporting workspace in the Service Manager console and verify you have a new reporting folder, as shown in Figure 13.5.

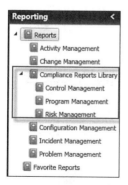

FIGURE 13.5   Reporting workspace additional reports.

Confirm that you have an extra button for Compliance and Risk Items in your Service Manager console, as shown in Figure 13.6, and verify that all components are present.

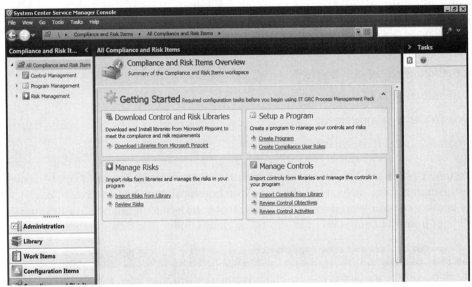

FIGURE 13.6   The IT GRC Process MP installed.

You have now installed the IT GRC Process MP basic components. You now have access to all libraries, views, templates, and reports included in the IT GRC Process MP SP1. The next part of this process is to add the IT Compliance Management Series into Service Manager 2010 SP 1.

Configuring the IT GRC Process MP

With the IT GRC Process MP installed, the next sections discuss how to use the MP after initial installation. The "Understanding the Governance, Risk, and Compliance Process" section discussed the requirement to define a GRC program to start the GRC Process. Starting to use the IT GRC Process MP is the same; you create a basic sample program for checking compliance on Microsoft Windows Server 2008 R2 systems.

NOTE: AUTOMATING GRC

Although you can start using the MP immediately after installation, the true automation can be achieved only when combining components as stated in the "Service Manager 2010 SP 1 and the GRC Process" section.

Before you begin creating a GRC program, import the necessary libraries. The libraries are part of the Compliance Solution Accelerators and can be downloaded from http://www.

microsoft.com/downloads/en/details.aspx?FamilyId=BD930882-0D39-4900-9A79-B91F213ED15D&displaylang=en. (At http://www.microsoft.com/downloads, search for "IT Compliance Management Series.")

After downloading the IT Compliance Management Series package, extract the libraries to a folder. At the time of this writing, the package contains four components:

- **Windows Server 2008 IT Compliance Management Library:** This library includes two add-ons for Service Manager 2010 SP 1 and Configuration Manager 2007 R2. These add-ons leverage automation between the two products by using manual and automated activities in Service Manager that interact with CIs in Configuration Manager for domain controllers running Windows 2008 Server.

- **Windows Server 2008 R2 IT Compliance Management Library:** This includes two add-ons for Service Manager 2010 SP 1 and Configuration Manager 2007 R2. These add-ons leverage automation between Service Manager 2010 SP 1 and Configuration Manager 2007 R2 by using manual and automated activities in Service Manager that interact with CIs in Configuration Manager for domain controllers running Windows Server 2008 R2.

- **Windows 7 IT Compliance Management Library:** This library includes two add-ons for Service Manager 2010 SP 1 and Configuration Manager 2007 R2. These add-ons leverage automation between the two products by using manual and automated activities in Service Manager that interact with CIs in Configuration Manager for domain clients running Windows 7.

- **System Center IT Compliance Management Library:** This includes the MP, which contains manual activities that support control objectives in the IT GRC Process MP. These activities are based on the System Center suite.

The first component you will want to import into Service Manager 2010 SP 1 is the System Center IT Compliance Management Library. Extract the contents of the file and import the MPB file Microsoft.ControlActivity.SystemCenter.Library.mpb into Service Manager.

NOTE: SYSTEM CENTER COMPLIANCE

You do not have to start with the System Center IT Compliance Management Library. However, when you want to implement compliance, it might as well be System Center in the first place and start from there. The library contains activities to maintain System Center and to maintain the processes within Service Manager 2010 SP 1, such as Incident Management, Asset Management, Change Management, Problem Management, and so on.

Navigate to **Administration -> Management Packs** in the Service Manager console and click **Import**. Browse to the location where you extracted the System Center IT Compliance Management Library and import the MP.

TIP: IMPORTING MANAGEMENT PACKS

When importing MPs, make sure you are using the correct file type; otherwise, no MPs are shown. For the library packs, the file extension is *.mpb.

After importing the MP, you should now have Manual Control Activity templates as shown in Figure 13.7. You can use these templates to create activities to make preventive or corrective changes to a system to be compliant.

ID	Name	Description
SYSCTR_MCA_00029	Maintain a Project Management Process	System Center: Use System Center Service Manager workflow capability to enforce project milestones within the cha
SYSCTR_MCA_00034	Manage Architectural Change Manage...	System Center: Use the change management workflow capability in System Center Service Manager to manage arch
SYSCTR_MCA_00023	Configure Event Logging	System Center: Log events that affect the health, security, availability, configuration status, and operational status o
SYSCTR_MCA_00028	Maintain a Change Management Policy	System Center: Enforce the organization's change management policy through the change and configuration manag
SYSCTR_MCA_00016	Configure Nonrepudiation Functionality	System Center: Ensure that reports are communicated in a manner that prevents denial of receipt when the report i
SYSCTR_MCA_00002	Configure Event Logging	System Center: Ensure that System Center Configuration Manager errors, faults, and account management actions a
SYSCTR_MCA_00018	Maintain a Risk Scoring Process	System Center: Ensure that your organization uses some form of risk management process to manage risks that mig
SYSCTR_MCA_00035	Configure Logging Functionality	System Center: Ensure that logging functionality is configured to accurately and securely record and store events wi
SYSCTR_MCA_00001	Configure Logging Functionality	System Center: Ensure that logging functionality is configured to accurately and securely record and store events wi
SYSCTR_MCA_00020	Maintain an Audit Program	System Center: Define the audit program term 'Material Weakness'.
SYSCTR_MCA_00033	Maintain a Change Management Process	System Center: Use the change management workflow capability in System Center Service Manager to manage ass
SYSCTR_MCA_00004	Change Vendor-Issued Authentication...	System Center: Ensure that default vendor values are changed if such values are used as part of an authentication r
SYSCTR_MCA_00021	Maintain a Controls Management Proc...	System Center: Use the System Center Service Manager GRC Pack to manage the applicability, requirements, assign
SYSCTR_MCA_00009	Configure Event Logging	System Center: Ensure that errors, faults, and account management actions are logged.
SYSCTR_MCA_00036	Configure Event Logging	System Center: Ensure that errors, faults, and account management actions are logged within System Center Opera

FIGURE 13.7   Manual Control Activity templates.

Not only are these activities prepopulated in the templates, but they also describe those procedures to follow and where to get external information. (This is what the IT GRC Process MP is about: to make your life easier.) Figure 13.8 shows the activity to maintain your Change Management process within Service Manager 2010 SP 1 and the information to have in the manual activity.

After importing the System Center IT Compliance Management Library, import the Windows Server 2008 R2 IT Compliance Management Library. This library contains the manual and automated activities required to set up a Windows Server 2008 R2 program.

Navigate to **Administration -> Management Packs** in the Service Manager console and click **Import**. Browse to the place where you extracted the Windows Server 2008 R2 IT Compliance Management Library and import the MP named Microsoft.ControlActivity.WinSrvr08R2.Library.mpb.

Check that all components are imported. Navigate to the Libraries workspace and look under Automated Control Activity Templates. There should be six templates for Windows Server 2008 R2. Under Manual Control Activity Templates, 25 Windows Server 2008 R2 activities should also be added.

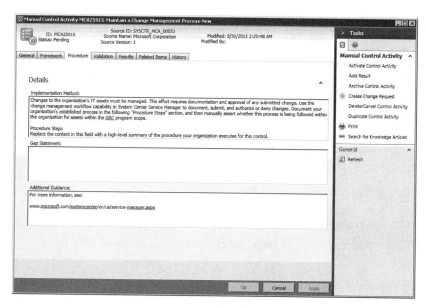

FIGURE 13.8   Maintain Change Process Activity.

To this point, all changes in your configuration have been made on the Service Manager 2010 SP 1 server. The next phase is to populate your Service Manager CMDB. There are several ways to populate your CMDB: manually; using a CSV file; or automatically with ConfigMgr, OpsMgr, or AD.

The favored method is automation, because automation is always the preferred approach. To set up the connector between OpsMgr or ConfigMgr, refer to Chapter 10, "Incident Management," to install the appropriate connector. Because you want to fully automate your IT GRC process, you should now configure DCM on your ConfigMgr server. Connect to your ConfigMgr server and open the ConfigMgr console. Navigate to Desired Configuration Management and select **Configuration Baselines**. In the Actions pane, click **Import Configuration Data**. Select the CAB file you extracted from the Windows Server 2008 R2 IT Compliance Management Library.

After importing the baseline, you need to assign it to a ConfigMgr collection. In the Configuration Manager console, navigate to Collections. Select the collection you want to have the baseline for, and in the Actions pane select **Assign Configuration Baseline**. You have now assigned your baseline to a collection and have completed creating a DCM workflow.

Now you have set up everything to start with the IT GRC Process MP and are ready to create your first program. To do so, follow these steps:

1. In the Service Manager console, navigate to the welcome screen in the Compliance and Risk Items pane, located at the root of All Compliance and Risk Items, as shown in Figure 13.9.

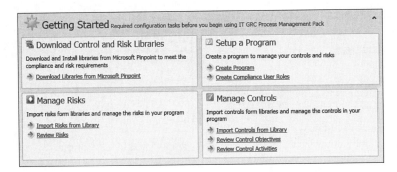

FIGURE 13.9   All Compliance and Risk Items screen.

2. Click the **Create Program** link to start creating your first IT GRC program.

3. When the program form opens, complete the necessary information. Here is an example:

   ▸ **Title of the program:** Example Windows 2008 R2 Sarbanes-Oxley Program.

   ▸ **Owner of the program:** Oskar Landman.

   ▸ **Business justification:** This example shows how the Sarbanes-Oxley requirements are implemented on Windows 2008 R2 servers.

   Click **Apply** to save the program.

4. Once you save the program, you can add controls from the libraries. Select **Create Controls from Library** and a wizard opens to let you add controls to your program. Only the owner of the program can add controls. Click **Next** in the wizard and verify you are adding controls to the correct program, Example Windows 2008 R2 Sarbanes-Oxley Program, and click **Next**.

5. Select the libraries you want to add: **Microsoft.ControlActivity.WinSrvr08R2.library** and **Microsoft.ControlObjective.Library**, click **Add**, and then click **Next**.

6. Now you can add the authority documents to the program. There are many authority documents. You can narrow down the results by category or search for "Sarbanes." Select the Sarbanes-Oxley authority document and click **Add**. You can select multiple documents if required. Click **Next**.

7. In the Control Objectives selection, based on the Sarbanes-Oxley authority document you have a preselected set of control objectives relevant to Sarbanes-Oxley. Change if necessary and click **Next**.

8. In the Selected Control Activities screen, based on the Control Objective selection, you now need to define which control activities you want to add to the program. Change if necessary and click **Next**.

9. Review the summary and click **Next** to save the program. Note the red remark saying that saving can take a long time when many objects are selected.

After saving the program, you should have a completion screen showing no failures.

You have now created an IT GRC Process MP program for measuring compliance on Windows Server 2008 R2 servers based on the Sarbanes-Oxley authority document. The next step is to publish the program. In the All Compliance and Risk Items pane, navigate to **Program Management -> All Programs** and select **Publish Program** from the Action pane.

NOTE: AUTHORITY DOCUMENTS, OBJECTIVE SELECTION, AND CONTROL ACTIVITIES

With the IT GRC Process MP in place, creating a GRC program in Service Manager 2010 is straightforward.

When creating the control activities, you can select different authority documents and control objectives, such as the Sarbanes-Oxley authority document. When you select this authority document, all objectives and control activities are based on Sarbanes-Oxley.

The selection is already made on those you selected. This is one of the benefits of the IT GRC Process MP: You don't have to read endlessly to determine which apply to your situation. The MP already selected those that needed to be applied.

With the IT GRC Process MP installed, you need to define user roles. By default, no roles are defined; you must create them manually.

Begin by defining the different roles required within your organization. The easiest way to do this is by using the list from the documentation, shown in Table 13.1.

TABLE 13.1   User Roles in the IT GRC Process MP

User Role	User Role Profile	Description
Administrator	Administrators	Responsible for installing the IT GRC Process MP, IT Compliance Management Libraries, and for ongoing management of systemwide configuration settings.
Compliance Program Manager	Compliance Program Manager	Responsible for the management of IT GRC programs within their organization and helps ensure that the organization is in compliance with authority document citations.
Compliance Program Implementer	Compliance Program Implementer	Responsible for management of control objectives, control activities, and risks. Also responsible for managing the day-to-day tasks, such as performing control activity compliance tests or updating risk information.
Compliance Program Read-Only Users	Read-Only Operators	Responsible for viewing IT GRC entities, such as programs, control objectives, control activities, and risks. Also responsible for creating compliance incidents.

TABLE 13.1   User Roles in the IT GRC Process MP

User Role	User Role Profile	Description
Library Author	Authors	Responsible for customizing the IT GRC Process MP and IT compliance management libraries. Also responsible for creating new MPs that work with the IT GRC Process MP. These users are also typically members of the Administrator user role profile in their authoring environment.

After defining which user roles apply to your organization, create the user roles. The procedure for doing this is the same as any other user role in Service Manager 2010.

For example, you can create the Compliance Program Manager user role. Open the Administration pane and navigate to **Security -> User Roles**. In the Action pane, select **Create User Role** and select the **Compliance Program Manager Role**.

Click the **Create Program** link to start creating your first IT GRC program. Perform the following steps:

1. After you select the Compliance Program Manager role, a wizard opens. You need to specify a name for the user role, such as **Compliance Program Manager**. You can optionally specify a description for the role, making it easier to define the purpose of the role in the future. Click **Next**.

2. Specify which MPs you want to filter for selection for the duration of the wizard. By selecting only the IT GRC packs, you narrow the results for the rest of the wizard, which makes the selections easier.

   Select the compliance MPs and click **Next**.

3. In the queues window, click **Next** if there are no queues; otherwise, select to which queues the role should have access, and then **Next**.

4. In the Groups window, there is only one group to be selected. This is based on the MPs selected earlier. Leave the default and click **Next**.

5. In the Tasks Window, select all tasks and click **Next**. In the Views window, you can select which views you want the role to be able to view. Select **All** and click **Next**. Use Form Templates to select the forms to access. Select **All** and click **Next**. You don't need to specify users; you can do so after creating the user role.

6. After selecting all areas to be accessed, save the user role. When the role is saved, you have created a user role to be used with the IT GRC Process MP.

To create other user roles, you can use the same procedure. (Just select a different base user role for the different IT GRC Process MP user roles.)

> **NOTE: SECURITY ROLES CREATION FOR IT GRC PROCESS MP SP1**
>
> In addition to using the console to create user roles, you can also use PowerShell to scope the user roles. The script can be found at *<SvcMgrInstallPath>*\IT GRC Process MP, and is named AddTypeToRoleScope.PS1. Use of the script is explained in the IT GRC Process MP documentation.
>
> For further information about user roles in Service Manager, see http://technet.microsoft.com/en-us/library/ff461151.aspx and http://scug.be/blogs/scsm/archive/2010/03/21/service-manager-role-based-security-scoping.aspx.

Using the IT GRC Process MP

Although you can use the MP in many ways, the discussion here focuses on creating and managing activities and reporting. There are two types of activities: manual activities that need to be set manually, and automatic activities that are automatically generated. For reporting, there are three types of reports: Control Management reports, Program Management reports, and Risk Management reports.

Using Manual Activities in the IT GRC Process MP

Control objectives must be met in order to be compliant. You can achieve compliance when these objectives are met. Figure 13.10 shows objectives currently in the console.

All Control Objectives 16												
Filter												
ID	Title	Status	Owner	Assigned To	Type	Level	Priority	Modified Date	Source Name	Source ID	Source Version	
CO14	Policy Needs Assessment	Draft			Process			3/30/2011 7:47...	Microsoft Corpo...	GRC_MCO_00044	1	
CO26	Event Logging	Draft	Administrator	Oskar Landman	Technical I...			3/30/2011 2:56...	Microsoft Corpo...	GRC_MCO_00002	1	
CO20	Assign Roles	Draft			Process			3/30/2011 7:47...	Microsoft Corpo...	GRC_MCO_00114	1	
CO28	Power Configuration	Draft			Process			3/30/2011 7:48...	Microsoft Corpo...	GRC_MCO_00074	1	
CO15	Risk and Vulnerability Ass...	Draft			Process			3/30/2011 7:47...	Microsoft Corpo...	GRC_MCO_00117	1	
CO22	Encryption Configuration	Draft			Technical I...			3/30/2011 7:47...	Microsoft Corpo...	GRC_MCO_00027	1	
CO19	License Management	Draft			Process			3/30/2011 7:47...	Microsoft Corpo...	GRC_MCO_00078	1	
CO18	Vision and Scope Docume...	Draft			Process			3/30/2011 7:47...	Microsoft Corpo...	GRC_MCO_00052	1	
CO24	Data Storage	Draft			Technical I...			3/30/2011 7:47...	Microsoft Corpo...	GRC_MCO_00084	1	
CO21	Data Access	Draft			Technical I...			3/30/2011 7:47...	Microsoft Corpo...	GRC_MCO_00011	1	
CO13	Policy Creation	Draft			Process			3/30/2011 7:47...	Microsoft Corpo...	GRC_MCO_00045	1	
CO17	Approve and Schedule Ch...	Draft			Process			3/30/2011 2:39...	Microsoft Corpo...	GRC_MCO_00107	1	
CO25	Report Management	Draft			Evidence			3/30/2011 7:47...	Microsoft Corpo...	GRC_MCO_00032	1	
CO16	Third Party Risk Managem...	Draft			Process			3/30/2011 7:47...	Microsoft Corpo...	GRC_MCO_00079	1	
CO27	Physical Environment Man...	Draft			Process			3/30/2011 7:48...	Microsoft Corpo...	GRC_MCO_00077	1	
CO23	Key Management	Draft			Process			3/30/2011 7:47...	Microsoft Corpo...	GRC_MCO_00030	1	

FIGURE 13.10   Objectives.

You have created a program based on Sarbanes-Oxley, and these objectives must be met according to Sarbanes-Oxley. Next, you need to specify the manual control activities on how the compliance can be met and controlled. After creating a program, the next phase is selecting activities to control compliance.

You can create a manual control activity based on the many templates available in the IT GRC Process MP or create a custom activity to control compliancy objects.

Select a template, fill in the details of the activity, and set the owner of the activity and the person to whom the activity should be assigned. Also, select the supported objective to combine the control to the objective.

After combining the object and control, you should also publish the objective and the control. Select the objective or control, and from the tasks, select **Publish**.

When you combine the activity with the object, you can start reporting on the compliancy of these objects. As these are manual activities, you need to check these manually.

Using Automatic Activities in the IT GRC Process MP

In addition to manual activities, there are also automated activities when you use Configuration Manager 2007 R2 or above and DCM. These activities are automatically created when systems are non-compliant.

Open the All Compliance and Risk Items pane, and navigate to **Control Management -> Control Activities -> Automated Control Activities -> All Automated Control Activities**. In the Tasks pane, select **Create Configuration Manager Control Activity from Template**.

A list of templates appears, and you can select the template for the automated activity. After selecting the template, fill in the same options as with the Manual template. After completing the information, you can select a supported control objective that needs to be met based on this activity. When all settings conform to your compliance program, select **Publish** to activate the activity.

TIP: AUTOMATED ACTIVITIES

Although the activity is "automated," this does not mean the activity will also automatically resolve the non-compliant system. It just checks automatically for non-compliant systems by using Configuration Manager. If you want to fully automate activities, you need Opalis to run those workflows for you.

The main difference is this activity is automatically checked with the integration of Configuration Manager. When a non-compliant system is detected, a workflow creates an incident based on the non-compliance.

Using Risk in the IT GRC Process MP

Risks can also be managed with the IT GRC MP. You can manage risks in the same way you set up your compliance. You can create a separate program for risks or use the same program as your compliance.

After setting up the program, you can start adding risks. Open the Compliance and Risk Items pane and navigate to **Risk Management -> All Risks**. From the Tasks pane, select Create Risk. A new form will open where you can fill in the information for the Risk, as stated in Table 13.2.

TABLE 13.2   Risk Information Table

Tab	Description
General	Contains basic information about the risk, including 　Title of the risk 　Description of the risk 　Owner of the risk 　User who the risk is assigned to 　Impact of the risk, which can be a value from 1 to 5, where 1 represents the least impact and 5 represents the greatest risk 　Likelihood of the risk, which can be a value from 1 to 5, where 1 represents the least likelihood and 5 represents the greatest likelihood 　Control level of the risk, which can be a value from 1 to 5, where 1 represents the least control and 5 represents the greatest control 　Risk Response, which can be a value of Accept, Avoid, Reduce, or Share 　Response plan for mitigating the risk 　Associated activities 　Due date
Framework	Contains a hierarchy of items within the program and buttons for adding the items, including program categories, risks, control objectives, and control activities.
Related Items	Contains other items managed in the Compliance and Risk Items pane that relate to this risk, including 　List of related Incidents 　List of supporting control activities 　List of supporting control objectives 　List of related work items 　List of attached files Note: On lower-resolution computer displays, you can click the arrow next to each item to collapse or expand the list of related items.
Approval	Contains a list of all the review activities.
History	Contains a list of all the changes made to the risk.

After you define the risks, you can add them to a program and begin to use them.

Reporting in the IT GRC Process MP

Reporting is a valuable part of the IT GRC MP, used to measure compliance within your organization, and to deliver reports for external audits on the GRC Process.

Reporting is activated when you first install the IT GRC Process MP in Service Manager 2010 SP 1. After successfully importing the MP, you will notice a new pane in reporting named Compliance Reports Library, as shown in Figure 13.11.

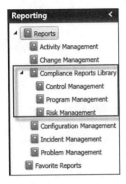

FIGURE 13.11   Compliance Reports.

There are three types of reports:

▶ **Control Management:** Includes reports on all control management components. This consists of Control Activities, Control Objectives, a Managed Entity Result list report, and a Control Management Change report.

▶ **Program Management:** Includes reports on your risk and compliance programs.

▶ **Risk Management:** Includes specifically for risk management.

You can run the reports from the Reporting pane and from the Compliance and Risk Items pane.

CAUTION: TRANSFERRING DATA TO DATA WAREHOUSE

Before you can start using the reports in the IT GRC Process MP, data must be transferred to the data warehouse. Particularly when you are just setting up your environment and testing, be aware that you must wait for the data to be transferred to get information in your reports.

Summary

This chapter discussed how to start using the IT GRC Process MP SP1 in Service Manager 2010 SP 1. When starting to implement the GRC process, there are a number of areas to consider. Most important is to define the key stakeholders in the organization to define the IT GRC process. The MP is just a tool; you need people and a process, as well, to be able to successfully implement the process.

Before configuring the MP, read the authority documents to understand what needs to be achieved, and discuss the documents with the Compliance Manager to verify you are on the right track. The Compliance Manager is responsible for establishing a compliance program. When the program is agreed on, you can begin adding systems to Service Manager by populating the CMDB.

The connector for Configuration Manager 2007 R2 automatically populates your CMDB by enabling automated activities. Once the CMDB is populated, add the GRC program to Service Manager. Set up the DCM connector with Configuration Manager 2007 R2 to leverage automatic activities by using DCM and the IT GRC MP. The activities are automatically checked, and if a non-compliant system is detected, you receive an Incident. To automate the process fully, integrate the Opalis Integration Server to trigger workflows for auto remediation of non-compliant systems.

The final step is running the IT GRC reports to measure, report, and audit compliance on a regular basis.

13

PART IV

Administering Service Manager

IN THIS PART

CHAPTER 14

Notification

A core feature of Service Manager 2010 is the Notification workflow, which is the engine underpinning all aspects of notification. You may want to utilize the notification feature when an incident or problem is created or a change request is approved. By using this feature, you can ensure that notifications are generated for almost any type of change or event in Service Manager.

Service Manager Notification workflow includes the following capabilities:

▶ Create and forward email messages

▶ Customize the messaging format at the user level

▶ Adapt the messaging format to the target's user language

▶ Multiple Simple Mail Transport Protocol (SMTP) server support for redundancy

▶ Support for custom classes and all default classes

Notification Overview

Here are the high-level steps to configure notification:

1. **Establish a notification channel.** In Service Manager 2010, the notification channel is via SMTP, using email.

2. **Create notification subscriptions.** Each subscription defines groups, classes, when to notify, and whom to notify. The subscription also includes

information regarding which template to use in the notification email. You establish subscriptions in the Service Manager console in the Administration workspace, under Notification and Subscriptions.

3. **Verify the notification account.** Service Manager uses the management server Workflow account. This account needs permissions to send emails with the SMTP server and email address specified in the notification channel. Be sure to give this account the appropriate rights for the notification channel it will use.

4. **Verify the notification template.** In the subscription, specify a notification template to use. You need to verify its format, message body, and subject. You also want to verify the language used in the template. The template can include a message and subject for each language. This is a nice capability to have when there are end users in different countries and you want to notify them in their local language.

TIP: WHERE ARE ALL THE RECIPIENTS?

If you have worked with Operations Manager, you most likely will miss one step available with that product: to create recipients. Service Manager does not create recipients, because it synchronizes users and email addresses from Active Directory. If the recipient is not in Active Directory, you can create a user object in Service Manager with the correct email address.

Notification Setup

Notification contains of a number of objects, recipients, channels, and a subscription. You must configure each of these correctly before notification emails can be sent. The next sections discuss those configurations.

Creating Recipients

Service Manager 2010 synchronizes user information from Active Directory, including the email address of the user. As Figure 14.1 shows, you can look at a user configuration item (CI) object and see the notification address. Do not modify this address in Service Manager, as the Active Directory connector will overwrite your changes next time it synchronizes. Should you need to change the address, modify it in Active Directory or Exchange. Service Manager uses the primary email address for the user. Should the user have multiple email addresses, only the primary address is synchronized.

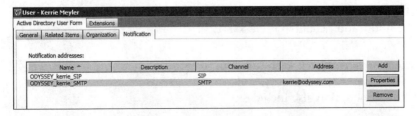

FIGURE 14.1   Notification address of a user CI; in this example, only an SMTP address.

For those intended recipients not in your Active Directory, you would create a user object in Service Manager so you can send a notification. For example, you might want to notify an external vendor when there is an issue with a product from that vendor. Follow these steps to create a user object for an external vendor. After you create a user according to this procedure, you can use it for notification, as shown in Figure 14.2.

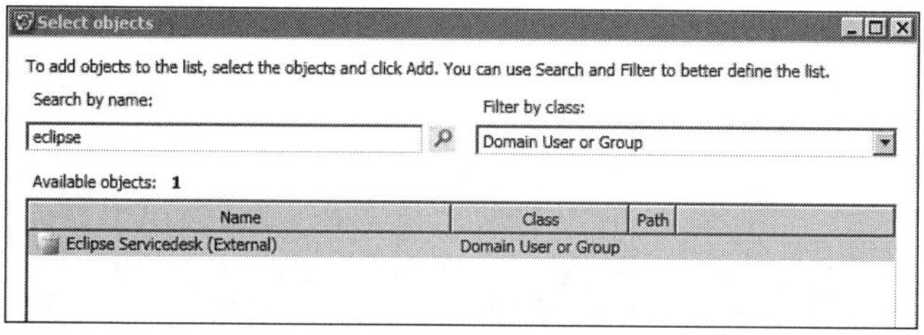

FIGURE 14.2   External recipient as member of a notification subscription.

1. In the Service Manager console, navigate to the Configuration Items workspace.
2. In the Navigation pane, click **Users**.
3. In the Tasks pane, click **Create User**.
4. In the User dialog box, input a first name and last name for the new user, such as the following (shown in Figure 14.3):

   ▶ **First name:** Eclipse Servicedesk

   ▶ **Last Name:** (External) (keyed in)

   ▶ **Company:** Eclipse

5. In the User dialog box, switch to the Notification tab.
6. In the User dialog box, Notification tab, click **Add**.

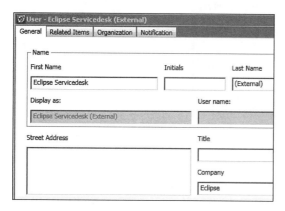

FIGURE 14.3   Configuration of external recipient in the CMDB.

7. In the User Notification dialog box, input the following:

   ▶ **Notification address name:**

     support@eclipse.com

   ▶ **Notification address description:** Eclipse ServiceDesk (external)

   ▶ **Delivery address for this notification channel:**

     support@eclipse.com

8. In the User Notification dialog box, click **OK.**

9. In the User dialog box, click **OK.**

NOTE: THE SMINTERNAL DOMAIN

Occasionally you may see a domain named SMINTERNAL in the Service Manager console. This is the default domain name used when you create users directly in Service Manager and do not synchronize from an Active Directory or other external source.

Service Manager 2010 supports incoming email out of the box. Service Manager 2010 can monitor a folder for new email items, and then generate a new incident for each email. Before generating the incident, it verifies that the From email address used in the email is in the configuration manager database (CMDB). If it is not in the CMDB, you will get an error such as the one shown in Figure 14.4.

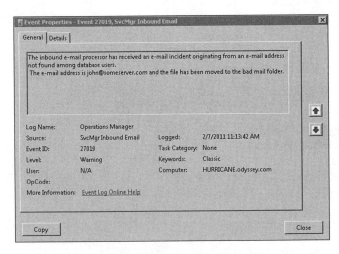

FIGURE 14.4   Event generated when From email address is missing in the CMDB.

If you want Service Manager to receive emails and generate incidents from email addresses not in the CMDB, you must create a user object for them as well, as described earlier in this section. The System Center Service Manager Exchange connector connects to

Exchange to process incoming email related to incidents and change requests. You can also use this connector to send notifications from the console. More information about the connector is available in Chapter 2, "Service Manager 2010 Overview."

Configuring a Notification Channel

Notification channels are the pipe by which notification messages are sent to recipients through a SMTP server. For Service Manager to send email, you must first configure a notification channel. Follow these steps to configure a notification channel in Service Manager 2010:

1. In the Service Manager Console, navigate to the Administration workspace.
2. In the Navigation pane, expand **Notifications** and click **Channels**.
3. In the Results pane, select **E-Mail Notification Channel**, and click **Properties** in the Tasks pane.
4. In the Configure E-Mail Notification Channel dialog box, check the **Enable e-mail notification** check box.
5. In the Configure E-Mail Notification Channel dialog box, click **Add**.
6. In the Add SMTP Server dialog box, input SMTP server (FQDN) (for example, **pioneer.odyssey.com**), as shown in Figure 14.5.

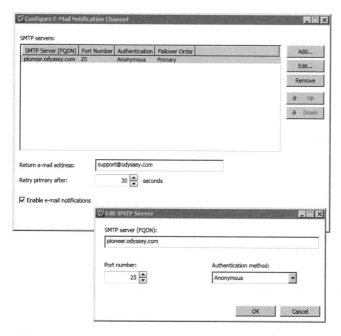

FIGURE 14.5   SMTP notification channel settings.

7. In the Add SMTP Server dialog box, select the authentication method from the drop-down menu and port number, depending on your mail server configuration. Click **OK**.

8. In the Configure E-Mail Notification Channel dialog box, input a return email address—in this example, **support@odyssey.com**. This email address is used as the From address when Service Manager sends notification. Ensure the Service Manager Workflow account is permitted to use this email address.

9. In the Configure E-Mail Notification Channel dialog box, verify your notification channel settings and click **OK**.

Service Manager 2010 only supports email notification channels. A solution for receiving Short Message Service (SMS) notification is to use gateway software that can receive email and convert those messages to SMS. Many mobile service operators provide this as a service to customers. Another solution for using notification in other channels could be to use Opalis Integration Server from Microsoft (http://www.microsoft.com/systemcenter/en/us/opalis.aspx). You can also use Opalis to connect Service Manager with other systems.

The authors recommend you have more than one SMTP server in your email notification channel. This provides fault tolerance.

Creating Notification Templates

Notification templates are used to format the notification email. You might want to use one format when you send notification to end users and another when you send notification to support teams within the IT department. The procedure in this section creates a notification template to be used when sending notification about assigned incidents to the Tier 2 support group. Follow these steps:

1. In the Service Manager console, navigate to the Administration workspace.

2. In the Navigation pane, expand **Notifications** and click **Templates**.

3. In the Tasks pane, click **Create E-Mail Template**.

4. In the Create E-Mail Notification Template wizard, General page, input
   - **Name:** Odyssey - Notification to Tier 2
   - **Target class:** Incident
   - **Management pack:** Select a suitable unsealed management pack (MP) or leave default value

5. On the General page of the Create E-Mail Notification Template wizard, click **Next**.

6. On the Template Design page, input the following:
   - **Message subject:** Incident assigned to Tier 2, priority [Trouble Ticket/Priority]
   - **Message body:** Incident [WorkItem/ID] has been assigned to Tier 2. The title of the incident is [WorkItem/Title].

Everything between [ ] are parameters you can insert using the Insert button. This inserts a dynamic value from the incident. Each time this template is used for notification, the parameter value is populated from the current incident. This configuration is shown in Figure 14.6.

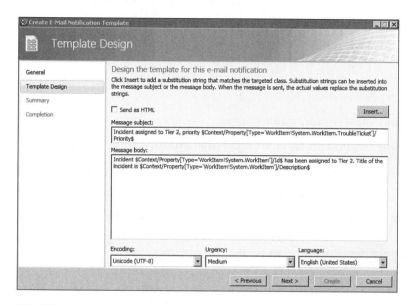

FIGURE 14.6   Configuration of an email notification template.

7. On the Template Design page of the Create E-Mail Notification Template wizard, click **Next**.

8. On the Summary page, review all settings and click **Create**.

9. On the Completion page, verify that the notification template was created successfully and click **Close**.

CAUTION: AVOID COPY/PASTE WITH SUBSTITUTION STRINGS BETWEEN TEMPLATES

Copying and pasting substitution strings from one notification template to another typically will not work. Avoid copy/paste between templates to prevent unnecessary errors with the text.

Creating Subscriptions

After you synchronize users, create a notification template, and configure a notification channel, your next step is to create a subscription for the users to receive email notification. The subscription controls what is sent to the recipient and the format. Follow these steps to configure a subscription for all new Tier 2 incidents in Service Manager 2010. The subscription in this example sends a notification when an incident is updated with Support group equals 2:

1. In the Service Manager console, navigate to the Administration workspace.

2. In the Navigation pane, expand **Notifications** and click **Subscriptions**.

3. In the Tasks pane, click **Create Subscription**.

4. In the Create E-Mail Notification Subscription wizard, Before You Begin page, click **Next**.

5. In the Create E-Mail Notification Subscription wizard, General page, input the following settings, also shown in Figure 14.7:

    ▶ **Notification subscription name:** Odyssey - Notification for Tier 2

    ▶ **Description:** Notification for all incidents updated to Tier 2

    ▶ **Target class:** Incident

    ▶ **When to notify:** When an object of the selected class is updated

    ▶ **Management pack:** Select a suitable unsealed MP or leave the default value.

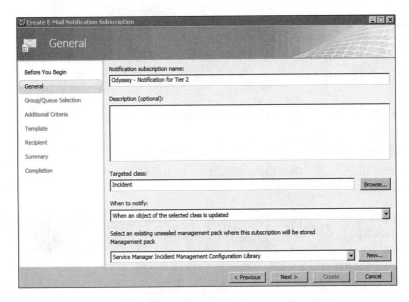

FIGURE 14.7   Configuration of E-Mail Notification subscription.

Notice that in the Targeted class dropdown, you choose the class for which you will be sending the notification. You can select any class here (for example, Change Request, Incident, or Manual Activity). The notification subscription feature is not limited to the default classes of the product.

6. Click **Next** on the General page of the Create E-Mail Notification Subscription wizard.

7. On the Group/Queue Selection page, select a queue or group to filter which objects to track. Then click **Next**.

   In Service Manager 2010, you can use both groups and queues. The capability is dependent upon whether you select a work item class or a configuration item class as the target class for your subscription.

   ▶ Groups are used to group objects, typically CIs. Groups can contain objects of the same class or of different classes.

   ▶ A queue is used to group work items, which meet specified criteria such as all change requests that are classified as email-related change requests.

   Both queue and group memberships can be dynamic and are periodically recalculated to ensure the membership list is correct.

8. On the Additional Criteria page, click the **Changed To** tab.

   Use the Changed To tab if you want to send notification when an incident is modified to this support group. If you want to be notified when an incident is changed from Tier 2 to another support group, use the Changed From tab.

NOTE: MORE CRITERIONS

In some scenarios, you might need to add criteria directly in the eXtended Markup Language (XML); say, when you need to use `2 does not equal` criteria. Travis Wright has written a blog post regarding this at http://blogs.technet.com/b/servicemanager/archive/2010/11/30/using-and-or-criteria-in-workflow-and-notification-subscriptions.aspx.

---

9. On the Additional Criteria page, in the property list, scroll down and select **Support Group**. Click **Add** to add it to the criteria field. In the criteria field, select Tier 2 in the drop-down menu, as shown in Figure 14.8. Click **Next**.

10. On the Template page, click the **Browse** button and select the **Odyssey - Notification to Tier 2** template in the Select E-Mail notification Template dialog box. Click **OK**.

11. Click **Add** in the Recipient page of the Create E-Mail Notification Subscription wizard. In the Select objects dialog box, select the recipient for the subscription. The authors recommend using shared mailboxes rather than sending individually to everyone in a team. You can also use distribution lists from Active Directory as recipients. Distribution lists will show up as instances of the Active Directory `Group` class. Click **Add** to add recipients and then click **OK**. Click **Next** to proceed to the next page of the wizard.

12. The Summary page gives you the opportunity to review your settings. Click **Create** to create the subscription.

14

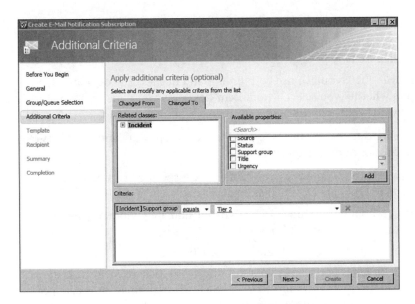

FIGURE 14.8   Configuration of email notification subscription.

13. At the Completion page, verify the subscription was successfully created, as in Figure 14.9. Click **Close**.

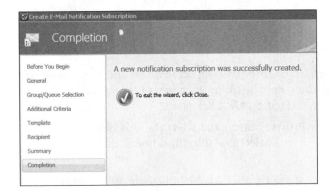

FIGURE 14.9   Subscription successfully created.

Working with Different Languages in Subscriptions

Some organizations require notification messages to be in the target user's native language. For example, if your organization has employees in France and Germany, you need to configure Service Manager to send notifications in either French or German depending on the target user. The language the user receives is controlled by the `Locale` attribute on the user CI, shown in Figure 14.10.

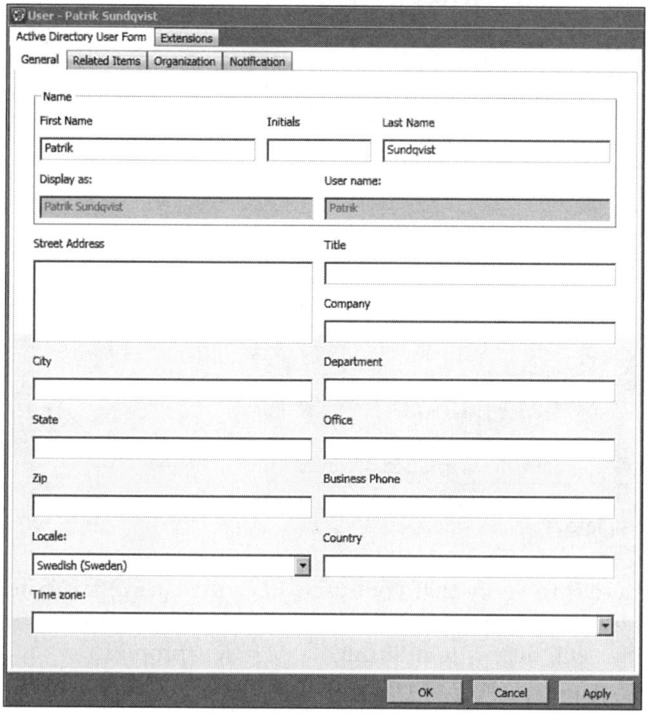

FIGURE 14.10   Locale attribute of a user CI.

To configure Service Manager to support different languages in notification emails, you must configure a notification template with the message body in each language. The following procedure updates the Odyssey - Notification to Tier 2 template:

1. In the Service Manager Console, navigate to the Administration workspace.

2. In the Navigation pane, expand **Notifications** and click **Templates**.

3. In the Results pane, select the **Odyssey - Notification Tier 2** template created earlier in the "Creating Notification Templates" section. From the Tasks pane, select **Properties**.

4. In the **Odyssey - Notification to Tier 2** dialog box, go to the Template Design page.

5. In the Odyssey - Notification to Tier 2 dialog box on the Template Design page, use the Language drop-down menu to select other languages. As you can see in Figure 14.11, both the message box and the message subject are blank when you select another language, such as French. Input your text in French, as shown in Figure 14.11, and then select **German** and input your German subject and message bodies. Click **OK**.

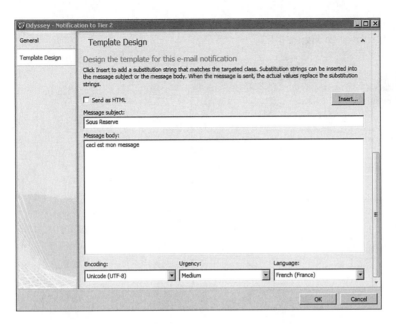

FIGURE 14.11   Configuring the template.

6. The final step in this procedure is to verify that your users have the `Locale` attribute configured. Remember that if you change the attribute value in Service Manager, the Active Directory connector will overwrite it during its next synchronization. The Active Directory connector will overwrite it even with a blank value; there will then be a blank value in Service Manager. Be sure to always update the attribute in Active Directory.

In some scenarios, you can see notification emails with a value such as `IncidentClassigicationEnum.Hardware`. In this example, the category parameter was inserted into the notification template. You could expect it to say Hardware problem, but the reason you see `IncidentClassificationEnum.Hardware` is because there is no display string for the category list value in that notification recipient language.

Table 14.1 shows you the result you will get depending on template language and user Locale property.

TABLE 14.1   Results Based on Template Language and the User's Locale Property

User Locale Property	Notification Template Language	Available Display String	Result in Email Notification
Sweden (Swedish)	Sweden (Swedish) (only language configured).	US-EN (Default)	Incorrect list values
English (United States)	Sweden (Swedish) (only language configured).	US-EN (Default)	Correct list values

TABLE 14.1   Results Based on Template Language and the User's Locale Property

User Locale Property	Notification Template Language	Available Display String	Result in Email Notification
English (United States)	Both English (United States) and Sweden (Swedish). Will use the English (United States) template body.	US-EN (Default)	Correct list values
Sweden (Swedish)	Both English (United States) and Sweden (Swedish). Will use the Sweden (Swedish) template body.	US-EN (Default)	Incorrect list values
Blank/null	Both English (United States) and Sweden (Swedish). Will use the Sweden (Swedish) template body that was first configured in the template. Swedish is also the local settings on the service	US-EN (Default)	Incorrect list values
Other language (example) Sweden (Finnish)	Both English (United States) and Sweden (Swedish).	US-EN (Default)	No email

To get the correct notification email message body for, say Swedish, you must add localization in the Service Manager Incident Management Configuration Library MP or the MP that contains the item, and configure the MP to support Swedish. Travis Wright has blogged about this; the article is available at http://blogs.technet.com/b/servicemanager/archive/2009/07/24/localizing-management-pack-content.aspx.

Here are the general steps to perform this:

1. Export the Service Manager Incident Management Configuration Library MP, or the MP where you stored your items.

2. Open it with an XML editor such as XML Notepad, downloadable from http://www.microsoft.com/downloads/en/details.aspx?familyid=72d6aa49-787d-4118-ba5f-4f30fe913628&displaylang=en. (At the Microsoft Download Center at http://www.microsoft.com/downloads, search for "XML Notepad.")

3. Add `languagepack` and localization `displaystrings` for your language. Both `LanguagePack` and `DisplayString` are XML tags.

4. Save the MP.

5. Import the MP back into Service Manager.

NOTE: SERVICE MANAGER LANGUAGE SUPPORT

With Service Manager 2010 Service Pack 1, Microsoft added language support for Czech, Danish, Greek, Finnish, Dutch, Norwegian, Polish, Portuguese, Swedish, and Turkish.

Culture XX is a Neutral Culture

If you try to send a notification email to a recipient with a `Locale` attribute value that the notification template does not support, an event is generated on your Service Manager server. The event will be in the Operations Manager log with Event ID 33880. The following text is an example of an event ID 33880. You can rectify this by ensuring you have the same language support in your MP and notification template as your user has as locale attribute value:

```
A Windows Workflow Foundation workflow failed during execution.
Workflow Type: Microsoft.EnterpriseManagement.ServiceManager.Incident.Workflows.
AutomaticIncidentChangeWorkflow
Workflow Identifier: 742dc6d1-90cf-9834-044f-9906bcf9dbf9
Exception Type: System.NotSupportedException
Exception Message: Culture 'en' is a neutral culture. It cannot be used in
formatting and parsing and
therefore cannot be set as the thread's current culture.
Exception Stack: at System.Globalization.CultureInfo.CheckNeutral
(CultureInfo culture)
at System.Globalization.CultureInfo.get_DateTimeFormat()
at System.DateTime.ToString(IFormatProvider provider)
at Microsoft.EnterpriseManagement.Notifications.Workflows.IReplaceableToken.
GetLocalizedPropertyValue(UserSettings settingsIn,
EnterpriseManagementObject instance)
at Microsoft.EnterpriseManagement.Notifications.Workflows.TokenizedMessage.
PopulateTokenValues(UserSettings userSettings,
EnterpriseManagementObject instance,
Dictionary`2 relationshipIdToInstanceToRelatedObjectMapping)
at Microsoft.EnterpriseManagement.Notifications.Workflows.RecipientGroupMessage.
PopulateTokenValues(UserSettings userSettings,
EnterpriseManagementObject instance, Dictionary`2
relationshipIdToInstanceToRelatedObjectMapping)
at Microsoft.EnterpriseManagement.Notifications.Workflows.SendNotificationsActivity.
Execute(ActivityExecutionContext executionContext)
at System.Workflow.ComponentModel.ActivityExecutor`1.Execute(T activity,
ActivityExecutionContext executionContext)
at System.Workflow.ComponentModel.ActivityExecutor`1.Execute(Activity activity,
ActivityExecutionContext executionContext)
at System.Workflow.ComponentModel.ActivityExecutorOperation.Run
(IWorkflowCoreRuntime workflowCoreRuntime)
at System.Workflow.Runtime.Scheduler.Run()
```

Workflows with Notification

Service Manager 2010 includes the functionality for you to configure a number of default workflows and author your own custom workflows. A workflow is a sequence of activities that automates a process; for example, it can pick information from a change request and carry out tasks in Active Directory based on the information in the change request. A workflow can also update and modify work items within Service Manager (such as change priority of an incident work item). Incident workflows can apply a template to an incident and send notification emails. You can use the Service Manager console to build workflows around

- ▶ Desired Configuration Management event workflow
- ▶ Activity event workflow
- ▶ Incident event workflow
- ▶ Change Request event workflow

You can use the Service Manager Authoring Tool to build custom workflows with other activities, an example of which is shown in Figure 14.12. You can also use the Authoring Tool to author new activities. System Center Opalis Integration Server (being rebranded as Orchestrator) includes an integration pack to connect to Service Manager, making it also possible to build Service Manager workflows in Opalis.

The following procedure configures a workflow that changes the impact of the incident and sends an email notification to the security team if an incident is created with a description containing the word *virus*. The procedure uses the High Priority Incident template, which is a default incident template in Service Manager 2010. You can modify the template; in this scenario, for example, add the modification of **assigned to**.

The High Priority Incident template changes the following settings of an incident:

- ▶ Impact changes to High.
- ▶ Urgency changes to High.
- ▶ Assigned to changes to Odyssey Antivirus Team.
- ▶ Support group changes to Tier 1.

Follow these steps:

1. In the Service Manager console, navigate to the Administration workspace.
2. In the Navigation pane, expand **Workflows**.
3. In the Navigation pane, click **Configuration**.
4. In the Results pane, select **Incident Event Workflow Configuration**.
5. In the Tasks pane, click **Properties**.
6. In the Configure Incident Event Workflows dialog box, click **Add**.

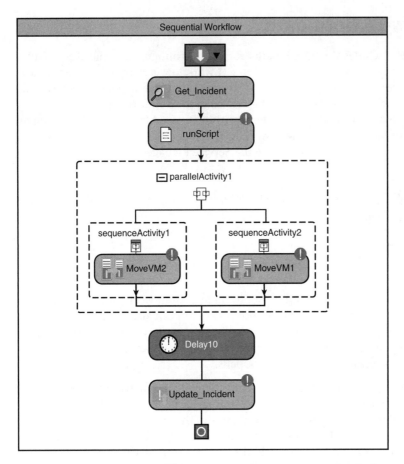

FIGURE 14.12 Workflow built in the Service Manager Authoring Tool.

7. On the Before you begin page of the Add Incident Event Workflow wizard, click **Next**.

8. On the Workflow Information page, input the following settings, also shown in Figure 14.13:

   ▶ **Name:** Update virus-related incidents.

   ▶ **Description:** For incidents that contain virus in the description, the priority would be increased and a notification e-mail sent.

   ▶ **Check for events:** When an incident is created.

   ▶ **Management pack:** Select a suitable unsealed MP or leave the default value.

9. On the Workflow Information page, click **Next**.

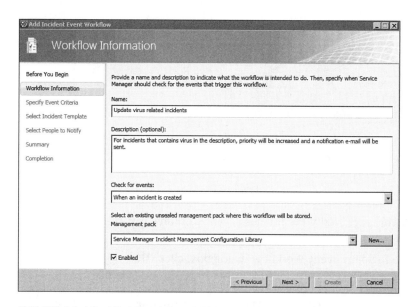

FIGURE 14.13   Workflow Information settings of an incident workflow.

10. On the Specify Event Criteria page, select the description property, click **Add**, and configure the criteria as **[Work Item] Description contains virus**. This is shown in Figure 14.14.

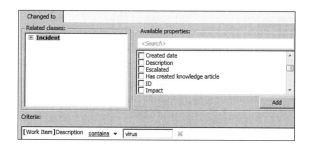

FIGURE 14.14   Event criteria of an incident workflow.

11. Click **Next** on the Specify Event Criteria page.

12. On the Select Incident Template page, select **Apply the following template**, and select **High Priority Incident Template** from the drop-down menu. Click **Next**.

13. On the Select People to Notify page, check the **Enable notification** check box. In the User drop-down menu, select **Assigned To User**. In the Message template drop-down menu, select **Assigned To User Notification Template**. Click **Add**. Figure 14.15 shows the notification settings. Click **Next**.

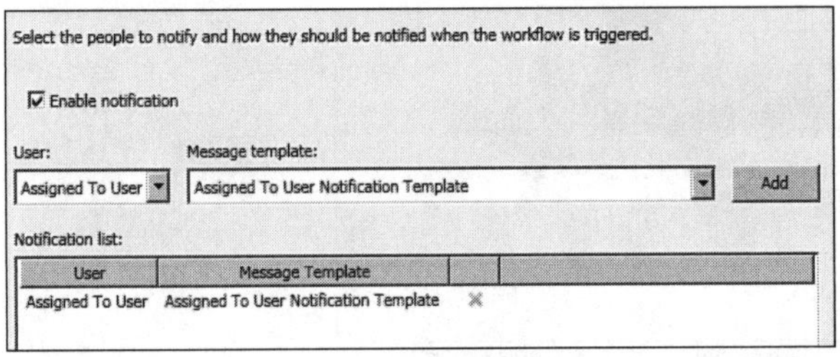

FIGURE 14.15   Notification settings of an incident workflow.

14. Click **Create** on the Summary page.

15. On the Completion page, verify the incident event workflow is successfully created. Then click **Close**.

16. In the Configure Incident Event Workflow dialog box, click **OK**.

When a new incident is created including the word *virus* in the description, this workflow will run and update the incident according to the template chosen in the Workflow wizard. The workflow also sends a notification email to the Odyssey antivirus team regarding the incident. You can see each workflow in the Service Manager console, under **Administration -> Workflows -> Configuration** node. This view can help to troubleshoot workflows and see when they last ran. Figure 14.16 shows information about the workflow created in this procedure. Figures 14.17 and 14.18 show the incident before and after the workflow ran. The workflow also sent a notification to the antivirus team.

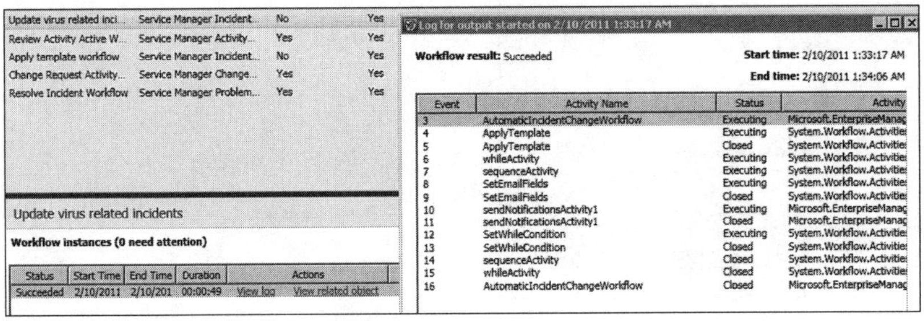

FIGURE 14.16   Workflow status.

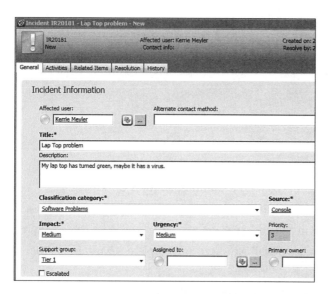

FIGURE 14.17   Incident before workflow has run.

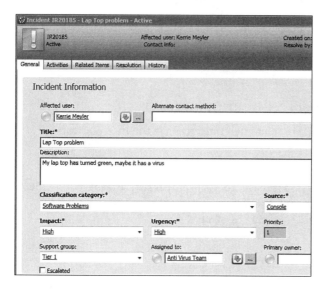

FIGURE 14.18   Incident after workflow has run; Impact, Urgency, and Assigned to are modified.

Notification for Review Activities

The next procedure configures notification for review activities to notify reviewers they need to review and approve or reject an activity in a change request. This procedure is divided into two areas:

▶ Create a notification template

▶ Configure Notification workflow

Follow these steps:

1. In the Service Manager console, navigate to the Administration workspace.

2. In the Navigation pane, expand **Notifications** and then click **Templates**.

3. Click **Create E-Mail Template** in the Tasks pane.

4. On the General page of the Create E-Mail Notification Template wizard, insert the following information:

   ▶ **Name:** Odyssey - Template for Reviewers Notification

   ▶ **Targeted class:** Review Activity (select class from menu)

   ▶ **Management pack:** (Optional) Choose a different MP.

5. On the General page, click **Next**.

6. On the Create E-Mail Notification Template wizard, Template Design page, insert the following information, also shown in Figure 14.19:

   ▶ **Send as HTML:** Checked

   ▶ **Message subject:** Activity to Review. ID: [WorkItem/ID]

   (Note that the WorkItem ID is a parameter inserted via the Insert button.)

   ▶ **Message Body:**
   ```
   Hi, <br>
   A review activity has been assigned to you for review. Please click the
   link to approve or reject the activity.
   <A HREF=http://server/analyst>Link to SCSM
   portal</A>
   <br>
   Thanks,
   ```

   Note that the URL in the text needs to be adapted to your environment. It should point to the Analyst Portal part of the Service Manager Self-Service portal (SSP). Then reviewers can simply click the link to access the activity to review.

7. On the Template Design page, click **Next**.

8. On the Summary page, click **Create**.

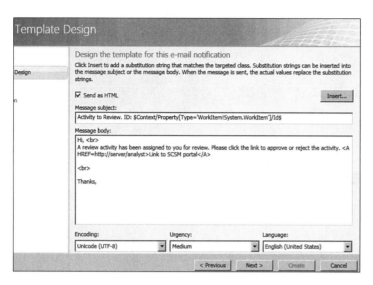

FIGURE 14.19   Message format of Reviewer Notification template.

9. On the Completion page, verify that the new E-Mail Notification template is successfully created. Then click **Close**.

Next, you configure a workflow to send notification when a review activity becomes active. Follow these steps to configure an activity event workflow that will send notification to reviewers:

1. In the Service Manager console, navigate to the Administration workspace.

2. In the Navigation pane, expand **Workflows** and select **Configuration**.

3. In the Results pane, select **Activity Event Workflow Configuration**.

4. In the Tasks pane, click **Configure Workflow Rules**.

5. In the Select a class dialog box, select **Review Activity**, and then click **OK**.

6. In the Configure Workflows dialog box, click **Add**.

7. On the Before you begin page of the Configure workflows for objects of class Review Activity wizard, click **Next**.

8. On the Workflow Information page of the wizard, input the information shown in Figure 14.20.

9. On the Workflow Information page, click **Next**.

10. On the Specify Criteria page, click the **Changed To** tab and configure as shown in Figure 14.21:

    ```
    [Activity] Status equals In Progress
    ```

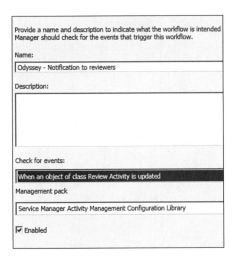

FIGURE 14.20   Workflow information.

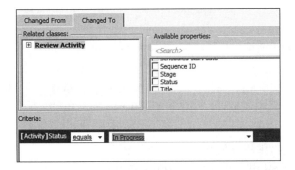

FIGURE 14.21   Changed To settings in workflow.

11. On the Specify the Criteria page, click the **Changed From** tab and configure the following (see Figure 14.22):

    Status does not equal In Progress

12. On the Specify the Criteria page, click **Next**.

13. On the Apply Template page, unselect **Apply the selected template**. Click **Next**.

14. On the Select People to Notify page, input the following settings, also shown in Figure 14.23:

   ▶ **Users:** Reviewers

   ▶ **E-Mail Template:** Odyssey - Template for Reviewers Notification

15. On the Select People to Notify page, click **Add**.

16. On the Select People to Notify page, click **Next**.

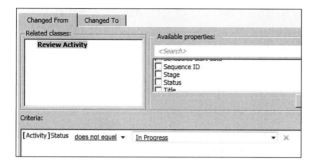

FIGURE 14.22   Changed From settings in workflow.

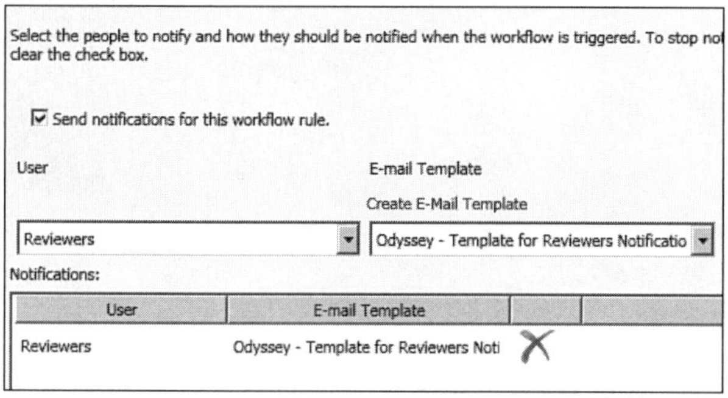

FIGURE 14.23   Notification settings in workflow.

17. Click **Create** at the Summary page.

18. At the Completion page, verify the workflow is successfully created. Then click **Close**.

19. In the Configure Workflows dialog box, click **OK**.

You now have configured a workflow that is triggered each time a Review activity goes from status Not in Progress to status In Progress. The workflow sends out a notification email to the reviewer in the Review activity.

Summary

This chapter did not include much clicking and navigation in the console; it focused on notification and the components that notification is built upon. The chapter discussed how to set up notification, including the different components. This included recipients, the notification channel used to send notification emails, and then how to configure a notification template and a subscription. The chapter also discussed configuring different notification formats for different languages. You can use this feature to configure the notification language based on the recipient's Locale setting.

You also learned how to use notification in workflows. The chapter discussed an example of when an antivirus-related incident was routed within Service Manager and a notification email was sent. The chapter also discussed how to configure notification for review activity. Notification is very useful in the review activity scenario. For change request reviewers who do not use the Service Manager console daily, it is a great way to receive information about a new review activity. The notification email can include a direct link to the Service Manager portal where they can work with the review activity.

The authors of this book recommend that you review all notification subscriptions and subscribers before activating them. Sending too many email notifications will often lead to an automatically delete rule in the recipient's email client.

CHAPTER 15

Service Manager Security

Similar to any enterprise systems management product implementation, you want to design, deploy, and maintain Service Manager with security in mind. Security is important for securing data based on business requirements, but it is also useful in optimizing the user experience for users based on their roles in an organization. Service Manager is unique in the Microsoft System Center family because of the many different types of people interacting with it:

▶ Tier 1 analysts

▶ Tier 2 and 3 advanced operators

▶ Managers

▶ End users

▶ Administrators

▶ Developers

▶ Change managers

Essentially, everyone in your organization interacts with Service Manager at some point. Because Service Manager is also a platform for Information Technology (IT) process automation, in addition to being secure, it needs to access systems securely. Service Manager is also a major datastore in an IT organization; other systems need to be able to access and update it. This chapter describes how to design a security model enabling these different uses without compromising on security.

Role-Based Security

Service Manager 2010 uses a security model founded on the concept of role-based access control (RBAC), where each user in an organization is classified according to his or her job function. Users with similar job functions are grouped together. These groups of users are then granted the least privileged permissions in the system required to perform these job functions.

Service Manager optimizes the user experience using this model such that users can see and operate on only those items relevant to their job function. This approach grants explicit permissions to users, although you can also grant implicit permissions based on the users' relationship to a given object.

Security Boundary Scoping

You secure permissions on objects by creating security boundaries around those objects. Here are the four different types of security boundaries:

- **Groups:** A collection of objects, typically configuration items (CIs) (for example, HRWeb servers).

- **Queues:** A collection of work items, such as HRWeb incidents.

- **Classes:** A type of item that you manage (for example, `Windows Computer`).

- **Properties:** A piece of information about an object defined at the class level, such as a computer's fully qualified domain name (FQDN).

Administrators may want to subdivide the CIs in the configuration management database (CMDB) into logical groups where users have access to perform actions based on their job function or other factors. For example, an administrator may want to create a group consisting of the HRWeb servers and grant permission to the HRWeb operations team to edit those servers. The administrator may want to give other groups of users permission to only view and not edit those servers, whereas other groups of users might not be allowed to view them at all because it is not related to their job function, or because the information needs to be secured.

Similarly, administrators may want to subdivide the work items into logical queues of work and assign those to different groups of users depending on their job role. For example, the HRWeb operations team would need to be able to view and edit incidents and change requests related to HRWeb, but other teams may only need to view them. The administrator may choose not to grant permission to that queue to some groups of users, improving the user experience for those users that have nothing to do with HRWeb while also securing the information about HRWeb work items.

Security boundaries are also defined at the class level. For example, only administrators should be able to view and edit objects of administrative classes such as notification settings, incident settings, or connectors. Another example is an incident resolver should be able to view and edit incidents, but only be able to view and not edit knowledge articles.

Lastly, Service Manager has the ability to secure properties of classes—meaning you have the granularity of deciding who has the permission to edit the value of a particular property on an object. You can grant a user permission to edit one property of a given object but not another one. (This security boundary only applies to edit and not viewing operations.) An example of this type of security boundary is that activity implementers can change the status or notes of a manual activity, but not any other properties such as the title or description.

User Experience Optimization Scoping

While groups, queues, classes, and properties can be used as security boundaries, other scoping methods exist that you can use simply to optimize the user experience for individuals in a particular job function. These scopes do not affect security in any way, but because they are defined by a user's role in the organization, they are specified at the same time you create a user role.

Here are the three additional scopes used for user experience optimization:

▶ **Console tasks:** These are actions a user can click on in the Tasks pane on the right side of the console or a form.

▶ **Views:** This is a query of data that is shown when the user selects a node from the navigation pane.

▶ **Templates:** Templates are partially completed objects that can be used to create a new object from or be applied to an existing object to set property values and add/remove relationships.

Given the job function for a particular group of users, an administrator may want to reduce the amount of information in the console to only what the users in that group need to be able to see and do. This decreases the cognitive load on the user and improves efficiency by minimizing the amount of time required to find information and perform actions. For example, the HRWeb incident resolver team probably does not need to have those incident views and templates used by the printing support team. Those views and templates would just be noise to an HRWeb incident resolver! Similarly, there may be console tasks specific to resolving printing incidents that are not necessary for an HRWeb incident resolver to be able to run.

Operations on the Data Access Service

The System Center Data Access Service is a Windows service running on each of the management servers deployed in a management group. It is a Windows Communication Foundation (WCF)-based web service through which all data access in Service Manager must pass. As such, it represents a single point of control for security authentication and authorization checks. The Data Access Service has a number of different operations that can be called on the application programming interface (API). Here are the four standard operations that are relevant to role-based security:

▶ **View:** Has permission to see information about an object.

▶ **Create:** Has permission to create an object of a certain class.

▶ **Edit:** Has permission to edit an object (or just some properties of an object).

▶ **Delete:** Has permission to delete an object from the database.

User Role Profiles

User role profiles are a predefined collection of operations that can be performed on certain classes, properties, and relationships. You cannot modify these user role profiles. They are intended to map to typical job functions in an organization according to Microsoft Operations Framework (MOF) and Information Technology Infrastructure Library (ITIL) best practices. Out of the box, Service Manager provides the user role profiles listed in Table 15.1.

TABLE 15.1   User Role Profiles Provided by Service Manager 2010

User Role Profile Name	User Role Profile Description
Report User	Report Users can view the Reporting workspace in the console and connect to the SQL Server Reporting Services (SRS) server. Security for individual reports or folders of reports is configured on the SRS server. Any user added to a user role based on the Report User profile must also be granted the Browser role, Publisher role, or Content Manager role on the SRS server for the System Center\Service Manager report folder.
End User	End Users can use the Self-Service portal (SSP) to create incidents, request software installation, view announcements, and search the knowledge base.
Read-Only Operator	Read-Only Operators have read-only access to work items in their queue scope and to CIs in their group scope.
Change Initiator	Change Initiators can create new change requests and activities for CIs in their assigned group scope. Change Initiators also have read-only access to other work items such as incidents, change requests, or problems that are in their assigned queue scope.
Incident Resolver	Incident Resolvers can edit and create incidents, problems, and manual activities that are in their queue scope. Incident Resolvers also have read-only access to other work items such as change requests in their queue scope and to CIs in their group scope.
Activity Implementer	Activity Implementers can edit only manual activities that are in their queue scope. They have read-only access to other work items in their queue scope and to CIs in their group scope.

TABLE 15.1   User Role Profiles Provided by Service Manager 2010

User Role Profile Name	User Role Profile Description
Problem Analyst	Problem Analysts can edit and create problems in their assigned queue scope. Problem Analysts also have read-only access to other work items such as change requests or incidents in their queue scope and to CIs in their group scope.
Change Owner	Change Owners can create and edit change requests and activity work items (such as review activities and manual activities) in their queue scope. Change Owners also have read-only access to other work items in their queue scope and to CIs in their group scope.
Advanced Operator	Advanced Operators can create or edit any work items that are in their queue scope and any CIs that are in their group scope. In the main console, they can also create, edit, and delete the announcements displayed on the Service Manager Self-Service portal.
Author	Authors can create or edit any work items in their queue scope and any CIs that are in their group scope. They may also create, edit, and delete announcements that are displayed on the Service Manager SSP. Authors can also make limited customizations that are stored in management packs (MPs). Such customizations can include creating, editing, and deleting list items, tasks, templates, views, and view folders.
Workflow	User roles based on the Workflow profile can create and edit any CI or work item.
Administrator	Administrators have full access to all operations. Similarly, their queue scope and their group scope contain all objects in the system and cannot be limited.

Table 15.1 orders the user role profiles in rough approximation of the scope of permissions, as users in a user role based on the Report User, End User, and Read-Only Operator user role profiles have the least privileges, and users in the Administrator user role (based on the Administrator user role profile) have the most.

Table 15.2 defines in detail those permissions granted to each user role profile. You can use this table to understand exactly which security scopes (classes, properties, and relationships) a user role profile has permission to perform each operation on.

When you deploy Service Manager with the data warehouse, there are two distinct management groups: the Service Manager management group and the Data Warehouse management group. Each has a different set of user role profiles installed as appropriate. For example, only the Administrators and the Report Users user roles are installed in the Data Warehouse management group, because they are the only user role profiles relevant to administering the data warehouse and using reporting.

TABLE 15.2   User Role Profiles Class and Relationship Permissions

Role	Operation	Class/Relationship Permissions
Report User	Read	MS.SC.RAL.SrsResourceStore
	Update	None
	Create	None
	Delete	None
End User	Read	All
	Update	None
		System.WorkItemCreatedByUser System.WorkItemAssignedToUser System.WorkItemCreatedForUser System.WorkItem.IncidentCallingUser System.WorkItemResolvedByUser System.FileAttachmentAddedByUser System.WorkItemRelatesToWorkItem System.WorkItemAboutConfigItem
	Create	System.WorkItem System.Reviewer System.WorkItem.Log System.FileAttachment
	Delete	None
Read-Only Operator	Read	All
	Update	None
		System.WorkItemAssignedToUser System.WorkItemCreatedForUser System.WorkItemRelatesToWorkItem System.WorkItemAboutConfigItem System.WorkItem.IncidentCallingUser
	Create	None
	Delete	None

TABLE 15.2   User Role Profiles Class and Relationship Permissions

Role	Operation	Class/Relationship Permissions
Change Initiator	Read	All
	Update	None

	Create	`System.WorkItem.ChangeRequest`
		`System.WorkItem.Activity`
		`System.FileAttachment`
		`System.WorkItem.Log`
		`System.Reviewer`
		
		`System.WorkItemCreatedByUser`
		`System.WorkItemAssignedToUser`
		`System.WorkItemCreatedForUser`
		`System.WorkItemResolvedByUser`
		`System.FileAttachmentAddedByUser`
		`System.WorkItemRelatesToWorkItem`
		`System.WorkItemAboutConfigItem`

	Delete	None
Activity Implementer	Read	All

	Update	`System.WorkItem.ManualActivity`
		(only the `.Status` and `.Notes` properties)
		
		`System.WorkItemResolvedByUser`

	Create	None
	Delete	None

15

TABLE 15.2   User Role Profiles Class and Relationship Permissions

Role	Operation	Class/Relationship Permissions
Incident Resolver	Read	All
	Update	System.WorkItem.Incident System.WorkItem.ManualActivity System.WorkItemCreatedByUser System.WorkItemAssignedToUser System.WorkItemCreatedForUser System.WorkItemResolvedByUser System.FileAttachmentAddedByUser System.WorkItemRelatesToWorkItem System.WorkItemAboutConfigItem System.WorkItem.IncidentCallingUser
	Create	System.WorkItem.Incident System.WorkItem.ManualActivity System.WorkItem.Log System.FileAttachment
	Delete	System.FileAttachment
Problem Analyst	Read	All
	Update	System.WorkItem.Problem System.WorkItemCreatedByUser System.WorkItemAssignedToUser System.WorkItemCreatedForUser System.WorkItemResolvedByUser System.FileAttachmentAddedByUser System.WorkItemRelatesToWorkItem System.WorkItemAboutConfigItem System.WorkItem.IncidentCallingUser
	Create	System.WorkItem.Problem System.WorkItem.Log System.FileAttachment
	Delete	System.FileAttachment

TABLE 15.2   User Role Profiles Class and Relationship Permissions

Role	Operation	Class/Relationship Permissions
Change Owner	Read	All
	Update–	System.WorkItem.ChangeRequest System.WorkItem.Activity System.Reviewer System.FileAttachment System.WorkItemCreatedByUser System.WorkItemAssignedToUser System.WorkItemCreatedForUser System.WorkItemResolvedByUser System.FileAttachmentAddedByUser System.WorkItemRelatesToWorkItem System.WorkItemAboutConfigItem
	Create	System.WorkItem.ChangeRequest System.WorkItem.Activity System.Reviewer System.FileAttachment
	Delete	System.Reviewer System.FileAttachment

15

TABLE 15.2 User Role Profiles Class and Relationship Permissions

Role	Operation	Class/Relationship Permissions
Advanced Operator	Read	All
	Update	-System.WorkItem System.ConfigItem System.Announcement.Item System.Reviewer System.WorkItem.Log System.FileAttachment System.WorkItemCreatedByUser System.WorkItemAssignedToUser System.WorkItemCreatedForUser System.WorkItemResolvedByUser System.FileAttachmentAddedByUser System.WorkItemRelatesToWorkItem System.WorkItemAboutConfigItem System.WorkItem.IncidentCallingUser
	Create	System.WorkItem System.ConfigItem System.Announcement.Item System.Reviewer System.WorkItem.Log System.FileAttachment
	Delete	System.Announcement.Item System.Reviewer System.FileAttachment

TABLE 15.2   User Role Profiles Class and Relationship Permissions

Role	Operation	Class/Relationship Permissions
Author	Read	All
	Update—	−System.WorkItem System.ConfigItem System.Announcement.Item System.Reviewer System.WorkItem.Log System.FileAttachment System.WorkItemCreatedByUser System.WorkItemAssignedToUser System.WorkItemCreatedForUser System.WorkItemResolvedByUser System.FileAttachmentAddedByUser System.WorkItemRelatesToWorkItem System.WorkItemAboutConfigItem System.WorkItem.IncidentCallingUser
	Create	System.WorkItem System.ConfigItem System.Announcement.Item System.Reviewer System.WorkItem.Log System.FileAttachment
	Delete	System.Announcement.Item System.Reviewer System.FileAttachment

15

TABLE 15.2   User Role Profiles Class and Relationship Permissions

Role	Operation	Class/Relationship Permissions
Workflow	Read	All
	Update	System.WorkItem System.ConfigItem System.Announcement.Item System.Reviewer System.WorkItem.Log System.FileAttachment
	Create	System.WorkItem System.ConfigItem System.Announcement.Item System.Reviewer System.WorkItem.Log System.FileAttachment
	Delete	MS.SC.CM.DCM_NonCompliance_CI
Administrator (Service Manager or Data Warehouse)	Read	All
	Update	All
	Create	All
	Delete	All

Object Permissions

In addition to the permissions listed in Table 15.2, all user role profiles (with any exceptions noted) have permission to:

▶ View global settings (System.GlobalSetting)

▶ View knowledge article ratings (System.StarRating), except Workflow

▶ Edit knowledge article ratings (System.StarRating), except Workflow, Report User, and Read-Only Operator

Console Workspace Access Permissions

Access to different workspaces of the Service Manager console is controlled by user role profiles, as defined in Table 15.3.

For example, compare the visibility of different workspaces between an incident resolver user and an administrator, as displayed in Figure 15.1.

TABLE 15.3   Workspace Access by User Role Profile

Profile	Work Items	Configuration Items	Authoring	Admin	Data Warehouse	Reports
Reporting User	No	No	No	No	No	Yes
End User	No	No	No	No	No	No
Read-Only Operator	Yes	Yes	No	No	No	No
Activity Implementer	Yes	Yes	No	No	No	No
Change Initiator	Yes	Yes	No	No	No	No
Incident Resolver	Yes	Yes	No	No	No	No
Problem Analyst	Yes	Yes	No	No	No	No
Change Owner	Yes	Yes	No	No	No	No
Advanced Operator	Yes	Yes	Yes	No	No	No
Author	Yes	Yes	Yes	No	No	No
Workflow	No	No	No	No	No	No
Service Manager Administrator	Yes	Yes	Yes	Yes	No	No
Data Warehouse Administrator	No	No	No	No	Yes	No

FIGURE 15.1   Workspaces visible to an incident resolver (left) and administrator user (right).

NOTE: WORKSPACES CREATED BY NON-MICROSOFT MANAGEMENT PACKS

Workspaces created by non-Microsoft MPs, such as the SLA Management workspace generated by importing the Cased Dimensions (a Microsoft partner) MP, are visible to users regardless of what user roles they are in.

Management Pack Elements Permissions

User role profiles determine what permissions a user has to create, edit, and delete MP elements. Only administrators and authors can create, edit, and delete the following MP elements:

▶ Templates

▶ Console tasks

▶ Views

▶ List items (in an existing list)

Administrators have full access to these MP elements regardless of their target class. You can scope authors to be allowed only to create, edit, or delete MP elements depending on those classes to which they are targeted. For example, you may want to allow the Tier 1 Help Desk Manager only to create incident templates for his team and not to create change request templates.

Queues and groups are also stored as MP elements. Because they are used as security boundaries, only administrators are allowed to create, edit, and delete them.

Mapping User Role Profiles with MOF/ITIL Roles

ITIL and the MOF are two of the most commonly used IT service management (ITSM) process frameworks in use today. Both frameworks define user roles in the IT organization and specify responsibilities of users in those organizational user roles. You can map these roles to user roles in Service Manager to grant users in those roles the appropriate permissions required to perform their jobs.

ITIL Role Types

ITIL defines several different user roles related to ITSM in the Service Operation phase. Several of these roles can be directly mapped to Service Manager user role profiles, shown in Table 15.4. Other roles are not as specific to a particular user role in a service desk tool and thus not included in this table. You can find specific information about what each role is responsible for in the ITIL documentation at http://www.best-management-practice. com. (Viewing this documentation requires an ITIL license.)

Microsoft Operations Framework Role Types

MOF 4.0 was first published in April 2008 and updated in July 2010. MOF 4.0 is an integrated set of best practices, principles, and guidelines for achieving high levels of service in an IT organization. It defines multiple phases of an IT service life cycle:

▶ Plan

▶ Deliver

▶ Operate

▶ (Continuously) Manage

TABLE 15.4   ITIL Role Types

Phase	Area	Role in ITIL	User Role Profile in Service Manager
Operation	Service Desk	Service Desk Manager	Advanced Operator
Operation	Service Desk	Service Desk Supervisor	Advanced Operator
Operation	Service Desk	Service Desk Analyst	Incident Resolver
Operation	Service Desk	Super Users	End User
Operation	Technical Management	Technical Managers / Team Leaders	Advanced Operator
Operation	Technical Management	Technical Analysts/Architects	Author
Operation	Technical Management	Technical Operator	Advanced Operator
Operation	IT Operations Management	IT Operations Manager	Advanced Operator
Operation	IT Operations Management	Shift Leader	Advanced Operator
Operation	IT Operations Management	IT Operations Analyst	Advanced Operator
Operation	Application Management	Application Manager / Team Leader	Advanced Operator (scoped to application)
Operation	Application Management	Application Analyst/Architect	Author (scoped to application)
Operation	Incident Management	Incident Manager	Advanced Operator
Operation	Incident Management	First, Second, and Third Line Support Group	Incident Resolver
Operation	Problem Management	Problem Manager	Advanced Operator
Operation	Problem Management	Problem Solving Group	Problem Analyst
Service Improvement	Service Management	Service Manager	Advanced Operator (scoped to service)
Service Improvement	Service Management	Service Owner	Advanced Operator (scoped to service)

15

TABLE 15.4   ITIL Role Types

Phase	Area	Role in ITIL	User Role Profile in Service Manager
Service Improvement	Service Management	Reporting Analyst	Reporting User
Service Transition	Service Transition Management	Service Transition Manager	Change Manager
Service Transition	Asset and Configuration Management	Service Asset Manager	Advanced Operator (scoped to assets related to the service)
Service Transition	Asset and Configuration Management	Configuration Manager	Advanced Operator
Service Transition	Asset and Configuration Management	Configuration Analyst	Advanced Operator
Service Transition	Asset and Configuration Management	Configuration Administrator	Advanced Operator
Service Transition	Configuration Control Board	Change Authority	Uses Implied Permissions
Service Transition	Configuration Control Board	Change Manager	Change Manager

Each phase contains service management functions (SMFs). Within each SMF, MOF defines the role types of people working in various job functions. Service Manager 2010 is primarily concerned with the Operate phase, which has four SMFs:

▶ Operations

▶ Service Monitoring and Control

▶ Customer Service

▶ Problem Management

Service Manager also provides support for the Change and Configuration Management SMF in the Manage layer. Tables 15.5, 15.6, and 15.7 in the next sections define the mapping of these MOF user role types to Service Manager user role profiles.

Operations and Service Monitoring and Control SMF Role Types
The primary team accountability that applies to the Build SMF is the Operations
Accountability. The role types within that accountability and their primary activities
within this SMF and their mapping to a Service Manager user role profile are listed in
Table 15.5.

TABLE 15.5   Description of Operations and Service Monitoring and Control SMF Role Types

Role Type	Responsibilities	Role in This SMF	User Role Profile in Service Manager
Operator	Executes tasks with predictable results based on instructions	Conducts planned operations tasks	Advanced Operator
Administrator	Executes tasks that are not well defined, requiring a deeper level of knowledge	Conducts unplanned or undefined operations tasks	Advanced Operator
Technology area manager	Owns short-term performance of components in a technology area Owns the work instructions Ensures operational requirements are met for the technology area	Ensures work instructions are carried out as intended	Advanced Operator
Monitoring manager	Responsible for Service Monitoring and Control SMF tasks Ensures that the right systems are monitored Facilitates effective monitoring mechanisms Is the expert on how to monitor, not what to monitor	Ensures needed monitoring information is generated	Advanced Operator
Scheduling manager	Plans schedule of individual activities within operations Owns timing decisions Plans operational work, including maintenance	Schedules operational work	Advanced Operator
Operations manager	Accountable for Operations and Service Monitoring and Control SMFs	Management oversight	Advanced Operator

15

TABLE 15.6   Customer Service SMF Role Types

Role Type	Responsibilities	Role in This SMF	User Role Profile in Service Manager
Customer service representative	Handles calls as the first contact with the user Registers and categorizes calls Determines supportability and dispatches calls	Interacts with customers, including recording, categorizing, classifying, resolving, and closing customer requests	Incident Resolver
Incident resolver	Diagnoses, investigates, and resolves	Resolves incident requests, including troubleshooting, escalating if necessary, and applying a fix or workaround	Incident Resolver
Incident coordinator	Is responsible for incident from beginning to end Owns quality control	Oversees all incident requests	Author
Problem analyst	Investigates and diagnoses	Investigates and resolves an underlying problem	Problem Analyst
Problem manager	Identifies problems from the incident list	Determines whether an underlying problem exists	Problem Analyst
Customer service manager	Is accountable for goals of Support Desk Covers incidents and problems	Oversees customer service	Author

TABLE 15.7   Change and Configuration SMF Role Types

Role Type	Responsibilities	Role in This SMF	User Role Profile in Service Manager
Change manager	Manages the activities of the change management process for the IT organization	Ensure changes are made with the least amount of risk and impact to the organization	Author
Configuration administrator	Tracks what is changing and its impact Tracks CIs, updates configuration management system (CMS)	Ensure a known state at all times	Advanced Operator

Customer Service SMF Role Types

The primary team accountability that applies to the Customer Service SMF is Support Accountability. Table 15.6 displays the role types within that accountability, primary activities within this SMF, and the mapping to a Service Manager user role profile.

Change and Configuration SMF Role Types

The chief team SMF accountability that applies to the Change and Configuration SMF is the Management Accountability. Table 15.7 lists the role types associated with the Management Accountability, as well as the responsibilities and roles and mapping to Service Manager user role profile for each role type.

User Roles

A user role is the combination of the following:

- User role profile
- Security scopes (group, queue, class; using class only for Author profile user roles)
- User experience optimization scopes (templates, views, console tasks)
- Assignment of users and user groups to the user role

You can assign users to the user roles provided out of the box or to custom user roles created by a Service Manager administrator. Any user can be a member of more than one user role, by either being directly assigned to multiple user roles or via membership in an Active Directory group assigned to a user role. If a user is a member of more than one user role, the user's resulting set of permissions is a union of permissions from all roles.

Out-of-the-Box User Roles

Out of the box in Service Manager 2010, there is one user role for each user role profile. Each of these roles is globally scoped in terms of its security and user experience optimization scopes, and appropriate to use in scenarios where custom user roles with more granular scopes based on queues or groups are not required. Out-of-the-box user roles cannot be deleted or modified in any way, except for assigning users to the roles.

When you install the Service Manager management group, the administrator account or group you specify during setup and the account of the user who ran the setup are added to the Administrators user role. Similarly, these accounts are added to the Administrators user role in the Data Warehouse management group during setup.

Setup also assigns the Authenticated Users group to the End Users user role. This ensures that all users in the organization that authenticate with Active Directory can use the functionality of the SSP out of the box.

Creating Custom User Roles

Before creating custom user role profiles, verify you have already created the custom groups, queues, classes, templates, console tasks, and views with which you will be scoping your new user role. As a best practice, group together related queues, groups, classes, views, console tasks, and templates in a single MP that will be assigned to a given user role. Doing so makes it easier to find and select those items when using the User Role wizard. To create a custom user role, follow these steps:

1. Navigate to the Administration workspace. With the exception of managing announcements, only administrators can manage configuration settings found in the Administration workspace.

2. In the Administration space, expand the **Security** node, and select the **User Roles view**.

3. Click the **Create User Role** link in the Tasks pane, and you are asked to choose which user role profile you want to base the new user role on. You can create custom user roles based on any of the user role profiles listed as Yes in the Create Custom User Role column in Table 15.8.

TABLE 15.8   User Role Profiles

User Role Profile	Create Custom User Role?
Report User	No
End User	No
Read-Only Operator	Yes
Change Initiator	Yes
Incident Resolver	Yes
Activity Implementer	Yes
Problem Analyst	Yes
Change Owner	Yes
Advanced Operator	Yes
Author	Yes
Workflow	No
Administrator	No

It is not necessary to have multiple Report User user roles, because that user role only controls access to the information about where the SQL SRS server is located. SQL SRS controls all report security. The Workflows user role is a special user role designed to give workflows the rights they need to perform typical workflow functions and thus there is no need for additional user roles based on that profile. Because the Administrator's user role profile has permissions to everything in the system, it doesn't make sense to create scoped custom user roles based on the Administrator profile; in fact, that isn't even possible. The End User's user role is specifically designed to give users the permissions they need to use the SSP and therefore is not designed to be used in custom user roles.

4. Select a user role profile to start the User Role wizard. You will see the same series of pages in the wizard for all user roles profiles except the Author user role profile. When you create a user role based on the Author user role profile, you may also optionally scope the user role by classes.

You can scope custom user roles based on the Author user role profile by classes. This determines the classes for which they are allowed to create templates, views, console tasks, and other MP elements.

TIP: USER ROLES ARE NOT TRANSPORTABLE

User roles are not stored in MPs and therefore cannot be transported from one environment to another. You must create user roles in each environment where they are needed.

Usage Examples

To better understand the concepts of user roles, let's go through a comprehensive example of setting up role-based security. You can use a table similar to Table 15.9 to map out your own business requirements to make implementing user roles in Service Manager very straightforward.

Suppose your organization has types of individuals and needs listed in Table 15.9. To implement the defined security model defined in this table, here are the actions an administrator should take before creating these user roles:

1. Create and populate User Groups in Active Directory with user accounts (or you may already have these groups):

   ▶ HRStaff

   ▶ T1SDStaff

   ▶ HRAppsSupport

   ▶ HRAppsDevTest

   ▶ HRAppsMgmt

2. Create work item queues for each type of work item for HR Apps:

   ▶ HR Apps incidents.

   ▶ HR Apps change requests.

   ▶ HR Apps problems.

   See Chapter 10, "Incident Management," for information on creating queues.

3. Create a CI group that contains all the HRWeb-related CIs such as servers, databases, websites, services, and so on. See Chapter 10 for information on creating groups.

4. Create views for HR application-related incidents, problems, change requests, and CIs. Chapter 10 includes information on creating views.

5. Create templates for HR application-related incidents, problems, and change requests. Chapter 10 includes information on creating templates.

TABLE 15.9   Mapping Security Requirements to User Roles

User Type	Users	Users' Requirements to Interact with the System	Role and Scope	Group/ Queue Scope	Views, Templates, Console Tasks Scope
End users	HRStaff Employees of HR department (because this is a pilot deployment only)	Create and edit incidents and change requests on the SSP Search and read the knowledge base View announcements	End Users user role	N/A	N/A
Tier 1 service desk staff	T1SDStaff	Create and edit all incidents in main console Search knowledge base Create change requests View all change requests	Incident Resolver user role Change Initiator user role	All	All
HR applications tier 2 and 3 support staff	HRAppsSupport	Create and edit all HR Apps incidents in main console Search knowledge base Create change requests View all change requests Create Problems Edit HR Apps Problems View only those CIs related to HRWeb apps	Custom Incident Resolver User Role Custom Problem Analyst User Role Change Initiator user role	HRApps Incident Queue HRApps Problem Queue HRApps Change Request Queue HRApps servers and services group	HRApps views HRApps templates

TABLE 15.9 Mapping Security Requirements to User Roles

User Type	Users	Users' Requirements to Interact with the System	Role and Scope	Group/ Queue Scope	Views, Templates, Console Tasks Scope
HR Application and Dev/Test team	HRAppsDevTest	Create and edit all types of work items related to HR Apps View only those CIs related to HRWeb Apps	Custom Advanced Operator user role	HRApps Incident Queue HRApps Problem Queue HRApps Change Request Queue HRApps Servers and Services Group	HRApps views HRApps templates
HR Apps Support Group managers	HRAppsMgmt	Create and edit all types of work items related to HR Apps View only those CIs related to HRWeb apps Create and edit templates, views, console tasks, and list items for incidents, problems, and change requests	Custom Author user role (Scoped to Problem, Incident, and Change request classes)	HRApps Incident Queue HRApps Problem Queue HRApps Change Request Queue HRApps Servers and Services Group	HRApps views HRApps templates

15

After completing these actions, the administrator can proceed with creating the user roles. In this scenario, the administrator needs to assign users to several of the out-of-the-box user roles and create four custom user roles.

The Active Directory user group HRStaff is added to the End Users user role. The group T1SDStaff is added to both the out-of-the-box Incident Resolvers and Change Initiator user role so that they will have global scope as additional departments are added into Service Manager following the initial pilot with the HR team. At this point, the administrator is ready to create the custom user roles. To create the custom Author user role for the HR Apps Support management team, follow these steps:

1. Starting in the User Roles view, click **Create User Role**. Select **Author** from the list of user role profiles.

2. Click **Next** on the Welcome page of the wizard.

3. Enter a name for the user role, such as **HR Apps Management**, shown in Figure 15.2. You can optionally enter a description. Click **Next** to continue.

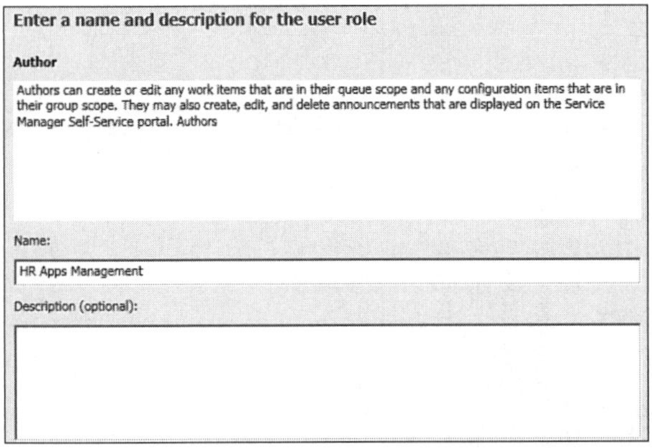

Enter a name and description for the user role

Author

Authors can create or edit any work items that are in their queue scope and any configuration items that are in their group scope. They may also create, edit, and delete announcements that are displayed on the Service Manager Self-Service portal. Authors

Name:

HR Apps Management

Description (optional):

FIGURE 15.2   Entering the name and description.

4. On the Management Packs page (see Figure 15.3), choose the MPs listed in this step so that the following pages in the wizard will be filtered to show only MP elements such as queues, groups, templates, and views from these MPs. This makes it much easier to choose the elements you need instead of trying to find them in a long list. Click **Next** to proceed to the next page.

   ▸ **HR Apps:** Contains the HR apps templates, views, queues, and groups already created.

   ▸ **Incident Management Library:** Contains the Incident class.

   ▸ **System Work Item Change Request Library:** Contains the Change Request class.

▶ **System Work Item Problem Library:** Contains the `Problem` class.

▶ **Service Manager Library Management Pack:** Contains the Templates, Tasks, Queues, Groups, and Lists views.

▶ **Service Manager Knowledge Management Configuration Library:** Contains the Knowledge views.

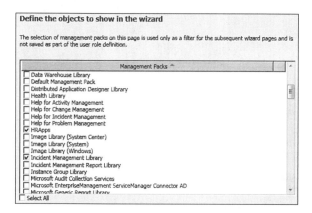

FIGURE 15.3   Filtering by MPs.

5. On the Classes page displayed in Figure 15.4, choose the `Problem`, `Change Request`, and `Incident` classes so that users in this user role can create additional templates and console tasks and manage lists for these classes. Notice only the classes in the MP selected on the previous page (refer to Figure 15.3) are shown, rather than the hundreds of classes actually in the system. Click **Next**.

TIP: USE THE COLUMN HEADERS TO SORT ITEMS

On any of the pages in the wizard where you can select MP elements, you can click the column headers to sort the items. By default, these lists are not sorted, making it difficult to find the item you are looking for. Sorting by element name or MP can make it much faster to find and select what you need.

---

6. On the Queues page (displayed in Figure 15.5), select all the queues shown. Click **Next**.

7. Similarly, on the Groups page (see Figure 15.6), select the group and click **Next**.

8. Figure 15.7 shows the Tasks page. Leave the All option selected. You can optionally optimize the user experience for users by scoping some of the tasks from view. Click **Next**.

15

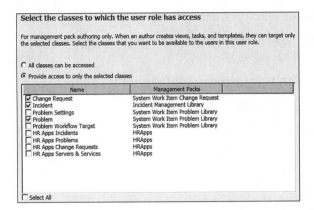

FIGURE 15.4   Selecting class scope.

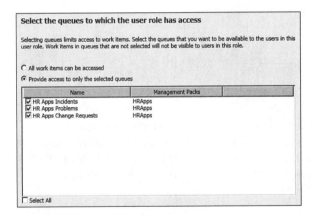

FIGURE 15.5   Selecting queue scope.

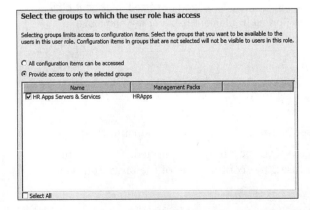

FIGURE 15.6   Selecting group scope.

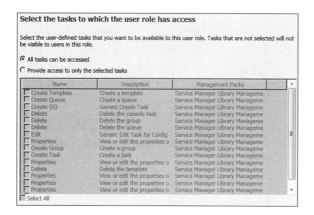

FIGURE 15.7   Selecting task scope.

9. On the Views page (shown in Figure 15.8), select just the views that are specifically created for the HR Apps support team, and then click **Next**. You could optionally select the Lists, Templates, and knowledge articles views if you want users in this role to be able to create and edit lists, templates, and knowledge articles.

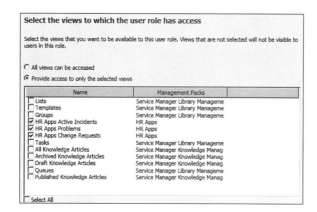

FIGURE 15.8   Selecting view scope.

10. On the Form Templates page displayed in Figure 15.9, select all the templates defined in the HR Apps MP. Those are the only templates the HR support team should need to use.

    After doing so, click **Next**.

11. On the Users page (shown in Figure 15.10), click the **Add** button and browse for and select those users or groups you want to assign to the user role, and then click **Next**.

12. Click **Create** on the Summary page and **Close** on the Completion page.

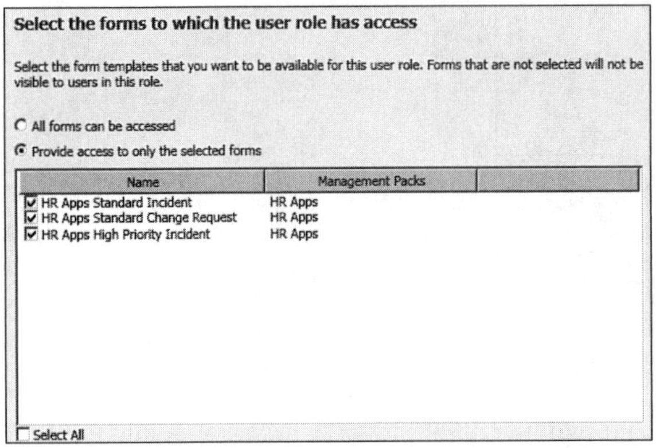

FIGURE 15.9   Selecting template scope.

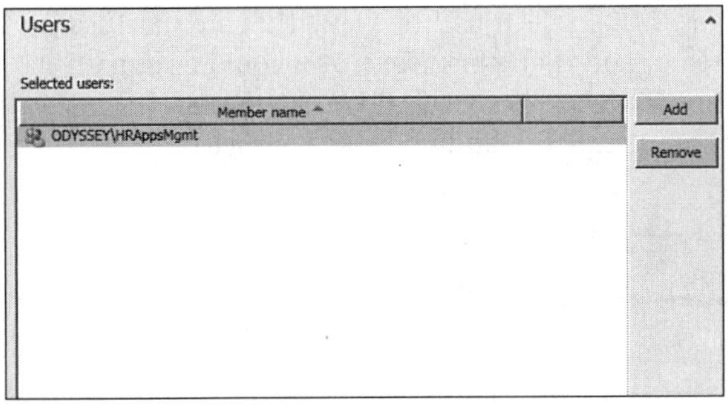

FIGURE 15.10   Adding users or user groups to the user role.

Once the user role is created, test it by adding a test user into the user role and then running the console as that user. You can do this by either logging in to a different Windows session or using the runas.exe utility in Windows to launch the console in a different process. Here is the syntax for the runas command to launch the console:

```
runas.exe /user:odyssey\testuser
Microsoft.EnterpriseManagement.ServiceManager.UI.Console.exe
```

(where odyssey\testuser is the domain and username for the test user)

Make sure that you run only one console process at a time. In addition, ensure that you log out of the test user session or close the console after making changes to the user roles to ensure the latest permissions are applied.

When you log in as the test user for this user role, you will notice that the user has a different experience than an administrator. For example, the test user cannot see the Administration, Reports, or Data Warehouse workspaces (see Figure 15.11).

FIGURE 15.11   Workspace buttons seen by a user in the new Author user role.

Figure 15.12 shows what the visible workspaces look like for a user in this role.

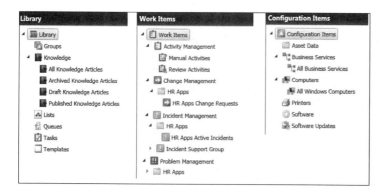

FIGURE 15.12   Workspace views seen by a user in the new Author user role.

REAL WORLD: SERVICE MANAGER 2010 AND VIEW SCOPING

Nodes in the tree such as Activity Management, Manual Activities, Review Activities, Incident Support Group, Business Services, Computers, Printers, Software, and Software Updates look like views but are in fact folders containing views. Each of these nodes in the tree does not have an expander next to it because there are no views contained in those folders that are visible to this test user. This is not the ideal user experience, because there is no action a user can take on those folder nodes in the tree, and the nodes just clutter up the user experience. Unfortunately, this is just the way Service Manager works in the 2010 version, but at least it is much better than showing all the folders and all the views.

If you will be creating many views and use user roles to scope the views, consider using a long list of views and few if any folders. The administrator's user experience will be terrible because the views will not be organized, but the other scoped users in the system will have a clutter-free experience without the useless folders appearing. There is one case where it is good to show the folders to a given user even if there are no views visible to the user in that folder—this is when the user is an author or administrator so the person can create new views in those folders.

The user can only see those views explicitly granted to him in the user role. Because the user role was not granted any CI views, only the folders will display. This could become an issue for people in this user role because it would be inconvenient to view the data. This oversight was intentional to illustrate the effect of not granting all the necessary views in all the workspaces. If you forget to add something like this, you can go back to the User Role properties dialog and add it. If you need to go back and edit the user role, though, you must sift through all of the templates, tasks, views, classes, queues, and groups. It is much more efficient to get it right using the MP filtering the first time through the wizard!

Data Warehouse and Reporting Security

The data warehouse and reporting platform used by Service Manager is designed as the long-term platform for all of System Center reporting. As such, it stands separate from Service Manager and simply uses Service Manager as a data source. The data warehouse will eventually consume data directly from other sources such as Operations Manager, Configuration Manager, and even user-defined data sources. Therefore, the data warehouse and reporting has its own security model and infrastructure. It is a combination of role-based security similar to what you find in Service Manager and the role-based security model of SRS. The data warehouse databases and workflow infrastructure are secured using the System Center common platform capabilities similar to Service Manager. The reports are secured using SRS. Differing from Operations Manager, Service Manager does not replace rights on the SRS.

Data Warehouse Administrators User Role

During setup of the data warehouse, the account or group specified during installation is placed into the Administrators role in the Data Warehouse management group. Here is the process used when determining whether a user is a data warehouse administrator and therefore should have visibility to the data warehouse workspace in the console:

1. The console connects to a Service Manager management group management server.

2. The console gets a global setting, which stores the name of the Data Warehouse management group management server name. Remember that any user can read the global settings.

3. The console attempts to connect to the Data Warehouse management group management server. The Data Warehouse workspace button is displayed if the user is in the Administrators user role in the Data Warehouse management group.

If necessary, you can manage the membership of the Data Warehouse management group Administrators user role from the User Roles view in the Data Warehouse workspace.

Granting Access to Reports

To get access to reports in the Service Manager main console, a user must be a member of the Report Users user role in the Data Warehouse management group. A data warehouse administrator can manage the membership of the Report Users user role from the User Roles view in the Data Warehouse workspace. The user also must be granted permissions in SRS to at least some of the reports under the System Center -> Service Manager folder.

Here are the conditions Service Manager uses to determine which reports to show to a user:

▶ Is the user in a Service Manager user role other than the End Users user role?

This determines whether the user can even open the Service Manager console.

▶ Is the Service Manager management group the console is connecting to associated with a data warehouse?

This determines whether the console should even attempt to display the Reports workspace.

▶ Is the user in the Report Users user role in the Data Warehouse management group?

This determines whether the console should show the Reports workspace and attempt to get the list of reports visible to the user from SRS.

▶ Does the user have permission to read any of the reports on the SRS instance associated with the data warehouse?

This list of reports/folders is what will be shown in the Service Manager console's Reports workspace.

Of course, users can access reports directly through the SRS browser interface, but they will still only be able to access those reports granted to them by the SRS administrator.

Here are some best practices for report security:

▶ SRS controls report security, not Service Manager. Just because somebody is not in the Report Users user role in Service Manager does not mean they cannot access the reports; they can always get around that by using the browser interface to SRS. The Report Users user role simply controls whether they can see the reports in the Service Manager console.

▶ Create a user group for each logical group of report users and grant these user groups access to the reports on SRS. Create a parent user group that contains all those user groups and put that in the Report Users user role and some other Service Manager user role so that they all will have access to use the reports through the Service Manager console. This enables you to manage just the membership of the child groups as people come and go. Ideally, you would use Forefront Identity Manager or similar software to delegate administration of these user groups to area owners.

▶ You cannot scope the data in the Service Manager data warehouse. Just because a user does not have permission to view some data in the Service Manager database doesn't mean that user cannot see it in the data warehouse. Do not give users scoped in Service Manager via user roles the access to run reports that are not scoped!

▶ You can create linked reports prescoped to some particular scope such as a queue or group and then grant users access to those linked reports only. For additional security, set up scheduled reports that are prescoped and deliver these to the user through email, SharePoint, or a file share (instead of allowing the user to run the reports on SQL SRS directly).

Advanced User Role Scenarios

Although not entirely obvious, there are ways to utilize user roles to fulfill commonly requested scenarios. These typically involve scoping access to SSP content. For example, it is common to want to display one set of announcements to one group of end users and show a different set of announcements to other end users. This could be because there are announcements pertinent only to a certain group of users because of location, the services they use, or their job function. Similarly, organizations often also want to filter the knowledge articles displayed on the portal or the list of software titles that can be requested based on the person's job role.

Scoping Knowledge Articles

Scoping knowledge articles is fairly easy to do using the existing data model for knowledge articles. Before starting, determine how to classify knowledge articles so that you can divide them into different groups of knowledge articles. You could use the Keywords field to enter special strings into, although that is somewhat error prone. A better choice is using the Category field. You can modify this list to contain options that make sense in your organization by going to the **Authoring workspace -> Lists -> Knowledge Article Category** and clicking **Properties** in the Tasks pane. Another option is to create your own custom field and customize the form to show it using the Service Manager Authoring Tool.

This example uses the Category field. The Category list (see Figure 15.13) has been modified to include just a few options that can be used to subdivide the knowledge base into articles based on the particular organization: Engineering, Finance, or Human Resources.

The next step is to create a series of groups that includes knowledge articles based on the Category being a certain value using dynamic membership rules. Create one group for each category. For example, you could create a group called Engineering Knowledge Articles, which would have criteria like that shown in Figure 15.14.

You will also need to create a group of all users in the database by creating a dynamic membership rule with the Domain User or Group class and no additional criteria. You could call it the All Users and Groups group.

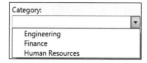

FIGURE 15.13   Knowledge form Category field after modification in the Lists view.

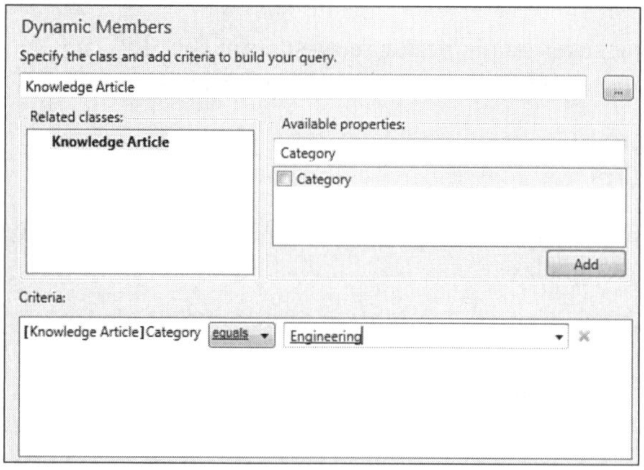

Dynamic Members

Specify the class and add criteria to build your query.

Knowledge Article

Related classes:

Knowledge Article

Available properties:

Category

☐ Category

[Add]

Criteria:

[Knowledge Article]Category [equals ▾] [Engineering   ▾] ✕

FIGURE 15.14   Creating the criteria for the Engineering knowledge article group.

Finally, modify and create the user roles as follows:

1. Remove the Authenticated Users user group from the End Users user role. This user group is placed in the End Users user role out of the box for convenience, but it also grants any member of that role to view all CIs, including knowledge articles.

2. Create a user group in Active Directory for each group of users in each organization: Engineering, Finance, or Human Resources.

3. Create a user role based on the Incident Resolver user role for each of the organizations. Do not grant the user role permission to any queues. Grant permission to the All Users and Groups group you just created and to the corresponding group of knowledge articles for each organization. For example, if you are creating the Engineering Incident Resolvers user role, grant permission to the Engineering Knowledge Articles group you created in this section. Add the Active Directory user group for the Engineering users.

4. Assuming you want end users to submit change requests from the portal, you need to create a user role based on the Change Initiator user role profile for each of the organizations. In this user role, don't grant any groups or queues.

Scoping Announcements

Scoping announcements is similar to scoping knowledge articles; the only difference is that there is not a good out-of-box field to categorize announcements by. You can add a new field based on the List data type to the Announcement class using the Authoring Tool. After importing the MP, you can add list values in the Lists view in the Authoring workspace. For example, you could add a new property called Organization with list items of Engineering, Finance, and Human Resources. Use the same pattern for creating groups and users roles to scope announcements as described in the "Scoping Knowledge Articles" section.

Scoping Software Packages

You can also scope the list of software packages available for request from the SSP. The approach is essentially the same as for announcements and knowledge articles, as follows:

1. Remove the Authenticated Users group from the End Users user role.

2. Create groups of software packages.

3. Follow the same approach as explained in the "Scoping Announcements" section by creating a new property on the Package class.

4. Create groups with dynamic membership rules. It might be more appropriate to select specific packages on the Included Members page of the wizard. Figure 15.15 shows selecting specific software packages to include in the group.

5. After creating the groups, you can assign them to the appropriate user roles.

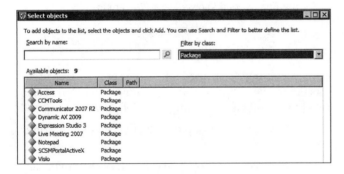

FIGURE 15.15   Selecting packages to include in a group.

When users log in to the SSP, they can select from only those software packages to which they have permission.

Run As Accounts

The concept of Run As Accounts has been carried over as part of the System Center common platform from Operations Manager. If you are familiar with Run As Accounts in Operations Manager, you have a head start on understanding them in Service Manager. With Run As Accounts, different workflows can run under the security context of specified user credentials.

Run As Account Usage Scenarios

Here are some scenarios where you can use Run As Accounts:

▶ System Run As Accounts are used to allow system workflows to access system resources such as the databases and local resources on the management servers. In some cases, system Run As Accounts are used to access resources outside of Service Manager.

▶ Run As Accounts can be specified when creating connectors to Operations Manager, Configuration Manager, or Active Directory. This enables the connectors to connect to those other systems as a user account that has the appropriate permissions required in those systems.

▶ You can create custom Run As Accounts to use when running your workflows. When the MPs containing the definition of those Run As Accounts are imported into the system, the administrator can specify the user account to use for that Run As Account.

▶ Similar to how organizations can create custom Run As Accounts, partners can declare Run As Accounts in their MPs. When the organization imports those MPs, the administrator can specify which user account to use for that partner's Run As Account.

System Run As Accounts

Two user accounts are specified to install Service Manager—the System account and the Workflow account:

▶ The account provided for the System account is used for the System Center Data Access Service and the System Center Management Configuration Windows services on the management server. It is also the account used for the Operational System Run As Account. This account is added to the local Administrators group on the management server. This account is effectively an administrator in Service Manager.

Any process that can run under this security context on the management server has complete control of Service Manager and the management server.

▶ The Workflow account is used only for the Workflow Run As Account. This account is added to the Workflows user role so that workflows running under this security context will have the permissions they need to query and update Service Manager.

The Workflow account is also used in the self-service software provisioning workflows. It is used to connect to the Configuration Manager database to put the requesting user's computer into the collection so the software can be distributed. In addition, the account is used in a workflow that queries Configuration Manager to see whether a requested software package has been delivered. Therefore, it needs to have the required level of permissions in Configuration Manager to query that information. This is separate from the permissions required by the Service Manager to Configuration Manager connector.

When new workflows are created using the Authoring Tool, they default to using the Operational System Run As Account for the `DataSourceModule` element, regardless of whether you use a `System.Scheduler` or a subscription data source module.

You can see this in the Extended Markup Language (XML). Here is what it will look like:

```
RunAs="SystemCenter!Microsoft.SystemCenter.DatabaseWriteActionAccount"
```

The MP alias `SystemCenter!` is for the `Microsoft.SystemCenter.Library` MP. Operational System Account is the display name for the `Microsoft.SystemCenter.DatabaseWriteActionAccount`.

The Operational System Run As Account is also used to submit the task that will actually execute the Windows Workflow Foundation workflow. All this should be essentially transparent to a workflow author because it just works!

A Windows Workflow Foundation workflow, command-line activity, VBScript, or PowerShell script module always executes under the security context of the Workflow Run As Account. In the XML, it looks like this:

```
RunAs="Core!Microsoft.SystemCenter.ServiceManager.WorkflowAccount"
```

The MP alias `Core!` is for the `ServiceManager.Core.Library` MP.

Therefore, if you are creating workflows in Service Manager using the Authoring Tool, you must consider three things given that the actual work will be done in the module of the workflow running as the Workflow Run As Account:

▶ Verify that the account has the permissions required to perform the actions you need in Service Manager itself. Out of the box, this account is added to the Workflows user role, which is based on the Workflows user role profile. Review the permissions granted to the Workflows user role profile in Table 15.2 to ensure the objects you want to query and update in Service Manager will be allowed to do so. If they are not allowed, add the account used for the Workflow Run As Account to the Administrators user role that has global access or to another user role that has the required permissions.

▶ If your workflow will be accessing resources locally on the management server (such as the Registry or event log), grant the account used for the Workflow Run As Account the local permissions required on the management server.

▶ If your workflow will be accessing resources on some other system such as querying another database or running PowerShell against Active Directory, verify that the Workflow Run As Account has the permissions required on those external systems.

Creating and Using Custom Run As Accounts

Sometimes it might not be feasible or appropriate to use the Workflow account to access remote resources (for instance, with domain trust issues or where a given user account is not allowed to access multiple secured resources because of separation-of-authority policies in an organization). In these cases, you can use a custom Run As Account.

To do this, first define a `SecureReference` element (also known as a Run As Profile in the Service Manager console) in your MP XML. Here is what the XML looks like:

```
<TypeDefinitions>
  <SecureReferences>
    <Secure Reference ID="MyRunAsAccount" Accessibility="Public"
➥Context="System!System.Entity"/>
  </SecureReferences>
</TypeDefinitions>
```

The `TypeDefinitions` section needs to appear immediately after the `Manifest` section:

▶ If you have an `EntityTypes` section inside the `TypeDefinitions` element, put the `<SecureReferences>` section immediately after the `EntityTypes` section.

▶ If you have a `ModuleTypes` section inside of `TypeDefinitions`, you need to place the `<SecureReferences>` section just before `ModuleTypes`.

The `System!` MP reference points to the `System.Library` MP. Make sure you also include a `DisplayString` in the appropriate `LanguagePack` section in the MP XML like this:

```
<DisplayString ElementID="MyRunAsAccount">
  <Name>My Run As Account</Name>
</DisplayString>
```

With a new Secure Reference defined, you now need to tell Service Manager to use that new Secure Reference. The following example shows how to tell Service Manager to use this new Secure Reference rather than the Workflow Run As Account. When you create a workflow in the Authoring Tool that uses a PowerShell script activity, behind the scenes the Authoring Tool creates a new `WriteActionModuleType` element in the MP XML. It looks something like this:

```
<WriteActionModuleType
ID="GetProcessUserWF.WindowsPowerShellScript.93c334f5_92cb_4b2f_b0dc_7ae92d344d31.MT"
Accessibility="Public"
RunAs="Core!Microsoft.SystemCenter.ServiceManager.WorkflowAccount"
➥Batching="false">
```

Change the `RunAs` attribute to use your new `SecureReference` ID:

```
<WriteActionModuleType
ID="GetProcessUserWF.WindowsPowerShellScript.93c334f5_92cb_4b2f_b0dc_7ae92d344d31.MT"
Accessibility="Public" RunAs="MyRunAsAccount" Batching="false">
```

15

Last, add a `Category` element that points to the `VisibleToUser` value in the `System.Library` MP:

```
<Category ID="MyRunAsAccountVisibleToUser" Target="MyRunAsAccount"
Value="System!VisibleToUser"/>
```

This ensures the Run As Account will be visible in the Run As Accounts view in the console so that you can set the actual credentials that will be used for this Run As Account.

After importing this MP into Service Manager, you need to initialize the credentials to use for this Run As Account. Unfortunately, the UI does not let you do this in the Run As Accounts view; you can use a special cmdlet called `Set-SCSMRunAsAccount` provided in the SMlets CodePlex project (http://smlets.codeplex.com). Set the credentials by running these two commands:

```
$cred = Get-Credential
Get-SCSMRunAsAccount -Name "My Run As Account" ¦ Set-SCSMRunAsAccount $cred
```

The `Get-Credential` cmdlet pops up a dialog box where you can securely enter the credentials; they are stored securely in the `$cred` variable in memory. The display name of the Run As Account should be passed to the `-Name` parameter of the `Get-SCSMRunAsAccount`. Don't forget that if the display name contains spaces, you must enclose the display name in quotes so the command-line parser doesn't get confused. The `Set-SCSMRunAsAccount` cmdlet securely stores the credentials in the Service Manager database and does all the magic required to make that Run As Account be effective in the system. From this point on, you can manage your custom Run As Account like any other Run As Account in the system.

Changing Run As Account Credentials

After a Run As Account has been created, you can manage it from the Administration workspace in the Security -> Run As Accounts view. There you can change the username and password for any Run As Account. As a security best practice, most organizations have a password expiration policy. Don't forget to update the password for Run As Accounts when the passwords expire and are changed!

Here are several special considerations for changing the Workflow and Operational System Run As Accounts:

▶ If you change the Workflow Run As Account, make sure that the new account you are using is added to the Workflows user role. You also need to verify the return email address for the account that is used to send emails from Service Manager is the same as the Workflow Account.

▶ If you change the Operational System Run As Account, you should also change the System Center Data Access Service and System Center Management Configuration Windows services to use the new account on each management server.

You also need to put that account in the sdk_users and configsvc_users database roles on the ServiceManager database.

Security Best Practices

This part of the chapter describes some security best practices that go beyond what is in the product documentation. These are intended to help you avoid common configuration mistakes that can leave you open for attack or data loss, or at least help you trace who did something.

Securing the Encryption Key and Passwords

Sensitive data such as Run As Account passwords are encrypted in the ServiceManager database (or DWStagingAndConfig database for the data warehouse management server) and transmitted between the database server and the management server in encrypted form using a symmetric key encryption scheme. The symmetric encryption key is generated the first time a management group (either Service Manager or data warehouse) is created by installing the first management server and a database. The first management server gets a copy of the symmetric encryption key, which is encrypted using a private encryption key for that management server.

Each time an additional management server or portal server is installed, it gets a copy of the symmetric encryption key for the management group. This copy of the symmetric encryption key is encrypted using a private encryption key generated for each management server or portal server.

Thus, there is a symmetric key for the entire management group, used to actually encrypt all the passwords, and a private key for each management server or portal server to encrypt the symmetric key for that server.

The account passwords provided during setup and any other Run As Account passwords later created are all encrypted using this same symmetric encryption key. Using that symmetric encryption key, the System Center Management service can decrypt the passwords at the appropriate time when running workflows so they can be used to log in to the local or to remote systems. The System Center Data Access Service can use the symmetric encryption key to encrypt the password when new Run As Accounts are created. The passwords are never passed on the wire in clear text, and only an administrator of the management server has access to the private encryption key and thus the symmetric encryption key.

If you need to reinstall a management server on the same server it was installed on previously, you need to first restore the symmetric encryption key by providing a backup of the private encryption key, as described in the product documentation in the disaster recovery guide (http://technet.microsoft.com/en-us/library/ff625768.aspx). If you have just one management server and it goes bad for any reason, and you do not have the private encryption key backup, the entire management group will be lost and you will need to reinstall the entire product.

Here are best practices for securing the private encryption key:

▶ Back up the private encryption key immediately after installing each management server and portal server in each management group (including the Data Warehouse management group). Setup recommends to do this immediately after setup is complete. Keep in mind that each management server or portal server has its own private encryption key, which must be backed up.

▶ Store the private encryption key backup file in a secure place with redundancy.

▶ Store the password to the private encryption key file in a secure location with redundancy, ideally in a separate place from the encryption key backup file. Because there is no way to recover the password, be very careful how you store it, so that you can retrieve it if necessary. Multiple people should know the password or have access to the password in the event people leave the organization, forget, and so on.

▶ Anyone who is a local administrator on a management server or portal server has access to the private encryption key and thus the symmetric encryption. If a person knows what he is doing, that person could retrieve any Run As Account passwords. Ensure only those individuals who would already have access to those passwords are allowed to be local administrators on these servers.

▶ Ideally, have more than one management server in a management group. Then, should the management server fail and you forget the password or lose the backup of the encryption key, you can install a new management server and get the encryption key from the secondary management server.

▶ If you forgot to back up your private encryption keys when you first installed the product, forgot the password, or misplaced the backup file, you can back them up at any time by running the encryption backup tool. Instructions are provided in the disaster recovery guide at http://technet.microsoft.com/en-us/library/ff631128.aspx.

Securing Database Access

All data, with the exception of the Run As Account passwords, is stored in plain text in the databases. This makes it important to minimize any direct access to the databases. You should scrutinize all users with the exception of Service Manager administrators to determine whether they need access to the databases.

During setup, the System Center Data Access Service and Management Configuration service accounts are granted appropriate permissions on the databases automatically. All access by non-Service Manager administrators should go through the Data Access Service. Workflows should never directly access the database either and should always go through the Data Access Service, which is secured by role-based security.

As a best practice, configure the Operational System Account to have a different account than the account used for the Workflow Account. Doing so ensures that even if a rogue workflow were to be executed in the system, it would not have full permissions over the Service Manager database.

Enabling Auditing

Service Manager out of the box stores a history of every new object created, every property value change, and every relationship add and removal. This history is visible on the forms on the History tab. For most organizations, this is an adequate trail of activity for auditing purposes. However, here are cases this does not cover:

▶ Conceivably, someone with access to the Service Manager databases such as a Service Manager administrator could delete the history records, thus covering his tracks.

▶ History keeps track of data changes only for objects. History is not maintained for other changes in the database, such as configuration settings, user roles, Run As Accounts, notification settings, or anything that goes into MPs, such as templates, views, or enumeration values.

▶ History is groomed periodically. Unless the data is configured to be archived in the data warehouse, history changes are deleted when they reach their expiration time.

If a more comprehensive and detailed audit trail is required, you can enable auditing on the System Center Data Access Service. When auditing is enabled, the System Center Data Access Service logs an event to the Windows Security event log for each operation called on the System Center Data Access Service. It will log who performed the action and which method was called at what time. You can aggregate and analyze these event logs using System Center Operations Manager Audit Collection Service (ACS).

To enable auditing on the System Center Data Acxcess Service on each management server, follow these steps:

1. On the Start menu, open **Administrative Tools** and select **Local Security Policy**.

2. In the Local Security Policy window, expand **Local Policies** and select **Audit Policy**.

3. Open **Audit Object Access** from the list and select **Success/Failure** depending on what you want to log in the event log. Click **OK**.

Once you enable auditing, the System Center Data Access Service starts logging events in the Security event log from the source MOMSDK Service Security. This source name is a residual effect of evolving the Microsoft Operations Manager (MOM) infrastructure to be the System Center common infrastructure platform that underlies Service Manager today. (The old name of the System Center Data Access Service was the SDK Service.)

Summary

The security model for Service Manager is flexible enough to meet the requirements of the most demanding organizations. It is also simple enough for those "configure and go" organizations with more basic requirements. Following the best practices outlined in this chapter will enable your organization to securely operate Service Manager and provide a user experience tailored to each person's role.

PART V

Beyond Service Manager

IN THIS PART

CHAPTER 16

Planning Your Customization

By now you have installed Service Manager 2010 (SvcMgr) and are familiar with the out-of-the-box functionality the product provides. This chapter discusses areas and strategies for customizing Service Manager, enabling you to increase the product's value for your organization.

Microsoft has invested considerable resources in making Service Manager easy to customize. While similar products often require a hard-to-find specialist familiar with that particular product, Service Manager provides tools you can use to perform typical customizations. For those advanced customizations requiring development resources, Service Manager offers an accessible platform built on known frameworks and technologies, making the product easy to work with for a wide range of developers.

Using the modular platform introduced by Operations Manager (OpsMgr) and further expanded by Service Manager, the product is customizable in every area (from the data layer through workflows to the presentation layer). This can require varying types of knowledge, depending on the area of the product under consideration. For example, when you are customizing the presentation layer in the Service Manager console, it is useful to know the basic concepts of Windows Presentation Foundation and its data-binding feature, and familiarity with PowerShell scripting makes it easy to provide console users with useful tools in the form of console tasks.

Before beginning to customize Service Manager, there are several areas of consideration. This chapter

▶ Describes those areas of the product that are customizable

▶ Highlights important questions to address before starting

▶ Increases your understanding of the knowledge required to customize the product in different ways

▶ Provides a basic understanding of some of the technologies that are core components in Service Manager

What You Can Customize

Service Manager incorporates the next generation of the common System Center architecture based on the OpsMgr platform. Similar to Operations Manager, Service Manager utilizes the concept of MPs (management packs) to give the product a roadmap of how it is to operate. Using MPs makes this architecture so modular that nearly everything in the product is customizable! This section discusses some of the different areas and examples of customizations.

Here are things you can customize from the console:

▶ The navigation structure, by creating folders

▶ Views

▶ Customizing existing views by adding or removing columns

▶ Groups

▶ Queues

▶ Console tasks

▶ Templates

▶ Notification templates

▶ Subscriptions

▶ Incident event workflows

▶ Problem event workflows

▶ Change event workflows

▶ Activity event workflows

▶ Lists

▶ User roles

▶ Run As Accounts

Figure 16.1 provides an example of the flexibility of the console presentation layer. The figure shows a custom view created using a Windows Presentation Foundation (WPF) browser control. The view is placed in a custom folder in the Navigation pane and the folder located in a custom workspace in the Service Manager console.

FIGURE 16.1   Service Manager console, custom view containing a web browser control.

NOTE: LEARN MORE ABOUT CUSTOMIZING THE CONSOLE

Chapter 17, "Management Packs," and Chapter 18, "Customizing Service Manager," discuss how to create your own workspaces and custom views.

Here are items you can customize in the Self-Service portal (SSP):

▶ Contact information for the Information Technology (IT) department

▶ Add/remove some of the action buttons on the first page (Request software, Reset password)

▶ Branding/logos

▶ Reuse the web parts on a SharePoint site

Figure 16.2 shows customized IT contact information. You can easily modify the information through the Service Manager console using the Administration workspace.

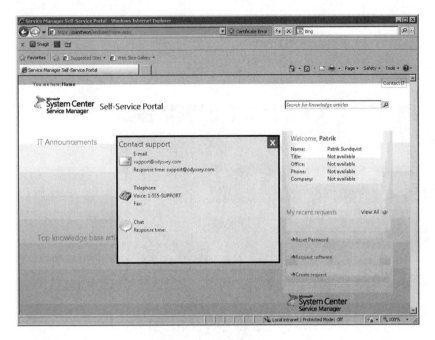

FIGURE 16.2   Customized SSP.

Using the Service Manager Authoring Tool, here are areas where you can further customize the product:

▶ Data models (Create new/Modify existing)

▶ Forms (Customize existing/Create new)

▶ Workflows

Figure 16.3 shows a custom workflow created with the Service Manager Authoring Tool. Chapter 18 discusses using the Service Manager Authoring Tool.

You can add additional customizations using the Software Development Kit (SDK) to develop custom components for Service Manager. Here are some examples of what you can customize:

▶ Advanced custom forms

▶ Custom connectors

▶ View types

▶ Workflow activities (extending the library provided out of the box)

▶ Advanced workflows

Because the Service Manager reporting infrastructure utilizes SQL Reporting Services (SRS), it is easy to deploy new reports.

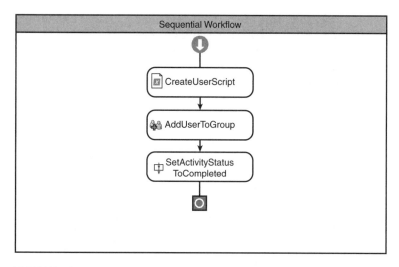

FIGURE 16.3   Custom workflow in the Authoring Tool.

Management Packs

MPs are eXtensible Markup Language (XML) files containing definitions that define not only data models but also objects such as views for the Service Manager console, work-flows, groups, queues, tasks, connectors, and so on. Chapter 17 discusses MP schema details, which are useful to know when customizing Service Manager. This section describes some general information regarding MPs that you need to consider before customizing

Consider MP structure when planning for customization; this being the relationship between and organization of MPs and resources within them. The most important areas to consider involve whether to seal MPs and which resources to place in each MP. Sealing an MP enables resources such as class types in the sealed MPs to be referenced in other MPs (sealed or unsealed). Here are examples of referencing scenarios:

▶ Extending an existing class type, this refers to using the existing class type as the base class for the new class type

▶ Customizing an existing form

▶ Defining a new relationship between an existing and a new class type

All these scenarios most often involve referencing resources in existing MPs. To be able to reference a resource in a different MP, the MP holding the referenced resource must be sealed.

TIP: MORE ABOUT MANAGEMENT PACKS

More information about MPs, including how to reference resources and how to seal MPs, is in Chapter 17 and Chapter 18.

An MP is sealed using a strong name key. This strong name key is a file created using the sn.exe tool. Similar to a certificate, a strong name key is unique and the individual sealing the MP should not distribute the key. The rationale behind sealing an MP is that the strong name key guarantees the integrity of the MP; only the owner of the key can change future versions of that MP. Sealing an MP gives the author control of the content within the MP and prevents others than the key holders from customizing it without breaking the identity of the MP. This enables the owner of the key to ensure consistency of the MP.

An example of when it is useful to use sealed MPs is when storing class types. Having a class type stored in a sealed MP means the class type definition (behavior, properties, and relationships) is owned by whoever controls the strong name key. This means the party sealing the MP can rely on the definition of the class type in all situations.

NOTE: SEALING ENABLES THE MP TO BE REFERENCED

As mentioned in this section, sealing an MP also enables other MPs to reference its resources. For example, you can add new properties in a third-party MP by using the concept of class extensions. Effectively, this makes it possible to protect resources (by sealing the MP holding them) without removing the capability of customizing them.

As part of the planning process, determine which resources to store in sealed MPs. Here are some questions and considerations for planning where to place resources:

▶ To what degree do you want to allow other parties to customize the resource?

▶ Do you need to be able to reference this resource in other MPs?

▶ How do you want to group functionality from a test and release management perspective?

TIP: MORE ON DEPLOYING CUSTOMIZATIONS

Chapter 17 describes strategies and considerations regarding deploying customizations (in form of MPs and related resources). The chapter also discusses how MPs are sealed, how they are used in the platform, what they can contain, and what is important to consider when working with them.

In a scenario where a vendor creates a boxed solution for multiple customers, here is an approach for organizing resources:

▶ Those resources important for core functionality of the delivered solution are stored within sealed MPs.

▶ Deliver those resources the customer should be able to modify to a high degree (for example, notification templates) in unsealed MPs.

Here are some general recommendations and best practices:

▶ Group related/similar customizations into MPs.

▶ Group related MPs using a naming standard. For example, when you have related customizations in both sealed and unsealed MPs, name those MPs using common naming conventions and elements to make them easy to identify. Figure 16.4 shows how Microsoft uses this concept to group functionality.

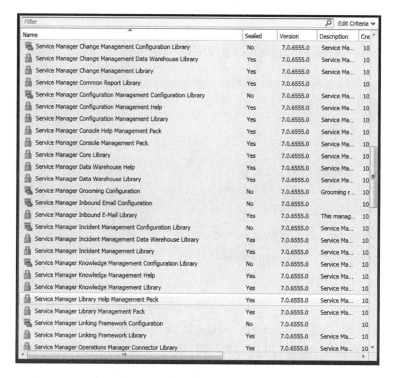

Name	Sealed	Version	Description	Cre
Service Manager Change Management Configuration Library	No	7.0.6555.0	Service Ma...	10
Service Manager Change Management Data Warehouse Library	Yes	7.0.6555.0	Service Ma...	10
Service Manager Change Management Library	Yes	7.0.6555.0	Service Ma...	10
Service Manager Common Report Library	Yes	7.0.6555.0		10
Service Manager Configuration Management Configuration Library	No	7.0.6555.0	Service Ma...	10
Service Manager Configuration Management Help	Yes	7.0.6555.0	Service Ma...	10
Service Manager Configuration Management Library	Yes	7.0.6555.0	Service Ma...	10
Service Manager Console Help Management Pack	Yes	7.0.6555.0	Service Ma...	10
Service Manager Console Management Pack	Yes	7.0.6555.0	Service Ma...	10
Service Manager Core Library	Yes	7.0.6555.0	Service Ma...	10
Service Manager Data Warehouse Help	Yes	7.0.6555.0	Service Ma...	10
Service Manager Data Warehouse Library	Yes	7.0.6555.0	Service Ma...	10
Service Manager Grooming Configuration	No	7.0.6555.0	Grooming r...	10
Service Manager Inbound Email Configuration	No	7.0.6555.0		10
Service Manager Inbound E-Mail Library	Yes	7.0.6555.0	This manag...	10
Service Manager Incident Management Configuration Library	No	7.0.6555.0	Service Ma...	10
Service Manager Incident Management Data Warehouse Library	Yes	7.0.6555.0	Service Ma...	10
Service Manager Incident Management Library	Yes	7.0.6555.0	Service Ma...	10
Service Manager Knowledge Management Configuration Library	No	7.0.6555.0	Service Ma...	10
Service Manager Knowledge Management Help	Yes	7.0.6555.0	Service Ma...	10
Service Manager Knowledge Management Library	Yes	7.0.6555.0	Service Ma...	10
Service Manager Library Help Management Pack	Yes	7.0.6555.0	Service Ma...	10
Service Manager Library Management Pack	Yes	7.0.6555.0	Service Ma...	10
Service Manager Linking Framework Configuration	No	7.0.6555.0		10
Service Manager Linking Framework Library	Yes	7.0.6555.0	Service Ma...	10
Service Manager Operations Manager Connector Library	Yes	7.0.6555.0	Service Ma...	10

FIGURE 16.4   Example of grouping MP functionality by name.

▶ To separate MPs from each other (and as shown in Figure 16.4), Microsoft often uses the Library suffix for sealed MPs, Configuration Library for unsealed MPs, and Data Warehouse Library for data warehouse resources.

▶ Store all model-related customizations in sealed MPs

Data Modeling

You can customize the SvcMgr configuration management database (CMDB) by extending existing data models or creating new models. This section highlights some important areas of the Service Manager modular database (the CMDB) and discusses how it can be customized, providing a complete picture of what is possible and required resources.

Chapter 4, "Looking Inside Service Manager," gives a basic introduction, and this discussion presents a deeper understanding of the modeling capabilities of the Service Manager CMDB.

For an object to be tracked in the CMDB, it must be described in a data model. A Service Manager data model consists of class types and relationships between these class types. The core part of the model and its properties is described using one or more class types that together describe the characteristics of the object.

Class Types

A *class type* in Service Manager is the description of an object type containing definitions of the different properties needed to describe objects of such type, excluding how such an object type relates to objects of other types. Table 16.1 lists examples of properties and their values.

TABLE 16.1   Class Type Properties: Examples

Name	Value
ID	IR101
Title	Printing problem
Description	User cannot print on local printer
Classification	Printing Problems - Local Printer
CreateDate	2011-01-04 20:00:00

Each property is defined using a set of parameters, such as Data Type, MinLength, MaxLength, and so on, ensuring the quality of the data stored in that property. You can use these parameters to mark a property as Required, meaning an object based on the class type containing the property cannot be saved to the CMDB without including a value set for the required property. You can also give the property a MaximumLength, to control the length of a string value stored in that property.

TIP: MORE ON DATA MODELS

Chapter 18 discusses how to put constraints on your data model and provides step-by-step instructions on how to create a new class type.

When defining the class types for a data model, all properties common to other types of objects are consolidated to separate those class types that can be re-used by other class types, using the concept of deriving classes.

A *derived class type* inherits all properties and relationships defined for its parent class type. Since almost all class types have properties or other definitions that are common to other class types, the first consideration when creating a new class type in Service Manager is which class type should be the new class type's *base class*. Figure 16.5 shows a simplified class type hierarchy example from Service Manager. (Additional class types are involved besides those illustrated in Figure 16.5.)

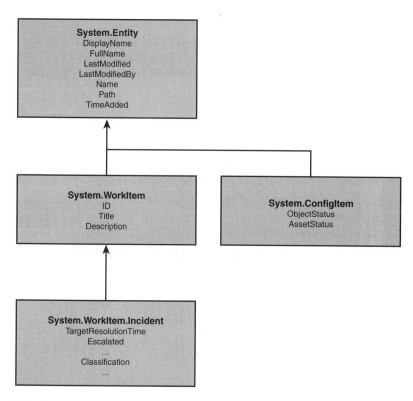

FIGURE 16.5   Class type hierarchy from Service Manager (simplified).

The diagram shows how the most common properties are defined by the class type System.Entity. Deriving from that class type is the System.ConfigItem and System. WorkItem, which inherit all properties and relationships defined by the System.Entity. At the bottom of the diagram is the class type System.WorkItem.Incident, which inherits all properties from System.Entity and System.WorkItem. Therefore, it is often said that the further down the hierarchy a class type is described, the more specialized is the type. This makes System.WorkItem.Incident a specialized version of System.WorkItem. Figure 16.5 displays this concept.

A class type in Service Manager can have different characteristics, based on how it is defined. Chapter 17 discusses defining a class type and available characteristics.

Relationships

After defining the required class types to describe the core part of the data model, the next task is to define how the class types relate to other class types. A data model is seldom complete without defining these relationships, which can, for example, document who is the owner of the object.

When defining a *relationship*, you must specify a source and a target class type. You must also specify the cardinality of the source and target, as this restricts how many instances of the two different class types can relate to each other. Cardinality is described using a minimum and maximum value for both the source and the target. By combining these in different ways, the relationship restricts how many instances of the class types can relate to each other.

Cardinality Example

Listing 16.1 contains the definition of the relationship called Affected User, which has the source class type work item (the base class type of class types such as an incident) and target class type user. This is the relationship used to show the affected user in the Incident form in the Service Manager console, as shown in Figure 16.6.

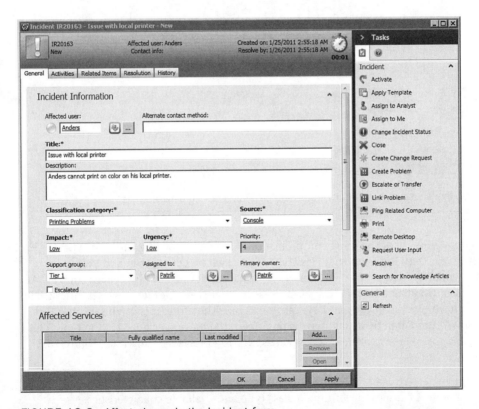

FIGURE 16.6   Affected user in the Incident form.

LISTING 16.1   Definition of Affected User Relationship

```
<RelationshipType ID="System.WorkItemAffectedUser" Accessibility="Public"
Abstract="false" Base="System!System.Reference">
    <Source ID="IsCreatedForUser" MinCardinality="0" MaxCardinality="2147483647"
    Type="System.WorkItem" />
    <Target ID="RequestedWorkItem" MinCardinality="0" MaxCardinality="1"
    Type="System!System.User" />
</RelationshipType>
```

> **NOTE: MEANING OF NUMBERS GREATER THAN 1**
>
> For Service Manager 2010, numbers larger than 1 in a cardinality statement are evaluated as "unlimited" when an MP is imported into Service Manager. This means that `MaxCardenality="2"` is the same as `MaxCardenality="2147483647"`. This constraint may be evaluated more strongly by the system in the future though, so be careful what you specify here.

In the Affected User relationship definition (Listing 16.1), the cardinality establishes several rules for the CMDB:

▶ `<Source ID="IsCreatedForUser" MinCardinality="0"`
`MaxCardinality="2147483647" Type="System.WorkItem" />`

From a user perspective, for a specific user, there can be zero or more work items where the user is the affected user.

▶ `<Target ID="RequestedWorkItem" MinCardinality="0" MaxCardinality="1"`
`Type="System!System.User" />`

From a work item perspective, for a specific work item, there can exist zero or one affected users.

Relationship Types

Service Manager has four core definitions of relationship types. You can use these types to define new relationships by using one of the four as a base when defining new relationships. Each type has its own characteristics, which affect the functionality and behavior inside the tool. It is important to know the differences of each type when planning for a new data model, as the different types can affect things such as how permissions are inherited between objects. Here are the four relationship types:

▶ **Reference:** The simplest type of relationship is the Reference relationship type. It is as simple as a pointer between two objects in the CMDB. The source and target receives no special dependency between each other by being part of this type of relationship. Deleting one of the objects (source or target) will remove the association/reference between these two objects, nothing more and nothing less.

16

Type behavior: The source and target of the relationship can be any class type defined.

Here's an example: An affected user in an incident is related to the incident using the relationship `System.WorkItemAffectedUser` (also known as Affected User), which is based on the `System.Reference` (also known as Reference) membership type.

▶ **Containment:** The Containment relationship type has the Reference relationship as base, meaning it inherits all the characteristics from that type. The Containment relationship introduces one new behavior that separates the Containment type from the Reference type.

Type behavior: The source and target of the relationship can be any class type defined.

If a user has permissions to manage the source (or container) object, the user automatically receives permissions to manage the target (or contained) object. In other words, permissions are cloned from the source to the target from a user perspective.

For example, if a user has permissions to edit a change request, he has permission to edit the contained activities.

▶ **Membership:** The Membership relationship type has the Containment relationship as base and thereby inherits all behaviors from the Containment and Reference type. The Membership relationship introduces one new behavior that separates the Membership type from the Containment type.

Type behavior: The source and target of the relationship can be any class type defined.

If a user has permissions to manage the source, the user automatically receives permissions to manage the target. In other words, permissions are cloned from source to target from a user perspective.

The target in the relationship has a dependency to the source of the relationship, if the source (or container) object is deleted the target (or contained) object will automatically be deleted, as well.

Here's an example: A file attachment is related to a configuration item (CI) or work item using relationships that uses `System.Membership` (also known as Membership) as the base and thereby inherits the characteristics of the Membership relationship type. When the configuration item is deleted, the file attachment is also deleted.

▶ **Hosting:** The Hosting relationship type has the Membership relationship as its base and thereby inherits all behaviors from the Containment, Reference, and Membership type. The Hosting relationship introduces three new behaviors that separate the Hosting type from the Membership type.

Type behavior: The source and target of the relationship can be any class type defined.

If a user has permissions to manage the source, the user automatically receives permissions to manage the target. In other words, permissions are cloned from source to target from a user perspective.

The target in the relationship has a dependency to the source of the relationship, if the source is deleted the target is automatically deleted, as well.

The target class type needs to be defined as hosted. This means that the target object cannot exist without a host object.

Hosted instances shares identity with the host, this means that there can be two hosted instances with the same key as long as they aren't hosted by the same host. In other words, uniqueness is only required within the host.

The target object in the relationship can only be related to one host source object using a hosting relationship type. The target object can be contained by other non-hosting relationship types.

For example, a `Microsoft.Windows.Computer` (represents a logical computer) is hosted by a `Microsoft.SystemCenter.ConfigurationManager.DeployedComputer` (represents the physical computer) through the relationship `LogicalComputerOn PhysicalComputer`. The `LogicalComputerOnPhysicalComputer` uses the `System. Hosting` base class, which means it inherits all the characteristics from the `System.Hosting` relationship class type.

Chapter 17 includes additional information describing relationship definitions regarding inheritance models.

Type Projections

Type projections, also known as *combination classes*, are commonly compared to database views because of their ability to combine data from several related objects and display this information as one object to the viewer. In this way, type projections are just like database views, but the big difference is that they are hierarchy aware.

A type projection object is defined using a type (a class type) and components (relationships where the type is either source or target). Within each included component, there can be other components; this lets the type projection expose data coming from objects related to related objects (nested objects). Listing 16.2 shows parts of the type projection `System.WorkItem.ChangeRequestProjection` that is defined in the `ServiceManager.ChangeManagement.Library` MP. The definition contains an example of nested components where it first includes the component `Activity` (relationship `System.WorkItemContainsActivity`) and within that component, includes components such as `ActivityAssignedTo` (relationship `System.WorkItemAssignedToUser`).

LISTING 16.2   Extract of `System.WorkItem.ChangeRequestProjection`

```
<TypeProjection ID="System.WorkItem.ChangeRequestProjection" Accessibility="Public"
Type="CoreChange!System.WorkItem.ChangeRequest">
<Component
Path="$Target/Path[Relationship='CoreActivity!System.WorkItemContainsActivity']$"
Alias="Activity">
    <Component
Path="$Target/Path[Relationship='CoreActivity!System.WorkItemContainsActivity'
    SeedRole='Target']$" Alias="ParentWorkItem" />
```

```
    <Component
Path="$Target/Path[Relationship='WorkItem!System.WorkItemCreatedByUser']$"
    Alias="ActivityCreatedBy" />
    <Component
    Path="$Target/Path[Relationship='WorkItem!System.WorkItemAssignedToUser']$"
    Alias="ActivityAssignedTo" />

    ...
</Component>
...
</TypeProjection>
```

One purpose of type projections is to provide a way for the user interface (the Service Manager console) to display data from related objects using a form. For example, the Incident form (target at a type projection) shows both data from the incident and the affected user. Type projections are also used to enable doing complex queries against the CMDB, which involves search criteria on related objects (all incidents with an affected user in department X).

Type projections are used in several places in Service Manager, one example of this is views. The next section, "Presenting Data," includes additional examples, and discusses why the view needs to target a type projection instead of a simple class.

When defining a new view in the Service Manager console (discussed in detail in Chapter 18), it is common to use type projections to enable showing data from related objects directly in the view and/or be able to define a search criteria based on a related item. For example, if you are creating a view for All Incidents with an affected user belonging to the HR Department, the view needs to target a type projection, which in its turn has the type of System.WorkItem.Incidents. The type projection needs to include the Affected User relationship (as a component).

The My Incidents view shown in Figure 16.7 is an example of a view that makes use of targeting a type projection to show data of related objects. As shown in the figure, the view shows the name of the affected user. This would not be possible if the view were not targeting a type projection. Most views do make use of targeting a type projection.

Presenting Data

Service Manager provides several channels to present data from the CMDB when interacting with the product. Table 16.2 lists these channels. When planning for customization, consider whether there is a need for custom implementations, such as a new view, to present model customizations. This will help to allocate the correct resources to create the customizations. The next sections describe some underlying techniques used for the different channels and the knowledge required to create custom implementations of them.

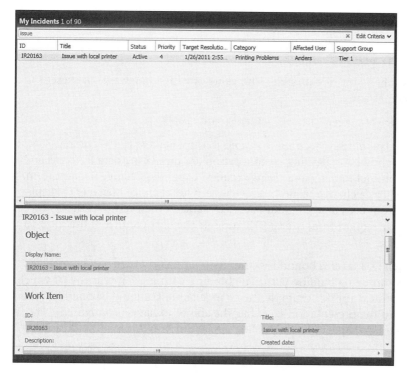

FIGURE 16.7   Type projections used in views.

TABLE 16.2   Presentation Channels

Channel	Description
Views	Shows data in table form where each row is supported by a type projection or a single configuration or work item
Forms	Shows data based on a type projection or a single configuration or work item
Reports	Shows data based on SQL queries
Web	Shows data based on custom queries and presentation based ASP.NET

Data Binding

To understand some of the underlying requirements for presenting data in Service Manager, you must understand the concept of *data binding*. The Service Manager console is built using a technology known as Windows Presentation Foundation. WPF uses data binding to display data in controls (text boxes, labels, data grids, and so on). Here are two terms to understand to explain data binding:

▶ **Data context:** An object that contains a data object that will be presented in a user interface (UI) or part of a UI.

Example in Service Manager: an incident.

▶ **Binding path:** The name of a property, the value of which one wants to present in a UI control such as a text box.

Example in Service Manager: Title of Incident (path=Title).

In Service Manager, a data-binding technique is used to display most of the content. The scenarios most important when planning customization are presenting data in forms and views. For example, consider looking at a change request using the Change Request form. When a user double-clicks a change request in a view, this tells Service Manager to display a form showing data from the change request. Service Manager then retrieves the object representing the change request from the CMDB and sets the data context of the form to the retrieved object.

The way a control such as a label is bound together with a property such as a change request description is through a binding path. The binding path is what tells the UI which property of the data context (in this example the change request) should be bound to the control. Each control in the presentation layer has the ability to have a configured binding path. Here is an example of how to define a data binding in a WPF application:

```
<TextBox Name="bodyText"
         Text="{Binding Path=Description}" />
```

This example could come from the Change Request form in the Service Manager console. The text box in the example would then show the description of the change request to which the form is currently bound.

TIP: MORE ON WPF DATA BINDING

Here are a couple of articles on WPF data binding to help you learn more about Windows Presentation Foundation:

▶ Windows Presentation Foundation Data Binding: Part 1, at http://msdn. microsoft.com/en-us/library/aa480224.aspx

▶ Windows Presentation Foundation Data Binding: Part 2, at http://msdn. microsoft.com/en-us/library/aa480226.aspx

---

Views

Views use the data binding technique described in the previous section. When selecting a view in the Service Manager console, the query configured for the specific view is executed against the Service Manager CMDB. When the result is presented in the view, each row in the table has a data context of the target type (type projection or class type). This means that if the view is configured to target type projections, each row represents an object of the projection targeted type wrapped in the given type projection. An example of this is the All Change Request view displayed in Figure 16.8. The view targets the type projection called `System.WorkItem.ChangeRequestViewProjection`, which has the seed class `System.WorkItem.ChangeRequest`. This means that each row has a data context of a change request wrapped in a type projection that includes other objects such as Assigned User, and so on. This makes it possible to display data not only for the change request but also data as the Display Name of the Assigned User.

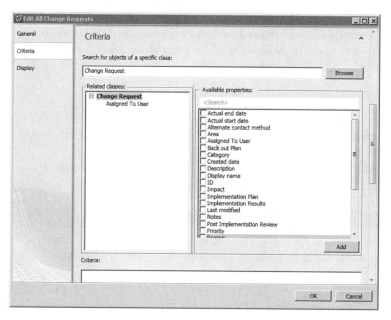

FIGURE 16.8   View configuration.

To show data of a related object, the binding path of the control (in this case the column of the view) must contain the full path to the property containing the value to be shown. The path to a related object is built up using the component alias from the targeted type projection. In the example just described, the column binding path can be seen in the `DisplayMemberBinding` attribute in Listing 16.3.

LISTING 16.3   All Change Requests: Assigned to User Display Name

```
<mux:Column Name="aDisplayName" DisplayMemberBinding="{Binding
Path=AssignedTo.DisplayName}" Width="200" DisplayName="Header_Owner"

Property="AssignedTo.DisplayName" DataType="s:String" />
```

Note that the binding path syntax is `<ComponentAlias>.<PropertyName>`. This means the type projection the view is targeting must have the Assigned User component (with the Alias `AssignedTo`); otherwise, the data would not be available for presentation in the view.

Creating new views to display data from the CMDB is simple and can be performed by almost anyone with permissions to do so using the Service Manager console. In some special cases when the wizard is not adequate, such as wanting to change the column header text, you can use someone with basic knowledge of MPs and WPF binding paths. You can first create the view in the Service Manager console, and then export the MP where the view is stored and modify it manually to display the correct text. Chapter 19 contains information about the view definition in an MP and modifying column names manually.

If there are special requirements to display data in other forms than a standard view in the console where you would normally use a view, you can use a more advanced approach. The individual tasked to do such a thing would need to be comfortable in WPF and have an in-depth knowledge of how to define MP elements. To learn more about how to accomplish this, read about custom views in Chapter 19.

Forms

Forms in Service Manager are built using standard WPF technology. Similar to how a view binds to properties in columns, the different controls on the form bind to properties of the underlying data context (such as a work item). Forms are stored in assemblies (dynamic link libraries, known as DLLs) that are bundled into MP bundles and bound together with class types or type projections using form definitions within MPs.

TIP: MORE ABOUT FORMS

Chapter 19 describes the process of creating a new form, associating this with a class type, bundling the MP and the assembly to an MP bundle (MPB) and importing it into Service Manager.

To understand some limitations of forms in Service Manager, you should understand the logic of how the product knows which form to use when displaying information about an object in the CMDB. Figure 16.9 describes the logic that determines which form is used. If you study the flowchart in this figure, you can draw the conclusion that there can only be one form associated to a given class type, even though it can be an indirect association through a type projection.

Following the flowchart in Figure 16.9 while considering the scenario of creating a change request, you can expect the following to happen:

1. Service Manager checks whether the currently selected view in the console is targeting a type projection or a class type.

2. If the current view is targeting a type projection, Service Manager locates the class type used as seed for the type projection. If not, Service Manager already has the class type.

3. Using the class type, Service Manager then tries to find a form that is targeted to the class type or a form that is targeting a type projection that has the class type as seed. If no form is found, Service Manager retrieves the parent class type (the class type

used as base for the current class type) and tries to find a form using that class type. Service Manager continues to retrieve a parent class until a form is found or no parent class is found.

4. If a form is located, Service Manager either wraps a new seed (instance) of the class type in the given type projection and uses the type projection as a data context for the form, or just uses the new class type seed as data context for the form. The decision is based on whether the form was targeting a class type or a type projection.

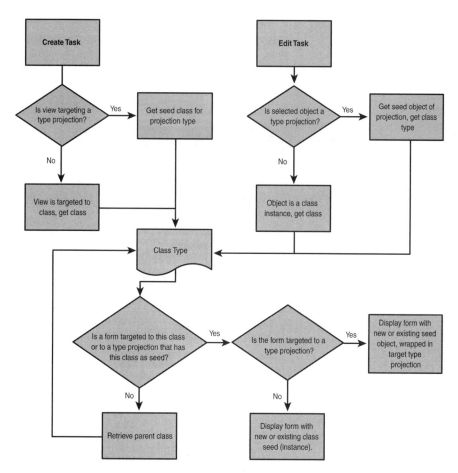

FIGURE 16.9   Determining which form is used.

Considering the flowchart (Figure 16.9) once more and the fact that the choice of form is always based on the class type, this means there can only be one form associated with a class type within Service Manager.

CAUTION: ONLY ONE FORM CAN BE ASSOCIATED WITH AN OBJECT

Service Manager 2010 only allows one form at a time to be associated with objects of a given class type. Even if you try to associate multiple forms with different type projections based on a given class, this will not work because the logic used to locate a form for a new or existing object is always based on a class type and not the type projection.

Generic Form

Service Manger can always locate a form, because the top class, System.Entity (also known as Object), is associated with a fallback form known as the Generic Form. The Generic Form is displayed in Figure 16.10, showing the properties of a custom class type called Building, which uses the Configuration Item class as base. The Generic Form is used because no other form is associated with the class in the environment where the picture comes from.

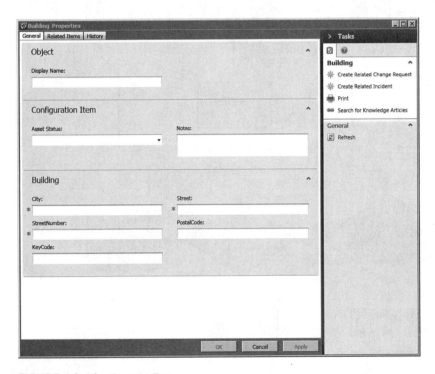

FIGURE 16.10   Generic Form.

The Generic Form is designed in runtime, where each class type in the class type hierarchy of the given object results in a separate panel in the form. The class type at the top of the hierarchy, known as the *most derived class type*, is represented in the first panel in the form where all the properties are listed. In Figure 16.10, the most derived class type is of the MP changes the ID of all the MP elements contained in that MP. This also means that MP elements have the same GUID in all installations of Service Manager.

For example, the incident class GUID is `A604B942-4C7B-2FB2-28DC-61DC6F465C68` in every installation of Service Manager. That GUID is a hash of the MP ID `System.WorkItem.Incident.Library` and the class ID `System.WorkItem.Incident`. If Microsoft were to change the MP ID of the MP that contains the incident class, change the incident class ID, or move the incident class from one MP to another, the GUID would change. This would break many different places in the code of the product itself and potentially any code that partners and other developers wrote against the Service Manager SDK. Therefore, as a best practice, ensure you choose the correct ID for your MP at the very beginning and don't change it over time. Here is a best practice for naming MPs:

`OrganizationName.ProductName.Area.SubArea`

Here are the conventions for adding `Library` or `Configuration` to the end of the MP name:

> ▶ If your MP contains model elements such as classes, properties, relationship types, and type projections and is a *sealed* MP, it is appropriate to add `Library` to the end of the ID and display name of the MP.

> ▶ If the MP is *unsealed* and contains MP elements that are intended to be modified or the MP is intended to store other customizations, it is appropriate to add `Configuration` to the end of the MP ID and display name.

The MP version must follow the format: `#.#.#.#` where each # must consist of numerals between 0 and 9 and can be from 1 to 10 digits long. For example, `1.0.0.0` is allowed. `1.0.1000000000.0` is allowed. `1.0` is not allowed. `1.1.123a.0`, with non-numeric characters, is not allowed.

Versions also control the upgradeability of MPs. If you try to import a lower version of a sealed MP on top of a higher version, the system rejects the import attempt. You can import a sealed MP only on top of an existing version of the same MP if the version you are importing is the same or higher. You can import any version of an unsealed MP on top of any version of the same unsealed MP, because the system treats that as a delete/import instead of an in-place upgrade. If you import a MP that has the same version as the same MP that already exists in the database, the System Center Management service will not be aware that there is in fact some new content in the MP that needs to be downloaded to the workflow engine. To avoid this situation, you should increment the version number before importing the MP. The same is true of MP synchronization to the data warehouse.

References

MPs can take a dependency on or "reference" another MP. An example of this is a view that is in one MP that is configured to show objects of a class defined in another MP. If the MP containing the class were deleted, the view in the other MP would be useless. In this case, the MP containing the view would take a dependency on the MP containing the

System.Entity (which has the display name Object), the second most derived class type is System.ConfigItem (also known as configuration item), which is therefore placed right below Object. As shown in Figure 16.10, the properties of the class types (definitions in Listing 16.4) are shown in each of the rendered panels of the Generic Form.

The reason why the property ObjectStatus is not in Figure 16.10 but is in Listing 16.4 is that it has been excluded from the form. You can accomplish this by adding properties to a special view type in SvcMgr. Chapter 18 explains how to use the special view type to prevent properties from being displayed in the Generic Form.

LISTING 16.4   Definition of System.Entity and System.ConfigItem

```
<ClassType ID="System.Entity" Accessibility="Public" Abstract="true" Hosted="false"

Singleton="false" Extension="false">
    <Property ID="DisplayName" Type="string" AutoIncrement="false" Key="false"
    CaseSensitive="false" MaxLength="4000" MinLength="0" Required="false" />
</ClassType>
<ClassType ID="System.ConfigItem" Accessibility="Public" Abstract="true"
Base="System.Entity" Hosted="false" Singleton="false" Extension="false">
    <Property ID="ObjectStatus" Type="enum" AutoIncrement="false" Key="false"

    CaseSensitive="false" MaxLength="256" MinLength="0" Required="false"
    EnumType="System.ConfigItem.ObjectStatusEnum"
    DefaultValue="System.ConfigItem.ObjectStatusEnum.Active" />
    <Property ID="AssetStatus" Type="enum" AutoIncrement="false" Key="false"
    CaseSensitive="false" MaxLength="256" MinLength="0" Required="false"
    EnumType="System.ConfigItem.AssetStatusEnum" />
    <Property ID="Notes" Type="richtext" AutoIncrement="false" Key="false"
    CaseSensitive="false" MaxLength="4000" MinLength="0" Required="false" />
</ClassType>
```

16

History

All objects within the CMDB are tracked when they change. For each change performed, the following data is stored in the CMDB:

▶ Who performed the change

▶ When was the change performed

▶ What was changed (from value, to value)

Figure 16.11 shows an example of how history is presented for a given object in the CMDB.

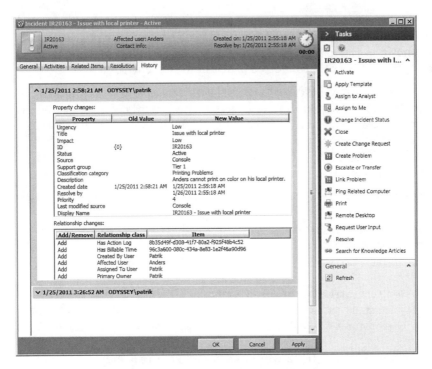

FIGURE 16.11   The History tab in the Change Request form.

The History tab is not visible when you create custom forms for Service Manager, although the history data will still be available for all CMDB objects (including custom objects). In fact, even though the Authoring Tool does not provide a way to add the control that is used to show the history data of an object, there are ways to reuse the control to show history data in a custom form.

TIP: MORE ABOUT REUSING BUILT-IN CONTROLS IN CUSTOM FORMS

Here is a blog post where you can learn how to re-use the related items and history control in your own custom forms: http://blogs.litware.se/?p=720.

Reports

Service Manager 2010 offers a reporting solution that exposes reports based on data from the data warehouse. A number of reports are available out of the box. Figure 16.12 lists some of these reports.

Chapter 20, "Reports, Dashboards, and Data Analysis," discusses the reporting infrastructure in detail. However, here is one important thing to know regarding reports when planning for customization; when you implement custom data models or extend existing models, the new data introduced to Service Manager isn't automatically available in the data warehouse for custom reports. One needs to "tell" the infrastructure this information should be available for reporting and in which way it should be available. To implement this involves defining Fact Tables, Dimensions, and Outriggers, discussed in Chapter 20.

As the reporting infrastructure is based on SQL SRS, you can easily add custom reports and publish these in the Service Manager console.

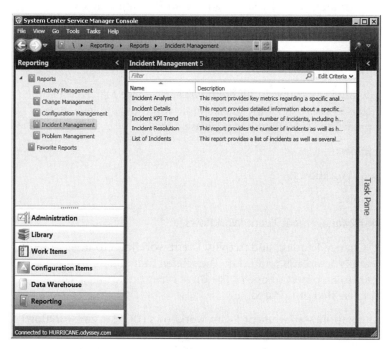

FIGURE 16.12   Out-of-the-box reports in Service Manager.

Web

The Self-Service portal and Analyst portal use ASP.NET to present data. The portals use the Service Manager SDK to interact with Service Manager, just as a third-party application would. Chapter 18 discusses how you can customize the portals.

Workflows

When planning a Service Manager implementation and approaches to customizing the product to provide the most value, you want to consider automating IT processes as an area where Service Manager 2010 can provide large time savings and increase your quality of service. By using the workflow engine to automate the most common IT processes, the IT department can move its focus from repetitive tasks such as resetting passwords to further bring business value by developing processes and services to better align itself with existing and future business needs.

The workflow engine is accessible to Service Manager implementers as a platform for automation. The workflow engine is built to support different types of workflows, with Windows Workflow Foundation (WF) the most accessible of the supported technologies. WF workflows are suitable to use when automating common IT tasks using Service Manager.

Here are the different ways you can trigger workflows in Service Manager:

- **Subscription based:** Example: Activity Status goes from Pending to Active.

- **Scheduled:** Example: Every 24h.

- **Task initiated:** Example: Synchronize now (as seen when selecting a configured connector).

You can implement user-defined workflows in different ways in Service Manager. Via the console, wizards are available to take care of the most simple workflow implementation scenarios. Here are some predefined workflows for your use:

- Incident Event Workflows

- Change Request Event Workflows

- Activity Event Workflows

- Desired Configuration Management Event Workflows

You can use the Incident, Change Request, and Activity Event workflows to trigger predefined workflows that can apply templates and notify the related individuals (as the affected user of an incident) to an object of one of the three types (incidents, change requests, or activities) being created or updated.

You can use Desired Configuration Management Event workflows (DCM event workflow) to control how noncompliance reports from System Center Configuration Manager should transform to Incidents by specifying Incident templates. With DCM event workflows, it is also possible to configure notifications for noncompliance reports.

TIP: MORE ABOUT INCIDENT AND CHANGE REQUEST MANAGEMENT

Read more about the Incident and Desired Configuration Management Event Workflows in Chapter 10, "Incident Management." To learn about Change Request Event Workflows, read Chapter 12, "Change Management."

Service Manager also includes predefined workflows for generic notifications.

Service Manager can have a huge impact when you use it to automate IT tasks. These tasks can be nearly any task executed in or using a computerized system. Anything from an internal maintenance job like Escalate all incident that has `Priority>5` is `Active` and (`CreateDate-Now`)>4days, to automating a request for a new user account.

You can build the workflows using the Service Manager Authoring Tool as shown in Figure 16.13. You could also write managed code to create the workflow, or create re-usable workflow activities you can import with the Authoring Tool and then use to build the complete workflow. Because Service Manager comes with an activity library containing some useful activities, you can begin automating without writing code, although to create the most useful workflows you will at a minimum need a resource capable of writing PowerShell scripts when using the built-in workflow engine.

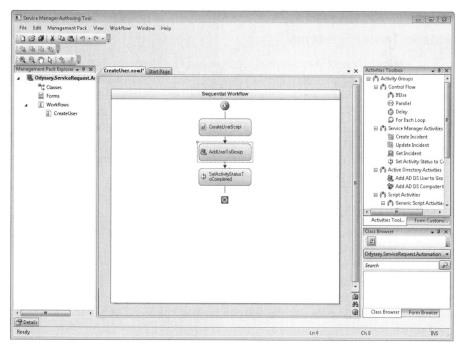

FIGURE 16.13   Service Manager Authoring Tool: Workflow Design Surface

TIP: USE SYSTEM CENTER OPALIS TO DO THE "DIRTY WORK" FOR SERVICE MANAGER

Consider exploring what System Center Orchestrator (previously known as Opalis Integration Server) can do when used in combination with Service Manager. The high number of integration packs that comes with the product enables you to automate a large number of tasks by just dragging and dropping the predefined activities. For example, you could use Service Manager to track change requests, but you can automate the process with Opalis using the drag-and-drop automation built into that product.

The skills required to create workflows that for example automate IT tasks can vary considerably, depending on the task to be automated. You can get far with having basic knowledge in PowerShell, although it doesn't hurt to have access to a .NET developer.

When planning customization in the area of workflows, it is not only enough to plan the tasks to automate and the human resources needed to implement the customization. You also need to consider areas such as account permissions and firewall ports.

16

TIP: LEARN MORE ABOUT SERVICE MANAGER WORKFLOWS

For more information about the Service Manager workflow infrastructure, see Chapter 4. For a step-by-step instruction on how to automate the task of creating new user accounts in Active Directory using workflows, see Chapter 19.

Permissions in Target Systems

All workflows in Service Manager are executed in the context of a service account. By default, this is the account specified as the Workflow account when installing the product. This is important to keep in mind when planning to automate IT tasks. For example, if you are automating the creation of user accounts, the Workflow account must have the necessary rights in Active Directory to create the account. If the new user account should be given an Exchange mailbox, the Workflow account needs to have the required rights in Exchange to create the mailbox. What this means is the Workflow account must be delegated the required access and permissions in each target system.

Firewall Configurations

Depending on what the custom workflows will do and the technology in use, the infrastructure must be configured to support the required access between the Service Manager management server (the first management server installed, which runs the workflows) and the target system. For instance, if a PowerShell script used in a workflow to automate a task in Configuration Manager is using Windows Management Instrumentation (WMI), you must configure firewalls in-between the systems and on the target server to allow the WMI traffic to pass through.

Scoping

The main purpose of groups is to limit the access to CIs (computers, printers, and so on). When you create a user role in Service Manager, you can use groups to limit the access of that role to members of the specified groups. The same goes for queues, although their main purpose is to limit access to work items (incidents, change requests, and such). If no group or queue is specified for a user role, the role will have access to all objects.

In addition to limiting access, here are some ways you can use groups and queues:

▶ As criteria when creating a custom report

▶ As target in a notification scenario

Groups and queues are managed directly in the Service Manager console in the Library workspace, shown in Figure 16.14.

When planning for customizations, you should understand scoping capabilities and limits to be able to achieve the desired access control on existing and new object types. Therefore, consider which scenarios you need to support, the user roles these include, and then the groups and queues necessary to build those roles.

FIGURE 16.14   The Library workspace of the Service Manager console.

Groups

Groups can contain CIs, and are used to limit access for a certain user role to the group members. You can specify the group members as

- ▶ Dynamic members

  Example: All objects of `Printer` class where `Manufacturer` property = "HP"

- ▶ Static members

  Example: Printer P12312, Printer P12315, Printer P12319

Note that a group can contain a mixture of static and dynamic members.

You specify the static members when creating the group in the console; these are located by searching for objects of a certain type, as shown in Figure 16.15.

NOTE: COMBINING DIFFERENT OBJECTS IN A GROUP

There is no limitation to the types of CIs that can be members of the same group. For example, a group can contain both computers and printers.

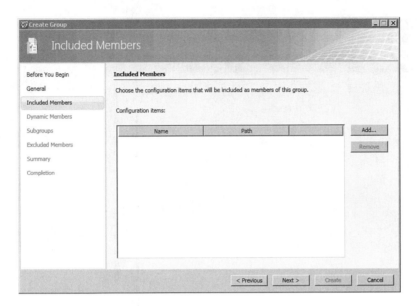

FIGURE 16.15   Adding static members to a group.

After you specify the static members of a group, there is an option to add a dynamic membership rule to the group definition, as shown in Figure 16.16. These rules are used to add dynamic members to a group. The rule is based on object-level properties. You can combine several rules to create a fine-grained filter.

The dynamic rules created in the console are sometimes called dynamic include rules. Should there be a need for dynamic exclude rules, you can manually define the rules by editing the XML of the MP files.

By using groups to limit the access for a user role, you could for example define a role giving a certain set of users access to all computers of a specific model. By combining multiple dynamic rules for the group, you could give the user role access to objects representing computers of multiple computer models.

Queues

Similar to groups, you can use queues to limit access to objects when defining new user roles in Service Manager. However, whereas groups are used to scope CIs, queues are used to scope work items such as incident, problems, and change requests, and so on. While groups have the capability to add both static and dynamic members, queues support only dynamic rules. (See Figure 16.17, which is missing the step for adding included members, the step for adding static members when creating a group.)

NOTE: WORKAROUND FOR STATIC RULES

Even though the usage is limited, you can achieve the functionality of a static rule by creating a dynamic rule and specifying something such as ID Equals IR101.

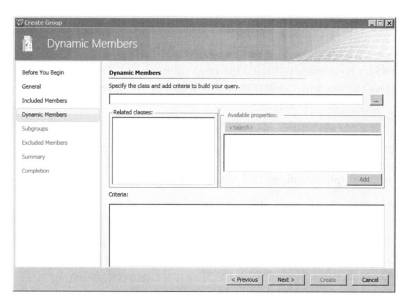

FIGURE 16.16   Adding dynamic members to a group.

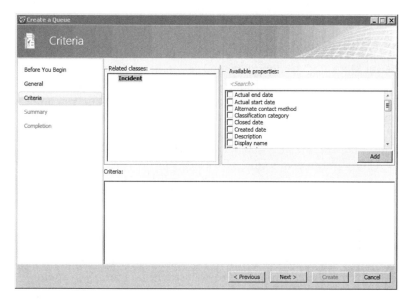

FIGURE 16.17   Specifying queue members.

For more information about creating user roles based on groups and queues, see Chapter 15, "Service Manager Security."

General Considerations

When planning for customization, you want to think through some general considerations early on in the project to avoid misjudging the need for resources. These include globalization as well as validation and constraints, discussed in the next sections.

Globalization

Because Service Manager supports multiple languages, a company implementing the product might decide or require the product is used in multiple languages within that organization. Supporting multiple languages affects some significant areas:

- ▶ Any notification templates you create will need to be translated to the supported languages.

- ▶ It becomes very important that you set the Locale property of the user CIs in the CMDB appropriately, because this is the language used when Service Manager sends notifications to a user. If a template exists in the specified language, that is the template used when sending the message.

- ▶ Creating custom list items will require exporting MPs for localized display strings to be added for the custom list items in the supported languages. Chapter 17 discusses display strings.

Validation and Constraints

As mentioned in the "Data Modeling" section, data models can be equipped with constraints such as properties with maximum lengths or are required fields. This ensures the data in the CMDB is guaranteed to have a particular level of quality. When you are using the Generic Form, the UI gives visual feedback of any data errors entered, such as showing a red star next to a text box bound to a required field. When you are planning to implement a custom form that will include visual feedback, the feedback should be implemented by the person creating the custom form.

Defining constraints similar to this can ensure a property value will exist when used by a custom workflow.

The other side of defining constraints is that you should not add constraints that are not absolutely necessary and valid in all scenarios. Generally, a better way to work with constraints is to add validation in custom forms (when possible). The rationale here is that should you later want to override the constraints, if the constraint in a form you could override those constraints using other methods to update the data (such as the CSV connector).

Summarizing Required Knowledge

To summarize the skills required for customization, the next sections discuss the different areas of Service Manager and recommended knowledge for customizing.

Console

You can perform many customizations directly in the console, such as creating new user roles, list items, templates, and so on. In addition to the knowledge available in this book and reading up on the product documentation, the authors suggest you know some basic Hypertext Markup Language (HTML), because this can prove useful when formatting notification templates.

Self-Service Portal

You can customize the Self-Service portal by following the product documentation, which describes in detail the steps required to take to change the customizable parts. SharePoint knowledge can also be useful if implementing the SSP web parts in an existing SharePoint infrastructure.

> **TIP: LEARN HOW TO CUSTOMIZE THE SELF-SERVICE PORTAL**
>
> Some modifications can be performed without any coding to the SSP. This is described in the System Center Service Manager 2010 SP1 Deployment Guide, located at http://technet.microsoft.com/en-us/library/ff461171.aspx.

Chapter 18 describes some further capabilities for customizing the SSP (for those who have access to a developer resource).

Data Modeling

Learning the concepts of data modeling discussed in this chapter as well as Chapter 4, Chapter 17, and Chapter 18 in addition to learning the Service Manager Authoring Tool will get you far. However, some scenarios will require manual editing of MPs. Chapters 17, 18, and 19 provide information on editing MPs.

Forms

Chapter 18 describes how to customize existing forms and how to create simple new ones. Knowing WPF enables you to use tools such as Microsoft Visual Studio and Expression Blend to create custom forms from scratch, making use of the full power in WPF.

Workflows

Learning the Authoring Tool is often enough for creating basic workflows. However, the authors recommend you know some basic PowerShell scripting. In addition, knowing Windows WF and being able to write managed code present endless possibilities.

Service Manager Authoring Tool

Chapter 18 provides a good base for the knowledge needed to master the Authoring Tool. The tool is designed for use by IT professionals and does not require the individual using it to know PowerShell or how to write code, although if you are creating advanced workflows it is best if you have capabilities in one of these areas.

Creating Custom Reports

When writing custom reports for Service Manager, you can use either the Report Builder or Business Intelligence Development Studio, tools provided with SQL Server. These tools provide drag-and-drop functionality and wizards to aid on building the reports. It is also useful to have some basic knowledge of Transact SQL (T-SQL) and SRS. See Chapter 20 for information on using the Business Intelligence Development Studio.

Summary

When planning for customization, you must consider a number of items. Here are the key things to remember from this chapter when planning your customizations:

▶ Different types of relationships can affect how permissions are cloned from object to objects. A user given permission on one object type can end up having permissions on a related object.

▶ Having resources in a sealed MP enables referencing those resources in other MPs. For example, it enables adding new properties through the concept of class extensions in a third-party MP.

▶ Sealing an MP protects the content of the MP, as it cannot be changed by anyone except the "key owners" without changing the identity of the MP.

▶ By using constraints when defining class types and properties, you can control the characteristics and thus the quality of data stored in Service Manager. However, it may be a better approach to validate data in the UI, leaving a door open for scenarios where the constraints end up being a problem.

▶ Type projections must be defined to enable creating search criteria containing properties of related objects. Type projections are also necessary to enable presentation of properties of related objects in views and forms.

▶ Locate the real cost drivers regarding IT processes, and consider automating these using the Service Manager workflow engine to save both time and money while increasing quality by removing the chance of human errors.

▶ When planning to automate IT tasks, include infrastructure requirements in your plan in terms of firewall configuration and service account permissions.

CHAPTER 17

Management Packs

Challenges faced by organizations implementing service desk products in the past usually were related to customizing the product and preserving those customizations from one upgrade to the next. Typically, this required hiring expensive consultants to navigate the process. Service Manager provides a unique approach to making customizations and ensuring preservation of those customizations during upgrades. Similar to the management packs (MPs) found in other System Center products such as Operations Manager, Service Manager MPs enable Microsoft and software partners to deliver additional value and for administrators to store customizations. Using MPs is key to alleviating many of the problems traditionally associated with customizing a service desk product. This chapter describes MP concepts, life cycle, and best practices.

Purpose of Management Packs

MPs serve two primary purposes:

▶ They provide storage of customizations.

▶ They are a packaging mechanism for Microsoft partners to deliver additional solutions on top of the Service Manager platform.

Most customizations made to Service Manager are stored in an MP. Extensions to the data model, form customizations, workflow rules, notification subscriptions, list items, views, templates, notification templates, groups, queues, console tasks, data warehouse extensions, reports, workflows, and new custom forms are all stored in MPs.

Microsoft software partners can deliver their solutions easily to customers using MPs. An analogy commonly used is that Service Manager is a platform similar to an Xbox. Partners deliver solution MPs much like game developers provide DVD games to play on the Xbox. Even the solutions provided by Microsoft out of the box such as change, incident, problem, configuration, and knowledge management are actually just MPs imported during setup.

There are several important advantages to storing customizations in MPs:

▶ Uninstallation

▶ Transportation

▶ Versioning

▶ Componentization

The next sections discuss these topics.

Uninstallation

When an MP is imported into Service Manager, it may extend the database schema and add additional content into the system such as forms, templates, and list items. One of the advantages of an MP is that it is extremely easy to revert those extensions and customizations by simply deleting the MP. If the database schema is extended to add new tables and fields when the MP is imported, those same tables and fields are deleted when the MP is deleted. It will be as if those schema extensions never happened and all the data stored in those tables and fields no longer exists. Any new forms, templates, console tasks, and so on defined in that MP are removed, as well. Here is how this is advantageous to Service Manager installations:

▶ It makes it very easy to try out a software partner's solution; should you decide not to move forward with it or want to start over, you can just delete the MPs.

▶ It is easy to remove the artifacts that were used to support a new process that is no longer needed for some reason. You can remove all of those artifacts by simply deleting the MP.

▶ If you suspect that a particular MP is causing some type of problem with a workflow or form, you can easily remove that offending MP until the problem can be determined.

Transportation

MPs are transportable in the form of an .xml, .mp, or .mpb file. This allows software partners to offer complete solutions that you can easily download from the web—similar to any other file—and import these into Service Manager. Administrators can also create and test all of their customizations to Service Manager in a preproduction environment, export

out the MPs, and then import them into production, alleviating the need to move complicated step-by-step code-based customizations from one environment to another. With
MPs, there is no complicated build or deployment process. This transportability also
enables Microsoft, partners, and administrators to share solutions easily with each other in
the community on sites such as blogs, CodePlex, or forums.

Versioning

MPs can be versioned over time as they are modified. This enables upgradeability of both
the Service Manager product itself and the partner and customer MPs created on top of
Service Manager. It also enables rollback. Administrators should treat MPs like source code
and use a source control system to control access, versioning, track history, and enable
rollback. Each version of the MP should be preserved so that at any point the customer
can roll back to a previous version of the MP or compare the differences between a previous version and the current version.

Componentization

Componentization is the concept of grouping together sets of customizations into an MP
(or set of MPs). For example, if you are adding a new automated process to provision new
users, you might want to store the data model extensions, forms, form customizations, list
items, views, templates, and queues associated with that process in a single MP. This
makes it easy to manage the artifacts of the complete solution in a single package that can
be transported, versioned, and easily uninstalled.

Sealed and Unsealed MPs

17

MPs can be either sealed (not modifiable) or unsealed (modifiable). Microsoft and software
partners and, in some cases, administrators will seal an MP to prevent modifications to the
MP itself. This ensures upgradeability without fear of breaking customizations the
customer may have applied, as the customizations are stored in another MP that references the sealed MP. Typically, these customizations are stored in unsealed MPs so they
can be easily modified at any time.

There are several other important characteristics to understand about sealed and unsealed
MPs. MPs can depend on each other but only so long as the MP that is being depended
upon is sealed:

▶ An MP (sealed or unsealed) can depend on a sealed MP.

▶ An MP (sealed or unsealed) cannot depend on an unsealed MP.

This dependency is called a *reference* and is discussed further in the "Management Pack
Schema" section of this chapter.

MPs that are sealed can be upgraded from one version to another without fear of losing any data, because the MP remains in place at all times. "Upgrading" an unsealed MP is effectively an uninstall and a reinstall; in some cases, it can result in data loss, particularly in cases where the MP contains data model extensions.

Also important to note is that only sealed MPs are synchronized from a Service Manager management group to the Data Warehouse management group. The exception to this is the following types of MP content, which are sent to the data warehouse even if part of an unsealed MP:

▶ List items (also known as enumerations)

▶ Groups

▶ Queues

In those cases, just those items are sent to the data warehouse, not the entire MP.

MPs can be sealed using either with a command-line utility called fastseal.exe or the Authoring Tool. Fastseal.exe is good for using with an automated MP build system, where you need to seal many MPs as part of the build of a complete solution that includes other code. You can download fastseal.exe from the Service Manager Engineering Team Blog at http://blogs.technet.com/servicemanager/archive/2009/12/25/sealing-management-packs.aspx. Run `fastseal.exe /?` to see usage. Here is some sample syntax:

```
fastseal.exe MyManagementPack.xml /Company "My Company"
/Copyright "Copyright 2011 My Company" /KeyFile MyKeyFile.snk
```

Alternatively, you can use the Service Manager Authoring Tool. Figure 17.1 shows how to start the Seal Management Pack dialog in the Authoring Tool by right-clicking the MP name in the Management Pack Explorer.

Once the Seal Management Pack dialog (see Figure 17.2) is open, you must provide the output directory (folder) for the .mp file, the .snk key file, and company information. A copyright can also optionally be included. Clicking the **Seal** button saves a sealed .mp file into the folder indicated as the output directory.

NOTE: ABOUT THE STRONG NAME FILE

To seal an MP, you need a strong name key file (.snk). You can create one using the Strong Name Tool (sn.exe), which is a tool in the Windows Software Development Kit (SDK) that you can download from http://www.microsoft.com/downloads/en/details.aspx?FamilyID=e6e1c3df-a74f-4207-8586-711ebe331cdc&displaylang=en.

Sealing an MP turns an MP from an .xml file to an .mp file, which is a binary representation of the MP instead of a human-readable XML file. This is not to protect intellectual property! It is solely to make it possible to digitally sign the file. Only binary files can be signed. Signing a binary ensures the receiver that the file was signed by the provider of the file and that it has not been modified.

FIGURE 17.1   Launching the sealing utility in the Service Manager Authoring Tool.

FIGURE 17.2   The Management Pack Sealing Tool in the Service Manager Authoring Tool.

Differences Between Management Pack Schema Version 1.0 and 1.1

Service Manager 2010 is built on a common technology platform that is shared with other Microsoft products such as Operations Manager, System Center Essentials, Virtual Machine Manager, and InTune. These other products are currently using the 1.0 version of the MP schema. Service Manager has introduced the 1.1 version of the schema. Other products built on the common technology platform will pick up this new version of the MP schema in future versions. Changes to the schema are additive.

Modeling Improvements

Version 1.1 of the MP schema introduces the concept of a class extension. When you extend a class, you can add new properties to that class and all other classes that derive from that class inherit those properties. You can only make class extensions to nonabstract classes.

The new schema also introduced new data types for properties, as follows:

▶ **Enumeration:** The enumeration data type allows you to constrain the data input for a property value to a predefined list of options.

▶ **RichText:** This data type is designed to store data that is formatted using Rich Text Format (RTF).

▶ **Binary:** The binary data type is for storing large chunks of data in binary format such as files.

Any string or number data type property can be set to auto-increment. The system increments the number of that property value for each new object of that class that is created. This is useful for creating a human-understandable unique identifier such as a work item ID. For example, the first incident that is created might have an ID of 1, the next incident would have an ID of 2, and so on.

Regular expressions are now supported as a means to validate a property value. The regular expression can be set on a `Property` element in the `RegEx` attribute.

`TypeProjection` is a new schema element. Type projections are similar to SQL Server views, and act as a query of multiple objects across relationship types. For example, most people looking at a computer record in Service Manager would want to see information about the physical make of the computer, such as manufacturer and model number. They would also want to see the logical and physical hardware in that computer, information about the operating system, and a list of installed software and software updates. In addition, they want to see the primary user of that computer and the asset owner. All of that information is actually modeled using about 10 different classes. Type projections make it possible to get all of those objects across multiple classes and return them as a single object. Type projections also make it possible to query for objects using related object properties in the criteria. For example, you could query Service Manager looking for all Incidents where the Assigned To User Domain property = Redmond. Nearly all forms and views in Service Manager out of the box are bound to type projections.

Data Warehouse Improvements

The 1.1 version of the schema introduces new elements to declare data warehouse extensions such as `Fact`, `Outrigger`, `Measure`, `Dimension`, `WarehouseModule`,

`DataWarehouseScript`, and `DataWarehouseDataSet`. These new elements allow a MP author to extend the data warehouse database schema to extract, transform, and load additional data from the Service Manager database. Facts, outriggers, and dimensions are discussed in Chapter 20, "Reports, Dashboards, and Data Analysis."

Other Improvements

The Resources section designed to catalog the satellite resource files such as assemblies, script files, and images is new in the 1.1 schema. The Categories section used to categorize other MP elements is also new, as are Templates. These new sections and elements are described in greater detail in the next section, "Management Pack Schema."

Management Pack Schema

MPs at their core are eXtensible Markup Language (XML) files that must match a particular schema. The schema can be broken down into the following main commonly used areas:

- ▶ Identity
- ▶ References
- ▶ Entity Types
- ▶ Secure References
- ▶ Categories
- ▶ Presentation
- ▶ Language Packs
- ▶ Resources

These areas are discussed in the following sections.

Identity

The Identity section uniquely identifies the MP by name and version:

```
<Identity>
  <ID>System.Library</ID>
  <Version>7.0.6555.0</Version>
</Identity>
```

The GUID ID of all the MP elements in the MP when they are imported into the database are a hash of the ID of the MP and the ID of the MP element. Therefore, changing the ID

class. The system enforces this dependency, and does not allow the MP containing the class to be removed until all MPs depending on it are removed.

MP dependencies are declared as References in the MP XML. To create a reference, the ID, version, and public key token for the MP that is being referenced must be provided. Here is an example of an MP reference:

```
<Reference Alias="System">
  <ID>System.Library</ID>
  <Version>7.0.6555.0</Version>
  <PublicKeyToken>31bf3856ad364e35</PublicKeyToken>
</Reference>
```

The ID is the same as the ID element in the referenced MP, which must also be the same as the MP filename. The version number in the reference is used to make sure that a certain version *or higher* of the referenced MP exists. For example, if an MP references an MP with version 7.0.6555.0 (Service Manager 2010 Service Pack 1), the MP is allowed to be imported if the referenced MP already exists that is version 7.0.6555.0 or 7.0.6555.1. The MP cannot be imported if the referenced MP that exists in the system is version 7.0.5826.0 (Service Manager 2010 English Edition).

The public key token is determined by the strong name key file (.snk) that is used to seal the MP. The public key token for all officially released Microsoft sealed MPs is 31bf3856ad364e35. If you need to look up the public key token or version for another MP that is already in the system, you can run this query in the ServiceManager database:

```
SELECT MPName, MPFriendlyName, MPVersion, MPKeyToken FROM ManagementPack
WHERE MPIsSealed = 1 ORDER BY MPName
```

The Alias of an MP reference is used as a shorthand way to point to that MP. For example, in this `RelationshipType` declaration the System MP alias `'System!'` is used.

```
<RelationshipType .... Base="System!System.Reference">
```

This is saying that this `RelationshipType` is based on the `System.Reference` `RelationshipType` contained in the MP with the alias `System`. The `System` alias is defined to point to the `System.Library` MP in the `Reference` XML example shown at the beginning of this section.

A reference can on be made only on MP elements that are configured to be publicly accessible. For example, the `System.Reference` `RelationshipType` in the `System.Library` MP looks like this:

```
<RelationshipType ID="System.Reference" Accessibility="Public" Abstract="true">
```

Accessibility being `Public` allows other MP elements in other MPs to refer to this `RelationshipType`. If the `Accessibility` attribute is set to `Internal`, other MP elements within the same MP can refer to it, but other MP elements in other MPs cannot. Setting the `Accessibility` to `Internal` is useful if you want to ensure that no other MPs ever depend on a MP element. You may want to set `Accessibility` to `Internal` if at some point you might want to remove that MP element.

Entity Types

The Entity Types section contains classes, properties on those classes, relationship types, type projections, and enumeration types. These concepts are described in detail in Chapter 18, "Customizing Service Manager."

Secure References

Secure References are described in detail in Chapter 15, "Service Manager Security."

Categories

Categories are used to categorize MP elements in the MP. The possibilities for how to use Categories are essentially limitless. Categories are used to categorize console tasks, icons, views, search options, and many other things. For example, adding this `Category` to an MP and importing it into Service Manager hides the Extensions tab on the incident form:

```
<Category
Value="Admin!Microsoft.EnterpriseManagement.ServiceManager.UI.Administration.
Enumeration.HideExtensionTab"
➥Target="Incident!System.WorkItem.Incident.ConsoleForm"
ID="HideIncidentFormExtensionTab"/>
```

A `Category` has a `Value` attribute and a `Target` attribute. The `Target` attribute is the MP element that is being categorized. The `Value` attribute is the category. Values typically point at an `EnumerationValue`, such as in the example in this section. You can create another `Category` that has the same `Value` attribute and a `Target` that points at the change request, computer, or other forms.

Templates

Templates are a new concept introduced into the common technology platform by Service Manager. You can think of templates as partially completed objects. Templates serve two purposes:

- ▶ They are used to create or update objects in a standardized way. For example, each time you create a change request to add more RAM to a server, the classification of that kind of change request, who it is assigned to, what the activities are to implement the change request, and such should be the same. Creating these types of change requests from the same template will help ensure standardized procedures are followed. The data will be more standardized and consistent, which improves searching and reporting.

▶ Templates are used to speed up data entry. Instead of filling out the same fields on a form over and over, a user can just choose to create an object from a template or update an object from a template that might fill out many of the fields on the form with several clicks.

Templates are also used to store notification templates in MPs. Notification templates are used to format email notifications that are sent by Service Manager. Administrators can insert properties of the object being notified into the subject or body of the message.

Templates are always targeted at a class or a type projection. When templates are targeted at a type projection, related objects can also be created or updated whenever an object is updated. A type projection always has a "seed" class. You can add components to the type projection by specifying the relationship type to traverse over. Here is an example:

```
<TypeProjection Type="System.WorkItem.Incident">
   <Component
Path="$Target/Path[Relationship='WorkItem!System.WorkItemAssignedToUser']$"
Alias="AssignedTo" />
   <Component
Path="$Target/Path[Relationship='WorkItem!System.WorkItemAffectedUser']$"
Alias="AffectedUser" />
   <Component
Path="$Target/Path[Relationship='WorkItem!System.WorkItemCreatedByUser']$"
Alias="CreatedBy" />
   <Component
Path="$Target/Path[Relationship='WorkItem!System.WorkItemRelatesToConfigItem']$"
Alias="RelatesToCI" />
</TypeProjection>
```

The "seed" class is specified in the Type attribute on the TypeProjection element. Components can then be added that specify which related objects to include. Each Component identifies a relationship type path over which to traverse.

Here is what a type projection object includes when it is returned by the System Center Data Access Service for this example type projection:

▶ The incident object as the "seed" object

▶ The user object that is assigned to the incident

▶ The user object that is the affected user

▶ The user object for the user that created the incident

▶ All the configuration item objects related to the incident

17

Presentation

The Presentation section of an MP is where forms, views, folders, console tasks, image references, and string resources are defined. Forms can be either a new form created in Visual Studio or Expression Blend, a customized form, or a simple form created using the Service Manager Authoring Tool. Views and folders are most easily created using the console because constructing them by hand in XML is pretty challenging!

It is possible to do things in views in XML that are not possible using the user interface (UI). After defining a view, you can export out the MP containing that view and modify column headings, for example. Image references are used to specify which icon should be used for views and console tasks. String resources are a layer of indirection used by forms and views to specify a localizable string shown in the UI, such as a label over a control on a form or a column header in a view.

Language Packs

Language packs store the localized display strings for all the user interface elements defined in MPs. Class names, property names, view names, template names, and many other things can be localized using language packs. An MP can contain many different language packs. Each language pack contains a display string and optionally a description for each MP element. An MP can also contain localized display strings for MP elements in other referenced MPs.

When something is created in the console, the name and description provided for that are stored in the language in which the console is running. Users viewing that item in a different language may see the ID of the item instead of the string the first user entered. The logic for determining what to show for each display string is to first look for a display string that is the same as the console (which is the same as the operating system). If a display string doesn't exist for that language, the console looks for a display string defined in a default language pack (typically English). If the display string doesn't exist in the default language pack, the console displays the ID of the MP element.

This is an example of a language pack and display string:

```
<LanguagePack ID="ENU" IsDefault="true">
  <DisplayStrings>
      <DisplayString ElementID="System.Library">
        <Name>System Library</Name>
        <Description>System Library: Root for all Management Packs. Contains
platform
independent definitions.</Description>
      </DisplayString>
```

The ID attribute of a language pack (ENU in the example) is a three-letter code for that language from ISO standard 639. You can see a list of those codes at http://www.sil.org/iso639-3/codes.asp. Each display string has an ElementID attribute that points to the MP element's ID. In this case, `System.Library` points to the ID of the MP itself. The `Name` element is required, although the `Description` element is optional.

Resources

The Resources section of the MP declares resource files that are external to the MP XML file itself. These include form assemblies, workflow assemblies, view type assemblies, console task handler assemblies, image files, SQL script files (.sql), report files (.rdl), and other files the MP author deems must be included with the MP for the MP to function correctly. Resources are declared as an `Assembly`, `Resource`, `ReportResource`, or `Image` resource element. When resources are declared in an MP, the associated files must be included in an MP bundle (described in the next section). When an MP bundle is imported into the system, the resource files are stored in the database and then deployed automatically to the appropriate location.

MP Bundles

MP bundles are used to group together an MP with its associated resources (assemblies, image files, or other files) or to group together multiple related MPs. An MP bundle is actually just an MSI file with an .mpb file extension. The .mpb file acts as a cabinet to bundle up multiple files (.xml, .mp, .dll, .sql, .png, and so on) into a single file for convenience. You can import .mpb files into Service Manager just as you do .mp or .xml files by using the MP Import dialog in the Management Packs view in the Service Manager console, or by using a PowerShell cmdlet such as `Import-SCSMManagementPack`.

To create an MP bundle, you first need to declare the MP resources in the MP XML. (See the "Management Pack Schema" section for additional information.) You then must place each of those resource files in the same folder as the MP file. Finally, you can use a PowerShell script such as `New-MBPFile.ps1` to create the MP bundle. Here is an example:

```
New-MPBFile.ps1 MyManagementPack.xml MyManagementPack
```

This command creates a file called MyManagementPack.mpb. You can download the `New-MPBFile.ps1` script from the Service Manager Engineering Team Blog at http://blogs.technet.com/b/servicemanager/archive/2009/09/04/introducing-management-pack-bundles.aspx.

After an MP bundle has been imported into Service Manager, the concept of a bundle is no longer present. The MPs imported as part of the bundle are independently managed.

MP Deployment

When an MP is imported into the system, it is shredded into its different parts and stored in the database. For example, any new views declared in the MP go into the Views table, new templates go into the ObjectTemplate table, and so on. Any new nonabstract classes or class extensions defined in the MP result in new tables being created in the database. Other parts of an MP will need to be deployed to other places in addition to the Service Manager database. Workflow assemblies must be manually copied to the %*ProgramFiles*%\Microsoft System Center\Service Manager 2010 folder.

View type assemblies, console task handler assemblies, and form assemblies are stored in the database during MP import. Later, when a user tries to use a view, console task, or form for which the console does not already have the assembly, the console requests the assembly from the System Center Data Access Service. The Data Access Service retrieves the requested file from the ServiceManager database and sends it to the console computer. The console caches that file in the C:\Users\%*UserName*%\AppData\Local\Microsoft\ System Center Service Manager 2010\%*ComputerName*% folder. Inside this folder, there is a folder for each unique MP version. The resource assemblies are stored in the version folder that corresponds to the version of the MP with which they are associated. The console always checks to make sure that it has the latest version of the required resource assembly. Thus, if a new version of the MP is imported that has a new assembly in it, the next time the console needs to use that assembly, it downloads and caches the new version of the assembly.

Image files are also stored in the database during MP import. The console downloads all required images when the console starts and caches them for quick access. Therefore, if you ever introduce new images via a MP import, you need to close and reopen the console to see the new images.

Data warehouse and reporting MP elements go through a special deployment process. The MP must be imported into the Service Manager management group first. Then a workflow called MPSync is triggered (every 60 minutes by default or on demand). The MPSync workflow takes all the sealed MPs from the Service Manager management group and imports them into the data warehouse management group. In addition to synchronizing all sealed MPs, the MPSync workflow synchronizes groups, queues, and enumeration values in unsealed MPs. Similar to when the MPs were imported into the Service Manager management group, importing these MPs extends the database schema of the DWStagingAndConfig database. This prepares that database to receive data from the Service Manager management group. The data is extracted from the ServiceManager data-base, and is staged in the DWStagingAndConfig database. It remains there until trans-formed and loaded into the DWRepository and DWDataMart databases.

When MPSync completes, the workflow begins the deployment. For each data warehouse element in the new MPs that have been imported, the workflow deploys the additional schema changes required to extend the DWRepository and DWDataMart databases to store the additional dimensions and facts. The .sql transform script resource files will also be deployed and the reports published to the SQL Server Reporting Services web service. Once these additional data warehouse artifacts are deployed, the next time the extract, transform, and load jobs run, the data starts to be populated in the new tables and shows up in the new reports.

Summary

MPs provide the essential value-added content that runs on the Service Manager platform. They make it easy to store, version, and transfer solutions and customizations. Administrators and partners can leverage content created in one MP in multiple System Center products when those products are built on the common System Center technology platform centered on MPs. Administrators and partners that become familiar with MP concepts and learn how to customize and extend one System Center product can immediately apply that knowledge to other System Center products. MPs simplify the deployment of complete solutions down to the simple step of importing an MP file being similar to inserting a game disk into an Xbox console.

17

Customizing Service Manager

When planning for your Service Manager (SvcMgr) implementation, you may determine there are customizations necessary to align Service Manager with your in-house processes. Chapter 16, "Planning Your Customization," covered a number of topics important to know before starting to customize; this chapter discusses the specifics of performing customizations.

The chapter goes through the steps required to achieve customizations such as creating new views, console tasks, classes, workflows, and forms.

Customizing the Console

As described in Chapter 16, most everything in the Service Manager console can be customized. The next sections describe the most common customizations you are able to perform directly in the console; although some scenarios may require a bit of eXtensible Markup Language (XML) editing.

Navigation Pane

You can customize the Navigation pane in the Service Manager console (shown in Figure 18.1) in several ways.

The most common scenarios are creating new views and modifying existing ones. When you create new views, these are placed in folders. You can place new folders and views in any of the out-of-the-box workspaces (Administration, Library, Work Items, Configuration Items, and so on). It is even possible to create custom workspaces; Figure 18.1 includes the Odyssey Workspace as an example.

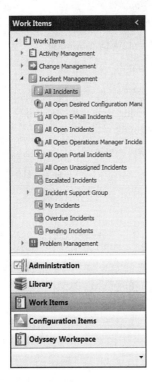

FIGURE 18.1   Navigation pane in Service Manager console.

Folders

You can create a folder in one of two ways:

▶ Within the console

▶ Editing the XML that defines a management pack (MP)

Where available, you can use the console Create Folder task, shown in Figure 18.2, to create a new folder below the currently selected folder.

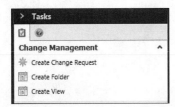

FIGURE 18.2   The Create Folder Console task.

The Create Folder task is only available in certain parts of the navigation tree; this is based on which folders have been associated with the Create Folder task. If the Create Folder task is unavailable where you want to create a folder, you can create the folder manually by editing an MP.

Folders created from the console can only be saved to unsealed MPs:

▶ Any views created beneath that folder must be saved to the same MP, as long as the MP defining the folder is left unsealed.

▶ If a folder is declared in a sealed MP (which enables external referencing), views stored in any MP can be placed beneath the folder.

Folders are declared in the `Presentation` element of an MP. The placement of the folder in the navigation tree is based on the `ParentFolder` attribute. Listing 18.1 shows the declaration of a `Folder` just below the Incident Management folder in the Work Items workspace.

LISTING 18.1   Management Pack Folder Declaration

```
<Presentation>
    <Folders>
        <Folder ID="Odyssey.Folders.MyCustomViews" Accessibility="Public"
        ParentFolder="IncidentManagement!ServiceManager.Console.IncidentManagement"
/>
    </Folders>
<Presentation>
```

> **NOTE: ABOUT MANAGEMENT PACK REFERENCES**
>
> `IncidentManagement!` in Listing 18.1 points to a reference `Alias`. For additional information about MP references, see Chapter 17, "Management Packs."

To make a folder appear in the Service Manager console, use a declaration similar to Listing 18.1. If you want a friendlier name to appear in the console or to enable localization, you should also declare a display string element folder. Chapter 17 discusses display strings.

Listing 18.2 builds on Listing 18.1, showing a more complete declaration of the custom folder. The listing includes an image reference to improve the appearance of the folder navigation pane and two `FolderItems` (`CreateGridView` and `CreateFolder`) to cause the Create View and Create Folder tasks to appear in the Folder Tasks section for the custom folder, as shown in Figure 18.2.

LISTING 18.2   Folder Declaration, Including Tasks

```
<Presentation>
    <Folders>
    <Folder ID="Odyssey.Folders.MyCustomViews" Accessibility="Public"
    ParentFolder="IncidentManagement!ServiceManager.Console.IncidentManagement"
      />
    </Folders>
    <FolderItems>
    <FolderItem ElementID="EnterpriseManagement!Microsoft.EnterpriseManagement.
      ServiceManager.UI.Console.Task.CreateGridView"
      ID="Odyssey.FolderItem.CreateView" Folder="Odyssey.Folders.MyCustomViews" />
      <FolderItem ElementID="EnterpriseManagement!Microsoft.EnterpriseManagement.
      ServiceManager.UI.Console.Task.CreateFolder"
      ID="Odyssey.FolderItem.CreateFolder" Folder="Odyssey.Folders.MyCustomViews " />
    </FolderItems>
    <ImageReferences>
      <ImageReference ElementID="Odyssey.Folders.MyCustomViews"
      ImageID="EnterpriseManagement!Microsoft.EnterpriseManagement.
      ServiceManager.UI.Console.Image.Folder" />
    </ImageReferences>
</Presentation>
```

Workspace

The lower portion of Figure 18.1 showed some of the built-in workspaces in Service Manager. The workspaces section in this figure was also extended with a custom workspace.

A workspace is defined as folder in an MP. What actually makes a custom folder a workspace is the parent folder used in the declaration of the custom folder. Using the built-in folder named ServiceManager.Console.RootFolder as the parent folder causes the custom folder to appear as a workspace.

In Listing 18.3, the custom folder with the ID Odyssey.Console.WorkSpace is declared as a workspace (shown in Figure 18.3 as Odyssey Workspace). The parent folder of the custom folder points at the built-in root folder (defined using a referenced MP Alias, shown in Listing 18.4); this is what makes the custom folder appear as a workspace. The folder called Odyssey.Console.WorkSpace.Root is then using the Odyssey Workspace folder as parent folder; this results in it being the root node in the Odyssey Workspace navigation tree, shown in Figure 18.3 as Workspace Root. The listing also includes several image references to make the nodes look more attractive, and a folder item to enable creating views in the folder named Folder in the figure. The names shown in Figure 18.3 are controlled by display strings, which enable localization.

FIGURE 18.3   Custom workspace.

LISTING 18.3   Workspace Declaration

```
<Presentation>
    <Folders>
      <Folder ID="Odyssey.Console.WorkSpace" Accessibility="Public"
    ParentFolder="EnterpriseManagement!ServiceManager.Console.RootFolder" />
      <Folder ID="Odyssey.Console.WorkSpace.Root" Accessibility="Public"
    ParentFolder="Odyssey.Console.WorkSpace" />
      <Folder ID="Odyssey.Folders.lvl1" Accessibility="Public"
    ParentFolder="Odyssey.Console.WorkSpace.Root" />
      <Folder ID="Odyssey.Folders.lvl2" Accessibility="Public"
    ParentFolder="Odyssey.Folders.lvl1" />
    </Folders>
    <FolderItems>
      <FolderItem ElementID=
    "EnterpriseManagement!Microsoft.EnterpriseManagement.
    ServiceManager.UI.Console.Task.CreateGridView"
    ID="Odyssey.FolderItem.CreateView" Folder="Odyssey.Folders.lvl1" />
    </FolderItems>
    <ImageReferences>
      <ImageReference ElementID="Odyssey.Console.WorkSpace"
    ImageID="SMWorkItem!WorkItemImage32x32" />
      <ImageReference ElementID="Odyssey.Console.WorkSpace"
    ImageID="SMWorkItem!WorkItemImage16x16" />
      <ImageReference ElementID="Odyssey.Console.WorkSpace.Root"
    ImageID="SMWorkItem!WorkItemImage16x16" />
      <ImageReference ElementID="Odyssey.Folders.lvl1"
    ImageID="EnterpriseManagement!Microsoft.EnterpriseManagement.
```

18

```
ServiceManager.UI.Console.Image.Folder" />
  <ImageReference ElementID="Odyssey.Folders.lvl2"
ImageID="EnterpriseManagement!Microsoft.
EnterpriseManagement.ServiceManager.UI.Console.Image.Folder" />
  </ImageReferences>
</Presentation>
```

LISTING 18.4   Required Reference

```
<Reference Alias="EnterpriseManagement">
    <ID>Microsoft.EnterpriseManagement.ServiceManager.UI.Console</ID>
    <Version>7.0.6555.0</Version>
    <PublicKeyToken>31bf3856ad364e35</PublicKeyToken>
</Reference>
```

After defining a workspace and a root folder for the workspace, you can add folders and views from within the console using console tasks (if these have been enabled using `Categories` and `FolderItems` as described in the "Folders" section).

Views

Folders have a single purpose in the Service Manager console, which is to act as containers for views. Using the Create View console task lets you easily create a view below the selected folder.

Starting the console task Create View launches the Create View wizard; Figure 18.4 shows the first step of this wizard.

In the General page of the wizard, enter the name of the view and choose the MP in which you will store the view. To learn more about choosing the correct MP in which to store customizations, see Chapters 16 and 17.

After specifying the name of the view and selecting the MP, specify criteria for the view in the second step in the wizard, shown in Figure 18.5. The criteria is basically a query definition used to query the configuration management database (CMDB) when the view is selected in the Navigation pane.

When specifying the view criteria, start by choosing a class to base the search on. The class is specifying which type of objects the search result should contain.

Clicking **Browse** opens the Select a Class dialog. This initially presents you with a list of frequently used basic classes, shown in the drop-down in Figure 18.6. Notice you can choose a combination class (also known as type projection) as the target for the view instead of a basic class. You would do this by selecting **Combination** classes in the View list, also shown in Figure 18.6. If the view criteria or the presented data contain information regarding related objects, you must build the criteria on a combination class rather than a basic class.

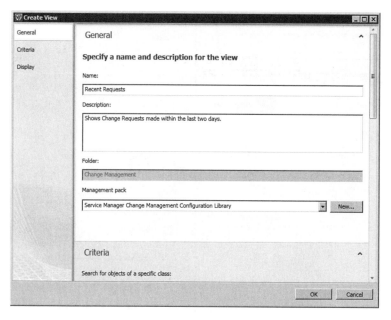

FIGURE 18.4   The General page of the Create View wizard.

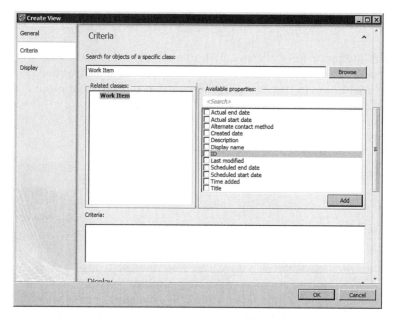

FIGURE 18.5   The Criteria page of the Create View wizard.

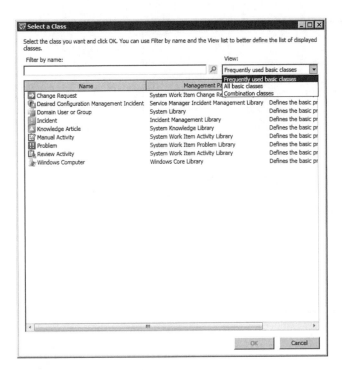

FIGURE 18.6   Select a Class.

Based on the class chosen, the properties associated with that class type are listed as available properties in the wizard. Selecting a property and clicking **Add** will add the property to the search criteria and enable you to specify a condition for that property that should be fulfilled by objects included in the view. This is shown in Figure 18.7.

FIGURE 18.7   The Criteria Builder dialog in the Create View wizard.

In most cases, building the criteria is self-explanatory. Based on the data type of a property, the criteria builder shows a suitable list of operators (equals, like, contains, and so on) that can be used. There is also functionality available to create a dynamic criteria, which requires some explanation. When specifying conditions in a criteria, there is a concept known as *tokens*. Tokens are placeholders; they are replaced with values at runtime. These are very useful as they give you the capability to have a criteria that is dynamically evaluated, based on factors such as time [Now] and who is using the view [me] (which user is running the console). To learn more about how to use tokens in a view criteria, see Chapter 19, "Advanced Customization Scenarios."

The final step in creating a view is to specify those properties to display in the view, shown in Figure 18.8. Each property selected is represented by a column in the finalized view. As mentioned earlier in this section, if you want a column showing a property value of a related object (such as the Assigned To user of an Incident), you must use a combination class as the base for the criteria.

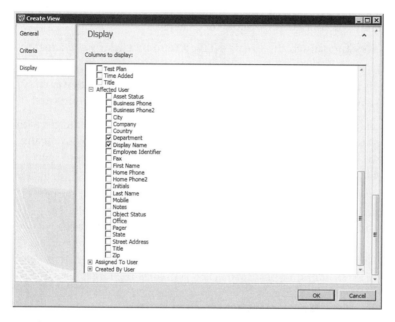

FIGURE 18.8   The Display page of the Create View wizard.

Console Tasks

In Service Manager, you can use console tasks to execute commands such as Ping Related Computer (see Figure 18.9) to simplify troubleshooting or automate repetitive tasks. Although there are quite a few useful tasks provided out of the box, you can also extend Service Manager with custom console tasks.

FIGURE 18.9   Console tasks example.

Console tasks can execute virtually anything that can be provided in a .NET Assembly
(.NET 3.5 is currently supported) or executed from a command line. This enables you to
write managed code, compile it into an assembly, and declare the use of this assembly in
an MP. This capability presents vast possibilities for adding useful console tasks.
Implementing custom console tasks does not have to include writing code! You can use
the create Console Task wizard in the console to create console tasks that execute any type
of useful command line, such as executing a custom script or executable.

As an example of creating a custom console task using the Create Task wizard, the next
procedure creates a custom console task that executes a Trace Route (`tracert`) command
against an Affected Computer in an incident. Follow these steps:

1. Go to **Library -> Tasks** and launch the Create a Task wizard by clicking the **Create
Task** console task.

2. At the second step in the wizard (see Figure 18.10), provide a name and description
for the console task. You also must specify a target class; this has several purposes:

   ▶ Specifying a target class associates the console task in the Service Manager with
   objects of the target class, or classes deriving from the target class. This means
   the console task will be available in the console whenever an object of specified class type is selected.

   ▶ Specifying a target class enables the use of target class properties, or properties
   of classes related to the target's class (when a combination class is used as
   target), as arguments in a command line executed by the console task.

   Because this example intends to execute the Trace Route command against an
   affected computer of an incident, the Incident class is used as the target class.

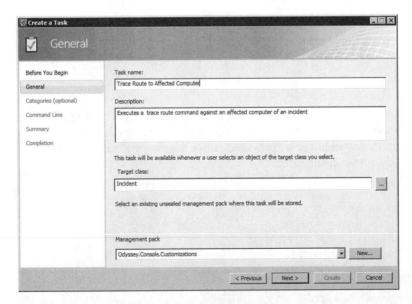

FIGURE 18.10   The General screen of the Create a Task wizard.

3. Now, select an MP in which to store the console task. Chapters 16 and 17 provide recommendations on storing your customizations and naming new MPs. Click **Next** to continue.

4. The next screen in the wizard (see Figure 18.11) enables the task to be added to categories that will associate it with folders. This makes the console task visible whenever a specified folder or child folder of the specified folder is selected in the Navigation pane. For example, selecting the Incident Management Folder Tasks category makes the task visible as a task for the Incident Management folder.

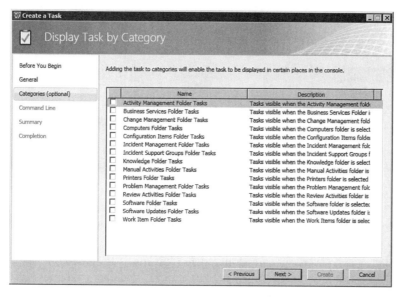

FIGURE 18.11   The Categories screen of the Create a Task wizard.

Because the Trace Route task requires that arguments be passed from a selected incident, this makes the console task unsuitable for other scenarios than when an incident is selected. For that reason, this particular example does not make use of any categories.

5. The Command Line step (see Figure 18.12) is where you specify which command should be executed, and which arguments that should be passed to the command.

Full path to command: lets you specify an executable to execute. This is in combination with specifying the optional Working directory (folder), identifying the exact path to the executable from the machine where the console task is used.

In the Trace Route example, the command that should be executed is tracert.exe. The working directory (folder) can therefore be left at its default value %windir%\system32, as this is where tracert.exe is placed.

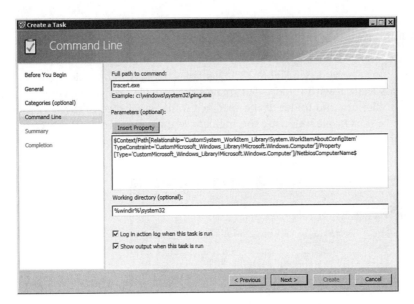

FIGURE 18.12   The Command Line screen of the Create a Task wizard.

The parameters section in Figure 18.12 enables you to pass arguments to the specified command. The arguments can be static arguments in the form of text as passed in a command in a console or an expression pointing to a class property and evaluated at runtime.

To assist in specifying the property expressions, there is an **Insert Property** button. This opens the Select Property dialog shown in Figure 18.13. The dialog enables you to select a property from the target class or classes related to the target class and add that as an argument to the command.

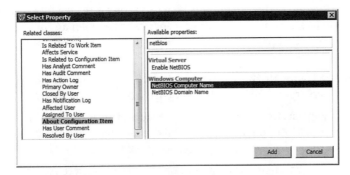

FIGURE 18.13   The Select Property dialog in the Create a Task wizard.

The Trace Route example passes the NetBIOS computer name of computers related via the About Configuration Item relationship.

6. After specifying the arguments, there are two options controlling whether output should be shown in a pop-up window when the task is executed and if the output should be logged in the Action log (such as the Incident Action log visible in the incident form).

   The Trace Route example makes use of both options, which means the output of the Trace Route task will be shown in a pop-up window and logged in the Incident Action log.

Figures 18.14, 18.15, and 18.16 show the result of implementing the console task described in this example. For additional console task examples, see Chapter 19.

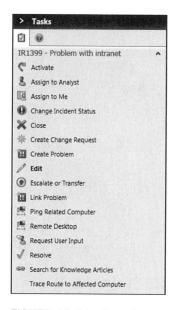

FIGURE 18.14   Trace Route to Affected Computer task.

18

FIGURE 18.15   Trace Route to Affected Computer output.

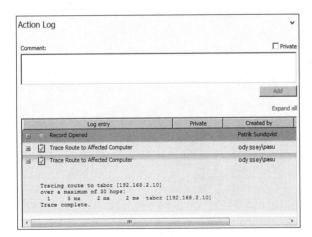

FIGURE 18.16   Trace Route to Affected Computer Action log.

Creating Data Models

In Service Manager, objects are stored as instances of classes. The classes define which properties and relationships you can use to describe an object. Chapter 16 describes the concepts of class types with associated class type properties, relationships, and how these together can form a data model describing an object and how it relates to other objects. It also describes the concept of inheritance between classes and relationships, and how this consolidates data model descriptions through the concept of base classes. This chapter puts the theory into practice to create new data models and customize existing ones. The chapter also delves further into the possibilities available for data modeling in Service Manager, describing the concept of singleton and abstract classes.

At a high level, here are the steps required to create a new data model for Service Manager:

1. Create an MP in which to store the model.
2. Create classes for the model.
3. Add properties to the classes.
4. Add relationships to the classes to describe how the classes relate to each other.
5. Seal the MP containing the data model.
6. Import the MP into Service Manager.

Sealing an MP containing a data model, or parts of it, is a best practice and a requirement if there are resources such as classes or relationships within it that will need to be referenced.

The next sections describe each step separately; see Chapter 19 for an end-to-end scenario creating a new data model.

Creating a Management Pack

To create a new MP using the Service Manager Authoring Tool, follow these steps:

1. To start the Service Manager Authoring Tool, click **Start -> All Programs -> Microsoft System Center -> Service Manager 2010 Authoring -> Service Manager Authoring Tool**.
2. In the Service Manager Authoring Tool, select **File -> New**.
3. In the New Management Pack dialog, enter a filename for the MP. Figure 18.17 shows an example.

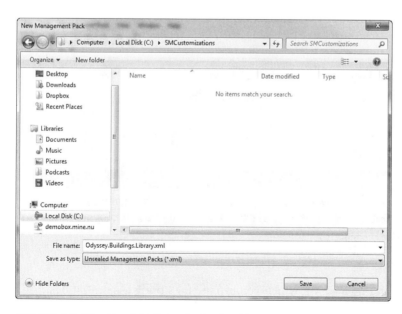

FIGURE 18.17   New MP dialog in Service Manager Authoring Tool.

4. In the New Management Pack dialog, click **Save**. The MP is created by the Authoring Tool and loaded into the Management Pack Explorer, shown in Figure 18.18.

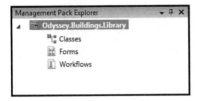

FIGURE 18.18   Management Pack Explorer in Service Manager Authoring Tool.

5. In the Management Pack Explorer, right-click the MP (**Odyssey.Buildings.Library**) and select **Properties**.

6. In the Details pane (shown in Figure 18.19), provide a description for the MP. Providing a description for an MP is a best practice.

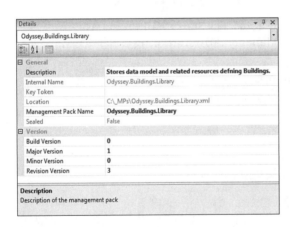

FIGURE 18.19   Details pane in Service Manager Authoring Tool.

7. Now, save the new Management Pack by selecting **File -> Save All**.

TIP: DETAILS OF SELECTED ITEM

The Details pane enables you to view and change the properties of the currently selected item, whether it is a selected node in the Management Pack Explorer or a workflow activity in the Workflow Designer.

You have now created an unsealed MP, which you can use for storing customizations.

Creating a New Class

Using the Service Manager Authoring Tool lets you easily define new classes for Service Manager. Follow these steps:

1. In the Service Manager Authoring Tool, create a new MP as described in the "Creating a Management Pack" section, or open an existing unsealed MP using **File -> Open**.

2. In the Management Pack Explorer, right-click the **Classes** node and select a base class by choosing one of the alternatives.

   ▶ Create Configuration Item Class

   ▶ Create Work Item Class

   ▶ Create Other Class

   Depending on the type of class you are creating, choose the most suitable option. For advice on choosing base class, see the "Choosing the Base Class" section, later in this chapter.

3. In the Create class dialog, enter an internal name for the class type and click **OK**. After you add a new class, all derived properties and relationships are visible in the Authoring pane, as shown in Figure 18.20.

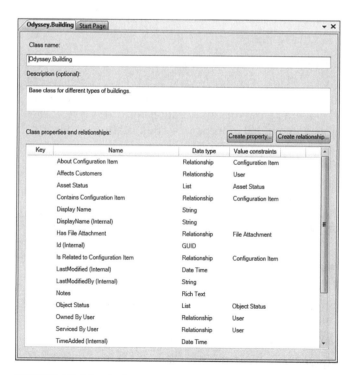

FIGURE 18.20   Authoring pane in Service Manager Authoring Tool.

4. In the Management Pack Explorer, right-click the new class below the Classes node. Select **Properties**.

5. In the Details pane (see Figure 18.21) showing the class type properties, enter a name and description for the class type. (The name is the display name shown in the Service Manager console.)

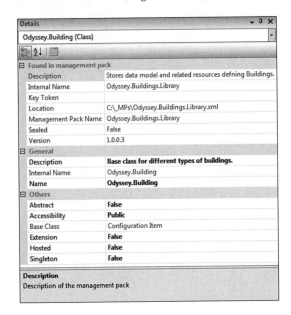

Details	▾ ⇩ ✕
Odyssey.Building (Class)	▾

Found in management pack	
Description	Stores data model and related resources defning Buildings.
Internal Name	Odyssey.Buildings.Library
Key Token	
Location	C:_MPs\Odyssey.Buildings.Library.xml
Management Pack Name	Odyssey.Buildings.Library
Sealed	False
Version	1.0.0.3
General	
Description	**Base class for different types of buildings.**
Internal Name	Odyssey.Building
Name	**Odyssey.Building**
Others	
Abstract	**False**
Accessibility	**Public**
Base Class	Configuration Item
Extension	**False**
Hosted	**False**
Singleton	**False**

Description
Description of the management pack

FIGURE 18.21   Details pane in Service Manager Authoring Tool.

6. In the Service Manager Authoring Tool, select **File -> Save All** to save the MP. You can now define the class is by adding properties and relationships. This is further described in the "Adding Properties and Relationships" section of this chapter.

Extending an Existing Class

To extend an existing class, follow these steps:

1. In the Service Manager Authoring Tool, open an existing unsealed MP, or create a new one using the procedure described in the "Creating a Management Pack" section of this chapter.

2. In the Management Pack Explorer, right-click the Classes node of the MP where you want to store the class extension, and select **Create Other Class**.

3. In the Base Class dialog, shown in Figure 18.22, locate and select the class you want to extend. Select the class, such as the Incident class, and click **OK**.

4. In the Create Class dialog, enter an internal name for the new class extension.

5. In the Management Pack Explorer, right-click the class node named in step 4 and select **Properties**.

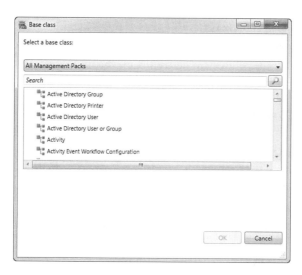

FIGURE 18.22   Base Class dialog in the Service Manager Authoring Tool.

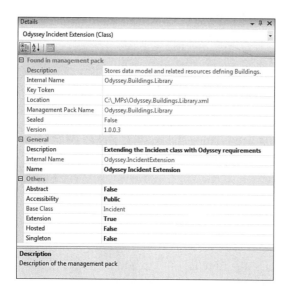

FIGURE 18.23   Details pane showing extension class.

6. In the Details pane, change the value of Extension to **True**, and enter a name and a description for the class extension. Figure 18.23 displays an example.

7. In the Service Manager Authoring Tool, select **File -> Save All** to save all changes. The class is now ready to be extended by adding properties and relationships. These are further described in the "Adding Properties and Relationships" section of the chapter.

Choosing a Base Class

When choosing a base class, base your decision on which characteristics you want the new class to inherit. Because all properties and relationships are derived from the base class, the type of object you want the class to describe should be the foundation for selecting a base class with suitable characteristics. Service Manager has out-of-the-box classes that fulfill the needs of most types, whether describing a physical or logical configuration item (CI) (such as a computer or an operating system) or describing a work item (such as a change request).

By reusing existing classes within Service Manager as base classes, your custom classes will gain useful characteristics other than derived data model characteristics such as properties and relationships. Here are some examples:

▶ Instances of the new class can be added to a relationship declaring a parent class as source or target. For example, if the new class derives from System.ConfigItem, it can be added to the Affected Items list in an incident.

▶ Instances of the new class are included in views targeting derived classes (as long as they fulfill the view criteria).

The next sections describe the most commonly used base classes.

Work Item

When defining a new work item for the Service Manager CMDB, use the class common for Incident, Change Request, and Problem, which is the Work Item class (internal name System.WorkItem). This gives you a good start in defining a new type of work item.

Choosing the Work Item class as base or using a class deriving from the Work Item class for a new class enables the use of existing lists of related work items to associate instances of the class with objects such as CIs or existing work items. Figure 18.24 shows an example of this, where an incident has been associated with a special request (a custom work item created to illustrate the example).

Configuration Item

When defining a new CI, such as a mobile phone, use the common class for all out-of-the-box CIs called Configuration Item. The Configuration Item class has the internal name System.ConfigItem.

By deriving from the Configuration Item class, the functionality to add instances of the class as related CIs in the change request form is automatically gained (see Figure 18.25).

Settings

In special cases, you might want to create a class to hold settings used by a workflow, an advanced console task, and so on. In these cases, you can use the class called Solution Settings (internal name System.SolutionSettings) as base. This scenario is also a perfect example of when a class should be marked as singleton, because you commonly only want one instance to exist of such a class.

Using the Solution Settings class, a base class causes instances of the class to appear in the Service Manager Settings view found in the Administration workspace. This is a good approach for managing all Service Manager-related settings in one place. Figure 18.26

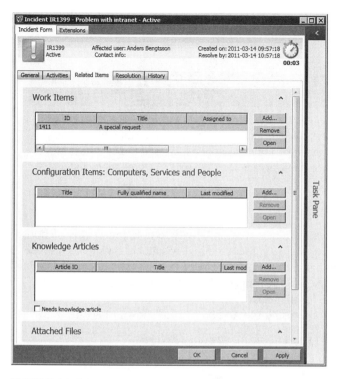

FIGURE 18.24   Incident related to custom work item.

FIGURE 18.25   Details pane showing extension class.

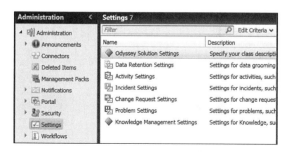

FIGURE 18.26   Settings view in Administration workspace.

shows how the Odyssey Solution Settings shows in the view by just using the Solution Settings class as base class.

TIP: LEARN HOW TO PROVIDE A GOOD USER EXPERIENCE FOR CUSTOM SETTINGS

Because the Settings view is not quite like the normal views in the Service Manager console, you need to register a task handler to be able to open up custom singleton instances in forms from the Settings view. For more information, see the blog post at http://blogs.technet.com/b/servicemanager/archive/2010/01/04/creating-a-custom-administration-setting.aspx.

Activities

In the special case when you are creating a new type of Activity to hold process instructions, such as the Manual Activity or Review Activity, there is a highly suitable class to use as base. This is the Activity class (internal name System.WorkItem.Activity), which is the base class for both of these out-of-the-box activities. Creating a class that derives from the Activity class and adding an object template for that class makes the template accessible from the Activity tab in the change request form (using the Add button), as shown in Figure 18.27.

Chapter 19 describes an end-to-end scenario using custom activities.

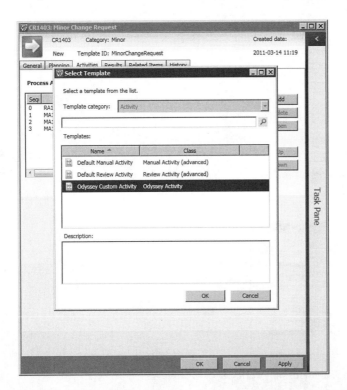

FIGURE 18.27   Template Picker showing custom activity template.

When deriving from the `Activity` class, you can use the Activity Event workflows for automation triggered by events from instances of your custom class. Figure 18.28 shows an example.

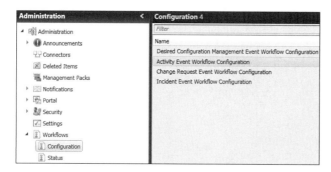

FIGURE 18.28   Activity Event Workflow for custom activities.

Adding Properties and Relationships

After preparing a new class or a class extension in the Service Manager Authoring Tool, follow these steps to add properties to the class:

1. In the Management Pack Explorer, right-click the class you want to add properties to and select **Edit**.

2. In the Authoring pane, click **Create Property**.

3. In the Create Property dialog, shown in Figure 18.29, enter an internal name for the new property.

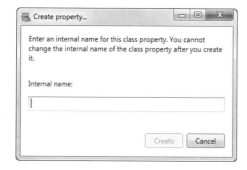

FIGURE 18.29   Create Property dialog in the Service Manager Authoring Tool.

4. Right-click the new property in the Authoring pane, and select **Properties**.

5. In the Details pane, enter a name and description of the property. Figure 18.30 shows an example.

6. This is also where you will define the characteristics of the property by defining the data type (string, integer, bool, and so on) and suitable constraints. For guidance, see the "Property Characteristics and Constraints" section.

FIGURE 18.30   Property details in the Service Manager Authoring Tool.

To add relationships, follow these steps:

1. In the Management Pack Explorer, right-click the new class you want to add a relationship to and select **Edit**.

2. In the Authoring pane, click **Create Relationship**.

3. In the Create Relationship dialog, enter an internal name for the relationship and click **OK**.

4. Right-click the newly added relationship in the Authoring pane, and select **Properties**.

5. In the Details pane, enter a name and description for the relationship. You can also define the characteristics of the relationship here, by defining the following relationship attributes:

   ▸ Relationship Type

   ▸ Abstract

   ▸ Source Class

   ▸ Source Class Min Cardinality

   ▸ Source Class Max Cardinality

   ▸ Target Class

   ▸ Target Class Min Cardinality

   ▸ Target Class Max Cardinality

Chapter 16 discusses these different attributes.

Property Characteristics and Constraints

When defining a new property for a class in Service Manager, the property has a number of attributes you can specify to provide different characteristics and constraints. All attributes except the RegEx attribute can be specified from the Service Manager Authoring Tool; specifying the RegEx attribute requires manually editing the MP XML.

The next sections describe the different attributes.

Data Type

To determine the data type of the property value, the Data Type attribute must be set to one of the supported data types. Supported data types are as follows:

▶ Integer

   Example: 1

▶ Decimal

   Example: 2.2

▶ Double

   Example: 2.2

▶ String

   Example: Printing Issue

▶ Date Time

   Example: 3/9/2010

▶ GUID (Globally Unique Identifier)

   Example: 26b70304-135f-4c77-af26-6bf952cd7caf

▶ Bool

   Example: True/False

▶ List

   Example: Low/Medium/High (Available values are determined by the value of the List Type attribute; see the "List Type" section for a description.)

▶ Rich Text (formatted text)

   Example: The user is having *problem*...

▶ Binary

   Example: 1011 1001...

Auto Increment

Setting `Auto Increment` to `True` causes the property to increase its value by 1 automatically for each new instance created in the CMDB. Setting `Auto Increment` is applicable only for data types `String` and `Integer`.

Case Sensitive

Marking a property as `Case Sensitive` makes the property value sensitive for case. This is applicable only for properties of data type `String`.

Default Value

All properties with a `Default Value` will have the `Default Value` as their value if nothing else is provided.

Key

Setting the `Key` to `True` makes the property part of the class identity, used to identify an instance uniquely among others. Therefore, marking a property as `Key` makes the property required.

Maximum Length

Setting `Maximum Length` is applicable only for properties with data type `String`. By specifying a number for `Maximum Length`, you prevent strings longer than the given value from being stored as property values in the CMDB.

Minimum Length

Setting `Minimum Length` is applicable only for properties with data type `String`. By specifying a number for `Minimum Length`, you prevent strings shorter than the given value from being stored as property values in the CMDB.

Maximum Value

Setting `Maximum Value` is applicable only for properties with data type `Integer`. By specifying a number for `Maximum Value`, you prevent values higher than the given value from being stored as property values in the CMDB.

Minimum Value

Setting `Minimum Value` is applicable only for properties with data type `Integer`. By specifying a number for `Minimum Value`, you prevent values lower than the given value from being stored as property values in the CMDB.

Required

Setting the `Required` attribute to `True` prevents instances without a given property value from being stored in the CMDB.

List Type

Use of the `List Type` attribute is valid only for data type `List` and used to specify which list to tie to the property value. Setting the `List Type` attribute ensures that only values from the given list are accepted as property values.

RegEx

The RegEx is the only valid attribute for data type String and used to enforce that a string stored as a property value follows a given pattern.

In Listing 18.5, the RegEx attribute is given a value of Room [0-9]+. This means that a string stored as property value in the property RoomName must start with the text Room followed by a whitespace and a number. The + means there can be any number of occurrences of the preceding character (which, in this example, is a digit between 0 and 9).

LISTING 18.5   Regular Expression Example

```
<Property ID="RoomName" Type="string" RegEx="Room [0-9]+" />
```

TIP: LEARN MORE ABOUT REGULAR EXPRESSIONS

To learn how to master the regular expression language, look at this excellent article at http://msdn.microsoft.com/en-us/library/28hw3sce.aspx, which introduces regular expressions.

List Types

Enumeration, also known as lists in Service Manager, is a special data type available for class type properties. Lists are frequently used as a data type, because it limits the possible values of a property to the list entries. This is the data type to use if planning to present a user with a list to choose the value from, as shown in the incident form in Figure 18.31.

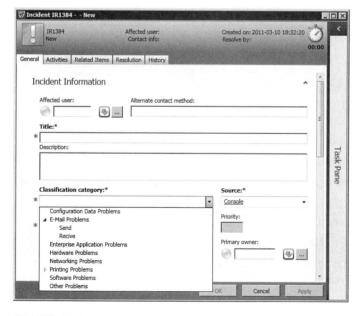

FIGURE 18.31   Example of List Type use.

As shown in Figure 18.31, lists in Service Manager have hierarchy support (parent - child support), which makes them even more useful. As an example of the usefulness of a list, suppose you want to describe the location of a server rack. You could create a list that looks like Listing 18.6 and use a list picker on the computer form for the user to pick a location. Alternatively, you could create new classes for `Buildings`, `Floors`, `Rooms`, and `Racks`, add hosting relationships between these, and use an object picker from the computer form to have the user pick an instance of the rack class to describe the location. The first alternative is extremely easy to implement compared to the second alternative and could probably fulfill the requirements of most scenarios. However, the second alternative, which is a more complex alternative, might be a better solution in some scenarios because it provides some advantages, such as

▶ The possibility to view all computers in a building, floor, room, or rack.

▶ Through derived or added relationships, you could create a change request related to a room.

▶ Ability to create reports based on the different classes.

LISTING 18.6   Example of List Hierarchy

```
Building 1
-- Floor 1
---- Room 1
------ Rack 1
-- Floor 2
---- Room 1
------ Rack 1
------ Rack 2
Building 2
```

To add a property of data type `List` to a class, follow these steps:

1. While adding properties to a new class or extending an existing class, click **Create Property**.

2. In the Create Property dialog, enter an internal name for the property and click **OK**.

3. In the Authoring pane, right-click the new property and click **Details**.

4. In the Details pane, give the property a description and change the data type to **List**.

5. In the Select a list dialog that opens (see Figure 18.32), select the list you want the property to be bound to and click **OK**.

   If there is not a suitable list, click **Create List**.

   In the Create List dialog, enter an internal name, a display name, a description for the new List, and click **Create**.

   Back in the Select a list dialog, select the new List and click **OK**.

6. Click **File -> Save All** to save the changes to the MP.

FIGURE 18.32   Select a list dialog in the Service Manager Authoring Tool.

All data model resources such as class definitions, including relationships and list type definitions (definition of the List root element), should be stored in sealed MPs, as discussed in Chapter 16.

When the MP containing a List definition is imported into Service Manager, you can add the list values using the console. To manage the values of a list, open the Service Manager console and go to **Library -> Lists**. If these are stored in an unsealed MP, list items you create from the console (in the Library workspace) will automatically be stored in the same unsealed MP. If you seal the MP where the List definition is stored, creating new list items for the list using the console will let you choose the unsealed MP into which to store the list items.

Singleton Classes

The singleton class type is special in the way that there always exists one, and no more than one, instance of a singleton class. When importing an MP containing a singleton class, an instance is immediately accessible in the CMDB. When looking in the CMDB, you will notice the class GUID (generated on import) and the instance ID are the same. Therefore, you can say "the single instance is the class." A common use for singleton classes is to store settings inside the CMDB, as shown in Administration -> Settings in the Administration workspace of the console.

To create a singleton class, follow the steps in the "Creating a New Class" section, and mark the class as Singleton = True using the Details pane in the Service Manager Authoring Tool.

NOTE: KEY NOT REQUIRED FOR A SINGLETON

A singleton does not require a Key property, because there can be only one instance of the class.

Abstract Classes

An abstract class is a class for which no instances can exist. The primary purpose of an abstract class is to consolidate common characteristics and act as a base class for deriving classes. The common characteristics (properties and relationships) do not always make sense in a standalone way, making it useful to be able to mark a class as abstract to ensure no instances are created using the class.

Even though an instance cannot be created of an abstract class, the abstract classes can be used as targets for views and workflows to make the views and workflows "hit" all instances of classes deriving from the abstract class.

To create an abstract class, follow the steps in the "Creating a New Class" section and mark the class as Abstract = True using the Details pane in the Service Manager Authoring Tool. The two most frequently used abstract classes in the CMDB are System.WorkItem (Work Item) and System.ConfigItem (Configuration Item).

Creating Workflows

As you might have noticed throughout this book, workflows come in many shapes within Service Manager. In earlier chapters (such as Chapter 10, "Incident Management") you learned how to use the event workflows configurable within the Service Manager console to notify users and apply object templates. This section looks at the possibilities of adding custom workflows to Service Manager.

Given the number of shapes a workflow can have in Service Manager, you can create and add them to the product in a number of ways. This part of the chapter describes how you can use the Service Manager Authoring Tool to create custom workflows for Service Manager. Chapter 19 includes an end-to-end example on how to use the Service Manager workflow engine to automate an IT (Information Technology) process.

On a high level, to implement a custom workflow into Service Manager using the Service Manager Authoring Tool you need to do the following:

1. Create an MP or open an existing (unsealed) MP to store the workflow.
2. Define the workflow, schedule, or when the object meets specified conditions.
3. Design the workflow using workflow activities.
4. Save the MP.
5. Deploy the workflow to Service Manager.

Using the Service Manager Authoring Tool, you can create two types of workflows, which do both the following:

- ▶ Run at a scheduled time or at scheduled intervals.

- ▶ Run only when a database object meets specified conditions.

Creating a Scheduled Workflow

Scheduled workflows are highly useful for doing maintenance jobs within your CMDB. For example, by scheduling a workflow to run on an interval you could check for incidents breaching a specific service level agreement (SLA) and take appropriate action.

To create a scheduled workflow, follow these steps:

1. Open the Service Manager Authoring Tool.

2. Open an existing or create a new MP (described in the "Creating a Management Pack" section).

3. In the Management Pack Explorer, right-click the **Workflows** node, and then select **Create**, as shown in Figure 18.33.

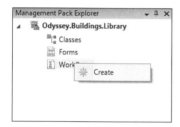

FIGURE 18.33   Create workflow: Service Manager Authoring Tool.

4. In the Create Workflow wizard shown in the General step in Figure 18.34, enter a name and description, and then click **Next**.

   Optionally, you can click the **Advanced** button, to adjust the retry and timeout limits of the workflow.

5. On the Trigger Condition step, leave the choice at Run at a scheduled time or at scheduled intervals, and click **Next**.

6. On the Trigger Criteria step, choose the schedule or interval on which you want to execute the workflow. Click **Next**.

7. On the Summary step, review the details and click **Create** and then **Close** to create the new scheduled workflow.

After you create the workflow, the Authoring pane shows the workflow design surface, and you are ready to add workflow activities to the design surface. The "Adding Workflow Activities and Setting Up the Required Properties" section discusses this process.

18

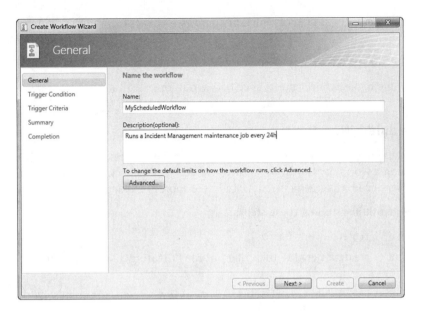

FIGURE 18.34   Create Workflow wizard: Service Manager Authoring Tool.

Creating a Workflow Triggered by a Database Change

Workflows triggered by a database change are used to react on a given state that is occurring in the CMDB. For example, you can use this to automate IT processes based on registration and approval of a standard change. If a manager were to request a user account for a new employee, this would normally be registered in a change request in the CMDB (or service request, which will be available as a work item in Service Manager 2012). When a review activity portion of the change request is approved, the status update can trigger a workflow to create the user account. For a step-by-step tutorial on building such a workflow, see Chapter 19.

To create a workflow triggered by a database change, follow these steps:

1. Open the Service Manager Authoring Tool.

2. Open an existing MP or create a new one (described in the "Creating a Management Pack" section).

3. In the Management Pack Explorer, right-click the **Workflows** node and select **Create**.

4. In the General step of the Create Workflow wizard, enter a name and description, and then click **Next**.

    Optionally, click the **Advanced** button to adjust the retry and timeout limits of the workflow.

5. On the Trigger Condition step, make sure that Run only when a database object meets specified conditions selection is chosen, and click **Next**.

6. On the Trigger Criteria step, click **Browse**.

7. In the Class Property dialog, choose which class to monitor in the CMDB and click **OK**.

The classes available to pick from are the classes stored in the MPs that are placed in the *%ProgramFiles%\Microsoft System Center\Service Manager 2010 Authoring\Library* folder, or in MPs currently loaded in the Management Pack Explorer.

8. Back in the Trigger Criteria step, choose which Change Event to monitor:

   ▶ When an object of the selected class is created

   ▶ When an object of the selected class is updated

   ▶ When an object of the selected class is deleted

9. Optionally, you can specify additional criteria by clicking **Additional Criteria** and specifying property values.

It is not possible to specify additional criteria for Delete Change Events. For Create Change Events, the new object that is created must fulfill the additional criteria; for the Updated Change Event, two criteria may be specified:

   ▶ One criteria for the pre-update state (Changed From) must be fulfilled by the object being updated before the change is applied

   ▶ One criteria for post-update state (Changed To) must to be fulfilled by the object after the change has been applied

This is shown in Figure 18.35.

When the criteria have been set, click **Next**.

FIGURE 18.35   Additional workflow criteria.

10. At the Summary screen, review the summary information and click **Create** and then **Close** to create the workflow.

After you create the workflow, the Authoring pane shows the workflow design surface, and you are ready to add workflow activities to the design surface. This is discussed in the "Adding Workflow Activities and Setting Up the Required Properties" section of this chapter.

Editing Workflow Details After Creation

To edit workflow details such as the workflow description after creating the workflow, follow these steps:

1. In the Management Pack Explorer, right-click the workflow you want to edit and select **Details**.

2. In the Details pane, select a property such as Description and click the ellipsis button (...) shown (marked by an arrow) in Figure 18.36. This opens the Workflow Properties dialog, where you can edit the workflow details.

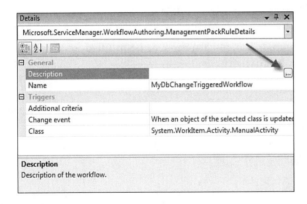

FIGURE 18.36   Workflow Details: Service Manager Authoring Tool.

Adding Workflow Activities and Setting Up the Required Properties

After you create a workflow with the Create Workflow wizard, it is time to design the workflow. The Service Manager Authoring Tool comes with a library of useful Windows workflow activities you can use to build the workflow. These out-of-the-box activities are shown in the Activities Toolbox in Figure 18.37.

The Service Manager Authoring Guide describes the different activities and instructions on how to extend the Activities Toolbox with custom activities. The guide is available at http://technet.microsoft.com/en-us/library/ff597545.aspx.

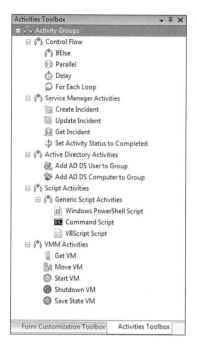

FIGURE 18.37   Activities Toolbox: Service Manager Authoring Tool.

Here is an example showing how to add a workflow activity to an empty workflow. Follow these steps:

1. Create a new workflow triggered by a data base change (instructions available in the "Creating a Workflow Triggered by a Database Change" section) using these trigger criteria:

   ▶ **Class name:** Incident

   ▶ **Change event:** When an object of the class is created

2. Select the **Command Script** activity in the Activity Toolbox.

3. Drag the activity onto the workflow design surface and drop the activity between the start (green arrow) and end point (red circle).

4. In the Authoring pane on the workflow design surface, right-click the newly dropped **Command Script** activity and select **Details**.

5. In the Details pane, enter the following:

   ▶ **Name:** CreateEvent

   ▶ **Description:** Writes Incident Id to the Application EventLog

6. Still in the Details pane, click the ellipses button (...) on the Script Body row.

7. In the Configure a Script Activity dialog, click the down arrow. This is indicated by an arrow in Figure 18.38.

FIGURE 18.38   The Configure a Script Activity dialog.

8. In the Configure a Script Activity dialog, in the area you expanded by clicking the down arrow, type:

   EventCreate /L Application /T Success /ID 1 /D "The Incident that triggered this workflow has the id: %1"

9. In the Configure a Script Activity dialog, click the **Script Properties** tab.

10. On the Properties tab, click **New**.

11. On the Properties tab, click the ellipses button (...) on the New Argument row.

12. In the Define input for the Activity dialog, select **Use a class property**.

13. In the Define input for the Activity dialog, select the **ID** property as shown in Figure 18.39, and click **OK**.

14. In the Configure a Script Activity dialog, click **OK**.

15. In the Service Manager Authoring Tool, click **File -> Save All** to save the MP and compile the workflow into an assembly.

16. Deploy the workflow using the instructions in the "Deploying Custom Workflows" section of this chapter.

To test the workflow, follow these steps:

1. In the Service Manager console, go to **Work Items -> Incident Management** and select the **Create Incident** task.

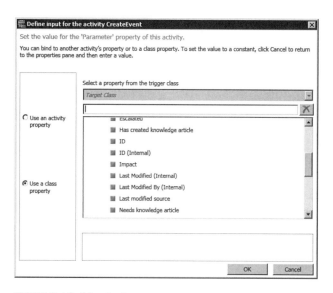

FIGURE 18.39   Define input for the activity dialog.

2. Enter required details and click **OK**.

3. On the Service Manager management server responsible for workflows, click **Start -> All Program -> Administrative Tools -> Event Viewer**.

4. In the Event Viewer, open the Application log and look for an event with source EventCreate, as shown in Figure 18.40.

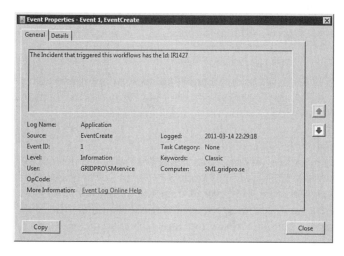

FIGURE 18.40   Workflow output in the Application log.

In this example, properties from the class instance that triggered the workflow were used as input. You can combine this with PowerShell or managed code, with no limit to what you can automate!

Deploying Custom Workflows

With your custom workflow built, it is time to deploy it to the Service Manager management server. Follow these steps to deploy a custom workflow built using the Service Manager Authoring Tool:

1. While still in the Service Manager Authoring Tool, click **File -> Save All** to save the MP and compile all workflows to assemblies.

2. Go to the folder where the MP is saved, and copy the assembly with the same name as the workflow you created in the Service Manager Authoring Tool.

3. Paste the assembly into the Service Manager 2010 installation folder, typically *%ProgramFiles%*\Microsoft System Center\Service Manager 2010 on the Service Manager management server responsible for workflows.

4. Open the Service Manager console.

5. Go to **Administration -> Management Packs**.

6. Click **Import**.

7. In the Select Management Packs to Import dialog, select the MP to import and click **Open**.

8. In the Import Management Packs dialog, click **Import** followed by **Close**.

TIP: IF THINGS GO BAD

If you are having problems compiling the workflow in the Service Manager Authoring Tool, click **View** and select **Output** to see the compiler output. This is the best place to look for errors caused when compiling workflows.

Customizing Forms

After creating new classes for Service Manager, you can create forms to support managing instances of the classes in the Service Manager console. It is not always necessary to create forms because Service Manager includes the Generic Form, previously described in Chapter 16. Chapter 16 also describes how the Generic Form is used when Service Manager is not aware of the existence of a specific form for a class. The Generic Form generates fields for all simple properties in a way that that is not customizable. Therefore, if the presentation demands are not too high, you may decide to use the Generic Form to create and manage instances of a custom class. However, if there are higher demands on presentation or the Generic Form is not able to deliver the functional requirements, you can create new forms using the Service Manager Authoring Tool, Visual Studio 2010, or Expression Blend.

TIP: LEARN MORE ABOUT FORMS IN SERVICE MANAGER

Chapter 16 describes the technology behind forms in Service Manager, and discusses how a form is bound to a class directly or indirectly through a type projection.

The Service Manager Authoring Tool not only enables creating new forms for new classes, it also allows you to customize existing out-of-the-box forms. Using the Authoring Tool, changes to a form can be "recorded" into an MP and imported into Service Manager. When a form is opened, Service Manager checks for customizations and applies these on top of the form by replaying all customizations before the form is visible to the user.

As described in Chapter 16, forms must target a type projection instead of a simple class to be able to show data on related objects. When you are using the Service Manager Authoring Tool to create a new form, the tool creates a type projection automatically if a control such as a User Picker is bound to a related object using the Authoring Tool. This means that when you use the Authoring Tool to create the new form, you generally do not need to be concerned about type projections.

The following sections show how to customize an existing form and create a new form for a custom class.

Creating New Forms

As mentioned in the previous section, you can create new forms using the Service Manager Authoring Tool, Visual Studio 2010, or Expression Blend. There are some differences in what you can accomplish with the Service Manager Authoring Tool versus the two other tools.

When using the Service Manager Authoring Tool to create a new form, you can use drag-and-drop to add controls. The tool provides a way to bind the values between the control and the underlying data model, consisting of the targeted class or type projection, through a user-friendly binding dialog (see Figure 18.41). The binding dialog makes it easy to bind a control such as a text box to a property in your data model.

However, the Authoring Tool limits you to from doing much more than that. You will be able to control visibility and binding mode (more on this in the example in this section on creating a new form), but doing more advanced customization will require use of Visual Studio.

Using Visual Studio to create new forms enables you to validate input and provide visual feedback of that validation result directly in the presentation layer. It also enables use of "code behind" to do things such as validating data against custom logic before submitting the data to the CMDB. Visual Studio enables use of the full range of controls available for Windows Presentation Foundation (WPF), including custom controls. Using Visual Studio to create new forms lets you do nearly anything with the form, only limited by the resources performing the development. Although the Authoring Tool enables someone unfamiliar to development and Visual Studio to create new forms with ease, Visual Studio 2010 and Expression Blend development will necessitate a developer familiar with WPF development.

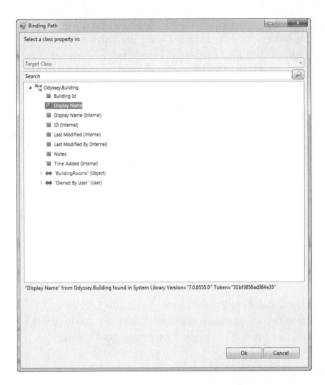

FIGURE 18.41   Binding dialog: Service Manager Authoring Tool.

To create a new form with the Service Manager Authoring Tool, follow these steps:

1. Open the Service Manager Authoring Tool.

2. Open an existing MP or create a new one where you will store the new form. Instructions for creating a new MP are in the "Creating a Management Pack" section in this chapter.

3. In the Management Pack Explorer, right-click the **Forms** node in the MP where you want to store the form and select **Create**.

4. In the Choose Base Class dialog, select the base class for the form and click **OK**.

   Choosing the base class associates the form to the chosen class and tells the Service Manager console to use this form to display data from instances of the chosen class.

5. In the Create Form dialog, enter an internal name for the form and click **Create**.

   After you click Create, the Authoring pane opens a form design surface for the new form.

6. In the Management Pack Explorer, right-click the new form and select **Properties**.

7. As a best practice, in the Properties pane, enter a name (a more user-friendly name than the internal name) and a description.

8. In the Service Manager Authoring Tool, click **File -> Save All** to save the new form to the MP.

A new form has now been created for the chosen base class and is ready to be populated with controls.

To add controls to the new form, follow these steps:

1. Using the Management Pack Explorer, right-click the new form and select **Customize**. The Authoring pane (if not already open) opens the form design surface.

2. In the Form Customization Toolbox, select and drag the **Text Box** control onto the Authoring pane, showing the new form.

3. In the Authoring pane, select the new **Text Box** control and make sure you have the Details pane showing the properties of the selected control.

TIP: MORE INFORMATION ON SERVICE MANAGER FORMS INFRASTRUCTURE

Chapter 16 describes the technology behind forms in Service Manager. It also discusses how a form is bound to a class directly or indirectly through a type projection.

---

4. In the Details pane, click the ellipses button (...) on the Binding Path row, shown in Figure 18.42.

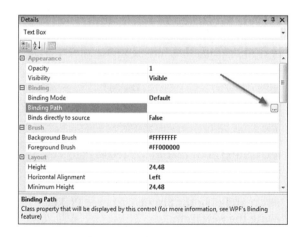

FIGURE 18.42   Control details: Service Manager Authoring Tool.

5. In the Binding path dialog that opens, select the property that you want to bind the text box to and click **OK**.

6. Repeat steps 3–5 to add more controls to the form.

    Some controls require special instructions; these are described in the "User Picker," "Single Instance Picker," and "List Picker" sections.

7. When satisfied with the form, click **File -> Save All** to save the form to the MP.

8. To deploy the form, open the Service Manager console and go to **Administration -> Management Packs**.

9. Click **Import**.

10. In the Select Management Packs to Import dialog box, select the MP to import and click **Open**.

11. In the Import Management Packs dialog, click **Import**, and then **Close**.

User Picker

A User Picker is used to bind user objects to the class instance currently being managed by the form. The User Picker lets you search for a user and updates the targeted relationship with the selected user object.

Follow these steps to add a User Picker to a form:

1. In the Form Customization Toolbox, select and drag the **User Picker** control onto the Authoring pane, showing the new form.

2. In the Authoring pane, select the new **User Picker** control and make sure you have the Details pane showing the properties of the selected control.

3. In the Details pane, click the ellipses button (...) on the Binding Path row, shown in Figure 18.42.

4. In the Binding path dialog box that appears, select the relationship you want to manage using the User Picker control and click **OK**.

The User Picker control only lets you choose relationships that have a source object class user and source max cardinality of 1 or target object class of User and a target max cardinality of 1.

Single Instance Picker

A Single Instance Picker is used to bind objects to each other using relationships. The control lets you choose an instance of given class and adds that as the related object.

Follow these steps to add a Single Instance Picker to a form:

1. In the Form Customization Toolbox, select and drag the **Single Instance Picker** control onto the Authoring pane, showing the new form.

2. In the Authoring pane, select the new **Single Instance Picker** control and make sure you have the Details pane showing the properties of the selected control.

3. In the Details pane, click the ellipses button (...) on the Instance Type row.

4. In the Select a class dialog, choose the class you want to use as a constraint for the Single Instance Picker and click **OK**. The control will only show instances of given type when used to select an instance.

5. In the Details pane, click the ellipses button (...) on the Binding Path row, shown in Figure 18.42.

6. In the Binding path dialog box that appears, select the relationship you want to bind the control to, and click **OK**.

The Single Instance Picker control only lets you choose relationships that have a source object class of specified type (or derives from that type) and source max cardinality of 1 or target object class of specified type (or derives from that type) and a target max cardinality of 1.

List Picker

A List Picker is used to manage properties with the data type List. To add a List Picker to a form, follow these steps:

1. In the Form Customization Toolbox, select and drag the **List Picker** control onto the Authoring pane, showing the new form.

2. In the Authoring pane, select the new **List Picker** control and make sure you have the Details pane showing the properties of the selected control.

3. In the Details pane, click the ellipses button (...) on the Binding Path row, shown in Figure 18.42.

4. In the Binding path dialog that pops up, select the property you want to bind the control to and click **OK**.

The Single Instance Picker control only lets you choose properties of data type List, for obvious reasons.

For a description of other controls such as the Tab Control available in the Form Customization Toolbox, read the Service Manager Authoring Guide at http://technet.microsoft.com/en-us/library/ff597545.aspx.

Customizing Built-In Forms

As mentioned in the "Customizing Forms" section, the Service Manager Authoring Tool allows for customization of out-of-the-box forms. To customize a form, follow these steps:

1. Open the Service Manager Authoring Tool.

2. In the Service Manager Authoring Tool, verify that the Form Browser is visible. If not, click **View -> Form Browser**.

3. In the Form Browser, search for and select the form you want to customize.

4. Right-click the form in the Form Browser, and then select **View**. This adds the MP hosting the form to the Management Pack Explorer.

5. In the Management Pack Explorer, right-click the form you want to customize and select **Customize**.

6. In the Target Management Pack dialog, select an MP into which to store the form customizations and click **OK**. (You have the option to create a new MP or browse for an existing one.)

7. In the Management Pack Explorer, right-click the **Form** node representing the customized form in the MP you chose to store the customizations and select Customize. The name of the MP will end with (Customized).

8. In the Authoring pane showing the form to be customized, add new controls as described in the "Creating New Forms" section of this chapter.

9. In the Authoring pane, select the existing controls and make required modifications using the Details pane.

10. After customizing the form, click **File -> Save All** to save your changes to the MP.

11. Import the MP containing the form customizations to Service Manager to begin using the customized forms.

TIP: ACTIVE TAB

When customizing forms that contain tabs, the tab where the last recorded modification took place is the one that will be selected when opening the customized form in the console.

Alternative Way to Add Controls to a Form

Using the Service Manager Authoring Tool, there is an alternative way to add controls to a form rather than dragging controls from the Forms Customization Toolbox. When a form design surface is visible in the Authoring pane, select the form by clicking the design surface. Ensure the Class Browser is visible (if not, click **View -> Class Browser**). When a form is selected in the Authoring pane, the Class Browser automatically shows the form base class and related classes. If you select a property from the base class or a related class and drag that onto the form design surface in the Authoring pane, the Service Manager Authoring Tool automatically chooses an appropriate control and sets the Binding Path of the control to the dragged property. Dragging a node representing a related objet, as shown in Figure 18.43, causes the Authoring Tool to create a User Picker on the form design surface and, again, will automatically set the Binding Path of the control.

FIGURE 18.43   Class Browser in Service Manager Authoring Tool.

Sealing Using the Service Manager Authoring Tool

Chapter 17 describes the process of sealing MPs using a tool called fastseal.exe. An alternative to this is using the Service Manager Authoring Tool to seal an MP. The process still requires you to create a strong name key, which you can create using sn.exe. Chapter 19 discusses the process of creating a strong name.

To seal an MP with the Authoring Tool, follow these steps:

1. Open the Service Manager Authoring Tool.

2. Open the unsealed MP using **File -> Open**.

3. Right-click the unsealed MP in the Management Pack Explorer, and select **Seal Management Pack**.

4. Perform the following actions in the Seal Management Pack dialog box, shown in Figure 18.44:

FIGURE 18.44   Seal Management Pack dialog in the Service Manager Authoring Tool.

▶ Select the output directory (folder).

▶ Locate the strong name key (created with sn.exe).

- ▸ Enter a company name.
- ▸ (Optional) Enter copyright text.
- ▸ Click **Seal**.

Web Portals

The Service Manager Self-Service and Analyst portals are built on ASP.NET technology. The ability to customize the portals was somewhat limited when Service Manager 2010 was initially released. Since then, Microsoft has released the portal source code to the public. If you have access to an ASP.NET developer, you can customize the portals to do nearly anything using the portal source code and the Service Manager Software Developer Kit (SDK).

The announcement of the portal source code availability and a download link is available at http://blogs.technet.com/b/servicemanager/archive/2011/03/02/service-manager-portal-source-code-released.aspx. Included in the download is a new version of the Self-Service portal that looks more SharePoint-like and therefore more suitable for incorporating in your current SharePoint implementation.

You can download the Service Manager 2010 SDK from http://www.microsoft.com/downloads/en/details.aspx?displaylang=en&FamilyID=1862b19e-9cc1-49b5-b121-eb567a7b2fee.

Several things are possible for customizing the web portals without using a developer, such as hiding the Reset Password link. For instructions on doing so, see the Service Manager Authoring Guide, available at http://technet.microsoft.com/en-us/library/ff597545.aspx.

Summary

This chapter discussed the specifics of less-advanced customizations for Service Manager. It went through the steps required to implement the different customizations, from customizing the console with new views and console tasks to creating classes, workflows, and forms. Chapter 19 takes this discussion to a deeper level.

CHAPTER 19

Advanced Customization Scenarios

The complexity of customizing Service Manager can vary. Chapter 18, "Customizing Service Manager," described the fundamental concepts you need to know for basic customization scenarios. This chapter utilizes those concepts already learned and applies them in an end-to-end scenario of automating an Information Technology (IT) process. It provides a data modeling example and describes several techniques for custom views. The chapter also includes an introduction to creating custom forms using Visual Studio and console tasks using PowerShell.

The online content available for this book at http://www.informit.com/store/product.aspx?isbn=0672334364 includes a management pack (MP) containing the custom workspace built using the step-by-step instructions in this chapter.

Custom Data Models

You can create or customize a data model in Service Manager by manually editing the eXtensible Markup Language (XML) of an MP or by using the Authoring Tool available for Service Manager. This chapter discusses how to use the Service Manager Authoring Tool.

To explain the concept of data modeling in Service Manager, the next sections discuss creating a data model you can use to describe different types of buildings in the Service Manager database. The example is a simplified version of how a real model would look; its purpose is to show what is possible to do within Service Manager, rather than to show how to define a perfect model for buildings.

Before creating your new model, you should identify the requirements of the model. This example identifies several common properties between the different kinds of buildings that the model should describe. All buildings should have these common properties, regardless of type, location, and so on. Here are the common properties:

▶ ID

▶ Description

▶ Address

▶ City

▶ State

▶ ZIP Code

In addition to common properties, several relationships are identified as common for all types of buildings:

▶ The building should have an owner defined that can be contacted if necessary. Using this relationship, the user owning the building can easily be looked up from the configuration management database (CMDB), and the contact information for that user shown.

▶ To describe the different rooms in a building, a class type describing the characteristics of a room and a relationship tying together the rooms to a building are added to the model. The relationship type used to relate rooms to a building should be of type `Hosting` to ensure a room cannot exist without a building in the CMDB.

▶ The room class type should have several basic properties:

    ▶ RoomNumber

    ▶ Availability

    ▶ SquareFeet

The different types of building described using this model will be represented by its own class type, deriving from a class containing the common properties for buildings and adding the unique properties for that type of building.

The model described to this point is visualized in Figure 19.1, where the `Odyssey.Building` class type has been equipped with the common properties for buildings.

The `System.User` class, which is an existing class type in Service Manager, is related to the `building` through the `BuildingHasOwner` relationship, which identifies the owner of the building. A class representing a room, `Odyssey.Building.Room`, is related to the `building` through the relationship called `BuildingHasRooms`, which describes the rooms of a building. Different types of buildings will be using the building class type as a base to derive all the properties and relationships from the `building` class type.

To begin working with the data model, you must create a MP in which to store the model. This is discussed in the next section.

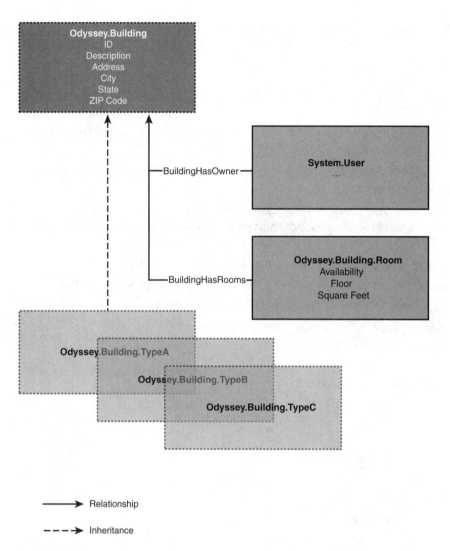

→ Relationship

- - -→ Inheritance

FIGURE 19.1   Data model sketch for Building.

Creating a Management Pack

To create an MP, follow these steps using the Service Manager Authoring Tool:

1. Create the folder **C:\Customizations**.

2. Open the Service Manager Authoring Tool.

3. Click **File -> New**.

4. In the New Management Pack dialog, go to C:\Customizations, enter the file name **Odyssey.Buildings.Library.xml**, and click **Save**.

With the new MP created, it is time to create the least specialized `Building` class that will be used as the base class for the different building types. This will be the class with all the common properties.

Creating Classes

To create the `Building` class, which contains the common properties and acts as the base for classes describing specific types of buildings, follow these steps:

1. In the Management Pack Explorer, right-click the **Classes** node and select **Create Configuration Item Class**.

   Service Manager 2010 provides a base class for Configuration Items that comes with a set of useful properties and relationships. You can use the Configuration Item class type as a base for all custom configuration items.

2. In the Create Class dialog, enter the name **Odyssey.Building.Base**.

3. In the Authoring pane, change the name (the display name) to **Building Base**.

4. In the Authoring pane, create the properties listed in Table 19.1.

   Should you require help in creating these properties, see the discussion in Chapter 18 on adding properties and relationships.

TABLE 19.1   Common Building Properties

Internal Name	Data Type	Other
ID	String	Key = True Auto Increment = True
Description	String	
Address	String	
City	String	
State	String	
ZIPCode	String	
Built	Integer	Description = The year the building was built

5. In the Authoring pane, delete the automatically added property named something similar to Property_4.

6. The chosen base class already has a relationship called `Owned By User` that will be used as the `BuildingHasOwner` relationship. However, you still must create the `BuildingHasRooms` relationship. In the Authoring pane, select **Create relationship**.

7. In the Create Relationship dialog, enter the name **BuildingHasOwner** and click **Create**.

This relationship will be modified later in this section, but let's leave it as is until the Room class is created.

8. Click **File -> Save** all to save the class to the MP.

You could mark the Building base class as abstract if it wouldn't make sense to create any instances of the generic building class type. An abstract class is used to consolidate characteristics that are common to multiple deriving classes. Because you cannot create instances of an abstract classes but it is possible to derive from them, using an abstract class to consolidate common properties enables consolidating the properties without risking creating instances of the class type.

To create the class representing a room, follow these steps:

1. In the Management Pack Explorer, right-click the **Classes** node and select **Create Configuration Item Class**.

2. In the Create Class dialog, enter the name **Odyssey.Building.Room**.

3. In the Authoring pane, change the name (the display name) to **Room**.

4. In the Management Pack Explorer, right-click the **Room** class and select **Details**.

5. In the Details pane, set Hosted equals **True**.

6. In the Management Pack Explorer, right-click the **Building Base** class and select **Edit**.

7. In the Authoring pane, right-click the **BuildingHasRooms** relationship and select Details.

8. In the Details pane, click the ellipses (...) button on the Target Class row.

9. In the Target Class dialog, select the **Odyssey.Building.Room** class and click **OK**.

10. In the Details pane, change the Relationship Type to **Hosting**.

11. In the Management Pack Explorer, right-click the **Room** class and select **Edit**.

12. In the Authoring pane, define the properties listed in Table 19.2.

TABLE 19.2   Room Properties

Internal Name	Data Type	Other
RoomNumber	String	Key = True
		Auto Increment = True
SquareFeets	Integer	MinValue = 0

13. In the Authoring pane, delete the automatically added property named something similar to Property_4.

14. In the Authoring Tool, click **File -> Save All** to save the two classes to the MP.

    Note the Room class is now hosted by the Building Base class. This means that a room cannot exist without a building hosting it. It also means that a room's key property value (room number) only needs to be unique within the host (the building).

15. In the Management Pack Explorer, right-click the **Rooms** class and select **Edit**.

16. In the Authoring pane, select **Add property**.

17. In the Create Property dialog, enter the internal name **Availability**.

18. In the Authoring pane, right-click the **Availability** property, and select **Details**.

19. In the Details pane, change the Data Type to **List**.

20. In the Select a List dialog, click **Create List**.

21. In the Create List dialog, enter the internal name **Room.Availability**.

22. In the Create List dialog, enter the display name **Room Availability** and click **Create**.

23. In the Select a List dialog, verify the Room Availability list is selected and click **OK**.

24. Click **File -> Save All**.

Should you require help in creating these properties, see the discussion on adding properties and relationships in Chapter 18.

You have now created the base for the model; type-specific classes can be created using this base.

To create a type-specific class, follow these steps:

1. In the Management Pack Explorer, right-click the **Classes** node and select Create other class.

2. In the Base Class dialog, select the Building Base class and click OK.

3. In the Create Class dialog, enter the internal name **Odyssey.Building.Bank** and click Create.

4. In the Authoring pane, change the class Name (the display name) to **Bank**.

5. In the Authoring pane, click **Add property**.

6. In the Create Property dialog, enter the internal name **VaultType** and click **Create**.

7. In the Authoring pane, delete the automatically added property named something similar to Property_11.

8. In the Authoring Tool, click **File -> Save All** to save all resources to the MP.

Note there was no need to add a key property, because this has been inherited from the Building base class.

To be able to reference the data models within this MP, you must seal the MP. The next section discusses sealing an MP.

Creating a Strong Name Key

Because this example includes sealing an MP, a strong name key is required. To create a new strong name key, follow these steps:

1. Open a new command prompt.

2. Type

   ```
   cd "C:\Program Files (x86)\Microsoft SDKs\Windows\v6.0A\Bin\"
   ```

   Then press **Enter** (on 32-bit systems, type "C:\Program Files\" rather than "C:\Program Files (x86)\").

3. To generate a key, type

   ```
   sn.exe /k C:\Customizations\mykey.snk
   ```

   and press **Enter**.

To seal the MP, follow these steps:

1. In the Management Pack Explorer, right-click **Odyssey.Buildings.Library**; then select **Seal Management Pack**.

2. In the Seal Management Pack dialog, set the output folder to C:\Customizations.

3. In the Seal Management Pack dialog, set the key file to C:\Customizations\mykey.snk.

4. In the Company field, enter **Odyssey**.

5. Click **Seal** followed by **Close**.

The model is now complete, and the MPs can be imported into Service Manager. Once the MP is imported, you may decide to add list items to the Availability list, such as Occupied, Available, or Under Repair. These list items would need to be stored in a different MP, because the MP has been sealed.

Using the Generic Form to manage this data model is hardly manageable; a custom form is required if you want to be able to work with relationships between buildings and owners. As described in Chapter 18, you can create custom forms with the Authoring Tool. Using the Authoring Tool, you could create a form for the Building base, which you could then use for all classes deriving from the class if no specific form was created for those classes.

You could also use the Authoring Tool to create a form for the Room class. However, because a Room is hosted, the Room must be associated with a Building in the same transaction as when the Room is created in the CMDB. Because this cannot be achieved using the Generic Form or a custom form built with the Authoring Tool, accomplishing this requires building a custom form with Visual Studio or Expression Blend for the Building base class (or a derived class). The form would include the logic for creating new rooms such that a room could be created and associated to a building at the same time as the building was updated.

If the resources needed to build such an advanced form for the Building base is lacking, you can still create new rooms using PowerShell, the Import from CSV file feature, or the CSV connector, and manage with the Generic Form or a custom form for both the buildings and the rooms.

19

Customizing Column Display Names

After creating a view using the Create View wizard, you might want to customize the generated column names. Figure 19.2 shows three columns with the text Display Name:

▶ One column shows the display name for the change request.

▶ One column shows the display name of the user that created the change request.

▶ One column shows the display name of the user assigned the change request.

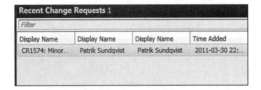

FIGURE 19.2   Change Request view.

It would make sense to change the column headers for the columns showing the display name for the "created by user" and "assigned to user" to something more descriptive, such as Created By and Assigned To.

The text presented in the column headers of a view is always stored in display strings in an MP. The trick in finding the correct display string to edit is to determine the MP the display string is stored in and the identifier the display string has. Once you know these two parameters, the display string can easily be located and manipulated to show a customized text.

To determine in which MP the display string and view are located, follow these steps:

1. Right-click the view in the Navigation pane, and select **Edit**.

2. In the Edit View wizard shown in Figure 19.3, note the text in the Name field and in the grayed-out Management Pack field.

To export the MP that contains the view and display string, follow these steps:

1. Go to **Administration -> Management Packs**.

2. Enter the noted MP name in the Search field and click **Search** (in this example, **Odyssey.Console.Customizations**).

3. Select the matching MP from the search result.

4. Click the **Export** console task in the Tasks pane.

5. Choose where to save the MP and click **OK**.

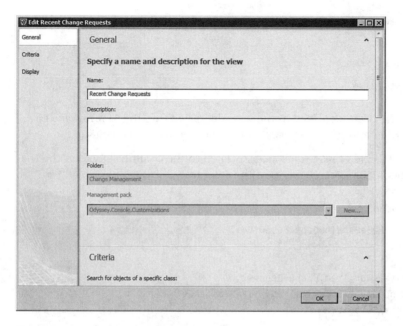

FIGURE 19.3   Edit View wizard.

To locate the identifier of the column header display string, you must locate the column definition stored in the view definition of the MP. Once you determine the correct column definition, you need to locate the correct ViewString. Based on the ViewString, you can locate a StringResource, which has the ID of the display string that should be modified.

Follow these steps to locate the view in the MP:

1. Search the XML using the name of the view noted when editing the view in the Service Manager console until a matching entry is found in the DisplayStrings section of the XML, as shown in Listing 19.1.

2. Copy the ElementID (in this example, View.b8d7852223e24b91b65dbe78ec66f541) of the DisplayString and create a new search in the XML until a matching entry is found in the Views section (shown in Listing 19.2).

LISTING 19.1   View **DisplayString**

```
<DisplayString ElementID="View.b8d7852223e24b91b65dbe78ec66f541">
    <Name>Recent Change Requests</Name>
</DisplayString>
```

To find the columns of interest, you must browse through the Columns section of the view definition and look for column elements with a property that matches the column value.

In this case, there are two property values of interest found in the view definition, shown in Listing 19.2:

▶ AssignedTo.DisplayName

▶ CreatedBy.DisplayName

When the columns have been identified in the view definition, use the DisplayName of the columns to go further and find the ViewString associated with each column.

As shown in Listing 19.2, the ViewStrings are associated to the columns based on the name of the MP element (the XML element) of the column.

LISTING 19.2   View Definition

```
<View ID="View.b8d7852223e24b91b65dbe78ec66f541"
Accessibility="Public"
Enabled="true"
Target="WorkItem!System.WorkItem.ChangeRequest"
TypeID="EnterpriseManagement!GridViewType" Visible="true">
    <Category>NotUsed</Category>
    <Data>
    ...
    </Data>
    <Presentation>
     <Columns>
       <mux:ColumnCollection >
         ...
         <mux:Column Name="AssignedTo.DisplayName" DisplayMemberBinding="{Binding
Path=AssignedTo.DisplayName}" Width="100"
DisplayName="DisplayName.656d9d340e6849078012a888506fafd8"
Property="AssignedTo.DisplayName" DataType="s:String" />
         <mux:Column Name="CreatedBy.DisplayName"
     DisplayMemberBinding="{Binding Path=CreatedBy.DisplayName}" Width="100"
DisplayName="DisplayName.822e216d004548eb9bc776f8311d943c"
Property="CreatedBy.DisplayName" DataType="s:String" />
         ...
       </mux:ColumnCollection>
     </Columns>
     <ViewStrings>
       ...
       <ViewString ID="DisplayName.656d9d340e6849078012a888506fafd8">$MPElement
[Name="DisplayName.656d9d340e6849078012a888506fafd8"]$</ViewString>
       <ViewString ID="DisplayName.822e216d004548eb9bc776f8311d943c">$MPElement
[Name="DisplayName.822e216d004548eb9bc776f8311d943c"]$</ViewString>
       ...
```

```
      </ViewStrings>
    </Presentation>
  </View>
```

Using the ID of the `ViewString`, the associated `StringResource` can be located (see Listing 19.3). Once the `StringResources` is located, the column display strings can be determined using the ID of the `StringResource` and finding a `DisplayString` with a matching `ElementID`. This is shown in Listing 19.4.

LISTING 19.3   StringResource

```
<StringResources>
    ...
    <StringResource ID="DisplayName.656d9d340e6849078012a888506fafd8" />
    <StringResource ID="DisplayName.822e216d004548eb9bc776f8311d943c" />
    ...
</StringResources>
```

LISTING 19.4   Column DisplayStrings

```
<DisplayStrings>
    ...
    <DisplayString ElementID="DisplayName.656d9d340e6849078012a888506fafd8">
      <Name>Display Name</Name>
      <Description>Display name of the object.</Description>
    </DisplayString>
    <DisplayString ElementID="DisplayName.822e216d004548eb9bc776f8311d943c">
      <Name>Display Name</Name>
      <Description>Display name of the object.</Description>
    </DisplayString>
    ...
</DisplayStrings>
```

When you create a view using the Service Manager console, `DisplayStrings` are added in the `LanguagePack` (the parent XML element of a `DisplayString`) matching the console language used when the view was created. This means that if the console is running English, a `DisplayString` in the `LanguagePack` with an ID of `ENU` is created. Matching `DisplayStrings` (`DisplayStrings` with the same `ElementID`) can be added to other `LanguagePacks` in the MP to provide translations of the column header in multiple languages.

By modifying the column display strings, you can achieve a more user-friendly result, as shown in Figure 19.4.

19

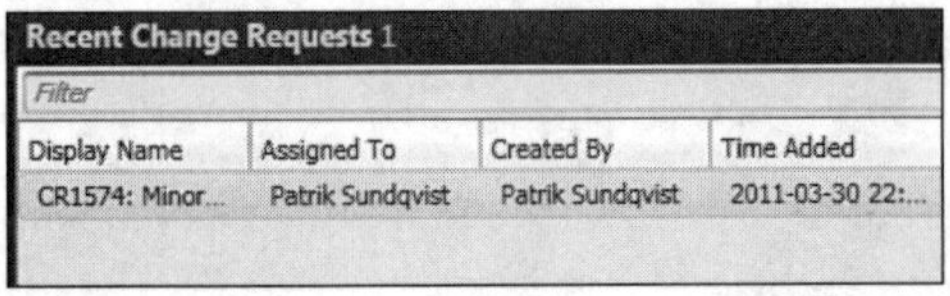

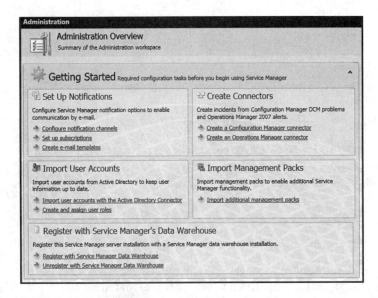

FIGURE 19.4   Customized column headers.

Custom Views

As discussed in Chapter 16, "Planning Your Customization," you can create custom views that can be implemented in the Service Manager console. The view shown in Figure 16.1 of Chapter 16 was based on the view type named Overview Type that is used by the Administration Overview screen shown in Figure 19.5. This section covers how to create custom views, which does require some basic knowledge of eXtensible Application Markup Language (XAML).

FIGURE 19.5   Administration Overview.

Although it is possible to create custom view types, using the predefined overview view type is a powerful and easy way to implement custom views in the Service Manager console. This view type can be used in several different ways to implement custom views:

▶ Designed directly in the MP using eXtensible Application Markup Language (XAML), which is the design language used by the Service Manager console.

▶ Defined in a Windows Presentation Foundation (WPF) User Control and compiled into an assembly referenced in a view definition in an MP. This enables you to add code that interacts with Service Manager through the Software Development Kit (SDK).

Because the second approach requires a full development environment and developer skills, this book discusses only the first alternative.

To declare a custom view in an MP using the Overview view type, follow these steps:

1. Declare a reference to the `Microsoft.EnterpriseManagement.ServiceManager.UI.Console` MP, as in Listing 19.5.

2. Define a `ViewType` as the one in Listing 19.6, which uses a view type defined in an assembly referenced in the MP referenced in step 1.

3. Once the `ViewType` has been defined, you can proceed to define the custom view as with the example in Listing 19.7. It is important that the `TypeID` is pointing at the `ID` given when you declared the overview type (as in Listing 19.7).

4. With the view defined, you can adjust the elements within the header and content tag to suit your needs. It helps to define the XAML code using a tool such as Visual Studio.

TIP: LIGHTWEIGHT ALTERNATIVE TO VISUAL STUDIO

If you do not have access to Visual Studio, you could use Kaxaml to design the XAML code. Kaxaml is a lightweight XAML editor that can render the result as you type the XAML code.

Kaxaml is available at http://www.kaxaml.com/.

5. After defining the view, it needs to be placed in a folder. This is accomplished with a `FolderItem` declaration as the example in Listing 19.7. The `FolderItem` ID must be a unique value, the `ElementID` should be set to the `ID` of the view (in this example `Odyssey.Views.CustomOverview`), and the `Folder` property should be set to the `ID` if it is a declared folder (in this example, `Odyssey.Folders.lvl2`).

The result of the MP XML listed in this section can be seen in Figure 19.6. Notice how the XAML elements from Listing 19.7 are rendered inside the Service Manager console.

LISTING 19.5   Required Reference

```
<Reference Alias="EnterpriseManagement">
    <ID>Microsoft.EnterpriseManagement.ServiceManager.UI.Console</ID>
    <Version>7.0.6555.0</Version>
    <PublicKeyToken>31bf3856ad364e35</PublicKeyToken>
</Reference>
```

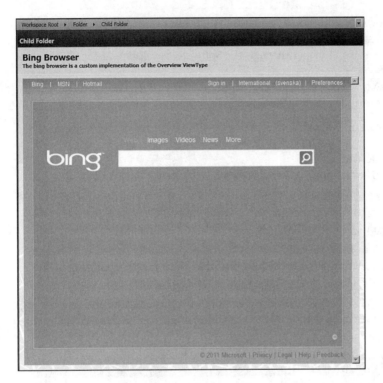

FIGURE 19.6   Custom view based on the `OverviewType`.

LISTING 19.6   Overview Type Declaration

```
<PresentationTypes>
 <ViewTypes>
  <ViewType ID="OverviewType" Accessibility="Public">
    <Configuration>
      <xsd:any minOccurs="0" maxOccurs="unbounded"
      processContents="skip" xmlns:xsd="http://www.w3.org/2001/XMLSchema" />
    </Configuration>
    <ViewImplementation>
    <Assembly>EnterpriseManagement!WpfViewsAssembly</Assembly>
    <Type>Microsoft.EnterpriseManagement.UI.WpfViews.Overview</Type>
    </ViewImplementation>
  </ViewType>
 </ViewTypes>
</PresentationTypes>
```

LISTING 19.7   Custom View

```
<Views>
<View ID="Odyssey.Views.CustomOverview" Accessibility="Public" Enabled="true"
Target="System!System.Entity" TypeID="OverviewType" Visible="true">
  <Category>Overview</Category>
  <Configuration>
    <Presentation>
    <Header >
    <UserControl Margin="10"
xmlns="http://schemas.microsoft.com/winfx/2006/xaml/presentation"
xmlns:x="http://schemas.microsoft.com/winfx/2006/xaml">
      <Grid>
      <Grid.RowDefinitions>
       <RowDefinition Height="Auto" />
       <RowDefinition Height="Auto" />
      </Grid.RowDefinitions>
      <Grid.ColumnDefinitions>
       <ColumnDefinition Width="*" />
       <ColumnDefinition Width="Auto" />
      </Grid.ColumnDefinitions>
      <TextBlock Text="Bing Browser" FontSize="18" FontWeight="DemiBold" />
      <TextBlock Grid.Row="1"
      Text="The bing browser is a custom implementation of the Overview ViewType"
      FontWeight="DemiBold" />
      </Grid>
      </UserControl>
      </Header>
    <Content>
    <UserControl Margin="10"
xmlns="http://schemas.microsoft.com/winfx/2006/xaml/presentation"
xmlns:x="http://schemas.microsoft.com/winfx/2006/xaml">
    <Grid>
      <WebBrowser Name="wb1" Source="http://www.bing.com" />
    </Grid>
    </UserControl>
    </Content>
  </Presentation>
  </Configuration>
</View>
</Views>
<Folders>
...
```

```
<Folder ID="Odyssey.Folders.lvl2" Accessibility="Public"
ParentFolder="Odyssey.Folders.lvl1" />
</Folders>
<FolderItems>
...
<FolderItem ElementID="Odyssey.Views.CustomOverview"
ID="FolderItem.ab59125f-452d-4212-9d38-40a32d367c27"
Folder="Odyssey.Folders.lvl2" />
</FolderItems>
```

Console Tasks Using PowerShell

Because you are able to use the full .NET Framework from a PowerShell script, you can
even render your own forms from the script and interact with the user running the task.
This section discusses an example of this by creating a console task that executes the script
in Listing 19.8. The script prompts the console user for a reason to force the status of
currently selected incident in the console to Status Active.

The PowerShell script used in this example requires that the community Service Manager
PowerShell cmdlets are installed on the machines where the console task is used. For more
information about the community Service Manager PowerShell cmdlets, see http://smlets.
codeplex.com/. Listing 19.8 and the material used in this section is also available in the
blog posting at http://blogs.litware.se/?p=646.

LISTING 19.8   PowerShell Script: Force Incident Status to Active

```
param($ID)
Import-module smlets -Force

[void] [System.Reflection.Assembly]::LoadWithPartialName("System.Drawing")
[void] [System.Reflection.Assembly]::LoadWithPartialName("System.Windows.Forms")

$objForm = New-Object System.Windows.Forms.Form
$objForm.Text = "Force Incident Status"
$objForm.Size = New-Object System.Drawing.Size(400,200)
$objForm.StartPosition = "CenterScreen"

$objForm.KeyPreview = $True
$objForm.Add_KeyDown({if ($_.KeyCode -eq "Enter")
    {$x=$objTextBox.Text;$objForm.Close()}})
$objForm.Add_KeyDown({if ($_.KeyCode -eq "Escape")
    {$objForm.Close()}})

$OKButton = New-Object System.Windows.Forms.Button
$OKButton.Location = New-Object System.Drawing.Size(125,120)
```

```
$OKButton.Size = New-Object System.Drawing.Size(75,23)
$OKButton.Text = "OK"
$OKButton.Add_Click({$x=$objTextBox.Text;$objForm.Close();$result="OK"})
$objForm.Controls.Add($OKButton)


$CancelButton = New-Object System.Windows.Forms.Button
$CancelButton.Location = New-Object System.Drawing.Size(200,120)
$CancelButton.Size = New-Object System.Drawing.Size(75,23)
$CancelButton.Text = "Cancel"
$CancelButton.Add_Click({$objForm.Close()})
$objForm.Controls.Add($CancelButton)


$objLabel = New-Object System.Windows.Forms.Label
$objLabel.Location = New-Object System.Drawing.Size(10,20)
$objLabel.Size = New-Object System.Drawing.Size(360,20)
$objLabel.Text = "Please enter a reason for forcing the incident status to Active:"
$objForm.Controls.Add($objLabel)


$objTextBox = New-Object System.Windows.Forms.TextBox
$objTextBox.Location = New-Object System.Drawing.Size(10,40)
$objTextBox.Size = New-Object System.Drawing.Size(360,60)
$objTextBox.Multiline = "True"
$objForm.Controls.Add($objTextBox)


$objForm.Topmost = $True


$objForm.Add_Shown({$objForm.Activate()})
[void] $objForm.ShowDialog()

if($result -eq "OK")
{
    Set-SCSMIncident -ID $ID -Status Active
    Write-Host "Incident status forced to Active"
    if($x -gt 0)
    {
    Write-Host "Reason for action: $x"
    }
    else
    {
    Write-Host "No reason provided"
    }
}
else
{
    Write-Host "Force to active status aborted"
}
```

19

To enable a console task to make use of a script, that script must be stored as a PowerShell script on the system running the Service Manager console. To prepare the script so it can be used by the console task, follow these steps:

1. If you haven't already done so, create a folder named **C:\Customizations**.

2. Create a file named **ForceActivate.ps1** in the folder created in step 1.

3. Open the file and paste the script from Listing 19.8; save and close the file.

Once the PowerShell script is created and available on the machines that will use the console task, follow these steps to create the console task:

1. Open the Service Manager console.

2. In the Service Manager console, go to **Library -> Tasks**.

3. Select **Create Task**.

4. In the Create Task wizard, click **Next** to begin creating the console task.

5. On the General page, enter the name **Force Activate**.

6. On the General page, browse and select the Incident class as **Target Class**.

7. On the General page, click **New** to create a new MP. Alternatively, if you already have a suitable MP for storing the console task, you can use that MP.

8. In the Create Management Pack wizard, enter the name **Odyssey.Customization.Configuration** and click **OK**.

9. On the General page, click **Next**.

10. On the Categories page, click **Next**.

11. On the Command Line page, enter **powershell.exe** in the field for Full path to command.

12. On the Command Line page, enter **&'.\ForceActivate.ps1'** in the Parameters text box. There should be a space after the **ps1'**.

13. On the Command Line page, select **Insert Property**.

14. In the Select Property dialog, enter **ID** in the search box as shown in Figure 19.7.

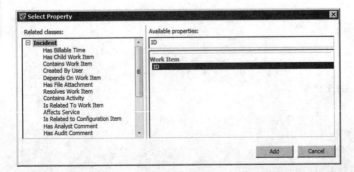

FIGURE 19.7   Insert Property value as argument in console task.

15. In the Select Property dialog, select **ID** and click **Add**.

16. On the Command Line page, set the Working Directory to **C:\Customizations**.

17. On the Command Line page, check both **Log in action log when this task is run** and **Show output when this task is run**.

18. Verify that the Command Line page looks like Figure 19.8 and click **Next**.

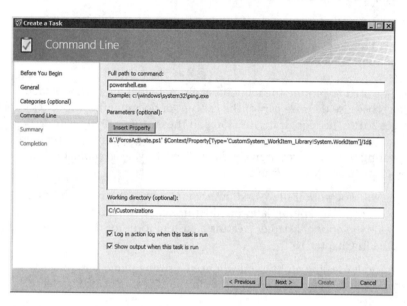

FIGURE 19.8   Insert Property value as an argument in the console task.

19. On the Summary page, click **Create** followed by **Close** to complete the creation of the console task.

To verify the console task, select an incident that status is closed. Run the Force Activate console task and see that the status is changed and the reason recorded in the Action log.

Automating an IT Process

Using the Service Manager workflow engine to automate IT processes is an effective way to cut costs while increasing the quality of service fulfillment. For an example of how a process can be automated, complete the step-by-step instructions that follow. The example shows how to automate the provisioning of a new Active Directory user based on a user request.

To support the automation of user account provisioning, you want to capture all details of such a request directly in the Service Manager console. By saving the details in the CMDB, you can then have the Service Manager workflow engine use those request details and fulfill the provisioning of the user account after any preceding activities, such as a review activity, are completed.

On a high level, the customizations needed to support the scenario are

▶ Creating a custom `Activity` class that can be used to store request details and trigger the workflow

▶ Creating the workflow that provisions the user account in Active Directory

▶ Creating a form for the custom activity (optional)

▶ Creating an object template for the custom `Activity` class

▶ Creating an object template for the `Change Request` class that specifies the process of a User Provisioning Request

A custom activity will be used to capture the request details. Activities are highly suitable for triggering workflows because they are part of the concept of documenting processes within Service Manager 2010. The request details stored in the custom activity will contain a username, a given name, and a surname. The automated workflow will then use these details when creating the user account in the Active Directory. Read more about Activities in Chapter 12, "Change Management."

Note that this example will not work if the Workflow account does not have permissions to create a new user account in the appropriate container in Active Directory. This example does not include the optional step of creating a custom form for the custom Activity; this is discussed in Chapter 18.

Because the example includes sealing an MP, you will need a strong name key. To create a new strong name key, follow the steps described earlier in the "Creating a Strong Name Key" section of this chapter.

Creating the Custom Activity

To be able to store the request details, you must create a custom activity. Using the `Activity` class as base for the custom activity makes it possible to use the internal workflows of Service Manager to manage status updates of the custom activity and to trigger the provisioning workflow. To create the custom activity, follow these steps:

1. Open the Service Manager Authoring Tool.

2. In the Service Manager Authoring Tool, click **File -> New**.

3. In the New Management Pack dialog, enter the name **Odyssey.Automation.Library.xml** and click **Save**.

4. In the Management Pack Explorer, right-click the **Classes** node and select **Create other class**.

5. In the Base Class dialog, choose the **Activity** class and click **OK**.

6. In the Create Class dialog, enter the class name **Odyssey.Activities.UserProvisioning** and click **OK**.

7. In the Authoring pane, change the class name to **User Provisioning Activity**.

8. In the Authoring pane, change the description to **Automates provisioning of a new Active Directory user account**.

9. In the Authoring pane, delete the automatically added property called Property_16 (or similar) by clicking the red X in the rightmost column on the row of the property.

10. In the Authoring pane, click **Create Property**.

11. In the Create Property dialog, enter the internal name **userName** and click **Create**.

12. In the Authoring pane, select the new property and press **F4** to show the Details pane.

13. In the Details pane, change the name (which sets the display name) of the property to **Username**.

14. Repeat steps 10 and 13 for properties gName (display name Given Name) and sName (display name Surname).

15. Click **File -> Save All** to save the new class to the MP file.

Building the User Provisioning Workflow

Once the status of the custom activity is updated by the internal workflows of Service Manager, a workflow must be triggered that will provision the user account. To create the workflow and the workflow trigger, follow these steps:

1. In the Management Pack Explorer, right-click the **Workflow** node and select **Create**.

2. In the Create Workflow Wizard, enter the name **ProvisionUserWF** and click **Next**.

3. On the Trigger Condition page, select **Run only when a database object meets specified conditions** and click **Next**.

4. On the Trigger Criteria page, browse and select the class named **User Provisioning Activity**.

5. On the Trigger Criteria page in the Change Event drop-down box, select the **When an object of the selected class is updated** option.

6. On the Trigger Criteria page, click the **Additional Criteria** button.

7. In the Additional Criteria dialog on the Changed From tab, select the **Status** property, click **Add**, and set the criteria to **Activity Status Equals Pending**.

8. On the Changed To tab, select the **Status** property, click **Add**, and set the criteria to **Activity Status Equals InProgress**.

9. In the Additional Criteria dialog, click **OK** to close the dialog.

10. On the Trigger Criteria step, click **Next**.

11. On the Summary page, confirm the settings and click **Create**.

12. Click **Close** to close the wizard and display the Workflow design surface in the Authoring pane.

13. Drag the Windows PowerShell activity from the Activities Toolbox onto the Workflow design surface, as shown in Figure 19.9.

19

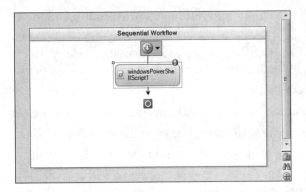

FIGURE 19.9   Workflow design.

14. On the workflow design surface, right-click the **windowsPowerShellScript1** activity and select **Details**.

15. In the Details pane, change the name to **CreateUser**.

16. In the Details pane, click the ellipses (...) button on the Script Body row.

17. In the Configure a Script Activity dialog, click the text **View or Edit Script**.

18. In the expanded area, enter the text in Listing 19.9.

19. In Configure a Script Activity, click the **Script Properties** tab.

20. On the Script Properties tab, click **New**.

21. On the new row, enter the name **userName** and click the ellipses (...) button in the rightmost column.

22. In the Define input for the Activity CreateUser dialog, select **Use a class property**.

23. Select **Username** in the list of class properties and click **OK**.

24. Repeat the steps 20–23 for parameters gName (selecting the Given name property) and sName (selecting the Surname property).

25. In the Configure a Script Activity dialog, click **OK** to close the dialog.

26. Drag the activity Set Activity Status to Completed from the Activities Toolbox onto the workflow design surface and drop it below the PowerShell activity.

27. On the workflow design surface, right-click **updateActivityStatusToCompleted1** and select **Details**.

28. In the Details pane, enter the name **UpdateActivityStatus**.

29. In the Details pane, click the ellipses (...) button on the Activity ID row.

30. In the Define input for the activity UpdateActivityStatus, select **Use a class property**.

31. In the list of class properties, select the **ID** (internal) property and click **OK**.

32. Click **File -> Save All** to save the MP and compile the workflow.

33. In the Management Pack Explorer, right-click the MP node **Odyssey.Automation.Library** and select **Seal Management Pack**.

34. In the Seal Management Pack dialog

- ▸ Enter an output folder of C:**Customizations**.

- ▸ Browse for the strong name key C:\Customizations\mykey.snk.

- ▸ Enter company name **Odyssey**.

- ▸ Click **Seal** followed by **Close** to close the dialog.

LISTING 19.9   Provision User PowerShell Script

```
param($userName,$gName,$sName)
$objOu = [ADSI]"LDAP://cn=Users,dc=odyssey,dc=com"
$user = $objOu.Create("user","cn=" + $userName)
$user.Put("sAMAccountName",$userName)
$user.Put("GivenName",$gName)
$user.Put("Sn",$lName)
$user.SetInfo()
```

You should modify "LDAP://cn=Users,dc=odyssey,dc=com" in Listing 19.9 to match your domain name and the organizational unit or container where you want to create the user.

Deploying the Solution

The solution at this point contains the MP with the custom `Activity` class and an assembly file containing the user provisioning workflow. To deploy the solution to Service Manager, you want to complete the following tasks.

To deploy the workflow assembly, do the following:

1. In the C:\Customizations folder, copy the ProvisionUserWF.dll file.

2. On the Service Manager management server running the workflows, paste the file into the folder C:\Program Files\Microsoft System Center\Service Manager 2010 (default folder).

To import the MP, follow these steps:

1. Open the Service Manager console.

2. Go to **Administration -> Management Packs** and select **Import**.

3. In the Select Management Pack to Import dialog, select
C:**Customizations\Odyssey.Automation.Library.mp** and click **Open**.

   You must change the drop-down box to be able to see the sealed MPs (*.mp) and not only the unsealed MPs.

4. In the Import Management Packs dialog, click **Import**.

5. In the Import Management Packs dialog, click **OK** to close the dialog.

Creating Object Templates

Before creating a custom Change Request template, you must create a template for the custom activity. This is to enable you to add the custom activity in the Activities tab in the custom Change Request template (only possible to pick from Activity templates).

To create a custom activity template, follow these steps:

1. Open the Service Manager console.
2. In the Service Manager console, go to **Library -> Templates**.
3. In the Service Manager console, click **Create Template**.
4. In the Create Template dialog, enter the name **User Provisioning Activity**.
5. In the Create Template dialog, click **Browse**
6. In the Select a class dialog, select **User Provisioning Activity** (it may be necessary to change the view to All basic classes) and click **OK**.
7. In the Select an unsealed MP section, click **New** to create a new MP.
8. In the Create Management Pack dialog, enter the name **Odyssey.Automation.Configuration** and click **OK**.
9. In the Create Template dialog, click **OK**.
10. In the User Provisioning Activity Properties form, enter **User Provisioning Activity** in the Title field and click **OK** to save the template.

To create a Change Request template, follow these steps:

1. Open the Service Manager console.
2. In the Service Manager console, go to **Library -> Templates**.
3. In the Service Manager console, click **Create Template**.
4. In the Create Template dialog, enter the name **User Provisioning Request**.
5. In the Create Template dialog, click **Browse**.
6. In the Select a class dialog, select the **Change Request** class, and click **OK**.
7. In the Select an unsealed management pack section, select the **Odyssey.Automation.Configuration** MP, and click **OK**.
8. In the Change Request Form, go to the Activities tab.
9. On the Activities Tab, click **Add** and choose the **Default Review Activity**, and then click **OK**.
10. In the Review Activity Form, enter the title **Please review**.
11. In the Review Activity Form, click **Add to add a reviewer**.
12. In the Reviewer dialog, click **OK**.

    You can specify a specific reviewer or leave the reviewer unspecified.
13. In the Review Activity Form, click **OK** to close the form and return to the Change Request Form.

14. On the Activities tab, click **Add** and choose the **User Provisioning Activity**.

15. In the User Provisioning Activity Properties Form, click **OK** to close it and go back to the Change Request Form.

16. In the Change Request Form, go to the General tab.

17. On the General tab, enter **User Provisioning Request** in the Title field.

18. In the Change Request Form, click **OK** to close the form and save the template.

Verifying the Solution

To verify the custom activity can be used to trigger a provisioning workflow that automates the provisioning of a user account, follow these steps:

1. In the Service Manager console, go to Work Items.

2. Select **Change Management**, and then select the **create Change Request** console task.

3. Select the **User Provisioning Request** template.

4. In the Change Request Form, go to the Activities tab.

5. Open the User Provisioning Activity and fill in a username, a given name, and a surname.

6. Click **OK** to close the Activity Form followed by **OK** to close the Change Request Form.

7. Wait a few seconds, and then refresh the view to see that the change request receives the status InProgress.

8. When the change request receives the status InProgress, this means the first activity has received the same status. Approve the review activity either through the Change Request Form or by viewing the review activity through the review activity views.

   Give the change request several seconds to update the status of the activities; when the review activity changes to Completed, the next activity in line will receive the status InProgress.

9. When the User Provisioning Activity receives the status InProgress, this triggers the provisioning workflow. Go to **Administration -> Workflow Status** and select **ProvisionUserWF**.

10. Select the **All instances** tab and verify there is a Success entry informing you that the workflow has succeeded.

11. Check in Active Directory and verify that a new account matching your request details has been created.

Creating Console Forms Using Visual Studio

Sometimes you want to reach further than the Authoring Tool can deliver in the sense of a user interface (UI) experience. With Visual Studio or Expression Blend, your custom form can be as customized as you like. Using one of these tools to create a form for Service Manager will enable you to add code to perform custom validation, as well as have total control over the XAML code used to generate the UI.

19

To create a custom form for Service Manager based on C# using Visual Studio, follow these steps:

1. If you haven't already, create the folder C:**Customizations**.

2. Start Visual Studio 2010.

3. Click **File -> New -> Project**.

4. In the New Project dialog, select the template C# -**Windows - WPF User Control Library**, as shown in Figure 19.10.

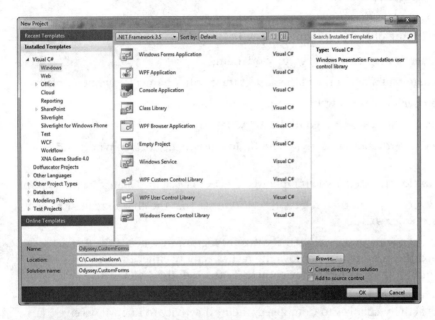

FIGURE 19.10   Visual Studio New Project wizard.

5. In the New Project dialog, enter the following details and then click **OK**:

   ▶ **Name:** Odyssey.CustomForms

   ▶ **Location:** C:\Customizations

   ▶ **Solution name:** Odyssey.CustomForms

6. In the Solution Explorer, right-click **UserControl1.xaml** and select **Delete**. Confirm that you want to delete the user control.

7. In the Solution Explorer, right-click **Odyssey.CustomForms** and click **Add -> User Control**.

8. In the Add New Item dialog, enter the file name **MyForm.xaml** and click **Add**.

9. In Visual Studio, make sure that the Toolbox is visible. If not, click **View -> Toolbox**.

10. Drag and drop a label from the Toolbox onto the design surface of MyForm.xaml as in Figure 19.11.

FIGURE 19.11   User Control design in Visual Studio.

11. Drag and drop a text box from the Toolbox onto the design surface of MyForm.xaml as in Figure 19.11.

12. On the design surface of MyForm.xaml, select the Label and press **F4** (to display the Details pane).

13. In the Details pane, set content to **Name**.

14. On the design surface of MyForm.xaml, right-click the **TextBox** and select **View XAML**.

15. In the XAML window, verify that the TextBox XAML has the following binding declared for the Text attribute: Text="{Binding Path=Name}".

16. In Visual Studio, click **Build -> Build Solution**.

17. Open the Service Manager Authoring Tool.

18. In the Authoring Tool, click **File -> New**.

19. In the New Management Pack dialog, enter the name **Odyssey.Customizations.Library.xml** and click **Save**.

20. In the Management Pack Explorer, right-click the **Classes** node and select the **Create Configuration Item** class.

21. In the Create Class dialog, enter the class name **Odyssey.ConfigItem.MyConfigItem** and click **OK**.

22. In the Authoring pane, change the class name to **My Configuration Item**.

23. In the Authoring pane, click **Create Property**.

24. In the Create Property dialog, enter the internal name **Name**, and click **Create**.

25. In the Authoring pane, select the new property and press **F4** to show the Details pane.

26. In the Details pane, mark the property as Key by setting Key = true.

19

27. In the Authoring pane, delete the automatically added property called Property_4 (or similar) by clicking the red X in the rightmost column on the row of the property.

28. In the Management Pack Explorer, right-click the **Forms** node, then select **Add Custom**.

29. In the Select Base Class dialog, select the **My Configuration Item** class.

30. In the Add custom form dialog, enter the internal name **Odyssey.Forms.MyConfigItem**.

31. In the Add custom form dialog, click **Browse**.

32. In the Open an Assembly dialog, go to C:\Customizations\Odyssey.CustomForms\Odyssey.CustomForms\bin\Debug\, select the file **Odyssey.CustomForms.dll**, and click **Open**.

33. In the Open an Assembly dialog, select **MyForm** in the Type drop-down list.

34. In the Add custom form dialog, click **Create** to associate the custom form created with Visual Studio with the class created in the Service Manager Authoring Tool.

Note: If prompted for the form's assembly file Odyssey.CustomForms.dll, just specify it again.

35. In the Authoring Tool, click **File -> Save**.

The MP now contains a form declaration with a pointer to the form in the assembly file. To ensure the assembly file is available when the custom form is called by the Service Manager console, the MP file needs to be bundled with the assembly file. Follow these steps:

1. In the Management Pack Explorer, right-click the MP node **Odyssey.Customization.Library**, and select **Seal Management Pack**.

2. In the Seal Management Pack dialog

   ▶ Enter the output folder C:**Customizations**.

   ▶ Browse for the strong name key C:\Customizations\mykey.snk created in the example in the "Creating a Strong Name Key" section of this chapter.

   ▶ Enter the company name **Odyssey**.

   ▶ Click **Seal** followed by **Close** to close the dialog.

3. Copy Odyssey.CustomForms.dll from C:\Customizations\Odyssey.CustomForms\Odyssey.CustomForms\bin\Debug\ to C:\Customizations.

4. Run the PowerShell script `New-MPBFile.ps1 Odyssey.Customization.Library.mp Odyssey.Customization.Library` from C:\Customizations.

TIP: LEARN MORE ABOUT MP BUNDLES

See Chapter 17 for information on MP bundles and where to find the PowerShell script that creates bundles.

---

5. Open the Service Manager console; go to **Administration** -> **Management Packs**.

6. Import the new MP bundle C:\Customizations\Odyssey.Customization.Library.mpb as described in the "Automating an IT Process" section.

7. Create a new view for My Configuration Items, as described in Chapter 18.

8. When the custom view is selected, select the task **Create My Configuration Item** to see the custom form, as shown in Figure 19.12.

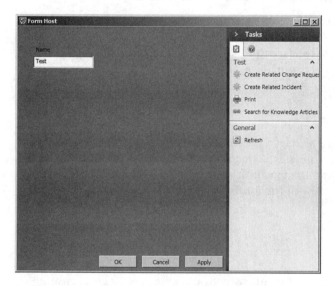

FIGURE 19.12   Custom form created using Visual Studio.

Other Scenarios

The customization scenarios around Service Manager are many, and most are covered in this book. To further aid you in the job of tailoring Service Manager to fulfill your needs, here are several additional valuable resources.

View Criteria Based on Tokens

Views in Service Manager can be based on *tokens*. A token is a placeholder that is replaced by a value at runtime when a view criteria is used to query the Service Manager database. Here are the tokens available in Service Manager:

▶ **[me]:** This token is replaced by the user identifier of the logged-on user running the console.

Example: Change Request - Created By User

▶ **[mygroups]:** This token is replaced by a list of groups that the logged-on user running the console is a member of.

▶ **[Now]:** This token is replaced by the current date and time at the time of the view querying the CMDB.

To learn how to use these tokens in a view criteria, see the blog post at http://blogs. technet.com/b/servicemanager/archive/2010/04/30/how-to-update-views-to-change-the-criteria-from-assigned-to-me-to-assigned-to-me-or-a-group-that-i-belong-to.aspx.

Building a Custom Web Application for Service Manager

Service Manager comes with an extensive SDK, enabling third-party applications to be built to interact with the product. To learn how to utilize the SDK to build a web application that interacts with Service Manager, see this blog post at http://blogs.technet.com/b/servicemanager/archive/2010/01/07/creating-browser-interfaces-to-service-manager-using-the-sdk.aspx.

Other Form Customizations

When a class is extended in Service Manager, the forms are equipped with a new tab that shows the values of all extension properties. To learn how to hide this tab, hide properties in the Generic Form, and more, read the blog post at http://blogs.technet.com/b/service-manager/archive/2010/02/08/overview-of-the-forms-infrastructure-and-the-generic-form.aspx

Summary

This chapter discussed how to use the different customization concepts such as creating classes and forms to build an end-to-end solution for automating IT processes. It also discussed how to fine-tune the Service Manager console by modifying custom views, by making column names more user friendly, and by adding new types of views. With the information available about creating custom forms for Service Manager in Visual Studio, you can pretty much do anything possible using Windows Presentation Foundation while integrating it into the Service Manager console.

The examples in Chapters 18 and 19 will prepare you for most of the customization scenarios in Service Manager.

CHAPTER 20

Reports, Dashboards, and Data Analysis

This chapter outlines how Service Manager reporting and dashboards work. It also introduces you to business intelligence basics, to the data warehouse available with Service Manager 2010, and will assist you in writing your own reports. The chapter will help you report on your Information Technology (IT) processes by using Service Manager's historical and analytical functions.

Reporting

Microsoft SQL Server Reporting Services (SRS) provides a complete server-based platform that is designed to support a wide variety of reporting needs, including managed enterprise reporting, ad hoc reporting, embedded reporting, and web-based reporting, to enable organizations to deliver relevant information where needed across the entire enterprise. SRS provides the tools and features necessary to author a variety of richly formatted reports from a wide range of data sources, and provides a comprehensive set of familiar tools to manage and secure an enterprise reporting solution. Reports are processed and delivered quickly and effectively, enabling users to receive reports automatically through subscriptions, to access reports from a central report repository on an ad hoc basis, or to consume reports in the context of their business processes through reports directly embedded into their business or web applications.

The Service Manager data warehouse and reporting features enable you to report on operational data in near real time. It also has historical and analytical functions to drive strategic service delivery and operations decision making. Three different elements make up data warehouse and reporting in Service Manager:

▶ **Data warehouse:** This is the processes and databases that manage the data from its raw source form to its end form that is used for reporting.

▶ **Reporting infrastructure:** The reporting infrastructure is the framework used for in-console reporting, which includes the custom controls used to support the interface between reports and the data warehouse.

▶ **Reports:** Reports are consumed by the end user for operational and analytical data.

SQL Reporting Explained

Although companies often collect and store large amounts of data, it is sometimes difficult to present that data in a meaningful way and provide insight into what is going on in the business to enable business decision makers to make relevant and timely decisions for the organization.

To be able to make effective business decisions, all types of users across the organization, from business managers to information workers, need easy access to informative and intuitive reports that combine data from the many data sources throughout the enterprise. Frequently these reports must combine detailed numeric and text-based information and analysis (often other reports) that provide a comprehensive account of business activity with graphic visualization to provide better view of trends and comparisons.

Data Warehouse Explained

The *data warehouse* is a set of databases and processes to populate those databases automatically. At a high level, the end goal is to populate the data mart where users will run reports and perform analyses to help them manage their business. The data is kept longer in the warehouse than in the configuration management database (CMDB) because of its usefulness for trending and analysis.

A data warehouse is optimized for aggregating and analyzing a considerable amount data simultaneously in many different and unpredictable ways. This differs from transactional processing systems, which are optimized for write access on few records in any given transaction (and those transactions are more predictable in behavior).

To optimize the data warehouse for performance and ease of use, Service Manager uses the Kimball approach to dimensional modeling. What this means to you is that tables in the DWDataMart database are logically grouped into subject matter areas that resemble a star when laid out in a diagram. So, these groupings are often called *star schemas*:

▶ In the center of the star is a Fact table. Fact tables represent relationships, measures, and key performance indicators (KPIs). They are normally long and skinny because they have relatively few columns but contain a large number of transactions.

▶ The Fact table joins to Dimension tables, which represent classes, properties, and enumerations. Dimension tables usually contain many fewer rows than fact tables but are wider because they have the interesting attributes by which users slice and dice reports (such as status, classifications, date attributes of a class such as Created Date or Resolved Date, and so on).

▶ An outrigger is a special kind of dimension table that hangs off another dimension table for performance/usability reasons.

Figure 20.1 shows a generalized representation of a star schema.

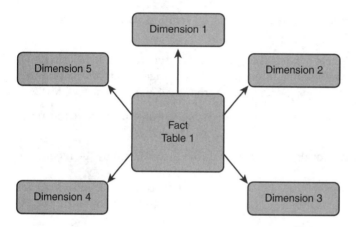

FIGURE 20.1   Generalized representation of a star schema.

Consider what a star schema for a local coffee shop might look like. The transactions are the coffee purchases themselves, whereas the dimensions might include some of the following areas:

▶ Date dimension (to roll up the transaction by both Gregorian and fiscal calendars)

▶ Customer dimension (bought the coffee)

▶ Employee dimension (made the coffee)

▶ Product dimension (espresso, drip, latte, breve, and so on)

▶ Store dimension

What measures might the fact table have? You could easily imagine these as some of those measures:

▶ Quantity sold

▶ Price per unit

▶ Total sales

▶ Total discounts

IT processes are not that different from the local coffee shop when it comes time to designing your dimensional model. A set of transactions occurs, such as incident creation/resolution/closure, which produces some interesting and useful metrics, such as time to resolution, resolution target adherence, billable time incurred by analysts, duration in status, and so on.

When thinking about extending and customizing your data warehouse, think about the business questions that you want to answer and read up on dimensional modeling for some tips on best practices.

Service Manager 2010 has three physical databases that make up its data warehouse, as follows:

▶ DWStagingAndConfig is where Service Manager stores all the management packs, ETL (extract, transform, and load) configuration, and other configuration information. It is also the initial store for the source data coming from the Service Manager CMDB.

▶ DWRepository is where the extracted source data is transformed into the reporting optimized structure.

▶ DWDataMart is the database for the published data that is consumed by the reports.

The Data Warehouse management server is the component that controls all the workflow processes associated with the data warehouse. There are three main processes:

▶ Management pack synchronization

▶ Data warehouse schema and report deployment

▶ ETL

These workflow processes are what make the data warehouse tick, from bringing the management packs in to deploying the reports out and everything in between.

Extract, Transform, and Load

Once the schema and reports are deployed, the database must be populated with some actual data for reporting purposes. This is accomplished by the three components of the ETL process, each of which serves its own specific purpose. Here are the components of that process:

▶ **Extract:** The extract process begins on a scheduled interval. Extract is the process that grabs the raw data from your online transaction processing (OLTP) store, which in this case is the Service Manager CMDB. Extract queries Service Manager for the changed (*delta*) data from its last run. This new data is written into the DWStagingAndConfig database in the same basic form as it is in the CMDB.

Extract is built specifically for processing high volumes of data from multiple sources and allows for moving the data into an area that is built for manipulating the data. For this reason, the data warehouse can have multiple Service Manager CMDBs reporting to it.

▶ **Transform:** The transform process begins on a scheduled interval. Transform takes the raw data from the staging area and does any cleansing, reformatting, aggregation, and so on that is required to get it into the final format for reporting. This transformed data is written into the DWRepository database.

Transform processes are built for optimization of complex logic and integration operations. This is where a lot of the heavy lifting occurs.

▶ **Load:** The load process begins on a scheduled interval. Load queries the data from the DWRepository database. The transformed data from DWRepository is inserted into the DWDataMart database. The DWDataMart is the database used for all end-user reporting needs.

Load is built for transferring the data that has already been processed into its target destination in a bulk manner.

There are several different reasons for having the three different databases, but one of the main reasons is so that you can optimize their hardware environment more easily. In high-volume environments, the DWStagingAndConfig and DWRepository databases need to be on hardware optimized for read/write input/output (I/O), whereas the DWDataMart should be optimized for read I/O. With that in mind, you can separate out the DWDataMart to a different server/drive from DWStagingAndConfig and DWRepository (these two must remain on the same server) with Service Manager 2010.

Management Pack Synchronization

The "Data Warehouse Explained" section discussed some of the components that make up the Service Manager data warehouse and reporting features. One of the data warehouse components is management pack synchronization. Because the structure and data within the data warehouse is driven by management packs within Service Manager, they must be regularly synchronized into the data warehouse.

Sequentially, here is how management pack (MP) synchronization works:

1. A management pack is imported into a Service Manager implementation that is registered as a source for the data warehouse.

2. On the Data Warehouse management server, the MPSync workflow kicks off on a set schedule.

3. The workflow grabs the source Service Manager names from the DWStagingAndConfig database, via the System Center Data Access Service. Service Manager accommodates multiple sources as a part of its multiple management group support within the data warehouse so that there is a consolidated location for all Service Manager reporting needs.

4. The Service Manager Data Warehouse management server connects to the source Service Manager instances and gets the list of their management packs. The data

warehouse specifically keys off the MP version number for changes to classes and relationships.

5. At this point, the MP list in the data warehouse is compared to the MP list in Service Manager for any action that MPSync should take. Here are potential actions:

   ▶ If the MP is new to that Service Manager instance but already exists in the data warehouse, there is only the need for the association between the source Service Manager and MP to be recorded within the data warehouse.

   ▶ If the MP is new or updated and does not exist within the data warehouse, the MP is exported from Service Manager and then imported into the DWStagingAndConfig database.

   ▶ If the MP has been deleted from that Service Manager instance, depending on how many sources have that MP, Service Manager either decrements the source counts within the data warehouse and removes the association to that source or removes the reference entirely if the source count will now be equal to zero.

NOTE: ONLY SEALED MANAGEMENT PACKS ARE SYNCHRONIZED TO THE DATA WAREHOUSE

Only sealed management packs are synchronized from Service Manager to the data warehouse. However, two exceptions apply:

▶ List items (also known as enumerations)

▶ Groups/queues

These are synchronized regardless of whether they are in a sealed or unsealed MP.

MPs that Service Manager brings over from a Service Manager instance will be both Service Manager specific and data warehouse specific. The Service Manager MPs give Service Manager awareness of what the Service Manager CMDB is structured like, and the data warehouse MPs drive the structure and processes of the data warehouse databases.

After those management packs have been synchronized between Service Manager and the data warehouse, Service Manager needs to get the data/reports deployed for user consumption.

Sequentially, here is how deployment works:

1. After all identified MPs have been synchronized with the data warehouse, MPSync triggers the report deployment workflow.

2. Because DWStagingAndConfig is the final destination of the MPs that have been synchronized, the deployment workflow queries the DWStagingAndConfig database for any new or changed reports to deploy or any reports to remove.

3. The deployment workflow then publishes any new or updated reports to the SQL Server Reporting Services server via the SRS web services.

4. SRS then stores the reports and appropriate metadata.

5. Schema deployment workflow is triggered by MPSync.

6. Once again, information that is driving schema changes is retrieved from the DWStagingAndConfig database based off the newly synchronized MPs that are driving the changes.

7. The schema changes are then deployed to the DWRepository.

8. Any necessary changes to ETL modules are made to the DWStagingAndConfig database.

MPs that contain only Service Manager-specific information do not trigger the execution of deployment activities. They are triggered only for new data warehouse/reporting-specific elements.

Subscribing to and Publishing Reports

A common requirement for service management is to be able to distribute reports to a wide variety of people. Often, managers who are accountable for a service want a daily or weekly report of specific work items, or perhaps other teams that are responsible for configuration items might want an updated history of work items related to the configuration items for which they are responsible. The next sections show two simple examples of publishing and subscribing to the built-in Computer Inventory report to get you started on report publishing and subscriptions. Service Manager uses SQL Reporting Services for its reporting engine, so you can leverage the built-in features of SRS to quickly enable report publishing and subscriptions.

Publishing Reports

Publishing reports refers to creating reports on a schedule and storing them on a file share for users to retrieve later. Reports published in this way can provide an easy method for people to get up-to-date information from a common location. You can also use file share security to control who can read reports from specific file shares.

Perform the following steps on the Service Manager data warehouse server:

1. Configure the SQL Agent Service on your Service Manager data warehouse server to start automatically and start the service if it is not already running. This is required to run the scheduled publishing and subscription activities.

2. Create the publishing share. Create a file share to which you will publish the report, and where your target users can retrieve it. You need a user account that can write to the share, and your users must have read rights.

3. Open a browser and navigate to http://localhost/reports (assuming you have not modified the default SRS URL). The first time you visit this URL, it might take a little longer to load.

4. Click **SystemCenter -> ServiceManager -> ServiceManager.Console.Reporting. ConfigurationManagement -> ServiceManager.Report. ConfigurationManagement.ComputerInventory**.

   You should now have the full Computer Inventory report displayed in the browser.

5. Click **Subscriptions**, then **New Subscription**.

6. Complete the form with your desired settings:

   ▶ **Delivered by:** Select **Windows File Share**.

   ▶ **File Name:** Enter the filename you want to save the report as.

   ▶ **Path:** Enter the path to the share you previously configured.

   ▶ **Render Format:** Select the format for the report from the list of XML, CSV, PDF, HTML, MHTML, Excel, RPL, TIFF, and Word.

   ▶ **Credentials used to access the file share:** Enter the username and password for an account that can write to the share.

   Complete the remaining options as you desire. During testing, it is helpful to set the schedule to publish frequently (for example, every 5 minutes) to test whether everything is working as expected.

7. At the bottom of the page, click **OK** to create the subscription.

8. Verify that the report is created in the publishing share, and you are done!

Subscribing to Reports

Perform the following steps to subscribe to reports on the Service Manager data warehouse server. These instructions assume you have a Simple Mail Transport Protocol (SMTP) server already available to send the email. If you have already configured an email notification channel for Service Manager, you should be fine.

1. If you haven't already, you need to configure the SQL Agent on your Service Manager data warehouse server to start automatically and also start the service if it is not already running. This is required to run the scheduled publishing and subscription activities.

2. Open the Reporting Services Configuration Manager and connect to the report server instance. (It will likely be populated with the correct default values already.)

3. Click **Email Settings** and enter the email address that you want to send the reports from and the SMTP server to use to send the email.

4. Click **Apply**, and then **Exit**.

5. Open a browser and navigate to http://localhost/reports (assuming you have not modified the default SRS URL). The first time you visit the URL, it might take a little longer to load.

6. Click **SystemCenter -> ServiceManager -> ServiceManager.Console. Reporting.ConfigurationManagement -> ServiceManager.Report. ConfigurationManagement.ComputerInventory**.

   You should now have the full Computer Inventory report displayed in the browser.

7. Click **Subscriptions**, and then **New Subscription**.

8. Complete the form with your desired settings:

   ▶ **Delivered by:** Select E-Mail.

   ▶ **To, Cc, Bcc, Reply To, Subject, Priority, Comment:** Enter the email details you want to use.

   ▶ **Render Format:** Select the format for the report from the list of XML, CSV, PDF, MHTML, Excel, RPL, TIFF, and Word.

   ▶ **Include Report:** Enabling (by checking) this check box will attach the report to the email.

   ▶ **Include Link:** Enabling this check box will include a link to the web-based report in the email message body.

   One of the nice features of published and subscribed reports is that you can config-ure them with specific report parameters. For example, if your environment contains multiple domains, you could email reports for specific domains to specific users. Any of the report parameters that are available interactively are available to configure for subscriptions. Custom reports will also expose their parameters.

9. Complete the remaining options as you desire. During testing, it is helpful to set the schedule to publish frequently (for example, every 5 minutes) to test whether every-thing is working as expected

10. At the bottom of the page, click **OK** to create the subscription.

11. Check your target inbox to see your report.

You can now email well-targeted reports directly to those who need the information related to incidents, problems, and configuration items automatically and on a regular basis. These report subscriptions can become an important part of your service manage-ment processes.

Troubleshooting

Troubleshooting the data warehouse can be a bit intimidating. Sometimes even determin-ing where to begin to look can prove difficult. This section should help make trou-bleshooting the data warehouse easier for you.

20

Depending on the type of issues you see, your start point will differ. Let's look at the general approach first. If you observe a failure or something just doesn't seem right, a general debugging process will have you looking in several different places, as follows:

1. Start by looking at the Operations Manager event log on the data warehouse server.

> **NOTE: EVENT LOG NAMES**
>
> Because System Center Service Manager uses the common System Center architecture first introduced by System Center Operations Manager, it uses the same names for the event log (for example, Operations Manager). The event log contains all the Service Manager-specific events.

This is the absolutely most important place to begin! Almost all errors from the data warehouse are output to this event log. Events in this log will have two different sources: Deployment and Data Warehouse.

Events with a source of Deployment are usually from MP deployment, which includes report deployment or building out the data warehouse (such as creating outriggers, dimensions, fact tables, and so on). If you see an error in the event log, it usually has instructions on how to recover from it. For example, it might indicate that you need to restart the services. In the Data Warehouse management server, there are three services similar to the Service Manager management server:

▸ System Center Data Access Service

▸ System Center Management

▸ System Center Management Configuration

It is usually best to recycle all these services at the same time.

Once your data warehouse is deployed, events are more likely to have a source of Data Warehouse. These events are written by jobs within the normal course of operations, like the ETL jobs, the MPSync job, and the DWMaintenance job. However, these all still write their events to the Operations Manager event log.

2. View the Data Warehouse workspace in the Service Manager console.

When you click **Data Warehouse Jobs** in the Data Warehouse workspace, you should see the ETL jobs and MPSync job status. If your deployment was successful and your data warehouse is correctly registered to at least one Service Manager management group, you will see at least five jobs. Every job should either be in a status of Running or Not Started.

If you see that a job is in Failed status, you can click this job and then click **Modules** in the Tasks pane to find out which job module has failed. However, to find out why it failed, the best place to get information is from the Operations Manager event log on the data warehouse server. You can also get more details from PowerShell cmdlets, which are discussed in step 3.

In the Data Warehouse workspace, you can also click the **Management Packs** link in the left pane. This is where you can see all the MPs in the data warehouse and the status of their deployment. When you import an MP to Service Manager, the MPSync job synchronizes it to the data warehouse (hence the name; MPSync means "management pack synchronization"). When you get the list of MPs in the data warehouse, you can determine whether your MP successfully deployed.

If your MP has defined data warehouse-specific elements such as outriggers, dimensions, fact tables, or reports, this MP must be deployed successfully before the new tables and reports will be ready to use.

3. Use PowerShell.

The PowerShell cmdlets provide much more detailed information about the data warehouse jobs than the console does. This will likely change in a future release, but for now, the authors strongly recommend that you learn how to use the following useful cmdlets:

▶ **Get-SCDWMgmtGroup**: This command tells you the sources that are currently registered with the data warehouse. You should expect to see at least two different DataSourceNames.

▶ **Get-SCDWJob**: This command tells you the status of all data warehouse jobs in the current batch.

When the MPSync job or DWMaintenance jobs start, they both disable all the ETL jobs, so you will see the IsEnabled column set to false for each of the ETL jobs. This means that even if the ETL job status shows it is running, it actually is not. When the MPSync job or DWMaintenance jobs complete, the ETL jobs are automatically enabled and resume processing.

A job normally is in the Not Started status, and if it is, you can assume the previous batch has completed. If you want, you can use the following commands to view the latest few batches of a specific job:

▶ **Get-SCDWJob -JobName <Specific job name> -NumberOfBatches <number>**: You will observe the latest MPSync job completed, when it started, and when it ended. If you want, you can calculate how long it ran and the next batch ID and status. The job batch ID is always incremental.

▶ **Get-SCDWJobModule**: This command provides detailed information about the specific modules within the job. This is very useful when you see that the job failed and want to find out what caused the failure.

20

Dashboards

In information systems, a *dashboard* is an executive information system user interface that (similar to an automobile's dashboard) is designed to be easy to read. For example, a product might obtain information from the local operating system in a computer, from one or more applications that may be running, and from one or more remote sites on the Web and present it as though it all came from the same source. Dashboards should not be confused with scorecards.

Technical Overview

The Service Manager 2010 Dashboard is a Windows SharePoint Services-based application that provides a view of multiple sets of Service Manager statistics on a single web page. Users can view data in the form of pie charts, graphs, or Dundas gauges.

The Service Manager Dashboard provides IT managers with a consolidated, near real-time view of the IT service management (ITSM) processes (including incidents, activities, and change control management) of their organization infrastructure, even if they do not have access to or knowledge of the Service Manager console application.

The Service Manager Dashboard is designed to work with an existing Service Manager 2010 infrastructure. The Dashboard queries the Service Manager data warehouse and uses the resulting data set to present key infrastructure metrics and KPIs in a graphical format.

The Service Manager Dashboard uses SharePoint web parts to manage and display data sets:

▶ **Microsoft Dashboard Configuration web part:** Use this web part to create and modify the SQL queries that produce the data sets and the other properties that govern how the Dashboard displays the data sets.

▶ **Microsoft Dashboard Viewer web part:** Use this web part to display the data sets. A Dashboard Viewer web part displays one data set at a time. The Service Manager Dashboard can contain multiple copies of the Dashboard Viewer web part simultaneously, each copy displaying a different data set. Be aware that as you add more copies of the web part to the site, and as you increase the amount of data displayed, the performance of the site may degrade.

Figure 20.2 shows how users can interact with the web parts to retrieve and display data.

The Service Manager Dashboard process flow involves the following sequence of activities:

1. An IT service manager requests a new data set.

2. The IT administrator uses the Dashboard Configuration web part to define the new data set.

3. The IT administrator stores the configuration information for the new data set. (The information is saved in the Windows SharePoint Services Content database.)

4. The IT administrator adds a new copy of the Dashboard Viewer web part to the default Service Manager Dashboard, and then modifies the web part to display the new data set.

5. The IT service manager browses to the Service Manager Dashboard site.

6. Windows SharePoint Services queries the Service Manager data warehouse as specified by the data set configuration.

7. Windows SharePoint Services renders the new data set using the Dashboard Viewer web part.

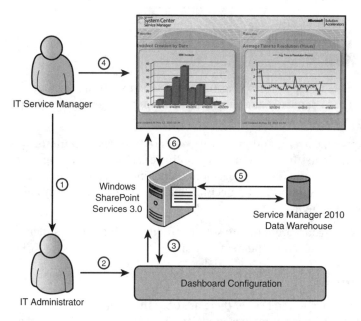

FIGURE 20.2   Interaction with the web parts.

Installation and Configuration Details

The Service Manager Dashboard integrates with an already functioning deployment of Service Manager 2010 and has no additional infrastructure requirements. It is assumed that Service Manager 2010 and the Service Manager data warehouse are configured in accordance with Microsoft installation guidance. (For additional information, see Chapter 6, "Planning Complex Configurations.")

Table 20.1 lists software requirements for the Service Manager Dashboard.

Install the Service Manager Dashboard on servers that run Windows SharePoint Services 3.0 Service Pack (SP) 2 or Microsoft Office SharePoint Server 2007 SP 2.

20

TABLE 20.1   Software Requirements for the Service Manager Dashboard

Component	Details
Operating system	Same requirements as for Service Manager 2010
Software	Service Manager 2010
	Windows SharePoint Services 3.0 Service Pack 2
	Microsoft SQL Server 2005 or 2008
	Microsoft .NET Framework 3.5
Browser	Microsoft Internet Explorer 7.0 or later

Business Intelligence

Business intelligence (BI) refers to computer-based techniques used in spotting, digging out, and analyzing data, such as IT service management processes by category, process, or by associated departments, for instance.

BI technologies provide historical, current, and predictive views of business operations. Common functions of BI technologies include reporting, online analytical processing, analytics, data mining, business performance management, benchmarking, text mining, and predictive analytics. BI aims to support better decision making. Therefore, a BI system can be called a decision support system.

System Center Service Manager's data warehouse uses BI techniques such as facts, dimensions, and outriggers. These are discussed in the next sections.

How the Data Model Works

No matter how many tables are in the warehouse, there are only three types of tables. It is important to understand what each type of table is used for. The next sections discuss the types of tables.

Dimensions

Dimensions represent the classes, where each row in the dimension is an instance of the class and each column is a property. Enum properties, however, are stored in outriggers, which are similar to dimensions except they have one row per item in a list that describes a class instance. See the "Outriggers" section for additional information.

Fact Tables

Fact tables are the most notable difference between a data warehouse and a transaction processing system. Generally, fact tables are used to track transactions, or things that happen, over time. These transactions are usually quantified and summarized, so they are represented as metrics (called *measures* in data warehousing terms).

In Service Manager 2010, there are two types of fact tables:

▶ **Relationship fact tables:** Relationship fact tables are used to track the relationships between instances of classes over time.

For example, in the Service Manager model, there is a relationship called WorkItemAssignedToUser that enables assigning a user to a `WorkItem`. As the `WorkItem` is assigned or reassigned to a user, a new row is inserted into the relationship WorkItemAssignedToUser fact table that targets this relationship.

Relationship fact tables also have CreatedDate and DeletedDate columns, which enable determining when the relationship was in effect. If the DeletedDate column is null, it is currently an active relationship.

All the code required to populate and maintain these fact tables are automatically generated once the fact table is defined in an MP. You can find more information about creating relationship fact tables in the blog post at http://blogs.msdn.com/b/scplat/archive/2010/03/29/a-deep-dive-on-creating-relationship-facts-in-the-data-warehouse.aspx.

▶ **Custom fact tables:** Custom fact tables are fact tables that a developer can write a custom code for and populate based on his specific business requirements.

Out of the box, several custom fact tables can be quite useful. One of them is the IncidentStatusDurationFact. This fact table tracks every time an incident's status changes. The measure in this fact table is the TotalTimeMeasure, which is the duration in minutes that the incident remained in that status.

This enables measuring both the total process time as the incident proceeds through its life cycle and the number of transitions (for example, how many times did the incident move from Active to Pending and how long was it Pending before being reactivated).

For custom fact tables, the Service Manager data warehouse infrastructure will automatically generate the code required to extract the data from Service Manager into the warehouse and to load the data mart from the Repository database. However, the developer creating the custom fact table must provide the transform code.

Outriggers

An *outrigger* describes an instance of a class. The Lists or Enum properties in Service Manager are used to populate outriggers, which describe their respective classes. For example, the IncidentClassification outrigger describes `Incidents`, the ChangeCategory outrigger describes `Change Requests`, the ProblemResolution outrigger describes `Problems`, and so on.

You can view the complete data warehouse schema in Visio format by visiting http://blogs.technet.com/cfs-file.ashx/__key/CommunityServer-Blogs-Components-WeblogFiles/00-00-00-62-41-DW/2425.DWDataMart.zip.

Viewing Data Using T-SQL

As mentioned in the "Dimensions" section, each dimension represents the classes. However, the dimensions help to abstract the complexity of the class hierarchy. For instance, there are several different types of Computer classes, but the Computer dimension represents each of them. Each dimension has a row for the class it targets and all the classes that extend or derive from that class.

For example, Incidents and Problems are classes that are types of TroubleTickets, which are in turn types of WorkItems, which in turn is a type of Entity. Each class in this hierarchy could have a dimension. Each dimension in this hierarchy contains a row not only for each instance of its class but also each of its descendant classes. Here are a few examples:

- ▶ EntityDimvw contains a row for every instance of all classes.

- ▶ WorkItemDimvw contains a row for each Incident and Problem (and other work items not reflected below).

- ▶ TroubleTicket does not have its own dimension.

- ▶ Incident and Problem both have their own dimensions (IncidentDimvw and ProblemDimvw, respectively).

Figure 20.3 shows a graphical representation of how the Incident and Problem class derive from the TroubleTicket class and their key properties.

What is interesting about this is that the EntityDimKey (the surrogate key of the EntityDim) and the BaseManagedEntityID are present in each dimension. This enables you to walk up the hierarchy to traverse fact tables that do no directly join to the dimensions you need.

A classic example of needing to traverse the hierarchy is the WorkItemAssignedtoUserFact. If you want to find out to whom an Incident is assigned, you can join IncidentDimvw > WorkItemDimvw > WorkItemAssignedtoUserFactvw > UserDimvw.

Here is a sample query:

```
Select Top 10 incident.Id, incident.Title, userdim.UserName as AssignedToUser
   From    IncidentDim incident
JOIN    WorkItemDim workitem on incident.EntityDimKey = workItem.EntityDimKey
JOIN    WorkItemAssignedToUserFactvw assignedtouser
        on workitem.WorkItemDimKey = assignedtouser.WorkItemDimKey
JOIN    UserDimvw userdim on assignedtouser.WorkItemAssignedToUser_UserDimKey =
        userdim.UserDimKey
Where   assignedtouser.DeletedDate is null
```

You can find additional examples and explanations on the System Center Service Manager blog at http://blogs.technet.com/b/servicemanager/archive/2011/03/14/service-manager-data-warehouse-schema-now-available.aspx.

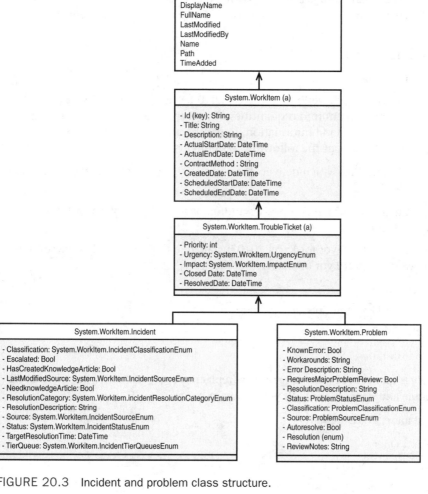

FIGURE 20.3   Incident and problem class structure.

Analyzing Data Using Excel PowerPivot

PowerPivot for Excel 2010 is a data analysis tool that delivers unmatched computational power directly within an application users already know: Microsoft Excel.

You can transform enormous quantities of data with incredible speed into meaningful information to get the answers you need in seconds. You can effortlessly share your findings with others. PowerPivot can even help your IT department improve operational efficiencies through SharePoint-based management tools.

PivotTables continue to be indispensable for allowing users to analyze their data flexibly and interactively. However, using a PivotTable that connects to an online analytical processing (OLAP) data source of course requires such a data source to exist.

The PowerPivot functionality is delivered by SQL Server's Analysis Services team in collaboration with the Excel team and is based on their experience delivering the Microsoft Business Intelligence platform over the past decade. There are two components of PowerPivot:

- ▶ PowerPivot for Excel 2010
- ▶ PowerPivot for SharePoint 2010

Designed for business users, PowerPivot for Excel 2010 leverages familiar Excel features, enabling users to transform enormous quantities of data from nearly any source with incredible speed into meaningful information, to get the answers they need in seconds. PowerPivot for Excel consists of the following components:

- ▶ The Excel 2010 add-in, which delivers the seamless PowerPivot user experience integrated within Excel.
- ▶ The VertiPaq engine, which compresses and manages millions of rows of data in memory with extremely fast performance.

Verify that you have PowerPivot for Excel 2010 installed, and then complete these steps to unleash the power of PowerPivot on Service Manager:

1. Open Excel 2010.
2. Start the PowerPivot window.
3. Choose the following:

   - ▶ From Database: SQL
   - ▶ Server name: **svcmgrdw.domain.com** (replacing **svcmgrdw** with your own server name and **domain.com** with your domain name)
   - ▶ Database: DWDataMart
   - ▶ Next: Query

4. Paste this query, replacing the date values:

```
DECLARE @StartDate date
    , @EndDate date


SET   @StartDate='1/1/2010'
SET   @EndDate='3/31/2010'


SELECT    Convert(date, i.CreatedDate) as Date
      , COUNT(*) as CreatedIncidents


FROM  IncidentDim i
WHERE i.CreatedDate between @StartDate and @EndDate
GROUP BY Convert(date, i.CreatedDate)
Order By Convert(date, i.CreatedDate)
```

5. Click **Finish**, and then **Close**.

6. Rename the tab to **Incidents**.

7. On the Home tab, click **PivotTable** and select **Single PivotChart**.

8. Select **Existing Worksheet** and click **OK**.

9. Configure the task pane:

   ▶ Check mark in **CreatedIncidents** box.

   ▶ Check mark in **Date** box.

10. Right-click **Chart** and select **Change Chart Type**.

11. Select **Line**, and then click **OK**.

12. Right-click **Chart Y-axis**, and then select **Format Axis**.

13. Set Maximum to **250**, and then click **OK**.

14. Click in the chart and select the **PowerPivot / Layout** tab.

15. Click **Trendline** in the Ribbon and then select **Linear Trendline**.

16. Also create Trendline for Incidents.

17. Drag **Date** under Alerts to Slicers Vertical in the task pane.

18. Show pivoting (for example, date from X to Y).

Customizing the Data Warehouse and Reporting

Dimensional modeling (DM) is the name of a set of techniques and concepts used in data warehouse design. It is considered to be different from entity-relationship modeling (ER). Dimensional modeling does not necessarily involve a relational database. The same modeling approach, at the logical level, can be used for any physical form, such as multi-dimensional database or even flat files. DM is a design technique for databases intended to support end-user queries in a data warehouse. It is oriented around understandability and performance. Dr. Kimball (see the "Data Warehouse Explained" section earlier in this chapter) goes on to state that although transaction-oriented ER is very useful for the trans-action capture, it should be avoided for end-user delivery.

Dimensional modeling always uses the concepts of facts (measures) and dimensions (context). Facts are typically (but not always) numeric values that can be aggregated, and dimensions are groups of hierarchies and descriptors that define the facts. For example, sales amount is a fact; timestamp, product, register#, store#, and so on are elements of dimensions. Dimensional models are built by business process area (store sales, inventory, claims, and so on). Because the different business process areas share some but not all dimensions, efficiency in design, operation, and consistency is achieved using conformed dimensions (that is, using one copy of the shared dimension across subject areas).

20

Because Service Manager is based on SQL Server technology, you can use the Business Intelligence Development Studio to author your own report. To author your own report, follow these steps:

1. Open SQL BI Studio.

2. Select **File -> Close Project**.

3. Select **File -> New Project**. Name it **My Custom Report** and click **OK**.

4. Create a new data source called **DWDataMart**. Populate it with the following information:

    ▶ **Server:** Fill in your Service Manager data warehouse server name

    ▶ **DB:** DWDataMart

5. Right-click the **Reports** node in Solution Explorer. Select **Add -> New Item**.

6. Select **Report as Template**, name it **My Custom Report.rdl**, and click **Add**.

7. In the Report Data Explorer, click **New**, **Dataset**. Provide the following information:

    ▶ **Name:** Incidents

    ▶ **Shared Datasource:** DWDataMart

    ▶ **Query:**
    ```
    exec ServiceManager_Report_IncidentManagement_SP_GetListOfIncidents
    @DateFilter=N'CreatedOn',@StartDate='2010-02-05 23:00:00',
    @EndDate='2010-03-05 23:00:00',@Source=N'-1',@AssignedTo=N'',
    @Status=N'-1',@Description=NULL,@ResolutionDescription=NULL,@Impact=N'-1',
    @ContactMethod=NULL,@Priority=N'-1',
    @Classification=N'-1',@SupportGroup=N'-1',
    @ResolutionCategory=N'-1',
    @RelatedCIs=N' ',@ID=NULL,@LanguageCode=N'ENU'
    ```
    (replacing the dates in query with alternative dates)

8. Resize the Report surface.

9. Drop a **Chart** item from the Toolbox onto the Report surface.

10. Select **Line** as type.

11. Drop **Date** from the Dataset onto the X-axis (Category).

12. Drop the **CreatedIncidents** from the Dataset onto the Z-axis (Data).

13. Resize the Chart.

14. Click the **Preview** tab.

15. Click the **Design** tab.

16. Drop a **Chart** item from the Toolbox onto the Report surface next to Chart.

17. Drop **Date** from the Dataset onto the First column.

18. Drop the **CreatedIncidents** from the Dataset onto the Second column.

19. Resize the Table.

20. Click the **Preview** tab.

21. Click the **Design** tab.

22. Drop an **Image** item from the Toolbox on the Report surface above Chart.

23. Resize the Image.

24. Right-click **My Custom Report (bold)** in Solution Explorer, and then select **Properties**. Enter the following information:

    ▶ DataSourceFolder: /SystemCenter/ServiceManager/Odyssey

    ▶ TargetFolder: /SystemCenter/ServiceManager/Odyssey

    ▶ ServerURL: http://*svcmgrdw*/reportserver

    (replacing *svcmgrdw* with your own server name)

25. In the Build menu, select **Deploy My Custom Report**.

26. Close and restart the Service Manager console.

27. Go to the **Reporting** workspace.

28. Expand the **Odyssey** node.

29. Run the **My Custom Report** report.

Summary

Service Manager 2010 provides a true data warehouse and an extensive reporting platform. Using the out-of-the-box management packs, you can introduce reports into the environment for all the key processes, such as incident, change, and problem management. Using custom management packs, you can extend the data warehouse to store additional CMDB data.

Using SQL Reporting Services as the underlying technology, Service Manager can provide you with extensive rendering options such as Word or PDF output and scheduling capabilities (for instance, through email or file share). The SQL Reporting Business Development Studio allows you to write your own reports, either from a report model or from scratch, using the well-documented data warehouse layout and T-SQL queries.

The Dashboard Solution Accelerator, a free download from the Microsoft download website, uses SharePoint to display key metrics (KPIs) on IT processes such as incident, change, and problem management. It is easy to set up and use and integrates well with the Service Manager console.

Using the new PowerPivot plug-in for Excel 2010, users can perform ad-hoc business intelligence tasks on the Service Manager data. Users can also report on data and pivot through it, to analyze how their processes are doing.

20

With the Service Manager 2012 release, Microsoft is making further investments in the System Center data warehouse. The System Center data warehouse will be able to pull data from Service Manager, Operations Manager, and Configuration Manager for a consolidated overview of your IT environment. In addition, it will be possible to publish directly to the data warehouse from custom sources such as SAP. Self-service reporting and dashboard authoring will be available using online analytical processing cubes—bringing in the Service Manager data in Excel (via a PowerPivot table) to where you can "slice and dice" it with the live data from the data warehouse.

PART VI
Appendixes

IN THIS PART

APPENDIX A

Reference URLs

This appendix includes a number of reference uniform resource locators (URLs) associated with System Center Service Manager 2010 (SvcMgr). URLs do change, and so although the authors have made every effort to verify these references as working links, there is no guarantee they will remain current. It is quite possible some will change or be "dead" by the time you read this book. Sometimes the Wayback Machine (http://www.archive.org/index.php) can rescue you from dead or broken links. This site is an Internet archive, and it will take you back to an archived version of a site (sometimes).

General Resources

A number of websites provide excellent resources for Service Manager:

▶ A great source of information is for all things System Center related, including Service Manager, is System Center Central (http://www.systemcentercentral.com).

▶ http://www.myITforum.com is a community of worldwide Information Technology (IT) professionals and a website established in 1999 by Rod Trent. myITforum includes topics on System Center and IT.

▶ Anders Bengtsson, a coauthor of this book, blogs extensively on Service Manager. For a list of his articles about Service Manager, see http://contoso.se/blog/?cat=25.

- If you are interested in understanding the Customer Improvement Program, Marnix Wolf has a great series of blog posts at http://thoughtsonopsmgr.blogspot.com/2010/02/ceip-odr-and-lot-what-are-they-and-why.html.

- http://www.techlog.nl/ is about everything Microsoft, maintained by Maarten Goet (a contributor to this book), Kenneth van Surksum, Steven van Loef, and Aad Noman.

- The System Center Virtual User Group is dedicated to providing educational resources and collaboration between users of System Center technologies worldwide. Bi-monthly meetings present topics from industry experts, including Microsoft engineers. These Live Meeting sessions are recorded for your convenience. To join the user group, go to http://www.linkedin.com/groupRegistration?gid=101906.

- The TechNet Manageability Center contains links to resources and TechNet Magazine articles, at http://technet.microsoft.com/en-us/default.aspx.

- Microsoft has published whitepapers on performance tuning guidelines for Windows Server 2008 at http://www.microsoft.com/whdc/system/sysperf/Perf_tun_srv.mspx.

Microsoft's Service Manager Resources

The following list includes some general Microsoft resources available for Service Manager 2010:

- Microsoft's Service Manager website is located at http://www.microsoft.com/systemcenter/en/us/service-manager.aspx.

- The Microsoft System Center website is at http://www.microsoft.com/systemcenter/.

- http://technet.microsoft.com/en-us/systemcenter/sm/ee923652 is the location of the Service Manager TechCenter.

- Service Manager webcasts are available at http://msevents.microsoft.com/CUI/WebCastEventDetails.aspx?culture=en-US&EventID=1032416974 and http://msevents.microsoft.com/CUI/WebCastEventDetails.aspx?culture=en-US&EventID=1032424297&CountryCode=US.

- The documentation library for Service Manager 2010 Service Pack (SP) 1 is available online at http://technet.microsoft.com/en-us/library/ff461010.aspx. This includes the planning guide, deployment guide, administrators guide, operations guide, authoring guide, upgrade guide, disaster recovery guide, a glossary, documentation on the cmdlets, and release notes.

- Microsoft's Service Manager Engineering Team blog is located at http://blogs.technet.com/b/servicemanager/.

- To use Operations Manager 2007 R2 to monitor Service Manager, download the management pack from http://www.microsoft.com/downloads/en/details.aspx?displaylang=en&FamilyID=82a6cd07-85aa-4739-9829-f1e7cdea7fe7.

▶ Here are some individual blogs by members of the engineering team:

  ▶ **Marc Umeno:** http://blogs.technet.com/b/umeno/

  ▶ **Jakub Olesky:** http://blogs.msdn.com/b/jakuboleksy/

  ▶ **Jim Truber:** http://jtruher3.wordpress.com/

▶ Microsoft's System Center Pack Catalog has multiple pages for Service Manager, Virtual Machine Manager, Operations Manager, Configuration Manager, Data Protection Manager, and Essentials. You can access the catalog at http://pinpoint. microsoft.com/en-US/systemcenter/managementpackcatalog.

▶ View a drilldown on Service Manager 2010 at http://www.msteched.com/2010/ NorthAmerica/MGT313. This TechEd session focuses on how Service Manager automates Change, Incident, Problem, and Configuration Management. It includes a discussion of the features and capabilities of Service Manager and discusses how to extend the product using the Authoring Tool and the Service Manager Software Development Kit (SDK).

▶ At the 2011 Microsoft Management Summit (MMS), Sean Christensen and Travis Wright delved deeply into automating the Information Technology Infrastructure Library (ITIL) and Microsoft Operations Framework (MOF) with Service Manager. You can view the presentation at http://www.mms-2011.com/topic/details/BB14.

▶ For information about System Center licensing, see http://www.microsoft.com/ systemcenter/en/us/pricing-licensing.aspx. Pricing for Service Manager is at http:// www.microsoft.com/systemcenter/en/us/service-manager/sm-pricing-licensing.aspx.

▶ Information regarding Windows Server Load Balancing is available in the Network Load Balancing Deployment guide at http://technet.microsoft.com/en-us/library/ cc754833(WS.10).aspx.

▶ http://technet.microsoft.com/en-us/library/cc732906(WS.10).aspx provides information on requesting an Internet Server certificate.

▶ If you are considering virtualizing Service Manager components, a good document on SQL Server 2008 virtualization is available at http://download.microsoft.com/ download/d/9/4/d948f981-926e-40fa-a026-5bfcf076d9b9/SQL2008inHyperV2008. docx.

▶ If you are looking at the product's history, Microsoft's announcement on the delayed release of Service Manager until 2010 is at http://blogs.technet.com/b/systemcenter/ archive/2008/02/07/system-center-service-manager-update.aspx.

▶ Want to know how grooming works? Travis Wright provides details at http://blogs. technet.com/b/servicemanager/archive/2009/09/18/data-retention-policies-aka-grooming-in-the-servicemanager-database.aspx.

▶ The Security Manager security matrix (discussed in Chapter 15, "Service Manager Security"), states that Administrators, Advanced Operators, and Authors can create announcements. However, the Announcement view by default is available only in the

Administration workspace, which is accessible only to Service Manager administrators. Travis Wright describes a solution for this at http://blogs.technet.com/b/servicemanager/archive/2010/12/01/faq-how-can-i-enable-non-admins-to-create-edit-delete-announcements.aspx.

▶ http://technet.microsoft.com/en-us/library/ff461151.aspx discusses user roles in Service Manager.

▶ Download the Service Manager Authoring Tool (SP 1) at http://www.microsoft.com/downloads/en/details.aspx?FamilyID=78dcb15b-8744-4a93-b3fa-6a7a40ffeaae&displaylang=en.

▶ http://blogs.technet.com/b/servicemanager/archive/2009/07/24/localizing-management-pack-content.aspx provides information on localizing Service Manager management packs.

▶ Management pack bundles are described at http://blogs.technet.com/b/servicemanager/archive/2009/09/04/introducing-management-pack-bundles.aspx.

▶ Use fastseal.exe to seal your management packs. You can download the utility from the Service Manager Engineering Team Blog at http://blogs.technet.com/servicemanager/archive/2009/12/25/sealing-management-packs.aspx.

▶ XML Notepad 2007 is an intuitive tool for browsing and editing extensible Markup Language (XML) documents. Read about it at http://msdn2.microsoft.com/en-us/library/aa905339.aspx, and download the tool from http://www.microsoft.com/downloads/details.aspx?familyid=72d6aa49-787d-4118-ba5f-4f30fe913628&displaylang=en.

▶ Virtual labs for System Center products including Service Manager, Operations Manager, Essentials, and Configuration Manager are located at http://technet.microsoft.com/en-us/bb539977.aspx.

▶ If you are ready to take a closer look at Service Manager, see Sean Christensen's videos at http://blogs.technet.com/b/systemcenter/archive/2011/04/01/system-center-service-manager-deep-dive-session-videos.aspx.

▶ If you are interested in learning about the Microsoft Operations Framework, you will want to check out version of 4.0 of the MOF at http://go.microsoft.com/fwlink/?LinkId=50015.

▶ Information on the MOF Deliver Phase is at http://technet.microsoft.com/en-us/library/cc506047.aspx.

▶ You can read about the MOF Envision service management function (SMF) at http://technet.microsoft.com/en-us/library/cc531013.aspx.

▶ For information on MOF 4.0 and the Manage layer, see http://technet.microsoft.com/en-us/library/cc506048.aspx.

▶ Information on the IO (Infrastructure Optimization) model is available at http://www.microsoft.com/technet/infrastructure.

▶ Details about the Microsoft Solutions Framework (MSF) are located at http://www.
microsoft.com/downloads/details.aspx?familyid=50DBFFFE-3A65-434A-A1DD-
29652AB4600F&displaylang=en and http://www.microsoft.com/downloads/
details.aspx?familyid=a71ac896-1d28-45a4-880c-8b0cc8265c63&displaylang=en.

▶ If you want to learn about Service Modeling Language (SML), see http://www.w3.
org/TR/sml/. For additional technical information about SML from Microsoft, visit
http://technet.microsoft.com/en-us/library/bb725986.aspx.

▶ Microsoft provides Solution Accelerators, which are guidelines and tools to leverage
the full functionality of Microsoft usage within your organization. The Solution
Accelerators are available for download at no cost at http://technet.microsoft.com/
en-us/solutionaccelerators/dd229342.

▶ The Compliance Solution Accelerators can be downloaded at http://www.
microsoft.com/downloads/en/details.aspx?FamilyId=BD930882-0D39-4900-9A79-
B91F213ED15D&displaylang=en.

▶ Microsoft provides a sizing helper for Service Manager. This utility can assist you in
determining the hardware required based on certain scenarios. Download
SM_jobaids.zip from http://go.microsoft.com/fwlink/?LinkId=186291.

▶ Travis Wright discusses the Allowed List at http://blogs.technet.com/b/
servicemanager/archive/2010/02/26/managing-the-allowed-list-for-the-operations-
manager-ci-connector-with-powershell.aspx.

▶ http://technet.microsoft.com/en-us/library/ff461125.aspx provides guidelines for
installing the Self-Service portal (SSP).

▶ Microsoft is providing the source code to the SSP, enabling you to create and
customize your own portal. Microsoft also added several new features to this version
such as being able to update an incident from the portal. The source code is at
http://www.microsoft.com/downloads/en/details.aspx?FamilyID=65fbe0a3-1928-
469f-b941-146d27aa6bac&displaylang=en. For more information and a preview of
how you could customize the portal, see http://blogs.technet.com/b/servicemanager/
archive/2011/03/02/service-manager-portal-source-code-released.aspx.

▶ If you are interested in customizing the data warehouse and reporting capabilities in
Service Manager, http://blogs.msdn.com/b/scplat/archive/2010/03/29/a-deep-dive-
on-creating-relationship-facts-in-the-data-warehouse.aspx provides details about
creating relationship facts in the data warehouse.

▶ View the complete data warehouse schema in Visio format at http://blogs.technet.
com/cfs-file.ashx/__key/CommunityServer-Blogs-Components-WeblogFiles/00-00-00-
62-41-DW/2425.DWDataMart.zip. A description is available at http://blogs.technet.
com/b/servicemanager/archive/2011/03/14/service-manager-data-warehouse-schema-
now-available.aspx.

▶ You can download the Service Manager 2010 SDK from http://www.microsoft. com/downloads/en/details.aspx?displaylang=en&FamilyID=1862b19e-9cc1-49b5-b121-eb567a7b2fee.

▶ To get started using the Service Manager SDK, see Jakub Olesky's article at http://blogs.msdn.com/b/jakuboleksy/archive/2008/12/03/getting-started-with-the-service-manager-sdk.aspx.

▶ Read how to use the SDK to build a web application that interacts with Service Manager at the blog posting at http://blogs.technet.com/b/servicemanager/archive/2010/01/07/creating-browser-interfaces-to-service-manager-using-the-sdk.aspx.

▶ You can download the Windows SDK from http://www.microsoft.com/downloads/en/details.aspx?FamilyID=e6e1c3df-a74f-4207-8586-711ebe331cdc&displaylang=en.

Other Service Manager Resources

Microsoft, of course, is not the only organization to discuss Service Manager. A number of websites provide excellent resources for Service Manager:

▶ An early look at the product that eventually became Service Manager 2010 is available at http://itservicemngmt.blogspot.com/2007/05/microsoft-system-center-service-manager.html.

▶ Thoughts on the product in early 2010 prior to its release are at http://plannetplc. wordpress.com/2010/02/17/microsoft-system-center-service-manager-2010-a-credible-challenger-in-the-service-management-software-market/.

▶ A Network World review of Service Manager 2010 is at http://www.networkworld. com/reviews/2011/012411-microsoft-system-center-test.html?source=NWWNLE_ nlt_daily_pm_2011-01-25.

▶ For a good overview of articles on the product, see http://scug.be/blogs/scsm/ archive/2010/07/13/system-center-service-manager-information-blog-overview.aspx.

▶ Tim Vanderderkoii writes about his experiences with the Service Manager test releases through December 2008 in a mid-sized business at http://timvanderkooi. wordpress.com/2008/12/05/service-managergreat-product-but-has-microsoft-missed-the-mid-sized-boat-again/.

▶ Matt Royer, Senior Technical Integration Engineer at Intel, talks about integration of 2010 Intel Core vPro processors with KVM Remote Control with Microsoft System Center Service Manager 2010. Matt shows how the combination allows IT to "get behind the user's keyboard-video-mouse (KVM)" through all PC states and see what their users see (even blue screens) when the operating system is starting up or shutting down. Watch his discussion on YouTube at http://www.youtube.com/ watch?v=nlWbXkirocc.

▶ Asset Management with Service Manager can be accomplished using Provance's IT Asset Management Pack. Read about it at http://www.nn4consultants.com/2010/05/asset-management-with-system-center-service-manager-and-sccm-be-safe-with-provance-the-8020-story/.

▶ To automatically delete objects in Pending Delete status, see http://blog.scsmfaq.ch/2011/03/16/automatically-delete-objects-in-status-pending-delete/.

▶ Read about the Exchange connector at http://bink.nu/news/system-center-service-manager-exchange-connector.aspx.

▶ To learn how to target announcements, read the blog posting by Anders Bengtsson at http://contoso.se/blog/?p=1243.

▶ Read about how to forward knowledge articles to specific users at a blog post by Anders Bengtsson at http://contoso.se/blog/?p=1262.

▶ Anders Bengtsson describes how to target software packages to specific users at http://contoso.se/blog/?p=1269.

▶ Anders Bengtsson also describes how to create a notification for an unassigned incident, at http://contoso.se/blog/?p=1875.

▶ http://scug.be/blogs/scsm/archive/2010/03/21/service-manager-role-based-security-scoping.aspx discusses role-based security scoping.

▶ Need to reset a user's password but haven't implemented Microsoft Forefront Identity Manager (FIM)? Anders Bengtsson describes one approach, which sends the user a new password in an email and creates a closed incident for the service desk to track the number of password-reset incidents. Read his post at http://contoso.se/blog/?p=1605.

Blogs

Here are some blogs the authors have used. Some are more active than others are, and new blogs seem to spring up overnight!

▶ A great source of information is System Center Central (http://www.systemcenter-central.com), managed by MVPs Pete Zerger, Rory McCaw, and Maarten Goet.

▶ If you're interested in keeping up with System Center Virtual Machine Manager (VMM), the VMM team has a blog at http://blogs.technet.com/scvmm/.

▶ See a blog by Stefan Stranger (former MVP and now at Microsoft) at http://blogs.technet.com/stefan_stranger/.

▶ http://systemscentre.blogspot.com/ is a blog by Steve Beaumont.

▶ http://bink.nu is managed by Steven Bink, former MVP for Windows Server Technologies. According to the blog, it "watches Microsoft like a hawk."

▶ You may want to look at the Acceleres Service Manager blog, http://blog.acceleres.com/. Acceleres, headed by coauthor David Pultorak, provides Service Manager implementation and training.

▶ http://blog.myscsm.com/ is by Chris Ross, a Senior Lead Consultant for Catapult Systems.

▶ Frederik Baert blogs at http://frederikbaert.wordpress.com/.

▶ http://itservicemngmt.blogspot.com/ is a blog discussing basic IT service management (ITSM) knowledge points for new people in ITIL.

▶ Kevin Sullivan's Management blog is at https://blogs.technet.com/kevinsul_blog/. (Kevin is a Technology Specialist at Microsoft focusing on management products.)

▶ http://www.systemcentercommunity.com/ is an OpsMgr 2007 forum with questions and answers about Service Manager. You must create a user ID to reply to the posts.

▶ http://www.techlog.org/ is all about everything Microsoft, by Maarten Goet (OpsMgr MVP), Kenneth van Surksum, Steven van Loef, and Sander Klaassen in the Netherlands.

▶ www.systemcenterguide.com is a System Center blog by Duncan McAlynn.

▶ Everything System Center Service Manager, http://blog.scsmfaq.ch, is a Service Manager blog run by Marcel Zehner and itnetx, a consulting and engineering company located in Switzerland.

▶ Walter Chomak's blog on System Center is at http://blogs.technet.com/wchomak/. Walter is a Senior Consultant with Microsoft MCS and a great technical resource.

▶ Ian Blyth, previously a Lead Technical Specialist for Microsoft UK, blogs at http://ianblythmanagement.wordpress.com/ on System Center Technologies.

Here are our own blogs:

▶ http://www.networkworld.com/community/meyler is a blog by Kerrie with general discussion topics, but concentrating on Microsoft management.

▶ Find coauthor and MVP Alexandre Verkinderen's blog at http://scug.be/blogs/scom/default.aspx.

▶ http://www.contoso.se/blog/ is the System Center blog by Anders Bengtsson, former MVP, now a PFE at Microsoft and coauthor of this book.

▶ http://blog.acceleres.com/, mentioned earlier in this section, is by coauthor David Pultorak.

▶ Coauthor Patrik Sundqvist's blog is found at http://blogs.litware.se/.

▶ Contributor and MVP Maarten Goet posts at http://blogs.inovativ.nl/auteur?u=maarten.

▶ Contributor Kurt Van Hoecke blogs at http://scug.be/blogs/scsm/default.aspx.

PowerShell and SMLets

You can find information on PowerShell itself at the following sites:

- The official PowerShell site is at http://www.microsoft.com/powershell.

- The Microsoft TechNet social forum covering general PowerShell discussions is at http://social.technet.microsoft.com/Forums/en-US/winserverpowershell/threads.

- Marco Shaw, PowerShell MVP, maintains a blog at http://marcoshaw.blogspot.com.

- You may want to check all the PowerShell webcasts by the Scripting Guys at http://www.microsoft.com/technet/scriptcenter/webcasts/ps.mspx.

- Direct from the PowerShell guy himself (Marc van Orsouw, PowerShell MVP) is located at http://thepowershellguy.com/blogs/posh/default.aspx.

- Find a PowerShell cheat sheet at http://blogs.msdn.com/powershell/archive/2007/01/25/powershell-cheat-sheet-redux-the-pdf-version.aspx.

- The Windows PowerShell team has its blog at http://blogs.msdn.com/powershell/.

- Find PowerShell script examples at http://www.microsoft.com/technet/scriptcenter/hubs/msh.mspx.

- PowerShell+ is a free PowerShell editing and debugging environment. You can get a free personal copy at http://www.powershell.com/downloads/psp1.zip.

- Read about using the Service Manager cmdlets for Windows PowerShell at http://technet.microsoft.com/en-us/library/ff461199.aspx.

- http://smlets.codeplex.com is your starting point for information on SMLets.

- Beta 3 of SMLets v3 was released in April 2011. The release includes 32 new cmdlets. Read Travis Wright's article on the release at http://blogs.technet.com/b/servicemanager/archive/2011/04/20/smlets-beta-3-released.aspx. There are several "breaking changes included," so be sure to read the article.

- Even more about PowerShell and examples of some of the constructs are available in an article by Don Jones at http://www.microsoft.com/technet/technetmag/issues/2007/01/PowerShell/default.aspx.

Connectors

Here are some useful references regarding connectors:

- To download the Exchange connector for Service Manager 2010 SP 1, see http://www.microsoft.com/downloads/en/details.aspx?FamilyID=0b48d1f1-434a-4ee6-8017-fc13f4c16785.

▶ You can download the CodePlex Service Manager CSV connector from http://
scsmcsvconnector.codeplex.com/. For a discussion by Travis Wright, see http://blogs.
technet.com/b/servicemanager/archive/2009/12/30/how-to-write-a-custom-
connector-csv-connector-example.aspx.

▶ For information about deleting a connector, see Kevin Holman's article at
http://blogs.technet.com/b/kevinholman/archive/2009/09/10/removing-an-old-
product-connector.aspx. Note that Microsoft does not officially support this process.

The System Center Family

Here are some references and articles regarding other components of Microsoft's System
Center family:

▶ Operations Manager is Microsoft's end-to-end service management product, and is
the cornerstone of the common system architecture used by other System Center
products, including Service Manager. A product overview is available at http://www.
microsoft.com/systemcenter/en/us/operations-manager/om-overview.aspx. Kerrie
Meyler discusses the common system architecture at http://www.networkworld.
com/community/blog/common-system-center-architecture.

▶ For an overview of Configuration Manager, see http://www.microsoft.com/system-
center/en/us/configuration-manager/cm-overview.aspx.

▶ For System Center Essentials (Essentials) deployment planning and installation, see
http://go.microsoft.com/fwlink/?LinkId=94444.

▶ The System Center Essentials Community TechCenter can be found at
http://technet.microsoft.com/en-us/sce/bb677155.aspx.

▶ One scenario for System Center Essentials is as a means for managing and monitoring assets of small organizations, tied to a centralized Operations Manager server.
Read John Joyner's take on Microsoft's direction for management tools in the mid-
sized market at http://www.eweek.com/article2/0,1895,1905780,00.asp.

▶ Opalis, being renamed as Orchestrator, was acquired by Microsoft in 2009 and is an
automation tool for System Center and third-party products. Charles Joy, one of the
"Opalis guys," gives an 8-minute product overview at
http://www.youtube.com/watch?v=Hmf6G7N7Tuk.

▶ Data Protection Manager (DPM) delivers data protection for SQL Server, Exchange,
SharePoint, Virtualization, file servers, and Windows desktops and laptops. For an
overview of the product, visit http://www.microsoft.com/systemcenter/en/us/
data-protection-manager/dpm-2010-overview.aspx.

Public Forums

If you need an answer to a question, the first place to check is the Microsoft public forums. Here's a list of the current Service Manager forums:

- **General:** http://social.technet.microsoft.com/Forums/en-us/ systemcenterservicemanager/threads

- **Setup:** http://social.technet.microsoft.com/Forums/en-US/setup/threads

- **Customization Using the SDK and Authoring Tool:** http://social.technet. microsoft.com/Forums/en-US/customization/threads

- **Data Warehouse, Reporting, and Dashboards:** http://social.technet.microsoft. com/Forums/en-US/dwreportingdashboards/threads

- **ITIL and MOF Processes – Incident, Problem, and Change Management:** http://social.technet.microsoft.com/Forums/en-US/itilmofprocesses/threads

- **Administration (User Roles, Notifications, Workflows, etc.):** http://social. technet.microsoft.com/Forums/en-US/administration/threads

- **System Center Integration, Opalis, and Connectors:** http://social.technet. microsoft.com/Forums/en-US/connectors/threads

- **Portals:** http://social.technet.microsoft.com/Forums/en-US/portals/threads

- **Documentation:** http://social.technet.microsoft.com/Forums/en-US/ documentation/threads

APPENDIX B
Available Online

Online content is available to provide add-on value to readers of *System Center Service Manager 2010 Unleashed*. This material, organized by chapter, can be downloaded from http://www.informit.com/store/product.aspx?isbn=0672334 364. This content is not available elsewhere. Note that the authors and publisher do not guarantee or provide technical support for the material.

PowerShell and SMLets

The PowerShell cmdlets developed for Service Manager 2010 assist in administrating Service Manager. The SMLets PowerShell module, an open source code project available on Codeplex, provides functionality for creating and maintaining configuration and work items. Chapter 4, "Looking Inside Service Manager," uses the _PS_Create_ChangeRequest.ps1 script, which is an example of using a PowerShell script that incorporates SMLets.

Building a Custom Workspace

Chapter 19, "Advanced Customization Scenarios," includes instructions for building a custom workspace. The scripts used to create this workspace are contained in the unsealed management pack Odyssey.Console.Customizations.xml.

Live Links

Reference uniform resource locators (URLs; see Appendix A, "Reference URLs") are provided as live links. These include more than 100 (clickable) hypertext links and references to materials and sites related to Service Manager and System Center.

A disclaimer and unpleasant fact regarding live links: URLs change! Companies are subject to mergers and acquisitions, pages move and change on websites, and so on. Although these links were accurate as of this writing (May 2011), it is possible some will change or be "dead" by the time you read this book. Sometimes the Wayback Machine (http://www. archive.org/index.php) can rescue you from dead or broken links. This site is an Internet archive, and it will take you back to an archived version of a site... sometimes.

Index

D

How can we make this index more useful? Email us at indexes@samspublishing.com

F

ITSM (Information Technology Service Management)

defined, 13-14

knowledge articles blog, 674

objectives, 19

strategies, 15

J–K

Jones, Don's article, 675

Joy, Charles, 676

Key attribute, 592

Key Performance Indicators (KPIs), 21

key stakeholders, 427

Kimball, Dr., 661

knowledge articles

blogs, 673

defined, 46

incidents, 309

Library workspace, 261

non-English, indexing, 225, 234

security, 506-507

users, targeting, 261

knowledge base, 6, 262

knowledge requirements

console, 549

customizations, 548-549

data modeling, 549

known errors

controlling, 368-369

defined, 44, 357

KPIs (Key Performance Indicators), 21

L

Landman, Oskar, xi

languages

column display names, customizing, 623

MPs, 562-563

notifications, 461-463

Locale attribute, 461

localization, adding, 463

template modifications, 461-462

values, 462-463

support, 53, 463

Library Author role, 442

Library workspace, 109, 261-263

groups, 261

knowledge articles, 261

knowledge base providers, adding, 262

lists, 262

queues, 263

licensing, 154-155

client versus server MLs, 157

CML, 157

costs

CML, 157

management server software, 157

management server software with SQL 2008 technology, 157

SML, 157

suite options, 156

management server software, 157

management server software with SQL 2008 technology, 157

MLs, 155

OSEs, 157

servers, 156

SML, 157

suite options, 155-156

M

Q

queues

defined, 41, 133

incidents, 310, 323-324

Library workspace, 263

scoping, 546-547

security boundaries, 476

R

RBAC (Role-Based Access Control), 476

reactive Problem Management, 361

Read-Only Operators

console workspace access, 487

defined, 478

permissions, 480

recipients

creating, 452-454

Active Directory users, 452

incoming emails, 454

non-Active Directory users, 453

SMInternal domain, 454

finding, 452

recording

changes, 78, 391-394

incidents, 312-314

problems, 364-366

recovering incidents, 318

recycling intervals (IIS), 272-273

redundancy

CMDB, 160

data warehouse management server, 160

log shipping, 169-170

management server, 160

SSP servers, 160

references, 558-560

secure, 560

relationships, 529-530

RegEx attribute, 593

registering data warehouses, 93, 226-231, 266

credentials, 228, 266

events, 230

management server selection, 227, 266

MP deployment, 230-231

Run As Accounts, creating, 228, 266

regular expressions, 593

regulations, 427-428

common, 427-428

resources, 428

related work items for the selected item property, 282

relationship fact tables, 657

relationships (data models), 528

Affected User, 529

cardinality example, 528-529

classes, adding, 590

types, 529-531

containment, 530

hosting, 530-531

membership, 530

reference, 529-530

release delays, 669

Remove-SCDWMgmtGroup cmdlet, 115

Remove-SCSMAllowListClass cmdlet, 115

reporting, 540-541

Change Management, 387

custom, creating, 550

customization planning, 541

data warehouse, 644

databases, 646

deployment, 648-649

management server, 646

SQL servers

assessing, 129

CMDB instances, 196-197

collation settings, 197

data warehouse management server installation, 208-209

high availability, 167-169

clustering, 167-168

fault tolerance, 168-169

instances, 167

log shipping, 169-170

Standard Edition versus Enterprise Edition, 167

memory, 183

minimizing, 95

performance planning, 180

disk throughput, 180-181

IOPS, 180-181

storage, 181-182

post-installation, 182

reporting services, assessing, 129

separate instances, benefits, 182

SRS (Server Reporting Services), 32, 643

configuring manually, 209-211

installation verification, 207-208

overview, 644

SSP (Self-Service Portal), 46, 98

administration, 244

analysts, 98

command-line installation, 223

customizations, 219, 521-522, 549, 612

data warehouse management server separation, 216

defined, 46

installing, 215-219, 671

location, 140

overview, 271

passwords, resetting, 272-274

post deployment configuration, 225

servers

adding, 141

high availability, 164-165

redundancy options, 160

virtualization, 171

slow response times, fixing, 272-273

software packages, targeting users, 272

software requests, 406-423

requirements, 419-420

software deployment change, creating, 420-422

software packages, publishing, 422-424

source code, 275, 671

users, 98

StagingAndConfig database, 160

stakeholders, 427

standard changes, 77, 386

standby servers, 162

star schemas, 644-646

Start-SCDWJob cmdlet, 116

static members, 546

status property, 281

storage

customizations in MPs, 552

encryption keys, 205

planning, 181-182

Stranger, Stefan's blog, 673

strong name keys, 618-619

Strong Name Tool, 554

subscriptions

notifications

creating, 458-460

languages, 461-463

reports, 650-651

Sullivan, Kevin's Management blog, 674

Sundqvist, Patrik's blog, 674

W

How can we make this index more useful? Email us at indexes@samspublishing.com

X–Z

UNLEASHED

Unleashed takes you beyond the basics, providing an exhaustive, technically sophisticated reference for professionals who need to exploit a technology to its fullest potential. It's the best resource for practical advice from the experts, and the most in-depth coverage of the latest technologies.

informit.com/unleashed

Microsoft SharePoint 2010 Unleashed
ISBN-13: 9780672333255

OTHER UNLEASHED TITLES

System Center Operations Manager (OpsMgr) 2007 R2 Unleashed
ISBN-13: 9780672333415

Microsoft System Center Enterprise Suite Unleashed
ISBN-13: 9780672333194

Windows Server 2008 R2 Unleashed
ISBN-13: 9780672330926

Microsoft Dynamics CRM 4 Integration Unleashed
ISBN-13: 9780672330544

Microsoft Exchange Server 2010 Unleashed
ISBN-13: 9780672330469

System Center Configuration Manager (SCCM) 2007 Unleashed
ISBN-13: 9780672330230

Microsoft SQL Server 2008 Reporting Services Unleashed
ISBN-13: 9780672330261

Microsoft SQL Server 2008 Integration Services Unleashed
ISBN-13: 9780672330322

Microsoft SQL Server 2008 Analysis Services Unleashed
ISBN-13: 9780672330018

C# 4.0 Unleashed
ISBN-13: 9780672330797

Silverlight 4 Unleashed
ISBN-13: 9780672333361

ASP.NET 4 Unleashed
ISBN-13: 9780672331121

Microsoft Visual Studio 2010 Unleashed
ISBN-13: 9780672330810

WPF 4 Unleashed
ISBN-13: 9780672331190

Visual Basic 2010 Unleashed
ISBN-13: 9780672331008

WPF Control Development Unleashed
ISBN-13: 9780672330339

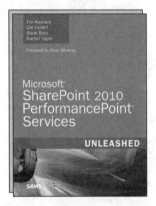

Microsoft SharePoint 2010 PerformancePoint Services Unleashed
ISBN-13: 9780672330940

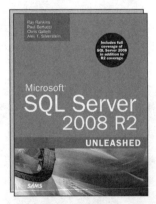

Microsoft SQL Server 2008 R2 Unleashed
ISBN-13: 9780672330568

SAMS

informit.com/sams

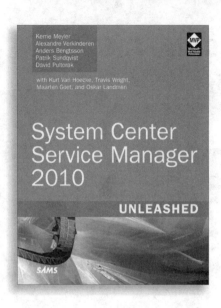